baac

11 07

Fodor's

TŌKYŌ

2nd edition

**Where to Stay and Eat
for All Budgets**

**Must-See Sights
and Local Secrets**

Ratings You Can Trust

Fodor's Travel Publications   New York, Toronto, London, Sydney, Auckland
www.fodors.com

FODOR'S TŌKYŌ

Editor: Alexis C. Kelly, Deborah Kaufman

Editorial Contributors: Brett Bull, Nicholas Coldicott, Oscar Johnson, Oliver Ormrod, Katherine Pham Do, Krista Kim Pickard

Editorial Production: Eric B. Wechter

Maps: David Lindroth, *cartographer*; Rebecca Baer and Robert Blake, *map editors*

Design: Fabrizio La Rocca, *creative director*; Guido Caroti, *art director*; Moon Sun Kim, *cover designer*; Melanie Marin, *senior picture editor*

Production/Manufacturing: Angela L. McLean

Cover Photograph (Shinjuku Ward, Tōkyō): Jasper James/Taxi/Getty Images

COPYRIGHT

Copyright © 2007 by Fodor's Travel, a division of Random House, Inc.

Fodor's is a registered trademark of Random House, Inc.

All rights reserved under International and Pan-American Copyright Conventions. Published in the United States by Fodor's Travel a division of Random House, New York, and simultaneously in Canada by Random House of Canada Limited, Toronto. Distributed by Random House, Inc., New York.

No maps, illustrations, or other portions of this book may be reproduced in any form without written permission from the publisher.

ISBN 978–1–4000–1780–5

ISSN 1554–5881

Second Edition

SPECIAL SALES

This book is available for special discounts for bulk purchases for sales promotions or premiums. Special editions, including personalized covers, excerpts of existing books, and corporate imprints, can be created in large quantities for special needs. For more information, write to Special Markets/ Premium Sales, 1745 Broadway, MD 6-2, New York, New York 10019, or e-mail specialmarkets@ randomhouse.com.

AN IMPORTANT TIP & AN INVITATION

Although all prices, opening times, and other details in this book are based on information supplied to us at press time, changes occur all the time in the travel world, and Fodor's cannot accept responsibility for facts that become outdated or for inadvertent errors or omissions. So **always confirm information when it matters,** especially if you're making a detour to visit a specific place. Your experiences—positive and negative—matter to us. If we have missed or misstated something, **please write to us.** We follow up on all suggestions. Contact the Tokyo editor at editors@fodors .com or c/o Fodor's at 1745 Broadway, New York, New York 10019.

PRINTED IN THE UNITED STATES OF AMERICA

10 9 8 7 6 5 4 3 2 1

Your opinion matters. It matters to us. It matters to your fellow Fodor's travelers, too. And we'd like to hear it. In fact, we *need* to hear it.

When you share your experiences and opinions, you become an active member of the Fodor's community. That means we'll not only use your feedback to make our books better, but we'll publish your name and comments whenever possible. Throughout our guides, look for "Word of Mouth," excerpts of your unvarnished feedback.

Here's how you can help improve Fodor's for all of us.

Tell us when we're right. We rely on local writers to give you an insider's perspective. But our writers and staff editors—who are the best in the business—depend on you. Your positive feedback is a vote to renew our recommendations for the next edition.

Tell us when we're wrong. We're proud that we update most of our guides every year. But we're not perfect. Things change. Hotels cut services. Museums change hours. Charming cafés lose charm. If our writer didn't quite capture the essence of a place, tell us how you'd do it differently. If any of our descriptions are inaccurate or inadequate, we'll incorporate your changes in the next edition and will correct factual errors at fodors.com *immediately.*

Tell us what to include. You probably have had fantastic travel experiences that aren't yet in Fodor's. Why not share them with a community of like-minded travelers? Maybe you chanced upon a beach or bistro or B&B that you don't want to keep to yourself. Tell us why we should include it. And share your discoveries and experiences with everyone directly at fodors.com. Your input may lead us to add a new listing or highlight a place we cover with a "Highly Recommended" star or with our highest rating, "Fodor's Choice."

Give us your opinion instantly at our feedback center at www.fodors.com/feedback. You may also e-mail editors@fodors.com with the subject line "Tōkyō Editor." Or send your nominations, comments, and complaints by mail to Tōkyō Editor, Fodor's, 1745 Broadway, New York, NY 10019.

You and travelers like you are the heart of the Fodor's community. Make our community richer by sharing your experiences. Be a Fodor's correspondent.

Itterasshai! (Or simply: Happy traveling!)

Tim Jarrell, Publisher

CONTENTS

MAPS

CONTENTS

ABOUT THIS BOOK

Our Ratings

Sometimes you find terrific travel experiences and sometimes they just find you. But usually the burden is on you to select the right combination of experiences. That's where our ratings come in.

As travelers we've all discovered a place so wonderful that its worthiness is obvious. And sometimes that place is so unique that superlatives don't do it justice: you just have to be there to know. These sights, properties, and experiences get our highest rating, **Fodor's Choice,** indicated by orange stars throughout this book.

Black stars highlight sights and properties we deem **Highly Recommended,** places that our writers, editors, and readers praise again and again for consistency and excellence.

By default, there's another category: any place we include in this book is by definition worth your time, unless we say otherwise. And we will.

Disagree with any of our choices? Care to nominate a place or suggest that we rate one more highly? Visit our feedback center at www.fodors.com/feedback.

Budget Well

Hotel and restaurant price categories from ¢ to $$$$ are defined in the opening pages of each chapter. For attractions, we always give standard adult admission fees; reductions are usually available for children, students, and senior citizens. Want to pay with plastic? **AE, D, DC, MC, V** following restaurant and hotel listings indicate whether American Express, Discover, Diner's Club, MasterCard, and Visa are accepted.

Restaurants

Unless we state otherwise, restaurants are open for lunch and dinner daily. We mention dress only when there's a specific requirement and reservations only when they're essential or not accepted—it's always best to book ahead.

Hotels

Hotels have private bath, phone, TV, and air-conditioning and operate on the European Plan (aka EP, meaning without meals), unless we specify that they use the Continental Plan (CP, with a Continental breakfast), Breakfast Plan (BP, with a full breakfast), or Modified American Plan (MAP, with breakfast and dinner) or are all-inclusive (including all meals and most activities). We always

list facilities but not whether you'll be charged an extra fee to use them, so when pricing accommodations, find out what's included.

Many Listings
- ★ Fodor's Choice
- ★ Highly recommended
- ✉ Physical address
- ✛ Directions
- ⌂ Mailing address
- ☎ Telephone
- 🖷 Fax
- 🌐 On the Web
- ✐ E-mail
- 🖾 Admission fee
- ☉ Open/closed times
- ▶ Start of walk/itinerary
- Ⓜ Metro stations
- 🖽 Credit cards

Hotels & Restaurants
- 🏨 Hotel
- ⟿ Number of rooms
- ☖ Facilities
- ¶◎¶ Meal plans
- ✗ Restaurant
- ☖ Reservations
- 🏛 Dress code
- ⤵ Smoking
- 🔞 BYOB
- ✗🏨 Hotel with restaurant that warrants a visit

Outdoors
- 🏌 Golf
- ⚠ Camping

Other
- Ⓒ Family-friendly
- 🎛 Contact information
- ⇨ See also
- ✉ Branch address
- ☞ Take note

HOKKAIDŌ
(see inset)

Hakodate

Tsugaru Peninsula

Shimokita Peninsula

NIHON–KAI
(Sea of Japan)

Aomori

Akita   Morioka

Tono

Tsuruoka

Sado Island

Niigata   Yamagata   **Sendai**

Noto Peninsula

Fukushima

Kanazawa   Toyama   Nikko

Fukui   Nagano   Utsunomiya

Matsumoto   Oyama

Takayama   Maebashi   Mito

Maibara   Kofu

Kyōto   Gifu   **Tōkyō**

...aka   **Nagoya**   *Fuji-san* ▲   Chiba

Nara   Tsu   Yokohama

...ma   Shizuoka   Kamakura

Koya-san ▲   Ise   *Izu Peninsula*   *Oshima*

...ngu

HONSHŪ

TAIHEIYŌ
(Pacific Ocean)

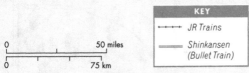

KEY
+—+— *JR Trains*
——— *Shinkansen (Bullet Train)*

0 ___ 50 miles
0 ___ 75 km

Japan

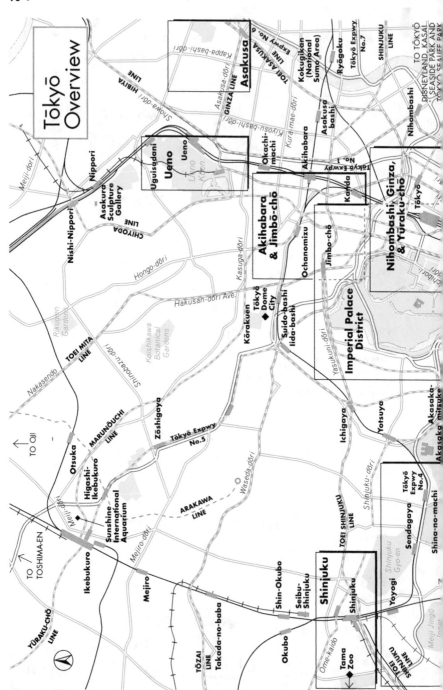

Tōkyō Overview

Asakusa

Ueno

Akihabara & Jimbō-chō

Nihombashi, Ginza, & Yūraku-chō

Imperial Palace District

Shinjuku

GINZA LINE

TOEI ASAKUSA LINE

HIBIYA LINE

CHIYODA LINE

TOEI MITA LINE

MARUNŌUCHI LINE

ARAKAWA LINE

TOEI SHINJUKU LINE

TŌZAI LINE

YŪRAKU-CHŌ LINE

SHINJUKU LINE

Kappa-bashi-dōri

Asakusa-dōri

Tōkyō Expwy No. 6

Kokugikan (National Sumō Area)

Ryōgoku

Tōkyō Expwy No. 7

SHINJUKU LINE

TO TŌKYŌ DISNEYLAND, KASAI SEASIDE PARK AND TOKYO CRUISE PARK

Kiyosu-bashi-dōri

Kura-mae-dōri

Asakusa-bashi

Nihombashi

Showa-dōri

Meiji-dōri

Nippori

Nishi-Nippori

Uguisudani

Ueno

Ueno Kōen

Asakura Sculpture Gallery

Okachi-machi

Akihabara

Tōkyō Expwy No. 1

Kanda

Ochanomizu

Jimbo-chō

Tōkyō

Shirobori

Hongo-dōri

Hakusan-dōri Ave.

Kasuga-dōri

Rikugien Gardens

Koishikawa Botanical Gardens

Kōrakuen

Tōkyō Dome City ◆

Suido-bashi

Iida-bashi

Yasukuni-dōri

Nakasendo

Shinobazu-dōri

← TO OJI

Otsuka

Zōshigaya

Tōkyō Expwy No. 5

Ichigaya

Yotsuya

Akasaka-mitsuke

Higashi-Ikebukuro

Sunshine International Aquarium

Waseda-dōri

TO TOSHIMA-EN

Ikebukuro

Mejiro-dōri

Mejiro

Okubo

Takada-no-baba

Shin-Okubo

Seibu-Shinjuku

Shinjuku

Yoyogi

Sendagaya

Shinjuku-dōri

Tōkyō Expwy No. 4

Shina-no-machi

Shinjuku Gyo-en

Ome-kaido

Tama Zoo ↓

Meiji Jingū

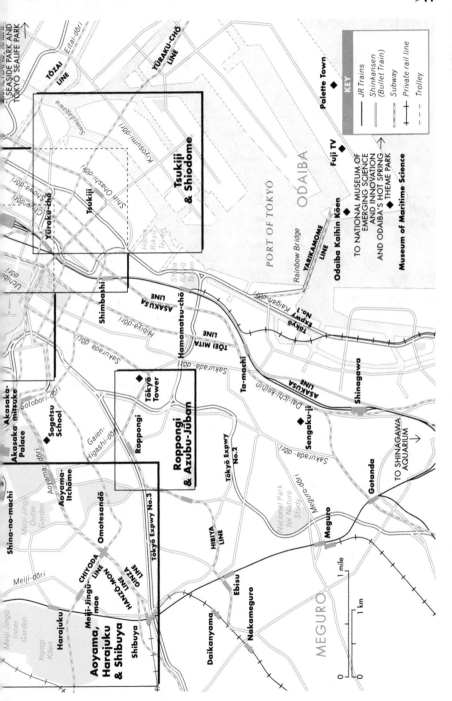

SEASIDE PARK AND
TOKYO SEALIFE PARK →

TŌZAI LINE
Eitai-dōri

YŪRAKU-CHŌ LINE

Sumidagawa

Kiyosumi-dōri

Shōwa-dōri

Shin Ōhashi-dōri

Chūō-dōri

Tsukiji & Shiodome

Yūraku-chō

Tsukiji

Uchibo-dōri

Hama Rikyū Tei-en

Shiba Rikyū Tei-en

Shimbashi

Hibiya-dōri

ASAKUSA LINE

Hamamatsu-chō

TŌEI MITA LINE

Sakurada-dōri

Sakurada-dōri

Ta-machi

Dai-ichi-keihin

ASAKUSA LINE

Shinagawa

PORT OF TOKYO

Rainbow Bridge

YARIKAMOME LINE

Ta-gan-dōri

Tōkyō Expwy No.1

ODAIBA

Palette Town ◆

Fuji TV ◆

Odaiba Kaihin Kōen ◆

TO NATIONAL MUSEUM OF
EMERGING SCIENCE
AND INNOVATION
AND ODAIBA'S HOT SPRING →
THEME PARK

Museum of Maritime Science ◆

Akasaka-
mitsuke

Akasaka Palace

Sogetsu School ◆

Sotobori-dōri

Aoyama-dōri

Gaien-Higashi-dōri

Tōkyō Tower ◆

Roppongi ◆

Roppongi & Azubu-Jūban

Tōkyō Expwy No.2

Sengaku-ji ◆

National Park for Nature Study

Meguro-dōri

Sakurada-dōri

Gotanda

Shinagawa

TO SHINAGAWA
AQUARIUM →

Shina-no-machi

Meiji Jingū Outer Garden

Aoyama-Itchōme

Omotesandō

CHIYODA LINE

GINZA LINE

Tōkyō Expwy No.3

HANZŌ-MON LINE

Meiji-dōri

Meiji Jingū Inner Garden

Harajuku

Meiji-Jingū-mae

Shibuya

Aoyama, Harajuku & Shibuya

HIBIYA LINE

Meguro

Ebisu

Daikanyama

Nakameguro

Yoyogi Kōen

MEGURO

1 mile

1 km

0

0

KEY

JR Trains

Shinkansen (Bullet Train)

Subway

Private rail line

Trolley

WHAT'S WHERE

Tōkyō commands a prominent position in the Kantō region on the southern coast of Honshū, Japan's largest island. Some 12 million people live in or within commuting distance of the capital and like most big cities, several colorful neighborhoods are stitched together, each with its own texture. A few of the most important neighborhoods for visitors are profiled below.

IMPERIAL PALACE DISTRICT

Kōkyo, the Imperial Palace, is at the center of Tōkyō where Edo Castle once stood. Although the imperial residence is only open two days a year, you can always explore the palace grounds and gardens. Near the palace are several important museums, Yasukuni Jinja shrine, the Japanese parliament and supreme court buildings, and the National Theater, as well as Tōkyō station.

AKIHABARA & JIMBŌ-CHŌ

Akihabara and Jimbō-chō are northeast of the Imperial Palace grounds. Akihabara is famed for its electronics wares—from big-box brand-name stores to do-it-yourself shops—as well as the comics, DVD, and memorabilia shops and cafés, where waitresses don maid attire and address patrons as *master*. The theme is more cerebral in Jimbō-chō. This neighborhood is filled with booksellers hawking anything printed including antique wood-block books, cheap dictionaries in every tongue, scrolls, and current literature. If you're inspired to compose your own prose, this is the place to stock up on everything from stationery to fancy pen sets.

UENO

Ueno Park, directly north of Akihabara, is home to three superb national museums, a university of fine arts, and a zoo. A stone's-throw south, just before Okachimachi, is Ameyoko market street. A throwback from its black-market origins during the U.S. occupation, the area is now geared more towards locals looking for legit Western wares. Its inviting eateries can be a nice reprieve between museum visits.

ASAKUSA

Asakusa, in the northeastern part of the city, is an essential Tōkyō experience. Here, the sacred merges with secular and ancient tradition meets modernity. The area is home to Tōkyō's oldest temple, the 13th-century Sensō-ji, as well as the Asakusa Jinja shrine. History just outside these hallowed grounds is no less rich. Once the city's suburban playground for urbanites, it's now home to artists, hipsters, and generations of locals fiercely proud of and loyal to their neighborhood.

TSUKIJI & SHIODOME	Tsukiji, in southeastern Tōkyō on the Sumida-gawa River, is home to the famed sumō stables, as well as what's purportedly the world's largest fish market—The Central Wholesale Market. With nearly 1,000 venders hawking some 2,000 metric tons of fish and seafood a day, this vivacious center of commerce contributes to the city's annual 600-billion-yen market. Shiodome, a bit farther inland, is a massive development zone, with plenty of fashionable shops and restaurants. Most of the area was built after 2000 and includes the Nippon Television Tower and the replica of the Shinbashi railway Station.
NIHOMBASHI, GINZA & YŪRAKU-CHŌ	Nihombashi, east of the Imperial Palace, lays claim to the geographical and financial center of Tōkyō. Follow the money slightly south to Ginza, where you'll find Tōkyō's traditional high-end department-store haven. Local big-name chains such as Matsuya, Matsuzakaya, and Mitsukoshi captivate with fashion, fine foods, and accessories alongside boutiques selling traditional and modern wares, plus hundreds of art galleries. Yūraku-chō, between Ginza and the Outer Garden of the Imperial Palace, flourished as black-market central during World War II. Today it's an upscale commercial area with shops, restaurants, and a Western-style park.
AOYAMA, HARAJUKU, & SHIBUYA	Aoyama and Harajuku, west of the Imperial Palace, were developed for the 1964 Olympics and today are chic neighborhoods saturated with designer and chain stores, independent boutiques, and malls where high fashion is the name of the game. To the south is Shibuya, which is more than a major transportation hub: it's an urban teen's dream. This loud, sprawling, neon jungle is packed with people, hip shops, mega-chain stores, and eateries.
ROPPONGI & AZABU-JŪBAN	Southeast of Shibuya is Roppongi, with a rich and sometimes sordid history of catering to foreign nightlife that dates back to the U.S. occupation. Here you'll find the massive Roppongi Hills development, which is comprised of high-end residences, restaurants, offices, and shops as well as some big-name businesses. However, this nightclub-saturated neighborhood, long home to ex-pats, U.S. military, and nearby embassies, is more notorious for its weekend revelers. Azabu-Jūban is located just south of Roppongi, within seven minute walking-distance from Roppongi Hills, or a short subway ride on the Toei Ōedo line to Azabu-Jūban station. It's a prestigious residential district with many embassies.

WHAT'S
WHERE

SHINJUKU	Shinjuku, northeast of Roppongi, is the seat of the city's government and home to, what is said to be, the busiest train station (of the same name) in the world. The station is adjacent to Takashimaya Times Square, a towering mall that includes department stores, shops, and restaurants. When the sun sets on Shinjuku, the area lights up like fireworks with bars, clubs, and the famed red-light district. Shinjuku is also home to the towering Tōkyō Tochō complex, whose observation platforms provide sweeping views, and the Tōkyō Dome, whose bleachers envelope thousands of passionate baseball fans.
SIDE TRIPS FROM TŌKYŌ	If Tōkyō were rows of Quonset huts, it would still be worth staying in for the side trips nearby. Start with lunch in **Yokohama's** Chinatown, where more than 150 restaurants serve every major regional Chinese cuisine and all things Chinese beckon from a warren of shops in narrow lanes. Far removed from such urban bustle lie **Nikkō** and the **Tōshō-gū** shrine complex, stirring in its sheer scale alone. Some call it sublime, some excessive, but no one finds it dull. At a nearby national park, **Chūzenji-ko (Lake Chūzenji)** and waterfalls like Kegon-no-taki nourish the spirit. The national park and resort area of **Hakone** puts you close to majestic **Fuji-san,** which you can climb in summer without special gear. In **Hase,** the 37-foot Daibutsu—the Great Buddha—has sat for seven centuries, serenely gazing inward. The temples and shrines of nearby **Kamakura,** 13th-century capital of Japan, remind you that this was an important religious as well as political center. Break away from the tourists and enjoy a moment of peace: the clamor of Tōkyō falls silent here in the ancient heart of Japan.

WHEN TO GO

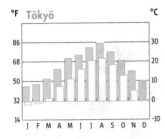

°F Tōkyō °C

The climate in Japan resembles that of the east coast of the United States, and the best time to visit Tōkyō is spring and fall. Spring is beautiful and much celebrated. The first harbingers are plum blossoms in early March, followed by the *sakura* (cherry blossoms) in early April, and festivals celebrating springtime last until June. Fall has clear blue skies and glorious foliage. Occasionally a few typhoons occur in early fall, but the storms are usually harmless and are as quick to disappear as they are to appear, leaving behind crystal clear skies.

Summer in Tōkyō can be unbearably hot in part due to the "heat island" effect, which occurs when exhausts from buildings in the crowded center affect the weather generally, raising the temperature and humidity to subtropical levels. It's also the rainy season, so avoid July and August if at all possible. Winter is gray and chilly. Western Japan receives plenty of snow, though Tōkyō and other areas along the Pacific Coast don't get much at all.

For the most part, Japanese cannot choose when they want to take their vacations and tend to do so on the same holiday dates. To avoid stifling crowds and long waits, do not plan a trip to Tōkyō for the few days before and after New Year's; Golden Week, which follows Greenery Day (April 29); and the Obon Festival (August 13 through 16). Airports, planes, trains, and hotels are usually booked far in advance for these dates and prices increase significantly. Also, many businesses, shops, and restaurants are closed during these holidays (except for tourist attractions outside the city).

🔲 Forecasts **Weather Channel** (🌐 www.weather.com).

Yahoo! Asia (🌐 http://asia.weather.yahoo.com).

QUINTESSENTIAL TŌKYŌ

Sushi

In Japan, sushi is a revered art form practiced only by the highly trained and licensed. You can not leave Tōkyō without having the essential sushi experience. Try *nigiri* (rice nuggets elegantly topped), *chirashi-zushi* (artfully capped rice bowls), *maki* (seaweed-wrapped sea treasures), or sashimi (fish sliced thin á la cart) with glutinous rice that's cooked to perfection, freshly grated wasabi root, and finely fermented *shōyū* (soy sauce). If you're feeling bold, try squid, sea urchin, or even raw horsemeat. If you're looking for something truly unique stop by a *kaiten* sushi restaurant, and get your sushi from a conveyor belt. Not all the dishes are pre-made and you can request something made-to-order. Major chains challenge even local sensibilities with mayo-topped sushi and meatballs or fried chicken wrapped with rice in seaweed.

Festivals

Untold eons before Buddhism came to Japan, Shinto, in its countless local expressions, was the dominant faith. These days, Shinto demigods share an equal place with bodhisattvas, or Buddhist deities, in the hearts and minds of locals. Most celebrants of Shinto festivals view them as cultural, not religious, and these *matsuri* are rare chances to see age-old tradition in postmodern Tokyo. Based on localized nature-centered customs, these festivals vary slightly. What they share is a ruckus, all-are-welcome block party where *mikoshi* (portable shrines) are boisterously paraded about by locals, and men sometimes clad only in loincloths. They include food, souvenirs, and kiddy game booths as well as plenty of libations. Virtually every neighborhood has one but the city's most famed are the **Kanda Festival**, at Kanda Myojin Shrine in Chiyoda-ku (May 15 every odd-numbered year) and the **Sanja Festival**, at Asakusa Jinja in the third week of May.

Shopping

In the capitol city of the world's second largest economy, shopping is a national pastime. No place better represents this than Harajuku, a fashion-conscious paradise of commerce and chic cafés. You won't hear the familiar barker's cry of *irasshaimase!* (welcome) here. Instead, white-gloved salespeople inside sleek edifices labeled Dior, Chanel, Tagheuer, and Ralph Lauren found along the main drag of Omotesando-dōri (street) are wont to pamper well-heeled patrons. Whether you aim to window shop or shop till you drop, this is your ultimate chance. Careen onto bustling Takashita Street, which caters to the less affluent, but equally fashion conscious, to see how local fashion is no judge of person—or pocketbook. Continue off the beaten path (literally and figuratively) to Harajuku Street and other winding byways where accessories and experiences can help you make a personalized fashion statement of your own.

Karaoke

When Japan's Daisuke Inoue accepted the 2004 Ig Nobel Prize for inventing the Karaoke machine and inspiring people, "to tolerate each other," he sang: "I'd like to teach the world to sing, in perfect harmony . . ." It may be marginally successful in other parts of the world but in Japan *karaōké* is a way of life. This national icebreaker and party favorite is the mainstay of many a social event and the focus of ubiquitous karaoke clubs frequented by locals from all walks of life. It's a social safe haven, allowing cut-loose crooning and nothing but applause from captive on-listeners. Most karaoke clubs offer private rooms, beverages, and snacks with a menu of Western and local pop favorites to choose from. Translations of familiar favorites may tempt a chuckle, but beware: if you're among locals, like it or not, you're next.

IF YOU LIKE

Nightlife

Wining and dining, cocktails with class, the sultry sounds of jazz or clubbing and carousing. You'll find it all and more beneath Tōkyō's neon-soaked night sky where the city's popular nightspots are open till the early morning hours. Tipping is uncustomary, but some upscale establishments may have extra service charges that range from a few hundred yen to a few thousand. Karaoke clubs and *Izakaya*, the traditional watering holes of office workers, are ubiquitous and a great way to mix with locals. All-night revelers might want to consider the likes of Shinjuku or Roppongi, but more tame entertainment is available in Shinjuku's many cinemas and theaters. Follow that up with a leisurely stroll through the bustling nightlife.

Kabuki-za, Ginza. There's no better place to catch a Kabuki performance than at this theater.

Montoak, Shibuya. This super-cool three-storied lounge in the Omotesandō high-fashion district offers cocktails and canapés to those in the know.

Sekirei, Akasaka. On sunny days nothing beats having a drink at this inexpensive outdoor bar on the grounds of the Meiji-Kinenkan complex.

Sweet Basil 139, Roppongi. Come for dinner or just a drink at this upscale club featuring a variety of musical performances, considered by many to be Tōkyō's best.

Natural Wonders

Tōkyō is an urban paradise for traveler and resident alike. That doesn't mean, however, that local Japanese sensibilities—steeped in centuries of cultural appreciation for nature—have been paved over.

Much like inner-city cherry blossom viewing, tiny veranda gardens, and well-groomed parks, nature's more awesome wonders are well preserved too—albeit just outside the concrete jungle. If you pine for more pristine surroundings follow the lead of the locals.

Every year roughly 300,000 Tōkyōites and visitors scale nearby Mt. Fuji during peak climbing season (July and August). It's an opportunity a local saying deems "foolish" to pass up (or to do more than once). While thousands take to Nikkō National Park to see Kegon Falls and other natural wonders, especially when foliage begins to bloom in spring.

Fuji-san, in Fuji-Hakone-Izu National Park, is well within reach of the big city. Whether you climb to the summit or view it from afar, beautiful, snow-capped Mt. Fuji is bound to make an impression.

Kegon Falls is about two hours from Tōkyō in Nikkō National Park. You can view Japan's most famous waterfall from either the top or the bottom of the 318-foot drop and make a day of enjoying this shrine-peppered scenic park.

Onsen

Japan is perched on a geothermal goldmine and *onsen* (hot-springs) are everywhere. Locals consider bathing in these hot springs to be a near ritual experience, with unique healing properties to the water. These baths are more about self-pampering than getting clean, but give yourself a thorough shower before your soak. Proper etiquette demands it.

There are indoor and outdoor pools of different sizes, with varying temperatures to choose from, but the ones outside are best if you want to admire the natural setting. Some places may also offer a sauna or professional massage. Afterwards, retire to the casual dinning room for a light meal or some saké and lounging at a low table on a *tatami* (straw mat) floor where even napping is permissible.

Oedo Onsen Monogatari, at Yurikamome Telecom Center in Odaiba, pays homage to this tradition at an Edo-period–style facility with all the trimmings; it's the city's finest.

Hakōné Kowakien Yunessun Resort is just 90 minutes by train from Tōkyō in the Kanagawa Prefecture. The area is famed for its abundance of onsen resorts and inns, from the budget to the lavish. The resort offers an exquisite traditional onsen, water amusement park, and bathing-suit-only grounds. Visitors can even soak in green tea and saké.

Kusatsu Onsen, three hours from Tōkyō and some 1,200 meters above sea level in Guma Prefecture, is for those with a generous itinerary. Japanese have flocked to it for centuries for all manner of cures including the most dreaded—lovesickness.

Baseball

It's fair to say that baseball is as much a national pastime in Japan as it is in the States. The Japanese have adopted and adapted this Western sport in a way that makes it a fascinating and easy-to-grasp microcosm of both their culture and their overall relationship to things Western. The team names alone—the Orix BlueWave and the Hiroshima Carp, for example—have an amusing appeal to Westerners accustomed to such monikers as the Yankees and the Indians, and the fans' cheers are chanted more in unison than in U.S. ballparks. The season runs from April through October. Same-day tickets are hard to come by; try the respective stadiums or the ticket agency Playguide (☎ 03/3561–8821). Depending on the stadium, the date, and the seat location, expect to pay from ¥1,700 to ¥8,000 for an afternoon at the ballpark.

Tōkyō Dome at Kōraku-en, which seats 45,600, is the place to see pro ball in the big city and it is home to one of Tōkyō's two home teams, the Yomiuri Giants. ✉ *1–3–61 Kōraku, Bunkyō-ku* ☎ *03/5800–9999* ⊕ *www.tokyo-dome.co.jp* Ⓜ *Marunouchi and Namboku lines, Kōraku-en Station (Exit 2); Toei Ōedo and Toei Mita lines, Kasuga Station (Exit A2); JR Chūō line, Suidō-bashi Station (West Exit).*

Meiji Jingū Baseball Stadium, in the Outer Gardens of Meiji Jingū, is the home turf of the Yakult Swallows, the city's second team. ✉ *13 Kasumigaoka, Shinjuku-ku* ☎ *03/ 3404–8999* Ⓜ *Ginza Line, Gaien-mae Station (Exit 2); JR Chūō line, Shinanomachi Station.*

GREAT ITINERARIES

TŌKYŌ IN 3 DAYS

You need three days just to take in the highlights of Tōkyō and still have time for some shopping and nightlife. With four or five days you can explore the city in greater depth, wander off the beaten path, and appreciate Tōkyō's museums at leisure. More time would allow for day trips to scenic and historical sights in communities outside the city.

Day 1

Start *very* early (5 AM) with a visit to the **Tōkyō Central Wholesale Market** (Tōkyō Chūō Oroshiuri Ichiba) in the Tsukiji district. (If you're feeling adventurous or can't sleep, take full advantage of your jetlag by starting your trip with nightlife in parts of the city that never sleep.) Direct train service starts around 5 AM from Shinjuku (Toei Oedo line) or Roppongi (Hibiya subway line) and gets you to Tsukiji or Tsukujishijo stations respectively in under 20 minutes. Or take a taxi. Then use the rest of the day for a tour of the **Imperial Palace** and environs.

Day 2

Spend the morning of Day 2 at **Sensō-ji** and adjacent **Asakusa Jinja** in Asakusa. If you're looking for souvenir gifts—sacred or secular—allow time and tote space for the abundant selection local vendors have to offer. From there, head to **Ueno** for an afternoon with its many museums, vistas, and historic sites.

Day 3

Start Day 3 with a morning stroll through **Ginza** to explore its fabled shops and *depāto* (department stores). Then hit a chic restaurant or café for lunch (more reasonably priced ones are easily found on the upper floor of most department stores). In the afternoon, see the Shintō shrine, **Meiji Jingū** and take a leisurely walk through the nearby Harajuku and Omotesandō fashion districts to the **Nezu Institute of Fine Arts**—a perfect oasis for your last impressions of the city.

TŌKYŌ IN 5 DAYS

Day 4

Follow the previous itinerary, adding to it a morning of browsing in **Akihabara,** Tōkyō's electronics quarter, and a visit to nearby Shintō **Kanda Myōjin.** Spend the afternoon on the west side of **Shinjuku,** Tōkyō's 21st-century model city; savor the view from the observation deck of architect Kenzō Tange's monumental **Tōkyō Metropolitan Government Office;** and cap off the day with a walk through the greenery of **Shinjuku Gyo-en National Garden.**

Day 5

The luxury of a fifth day would allow you to fill in the missing pieces: the Buddhist temple, **Sengaku-ji** in Shinagawa, the remarkable **Edo-Tōkyō Hakubutsukan** in **Ryōgoku,** a tea ceremony, kabuki play, or any of the shops you passed by. See a sumō tournament, if there's one in town. Or just visit the **Kokugikan,** National Sumō Arena, in the Ryōgoku district, and some of the sumō stables in the neighborhood.

If You Have More Time

With a week or more, you can make Tōkyō your home base for a series of side trips (⇨ Chapter 6). After getting your fill of Tōkyō, take a train out to **Yokohama,** with its scenic port and Chinatown. A bit farther away but still easily accessible by train is **Kamakura,** the 12th-century military capital of Japan. The **Great Buddha** (Daibutsu) of the **Kōtoku-in** is but one of the National Treasures of art and architecture here that draw millions of visitors a year. For both Yokohama and Kamakura, an early morning start will allow you to see most of the important sights in a full day and make it

back to Tōkyō by late evening. As Kamakura is one of the most popular of excursions from Tōkyō, avoid the worst of the crowds by making the trip on a weekday, but time it to avoid rush-hour commuting that peaks roughly at 8 AM and just after 6 PM.

Still farther off, but again an easy train trip, is **Nikkō,** where the founder of the Tokugawa Shōgun dynasty is enshrined. **Tōshō-gū** is a monument unlike any other in Japan, and the picturesque **Lake Chūzen-ji** is in a forest above the shrine. Two full days, with an overnight stay, would allow you an ideal, leisurely exploration of both. Yet another option would be a trip to **Hakone** where you can soak in a traditional onsen or venture a climb to the summit of **Fuji-san** (Mt. Fuji).

ON THE CALENDAR

Matsuri (festivals) are very important to the Japanese, and hundreds of them are held throughout the year. Many originated in folk and religious rituals and date back hundreds of years. Gala matsuri often take place annually at Buddhist temples and Shintō shrines, and many are associated with the seasons.

To find out specific matsuri dates, contact the **Japan National Tourism Organization** (☎ 212/757–5640 in U.S., 03/3201–3331 in Tōkyō).

Note: When national holidays fall on Sunday, they are celebrated on the following Monday. Museums, embassies, and government offices are often closed on these days.

WINTER January 1	New Year's Day, along with the days preceding and following, is the festival of festivals for the Japanese. Some women dress in traditional kimonos, and many people visit shrines and hold family reunions. Streets are often decorated with pine twigs, plum branches, and bamboo stalks.
January 2	On the days immediately following New Year's, join the early morning lines outside budget shops and high-end department stores for the annual *fūkūbūkūrō* craze. These traditional grab-bag bonanzas allow stores to clear out their year-end inventories and shoppers can purchase items at rock-bottom prices.
2nd Monday of January	Coming of Age Day honors those reaching adulthood at the age of 20, earning the right to vote, drink, and more. It's a time to see a more traditional side of modern Tōkyō. Men in suits and kimono-clad women go to and from events marking their right of passage.
SPRING April 29	Greenery Day marks the first day of Golden Week and the worst time to travel in Japan.
SUMMER August 13–16	During the Obon Festival, a Buddhist tradition honoring ancestors, many Japanese travel to their hometowns or vacation spots. Avoid travel on these days.
FALL December 23	On Tennō Tanjobi (the Emperor's birthday) Emperor Akihito makes an appearance on the balcony of the Imperial Palace. It's a rare event, so if you're in town don't miss it.
December 27	The city starts to wind down, and temples and shrines start to gear up for New Year's celebrations. Travel is *not* advised.

Exploring Tōkyō

WORD OF MOUTH

"There are many things that I love about Tōkyō, especially the food and the juxtaposition of the new and old."

—KMLoke

"One of my favorite memories of Tōkyō is that one minute you can be in the middle of the most up-to-date high-tech, high-fashion, high-everything shopping districts and then you can wander down a small street and come to a 1,000-year-old temple or even just a tiny traditional *okonomiyaki* restaurant."

—jules39

Updated by
Krista Kim-
Pickard

TŌKYŌ IS A CITY OF CONSTANT STIMULI. Complex, big, and always on the move, it's a place where opposites attract, and new trends come and go like the tide. The Japanese like harmony, which is reflected in a city that is both ancient and modern. It's a place where youth culture affects world trends; yet age-old traditions are deeply rooted. Tōkyōites aren't phased by complexity and change, which is why this city is in constant flux.

Greater Tōkyō incorporates 23 wards, 26 smaller cities, 7 towns, and 8 villages—altogether sprawling 88 km (55 mi) from east to west and 24 km (15 mi) from north to south with a population of 35 million people. The wards alone enclose an area of 590 square km (228 square mi), which comprise the city center and house 8 million residents. Chiyoda-ku, Chuo-ku, Shinju-ku, and Minato-ku are the four central business districts. Because of the easy access to the public transportation system, 48% of residents are transit commuters; only 32% drive to work. Most people live in the suburbs and average a 56-minute commute. During rush hour, an immense tidal wave of people floods all major transportation hubs, through which approximately 3 million people pass each day.

Why must the majority of people commute for almost an hour? Because space is the greatest luxury in Tōkyō and affordable housing is only found in the suburbs. An average Tōkyō resident probably lives in a cramped apartment that averages 80 square meters. A 62.25 square-meter apartment situated on top of the Omotesandō Hills complex is approximately ¥1 million per month to rent (around $8,500).

Tōkyō is a state-of-the-art financial marketplace, where billions of dollars are whisked electronically around the globe at the blink of an eye. However, most ATMs in the city shut down by 9 PM, so be sure to get enough cash when you find one. Most Citibank, Shinsei Bank (in most subway stations), and Japan Postal Savings ATMs allow international bank card transactions, but they are not always accessible. Tōkyō is a safe city, so you may carry cash without fear of street crime.

It's also a city of astonishing beauty, with a strong sense of tradition. On the flip side, it's also the center of futuristic design, lifestyle, and cutting edge urban trends. Each area of this city is distinct in its commercial and social activities.

Each city ward has its own pace and style, which is reflected in its history, architecture, by-laws, and atmosphere. You may smoke on the streets of Shinjuku, but not on the streets of Ginza (there's a ¥50,000 fine). Residents of Roppongi wear European designer fashion and drive luxury cars; residents of Asakusa are more traditional and ride the subway.

Widespread postwar construction had given the city an uneven look that is being replaced with large scale, designer architectural projects. Mori Building is at the forefront with its progressive Roppongi Hills (2003) and Omotestando Hills (2006) developments, and Mitsui Fudosan Co. Ltd., has joined in with the Midtown Project (2007) in Roppongi. Not only is this planned to be the tallest building in Tōkyō at 565 feet, it is also a collaboration of such famous designers as Pritzker Prize–winning architect Tadao Ando and fashion designer Issey Miyake and will house the Ritz-Carlton Hotel, a Johns Hopkins affiliated medical clinic, a conference center, and luxury residences.

Tōkyō is a vanguard of international cultural events and entertainment, attracting stars like Tom Cruise and Madonna, and world-class performances like the Berlin Philharmonic. Michelin-star chefs like Alain Ducasse and Pierre Gagnaire have launched restaurants here, making this city a top gourmet destination. If you're a foodie, artist, design lover, or cultural adventurer, then Tōkyō, a city of inspiration and ideas, is for you.

> ### DISCOUNTED MUSEUM ADMISSION
>
> If you plan on visiting a lot of the city's sites, purchasing a **GRUTT Pass** (⊕ www.museum.or.jp/grutto) is the way to go. The pass, which is only ¥2,000, gives visitors free or discounted admission to 49 sites throughout the city including museums, zoos, aquariums, and parks. Passes can be purchased at all participating sites, as well as the Tōkyō Tourist Information Center, or Family Mart and SevenEleven convenience stores. Keep in mind that passes expire two months after date of purchase.

IMPERIAL PALACE AND GOVERNMENT DISTRICT

The district of *Nagata-chō* is the core of Japan's government. It is primarily comprised of the Imperial Palace (*Kōkyo-gaien*), the Diet (national parliament building), the Prime Minister's residence (*Kantei*), and the Supreme Court. The Imperial Palace and the Diet are both important to see, but the Supreme Court is non-descript. Unfortunately, the Prime Minister's residence is only viewable from afar, hidden behind fortified walls and trees.

The Imperial Palace was built by the order of Ieyasu Tokugawa, who chose the site for his castle in 1590. The castle had 99 gates (36 in the outer wall), 21 watchtowers (of which three are still standing), and 28 armories. The outer defenses stretched from present-day Shimbashi Station to Kanda. Completed in 1640 (and later expanded), it was at the time the largest castle in the world. The Japanese Imperial Family resides in heavily blockaded sections of the palace grounds. Tours are conducted by reservation only, and restricted to designated outdoor sections, namely, the palace grounds and the East Gardens. The grounds are open to the general public only twice a year: on January 2 and December 23 (the Emperor's birthday), when thousands of people assemble under the balcony to offer their good wishes to the Imperial Family.

Numbers in the margin correspond to the Imperial Palace map.

Where's MapQuest When You Need It?

THE SIMPLEST WAY TO DECIPHER a Japanese address is to break it into parts. For example: 6-chōme 8–19, Chūō-ku, Fukuoka-shi, Fukuoka-ken. In this address the "chōme" indicates a precise area (a block, for example), and the numbers following "chōme" indicate the building within the area. Note that buildings aren't always numbered sequentially; numbers are often assigned as buildings are erected. Only local police officers and mail carriers in Japan seem to be familiar with the area defined by the chōme. Sometimes, instead of "chōme," "machi" (town) is used.

Written addresses in Japan have the opposite order of those in the West, with the city coming before the street. "Ku" refers to a ward (a district) of a city, "shi" refers to a city name, and "ken" indicates a prefecture, which is roughly equivalent to a state in the United States. It's not unusual for the prefecture and the city to have the same name, as in the above address. There are a few geographic areas in Japan that are not called ken. One is greater Tōkyō, which is called Tōkyō-to. Other exceptions are Kyōto and Ōsaka, which are followed by the suffix "-fu"–Kyōto-fu, Ōsaka-fu. Hokkaidō, Japan's northernmost island, is also not considered a ken. Not all addresses conform exactly to the above format. Rural addresses, for example, might use "gun" (county) where city addresses have "ku" (ward).

Even Japanese people cannot find a building based on the address alone. If you get in a taxi with a written address, do not assume the driver will be able to find your destination. Usually, people provide very detailed instructions or maps to explain their exact locations. It's always good to know the location of your destination in relation to a major building or department store.

Orientation & Planning

ORIENTATION The Imperial Palace is located in the heart of central Tōkyō and the city's other neighborhoods branch out from here. The palace, in which the Imperial Family still resides, is surrounded by a moat that connects through canals to Tōkyō Bay and Sumida river (*Sumida-gawa*) to the east. Outside the moat, large four-lane roads trace its outline, as if the city expanded from this primary location.

PLANNING The best way to discover the Imperial Palace is to take part in one of the free tours offered by the **Imperial Household Agency** (☎ 03/3213–1111 ⊕ www.kunaicho.go.jp), which manages matters of the state. There are four different tours: Imperial Palace Grounds, the East Gardens (*Higashi Gyo-en*), Sannomaru Shozokan, and Gagaku Performance (in autumn only). All tours require registration a day in advance and hours change according to the season.

If you are exploring on your own, allow at least an hour for the East Garden and Outer Garden of the palace itself. Plan to visit Yasukuni Jinja after lunch and spend at least an hour there. The Yūshūkan (at Yasukuni Jinja) and Kōgeikan museums are both small and should engage you for no more than a half hour each, but the modern art mu-

TOP REASONS TO VISIT

A City Oasis Located in the middle of the city, the Imperial Palace East Gardens is a wonderful place to escape the hustle and bustle of the city.

House of Parliament Looking something like a squat pyramid, the National Diet Building houses Japan's parliament.

A Peaceful Shrine? The Yasukuni Shrine (Shrine of Peace for the Nation), which represents Japan's

militaristic past, has long been the source of political tension between Japan and its neighbors, Korea and China.

Art Abounds The finest collection from Japanese modern artists are housed in the National Museum of Modern Art, including works by such renowned painters as Taikan Yokoyama, Gyoshū Hayami, Kokei Kobayashi, and Gyokudō Kawai.

seum requires a more leisurely visit—particularly if there's a special exhibit. The best time to visit is during the spring when the *ōhanami* (cherry trees) are in bloom between late March and early April, or during the Yasukuni Spring festival (April 21–23), which pays homage to the war-dead and shrine deities.

■ TIP→ Avoid visiting the Imperial Palace on Monday, when the East Garden and museums are closed; the East Garden is also closed Friday. In July and August, heat will make the palace walk grueling—bring hats and bottled water.

The best way to get to the Imperial Palace is by subway. Take the Nijubashimae (Chiyoda line) Exit 6 or Tōkyō (JR line) Exit to Maranouchi Central. There are three entrance gates—Ōte-mon, Hirakawa-mon, and Kita-hane-bashi-mon. You can easily get to any of the three from the Ōte-machi or Takebashi subway station.

What to See

❶ **Chidori-ga-fuchi National Memorial Garden.** High on the edge of the Imperial Palace moat, this park is famous for its cherry tree blossoms, which appear in spring. The most popular activity in this garden is renting rowboats on the moat at the **Chidori-ga-fuchi Boathouse.** The entrance to the garden is near Yasukuni Jinja. ⊠ *Chiyoda-ku* ☎ *03/3234–1948* ⊠ *Park free, boat rental ¥500 for 30 min during regular season, and ¥800 for 30 min during cherry blossom season* ⊙ *Park daily sunrise–sunset, boathouse daily 9:30–4, usually late Mar.–early Apr.* Ⓜ *Hanzō-mon and Shinjuku subway lines, Kudanshita Station (Exit 2).*

❽ **Hanzō-mon** (Hanzō Gate). The house of the legendary Hattori Hanzō (1541–1596) once sat at the foot of this small wooden gate. Hanzō was a legendary leader of Ieyasu Tokugawa's private corps of spies and infiltrators—and assassins, if need be. They were the menacing, black-clad ninja—perennial material for historical adventure films and television dramas. The gate is a minute's walk from the subway. ⊠ *Chiyoda-ku* Ⓜ *Hanzō-mon subway line, Hanzō-mon Station (Exit 3).*

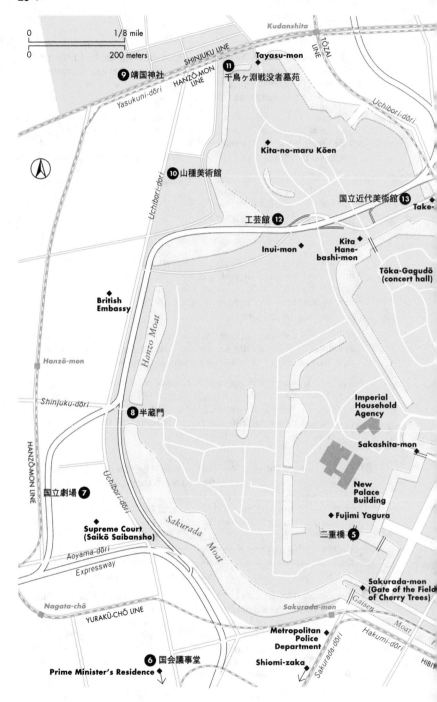

0

0

1/8 mile

200 meters

Kudanshita

SHINJUKU LINE

Yasukuni-dōri

HANZŌ-MON LINE

9 靖国神社

Uchibori-dōri

TŌZAI LINE

Tayasu-mon

11 千鳥ヶ淵戦没者墓苑

Uchibori-dōri

Kita-no-maru Kōen

10 山種美術館

国立近代美術館 **13**

Take-

工芸館 **12**

Inui-mon

Kita
Hane-
bashi-mon

Tōka-Gagudō
(concert hall)

British
Embassy

Hanzo Moat

Hanzō-mon

Shinjuku-dōri

8 半蔵門

Imperial
Household
Agency

Sakashita-mon

HANZŌ-MON LINE

Uchibori-dōri

国立劇場 **7**

New
Palace
Building

Fujimi Yagura

Supreme Court
(Saikō Saibansho)

Sakurada Moat

二重橋 **5**

Aoyama-dōri

Expressway

Sakurada-mon
(Gate of the Field
of Cherry Trees)

Nagata-chō

YURAKŪ-CHŌ LINE

Sakurada-mon

Gaisen

Moat

Hakumi-dōri

Metropolitan
Police
Department

6 国会議事堂

Shiomi-zaka

Prime Minister's Residence ↓

Sakurada-dōri

HIBIY

Imperial Palace & Government District

⓮ **Hirakawa-mon** (Hirakawa Gate). The approach to this gate crosses the only wooden bridge that spans the Imperial Palace moat. The gate and bridge are reconstructions, but Hirakawa-mon is especially beautiful, looking much as it must have when the shōgun's wives and concubines used it on their rare excursions from the seraglio. ⊠ *Chiyoda-ku* Ⓜ *Tōzai subway line, Takebashi Station (Exit 1A).*

❸ **Imperial Palace East Garden** (Kōkyo Higashi Gyo-en). The entrance to
FodorśChoice the East Garden is the ⇨ Ōte-mon, once the main gate of Ieyasu Toku-
★ gawa's castle. Here, you will come across National Police Agency dōjō (martial arts hall) and the Ōte Rest House, where for ¥100 you can buy a simple map of the garden.

The **Hundred-Man Guardhouse** was once defended by four shifts of 100 soldiers each. Past it is the entrance to what was once the **ni-no-maru,** the "second circle" of the fortress. It's now a grove and garden. At the far end is the **Suwa Tea Pavilion,** an early-19th-century building relocated here from another part of the castle grounds.

The steep stone walls of the **hon-maru** (the "inner circle"), with the Moat of Swans below, dominate the west side of the garden. Halfway along is **Shio-mi-zaka,** which translates roughly as "Briny View Hill," so named because in the Edo period the ocean could be seen from here.

Head to the wooded paths around the garden's edges for shade, quiet, and benches to rest your weary feet. In the southwest corner is the Fujimi Yagura, the only surviving watchtower of the hon-maru; farther along the path, on the west side, is the **Fujimi Tamon,** one of the two remaining armories.

The odd-looking octagonal tower is the **Tōka-Gakudō** (concert hall). Its mosaic tile façade was built in honor of Empress Kojun in 1966. ⊠ *Chiyoda-ku* ⊡ *Free* ⊙ *Mar.–Oct., weekends and Tues.–Thurs. 9–4; Nov.–late Dec. and early Jan. and Feb., weekends and Tues.–Thurs. 9–3:30* Ⓜ *Tōzai, Marunouchi, and Chiyoda subway lines, Ōte-machi Station (Exit C13b).*

❹ **Imperial Palace Outer Garden** (Kōkyo-Gaien). When the office buildings of the Meiji government were moved from this area in 1899, the whole expanse along the east side of the palace was turned into a public promenade and planted with 2,800 pine trees. The Outer Garden affords the best view of the castle walls and their Tokugawa-period fortifications: Ni-jū-bashi and the Sei-mon, the 17th-century Fujimi Yagura watchtower, and the Sakurada-mon. ⊠ *Chiyoda-ku* ⊡ *Free* Ⓜ *Chiyoda subway line, Ni-jū-bashi-mae Station (Exit 2).*

⓬ **Kōgeikan** (Crafts Gallery of the National Museum of Modern Art). For those who are interested in modern and traditional Japanese crafts, this museum is worth seeing. Built in 1910, the Kōgeikan, once the headquarters of the Imperial Guard, is a Gothic Revival red brick building. The exhibits are all too few, but many master artists are represented here in the traditions of lacquerware, textiles, pottery, bamboo, and metalwork. The most direct access to the gallery is from the Takebashi subway station on the Tōzai Line (Exit 1B). ⊠ *1–1 Kita-no-maru Kōen,*

Chiyoda-ku ☎ *03/3211–7781* 🎫 *¥200, admission to National Museum of Modern Art is separate; additional fee for special exhibits; free 1st Sun. of month* ⊘ *Tues.–Sun. 10–5* Ⓜ *Hanzō-mon and Shinjuku subway lines, Kudanshita Station (Exit 2); Tōzai subway line, Takebashi Station (Exit 1b).*

❻ National Diet Building (Kokkai-Gijidō). This building, which houses the Japanese parliament, is the perfect example of post-WWII Japanese architecture; on a gloomy day it seems as if it might have sprung from the screen of a German Expressionist movie. Started in 1920, construction took 17 years to complete. The Prime Minister's residence, *Kantei*, is across the street. ✉ *1–7–1 Nagata-chō, Chiyoda-ku* Ⓜ *Marunouchi subway line, Kokkai-Gijidō-mae Station (Exit 2).*

⓭ National Museum of Modern Art, Tōkyō (Tōkyō Kokuritsu Kindai Bijutsukan). Founded in 1952 and moved to its present site in 1969, this was Japan's first national art museum. Twentieth- and 21st-century Japanese and Western art is featured throughout the year, but the museum tends to be rather bland about how these exhibitions are organized and presented, and they're seldom on the cutting edge. The second through fourth floors house the permanent collection, which includes the painting, prints, and sculpture by Rousseau, Picasso, Tsuguji Fujita, Ryūzaburo Umehara, and Taikan Yokoyama. ✉ *3–1 Kita-no-maru Kōen, Chiyoda-ku* ☎ *03/ 3214–2561* ⊕ *www.momat.go.jp* 🎫 *¥420, includes admission to the Kōgeikan; free 1st Sun. of month* ⊘ *Tues.–Thurs. and weekends 10–5, Fri. 10–8* Ⓜ *Tōzai subway line, Takebashi Station (Exit 1b); Hanzō-mon and Shinjuku subway lines, Kudanshita Station (Exit 2).*

❼ National Theater (Kokuritsu Gekijō). Architect Hiroyuki Iwamoto's winning entry in the design competition for the National Theater building (1966) is a rendition in concrete of the ancient *azekura* (storehouse) style, invoking the 8th-century Shōsōin Imperial Repository in Nara. The large hall seats 1,746 and presents primarily Kabuki theater, ancient court music, and dance. The small hall seats 630 and is used mainly for Bunraku puppet theater and traditional music. The building is nice to see, but all performances are in Japanese, so it can be difficult to sit through an entire show. Catch a show at the ⇨ **Kabukiza** in Ginza, where English earphones are offered. ✉ *4–1 Hayabusa-chō, Chiyoda-ku* ☎ *03/ 3265–7411* 🎫 *Varies depending on performance* Ⓜ *Hanzō-mon subway line, Hanzō-mon Station (Exit 1).*

❷ Ōte-mon (Ōte Gate). The main entrance to the Imperial Palace East Garden, Ōte-mon was in former days the principal gate of Ieyasu Tokugawa's castle. Most of the gate was destroyed in 1945 but was rebuilt in 1967 on the original plans. The outer part of the gate survived, and today it houses a fascinating photo collection of before-and-after photographs of the castle, taken about 100 years apart. ✉ *Chiyoda-ku* Ⓜ *Tōzai, Marunouchi, and Chiyoda subway lines, Ōte-machi Station (Exit C10).*

❶ Tōkyō Station. The work of Kingo Tatsuno, one of Japan's first modern architects, Tōkyō Station was completed in 1914. Tatsuno modeled his creation on Amsterdam's railway station. The building lost its original

Stretch Your Legs

THE VENUE OF CHOICE for runners is the **Imperial Palace Outer Garden.** At the west end of the park, Sakurada-mon's (Gate of the Field of Cherry Trees) small courtyard is the traditional starting point for the 5-km (3-mi) run around the palace—though you can join in anywhere along the route. Jogging around the palace is a ritual that begins as early as 6 AM and goes on throughout the day, no matter what the weather. Almost everybody runs the course counterclockwise, but now and then you may spot someone going the opposite way.

Looking for a challenge? Japan is a marathon mecca and one of the most famous is the **Tōkyō Big Marathon,** (⊕ www.tokyo42195.org) which is held every February. Plan ahead if you're going to sign up, because the registration deadline is in August of the previous year (most of the country's running events require signing up and qualifying far more in advance than their counterparts on other shores). The Big Marathon starts at one of Tōkyō's most prominent landmarks, the Tōkyō Metropolitan Government Office in Shinjuku-ku, winds its way through the Imperial Palace, past the Tōkyō Tower and Asakusa Kaminarimon Gate, and finishes at Tōkyō Big Sight Exhibition Center in Ariake-ku. Remember to pack your long-johns—the weather can be harsh.

---

top story in the air raids of 1945, but was promptly repaired. In the late 1990s, a plan to demolish the station was impeded by public outcry. Inside, it has been deepened and tunneled and redesigned any number of times to accommodate new commuter lines, but the lovely old redbrick facade remains untouched. The best thing about the place is the historical **Tōkyō Station Hotel,** on the west side on the second and third floors. ⊠ *1–9–1 Marunouchi, Chiyoda-ku* ☎ *03/3231–2511.*

NEED A BREAK?

Stop by the **Wadakura Fuusui Koen Restaurant** for pasta, sandwiches, and soup with lovely water fountain views. English menus are available by request, but the signs are only in Japanese. Lunch set menus range from ¥1,000 to ¥2,000. ⊠ *3-1 Imperial Palace Outer Garden, Chiyoda-ku* Ⓜ *Otemachi Station (Exit D2, D3)* ☎ *03/3214-2286.*

⑤ Two-Tiered Bridge (Ni-jū-bashi). Making a graceful arch across the moat, this bridge is surely the most photogenic spot on the grounds of the former Edo Castle. Mere mortals may pass through only on December 23 and January 2 to pay their respects to the Imperial family. The guards in front of their small, octagonal, copper-roof sentry boxes change every hour on the hour—alas, with nothing like the pomp and ceremony of Buckingham Palace. ⊠ *Chiyoda-ku* Ⓜ *Chiyoda subway line, Ni-jū-bashi-mae Station (Exit 2).*

⑩ Yamatane Museum of Art (Yamatane Bijutsukan). The museum, which specializes in *Nihon-ga*—traditional Japanese painting—from the Meiji period and later, has a private collection of masterpieces by such painters as Taikan Yokoyama, Gyoshū Hayami, Kokei Kobayashi, and Gyokudō Kawai. The exhibits, which sometimes include works borrowed from other collections, change every two months. The décor and displays make this museum an oasis of quiet elegance. Buy the lavish catalog of the collection as a stylish coffee table souvenir. The interior garden was designed by architect Yoshio Taniguchi, who also did the Museum of Modern Art. ⊠ *2 Samban-chō, Chiyoda-ku* ☎ *03/3239–5911* 🖶 *03/ 3239–5913* ✉ *¥500* ☉ *Tues.–Sun. 10–4:30* Ⓜ *Tōzai and Shinjuku subway lines, Kudanshita Station (Exit 2).*

★ ❾ **Yasukuni Jinja** (Shrine of Peace for the Nation). This shrine is not as impressive as Asakusa Shrine and Meiji Jingu Shrine, so if you must choose between the three, visit the latter. Founded in 1869, this shrine is dedicated to approximately 2.5 million Japanese, Taiwanese, and Koreans who have died since then in war or military service. Since 1945 Yasukuni has been a center of stubborn political debate given that the Japanese constitution expressly renounces both militarism and state sponsorship of religion. Several prime ministers have visited the shrine since 1979, causing a political chill between Japan and its close neighbors, Korea and China—who suffered under Japanese colonialism. Despite all this, hundreds of thousands of Japanese come here every year, simply to pray for the repose of friends and relatives they have lost.

The shrine is not one structure but a complex of buildings that include the **Main Hall** and the **Hall of Worship**—both built in the simple, unadorned style of the ancient Shintō shrines at Ise—and the **Yūshūkan,** a museum of documents and war memorabilia. Also here are a Nō theater and, in the far western corner, a sumō-wrestling ring. Sumō matches are held at Yasukuni in April, during the first of its three annual festivals. You can pick up a pamphlet and simplified map of the shrine, both in English, just inside the grounds.

Refurbished in 2002, the Yūshūkan presents Japan at its most ambivalent—if not unrepentant—about its more recent militaristic past. Critics charge that the newer exhibits glorify the nation's role in the Pacific War as a noble struggle for independence; certainly there's an agenda here that's hard to reconcile with Japan's firm postwar rejection of militarism as an instrument of national policy. Many Japanese visitors are moved by such displays as the last letters and photographs of young kamikaze pilots; visitors from other countries tend to find the Yūshūkan a cautionary, rather than uplifting, experience.

Although some of the exhibits have English labels and notes, the English is not very helpful; most objects, however, speak clearly enough for themselves. Rooms on the second floor house an especially fine collection of medieval swords and armor. Perhaps the most bizarre exhibit is the *kaiten* (human torpedo) on the first floor. ⊠ *3–1–1 Kudankita, Chiyoda-ku* ☎ *03/3261–8326* ✉ *¥800* ☉ *Grounds daily, usually 9–9. Museum Mar.–Oct., daily 9–5; Nov.–Feb., daily 9–4:30* Ⓜ *Hanzō-mon and Shinjuku subway lines, Kudanshita Station (Exit 1).*

Etiquette & Behavior

PROPRIETY IS AN IMPORTANT part of Japanese society. Many Japanese expect foreigners to behave differently and are tolerant of faux pas, but they are pleasantly surprised when people acknowledge and observe their customs. The easiest way to ingratiate yourself with the Japanese is to take time to learn and respect Japanese ways.

Bow upon meeting someone.

Don't be offended if you're not invited to someone's home. Most entertaining is done in restaurants and bars.

Upon entering a home, **remove your shoes** and put on the slippers that are provided.

Oshibori is a small hot towel provided in Japanese restaurants. **This is to wipe your hands but not your face.** If you must use it on your face, wipe your face first, then your hands and never toss it on the table: fold or roll it up.

When eating with chopsticks, **do not use the part that has entered your mouth to pick up food.** Instead, use the end that you have been holding in your hand. Always rest chopsticks on the edge of the tray, bowl, or plate; sticking upright in your food is how rice is arranged at funerals.

Meishi (business cards) are **mandatory.** Remember to place those you have received in front of you during the meeting. It's also good to have one side of your business card printed in Japanese.

Be prompt for social and business occasions.

Stick to last names and use the honorific *-san* after the name, as in *Tanaka-san* (Mr. or Mrs. Tanaka). Also, respect the hierarchy, and as much as possible address yourself to the most senior person in the room.

Don't express anger or aggression. Losing one's temper is equated with losing face.

Stick to neutral subjects in conversation. The weather doesn't have to be your only topic, but you should take care not to be nosy.

It's not customary for Japanese businessmen to bring wives along. If you are traveling with your spouse, **do not assume that an invitation includes both of you.** If you must ask if it's acceptable to bring your spouse along, do so in a way that eliminates the need for a direct, personal refusal.

Don't pour your own drink, and always fill a companion's empty glass. If you would rather not drink, do not refuse a refill, but rather sip, keeping your glass at least half full.

Remember that because many Japanese women do not have careers, many Japanese businessmen still don't know how to interact with Western businesswomen. Be patient and, if the need arises, gently remind them that, professionally, you expect to be treated as any man would be.

Avoid too much eye contact when speaking. Direct eye contact is a show of spite and rudeness.

Refrain from speaking on your mobile phone in restaurants or public transportation.

Avoid physical contact. A slap on the back or hand on the shoulder would be uncomfortable for a Japanese person.

Do not blow your nose in public. Seriously.

TOP REASONS TO VISIT

Hello Master At Maid Cafés, an Akihabara phenomenon, waitresses dress in maid costumes and address patrons as *master*, and cater to the festishes of Japanese *otaku* (nerds).

Dancing in the Streets A visit during May must include the Kanda Festival—one of Tōkyō's major street celebrations. More than 200 portable shrines are carried in a parade towards the ground of the Kanda Jinja Shrine.

Toys without Tax Purchase the best and most up-to-date electronics at the LAOX Duty Free store.

Want to be a Superhero? See the greatest collection of Japanese comic character costumes at Cosa Gee Store.

An Eccentric Collection Check out the collection of toys, electronic gadgets, and hobby items at Radio Kaiken.

Read All About It Browse an impressive variety of specialty bookstores in Jimbō-chō.

AKIHABARA & JIMBŌ-CHŌ

Akihabara is techno-geek heaven. Also known as Akihabara Electric Town, this district, which was once all about electronics, is becoming a wacky fetish district where *otaku* (nerds) can indulge in Japanese anime computer game fantasies, hang out in kinky cafés, and buy anime comics. Visitors don't just come here to buy digital cameras, but to observe the bizarre subculture of this tech-savvy country.

If you're looking for something a little more cerebral, head to Jimbō-chō where family-run specialy bookstores of every genre abound including rare antiquarian and Japanese manga. The area is also home to Meiji University and Nihon Daigaku (university).

Numbers in the margin correspond to the Akihabara & Jimbō-chō map.

Orientation & Planning

ORIENTATION Akihabara is east of the Imperial Palace, right below Ueno and Asakusa. Akihabara Station is located north of Tōkyō Station, on the JR Yamanote line, Hibiya line, and Tsukuba line. It is right below Asakusa and Ueno districts.

Located just to the west of Akihabara, Jimbō-chō should be a very short stopover either before or after an excursion to Akihabara. The best way to get there is by taxi, which should cost about ¥800 to or from Akihabara station.

PLANNING Take the train to Akihabara Station on the JR Yamanote line. Akihabara is a 30–40 min. ride from most tourist hotels in Shinjuku or Minato-ku. This is a rougher part of Tōkyō, so mind your bags and wallets. Credit cards are accepted at all major electronics superstores, but bring enough

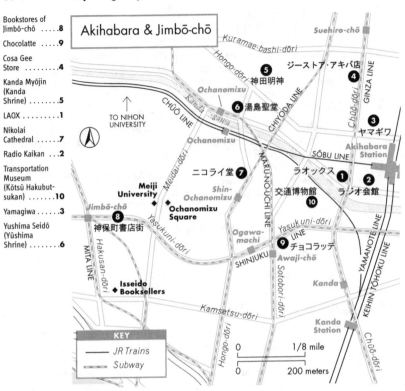

Akihabara & Jimbō-chō

cash to get around, because ATMs are difficult to find. Keep in mind that most stores in Akihabara do not open until 10 AM. Weekends draw hordes of shoppers, especially on Sunday, when the four central blocks of Chūō-dōri are closed to traffic and become a pedestrian mall. That's when the geeks come out.

What to See

8 Bookstores of Jimbō-chō. For the ultimate browse through art books, catalogs, scholarly monographs, secondhand paperbacks, and dictionaries in almost any language, the bookstores of Jimbō-chō are the place to go. A number of the antiquarian booksellers here carry rare typeset editions, wood-block-printed books of the Edo period, and individual prints. At shops like **Isseidō** and **Ohya Shōbō**, both open Monday–Saturday 10–6, it's still possible to find genuine 19th- and 20th-century prints—not always in the best condition—at affordable prices. Many of Japan's most prestigious publishing houses make their home in this area as well. The bookstores run for ½ km (¼ mi) on Yasukuni-dōri beginning at the Surugadai-shita intersection. ⊠ *Isseidō: 1–7–4 Kanda Jimbō-chō, Chiyoda-ku* ☎ *03/3292–0071* ⊠ *Ohya Shōbō: 1–1 Kanda Jimbō-chō, Chiyoda-ku, Jimbō-chō* ☎ *03/3291–0062* Ⓜ *Shinjuku and Mita subway lines, Jimbō-chō Station (Exit A7).*

⑨ Chocolatte. This maid café is not exceptional by any standards, but it is a glimpse inside the otaku world and definitely a one-of-a-kind Tōkyō experience. Beer, cocktails, tea, pasta, coffee, and desserts are served on the 2nd floor and are cheap by Tōkyō standards. If you need to check in with the folks at home, be sure to stop by the relaxing Internet café on the third floor. Coffee is ¥400 and pasta ¥800. ⊠ *1-2-1 Suda-chō Kanda-ku* ☎ *03/3251–7755* ⊙ *Weekdays 7:30–10, Weekends 10–9.*

④ Cosa Gee Store. Fans of anime will enjoy this zany Japanese costume shop experience. It's like no other in the world and is a good place to pick up an original costume for Halloween. ⊠ *2F MN building, 3-15-5 Soto-Kanda, Chiyoda-ku* ☎ *03/3526–6877* ⊙ *Daily, 11–7.*

⑤ Kanda Myōjin. (Kanda Shrine). You will never be able to see every shrine in the city and the ones in Akihabara are of minor interest, unless you are around for the Kanda festival. This shrine is said to have been founded in 730 in a village called Shibasaki, where the Ōte-machi financial district stands today. The shrine itself was destroyed in the Great Kantō Earthquake of 1923, and the present buildings reproduce in concrete the style of 1616.

Some of the smaller buildings you see as you come up the steps and walk around the main hall contain the *mikoshi*—the portable shrines that are featured in one of Tōkyō's three great blowouts, the **Kanda Festival.** (The other two are the Sannō Festival of Hie Jinja in Nagata-chō and the Sanja Festival of Asakusa Shrine.) Kanda Myōjin is on Kuramae-bashi-dōri, about a five-minute walk west of the Suehiro-chō subway stop. ⊠ *2–16–2 Soto Kanda, Chiyoda-ku* ☎ *03/3254–0753* Ⓜ *Ginza subway line, Suehiro-chō Station (Exit 3).*

① LAOX. Of all the discount stores in Akihabara, LAOX has the largest and most comprehensive selection, with four buildings in this area—one exclusively for musical instruments, another for duty-free appliances—and outlets in Yokohama and Narita. This is a good place to find the latest in digital cameras, watches, and games. ⊠ *1–2–9 Soto Kanda, Chiyoda-ku* ☎ *03/3253–7111* ⊙ *Mon.–Sat. 10–8, Sun. 10–7:30* Ⓜ *JR Akihabara Station (Nishi-guchi/West Exit).*

⑦ Nikolai Cathedral. It is curious that a Russian Orthodox cathedral was built in Tōkyō's Electric Town, but Tōkyō Resurrection Cathedral is a great place to stop for a quick snapshot. Its common name, Nikolai Cathedral, was derived from its

SHRINE FESTIVAL ESSENTIALS

The Shrine Festival is a procession in which the gods, housed in their mikoshi, are passed through the streets. The floats that lead the procession move in stately measure on wheeled carts, attended by the priests and officials of the shrine dressed in Heian-period (794–1185) costume. The mikoshi, some 70 of them, follow behind, bobbing and weaving, carried on the shoulders of the townspeople. Shrine festivals are a peculiarly competitive form of worship: piety is a matter of who can shout the loudest, drink the most beer, and have the best time.

founder, St. Nikolai Kassatkin (1836–1912), a Russian missionary who came to Japan in 1861 and spent the rest of his life here. The building, planned by a Russian engineer and executed by a British architect, was completed in 1891. Heavily damaged in the earthquake of 1923, the cathedral was restored with a dome much more modest than the original. Even so, it endows this otherwise featureless part of the city with unexpected charm. ⊠ *4–1 Surugadai, Chiyoda-ku* ☎ *03/3291–1885* Ⓜ *Chiyoda subway line, Shin-Ochanomizu Station (Exit B1).*

❷ **Radio Kaikan.** Eight floors featuring a variety of vendors selling mini spy cameras, cell phone disguised stun guns, anime comics, adult toys, gadgets, and odd-ball hobby supplies is a shopping mecca for otaku and visitors alike. Start browsing from the top floor and work your way down. ⊠ *1-15-16 Soto-Kanda, Chiyoda-ku* ☺ *Daily 11–7.*

🌀 ❿ **Transportation Museum** (Kōtsū Hakubutsukan). There seems to be a niche museum on almost every topic in Japan, including their transportation system. It's an activity for families in Akihabara district—displays explain the early development of the railway system and include a miniature layout of the rail services, as well as Japan's first airplane, which took off in 1903. To get here from JR Akihabara Station, cross the bridge on Chūō-dōri over the Kanda River, and turn right at the next corner. ⊠ *1–25 Kanda Sudachō, Chiyoda-ku* ☎ *03/3251–8481* 💲 *¥310* ☺ *Tues.–Sun. 9:30–5* Ⓜ *JR Akihabara Station (Denki-gai Exit).*

❸ **Yamagiwa.** This discount superstore is for die-hard electronic shoppers. Entire floors are devoted to computer hardware and software, fax machines, and copiers. Yamagiwa has a particularly good selection of lighting fixtures, most of them 220 volts, but the annex has export models of the most popular appliances and devices, plus an English-speaking staff to assist you with selections. You should be able to bargain prices down a bit—especially if you're buying more than one big-ticket item. ⊠ *1–5–10 Soto Kanda, Chiyoda-ku* ☎ *03/3253–5111* ☺ *Weekdays 11–7:30, weekends 10:30–7:30* Ⓜ *JR Akihabara Station (Nishi-guchi/West Exit).*

❻ **Yushima Seido** (Yushima Shrine). Again, Akihabara shrines are of minor interest in comparison to the Asakusa Shrine, Yasukuni Shrine, and Meiji Jingu Shrine. If you have time to kill, then perhaps a short stroll through this shrine will do. The origins of this shrine date to a hall, founded in 1632, for the study of the Chinese Confucian classics. Its headmaster was Hayashi Razan, the official Confucian scholar to the Tokugawa government. Moved to its present site in 1691 (and destroyed by fire and rebuilt six times), the hall became an academy for the ruling elite. In a sense, nothing has changed: in 1872 the new Meiji government established the country's first teacher-training institute here, and that, in turn, evolved into Tōkyō University—the graduates of which still make up much of the ruling elite. The hall looks like nothing else you're likely to see in Japan: painted black, weathered and somber, it could almost be in China. ⊠ *1–4–25 Yushima, Bunkyō-ku* ☎ *03/3251–4606* 💲 *Free* ☺ *Apr.–Sept., Fri.–Wed. 10–5; Oct.–mid-Dec. and Jan.–Mar., Fri.–Wed. 10–4* Ⓜ *Marunouchi subway line, Ochanomizu Station (Exit B2).*

UENO

JR Ueno Station is Tōkyō's version of the Gare du Nord: the gateway to and from Japan's northeast provinces. Since its completion in 1883, the station has served as a terminus in the great migration to the city by villagers in pursuit of a better life.

Ueno was a place of prominence long before the coming of the railroad. Since Ieyasu Tokugawa established his capital here in 1603, 36 subsidiary temples were erected surrounding the Main Hall, and the city of Edo itself expanded to the foot of the hill where Kan-ei-ji's main gate once stood.

The Meiji government turned Ueno Hill into one of the nation's first public parks. It would serve as the site of trade and industrial expositions; it would have a national museum, a library, a university of fine arts, and a zoo. The modernization of Ueno still continues, but the park is more than the sum of its museums. The Shōgitai failed to take everything with them: some of the most important buildings in the temple complex survived or were restored and should not be missed.

Numbers in the margin correspond to the Ueno map.

Orientation & Planning

ORIENTATION Ueno and Asakusa make up the historical enclave of Tōkyō. Traditional architecture and way of life are preserved here at the northeastern reaches of the city. Both areas can be explored in a single day, though if you have the time, it is also a good idea to devote an entire day to this place to fully appreciate its many museum exhibits and shrines.

PLANNING Exploring Ueno can be one excursion or two: an afternoon of cultural browsing or a full day of discoveries in one of the great centers of the city. ■ TIP→ Avoid Monday, when most of the museums are closed. Ueno out of doors is no fun at all in February or the rainy season (late June–mid-July); mid-August can be brutally hot and muggy. In April, the cherry blossoms of Ueno Kōen are glorious.

Ueno Station can be accessed by train on the Hibiya line, Ginza line, and JR Yamanote line (Kōen Entrance). Be sure to avoid morning (8–9) and evening rush hour (7–9) and bring plenty of cash for admission to museums and food for the day; there are no ATMs. To purchase souvenirs, museum stores accept all major credit cards.

What to See

🕼 **Ame-ya Yoko-chō Market.** Not much besides Ueno Station survived the bombings of World War II and anyone who could make it here from the countryside with rice and other small supplies of food could sell them at exorbitant black-market prices. Sugar was a commodity that couldn't be found at any price in postwar Tōkyō. Before long, there were hundreds of stalls in the black market selling various kinds of *ame* (confections), most of them made from sweet potatoes. These stalls gave the market its name Ame-ya Yoko-chō (often shortened to Ameyoko),

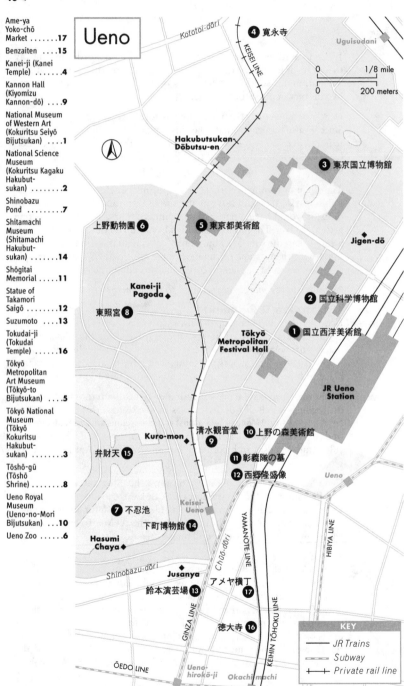

Ueno

Kototoi-dōri

KEISEI LINE

Uguisudani

4 寛永寺

0   1/8 mile

0   200 meters

Hakubutsukan-Dōbutsu-en

3 東京国立博物館

Shinobazu Pond

上野動物園 **6**

5 東京都美術館

Jigen-dō

Kanei-ji Pagoda ◆

東照宮 **8**

2 国立科学博物館

1 国立西洋美術館

Tōkyō Metropolitan Festival Hall

JR Ueno Station

Kuro-mon ◆

弁財天 **15**

清水観音堂 **9**

10 上野の森美術館

11 彰義隊の墓

12 西郷隆盛像

Ueno

Keisei-Ueno

7 不忍池

下町博物館 **14**

Hasumi Chaya ◆

Shinobazu-dōri

Chūō-dōri

YAMANOTE LINE

HIBIYA LINE

Jusanya ◆

鈴本演芸場 **13**

アメヤ横丁 **17**

GINZA LINE

KEIHIN TŌHOKU LINE

徳大寺 **16**

ŌEDO LINE

Ueno-hirokō-ji

Okachi machi

TOP REASONS TO VISIT

All That Art! If you want to explore Tōkyō's top museums, then head to Ueno where you'll find the Tōkyō National Museum and the National Museum of Western Art, among many others.

Shining Shrine Dating back to 1627, the Tōshō-gū Shrine is a national treasure that houses a priceless collection of historical art and is one of the few last remaining early Edo-period buildings in Tōkyō—it survived the 1868 revolt, the 1923 earthquake, and the 1945 bombings.

Cute & Cuddly Even if you don't have kids in tow, it might be hard to pass up the chance to see the resident Giant Pandas, Tong Tong and Ling Ling, at the Ueno Zoo.

Beautiful Bloom From mid-June through August, *Shinobazu-ike* (Shinobazu Pond) is the only place in Tōkyō where you'll see such a vast expanse of lotus flowers in bloom—the flowers stretch over the entire pond and are definitely worthy of a few photographs.

which means "Confectioners' Alley." Shortly before the Korean War, the market was legalized, and soon the stalls were carrying watches, chocolate, ballpoint pens, blue jeans, and T-shirts that had somehow been "liberated" from American PXs. In years to come the merchants of Ameyoko diversified still further—to fine Swiss timepieces and fake designer luggage, cosmetics, jewelry, fresh fruit, and fish. The market became especially famous for the traditional prepared foods of the New Year, and during the last few days of December, as many as half a million people crowd into the narrow alleys under the railroad tracks to stock up for the holiday. ⊠ *Ueno 4-chōme, Taitō-ku* ☯ *Most shops and stalls daily 10–7* Ⓜ *JR Ueno Station (Hirokō-ji Exit).*

⑮ **Benzaiten.** Perched in the middle of Shinobazu Pond, this shrine is dedicated to the goddess Benten, one of the Seven Gods of Good Luck that evolved from a combination of Indian, Chinese, and Japanese mythology. As matron goddess of the arts, she is depicted holding a lutelike musical instrument called a *biwa.* The shrine, which was built by Abbot Tenkai, was destroyed in the bombings of 1945; the present version, with its distinctive octagonal roof, is a faithful copy. You can rent rowboats and pedal boats at a nearby boathouse. ⊠ *Taitō-ku* ☎ *03/3828–9502 for boathouse* 🕹 *Rowboats ¥600 for 1 hr, pedal boats ¥600 for 30 min, swan boats ¥700 for 30 min* ☯ *Boathouse daily 10–5:30* Ⓜ *JR Ueno Station (Kōen-guchi/Park Exit); Keisei private rail line, Keisei-Ueno Station (Ikenohata Exit).*

❹ **Kan-ei-ji** (Kanei Temple). In 1638 the second Tokugawa shōgun, Hidetada, commissioned the priest Tenkai to build a temple on the hill known as Shinobu-ga-oka in Ueno to defend his city from evil spirits. The only remarkable remaining structure here is the ornately carved vermilion gate to what was the mausoleum of Tsunayoshi, the fifth shōgun. Tsunayoshi is famous for his disastrous fiscal mismanagement and his

Shōrui Awaremi no Rei (Edicts on Compassion for Living Things), which, among other things, made it a capital offense for a human being to kill a dog. ✉ *1–14–11 Ueno Sakuragi, Taitō-ku* ☎ *03/3821–1259* 🖼 *Free, contributions welcome* 🕙 *Daily 9–5* Ⓜ *JR Ueno Station (Kōen-guchi/Park Exit), JR Uguisudani Station.*

❾ Kannon Hall (Kiyomizu Kannon-dō). This National Treasure was a part of Abbot Tenkai's attempt to build a copy of Kyōto's magnificent Kiyomizu-dera in Ueno. His attempt was honorable, but failed to be as impressive as the original. The principal Buddhist image of worship here is the Senjū Kannon (Thousand-Armed Goddess of Mercy). Another figure, however, receives greater homage. This is the Kosodate Kannon, who is believed to answer the prayers of women having difficulty conceiving children. If their prayers are answered, they return to Kiyomizu and leave a doll, as both an offering of thanks and a prayer for the child's health. In a ceremony held every September 25, the dolls that have accumulated during the year are burned in a bonfire. ✉ *1–29 Ueno Kōen, Taitō-ku* ☎ *03/3821–4749* 🖼 *Free* 🕙 *Daily 7–5* Ⓜ *JR Ueno Station (Kōen-guchi/Park Exit).*

★ ❶ National Museum of Western Art (Kokuritsu Seiyō Bijutsukan). Along with castings from the original molds of Rodin's *Gate of Hell, The Burghers of Calais,* and *The Thinker,* the wealthy businessman Matsukata Kojiro (1865–1950) acquired some 850 paintings, sketches, and prints by such masters as Renoir, Monet, Gauguin, van Gogh, Delacroix, and Cézanne. Matsukata kept the collection in Europe, but he left it to Japan in his will. The French government sent the artwork to Japan after World War II, and the collection opened to the public in 1959 in a building designed by Swiss-born architect Le Corbusier. Since then, the museum has diversified a bit; more recent acquisitions include works by Reubens, Tintoretto, El Greco, Max Ernst, and Jackson Pollock. The Seiyō is one of the best-organized, most pleasant museums to visit in Tōkyō. ✉ *7-7 Ueno Kōen, Taitō-ku* ☎ *03/3828–5131* ⊕ *www.nmwa. go.jp* 🖼 *¥420; additional fee for special exhibits* 🕙 *Tues.–Thurs. and weekends 9:30–4:30, Fri. 9:30–7:30* Ⓜ *JR Ueno Station (Kōen-guchi/ Park Exit).*

☪ ❷ National Science Museum (Kokuritsu Kagaku Hakubutsukan). The six buildings of the complex house everything from fossils to moon rocks—the 30-meter model of a blue whale perched at the museum's entrance is a huge hit with kids. And what self-respecting institution of its kind would be without a dinosaur collection? Look for them in the B2F Exhibition Hall, in the newest annex. Although the museum occasionally outdoes itself with special exhibits, it's pretty conventional, and provides relatively little in the way of hands-on learning experiences. Kids seem to like it anyway—but this is not a place to linger if your time is short. ✉ *7–20 Ueno Kōen, Taitō-ku* ☎ *03/3822–0111* ⊕ *www.kahaku. go.jp* 🖼 *¥420; additional fees for special exhibits* 🕙 *Tues.–Thurs. 9–5, Fri. 9–8, weekends 9–6* Ⓜ *JR Ueno Station (Kōen-guchi/Park Exit).*

☪ ❼ Shinobazu Pond. Shinobazu was once an inlet of Tōkyō Bay. When the area was reclaimed, it became a freshwater pond. Abbot Tenkai, founder of Kan-ei-ji on the hill above the pond, had an island made in the middle of it, which he built for ⇨ **Benzaiten** the goddess of the arts. Later improvements included a causeway to the island, embankments, and even a racecourse (1884–93). Today the pond is in three sections. The first, with its famous lotus plants, is a wildlife sanctuary. Some 5,000 wild ducks migrate here from as far away as Siberia, sticking around from September to April. The second section, to the north, belongs to Ueno Zoo; the third, to the west, is a small lake for boating. ⊠ *Shinobazu-dōri, Taitō-ku* ☎ *Free* ☉ *Daily sunrise–sunset* Ⓜ *JR Ueno Station (Kōen-guchi/Park Exit); Keisei private rail line, Keisei-Ueno Station (Higashi-guchi/East Exit).*

NEED A BREAK?

Hasumi Chaya, a charming Japanese teahouse located on the bank of the pond, is only opened during the summer when the lotus flowers cover Shinobazu Pond. It is an open, airy café that offers perfect views of the blooms and serves lunch and dinner sets: for lunch, you can get a set of tea and snacks for ¥900; for dinner you can get a set of cold beer and snacks for ¥1,000. English is not spoken, but sets are displayed in plastic models at the entrance to make ordering easier. ⊠ *Shinobazu-dōri, Taitō-ku* ☎ *03/3833-0030 (Mon.-Sat)* ☉ *Jun. 17–Aug. 31, Daily 12–4, 5–9.* Ⓜ *Toei Oedo line, Ueno-Okachimachi Station (Exit 2), JR Yamanote Line, Ueno Station (Exit 6).*

★ ☾ ⑭ **Shitamachi Museum** (Shitamachi Hakubutsukan). Japanese society in the days of the Tokugawa shōguns was rigidly stratified. Some 80% of the city's land was allotted to the warrior class, temples, and shrines. The remaining 20%—between Ieyasu's fortifications on the west, and the Sumida-gawa on the east—was known as Shitamachi, literally, "downtown" or the "lower town" (as it expanded, Shitamachi came to include what today constitutes the Chūō, Taitō, Sumida, and Kōtō wards). It was here that the common, hard-working, free-spending folk, who made up more than half the population, lived. The Shitamachi Museum preserves and exhibits what remained of that way of life as late as 1940.

The two main displays on the first floor are a merchant house and a tenement, intact with all their furnishings. This is a hands-on museum: you can take your shoes off and step up into the rooms. On the second floor are displays of toys, tools, and utensils donated, in most cases, by people who had grown up with them and used them all their lives. There are also photographs and video documentaries of craftspeople at work. Occasionally various traditional skills are demonstrated, and you're welcome to take part. This don't-miss museum makes great use of its space, and there are even volunteer guides (available starting at 10) who speak passable English. ⊠ *2–1 Ueno Kōen, Taitō-ku* ☎ *03/3823–7451* ☞ *¥300* ☉ *Tues.–Sun. 9:30–4:30* Ⓜ *JR Ueno Station (Kōen-guchi/Park Exit); Keisei private rail line, Keisei-Ueno Station (Higashi-guchi/East Exit).*

⑪ **Shōgitai Memorial.** Time seems to heal wounds very quickly in Japan. Only six years after the Shōgitai had destroyed most of Ueno Hill in 1868, the Meiji government permitted these Tokugawa loyalists to be honored with a gravestone, erected on the spot where their bodies had been cremated. ⊠ *Taitō-ku* Ⓜ *JR Ueno Station (Kōen-guchi/Park Exit); Keisei private rail line, Keisei-Ueno Station (Higashi-guchi/East Exit).*

⑫ Statue of Takamori Saigō. As chief of staff of the Meiji imperial army, Takamori Saigō (1827–77) played a key role in forcing the surrender of Edo and the overthrow of the shogunate. Ironically, Saigō himself fell out with the other leaders of the new Meiji government and was killed in an unsuccessful rebellion of his own. The sculptor Takamura Kōun's bronze, made in 1893, sensibly avoids presenting Saigō in uniform. ✉ *Taitō-ku* Ⓜ *JR Ueno Station (Kōen-guchi/Park Exit); Keisei private rail line, Keisei-Ueno Station (Higashi-guchi/East Exit).*

⑬ Suzumoto. Originally built around 1857 for Japanese comic monologue performances called *rakugo*, Suzumoto is the oldest theater operation of its kind in Tōkyō. The theater is on Chūō-dōri, a few blocks north of the Ginza Line's Ueno Hirokō-ji stop. ✉ *2–7–12 Ueno, Taitō-ku* ☎ *03/ 3834–5906* 💴 *¥2,000* ☉ *Continual performances daily 12:20–4:30 and 5:20–9:10* Ⓜ *Ginza subway line, Ueno Hirokō-ji Station (Exit 3).*

⑯ Tokudai-ji (Tokudai Temple). This is a curiosity in a neighborhood of curiosities: a temple on the second floor of a supermarket. Two deities are worshipped here. One is the bodhisattva Jizō, and the act of washing this statue is believed to safeguard your health. The other is of the Indian goddess Marici, a daughter of Brahma; she is believed to help worshippers overcome difficulties and succeed in business. ✉ *4–6–2 Ueno, Taitō-ku* Ⓜ *JR Yamanote and Keihin-tōhoku lines, Okachi-machi Station (Higashi-guchi/East Exit) or Ueno Station (Hirokō-ji Exit).*

⑤ Tōkyō Metropolitan Art Museum (Tōkyō Bijutsukan). The museum displays its own collection of modern Japanese art on the lower level and rents out the remaining two floors to various art institutes and organizations. At any given time, there can be at least five exhibits in the building: international exhibitions, work by local young painters, or new forms and materials in sculpture or modern calligraphy. ✉ *8–36 Ueno Kōen, Taitō-ku* ☎ *03/3823–6921* ⊕ *www.tobikan.jp* 🖼 *Permanent collection free; fees vary for other exhibits (usually ¥800–¥1,400)* ☉ *Daily 9–5; closed 3rd Mon. of month* Ⓜ *JR Ueno Station (Kōen-guchi/Park Exit).*

③ Tōkyō National Museum (Tōkyō Kokuritsu Hakubutsukan). This complex of four buildings grouped around a courtyard is one of the world's great repositories of East Asian art and archaeology. Altogether, the museum has some 87,000 objects in its permanent collection, with several thousand more on loan from shrines, temples, and private owners.

FodorśChoice
★

The Western-style building on the left (if you're standing at the main gate), with bronze cupolas, is the **Hyōkeikan.** Built in 1909, it was devoted to archaeological exhibits; aside from the occasional special exhibition, the building is closed today. The larger **Heiseikan,** behind the Hyōkeikan, was built to commemorate the wedding of crown prince Naruhito in 1993 and now houses Japanese archaeological exhibits. The second floor is used for special exhibitions.

In 1878, the 7th-century Hōryū-ji (Hōryū Temple) in Nara presented 319 works of art in its possession—sculpture, scrolls, masks, and other objects—to the Imperial Household. These were transferred to the National

CLOSE UP

A Day on the Green

1

TŌKYŌ HAS 21 GOLF COURSES

within its borders and a vast selection beyond city limits. Though some are private, private doesn't always mean non-members can't play. Bear in mind that you may pay twice what you would on weekdays for weekends and holidays and just because facilities are open to tourists doesn't mean they have bilingual staff. Luckily, most have self-service systems or friendly staff. Looking for courses or to book tee-times? Visit the online guide *Golf in Japan* (⊕ www.golf-in-japan.com). Don't feel like lugging your clubs? Most courses rent sets.

IN TOWN

Showanomori Golf Course, Akishima-shi. Originally built during the U.S. occupation, this public course offers wide fairways, a remote control monorail cart, and some English-speaking staff, but no caddies. *⅄ 18 holes, Par 72* ☎ *042/543-1273* 🏌 *Fees ¥11,000–¥16,500; clubs rentals ¥2,000* Ⓜ *JR Ome Line, Akishima Station.*

Yomiuri Golf Club, Inagi-shi. Expect a strict dress code at this private club, which hosts the annual Salonpas World Ladies Championships in May. It's open to the public, you can rent golf-carts, and caddies are a must, but don't count on a bilingual staff. *⅄ 18 holes, Par 72* 🏌 *Fees ¥26,850–¥40,000; club rentals ¥5,250* ☎ *044/966-1141* Ⓜ *Odakyu Line Semi Express, Shin Yurigaoka Station.*

Wakasu Golf Links, Koto-ku. If convenience is what you seek, this centrally located public course is for you. Reservations are required, but carts and caddies are optional. *⅄ 18 holes, Par 72* 🏌 *Fees ¥13,745–¥22,745; club rentals ¥5,250* ☎ *03/3647-9111* Ⓜ *Yūracuchō Line, Shin Kiba Station.*

OUT OF TOWN

Gotemba and Belle View Nagao golf clubs, Gotemba-shi, Shizuoka. Located at the foot of Mount Fuji, these courses will challenge your skills and stamina, especially on foggy days when the mountain and your ball will be hard to see. *⅄ 18 holes, Par 72* 🏌 *Fees ¥5,000 for 9 holes; ¥19,000 for 18 holes; club rentals ¥3,675* ☎ *090/9892-4319* Ⓜ *Odakyu Asagiri Romance car from Shinjuku Station to Gotemba Station, 1 hour and 40 minutes.*

Kasumigaura Country Club, Kasumigaura, Ibaraki. Loaded with water hazards and sand traps, this course will make you curse and sweat. The spacious clubhouse, high-end restaurant, and other luxurious facilities will make up for it though. *⅄ 18 holes, Par 72* 🏌 *Fees ¥8,000–¥13,000; club rentals ¥4,200* ☎ *029/55-2311* Ⓜ *JR Fresh Hitachi No. 48 from Ueno Station to Ishioka Station, 1 hour.*

ANOTHER OPTION

Can't make it to a course? Try one of the city's 78 driving ranges. Most are open from 11 AM to 7 or 8 PM and will rent you a club for around ¥200. The granddaddy of them all, **Lŏttè Kasai Golf,** sports 300 bays and a 250-yard field. (✉ 2-4-2 Rinkai-cho, Edogawa-ku ☎ 03/5658-5600 🏌 ground-level bays ¥80 per ball; three stories up ¥60 per ball; prepaid cards ¥3,000–¥20,000 🕐 Daily 24 hours Ⓜ JR Keiyō line, Kasai-Rinkai-Koen Station). No weekday wait and an easy-to-navigate self-service system make **Meguro Gorufu-jō** another great choice. (✉ 5-6-22 Kami-Meguro, Meguro-ku ☎ 03/3713-2805 🏌 prepaid card for 50 balls ¥2,000 Ⓜ Hibiya line, Naka-Megurō Station.)

Museum in 2000 and now reside in the **Hōryū-ji Hōmotsukan** (Gallery of Hōryū-ji Treasures), which was designed by Yoshio Taniguchi. There's a useful guide to the collection in English, and the exhibits are well explained. Don't miss the hall of carved wooden *gigaku* (Buddhist processional) masks.

The central building in the complex, the 1937 **Honkan,** houses Japanese art exclusively: paintings, calligraphy, sculpture, textiles, ceramics, swords, and armor. Also here are 84 objects designated by the government as National Treasures. The Honkan rotates the works on display several times during the year. It also hosts two special exhibitions annually (April and May or June, and October and November), which feature important collections from both Japanese and foreign museums. These, unfortunately, can be an ordeal to take in: the lighting in the Honkan is not particularly good, the explanations in English are sketchy at best, and the hordes of visitors make it impossible to linger over a work you especially want to study. The more attractive **Tōyōkan,** to the right of the Honkan, completed in 1968, is devoted to the art and antiquities of China, Korea, Southeast Asia, India, the Middle East, and Egypt. ✉ *13–9 Ueno Kōen, Taitō-ku* ☎ *03/3822–1111* ⊕ *www.tnm.go.jp* ✉ *Regular exhibits¥420, special exhibits approx. ¥1,500* ◷ *Tues.–Sat. 9:30–5, Sun. 9:30–6* Ⓜ *JR Ueno Station (Kōen-guchi/Park Exit).*

★ ❽ **Tōshō-gū** (Tōshō Shrine). This shrine, built in 1627, is dedicated to Ieyasu, the first Tokugawa shōgun. It miraculously survived all major disasters that destroyed most of Tōkyō's historical structures—the fires, the 1868 revolt, the 1923 earthquake, the 1945 bombings—making it one of the only early-Edo-period buildings left in Tōkyō. The shrine and most of its art are designated National Treasures.

Two hundred *ishidōrō* (stone lanterns) line the path from the stone entry arch to the shrine itself. One of them, just outside the arch to the left, is more than 18 feet high, called *obaketōrō* (ghost lantern). Legend has it that one night a samurai on guard duty slashed at a ghost (*obake*) that was believed to haunt the lantern. His sword was so strong, it left a nick in the stone, which can be seen today.

The first room inside the shrine is the **Hall of Worship;** the four paintings in gold on wooden panels are by Tan'yū, a member of the famous Kano family of artists, during the 15th century. Behind the Hall of Worship, connected by a passage called the *haiden,* is the sanctuary, where the spirit of Ieyasu is said to be enshrined.

The real glories of Tōshō-gū are its so-called **Chinese Gate,** which you reach at the end of the building, and the fence on either side that has intricate carvings of birds, animals, fish, and shells of every description. The two long panels of the gate, with their dragons carved in relief, are attributed to Hidari Jingoro—a brilliant sculptor of the early Edo period whose real name is unknown (*hidari* means "left"; Jingoro was reportedly left-handed). The lifelike appearance of his dragons has inspired a legend. Every morning they were found mysteriously dripping with water and it was believed that the dragons were sneaking out at night to drink from the nearby Shinobazu Pond. Wire cages were put up to curtail this disquieting habit. ⊠ *9–88 Ueno Kōen, Taitō-ku* ☎ *03/3822–3455* ✆ *¥200* ⊙ *Daily 9–5* Ⓜ *JR Ueno Station (Kōen-guchi/Park Exit).*

❿ Ueno Royal Museum (Ueno-no-Mori Bijutsukan). Although the museum has no permanent collection of its own, it makes its galleries available to various groups, primarily for modern painting and calligraphy.

> **THE RAKUGO TRADITION**
>
> Though rakugo is not the most popular form of Japanese theater, even among the Japanese, it is traditional and features stories that have been handed down for centuries. A kimono-clad comedian sits on a purple cushion in the middle of the audience and tells stories using only a few simple props—a fan, a pipe, a handkerchief—that transform the storyteller into a whole cast of characters. There's no English interpretation and the monologues are difficult to follow, even for the Japanese—but don't let that deter you. For a slice of traditional pop culture, rakugo at Suzumoto is worth seeing, even if you don't understand a word.

⊠ *1–2 Ueno Kōen, Taitō-ku* ☎ *03/3833–4191* ✆ *Prices vary depending on exhibition, but usually ¥400–¥1500* ⊙ *Sun.–Wed. 10–5, Thurs.–Sat. 10–7:30* Ⓜ *JR Ueno Station (Kōen-guchi/Park Exit).*

❻ Ueno Zoo (Onshi Ueno Dōbutsuen). First built in 1882, this is Japan's first zoo. It houses more than 900 species including an exotic mix of gorillas, tigers, and the main attraction, Tong Tong and Ling Ling the Giant Pandas. The resident Giant Pandas are so popular that the Ueno JR station 3rd floor connection concourse has a panda statue, which is a landmark meeting spot. On a pleasant Sunday afternoon, you can expect upwards of 20,000 Japanese clamoring to see the pandas, so be prepared for large crowds and line-ups. The process of the zoo's expansion somehow left within its confines the 120-foot, five-story Kan-ei-ji Pagoda, built in 1631 and rebuilt after a fire in 1639. ⊠ *9–83 Ueno Kōen, Taitō-ku* ☎ *03/3828–5171* ✆ *¥600. Free on Mar. 20, Apr. 29, and Oct. 1* ⊙ *Tues.–Sun. 9:30–4* Ⓜ *JR Ueno Station (Kōen-guchi/Park Exit); Keisei private rail line, Ueno Station (Dōbutsu-en Exit).*

ASAKUSA

Historically, Asakusa has been the hub of the city's entertainment. The area blossomed when Ieyasu Tokugawa made Edo his capital, becoming the 14th-century city that never slept. For the next 300 years it was the wellspring of almost everything we associate with Japanese culture. In the mid-1600s, it became a pleasure quarter in its own right with stalls selling toys, souvenirs, and sweets; acrobats, jugglers and strolling musicians; and saké shops and teahouses—where the waitresses often pro-

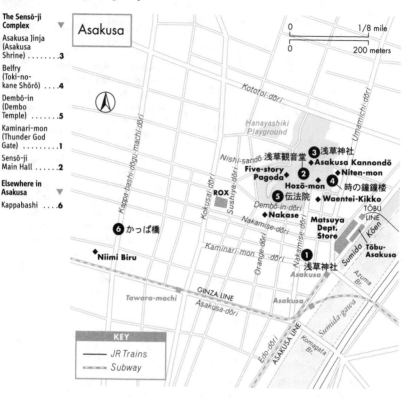

vided more than tea. Then, in 1841, the Kabuki theaters moved to Asakusa. It was only for a short time, but that was enough to establish it as *the* entertainment quarter of the city—a reputation it held unchallenged until World War II, when most of the area was destroyed. Though it never fully recoved as an entertainment district, the area today is home to artisans and small entrepreneurs, children and grandmothers, hipsters, hucksters, and priests. If you have any time to spend in Tōkyō, make sure you devote at least a day to exploring Asakusa.

Numbers in the margin correspond to the Asakusa map.

DID YOU KNOW?

Kuremutusu, the first drinking establishment in Japan to call itself a "bar," was started in Asakusa in 1880. It still stands today, under new ownership (of course) and a new name, Waentei-Kikko.

Orientation & Planning

ORIENTATION Rich in history and traditional culture, this northeastern area of Tōkyō should be top on your list of destinations. Asakusa is a border city ward that separates central Tōkyō from suburban areas beyond. It is a unique spiritual and commercial, tourist and residential area, where locals walk

1

TOP REASONS TO VISIT

Make a Wish Visit the **Asakusa Jinja** where the souls of the three men who built Sensō-ji are enshrined. If you have a special wish, purchase a wooden placard, write your message on it, and leave it for the gods.

A Japanese Party Half-naked drunken people? Loud Crowds? Brilliant colors? It's all part of the **Sanja Festival**, which happens every May in the streets of Asakusa.

Photo Op Want to show your friends that you saw the Thunder God Gate?

Then make sure you take a photograph in front of the giant red-paper lantern of **Kaminari-mon.**

Don't Eat That! Discover the delight of Japanese plastic food in **Kappabashi.**

Shop Till You Drop Looking for trinkets or gifts to bring home? Visit more than 80 shops on Nakamise-dori that sell everything from rice crackers to *kiriko* (traditionally cut and colored glassware whose style was developed in the Edo period).

their dogs on the Asakusa Jinja grounds or give offerings and pray at Kannon Temple. Life in this area is slow-paced and uncomplicated.

Asakusa is just east of Ueno and can be explored thoroughly in a half-day, whether you go straight from Ueno or on a separate excursion. Getting there by subway from Ueno Station (Ginza line, Ueno Station to Asakusa Station, ¥160) or taxi (approximately ¥900) is most convenient. Asakusa is the last stop (eastbound) on the Ginza subway line.

PLANNING   Unlike most of the other areas to explore on foot in Tōkyō, Sensō-ji is admirably compact. You can easily see the temple and environs in a morning. The garden at Dembō-in is worth a half hour. If you decide to include Kappabashi, allow yourself an hour more for the tour. Some of the shopping arcades in this area are covered, but Asakusa is essentially an outdoor experience. Be prepared for rain in June and heat and humidity in July and August.

Another way get to Asakusa is by river bus ferry from Hinode Pier, which stops at the southwest corner of Sumida Kōen.

The Asakusa Tourist Information Center (Asakusa Bunka Kankō Center) is across the street from Kaminari-mon. A volunteer with some English knowledge is on duty here daily 10–5 and will happily load you down with maps and brochures.

What to See

The Sensō-ji Complex

FodorsChoice   Dedicated to the goddess Kannon, the Sensō-ji Complex is the heart and
★   soul of Asakusa. Come for its local and historical importance, its garden, its 17th-century Shintō shrine, and the wild Sanja Festival in May.
⊠ *2–3–1 Asakusa, Taitō-ku* ☎ *03/3842–0181* 📧 *Free* ☺ *Temple*

grounds daily 6–sunset Ⓜ *Ginza subway line, Asakusa Station (Exit 1/Kaminari-mon Exit).*

❸ **Asakusa Jinja** (Asakusa Shrine). Several structures in the temple complex survived the bombings of 1945. The largest, to the right of the Main Hall, is this Shintō shrine to the Hikonuma brothers and their master, Naji-no-Nakamoto—the putative founders of Sensō-ji. In Japan, Buddhism and Shintōism have enjoyed a comfortable coexistence since the former arrived from China in the 6th century. The shrine, built in 1649, is also known as Sanja Sama (Shrine of the Three Guardians). Near the entrance to Asakusa Shrine is another survivor of World War II: the east gate to the temple grounds, **Niten-mon,** built in 1618 for a shrine to Ieyasu Tokugawa and designated by the government as an Important Cultural Property. ✉ *Taitō-ku.*

> ### THREE WISE MEN
>
> The Sanja Festival, held annually on May 17–20, is said to be the biggest, loudest, wildest party in Tōkyō. Each of the neighborhoods under Sanja Sama's protection has its own **mikoshi** (portable Shintō shrines), and on the second day of the festival, these palanquins are paraded through the streets of Asakusa to the shrine. Many of the "parishioners" take part naked to the waist, or with the sleeves of their tunics rolled up, to expose fantastic red-and-black tattoo patterns that sometimes cover their entire backs and shoulders. These are the tribal markings of the Japanese underworld.

❹ **Belfry** (Toki-no-kane Shōrō). The tiny hillock Benten-yama, with its shrine to the goddess of good fortune, is the site of this 17th-century belfry. The bell here used to toll the hours for the people of the district, and it was said that you could hear it anywhere within a radius of some 6 km (4 mi). The bell still sounds at 6 AM every day, when the temple grounds open. It also rings on New Year's Eve—108 strokes in all, beginning just before midnight, to "ring out" the 108 sins and frailties of humankind and make a clean start for the coming year. Benten-yama and the belfry are at the beginning of the narrow street that parallels Nakamise-dōri. ✉ *Taitō-ku.*

NEED A BREAK? Originally a teahouse, **Waenti-Kikko,** which used to be Kuremuttsu, is now a cosy country style Japanese restaurant and bar. The new owner, Fukui Kodai, is a traditional Japanese *Tsugaru Shamisen* (string instrument) musician, who performs at scheduled times throughout the day. Narrow your field of vision, shut out the world outside, and you could be back in the waning days of Meiji-period Japan. This pub specializes in premium sake, with set courses of food and drink for lunch (¥1,890 to ¥3,500) and dinner (¥6,300 to ¥12,600). There is a 10% service charge for dinner. ✉ *2-2-13 Asakusa, Taitō-ku* ☎ *03/5828-8833* ⊕ *www.waentei-kikko.com* ⊙ *Daily 11:30–2 and 5–10.*

★ ❺ **Dembō-in** (Dembo Temple). Believed to have been made in the 17th century by Kōbori Enshū, the genius of Zen landscape design, the garden of Dembō-in, part of the living quarters of the abbot of Sensō-ji, is the best-kept secret in Asakusa. The garden of Dembō-in is usually empty and always utterly serene, an island of privacy in a sea of pilgrims. Spring, when the wisteria blooms, is the ideal time to be here.

A sign in English on Dembō-in-dōri, about 150 yards west of the intersection with Nakamise-dōri, indicates the entrance, through the side door of a large wooden gate. ■ TIP→ **For permission to see the abbot's garden, you must first apply at the temple administration building, between Hōzō-mon and the Five-Story Pagoda, in the far corner.** ⊠ *Taitō-ku* ☎ *03/3842–0181 for reservations* ≊ *Free* ⊙ *Daily 9–4; may be closed if abbot has guests.*

NEED A BREAK?

Nakase is a lovely retreat from the overbearing crowds at Asakusa Kannon. The building, which is 130 years old, lends to a truly authentic Japanese experience: food is served in lacquerware bento boxes and there's an interior garden and pond, which is filled with carp and goldfish. Across Orange-dōri from the red-brick Asakusa Public Hall, Nakase is expensive (lunch at the tables inside starts at ¥3,000; more elaborate meals by the garden start at ¥7,000), but the experience is worth it. ⊠ *1–39–13 Asakusa, Taitō-ku* ☎ *03/3841–4015* ▭ *No credit cards* ⊙ *Wed.–Mon. 11–3, 5–8.*

❶ Kaminari-mon (Thunder God Gate). This is the proper Sensō-ji entrance, with its huge red-paper lantern hanging in the center—a landmark of Asakusa, and picture perfect. The original gate was destroyed by fire in 1865; the replica you see today was built after World War II. Traditionally, two fearsome guardian gods are installed in the alcoves of Buddhist temple gates to ward off evil spirits. The Thunder God (Kaminari-no-Kami) is on the left with the Wind God (Kaze-no-Kami) on the right. ■ TIP→ **Looking to buy some of Tōkyō's most famous souvenirs? Stop at Tokiwa-dō, the shop on the west side of the gate for** *kaminari okoshi* **(thunder crackers), made of rice, millet, sugar, and beans.**

Kaminari-mon also marks the southern extent of **Nakamise-dōri**, the Street of Inside Shops. The area from Kaminari-mon to the inner gate of the temple was once composed of stalls leased to the townspeople who cleaned and swept the temple grounds. This is now kitsch-souvenir central, so be prepared to buy a few key chains and snacks. ⊠ *Taitō-ku.*

❷ Sensō-ji Main Hall. The Main Hall and Five-Story Pagoda of Sensō-ji are both faithful copies in concrete of originals that burned down in 1945. During a time when most of the people of Asakusa were still rebuilding after the fire raids, it took 13 years to raise money for the restoration of their beloved Sensō-ji. To them, and those in the entertainment world, this is much more than a tourist attraction: Kabuki actors still come here before a new season of performances, and sumō wrestlers visit before a tournament to pay their respects. The large lanterns in the Main Hall were donated by the geisha associations of Asakusa and nearby Yanagi-bashi. Most Japanese stop at the huge bronze incense burner, in front of the Main Hall, to bathe their hands and faces in the smoke—it's a charm to ward off illnesses—before climbing the stairs to offer their prayers.

CLOSE UP

Is That Edible?

THE CUSTOM OF PUTTING models of the food served in the restaurant's windows dates back to the Meiji Restoration period, but the food wasn't always plastic. In fact, the idea first came to Japan from the wax models that were used as anatomical teaching aids in the new schools of Western medicine. A businessman from Nara decided that wax models would also make good point-of-purchase advertising for restaurants. He was right: the industry grew in a modest way at first, making models mostly of Japanese food. In the boom years after 1960, restaurants began to serve all sorts of dishes most people had never seen before, and the models provided much-needed reassurance: "So *that's* a cheeseburger. It doesn't look as bad as it sounds. Let's go in and try one." By the mid-1970s, the makers of plastic food were turning out creations of astonishing virtuosity and realism. If you're looking for what some have deemed a form of pop art, then head to Kappabashi.

The Main Hall, about 115 feet long and 108 feet wide, is not an especially impressive work of architecture. Unlike many other temples, part of the inside has a concrete floor, so you can come and go without removing your shoes. In this area hang Senso-ji's chief claims to artistic importance: a collection of 18th- and 19th-century votive paintings on wood. Plaques of this kind, called *ema,* are still offered to the gods at shrines and temples, but they are commonly simpler and smaller. The worshipper buys a little tablet of wood with the picture already painted on one side and inscribes a prayer on the other. The temple owns more than 50 of these works, which were removed to safety in 1945 to escape the air raids. Only eight of them, depicting scenes from Japanese history and mythology, are on display. A catalog of the collection is on sale in the hall, but the text is in Japanese only.

Lighting is poor in the Main Hall, and the actual works are difficult to see. One thing that visitors cannot see at all is the holy image of Kannon itself, which supposedly lies buried somewhere deep under the temple. Not even the priests of Senso-ji have ever seen it, and there is in fact no conclusive evidence that it actually exists.

Hōzō-mon, the gate to the temple courtyard, is also a repository for sutras (Buddhist texts) and other treasures of Senso-ji. This gate, too, has its guardian gods; should either god decide to leave his post for a stroll, he can use the enormous pair of sandals hanging on the back wall—the gift of a Yamagata Prefecture village famous for its straw weaving. ⊠ *Taitō-ku.*

Elsewhere in Asakusa

★ ❻ **Kappabashi.** In the 19th century, according to local legend, a river ran through the present-day Kappabashi district. The surrounding area was poorly drained and was often flooded. A local shopkeeper began a project to improve the drainage, investing all his own money, but met with little success until a troupe of *kappa*—mischievous green water sprites—

emerged from the river to help him. A more prosaic explanation for the name of the district points out that the lower-ranking retainers of the local lord used to earn extra money by making straw raincoats, also called *kappa,* that they spread to dry on the bridge.

Today, Kappabashi's more than 200 wholesale dealers sell everything the city's restaurant and bar trade could possibly need to do business, from paper supplies and steam tables to their main attraction, plastic food. It is baffling to most Japanese that Kappabashi is a hot tourist attraction. ⊠ *Nishi-Asakusa 1-chōme and 2-chōme, Taitō-ku* ⊗ *Most shops daily 9–6* Ⓜ *Ginza subway line, Tawara-machi Station (Exit 1).*

TSUKIJI & SHIODOME

Although it's best known today as the site of the largest fish market in Asia, Tsukiji is also a reminder of the awesome disaster of the great fire of 1657. In the space of two days, it killed more than 100,000 people and leveled almost 70% of Ieyasu Tokugawa's new capital. Ieyasu was not a man to be discouraged by mere catastrophe, however; he took it as an opportunity to plan an even bigger and better city, one that would incorporate the marshes east of his castle. Tsukiji, in fact, means "reclaimed land," and a substantial block of land it was, laboriously drained and filled, from present-day Ginza to the bay.

The common people of the tenements and alleys, who had suffered most in the great fire, did not benefit from this land project as it was first allotted to feudal lords and temples. After 1853, when Japan opened its doors to the outside world, Tsukiji became Tōkyō's first foreign settlement—the site of the American delegation and an elegant two-story brick hotel, and home to missionaries, teachers, and doctors.

To the west of Tsukiji lie Shiodome and Shimbashi. In the period after the Meiji Restoration, Shimbashi was one of the most famous geisha districts of the new capital. Its reputation as a pleasure quarter is even older. In the Edo period, when there was a network of canals and waterways here, it was the height of luxury to charter a covered boat (called a *yakata-bune*) from one of the Shimbashi boathouses for a cruise on the river; a local restaurant would cater the excursion, and a local geisha house would provide companionship. Almost nothing remains in Shimbashi to recall that golden age, but as its luster has faded, adjacent Shiodome has risen—literally—in its place as one of the most ambitious redevelopment projects of 21st-century Tōkyō.

Shiodome (literally "where the tide stops") was an area of saltwater flats on which in 1872 the Meiji government built the Tōkyō terminal—the original Shimbashi Station—on Japan's first railway line, which ran for 29 km (18 mi) to nearby Yokohama. The area eventually became Japan Rail's (JR) most notorious white elephant: a staggeringly valuable hunk of real estate, smack in the middle of the world's most expensive city that JR no longer needed and couldn't seem to sell. By 1997 a bewildering succession of receivers, public development corporations, and zoning commissions had evolved an urban renewal plan for the area, and the land was auctioned off. Among the buyers were Nippon Television

TOP REASONS TO VISIT

Urban Oasis Discover a lovely traditional garden oasis and old teahouse surrounded by skycrapers and concrete at **Hama Rikyū Tei-en**.

Got Fish? You'll dine on the freshest sushi in the world at **Tsukiji fish market**.

Off the Beaten Path Discover the local charm of old sushi and sashimi restaurants, and small markets in the **backstreets of Tsukiji**.

Kabuki Krazy Kabuki-za is the only Kabuki show in Tōkyō with English dubbing available.

and Dentsū, the largest advertising agency in Asia and the fourth largest in the world.

In 2002 Dentsū consolidated its scattered offices into the centerpiece of the Shiodome project: a 47-story tower and annex designed by Jean Nouvel. With the annex, known as the Caretta Shiodome, Dentsū aspired not just to a new corporate address, but an "investment in community": a complex of cultural facilities, shops, and restaurants that has turned Shiodome into one of the most fashionable places in the city to see and be seen. The 1,200-seat Dentsū Shiki Theater SEA has become one of Tōkyō's major venues for live performances; its resident repertory company regularly brings long-running Broadway hits like *Mamma Mia* to eager Japanese audiences.

Numbers in the margin correspond to the Tsukiji & Shiodome map.

Orientation & Planning

ORIENTATION Shiodome is the southeastern transportation hub of central Tōkyō and the area is easily accessed by public transport: JR Yurikome Line Shimbashi Station, Toei-Ōedo Shiodome Line Station, Toei-Asakusa Line Shimbashi Station, and Ginza Line Shimbashi Station. The connection station to the Yuikamome Monorail, a scenic ride that takes you to Odaiba in approximately 30 minutes, is also here. You can also get around quite easily on foot. There are sophisticated walkways in the sky that connect all the major buildings and subway and train stations.

Tsukiji, located just east of Shiodome, is a sushi-lover's dream. Perhaps getting up at 5 AM to eat fish at the market isn't your idea of breakfast, but this is definitely an excellent place to taste the freshest sushi on earth.

PLANNING Tsukiji has few places to spend time *in*; getting from point to point, however, can consume most of a morning. The backstreet shops will probably require no more than an hour. Allow yourself about an hour to explore the fish market; if fish in all its diversity holds a special fascination for you, take two hours. Remember that in order to see the fish auction in action, you need to get to the market before 6:30 AM; by 9 AM the business of the market is largely finished for the day.

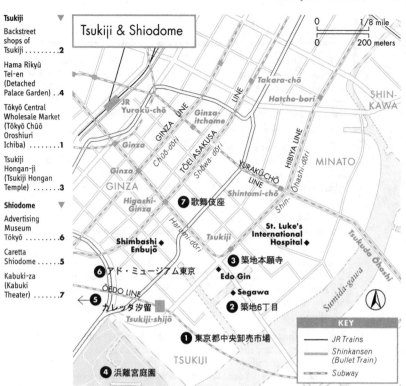

Take the subway to Tsukiji Station, which will always be the more dependable and cost efficient option. To take the train there and back (depending on where you are staying), it will cost between ¥160 and ¥600. Sushi and sashimi will be cheaper here than other parts of Tōkyō, with sushi sets at most sushi stalls costing between ¥1,000 to ¥2,100.

This part of the city can be brutally hot and muggy in August; during the O-bon holiday, in the middle of the month, Tsukiji is comparatively lifeless. Mid-April and early October are best for strolls in the Hama Rikyū Tei-en.

What to See

❻ **Advertising Museum Tōkyō.** ADMT puts the unique Japanese gift for graphic and commercial design into historical perspective, from the sponsored "placements" in 18th-century wood-block prints to the postmodern visions of fashion photographers and video directors. The museum is maintained by a foundation established in honor of Hideo Yoshida, fourth president of the mammoth Dentsū Advertising Company, and includes a digital library of some 130,000 entries on everything you ever wanted to know about hype. There are no explanatory panels in English—but this in itself is a test of how well the visual vocabulary of consumer media

CLOSE UP

Gooooaaaallll!!!!

THE J. LEAGUE, JAPAN'S FIRST professional soccer league, was started in 1993 and has 26 teams in two divisions. Tōkyō hosts two of those professional soccer teams, FC Tōkyō and Tōkyō Verde.

When: The J. League's preseason has two 15-week schedules, one beginning in mid-March and the other in mid-August; visitors to Tōkyō have a pretty fair window of opportunity to see a match.

Where: Both of Tōkyō's teams play at the 50,000-seat **Ajinomoto Stadium.** ✉ *376–3 Nishi-machi, Chōfu City* ☎ *0424/88–6255* Ⓜ *JR Keiō Line, Tobitakyū Station.*

How: Tickets cost ¥1,500–¥6,000 and can be ordered through **Playguide** (☎ 03/3561–8821) or purchased directly at the stadium or most Seven-Eleven, Family Mart, or Lawson convenience stores.

can communicate across cultures. ✉ *1–8–2 Higashi-Shimbashi, Caretta Shiodome B1F–B2F, Chūō-ku* ☎ *03/6218–2500* ⊕ *www.admt.jp* 🎫 *Free* ◷ *Tues.–Fri. 11–6:30, Sat. 11–4:30* Ⓜ *Ōedo subway line, Shiodome Station (Exit 7); JR (Shiodome Exit) and Asakusa and Ginza lines (Exit 4), Shimbashi Station.*

❷ Backstreet shops of Tsukiji. Tōkyō's markets provide a vital counterpoint

FodorśChoice ★ to the museums and monuments of conventional sightseeing: they let you see how people really live in the city. If you have time for only one market, this is the one to see. The three square blocks between the Tōkyō Central Wholesale Market and Harumi-dōri have, naturally enough, scores of fishmongers, but also shops and restaurants. Stores sell pickles, tea, crackers and snacks, cutlery (what better place to pick up a professional sushi knife?), baskets, and kitchenware. Hole-in-the-wall sushi bars here have set menus ranging from ¥1,000 to ¥2,100; look for the plastic models of food in glass cases out front. The area includes the row of little counter restaurants, barely more than street stalls, under the arcade along the east side of Shin-Ōhashi-dōri, each with its specialty. If you haven't had breakfast by this point in your walk, stop at **Segawa** for *maguro donburi*—a bowl of fresh raw tuna slices served over rice and garnished with bits of dried seaweed (Segawa is in the middle of the arcade, but without any distinguishing features or English signage; your best bet is to ask someone). ■ TIP→ **Some 100 of the small retailers and restaurants in this area are members of the Tsukiji Meiten-kai (Association of Notable Shops), and promote themselves by selling illustrated maps of the area for ¥50; the maps are all in Japanese, but with proper frames they make great souvenirs.** ✉ *Tsukiji 4-chōme, Chūō-ku* Ⓜ *Ōedo subway line, Tsukiji-shijō Station (Exit A1); Hibiya subway line, Tsukiji Station (Exit 1).*

❺ Caretta Shiodome. This 51-story skyscraper (◷ 11–8) houses the offices of advertising giant Dentsū, as well as other offices, restaurants, and shopping. The sky restaurants on the building's top floors have scenic views of Tōkyō Bay and are a good place to have lunch or dinner. Try Bice

Tōkyō (☎ 03/5537–1926 ⊘ Weekdays lunch 11–5, dinner 5:30–9:30, weekend dinner starts at 5:30) on the 47th floor, which serves a European set lunch (¥4,000) and dinner (¥12,000) menus. ✉ *1-8-1 Higashi Shimbashi Minato-ku.*

★ ❹ **Hama Rikyū Tei-en** (Detached Palace Garden). Like a tiny sanctuary of Japanese tradition and nature that's surrounded by towering glass buildings, this garden is worth a visit. The land here was originally owned by the Owari branch of the Tokugawa family from Nagoya, and it extended to part of what is now the fish market. When one of the family became shōgun in 1709, his residence was turned into a shōgunal palace—with pavilions, ornamental gardens, pine and cherry groves, and duck ponds. The garden became a public park in 1945, although a good portion of it is fenced off as a nature preserve. None of the original buildings have survived, but on the island in the large pond is a reproduction of the pavilion where former U.S. president Ulysses S. Grant and Mrs. Grant had an audience with the emperor Meiji in 1879. The building can now be rented for parties. The path to the left as you enter the garden leads to the "river bus" ferry landing, from which you can leave this excursion and begin another: up the Sumida-gawa to Asakusa. ⚠ Note that you must pay the admission to the garden even if you're just using the ferry. ✉ *1–1 Hamarikyū–Teien, Chūō-ku* ☎ *03/3541–0200* ⚑ *¥300* ⊘ *Daily 9–4:30* Ⓜ *Ōedo subway line, Shiodome Station (Exit 8).*

★ ❼ **Kabuki-za** (Kabuki Theater). Soon after the Meiji Restoration and its enforced exile in Asakusa, Kabuki began to reestablish itself in this part of the city. The first Kabuki-za was built in 1889, with a European facade. In 1912 the Kabuki-za was taken over by the Shochiku theatrical management company, which replaced the old theater building in 1925. Designed by architect Shin'ichirō Okada, it was damaged during World War II but was restored soon thereafter. Tickets are only sold at the theater's ticket booth. Reservations by phone are recommended. If you want to see what all of the hype is about, this is the place to see a Kabuki show. English Earphone Guides are available for a small fee and provide explanations and comments in English about the performance. ✉ *4–12–15 Ginza, Chūō-ku* ☎ *03/5565–6000* ⚑ *¥2,500 to ¥17,000* ⊘ *Box office open daily 10–4* ⊕ *www.shochiku.co.jp/play/kabukiza/ theater* Ⓜ *Hibiya subway line, Higashi-Ginza Station (Exit 3).*

NEED A BREAK?
Edo-Gin, one of the area's older sushi bars, founded in 1924, is legendary for its portions—slices of raw fish that almost hide the balls of rice on which they sit. The set menu at lunch is a certifiable *bāgen* (bargain) at ¥1,050, and sushi dinner sets are only ¥2,800, including beer or sake. Walk southwest on Shin-Ōhashi-dōri from its intersection with Harumi-dōri. Take the first right and look for Edo-Gin just past the next corner, on the left. ✉ *4–5–1 Tsukiji, Chūō-ku* ☎ *03/ 3543–4401* ▭ *AE, MC, V* ⊘ *Closed early Jan.* Ⓜ *Hibiya subway line, Tsukiji Station (Exit 1); Ōedo subway line, Tsukiji-shijō Station (Exit A1).*

★ ❶ **Tōkyō Central Wholesale Market** (Tōkyō Chūō Oroshiuri Ichiba). The city's fish market used to be farther uptown, in Nihombashi. It was moved to Tsukiji after the Great Kantō Earthquake of 1923, and it occupies

Fish Mongers Wanted

WHY GO TO THE TSUKIJI FISH market? Quite simply, because of how the fish is sold—auction. The catch—more than 100 varieties of fish in all, including whole frozen tuna, Styrofoam cases of shrimp and squid, and crates of crabs—is laid out in the long covered area between the river and the main building. Then the bidding begins. Only members of the wholesalers' association can take part. Wearing license numbers fastened to the front of their caps, they register their bids in a kind of sign language, shouting to draw the attention of the auctioneer and making furious combinations in the air with their fingers. The auctioneer keeps the action moving in a hoarse croak that sounds like no known language, and spot quotations change too fast for ordinary mortals to follow.

Different fish are auctioned off at different times and locations, and by 6:30 AM or so, this part of the day's business is over, and the wholesalers fetch their purchases back into the market in barrows. Restaurant owners and retailers arrive about 7, making the rounds of favorite suppliers for their requirements. Chaos seems to reign, but everybody here knows everybody else, and they all have it down to a system.

⚠ The 52,000 or so buyers, wholesalers, and shippers who work at the market may be a lot more receptive to casual visitors than they were in the past, but they are not running a tourist attraction. They're in the fish business, moving more than 600,000 tons of it a year to retailers and restaurants all over the city, and this is their busiest time of day. The cheerful banter they use with each other can turn snappish if you get in their way. Also bear in mind that you are not allowed to take photographs while the auctions are under way (flashes are a distraction). The market is kept spotlessly clean, which means the water hoses are running all the time. Boots are helpful, but if you don't want to carry them, bring a pair of heavy-duty trash bags to slip over your shoes and secure them above your ankles with rubber bands.

the site of what was once Japan's first naval training academy. Today the market sprawls over some 54 acres of reclaimed land and employs approximately 15,000 people, making it the largest fish market in the world. Its warren of buildings houses about 1,200 wholesale shops, supplying 90% of the seafood consumed in Tōkyō every day—some 2,400 tons of it. Most of the seafood sold in Tsukiji comes in by truck, arriving through the night from fishing ports all over the country. ⊠ *5–2–1 Tsukiji, Chūō-ku* ☎ *03/3542–1111* ⊕ *www.shijou.metro.Tōkyō.jp* ▨ *Free* ☉ *Business hrs Mon.–Sat. (except 2nd and 4th Wed. of month) 5 AM–3 PM* Ⓜ *Ōedo subway line, Tsukiji-shijō Station (Exit A1); Hibiya subway line, Tsukiji Station (Exit 1).*

❸ **Tsukiji Hongan-ji** (Tsukiji Hongan Temple). Disaster seemed to follow this temple, the main branch in Tōkyō of Kyōto's Nishi Hongan-ji, since it was first located here in 1657: it was destroyed at least five times, and reconstruction in wood was finally abandoned after the Great Kantō Earthquake of 1923. The present stone building dates from 1935. It was designed by Chūta Ito, a pupil of Tokyo Station architect Tatsuno Kingo. Ito's other credits include the Meiji Shrine in Harajuku; he also lobbied for Japan's first law for the preservation of historic buildings. Ito traveled extensively in Asia; the evocations of classical Hindu architecture in the temple's domes and ornaments were his homage to India as the cradle of Buddhism. But with stained-glass windows and a pipe organ as well, the building is nothing if not eclectic. ✉ *3–15–1 Tsukiji, Chūō-ku* ☎ *03/3541–1131* ✉ *Free* 🕐 *Daily 6 AM–4 PM* Ⓜ *Hibiya subway line, Tsukiji Station (Exit 1).*

NIHOMBASHI, GINZA & YŪRAKU-CHŌ

Tōkyō is a city of many centers. The municipal administrative center is in Shinjuku. The national government center is in Kasumigaseki. Nihombashi is the center of banking and finance and Ginza is the center of commerce.

When Ieyasu Tokugawa had the first bridge constructed at Nihombashi, he designated it the starting point for the five great roads leading out of his city, the point from which all distances were to be measured. His decree is still in force: the black pole on the present bridge, erected in 1911, is the Zero Kilometer marker for all the national highways and is considered the true center of Tōkyō.

The early millionaires of Edo built their homes in the Nihombashi area. Some, like the legendary timber magnate Bunzaemon Kinokuniya, spent everything they made in the pleasure quarters of Yoshiwara and died penniless. Others founded the great trading houses of today—Mitsui, Mitsubishi, Sumitomo—which still have warehouses nearby.

When Japan's first corporations were created and the Meiji government developed a modern system of capital formation, the Tōkyō Stock Exchange (Shōken Torihikijo) was established on the west bank of the Nihombashi-gawa (Nihombashi River). The home offices of most of the country's major securities companies are only a stone's throw from the exchange.

In the Edo period there were three types of currency in circulation: gold, silver, and copper. Ieyasu Tokugawa started minting his own silver coins in 1598 in his home province of Suruga, even before he became shōgun. In 1601 he established a gold mint; the building was only a few hundred yards from Nihombashi, on the site of what is now the Bank of Japan. In 1612 he relocated the Suruga plant to a patch of reclaimed land west of his castle. The area soon came to be known informally as Ginza (Silver Mint).

Currency values fluctuated during this time and eventually businesses fell under the control of a few large merchant houses. One of the most successful of these merchants was a man named Takatoshi Mitsui, who by the end of the 17th century created a commercial empire—in retail-

CLOSE UP

Need to Get Physical?

THE VAST MAJORITY OF POOLS and fitness centers in Tōkyō are for members only, but the fitness center at **Bigbox Seibu Athletic Club** is open to nonmembers for ¥4,200; use of the six-lane, 25-meter-long pool, which is only available to nonmembers on Sundays and Mondays 10–6, is an additional ¥1,575. (✉ 1–35–3 Takadano-baba, Shinjuku-ku ☎ 03/5272–5204).

The various wards of Tōkyō operate public facilities that are usually for residents only. A few do allow visitor use but the registration formalities can be a hassle, so make sure you bring your passport or a photo ID, and if you don't speak Japanese, be prepared to improvise. One of the best is the recently renovated **Shiba Swimming Pool** at **Minato City Sports Center,** (✉ 2–7–2 Shiba Kōen, Minato-ku ☎ 03/3452–4151), which is

open to non-residents daily 9 to 9 except for the first and third Sunday and Monday of each month. The pool charges ¥700 for two hours of swimming.

Another option is Tōkyō's best-kept secret: international amateur sports clubs. Often started by ex-pats, they range from seriously competitive soccer or rugby to just-for-fun volleyball or cycling. Most meet regularly on weekends and evenings, welcome walk-ins, and are likely to have some English-speaking members. One-time fees vary but are rarely more than ¥2,000 for one to two hours of play or practice. Many are listed in local English-language magazines or Web sites. *Fitness Japan* is a comprehensive source with contact info, a directory, and an events calendar. ⊕ www.fitnessjp.com.

ing, banking, and trading—known today as the Mitsui Group. Not far from the site of Echigo-ya stands its direct descendant: Mitsukoshi department store.

The district called Yūraku-chō—the Pleasure (*yūraku*) Quarter (*chō*)— lies west of Ginza's Sukiya-bashi, stretching from Sotobori-dōri to Hibiya Kōen and the Outer Garden of the Imperial Palace. The "pleasures" associated with this district in the early postwar period stemmed from a number of the buildings that survived the air raids of 1945 and requisitioned by the Allied forces. Yūraku-chō quickly became the haunt of the so-called *pan-pan* women, who kept the GIs company. Because it was so close to the military post exchange in Ginza, the area under the railroad tracks became one of the city's largest black markets. Later, the black market gave way to clusters of cheap restaurants, most of them little more than a counter and a few stools, serving *yakitori* (skewered grilled chicken) and beer. Office workers on meager budgets and journalists from the nearby *Mainichi, Asahi,* and *Yomiuri* newspaper headquarters would gather here at night. Yūraku-chō-under-the-tracks was smoky, loud, and friendly—a kind of open-air substitute for the local taproom. The area has long since become upscale, and no more than a handful of the yakitori stalls remain.

Numbers in the margin correspond to the Nihombashi, Ginza, & Yūraku-chō map.

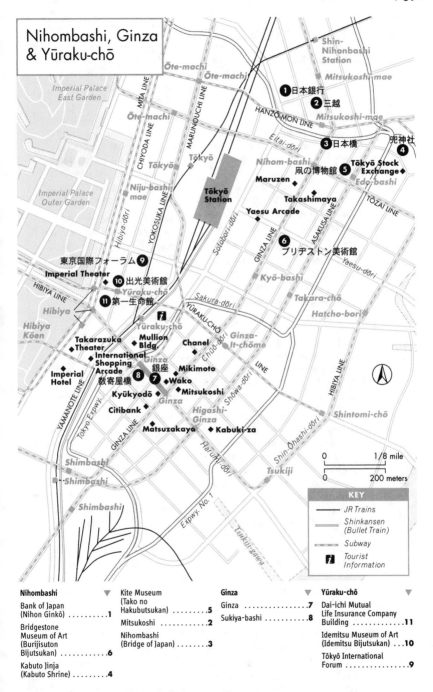

Nihombashi, Ginza & Yūraku-chō

TOP REASONS TO VISIT

A Yen for Yen See where the history of the yen began, in the **Bank of Japan and Currency Museum,** which houses a collection of rare historical Asian currencies.

Japanese Impressions Go to the **Bridgestone Museum of Art,** one of Japan's best private collections of French impressionist art and sculpture and of post-Meiji Japanese painting in Western styles by such artists as Shigeru Aoki and Tsuguji Fujita.

Tang and Song The **Idemitsu Museum of Art** houses a collection of Tang- and Song-dynasty Chinese porcelain and Japanese ceramics— including works by Nonomura

Ninsei and Ogata Kenzan. Also on display are masterpieces of Old Seto, Oribe, Old Kutani, Karatsu, and Kakiemon ware.

A Leisurely Stroll On weekends, the main roads of Ginza are closed off for pedestrians, so you can see the historical **Wako** department store, and explore the small side streets of this old shopping district without fearing the crazy drivers.

Feeding Frenzy Check out the basement food halls in **Mitsukoshi** department store, in Nihombashi and Ginza, where you will find hundreds of delicious desserts and prepared foods of many varieties.

Orientation & Planning

ORIENTATION The combined areas of Yūraku-chō, Ginza, and Nihombashi are located beside the Imperial Palace district, to the southeast side of central Tōkyō. Yūraku-chō lies west of Ginza's Sukiya-bashi, stretching from Sotobori-dōri to Hibiya Kōen and the Outer Garden of the Imperial Palace.

PLANNING There's something about this part of Tōkyō—the traffic, the number of people, the way it urges you to keep moving—that can make you feel you've covered a lot more ground than you really have. Attack this area early in the morning but avoid rush hour (8–9) if you plan on taking the subway. None of the area's sites, with the possible exception of the Bridgestone and Idemitsu museums, should take you more than 45 minutes. The time you spend shopping, of course, is up to you. In summer make a point of starting early or in the late afternoon, because by midday the heat and humidity can be brutal. Make sure to carry bottled water. On weekend afternoons (October–March, Saturday 3–5 and Sunday noon–5; April–September, Saturday 2–6 and Sunday noon–6), Chūō-dōri is closed to traffic from Shimbashi all the way to Kyō-bashi and becomes a pedestrian mall with tables and chairs set out along the street. Keep in mind that some of the museums and other sights in the area close on Sunday.

What to See

❶ **Bank of Japan** (Nihon Ginkō). The older part of the Bank of Japan is the work of Tatsuno Kingo, who also designed Tōkyō Station. Completed in 1896, on the site of what had been the Edo-period gold mint, the bank is one of the few surviving Meiji-era Western buildings in the city. The annex building houses the **Currency Museum,** a historical collection of rare gold and silver coins from Japan and other East Asian countries. There's little English information here, but the setting of muted lighting and plush red carpets evokes the days when the only kind of money around was heavy, shiny, and made of precious metals. ⊠ *2–1–1 Nihombashi Hongoku-chō, Chūō-ku* ☎ *03/3279–1111 bank, 03/3277–3037 museum* ⊕ *www.boj.or.jp* 🎫 *Free* ⊙ *Tues.–Sun. 9:30–4:30* Ⓜ *Ginza (Exit A5) and Hanzō-mon (Exit B1) subway lines, Mitsukoshi-mae Station.*

❻ Bridgestone Museum of Art (Burijisuton Bijutsukan). This is one of Japan's best private collections of French impressionist art and sculpture and of post-Meiji Japanese painting in Western styles by such artists as Shigeru Aoki and Tsuguji Fujita. The collection, assembled by Bridgestone Tire Company founder Shōjiro Ishibashi, also includes work by Rembrandt, Picasso, Utrillo, and Modigliani. The small gallery devoted to ancient art has a breathtaking Egyptian cat sculpture dating to between 950 and 660 BC. The Bridgestone also puts on major exhibits from private collections and museums abroad. ⊠ *1–10–1 Kyō-bashi, Chūō-ku* ☎ *03/3563–0241* ⊕ *www.bridgestone-museum.gr.jp* 🎫 *¥800* ⊙ *Tues.–Sat. 10–8, Sun. 10–6 (entrance up to 30 min. before closing)* Ⓜ *Ginza subway line, Kyō-bashi Station (Meijiya Exit) or Nihombashi Station (Takashimaya Exit).*

⓫ Dai-ichi Mutual Life Insurance Company Building. Built like a fortress, this edifice survived World War II virtually intact and was taken over by the Supreme Command of the Allied powers. From his office here, General Douglas MacArthur directed the affairs of Japan from 1945 to 1951. The room is kept exactly as it was then. Individuals and small groups can visit without appointment; you need only to sign in at the reception desk in the lobby. ⊠ *1–13–1 Yūraku-chō, Chiyoda-ku* ☎ *03/3216–1211* 🎫 *Free* ⊙ *Weekdays 10–4:30* Ⓜ *Hibiya subway line, Hibiya Station (Exit B1).*

❼ Ginza. With more history as a shopping district than trendier Omotesandō and Harajuku, Ginza is where high-end shopping first took root in Japan and now it's where Japanese "ladies who lunch" shop. But this area didn't always have the cachet of wealth and style. In fact, it wasn't until a fire in 1872 destroyed most of the old houses here and that the area was rebuilt as a Western quarter. It had two-story brick houses with balconies, the nation's first sidewalks and horse-drawn streetcars, gaslights, and, later, telephone poles. Before the turn of the 20th century, Ginza was home to the great mercantile establishments that still define its character. The **Wako** department store, for example, on the northwest corner of the 4-chōme intersection, established itself here as Hattori, purveyors of clocks and watches. The clock on the present building was first installed in the Hattori clock tower, a Ginza landmark, in 1894.

Many of the nearby shops have lineages almost as old, or older, than Wako's. A few steps north of the intersection, on Chūō-dōri, **Mikimoto** sells the famous cultured pearls first developed by Kōkichi Mikimoto in 1883. His first shop in Tōkyō dates to 1899. South of the intersection, next door to the Sanai Building, **Kyūkyodō** carries a variety of handmade Japanese papers and traditional stationery goods. Kyūkyodō has been in business since 1663 and on Ginza since 1880. Across the street and one block south is the **Matsuzakaya** department store, which began as a kimono shop in Nagoya in 1611. And connected to the Ginza line Ginza Station is the **Mistukoshi** department store, where the basement food markets are a real attraction.

There's even a name for browsing this area: Gin-bura, or "Ginza wandering." The best times to wander here are Saturday afternoons and Sunday from noon to 5 or 6 (depending on the season), when Chūō-dōri is closed to traffic between Shimbashi and Kyō-bashi. ⊠ *Chūō-ku* Ⓜ *Ginza and Hibiya subway lines, Ginza Station.*

★ ⑩ **Idemitsu Museum of Art** (Idemitsu Bijutsukan). The strength of the collection in these four spacious, well-designed rooms lies in the Tang- and Song-dynasty Chinese porcelain and in the Japanese ceramics—including works by Nonomura Ninsei and Ogata Kenzan. On display are masterpieces of Old Seto, Oribe, Old Kutani, Karatsu, and Kakiemon ware. The museum also houses outstanding examples of Zen painting and calligraphy, wood-block prints, and genre paintings of the Edo period. Of special interest to scholars is the resource collection of shards from virtually every pottery-making culture of the ancient world. The museum is on the ninth floor of the Teikoku Gekijō building. ⊠ *3–1–1 Marunouchi, Chiyoda-ku* ☎ *03/3213–9402* ✎ *¥800* ⊘ *Tues.–Sun. 10–4:30* Ⓜ *Yūraku-chō subway line, Yūraku-chō Station (Exit A1).*

❹ **Kabuto Jinja** (Kabuto Shrine). This is a minor shrine, so if you have had your fill of shrine-viewing, this one can be overlooked. But like the Nihombashi itself, it is another bit of history lurking in the shadows of the expressway. Legend has it that a noble warrior of the 11th century, who had been sent by the Imperial Court in Kyōto to subdue the barbarians of the north, stopped here and prayed for assistance. His expedition was successful, and on the way back he buried a *kabuto*, a golden helmet, on this spot as an offering of thanks. Few Japanese are aware of this legend, and the monument of choice in Kabuto-chō today is the nearby Tōkyō Stock Exchange. ⊠ *1–8 Kabuto-chō, Nihombashi, Chūō-ku* Ⓜ *Tōzai subway line, Kayaba-chō Station (Exit 10).*

☪ ❺ **Kite Museum** (Tako no Hakubutsukan). Kite flying is an old tradition in Japan. The collection here includes examples of every shape and variety from all over the country, hand-painted in brilliant colors with figures of birds, geometric patterns, and motifs from Chinese and Japanese mythology. You can call ahead to arrange a kite-making workshop (in Japanese) for groups of children. ⊠ *1–12–10 Nihombashi, Chūō-ku* ☎ *03/ 3271–2465* ⊕ *www.tako.gr.jp* ✎ *¥210* ⊘ *Mon.–Sat. 11–5* Ⓜ *Tōzai subway line, Nihombashi Station (Exit C5).*

★ ❷ **Mitsukoshi.** Takatoshi Mitsui made his fortune by revolutionizing the retail system for kimono fabrics. The emergence of Mitsukoshi as Tōkyō's first *depāto* (department store), also called *hyakkaten* (hundred-kinds-of-goods emporium), actually dates to 1908, with the construction of a three-story Western building modeled on Harrods of London. This was replaced in 1914 by a five-story structure with Japan's first escalator.

The present flagship store is vintage 1935. Even if you don't plan to shop, this branch merits a visit. Two bronze lions, modeled on those at London's Trafalgar Square, flank the main entrance and serve as one of Tōkyō's best-known meeting places. Inside, a sublime statue of Magokoro, a Japanese goddess of sincerity, rises four stories through the store's central atrium. Check out the basement floors for a taste of the food market culture of Japanese department stores and grab a quick meal-to-go while you're there. Delicious local and international prepared food is sold here at premium prices: intricately designed *mochi* (sweet red bean) cakes, Japanese bento boxes, sushi sets, and square watermelons (yes, square) all sell for approximately ¥10,000. ⊠ *1–4–1 Nihombashi Muromachi, Chūō-ku* ☎ *03/3241–3311* ⊕ *Daily 10–7:30* Ⓜ *Ginza and Hanzō-mon subway lines, Mitsukoshi-mae Station (Exits A3 and A5).*

❸ Nihombashi (Bridge of Japan). Why the expressway *had* to be routed directly over this lovely old landmark back in 1962 is one of the mysteries of Tōkyō and its city planning—or lack thereof. There were protests and petitions, but they had no effect. At that time, Tōkyō had only two years left to prepare for the Olympics, and the traffic congestion was out of control. So the bridge, originally built in 1603, with its graceful double arch, ornate lamps, and bronze Chinese lions and unicorns, was doomed to bear the perpetual rumble of trucks overhead—its claims overruled by concrete ramps and pillars. ⊠ *Chūō-ku* Ⓜ *Tōzai and Ginza subway lines, Nihombashi Station (Exits B5 and B6); Ginza and Hanzō-mon subway lines, Mitsukoshi-mae Station (Exits B5 and B6).*

❽ Sukiya-bashi. The side streets of the Sukiya-bashi area are full of art galleries, which operate a bit differently here than they do in most of the world's art markets. A few, like the venerable **Nichidō** (5–3–16 Ginza), **Gekkōso** (7–2–8 Ginza), **Yoseidō** (5–5–15 Ginza), and **Kabuto-ya** (8–8–7 Ginza), actually function as dealers, representing particular artists, as well as acquiring and selling art. The majority, however, are rental spaces. Artists or groups pay for the gallery by the week, publicize their shows themselves, and in some cases even hang their own work. You might suspect, and with good reason, that some of these shows are vanity exhibitions by amateurs with money to spare, even in a prestigious venue like Ginza; thankfully, that's not always the case. ⊠ *Chiyoda-ku* Ⓜ *Ginza, Hibiya, and Marunouchi subway lines, Ginza Station (Exit C4).*

★ ❾ Tōkyō International Forum. This postmodern masterpiece, the work of Uruguay-born American architect Raphael Viñoly, is the first major convention and art center of its kind in Tōkyō. Viñoly's design was selected in a 1989 competition that drew nearly 400 entries from 50 countries. The plaza of the Forum is that rarest of Tōkyō rarities: civilized open space. There's a long central courtyard with comfortable benches shaded by trees. Freestanding sculpture, triumphant architecture, and people strolling—actually *strolling*—are all here. The Forum itself is actually two buildings. On the east side of the plaza is Glass Hall, the main exhibition space, and the west building has six halls for international conferences, exhibitions, receptions, and concert performances. ⊠ *3–5–1 Marunouchi, Chiyoda-ku* ☎ *03/5221–9000* ⊕ *www.t-i-forum.co.jp* Ⓜ *Yūraku-chō subway line, Yūraku-chō Station (Exit A-4B).*

NEED A BREAK?

Amid all of Tōkyō's bustle and crush, you actually can catch your breath in the Tōkyō International Forum—cafés and Italian, Japanese, and French restaurants are located throughout the complex. Maps are available, so pick and choose. There are also ATM machines on the 3rd floor. A reasonably priced and delicious Kyoto-style vegetarian restaurant to try is Tsuruhan. Lunch sets start at ¥1,000 and dinner ¥3,000. ✉ 3-5-1 Marunouchi, Chiyoda-ku ☎ 03/3214-2260 ⊕ www.t-i-forum.co.jp.

AOYAMA, HARAJUKU & SHIBUYA

Who would have known? As late as 1960, this was as unlikely a candidate as any area in Tōkyō to develop into the chic capital of Tōkyō. Between Meiji shrine and the Aoyama Cemetery to the east, the area was so boring that the municipal government zoned a chunk of it for low-cost public housing. Another chunk, called Washington Heights, was being used by U.S. occupation forces who spent their money elsewhere. The few young Japanese people in Harajuku and Aoyama were either hanging around Washington Heights to practice their English or attending the Methodist-founded Aoyama Gakuin (Aoyama University)—seeking entertainment farther south in Shibuya.

When Tōkyō won its bid to host the 1964 Olympics, Washington Heights was turned over to the city for the construction of Olympic Village. Aoyama-dōri, the avenue through the center of the area, was renovated and the Ginza Line subway and Hanzō-mon Line were build under it. Suddenly, Aoyama became attractive for its Western-style fashion houses, boutiques, and design studios, and it became a hip neighborhood. By the 1980s the area was positively *smart*. Today, most of the low-cost public housing along Omotesandō, are long gone, and in their place are the glass-and-marble emporia of *the* preeminent fashion houses of Europe: Louis Vuitton, Chanel, Armani, and Prada. Their showrooms here are cash cows of their worldwide empires. Superb shops, restaurants, and amusements in this area target a population of university students, wealthy socialites, young professionals, and people who like "to see and be seen."

Numbers in the margin correspond to the Aoyama, Harajuku & Shibuya map.

TEENYBOPPER SHOPPERS OF HARAJUKU

On weekends the heart of Harajuku, particularly the street called Takeshita-dōri, belongs to high school and junior high school shoppers, who flock there for the latest trends. Entire industries give themselves convulsions just trying to keep up with adolescent styles. Stroll through Harajuku—with its outdoor cafés, its designer ice-cream and Belgian-waffle stands, its profusion of stores with names like Rap City and Octopus Army, its ever-changing profusion of mascots and logos—and you may find it impossible to believe that Japan is in fact the most rapidly aging society in the industrial world.

TOP REASONS TO VISIT

Trendy Togs and Tots Observe the trendy Japanese youth street fashions of **Harajuku Street**.

National Treasures The **Nezu Institute of Fine Arts** houses an extensive collection of painting, calligraphy, and ceramics that includes some Japanese treasures.

What's Your Hobby? Whether you're a fan of woodworking, painting, do-it-yourself home improvement projects, traveling, or even jewelry making, you're sure to find something you'll need at **Tōkyū Hands**.

You Ain't Nothing But a Hound Dog Every Sunday watch a large groups of dancing Elvis impersonators who meet at the entrance of **Yoyogi Park** to dance to a little rock'n roll.

Orientation & Planning

ORIENTATION Aoyama, Omotesandō, and Harajuku, west of the Imperial Palace and just north of Roppongi, are the trend-setting areas of youth culture and fashion. Omotesandō and Aoyama contain a laundry list of European fashion houses' flagship stores. Harajuku is a bohemian and younger fashion district that inspired Gwen Stefani to write a hit song, "Harajuku Girls," and create a "Harajuku Lovers" fashion line in 2005.

Just north of Omotesandō and Aoyama, in front of the Harajuku JR Station, is Harajuku's Meiji Jingu Shrine, which is a famous hang out for dressed-up teens and crowds of on-lookers.

Because it is the entertainment district for Japanese youth, Shibuya is not as clean or sophisticated as Tōkyō's other neighborhoods. Rarely will you see an elderly person on the streets. Shops, cheap restaurants, karaoke lounges, bars, theaters, concert halls, and nightclubs are everywhere. With Shibuya station connecting thousands of passengers from the suburbs into the heart of the city, it is the western frontier of central Tōkyō, and the last stop of the Ginza Line.

PLANNING Trying to explore Aoyama and Harajuku together will take a long time because there is a lot of area to cover. Ideally, you should devote an entire day here, giving yourself plenty of time to browse in shops. You can see Meiji Shrine in less than an hour; the Nezu Institute warrants a leisurely two-hour visit. Spring is the best time of year for the Meiji Jingū Inner Garden. Just like everywhere else in this city, June's rainy season is horrendous, and the humid heat of midsummer can quickly drain your energy and add hours to the time you need to comfortably explore. The best way to enjoy this area is to explore the tiny shops, restaurants, and cafés in the back streets.

Shibuya seems chaotic and intimidating at first, but it is fairly compact, so you can easily cover it in about two hours. Be prepared for huge crowds and some shoulder bumping. Shibuya crossing is one of the busiest in the world and at one light change, hundreds rush to reach the other side.

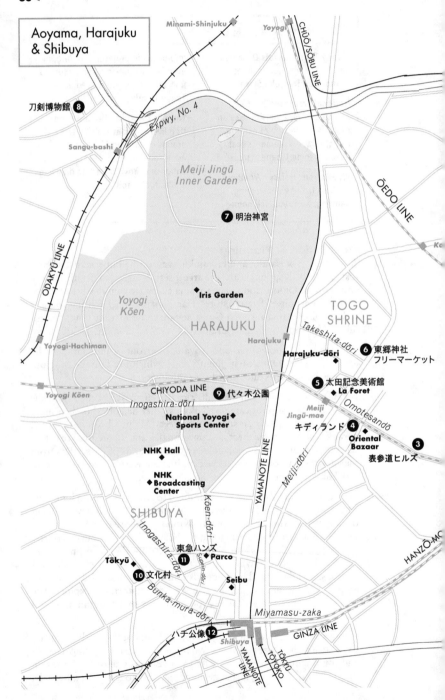

Unless you switch into shopping mode, no particular stop along the way should occupy you for more than a half hour; allow a full hour for the NHK Broadcasting Center, however, if you decide to take the guided tour. Spring is the best time of year for Yoyogi Kōen, and Sunday is the best day. The area will be crowded, but Sunday affords the best opportunity to observe Japan's younger generation on display. Two subway lines, three private railways, the JR Yamanote Line, and two bus terminals move about a million people a day through Shibuya.

What to See

⑩ Bunka-mura. One of the liveliest venues in Tōkyō for music and art, this six-story theater-and-gallery complex, a venture of the next-door Tōkyū department store, hosts everything from science-fiction film festivals and opera to ballet and big bands. The museum on the lower-level Garden Floor often has well-planned, interesting exhibits on loan from major European museums. ⌧ *2–24–1 Dōgen-zaka, Shibuya-ku* ☎ *03/ 3477–9111, 03/3477–9999 ticket center* ✆ *Theater admission and exhibit prices vary with events* ⏱ *Lobby ticket counter daily 10–7* Ⓜ *JR Yamanote Line, Ginza and Hanzō-mon subway lines, and private rail lines; Shibuya Station (Exits 5 and 8 for Hanzō-mon subway line, Kitaguchi/North Exit for all others).*

NEED A BREAK? **Les Deux Magots,** sister of the famed Paris café, in the Bunka-mura complex, serves a good selection of beers and wines, sandwiches, salads, quiches, tarts, and coffee. There's a fine-arts bookstore next door, and the tables in the courtyard are perfect for people-watching. ⌧ *Bunka-mura, lower courtyard, 2–24–1 Dōgen-zaka, Shibuya-ku* ☎ *03/3477–9124* Ⓜ *JR Yamanote Line, Ginza and Hanzō-mon subway lines, and private rail lines; Shibuya Station (Exits 5 and 8 for Hanzō-mon subway line, Kita-guchi/North Exit for all others).*

★ **⑧ Japanese Sword Museum** (Tōken Hakubutsukan). It's said that in the late 16th century, before Japan closed its doors to the West, the Spanish tried to establish a trade here in weapons made from famous Toledo steel. The Japanese were politely uninterested; they had been making blades of incomparably better quality for more than 600 years. At one time there were some 200 schools of sword making in Japan; swords were prized not only for their effectiveness in battle but for the beauty of the blades and fittings and as symbols of the higher spirituality of the warrior caste. There are few inheritors of this art today. ⌧ *4–25–10 Yoyogi, Shibuya-ku* ☎ *03/3379–1386* ✆ *¥525* ⏱ *Tues.–Sun. 10–4:30* Ⓜ *Odakyū private rail line, Sangū-bashi Station.*

④ Kiddy Land. With six floors full of toys, kids will go wild—they'll spend hours shopping if it's up to them. You might, too: there's something for the kid in all of us, including a complete collection of Hello Kitty and Mickey Mouse paraphernalia, as well as home planetariums. ⌧ *6-1-9 Jingumae Shibuya-ku* ☎ *03/3409–3491* ⏱ *Daily, 10-9* Ⓜ *Ginza Line, Chiyoda Line, Hanzomon Line, Omotesandō Station (Exit A1).*

⑦ Meiji Shrine (Meiji Jingū). The Meiji Shrine honors the spirits of Emperor Meiji, who died in 1912, and Empress Shōken. It was established by a resolution of the Imperial Diet the year after the emperor's death to commemorate his role in ending the long isolation of Japan under the Tokugawa Shōgunate and setting the country on the road to modernization. Completed in 1920 and virtually destroyed in an air raid in 1945, it was rebuilt in 1958.

A wonderful spot for photos, the mammoth entrance gates (*torii*), rising 40 feet high, are made from 1,700-year-old cypress trees from Mt. Ari in Taiwan; the crosspieces are 56 feet long. Torii are meant to symbolize the separation of the everyday secular world from the spiritual world of the Shintō shrine. The buildings in the shrine complex, with their curving green copper roofs, are also made of cypress wood. The surrounding gardens have some 100,000 flowering shrubs and trees.

An annual festival at the shrine takes place on November 3, Emperor Meiji's birthday, which is a national holiday. On the festival and New Year's Day, as many as one million people come to offer prayers and pay their respects. Several other festivals and ceremonial events are held here throughout the year; check by phone or on the shrine Web site to see what's scheduled during your visit. Even on a normal weekend the shrine draws thousands of visitors, but this seldom disturbs its mood of quiet serenity.

The peaceful **Inner Garden** (Jingū Nai-en), where the irises are in full bloom in the latter half of June, is on the left as you walk in from the main gates, before you reach the shrine. Beyond the shrine is the **Treasure House,** a repository for the personal effects and clothes of Emperor and Empress Meiji—perhaps of less interest to foreign visitors than to the Japanese. ✉ *1–1 Kamizono-chō, Yoyogi, Shibuya-ku* ☎ *03/3379–9222* ⊕ *www.meijijingu.or.jp* ✉ *Shrine free, Inner Garden ¥500, Treasure House ¥500* ☉ *Shrine daily sunrise–sunset; Inner Garden Mar.–Nov., daily 9–4; Treasure House daily 10–4; Closed 3rd Fri. of month* Ⓜ *Chiyoda subway line, Meiji-jingū-mae Station; JR Yamanote Line, Harajuku Station (Exit 2).*

❶ **Meiji Shrine Outer Gardens** (Meiji Jingū Gai-en). This rare expanse of open space is devoted to outdoor sports of all sorts. The Yakult Swallows play at **Jingū Baseball Stadium** (✉ 13 Kasumigaoka, Shinjuku-ku ☎ 03/3404–8999); the Japanese baseball season runs from April to October. The main venue of the 1964 Summer Olympics, **National Stadium** (✉ 10 Kasumigaoka, Shinjuku-ku ☎ 03/3403–1151) now hosts soccer matches. Some of the major World Cup matches were played here when Japan cohosted the event with Korea in autumn 2002. The **Meiji Memorial Picture Gallery** (Kaigakan) (✉ 9 Kasumigaoka, Shinjuku-ku, Aoyama ☎ 03/3401–5179), across the street from the National Stadium, doesn't hold much interest unless you're a fan of Emperor Meiji and don't want to miss some 80 otherwise undistinguished paintings depicting events in his life. It's open daily 9–4:30 and costs ¥500. ✉ *Shinjuku-ku* Ⓜ *Ginza and Hanzō-mon subway lines, Gai-en-mae Station (Exit 2); JR Chūō Line, Shina-no-machi Station.*

❷ **Nezu Institute of Fine Arts** (Nezu Bijutsukan). This museum houses the
Fodor'sChoice private art collection of Meiji-period railroad magnate and politician
★ Kaichirō Nezu. The permanent display in the main building and the annex
includes superb examples of Japanese painting, calligraphy, and ceramics—some of which are registered as National Treasures—plus Chinese
bronzes, sculpture, and lacquerware. The institute also has one of
Tōkyō's finest gardens, with more than 5 acres of shade trees and flowering shrubs, ponds, and waterfalls, as well as seven tea pavilions.
⊠ 6–5–1 Minami-Aoyama, Minato-ku ☎ 03/3400–2536 ⊕ www.nezu-
muse.or.jp ☑ ¥1,000 ☉ Tues.–Sun. 9–4 Ⓜ Ginza and Hanzō-mon
subway lines, Omotesandō Station (Exit A5).

★ **❸** **Omotesandō Hills.** This curious shopping mall was designed by Pritzker
Prize–winning architect Tadao Ando. Despised and adored with equal
zeal, this controversial project demolished the charming, yet antiquated
Dojunkai Aoyama Apartments along the Omotesandō Avenue. Filled
with high end boutiques and designer flagship stores for Dolce & Gab-
bana and Yves Saint Laurent, it's worth a stroll to see the latest in Japanese haute couture. Restaurants and cafés can also be found here, but
beware of long lines. ⊠ 4-12-10 Jingumae Shibuya-ku ☎ 03/3497–0310
☉ Daily 11–9 Ⓜ Ginza Line, Chiyoda Line, Hanzomon Line Omotesandō Station (Exit A2).

**NEED A
BREAK?** Relax "Omotesandō style" at **Anniversaire**–it's just like stepping into a Parisian
café. This charming venue is part of a wedding center and hall and has outdoor
seating under a red awning. It's a perfect resting spot in spring and early summer. On weekends, the chapel doors open and newlyweds walk in procession in
front of onlookers sitting in the café, who ring little bells to wish them well. Champagne by the glass costs ¥1,000; strong coffee, ¥1,000; delicious sandwiches, ¥1,200;
and desserts ¥800. ⊠ 3-5-30 Kita Aoyama, Minato-ku ☎ 03/5411–5988 Ⓜ Ginza,
Chiyoda, and Hanzō-mon subway lines, Omotesandō Station (Exit A2).

★ **❺** **Ōta Memorial Museum of Art** (Ōta Kinen Bijutsukan). The gift of former
Tōhō Mutual Life Insurance chairman Seizō Ōta, this is probably the
city's finest private collection of ukiyo-e, traditional Edo-period wood-
block prints that flourished in the 18th and 19th centuries. The works
on display are selected and changed periodically from the 12,000 prints
in the collection, which include some extremely rare work by artists such
as Hiroshige, Hokusai, Sharaku, and Utamaro. Be sure to verify opening hours on their official Web site or call ahead. ⊠ 1–10–10 Jingū-mae,
Shibuya-ku ☎ 03/3403–0880 ⊕ www.ukiyoe-ota-muse.jp
☑ ¥700–¥1,000, depending on exhibit ☉ Tues.–Sun. 10:30–5; closed
from the 26th or 27th to the last day of each month.

⓬ **Statue of Hachiko.** Hachiko is the Japanese version of Lassie; he even starred
in a few heartwrenching films. Every morning, Hachiko's master, a professor at Tōkyō University, would take the dog with him as far as
Shibuya Station and Hachiko would go back to the station every evening
to greet him on his return. In 1925 the professor died of a stroke. Every
evening for the next seven years, Hachiko would go to Shibuya and wait
there until the last train had pulled out of the station. When loyal

Hachiko died, his story made headlines. A handsome bronze statute of Hachiko was installed in front of the station, funded by fans from all over the country. The present version is a replica—the original was melted down for its metal in World War II. This Shibuya landmark is a meeting place for many. ⊠ *JR Shibuya Station, West Plaza, Shibuya-ku.*

❻ Tōgō Jinja Flea Market. To find some Japanese antiques and knick knacks, come to this shrine the first Sunday of every month. It's located near the intersection of Takeshita-dōri and Meiji-dori in Harajuku. ⊠ *1-5 Jingū-mae Shibuya-ku* ☎ *03/3425–7965* ⊗ *Daily 11-7* Ⓜ *JR Yamanote Line, Harajuku Station (Takeshita Entrance).*

★ **⓫ Tōkyū Hands.** This is a hobbyist's fantasy store. Everything anyone would ever need, and plenty of things we don't, is here: tools for woodworking, painting, do-it-yourself home improvement, travel accessories, and jewelry making. Their slogan is "creative life store," and they truly are: seven floors of cool stuff that can take two hours at least to fully browse. This superstore is worth a visit, especially for souvenir shopping. ⊠ *12-18 Udagawacho Shibuya-ku* ☎ *03/5489–5111* ⊗ *Daily 11-7.*

Ⓒ **❾ Yoyogi Kōen** (Yoyogi Park). This is the perfect spot to have a picnic on a sunny day. On Sundays, people come here to play music, practice martial arts, and ride bicycles on the bike path (rentals are available). Be sure to look out for a legendary group of dancing Elvis impersonators, who meet at the entrance every Sunday and dance to classic rock'n'roll music. There is also a community of homeless people who live in orderly, clean camps along the periphery. Sundays and holidays, there's a flea market along the main thoroughfare that runs through the park, opposite the National Yoyogi Sports Center. ⊠ *Jinnan 2-chōme, Shibuya-ku* Ⓜ *Chiyoda subway line, Meiji Jingū-mae Station (Exit 2); JR Yamanote Line, Harajuku Station (Omotesandō Exit).*

ROPPONGI & AZABU-JŪBAN

During the last quarter of the 20th century, Roppongi was a better-heeled, better-behaved version of Shinjuku or Shibuya, without the shopping: not much happens by day, but by night the area is an irresistible draw for young clubbers with foreign sports cars and wads of disposable income.

Today, this area has become an entertainment capital, attracting tourists to its bustling bar, restaurant, and nightclub scenes; English is spoken at most restaurants and shops. It's also the most prestigious address in town including the developments known as Roppongi Hills and Tōkyō Midtown, where residents are rumored to be politicians, celebrities, and businessmen. The famous Mori Tower houses the headquarters for high-rolling banking and IT companies like Goldman Sachs Japan, Lehman Brothers Japan, and Livedoor, founded by disgraced renegade businessman, Takafumi Horie.

Azabu-Jūban is a prestigious residential district with many embassies in Minato-ku. Before the fire raids of 1945, Azabu-Jūban, like Roppongi nearby, was a famous entertainment disctrict with department stores, a red-light quarter, and theaters. The fires destroyed the entire neighbor-

---

TOP REASONS TO VISIT

A Day's Trip Visit Mori Building company's apex development, **Roppongi Hills** to see the Mori Museum, watch a film, do some shopping, have a bite to eat, see some art, or see the best view of Tōkyō on the observation deck.

Lofty Aspirations The **Tōkyō MidTown** is the tallest building in

Tōkyō and offers excellent restaurants, striking architecture and design, art exhibitions, shopping, and views of the city.

How the Locals Do It Enjoy observing everyday life for Tōkyō residents in **Azabu-Jūban,** where good food and cafés are plentiful.

---

hood, and it was reborn as a residential area. Though the apartments may be small and dilapidated, this is one of the most expensive areas of the city and many famous celebrities, artists, and businesspeople reside here too.

Numbers in the text correspond to numbers in the margin and on the Roppongi & Azabu-Jūban map.

Orientation & Planning

ORIENTATION Roppongi is located just south of Shibuya and Aoyama, and west of the Imperial Palace. The best way to get to Roppongi is by subway, though the trains stop running at midnight. Azabu-Jūban is located just south of Roppongi, within seven-minute walking distance from Roppongi Hills, or a short subway ride on the Toei Ōedo line to Azabu-Jūban station.

PLANNING Roppongi is a very central area, located in between Shibuya and the Imperial Palace. The best way to get here is by subway, and there are two stations: Hibiya line Roppongi Station (takes you right into the complex of Roppongi Hills), and Toei Ōedo line Roppongi Station. At Roppongi Hills Complex, there are ATMs and Currency Exchange services, as well as family- and kid-friendly activities.

Azabu-Jūban is a quick visit, and a good place to sit in a café and people watch. The best time to visit is in August, during the **Azabu-Jūban Summer Festival,** one of the biggest festivals in Minato-ku. The streets, which are closed to car traffic, are lined with food vendors selling delicious international fare and drinks. Everyone wears their nicest summer kimonos and watches live performances. Check the online *Minato Monthly* newsletter (⊕ www.city.minato.tokyo.jp) in August for a list of summer festivals. Only a short 10 minute walk from Roppongi, you can also take the Toei Ōedo Line from Roppongi, to Azabu-Jūban Station (Exit 5), just one stop away for ¥160.

What to See

⑤ Don Quijote. This is perhaps the weirdest 24-hour discount store on earth, complete with aquariums featuring the ugliest giant fish you've ever seen; a half-pike rollercoaster on the rooftop that has never operated (angry neighbors signed a petition, forcing them to drop the idea); the constantly looping "Don Quixote" theme song; and cheesy merchandise like vinyl

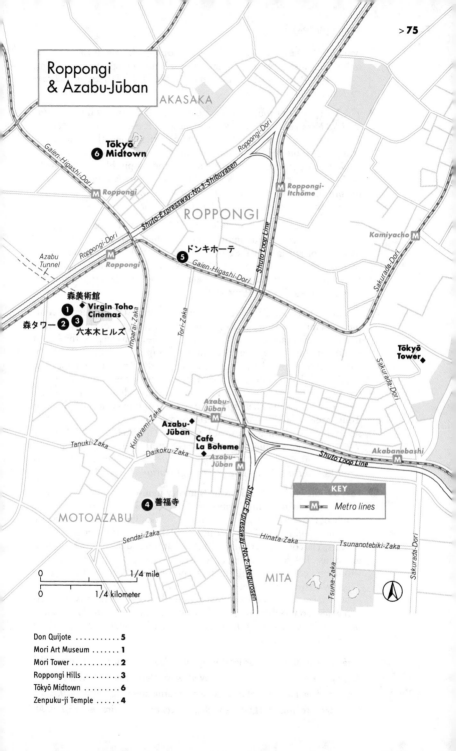

Roppongi & Azabu-Jūban

AKASAKA

6 Tōkyō Midtown

Gaien-Higashi-Dori

Ⓜ Roppongi

Roppongi-Dori

Shuto Expressway-No.3-Shibuyasen

ROPPONGI

Roppongi-Itchōme Ⓜ

Kamiyacho Ⓜ

Sakurada-Dori

Azabu Tunnel

Ⓜ Roppongi

5 ドンキホーテ

Gaien-Higashi-Dori

Shuto Loop Line

森美術館
1 ♦ Virgin Toho Cinemas

森タワー **2** **3**

Imoarai-Zaka

Tori-Zaka

六本木ヒルズ

Tōkyō Tower ♦

Sakurada-Dori

Kurayami-Zaka

Azabu-Jūban Ⓜ

Tanuki-Zaka

Azabu-Jūban ♦

Daikoku-Zaka

Café La Boheme ♦ Azabu-Jūban Ⓜ

Akabanebashi

Shuto Loop Line

KEY

Ⓜ Metro lines

4 善福寺

MOTOAZABU

Shuto Expressway-No.2-Megurosen

Sendai-Zaka

Hinata-Zaka

Tsunanotebiki-Zaka

MITA

Tsuna-Zaka

Sakurada-Dori

0 ___ 1/4 mile
0 ___ 1/4 kilometer

pants and wigs. Not convinced that you can find almost anything here? They also have second-hand Louis Vuitton bags and deodorant. ✉ *3-14-10 Roppongi Minato-ku* ☎ *03/5786–0811* ⊕ *www.donki.com* ⊘ *Daily 11–10.*

❶ The Mori Tower promenade encircles three of the nine galleries of the **Mori Art Museum**, which is now one of the leading contemporary art showcases in Tōkyō. You enter the six main galleries, where the major exhibitions are mounted, from the floor above. The Mori is well-designed, intelligently curated, diverse in its media, and hospitable to big crowds. ✉ *Minato-ku* ☎ *03/5777–8600* ⊕ *http://mori.art.museum/jp* ✐ *Admission fees vary with each exhibit* ⊘ *Wed.–Mon. 10–10; Tues. 10–5* Ⓜ *Hibiya subway line, Roppongi Station (Exit 1C).*

❷ At the center of Roppongi Hills is the 54-story **Mori Tower**. On a clear day, you can see Mt. Fuji in the distance from the Tōkyō City View observation promenade on the 52nd floor, and by night the panoramic view of the city is spectacular. ✉ *Minato-ku* ☎ *03/5777–8600* ⊕ *www.tokyocityview.com* ✐ *¥1,500* ⊘ *Daily 9 AM–1 PM* Ⓜ *Hibiya subway line, Roppongi Station (Exit 1C).*

✋ ❸ **Roppongi Hills.** In 2003, Mori Building Company—Japan's biggest commercial landlord—created Roppongi Hills, a complex of shops, restaurants, residential and commercial towers, a nine-screen cineplex, the Grand Hyatt hotel, and a major art museum—all wrapped around the TV Asahi studios and sprawled out in five zones from the Roppongi intersection to Azabu-Jūban. To navigate this mini-city, go to the information center to retrieve a 12-page floor guide with color-coded maps in English; most of the staff members speak a modicum of English as well. **English Tours** are available from the information center, which you must book seven days in advance online or by phone. (☎ *03/6406–6677* ⊘ *Daily 9–6* ✐ *Roppongi Hills walking tour (45 min) ¥1,500; Quick tour (30 min) ¥1,000* ✉ *6–10–1 Roppongi, Minato-ku* ⊕ *www.roppongihills .com* Ⓜ *Hibiya subway line, Roppongi Station (Exit C-1).*

❻ **Tōkyō Midtown.** The trend towards luxury mini-city development projects, which started with Roppongi Hills in 2003, is improving the dynamic of the city. With Tōkyō Midtown, Mitsui Fudosan aims to create the tallest building in Tōkyō, using a collaboration of international architects. The complex will include a Ritz-Carlton and the Midtown Tower, and house Tōkyō businesses, upscale residences, museums, restaurants, shops, and convention halls in adjacent buildings. The top floor of the Midtown Tower will offer a spectacular view of Tōkyō. For locals, the new medical center associated with Johns Hopkins University is a welcome addition to Roppongi. ✉ *9-chome Akasaka Minato-ku* ⊕ *www .tokyo-midtown.com* Ⓜ *Toei Ōedo Line, Roppongi Station; Hibiya Line, Roppongi Station.*

NEED A BREAK?

Café La Boheme A popular local hangout in Azabu-Jūban at all hours of the day, this café is open until 5 AM. They serve Western food for lunch, a coffee break, or dinner in 19th century Czech dining surroundings. Coffee is ¥420, pasta lunch sets are around ¥1,000, and dinner sets are approximately ¥5,250. All major credit cards accepted. ✉ *2-3-7 Azabu-Jūban, Minato-ku* ☎ *03/6400-3060* 🌐 *www.boheme.jp* 🕐 *Daily: lunch 11:30-2; dinner 2 PM-5 AM.*

❹ **Zenpuku-ji Temple.** This temple, just south of the Ichinohashi Crossing, dates back to the 800s. In the 1200s, the temple was converted to the Shinran school of Buddhism. When Consul-General Townsend Harris arrived from the Americas in 1859, he lived on the temple grounds. ✉ *1-6 Moto-Azabu, Minato-ku* ☎ *03/3451-7402* Ⓜ *Toei Ōedo Line, Azabu-Jūban Station (Exit 1).*

SHINJUKU

If you have a certain sort of love for big cities, you're bound to love Shinjuku. Come here, and for the first time Tōkyō begins to seem *real:* all the celebrated virtues of Japanese society—its safety and order, its grace and beauty, its cleanliness and civility—fray at the edges.

To be fair, the area has been on the fringes of respectability for centuries. When Ieyasu, the first Tokugawa shōgun, made Edo his capital, Shinjuku was at the junction of two important arteries leading into the city from the west. It became a thriving post station, where travelers would rest and refresh themselves for the last leg of their journey; the appeal of this suburban pit stop was its "teahouses," where the waitresses dispensed a good bit more than sympathy with the tea.

When the Tokugawa dynasty collapsed in 1868, 16-year-old Emperor Meiji moved his capital to Edo, renaming it Tōkyō, and modern Shinjuku became the railhead connecting it to Japan's western provinces. As the haunt of artists, writers, and students, it remained on the fringes of respectability; in the 1930s Shinjuku was Tōkyō's bohemian quarter. The area was virtually leveled during the firebombings of 1945—a blank slate on which developers could write, as Tōkyō surged west after the war. By the 1970s property values in Shinjuku were the nation's highest, outstripping even those of Ginza.

After the Great Kantō Earthquake of 1923, Nishi-Shinjuku was virtually the only part of Tōkyō left standing; the whims of nature had given this one small area a gift of better bedrock. That priceless geological stability remained largely unexploited until the late 1960s, when technological advances in engineering gave architects the freedom to soar. Some 20 skyscrapers have been built here since then, including the Tōkyō Metropolitan Government Office complex, and Nishi-Shinjuku has become Tōkyō's 21st-century administrative center.

By day the quarter east of Shinjuku Station is an astonishing concentration of retail stores, vertical malls, and discounters of every stripe and description. By night it's an equally astonishing collection of bars and clubs, strip joints, hole-in-the-wall restaurants, pinball parlors, and peep shows—just about anything that amuses, arouses, alters, or intoxicates is for sale in Higashi-Shinjuku, if you know where to look. Drunken fistfights are hardly unusual here, and petty theft is not unknown. Not surprisingly, Higashi-Shinjuku has the city's largest—and busiest—police substation.

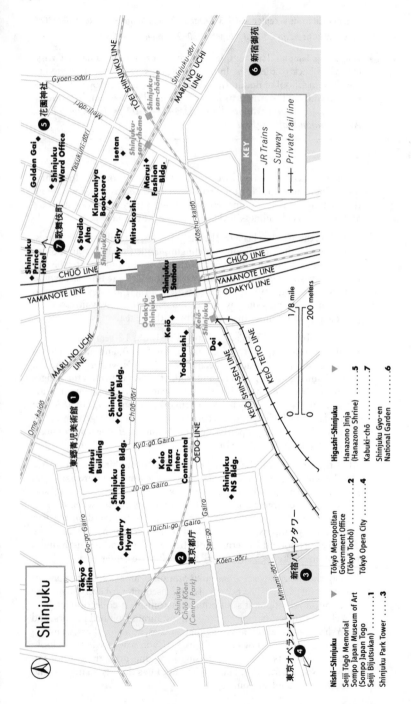

Shinjuku

KEY

— JR Trains

=== Subway

—+— Private rail line

1/8 mile

200 meters

MARU NO UCHI LINE

TOEI SHINJUKU LINE

MARU NO UCHI LINE

Gyoen-odori

Meiji-dori

Yasukuni-dori

Shinjuku-dori

Shinjuku-san-chōme

⑤ 花園神社

⑥ 新宿御苑

Golden Gai ◆

⑤ Shinjuku Ward Office ◆

⑦ 歌舞伎町

Iseten ◆

Shinjuku-san-chōme

Marui Fashion Bldg. ◆

Kinokuniya Bookstore ◆

Mitsukoshi ◆

Studio Alta ◆

My City ◆

Shinjuku Prince Hotel ◆

Shinjuku

CHŪO LINE

CHŪO LINE

YAMANOTE LINE

Shinjuku Station

YAMANOTE LINE

ODAKYŪ LINE

Kōshu-kaidō

Odakyū-Shinjuku

Keiō ◆

Keiō-Shinjuku

Yodobashi ◆

Doi ◆

KEIŌ SHIN-SEN LINE

KEIŌ TEITO LINE

MARU NO UCHI LINE

Ome-kaidō

東郷青児美術館 ①

Shinjuku Center Bldg. ◆

Chūo-dōri

Mitsui Building ◆

Shinjuku Sumitomo Bldg. ◆

Kyū-go Gairo

Keio Plaza Inter-Continental ◆

Shinjuku NS Bldg. ◆

Jū-go Gairo

Century Hyatt ◆

Jūichi-go Gairo

Go-go Gairo

OEDO LINE

Gairo

San-go

② 東京都庁

Kōen-dōri

③ 新宿パークタワー

Minami-dōri

Tōkyō Hilton ◆

Shinjuku Chūo Kōen (Central Park)

④ 東京オペラシティ

Nishi-Shinjuku

Seiji Tōgō Memorial
Sompo Japan Museum of Art
(Sompo Japan Togo
Seiji Bijutsukan) **1**

Tōkyō Metropolitan
Government Office
(Tōkyō Tochō) **2**

Tōkyō Opera City **4**

Shinjuku Park Tower **3**

Higashi-Shinjuku

Hanazono Jinja
(Hanazono Shrine) **5**

Kabuki-chō **7**

Shinjuku Gyo-en
National Garden **6**

TOP REASONS TO VISIT

On a Clear Day The observation deck of **Tōkyō Metropolitan Government Office** has a great view of Mount Fuji and the complex hosts open-air concerts and exhibitions.

Priceless Art The **Seiji Tōgō Memorial Sompo Japan Museum of Art** has van Gogh's *Sunflowers*,

and the work of Japanese painter Seiji Tōgō.

Take a Wrong Turn? No, you haven't fallen down the rabbit hole: the famous New York Bar now calls the **Park Hyatt** home. You might recognize it from the movie *Lost in Translation*.

Numbers in the text correspond to numbers in the margin and on the Shinjuku map.

Orientation & Planning

ORIENTATION By day, Shinjuku is a bustling center of business and government where office workers move in droves during rush hour. By night, people are inundated with flashing signs, and a darker side of Tōkyō emerges, where druken hordes leave their offices to go out for drinks, food, and sometimes, sex. Perhaps this is a rougher side of town, but Shinjuku is a fascinating place to discover at night.

PLANNING Every day three subways, seven railway lines, and more than 3 million commuters converge on Shinjuku Station, making this the city's busiest and most heavily populated commercial center. The hub at Shinjuku— a vast, interconnected complex of tracks and terminals, department stores and shops—divides the area into two distinctly different subcities, Nishi-Shinjuku (West Shinjuku) and Higashi-Shinjuku (East Shinjuku).

Plan at least a full day for Shinjuku if you want to see both the east and west sides. Subway rides can save you time and energy as you're exploring, but don't rule out walking. The Shinjuku Gyo-en National Garden is worth at least an hour, especially if you come in early April during *sakura* (cherry blossom) season. The Tōkyō Metropolitan Government Office complex can take longer than you might expect; lines for the elevators to the observation decks are often excruciatingly long. Sunday, when shopping streets are closed to traffic, is the best time to tramp around Higashi-Shinjuku. The rainy season in late June and the sweltering heat of August are best avoided.

What to See

❺ **Hanazono Jinja** (Hanazono Shrine). Constructed in the early Edo period, Hanazono is not among Tōkyō's most imposing shrines, but it does have one of the longest histories. Prayers offered here are believed to bring prosperity in business. The shrine is a five-minute walk north on Meiji-dōri from the Shinjuku-san-chōme subway station. The block just to the west (5-chōme 1) has the last embattled remaining bars of the "Golden-Gai": *See* Golden Gai in Chapter 4, a district of tiny, unpretentious, even seedy, *nomiya* (bars) that in the '60s and '70s commanded the fierce loyalty of fiction writers, artists, freelance journalists, and expat Japanophiles—the city's hard-core outsiders. ⊠ *5–17–3 Shinjuku, Shinjuku-ku* ☎ *03/3209–5265* 🖼 *Free* ⊙ *Daily sunrise–sunset* Ⓜ *Marunouchi subway line, Shinjuku-san-chōme Station (Exits B2 and B3).*

❼ **Kabuki-chō.** In 1872 the Tokugawa-period formalities governing geisha entertainment were dissolved, and Kabuki-chō became Japan's largest center of prostitution. Later, when

> ### HE SAID WHAT?
>
> Yasuda Fire & Marine Insurance Company CEO Yasuo Gotō acquired *Sunflowers* in 1987 for ¥5.3 billion—at the time the highest price ever paid at auction for a work of art. He later created considerable stir in the media with the ill-considered remark that he'd like the painting cremated with him when he died.

vice laws got stricter, prostitution just went a bit deeper underground, where it remains—deeply deplored and widely tolerated.

⚠ **Kabuki-chō means unrefined nightlife at its best and raunchy seediness at its worst. Neon signs flash; shills proclaim the pleasures of the places you particularly want to shun. Even when a place looks respectable, ask about prices first: *bottakuri*—overcharging for food and drink—is the regional sport here, and watered-down drinks can set you back ¥5,000 or more in a hostess club. Avoid the cheap nomiya under the railway tracks; chances are there's a client in at least one of them looking for a fight. All that said, you needn't be intimidated by the area: use your street-smarts, and it *can* be fun.**

In an attempt to change the area's image after World War II, plans were made to replace Ginza's fire-gutted Kabuki-za with a new one in Shinjuku. The plans were never realized, however, as the old theater was rebuilt. But the project gave the area its present name. Kabuki-chō's own multipurpose theater is the 2,000-seat **Koma Gekijō** (⊠ *1–19–1 Kabuki-chō, Shinjuku-ku* ☎ *03/3200–2213*). The building, which also houses several discos and bars, is a central landmark for the quarter. ⊠ *Shinjuku-ku* Ⓜ *JR (Higashi-guchi/East Exit) and Marunouchi subway line (Exits B10, B11, B12, and B13), Shinjuku Station.*

❶ **Seiji Tōgō Memorial Sompo Japan Museum of Art** (Sompo Japan Togo Seiji Bijutsukan). The painter Seiji Tōgō (1897–1978) was a master of putting on canvas the grace and charm of young maidens. More than 100 of his works from the museum collection are on display here at any given time, along with other Japanese and Western artists. The museum also houses van Gogh's *Sunflowers.* The gallery has an especially good view of the old part of Shinjuku. ⊠ *Yasuda Fire and Marine Insurance Bldg., 42nd fl., 1–26–1 Nishi-Shinjuku, Shinjuku-ku* ☎ *03/5777–8600* ⊕ *www. sompo-japan.co.jp/museum* 🖼 *¥500; additional fees for special exhibits* ⊙ *Tues.–Sun. 10–6* Ⓜ *Marunouchi and Shinjuku subway lines, JR, and Keiō Shin-sen and Teitō private rail lines; Shinjuku Station (Exit A18 for subway lines, Nishi-guchi/West Exit or Exit N4 from the underground passageway for all others).*

★ ❻ **Shinjuku Gyo-en National Garden.** This lovely 150-acre park was once the estate of the powerful Naitō family of feudal lords, who were among the most trusted retainers of the Tokugawa shōguns. After World War II, the grounds were finally opened to the public. It's a perfect place for leisurely walks: paths wind past ponds and bridges, artificial hills, thoughtfully placed stone lanterns, and more than 3,000 kinds of plants, shrubs, and trees. There are different gardens in Japanese, French, and English styles, as well as a greenhouse (the nation's first, built in 1885) filled with tropical plants. The best times to visit are April, when 75 different species of cherry trees—some 1,500 trees in all—are in bloom, and the first two weeks of November, during the chrysanthemum exhibition. ⊠ *11 Naitō-chō, Shinjuku-ku* ☎ *03/3350–0151* 🎟 *¥200* 🕐 *Tues.–Sun. 9–4; also open Mon. 9–4 in cherry-blossom season (Mar. 25–Apr. 24) and for chrysanthemum show (Nov. 1–15)* Ⓜ *Marunouchi subway line, Shinjuku Gyo-en-mae Station (Exit 1).*

❸ **Shinjuku Park Tower Building.** The Shinjuku Park Tower has in some ways the most arrogant, hard-edged design of any of the skyscrapers in Nishi-Shinjuku, but it does provide any number of opportunities to rest and refuel. Some days there are free chamber-music concerts in the atrium. There are many restaurants to choose from in the building, with a variety of international and Japanese restaurants. In the afternoon, you can ride up to the skylighted bamboo garden of the Peak Lounge on the 41st floor of the **Park Hyatt Hotel** (☎ 03/5322–1234). This is the set location of the Oscar-winning film, *Lost in Translation*; the rates at Park Hyatt skyrocketed after the film became a hit and Sofia Coppola accepted the Oscar in 2003 for best screenplay. Just for kicks, have a Suntory whiskey at the New York Bar on the 41st floor. Also come for high tea, allegedly the best Sunday brunch in the city, and a spectacular view. ⊠ *3–7–1 Nishi-Shinjuku, Shinjuku-ku* Ⓜ *JR Shinjuku Station (Nishi-guchi/West Exit).*

★ ❷ **Tōkyō Metropolitan Government Office** (Tōkyō Tochō). Dominating the western Shinjuku skyline and built at a cost of ¥157 billion, Kenzō Tange's grandiose city hall complex is clearly meant to remind observers that Tōkyō's annual budget is bigger than that of the average developing country. The late-20th-century complex consists of a main office building, an annex, the Metropolitan Assembly building, and a huge central courtyard, often the venue of open-air concerts and exhibitions. The building design has raised some debate: Tōkyōites either love it or hate it. On a clear day, from the observation decks on the 45th floors of both towers, you can see all the way to Mt. Fuji and to the Bōsō Peninsula in Chiba Prefecture. Several other skyscrapers in the area have free observation floors—among them the Shinjuku Center Building, the Shinjuku Nomura Building, and the Shinjuku Sumitomo Building—but city hall is the best of the lot. The Metropolitan Government Web site, incidentally, is an excellent source of information on sightseeing and current events in Tōkyō. ⊠ *2–8–1 Nishi-Shinjuku, Shinjuku-ku* ☎ *03/5321–1111* ⊕ *www.metro.tokyo.jp* 🎟 *Free* 🕐 *North observation deck daily 9:30–10:30; south observation deck daily 9:30–5:30* Ⓜ *Marunouchi and Shinjuku subway lines, JR, Keiō Shin-sen and Teitō private rail lines; Shinjuku Station (Nishi-guchi/West Exit).*

❹ Tōkyō Opera City. Completed in 1997, this is certain to be the last major cultural project in Tōkyō for the foreseeable future. The west side of the complex is the New National Theater (Shin Kokuritsu Gekijō), consisting of the 1,810-seat Opera house, the 1,038-seat Playhouse, and an intimate performance space called the Pit, with seating for 468. Architect Helmut Jacoby's design for this building, with its reflecting pools, galleries, and granite planes of wall, deserves real plaudits.

The east side of the complex consists of a 54-story office tower flanked by a sunken garden and art museum on one side and a concert hall on the other. The museum focuses rather narrowly on post–World War II Japanese abstract painting. The 1632-seat concert hall is arguably the most impressive classical-music venue in Tōkyō, with tiers of polished-oak panels, and excellent acoustics despite the venue's daring vertical design. ⊠ *3–20–2 Nishi-Shinjuku, Shinjuku-ku* ☎ *03/5353–0700 concert hall, 03/5351–3011 New National Theater* ⊕ *www.operacity.jp* Ⓜ *Keiō Shin-sen private rail line, Hatsudai Station (Higashi-guchi/East Exit).*

ODAIBA

Tōkyō's "offshore" leisure and commercial-development complex rises on more than 1,000 acres of landfill, connected to the city by the Yurikamome monorail from Shimbashi. People come here for the arcades, shopping malls, and museums, as well as the city's longest (albeit artificial) stretch of sand beach, along the boat harbor—swimming is not recommended because of high levels of pollution. There's also the Great Ferris Wheel of Diamonds and Flowers—a neon phantasmagoric beacon for anyone driving into the city across the Rainbow Bridge. With hotels and apartment buildings as well, this is arguably the most successful of the megaprojects on Tōkyō Bay.

Orientation & Planning

ORIENTATION Located on the southernmost point of Tōkyō, this is a popular weekend destination for families. The lack of historical monuments or buildings in Odaiba separates it from Tōkyō's other districts.

PLANNING If you can, visit Odaiba during the week, as weekends are frenzied and crammed with families. The best way to get here is by monorail, which will also be packed on weekends. From Shimbashi Station you can take the JR, Karasumori Exit; Asakusa subway line, Exit A2; or the Ginza subway line, Exit 4—follow the blue seagull signs to the monorail. You can pick up a map of Odaiba in English at the entrance. The Yurikamome Line makes 10 stops between Shimbashi and the terminus at Ariake; fares range from ¥310 to ¥370, but the best strategy is to buy a ¥1,000 prepaid card that allows you to make multiple stops at different points in Odaiba. The monorail runs every three to five minutes from 5:46 AM to 11:56 PM.

What to See

Architecture buffs should make time for Daiba if only to contemplate the futuristic **Fuji Television Nippon Broadcasting Building.** From its fifth-floor Studio Promenade, you can watch programs being produced. The

TOP REASONS TO VISIT

Another World Check out the **Odaiba Kaihin Kōen** for shopping, arcades, and Chinese food in Little Hong Kong.

Lights, Camera, Action Don't miss the **Fuji Television Nippon Broadcasting Building,** Odaiba's modern architectural landmark.

Buff Bathing: Odaiba's **Hot Spring Theme Park** is a memorable onsen

experience in Edo-era surroundings; that is, if you don't mind being naked in a crowd.

Amazing ASIMO Meet Honada's famous humanoid robot at the **National Museum of Emerging Science and Innovation.**

observation deck on the 25th floor affords a spectacular view of the bay and the graceful curve of the Rainbow Bridge. ⊠ *2–4–8 Daiba, Minato-ku* ☎ *03/5500–8888* 🎫 *¥500* ◷ *Tues.–Sun. 10–8.*

The **Museum of Maritime Science** (Fune-no-Kagakukan) houses an impressive collection of models and displays on the history of Japanese shipbuilding and navigation. Built in the shape of an ocean liner, the museum is huge; if you're interested in ships, plan at least an hour here to do it justice. There are no English-language explanations at the museum. Anchored alongside the museum are the ferries: *Yōtei-maru,* which for some 30 years plied the narrow straits between Aomori and Hokkaidō, and the icebreaker *Sōya-maru,* the first Japanese ship to cross the Arctic Circle. ⊠ *3–1 Higashi-Yashio, Shinagawa-ku* ☎ *03/5500–1111* ⊕ *www.funenokagakukan.or.jp* 🎫 *¥1,000* ◷ *Weekdays 10–5, weekends 10–6.*

The **National Museum of Emerging Science and Innovation** (Nihon Gagaku Miraikan) is known locally as Miraikan. Make sure to stop by the third floor, where you will meet the most famous intelligent robot in the world, ASIMO, and a host of other experimental robots in development. This museum has four different themes, "Earth, Environment and Frontiers," "Innovation and the Future," "Information Science and Technology for Soceity," and "Life Science." The rest of the museum is what the Japanese call *ō-majime* (deeply sincere)—five floors of thematic displays on environment-friendly technologies, life sciences, and the like with high seriousness and not much fun. The director of this facility, Dr. Mamoru Mohri, was Japan's first astronaut, who in 1992 logged some 460 hours in space aboard the NASA Spacelab-J *Endeavor.* Some of the exhibits have English-language explanations. It's a short walk here from the Museum of Maritime Science. ⊠ *2–41 Aomi, Kōtō-ku* ☎ *03/3570–9151* ⊕ *www.miraikan.jst.go.jp* 🎫 *¥500* ◷ *Mon. and Wed.–Sat. 10–7, Sun. 10–5.*

A two-minute walk south from the Telecom Center, brings you to **Odaiba's Hot Spring Theme Park** (Ōedo Onsen Monogatari). Once upon a time, when bathtubs in private homes were a rarity, the great defining social institution of Japanese urban life was the *sento:* the local public bath. At the end of a hard day of work, there was no pleasure like sinking to your neck in hot water with your friends and neighbors, soaking your cares away, and sitting around afterward for soba, beer, and gossip. And if the sento was also an *onsen*—a thermal spring—with waters drawn from some mineral-rich underground supply, the delight was even greater. No more than a handful of such places survive in Tōkyō, but the Ōedo Onsen managed to tap a source some 4,600 feet below the bay. Visitors can choose from several indoor and outdoor pools, each with different temperatures and motifs—but remember that you must soap up and rinse off (including your hair) before you enter any of them. Follow your soak with a massage and a stroll through the food court—modeled after a street in Yoshiwara, the licensed red-light district of the Edo period—for sushi or noodles and beer. Charges include the rental of a *yukata* (cotton robe) and a towel. ⊠ *2–57 Ōmi, Kōtō-ku* ☎ *03/5500–1126* ◷ *Daily 11 AM–9 AM; front desk closes at 2 AM* ✎ *¥2,700; ¥1,500 surcharge for entrance after midnight.*

Odaiba Kaihin Kōen is the closest point to the beach and the site of two massive shopping complexes. Aqua City has four floors of boutiques, movie theaters, cafés, and eateries—including a Starbucks and Hanashibe, an excellent sake-brewery restaurant on the third level. Overlooking the harbor is Decks Tōkyō Beach, a five-story complex of shops, restaurants, and boardwalks in two connected malls. Daiba Little Hong Kong, on the sixth and seventh floors of the Island Mall, has a collection of Cantonese restaurants and dim sum joints on neon-lighted "streets" designed to evoke the real Hong Kong. At the Seaside Mall, a table by the window in any of the restaurants affords a delightful view of the harbor, especially at sunset, when the *yakatabune* (traditional roofed pleasure boats) drift down the Sumida-gawa from Yanagibashi and Ryōgoku.

Palette Town is a complex of malls and amusements at the east end of the island. The uncontested landmark here is the the 377-foot-high Giant Sky Wheel, modeled after the London Eye, the biggest in the world; it's open daily 10–10 and costs ¥900. Adjacent to the Ferris wheel is Mega Web, a complex of rides and multimedia amusements that's also a showcase for the Toyota Motor Corporation. You can ride a car (hands off—the ride is electronically controlled) over a 1-km (½-mi) course configured like a roller coaster but moving at a stately pace. You can drive any car you want, of course, as long as it's a Toyota. The shopping mall **Venus Fort** (⊠ Palette Town 1-chōme, Aomi, Kōtō-ku ☎ 03/ 3599–0700) at Aomi consists of galleries designed to suggest an Italian Renaissance palazzo, with arches and cupolas, marble fountains and statuary, and painted vault ceilings. The mall is chock-full of boutiques by the likes of Jean Paul Gaultier, Calvin Klein, Ralph Lauren, and all the other usual suspects.

ELSEWHERE IN TŌKYŌ

The sheer size of the city and the diversity of its institutions make it impossible to fit all of Tōkyō's interesting sights into neighborhoods.

Plenty of worthy places—from Tōkyō Disneyland to sumō stables to the old Ōji district—fall outside the city's neighborhood repertoire. Yet no guide to Tōkyō would be complete without them.

Amusement Centers

🕙 **Kasai Seaside Park.** With two artificial beaches, a bird sanctuary, and the ➪ **Tōkyō Sea Life Park** aquarium spread over a stretch of landfill between the Arakawa and the Kyū-Edogawa rivers, Kasai Seaside Park is one of the major landmarks in the vast effort to transform Tōkyō Bay into Fun City. The **"Diamonds and Flowers Ferris Wheel"** (Daia to Hana no Dai-kanransha), the tallest Ferris wheel in Japan, takes passengers on a 17-minute ride to the apex, 384 feet above the ground, for a spectacular view of the city. One rotation takes 70 minutes. On a clear day you can see all the way to Mt. Fuji; at night, if you're lucky, you reach the top just in time for a bird's-eye view of the fireworks over the Magic Kingdom, across the river. To get here, take the JR Keiyo Line local train from Tōkyō Station to Kasai Rinkai Kōen Station; the park is a five-minute walk from the south exit. ✉ *Rinkai-chō, Edogawa-ku* ☎ *03/ 3686–6911* 🎫 *Free, Ferris wheel ¥700* 🕙 *Ferris wheel Sept.–July, Tues.–Fri. 10–8, weekends 10–9; Aug., weekdays 10–8, weekends 10–9.*

🕙 **Tōkyō Dome City.** The Kōrakuen stop on the Marunouchi subway line, about 10 minutes from Tōkyō Station, lets you out in front of the **Tōkyō Dome,** Japan's first air-supported indoor stadium, built in 1988 and home to the Tōkyō Yomiuri Giants baseball team. Across from the stadium is Tōkyō Dome City, a combination of family amusement park, shopping mall, restaurants, and a natural spring spa. **The Amusement Park** (🕙 Mon.–Sat. 10–8:30; Sat and holidays, 9–8:30 🎫 Four roller-coaster rides are between ¥600–¥800) has three stomach-churning roller coasters, a haunted house, and a merry-go-round. **The La Qua Shopping Center** holds 70 shops and restaurants. Shops are open daily from 11–9, and restaurants are open 11–11. **La Qua Spa** (🎫 ¥2,565; ¥315 more on holidays; and ¥1,890 surcharge midnight–6 AM; ¥525 surcharge for Healing Room 🕙 Daily 11 AM–9 AM), is a natural hot spring for adults, more like an amusement park in itself. There are four floors of pampering and hot springs with high concentrations of sodium-chloride, which is believed to increase blood circulation. ✉ *1–3–61 Kōraku, Bunkyō-ku* ☎ *03/5800–9999* ⊕ *www.tokyo-dome.co.jp.*

🕙 **Tōkyō Disneyland.** At Tōkyō Disneyland, Mickey-san and his coterie of Disney characters entertain just the way they do in the California and Florida Disney parks. When the park was built in 1983 it was much smaller than its counterparts in the United States, but the construction in 2001 of the adjacent DisneySea, with its seven "Ports of Call" with different nautical themes and rides, added more than 100 acres to this multifaceted Magic Kingdom.

There are several types of admission tickets. Most people buy the One-Day Passport (¥5,800), which gives you unlimited access to the attractions and shows at one or the other of the two parks; also available are a weekday after–6 PM pass, at ¥3,100, and a weekend (and national holiday) after–3 PM pass, at ¥4,700 (check online for updates). There's also a two-day pass, good for both parks, for ¥10,000. You can buy tickets in advance in Tōkyō Station, near the Yaesu North Exit—look for red-jacketed attendants standing outside the booth—or from any local travel agency, such as the Japan Travel Bureau (JTB).

The simplest way to get to Disneyland is by JR Keiyō Line from Tōkyō Station to Maihama; the park is just a few steps from the station exit. From Nihombashi you can also take the Tōzai subway line to Urayasu and walk over to the Tōkyō Disneyland Bus Terminal for the 25-minute ride, which costs ¥230. ☒ *1–1 Maihama, Urayasu-shi* ☏ *Information 0570/00–8632, reservations 045/683–3333* ⊕ *www.tokyodisneyresort. co.jp* ⊙ *Daily 9–10; seasonal closings in Dec. and Jan. may vary, so check before you go.*

☺ **Tōkyō Tower.** In 1958 Tōkyō's fledgling TV networks needed a tall antenna array to transmit signals. Trying to emerge from the devastation of World War II, the nation's capital was also hungry for a landmark—a symbol for the aspirations of a city still without a skyline. The result was the 1,093-foot-high Tōkyō Tower, an unabashed knockoff of Paris's Eiffel Tower, but with great views of the city. The Grand Observation Platform, at an elevation of 492 feet, and the Special Observation Platform, at an elevation of 820 feet, quickly became major tourist attractions; they still draw some 3 million visitors a year, the vast majority of them Japanese youngsters on their first trip to the big city. A modest art gallery and a wax museum round out the tower's appeal as an amusement complex. Enjoy live music and stunning views on the main observation floor café during **Club 333**, an in-house radio show, featuring live jazz, R&B, and bossa nova performances on Wednesday evenings and a live DJ show on Friday evenings; both are from 7–9 and at no extra charge. ☒ *4–2–8 Shiba-Kōen, Minato-ku* ☏ *03/3433–5111* 🖾 *¥920 for Grand Observation Platform, ¥600 extra for Special Observation Platform; aquarium ¥1,000; wax museum ¥870* ⊙ *Tower, daily 9–10. Wax museum, daily 10–9. Aquarium, Sept.–July, daily 10–7; Aug., daily 10–8* Ⓜ *Hibiya subway line, Kamiyachō Station (Exit 2).*

☺ **Toshima-en.** This large, well-equipped amusement park in the northwestern part of Tōkyō has four roller coasters, a haunted house, and seven swimming pools. What makes it special is the authentic Coney Island carousel—left to rot in a New York warehouse, discovered and rescued by a Japanese entrepreneur, and lovingly restored down to the last gilded curlicue on the last prancing unicorn. From Shinjuku, the Ōedo subway line goes directly to the park. ☒ *3–25–1 Koyama, Nerima-ku* ☏ *03/ 3990–3131* 🖾 *Day pass ¥3,800* ⊙ *Thurs.–Mon. 10–6.*

Zoo & Aquariums

☺ **Shinagawa Aquarium** (Shinagawa Suizokukan). The fun part of this aquarium in southwestern Tōkyō is walking through an underwater glass tunnel while some 450 species of fish swim around and above you. There are no pamphlets or explanation panels in English, however, and do your

1

best to avoid Sundays, when the dolphin and sea lion shows draw crowds in impossible numbers. Take the local Keihin-Kyūkō private rail line from Shinagawa to Ōmori-kaigan Station. Turn left as you exit the station and follow the ceramic fish on the sidewalk to the first traffic light; then turn right. You can also take the JR Tōkaidō Line to Oimachi Station; board a free shuttle to the aquarium from the No. 6 platform at the bus terminal just outside Oimachi Station. ✉ *3–2–1 Katsushima, Shinagawa-ku* ☎ *03/3762–3431* 🎫 *¥1,100* ☉ *Wed.–Mon. 10–4:30; dolphin and sea lion shows 3 times daily, on varying schedule.*

🐧 **Sunshine International Aquarium.** This aquarium has some 750 kinds of sea creatures on display, plus sea lion performances four times a day (except when it rains). An English-language pamphlet is available, and most of the exhibits have some English explanation. If you get tired of the sea life, head to the newly refurbished Sunshine Starlight Dome planetarium, where you can see 400,000 stars. And if that still isn't enough to keep you occupied, head to the 60th floor observatory to take in some great views of the city. To get there, take the JR Yamanote Line to Ikebukuro Station (Exit 35) and walk about eight minutes west to the Sunshine City complex. You can also take the Yūraku-chō subway to Higashi-Ikebukuro Station (Exit 2); Sunshine City and the aquarium are about a three-minute walk north. ✉ *3–1–3 Higashi-Ikebukuro, Toshima-ku* ☎ *03/3989–3331* 🎫 *Aquarium ¥1,600; planetarium ¥800; observatory ¥620; tickets may be purchased in combination* ☉ *Aquarium open weekdays 10–6, weekends 10–6:30; Planetarium open daily 11–7; Observation deck open daily 10–9:30.*

🐧 **Tama Zoo** (Tama Dōbutsu Kōen). More a wildlife park than a zoo, this facility in western Tōkyō gives animals room to roam; moats typically separate them from you. You can ride through the Lion Park in a minibus. To get here, take a Keiō Line train toward Takao from Shinjuku Station and transfer at Takahata-Fudō Station for the one-stop branch line that serves the park. ✉ *7–1–1 Hodokubo, Hino-shi* ☎ *0425/91–1611* 🎫 *¥600* ☉ *Thurs.–Tues. 9:30–4.*

🐧 **Tōkyō Sea Life Park.** The three-story cylindrical complex of this aquarium houses more than 540 species of fish and other sea creatures within three different areas: "Voyagers of the Sea" ("Maguro no Kaiyū"), with migratory species; "Seas of the World" ("Sekai no Umi"), with species from foreign waters; and the "Sea of Tōkyō" ("Tōkyō no Umi"), devoted to the creatures of the bay and nearby waters. To get here, take the JR Keiyō Line local train from Tōkyō Station to Kasai Rinkai Kōen Station; the aquarium is a 10-minute walk or so from the south exit. ✉ *6–2–3 Rinkai-chō, Edogawa-ku* ☎ *03/3869–5152* 🎫 *¥700* ☉ *Thurs.–Tues. 9:30–5.*

Off the Beaten Path

Asakura Sculpture Gallery. Outsiders have long since discovered the Nezu and Yanaka areas of Shitamachi—much to the dismay of the handful of foreigners who have lived for years in this charming, inexpensive section of the city. Part of the areas' appeal lie in the fact that some of the giants of modern Japanese culture lived and died here, including novelists Ōgai Mori, Sōseki Natsume, and Ryūnosuke Akutagawa; scholar Tenshin Okakura, who founded the Japan Art Institute; painter Taikan Yokoyama; and sculptors Kōun Takamura and Fumio Asakura. If there's one single attraction here, it's probably Asakura's home and studio, which was converted into a gallery after his death in 1964 and now houses many of his most famous pieces. The tearoom on the opposite side of the courtyard is a quiet place from which to contemplate his garden.

From the north wicket (Nishi-guchi/West Exit) of JR Nippori Station, walk west—Tennō-ji temple will be on the left side of the street—until you reach a police box. Turn right, then right again at the end of the street. The gallery is a three-story black building on the right, a few hundred yards from the corner. ✉ 7–18–10 Yanaka, Taitō-ku ☎ 03/ 3821–4549 ▦ ¥400 ✿ Tues.–Thurs. and weekends 9:30–4:30.

Fodor'sChoice   **Ryōgoku.** Two things make this working-class Shitamachi neighbor-
★   hood worth a special trip: this is the center of the world of sumō wrestling as well as the site of the extraordinary Edo-Tōkyō Museum. Five minutes from Akihabara on the JR Sōbu Line, Ryōgoku is easy to get to, and if you've budgeted a leisurely stay in the city, it's well worth a morning's expedition.

The **Edo-Tōkyō Museum** (✉ 1–4–1 Yokoami, Sumida-ku ☎ 03/ 3626–9974 ⊕ www.edo-tokyo-museum.or.jp ▦ ¥600; additional fees for special exhibits ✿ Tues., Wed., and weekends 9:30–5; Thurs. and Fri. 9:30–8; closed Tues. when Mon. is a national holiday) opened in 1993, more or less coinciding with the collapse of the economic bubble that had made the project possible. Money was no object in those days; much of the large museum site is open plaza—an unthinkably lavish use of space. From the plaza the museum rises on massive pillars to the permanent exhibit areas on the fifth and sixth floors. The escalator takes you directly to the sixth floor—and back in time 300 years. You cross a replica of the Edo-period Nihombashi Bridge into a truly remarkable collection of dioramas, scale models, cutaway rooms, and even whole buildings: an intimate and convincing experience of everyday life in the capital of the Tokugawa shōguns. Equally elaborate are the fifth-floor re-creations of early modern Tōkyō, the "enlightenment" of Japan's headlong embrace of the West, and the twin devastations of the Great Kantō Earthquake and World War II. If you only visit one non-art museum in Tōkyō, make this it.

To get to the museum, leave Ryōgoku Station by the west exit, immediately turn right, and follow the signs. The moving sidewalk and the stairs bring you to the plaza on the third level; to request an English-speaking volunteer guide, use the entrance to the left of the stairs instead, and ask at the General Information counter in front of the first-floor Special Exhibition Gallery.

Walk straight out to the main street in front of the west exit of Ryōgoku station, turn right, and you come almost at once to the Kokugikan (Na-

CLOSE UP

A Mostly Naked Free-For-All

SUMŌ WRESTLING DATES BACK some 1,500 years. Originally it was not just a sport but a religious rite performed at shrines to entertain the harvest gods. To the casual spectator, a match may seem like a fleshy free-for-all, but to the trained eye, it's a refined battle. Two wrestlers square off in a dirt ring about 15 feet in diameter and charge straight at each other in nothing but silk loincloths. There are various techniques of pushing, gripping, and throwing, but the rules are simple: except for hitting below the belt (which is nearly all a sumō wrestler wears), grabbing your opponent by the hair (which would certainly upset the hairdresser that accompanies every sumō ringside), or striking with a closed fist, almost anything goes. If you are thrown down or forced out of the ring, you lose. There are no weight divisions and a runt of merely 250 pounds can find himself facing an opponent twice his size.

To compete, you must belong to one of the 30 *heya* (stables) based in Tōkyō; there are no free agents. The stables are run by retired wrestlers who have purchased the right from the Japan Sumō Association. Sumō is very much a closed world, where hierarchy and formality rule. Youngsters recruited into the sport live in the stable dormitory and do all the community chores, as well as wait on their seniors. When they rise high enough in tournament rankings, they acquire servant-apprentices of their own.

When: Of the six Grand Sumō Tournaments (called *basho*) that take place during the year, Tōkyō hosts three: in early January, mid-May, and mid-September. Matches go from early afternoon, when the novices wrestle, to the titanic clashes of the upper ranks at around 6 PM.

Where: The tournaments are held in the Kokugikan, the National Sumō Arena, in Ryōgoku, a district in Sumida-ku also famed for its clothing shops and eateries that cater respectively to sumō sizes and tastes.
✉ *1–3–28 Yokoami, Sumida-ku*
☎ *03/3623–5111* ⊕ *www.sumo.or.jp*
Ⓜ *JR Sōbu Line, Ryōgoku Station (West Exit).*

How: The price of admission buys you a whole day of sumō; the most expensive seats, closest to the ring, are tatami-carpeted loges for four people, called *sajiki*. The loges are terribly cramped, but the cost (¥9,200–¥11,300 per person) includes all sorts of food and drink and souvenirs, brought around to you by Kokugikan attendants in traditional costume. The cheapest seats cost ¥3,600 for advance sales, ¥2,100 for same-day box office sales. The latter includes discount children's tickets, which makes for an ideal family adventure. For same-day box office sales you should line up an hour in advance of the tournament. You can also reserve tickets through **Playguide** (☎ 03/5802–9999) or at Seven-Eleven, Family Mart, or Lawson convenience stores.

tional Sumō Arena), with its distinctive copper-green roof. If you can't attend one of the Tōkyō sumō tournaments, you may want to at least pay a short visit to the **Sumō Museum** (✉ 1–3–28 Yokoami, Sumida-ku ☎ 03/3622–0366 ⌨ Free ☉ Weekdays 10–4:30), in the south wing of the arena. There are no explanations in English, but the museum's collection of sumō-related wood-block prints, paintings, and illustrated scrolls includes some outstanding examples of traditional Japanese fine art.

Wander this area when the wrestlers are in town (January, May, and September are your best bets) and you're more than likely to see some of them on the streets, in their wood clogs and kimonos. Come 7 AM–11 AM, and you can peer through the doors and windows of the stables to watch them in practice sessions. One of the easiest to find is the **Tatsunami Stable** (⊠ 3–26–2 Ryōgoku), only a few steps from the west end of Ryōgoku Station (turn left when you go through the turnstile and left again as you come out on the street; then walk along the station building to the second street on the right). Another, a few blocks farther south, where the Shuto Expressway passes overhead, is the **Izutsu Stable** (⊠ 2–2–7 Ryōgoku).

★ **Sengaku-ji** (Sengaku Temple). In 1701, a young provincial baron named Asano Takumi-no-Kami attacked and seriously wounded a courtier named Yoshinaka Kira. Asano, for daring to draw his sword in the confines of Edo Castle, was ordered to commit suicide so his family line was abolished and his fief confiscated. Forty-seven of Asano's loyal retainers vowed revenge; the death of their leader made them *rōnin*—masterless samurai. On the night of December 14, 1702, Asano's rōnin stormed Kira's villa in Edo, cut off his head, and brought it in triumph to Asano's tomb at Sengaku-ji, the family temple. The rōnin were sentenced to commit suicide—which they accepted as the reward, not the price, of their honorable vendetta—and were buried in the temple graveyard with their lord.

Through the centuries this story has become a national epic and the last word on the subject of loyalty and sacrifice, celebrated in every medium from Kabuki to film. The temple still stands, and the graveyard is wreathed in smoke from the bundles of incense that visitors still lay reverently on the tombstones. There is a collection of weapons and other memorabilia from the event in the temple's small museum. One of the items dispels forever the myth of Japanese vagueness and indirection in the matter of contracts and formal documents. Kira's family, naturally, wanted to give him a proper burial, but the law insisted this could not be done without his head. They asked for it back, and Ōishi—mirror of chivalry that he was—agreed. He entrusted it to the temple, and the priests wrote him a receipt, which survives even now in the corner of a dusty glass case. "Item," it begins, "One head."

Take the Asakusa subway line to Sengaku-ji Station (Exit A2), turn right when you come to street level, and walk up the hill. The temple is past the first traffic light, on the left. ⊠ *2–11–1 Takanawa, Minato-ku* ☎ *03/3441–5560* 🖃 *Temple and grounds free, museum ¥200* ⊙ *Temple Apr.–Sept., daily 7–6; Oct.–Mar., daily 7–5. Museum daily 9–4.*

Sōgetsu Ikebana School (Sōgetsu Kaikan). The schools of *Ikebana*, like those of other traditional arts, are highly stratified organizations. Students rise through levels of proficiency, paying handsomely for lessons and certifications as they go, until they can become teachers themselves. At the top of the hierarchy is the *iemoto*, the head of the school, a title usually held within a family for generations. The Sōgetsu school of flower arrangement is a relative newcomer to all this. It was founded by Sōfū Teshigahara in 1927, and, compared to the older schools, it espouses a style flamboyant, free-form, and even radical. Introductory lessons in flower arrangement are given in English on Mondays from 10 to noon. Reservations must be made a day in advance. The main hall of the Sōgetsu Kaikan, created by the late Isamu Noguchi, one of the masters of modern sculpture, is well worth a visit. It is a 10-minute walk west on Aoyama-dōri from the Akasaka-mitsuke intersection or east from the Aoyama-itchōme subway stop. ⊠ *7–2–21 Akasaka, Minato-ku* ☎ *03/ 3408–1151* ⊕ *www.sogetsu.or.jp* Ⓜ *Ginza and Marunouchi subway lines, Akasaka-mitsuke Station; Ginza and Hanzō-mon subway lines, Aoyama-itchōme Station (Exit 4).*

Ōji. Want to take a trip back in time? Take the JR Yamanote Line to Ōtsuka, cross the street in front of the station, and change to the Toden Arakawa Line—Tōkyō's last surviving trolley. Heading east, for ¥160 one-way, the trolley takes you through the back gardens of old neighborhoods on its way to Ōji—once the site of Japan's first Western-style paper mill, built in 1875 by Ōji Paper Company, the nation's oldest joint-stock company. The mill is long gone, but the memory lingers on at the **Asuka-yama Ōji Paper Museum.** Some exhibits here show the process of milling paper from pulp. Others illustrate the astonishing variety of products that can be made from paper. The museum is a minute's walk from the trolley stop at Asuka-yama Kōen: you can also get here from the JR Ōji Station (Minami-guchi/South Exit) on the Keihin–Tōhoku Line, or the Nishigahara Station (Asuka-yama Exit) on the Namboku subway line. ⊠ *1–1–3 Ōji, Kita-ku* ☎ *03/3916–2320* ✉ *¥300* ⊘ *Tues.–Sun. 10–4:30.*

Points of Interest

SITES/AREAS	JAPANESE CHARACTERS
Advertising Museum Tōkyō	アド・ミュージアム東京
Akihabara	秋葉原
Ame-ya Yoko-chō Market	アメヤ横丁
Aoyama	青山
Asakura Sculpture Gallery	朝倉彫刻館
Asakusa	浅草
Asakusa Shrine (Asakusa Jinja)	浅草神社
Azabu-Jūban	麻布十番
Backstreet shops of Tsukiji	築地6丁目
Bank of Japan (Nihon Ginkō)	日本銀行
Belfry (Toki-no-kane Shōrō)	時の鐘鐘楼
Benzaiten	弁財天
Bookstores of Jimbō-chō	神保町書店街
Bridge of Japan (Nihombashi)	日本橋
Bridgestone Museum of Art (Burijisuton Bijutsukan)	ブリヂストン美術館
Bunka-mura	文化村
National Memorial Garden (Chidori-ga-fuchi)	千鳥ヶ淵戦没者墓苑
Chocolatte	ショコラッテ
Crafts Gallery of the National Museum of Modern Art (Kōgeikan)	工芸館
Dai-ichi Mutual Life Insurance Company Building	第一生命館
Dembo Temple (Dembō-in)	伝法院
Detached Palace Garden (Hama Rikyū Tei-en)	浜離宮庭園
Edo-Gin	江戸銀
Fuji Television Nippon Broadcasting Building	フジテレビ
Ginza	銀座
Hanazono Shrine (Hanazono Jinja)	花園神社
Hanzō Gate (Hanzō-mon)	半蔵門
Harajuku	原宿
Hasumi Chaya	蓮見茶屋
Hirakawa Gate (Hirakawa-mon)	平川門
Idemitsu Museum of Art (Idemitsu Bijutsukan)	出光美術館

Imperial Palace and Government District	皇居近辺
Imperial Palace East Garden (Kōkyo Higashi Gyo-en)	皇居東御苑
Imperial Palace Outer Garden (Kōkyo-Gaien)	皇居外苑
Japanese Sword Museum (Tōken Hakubutsukan)	刀剣博物館
Jimbō-chō	神保町
Kabuki-chō	歌舞伎町
Kabuki Theater (Kabuki-za)	歌舞伎座
Kabuto Shrine (Kabuto Jinja)	兜神社
Kanda Shrine (Kanda Myōjin)	神田明神
Kan-ei Temple (Kan-ei-ji)	寛永寺
Kannon Hall (Kiyomizu Kannon-dō)	清水観音堂
Kappabashi	かっぱ橋
Kasai Seaside Park	葛西臨海公園
Kite Museum (Tako no Hakubutsukan)	凧の博物館
LAOX	ラオックス
Les Deux Magots	ドゥ・マゴ・パリ
Meiji Shrine (Meiji Jingū)	明治神宮
Meiji Shrine Outer Gardens (Meiji Jingū Gai-en)	明治神宮外苑
Mitsukoshi	三越
Mori Tower	森タワー
Museum of Maritime Science (Fune-no-Kagakukan)	船の科学館
Nakase	中瀬
National Diet Building (Kokkai-Gijidō)	国会議事堂
National Museum of Emerging Science and Innovation (Nihon Kagaku Miraikan)	日本科学未来館
National Museum of Modern Art, Tōkyō (Tōkyō Kokuritsu Kindai Bijutsukan)	国立近代美術館
National Museum of Western Art (Kokuritsu Seiyō Bijutsukan)	国立西洋美術館
National Science Museum (Kokuritsu Kagaku Hakubutsukan)	国立科学博物館
National Theater (Kokuritsu Gekijō)	国立劇場
Nezu Institute of Fine Arts (Nezu Bijutsukan)	根津美術館
Nikolai Cathedral	ニコライ堂

Odaiba	お台場
Odaiba Kaihin Kōen	お台場海浜公園
Odaiba's Hot Spring Theme Park (Ōedo Onsen Monogatari)	大江戸温泉物語
Ōta Memorial Museum of Art (Ōta Kinen Bijutsukan)	太田記念美術館
Ōte Gate (Ōte-mon)	大手門
Roppongi	六本木
Roppongi Hills	六本木ヒルズ
Ryōgoku	両国
Seiji Tōgō Memorial Sompo Japan Museum of Art (Sompo Japan Tōgō Seiji Bijutsukan)	東郷青児美術館
Sengaku Temple (Sengaku-ji)	泉岳寺
Sensō-ji Complex	浅草寺
Sensō-ji Main Hall	浅草観音堂
Shibuya	渋谷
Shinagawa Aquarium (Shinagawa Suizokukan)	しながわ水族館
Shinjuku	新宿
Shinjuku Gyo-en National Garden	新宿御苑
Shinjuku Park Tower Building	新宿パークタワー
Shinobazu Pond (Shinobazu-ike)	不忍池
Shiodome	汐留
Shitamachi Museum (Shitamachi Hakubutsukan)	下町博物館
Shōgitai Memorial	彰義隊の墓
Shrine of Peace for the Nation (Yasukuni Jinja)	靖国神社
Sōgetsu Ikebana School (Sōgetsu Kaikan)	草月会館
Statue of Hachikō	ハチ公像
Statue of Takamori Saigō	西郷隆盛像
Sukiya-bashi	数寄屋橋
Sunshine International Aquarium	サンシャイン国際水族館
Suzumoto	鈴本演芸場
Tama Zoo (Tama Dōbutsu Kōen)	多摩動物公園
Thunder God Gate (Kaminari-mon)	雷門
Toden Arakawa Line	都電荒川線
Tōkyō Central Wholesale Market (Tōkyō Chūō Oroshiuri Ichiba)	東京都中央卸売市場

Tokudai Temple (Tokudai-ji)	徳大寺
Tōkyō Disneyland	東京ディズニーランド
Tōkyō International Forum	東京国際フォーラム
Tōkyō Metropolitan Art Museum (Tōkyō-to Bijutsukan)	東京都美術館
Tōkyō Metropolitan Government Office (Tōkyō Tochō)	東京都庁
Tōkyō National Museum (Tōkyō Kokuritsu Hakubutsukan)	東京国立博物館
Tōkyō Opera City	東京オペラシティ
Tōkyō Sea Life Park	葛西臨海水族園
Tōkyō Station	東京駅
Tōkyō Tower	東京タワー
Tōshō Shrine (Tōshō-gū)	東照宮
Toshima-en	としまえん
Transportation Museum (Kōtsū Hakubutsukan)	交通博物館
Tsukiji	築地
Tsukiji Hongan Temple (Tsukiji Hongan-ji)	築地本願寺
Two-Tiered Bridge (Ni-jū-bashi)	二重橋
Ueno	上野
Ueno Royal Museum (Ueno-no-Mori Bijutsukan)	上野の森美術館
Ueno Zoo (Onshi Ueno Dōbutsuen)	上野動物園
Wadakura Fuusui Koen Restaurant	和田倉噴水公園レストラン
Waentei-Kikkō	和えん亭 吉幸
Yamagiwa	ヤマギワ
Yamatane Museum of Art (Yamatane Bijutsukan)	山種美術館
Yoyogi Park (Yoyogi Kōen)	代々木公園
Yūraku-chō	有楽町
Yushima Shrine (Yushima Seidō)	湯島聖堂
Zenpuku Temple (Zenpuku-ji)	麻布山善福寺

Where to Eat

WORD OF MOUTH

"If you see a small place with a bunch of young guys chowing down, go there."

—mrwunrfl

"There was a vendor at the base of Tōkyō Tower who had baked sweet potatoes in a wood-fired oven on his little roasting cart. Seeing this cart and little old man and fire embers late at night was magical."

—emd

"Try Maisen, a restaurant in a converted bathhouse in Aoyama Dori for the most amazing deep-fried pork chops called *tonkatsu*."

—hobbes

Updated by
Katherine
Pham Do

THOUGH TŌKYŌ IS STILL STUBBORNLY PROVINCIAL in many ways, whatever the rest of the world has pronounced good in the realm of dining eventually makes its way here: French, Italian, Chinese, Indian, Middle Eastern, Latin American. And at last count, there were more than 200,000 bars and restaurants in the city.

Restaurants in Japan naturally expect most of their clients to be Japanese, and the Japanese are the world's champion modifiers. Only the most serious restaurateurs refrain from editing some of the authenticity out of foreign cuisines; in areas like Shibuya, Harajuku, and Shinjuku, too many of the foreign restaurants cater to students and young office workers who come mainly for the *fun'iki* (atmosphere). Choose a French bistro or Italian trattoria in these areas carefully, and expect to pay dearly for the real thing. That said, you can count on the fact that the city's best foreign cuisine is world-class. Several of France's two- and three-star restaurants, for example, have established branches and joint ventures in Tōkyō, and they regularly send their chefs over to supervise. The style almost everywhere is nouvelle cuisine: small portions, with picture-perfect garnishes and light sauces. More and more, you find interesting fusions of French and Japanese culinary traditions served in poetically beautiful presentations. Recipes make imaginative use of fresh Japanese ingredients, like *shimeji* (mushrooms) and local wild vegetables.

Tōkyō has also embraced the range and virtuosity of Italian cuisine; chances are good that the finer trattorias here will measure up to even Tuscan standards. Indian food is also consistently good—and relatively inexpensive. Chinese food is the most consistently modified; it can be very good, but it pales in comparison to fare in Hong Kong or Beijing.

A few pointers are in order on the geography of food and drink. The farther "downtown" you go—into Shitamachi—the less likely you are to find the real thing in foreign (that is, non-Japanese) cuisine. There's superb Japanese food all over the city, but aficionados of sushi swear (with excellent reason) by Tsukiji, where the fish market supplies the neighborhood's restaurants with the freshest ingredients; the restaurants in turn serve the biggest portions and charge the most reasonable prices. Asakusa takes pride in its tempura restaurants, but tempura is reliable almost everywhere, especially at branches of the well-established, citywide chains like Tenya and Tsunahachi.

Tōkyōites love to wine and dine at first-rate establishments, some of which are grotesquely expensive. But have no fear: the city has a fair number of bargains too—good cooking of all sorts that you can enjoy on even a modest budget. Every department store and skyscraper office building devotes at least one floor to

CHECK IT OUT!

English OK! (⊕ www.englishok.jp) lists restaurants where English is spoken so people with limited or no Japanese can order food without worrying about the language barrier. Before heading out, check the Web site for maps, sample menus, and printable coupons.

KNOW-HOW

DRESS

Dining out in Tōkyō does not ordinarily demand a great deal in the way of formal attire. If it's a business meal, of course, and your hosts or guests are Japanese, dress conservatively: for men, a suit and tie; for women, a dress or suit in a basic color and a minimum of jewelry. On your own, follow the unspoken dress codes you'd observe at home and you won't go wrong. We mention dress only when men are required to wear a jacket or a jacket and tie.

For Japanese-style dining on tatami floors, keep two things in mind: wear shoes that slip on and off easily and presentable socks, and choose clothing you'll be comfortable in for a few hours with your legs gathered under you.

RESERVATIONS

Unless otherwise noted, the restaurants listed in this guide are open daily for lunch and dinner. Reservations are always a good idea: we mention them only when they're essential or not accepted. Book as far ahead as you can, and reconfirm as soon as you arrive.

PRICES

Eating at hotels and famous restaurants is costly; however, you can eat well and reasonably at standard restaurants that may not have signs in English. Many less expensive restaurants display in their front windows plastic replicas of the dishes they serve, so you can always point to what you want if the language barrier is insurmountable. Good places to look for moderately priced dining spots are in the restaurant concourses of department stores, usually on the first and/or second basement levels and the top floors.

The restaurants we list are the cream of the crop in each price category. Price-category estimates are based on the cost of a main course at dinner, excluding drinks, taxes, and service charges. Japanese-style restaurants often serve set meals, which may include rice, soup, and pickled vegetables in addition to the main course—this can drive up the cost. You can sometimes request the main dish without the sides, but then you'd be missing out on the beauty and harmony of a Japanese meal. Credit cards are generally accepted at cheaper establishments, but definitely check before sitting down.

WATER & REST ROOMS

Japanese restaurants are very clean (standards of hygiene are high), and tap water is safe to drink. Restaurants may have Japanese-style toilets, with bowls recessed into the floor, over which you must squat.

WHAT IT COSTS In yen				
	$$$$	$$$	$$	$	¢
AT DINNER	over 3,000	2,000–3,000	1,000–2,000	800–1,000	under 800

Prices are per person for a main course.

restaurants; none of them stand out, but all are inexpensive and quite passable places to lunch. Food and drink, even at street stalls, are safe wherever you go. ■ TIP→ **When in doubt, note that Tōkyō's top-rated international hotels also have some of the city's best places to eat and drink.**

Akasaka

Indian

★ **$$** ╳ **Moti.** Vegetarian dishes at Moti, especially the lentil and eggplant curries, are very good; so is the chicken marsala, cooked in butter and spices. The chefs here are recruited from India by a family member who runs a restaurant in Delhi. As its reputation for reasonably priced North Indian cuisine grew, Moti established branches in nearby Akasaka-mitsuke, Roppongi, and farther away in Yokohama. They all have the inevitable Indian friezes, copper bowls, and white elephants, but this one—popular at lunch with the office crowd from the nearby Tōkyō Broadcasting System headquarters—puts the least into decor. ⊠ *Kimpa Bldg., 3rd fl., 2–14–31 Akasaka, Minato-ku* ☎ *03/3584–6640* ⊟ *AE, DC, MC, V* Ⓜ *Chiyoda subway line, Akasaka Station (Exit 2).*

Italian

$$$–$$$$ ╳ **La Granata.** Located in the Tōkyō Broadcasting System Garden building, La Granata is very popular with the media crowd, and deservedly so: the chefs prepare some of the most accomplished Italian food in town. La Granata is decked out in trattoria style, with brickwork arches, red-checker tablecloths, and a display of antipasti to whet the appetite. Whether you order the *tagliolini* (thin ribbon noodles) with porcini mushrooms, the spaghetti with garlic and red pepper, or any of the other menu offerings as your main meal, start with the wonderful batter-fried zucchini flowers filled with mozzarella and asparagus as an appetizer. ⊠ *TBS Garden, 1F, 5–1–3 Akasaka, Minato-ku* ☎ *03/ 3582–3241* ⊟ *AE, MC, V* Ⓜ *Chiyoda subway line, Akasaka Station (Exit 1A).*

Japanese

$$$$ ╳ **Kisoji.** The specialty here is shabu-shabu: thin slices of beef cooked at your table. Normally this is an informal sort of meal; after all, you do get to play with your food a bit. Kisoji, however, adds a dimension of posh to the experience, with all the tasteful appointments of a traditional *ryōtei*—private dining rooms with tatami seating (at a 10% surcharge), elegant little rock gardens,

---

THE QUINTESSENTIAL JAPANESE RESTAURANT

Most often walled off from the outside world, a *ryōtei* is like a villa that has been divided into several small, private dining rooms. These rooms are traditional in style, with tatami-mat floors, low tables, and a hanging scroll or a flower arrangement in the alcove. Servers are assigned to each room to present the meal's many dishes (which likely contain foods you've never seen before), pour sake, and provide light conversation. Many parts of the city are proverbial for their ryōtei; the top houses tend to be in Akasaka, Tsukiji, Asakusa, and nearby Yanagibashi, and Shimbashi.

and alcoves with flower arrangements. ✉ *3–10–4 Akasaka, Minato-ku* ☎ *03/3588–0071* 🚫 *AE, MC, V* 🕙 *Closed Sun.* Ⓜ *Ginza and Marunouchi subway lines, Akasaka-mitsuke Station (Belle Vie Akasaka Exit).*

$$$$ ✕ **Jidaiya.** Like the Jidaiya in Roppongi, these two Akasaka branches serve various prix-fixe courses, including shabu-shabu, tempura, sushi, and steamed rice with seafood. The food isn't fancy, but it's delicious and filling. ✉ *Naritaya Bldg. 1F, Akasaka 3–14–3, Minato-ku* ☎ *03/3588–0489* 🚫 *AE, DC, MC, V* 🕙 *No lunch weekends* Ⓜ *Ginza and Marunouchi subway lines, Akasaka-mitsuke Station (Belle Vie Akasaka Exit)* ✉ *Isomura Bldg. B1, Akasaka 5–1–4, Minato-ku* ☎ *03/3224–1505* 🚫 *AE, DC, MC, V* 🕙 *No lunch weekends* Ⓜ *Chiyoda subway line, Akasaka Station (Exit 1A).*

Akasaka-mitsuke

Japanese

$$$–$$$$ ✕ **Ninja.** In keeping with the air of mystery you'd expect from a ninja-theme restaurant, a ninja-costumed waiter leads you through a dark underground maze to your table in an artificial cave. The menu has more than 100 choices, including some elaborate set courses that are extravagant in both proportion and price. Among the impressively presented dishes are "jack-in-the-box" seafood salad, tuna and avocado tartar with mustard and vinegar-miso paste, and the life-size bonsai-tree dessert made from cookies and green-tea ice cream. Magical tricks are performed at your table during dinner—it's slightly kitschy but entertaining nonetheless. ✉ *Akasaka Tokyu Plaza, 2–14–3 Nagata-cho, Minato-ku* ☎ *03/5157–3936* ⚑ *Reservations essential* 🚫 *AE, MC, V* Ⓜ *Ginza and Marunouchi subway lines, Akasaka-mitsuke Station (Tokyo Plaza Exit).*

¢–$$ ✕ **Sawanoi.** The homemade udon noodles, served in a broth with seafood, vegetables, or chicken, make a perfect light meal or midnight snack. Try the *inaka* (country-style) udon, which has bonito, seaweed flakes, radish shavings, and a raw egg dropped in to cook in the hot broth. For a heartier meal, chose the *tenkama* set: hot udon and shrimp tempura with a delicate soy-based sauce. A bit rundown, Sawanoi is one of the last remaining neighborhood shops in what is now an upscale business and entertainment district. It stays open until 3 AM, and a menu is available in English. ✉ *Shimpo Bldg., 1st fl., 3–7–13 Akasaka, Minato-ku* ☎ *03/3582–2080* 🚫 *No credit cards* 🕙 *Closed Sun.* Ⓜ *Ginza and Marunouchi subway lines, Akasaka-mitsuke Station (Belle Vie Akasaka Exit).*

Aoyama

Japanese

$$$ ✕ **Higo-no-ya.** The specialty of the house is *kushi-yaki*: small servings of meat, fish, and vegetables cut into bits and grilled on bamboo skewers. There's nothing ceremonious or elegant about kushi-yaki; it resembles the more familiar yakitori, with somewhat more variety to the ingredients. Higo-no-ya's helpful English menu guides you to other delicacies like shiitake mushrooms stuffed with minced chicken; bacon-wrapped scallops; and bonito, shrimp, and eggplant with ginger. The

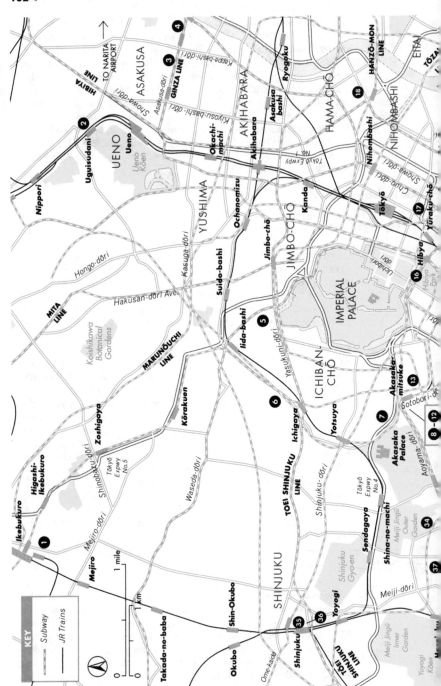

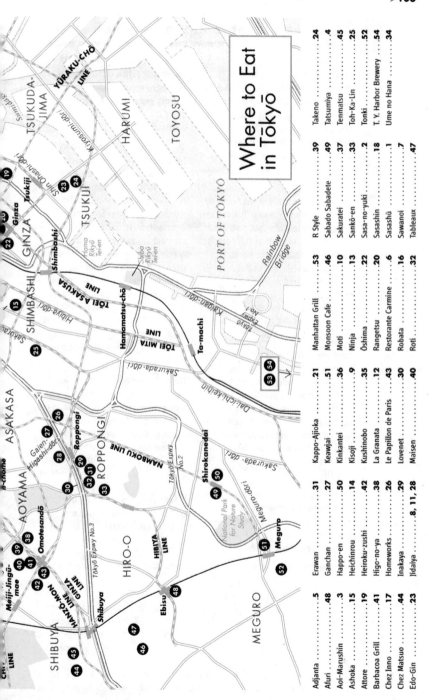

Where to Eat in Tōkyō

The Essentials of a Japanese Meal

THE BASIC FORMULA FOR A traditional Japanese meal is deceptively simple. It starts with soup, followed by raw fish, then the entrée (grilled, steamed, simmered, or fried fish, chicken, or vegetables), and ends with rice and pickles, with perhaps fresh fruit for dessert, and a cup of green tea. It's as simple as that—almost.

There are, admittedly, a few twists to the story. Beyond the raw fish, it's the incredible variety of vegetation used in Japanese cooking that still surprises the Western palate: *take-no-ko* (bamboo shoots), *renkon* (lotus root), and the treasured *matsutake* mushrooms (which grow wild in jealously guarded forest hideaways and sometimes sell for more than $60 apiece), to name a few.

There are also ground rules. Absolute freshness is first. To a Japanese chef, this is an unparalleled virtue, and much of a chef's reputation relies on the ability to obtain the finest ingredients at the peak of season: fish brought in from the sea this morning (not yesterday) and vegetables from the earth (not the hothouse), if at all possible.

Simplicity is next. Rather than embellishing foods with heavy spices and rich sauces, the Japanese chef prefers flavors au naturel. Flavors are enhanced, not elaborated, accented rather than concealed. Without a heavy sauce, fish is permitted a degree of natural fishiness–a garnish of fresh red ginger will be provided to offset the flavor rather than to disguise it.

The third prerequisite is beauty. Simple, natural foods must appeal to the eye as well as to the palate. Green peppers on a vermilion dish, perhaps, or an egg custard in a blue bowl. Rectangular dishes for a round eggplant. So important is the seasonal element in Japanese cooking that maple leaves and pine needles will be used to accent an autumn dish. Or two small summer delicacies, a pair of freshwater *ayu* fish, will be grilled with a purposeful twist to their tails to make them "swim" across a crystal platter and thereby suggest the coolness of a mountain stream on a hot August night.

Not to be forgotten is mood, which can make or break the entire meal. Japanese connoisseurs will go to great lengths to find the perfect yakitori stand–a smoky, lively place–an environment appropriate to the occasion, offering a night of grilled chicken, cold beer, and camaraderie. In fancier places, mood becomes a fancier problem, to the point of quibbling over the proper amount of "water music" trickling in the basin outside your private room.

---

restaurant is a postmodern–traditional cross, with wood beams painted black, paper lanterns, and sliding paper screens. There's tatami, table, and counter seating. ⊠ *AG Bldg. B1, 3–18–17 Minami-Aoyama, Minato-ku* ☎ *03/3423–4461* ▤ *AE, DC, MC, V* ⊗ *No lunch* Ⓜ *Ginza, Chiyoda, and Hanzō-mon subway lines, Omotesandō Station (Exit A4).*

$$–$$$ ✕ **Maisen.** Converted from a *sentō* (public bathhouse), Maisen still has the old high ceiling (built for ventilation) and the original signs instructing bathers where to change. Bouquets of seasonal flowers help transform the large, airy space into a pleasant dining room. Maisen's specialty is the *tonkatsu* set: tender, juicy, deep-fried pork cutlets served with a spicy sauce, shredded cabbage, miso soup, and rice. A popular alternative is the *Suruga-zen* set, a main course of fried fish served with sashimi, soup, and rice. There are no-smoking rooms upstairs. ⊠ *4–8–5 Jingū-mae, Shibuya-ku* ☎ *03/3470–0071* ▭ *AE, DC, MC, V* Ⓜ *Ginza, Chiyoda, and Hanzō-mon subway lines, Omotesandō Station (Exit A2).*

¢–$$
FodorsChoice
★
✕**Ume no Hana.** The exclusive specialty here is tofu, prepared in more ways than you can imagine—boiled, steamed, stir-fried with minced crabmeat, served in a custard, wrapped in thin layers around a delicate whitefish paste. Tofu is touted as the perfect high-protein, low-calorie health food; at Ume no Hana it is raised to the elegance of haute cuisine. Enter this restaurant from a flagstone walk lined with traditional stone lanterns, and remove your shoes when you step up to the main room. Latticed wood screens separate the tables. Private dining rooms have tatami seating with recesses under the tables so you can stretch your legs. Prix-fixe meals include a complimentary aperitif. ⊠ *2–14–6 Kita-Aoyama, Bell Commons 6F, Minato-ku* ☎ *03/3475–8077* ▭ *AE, DC, MC, V* ⭗ *No smoking except in private rooms* Ⓜ *Ginza Line, Gaien-mae Station (Exit 3).*

Asakusa

Japanese

$$
FodorsChoice
★
✕**Aoi-Marushin.** The largest tempura restaurant in Tōkyō, with six floors of tables and tatami seating, welcomes foreign customers and makes a visit easy with English menus. This is a family restaurant. Don't expect much in the way of decor—just lots of food at very reasonable prices. Asakusa is a must on any itinerary, and tempura *teishoku* (an assortment of delicate batter-fried fish, seafood, and fresh vegetables) is the specialty of the district. Aoi-Marushin's location, just a few minutes' walk from the entrance to Sensō-ji temple, makes it an obvious choice after a visit to the temple. ⊠ *1–4–4 Asakusa, Taitō-ku* ☎ *03/3841–0110* ▭ *AE, MC, V* Ⓜ *Ginza and Asakusa subway lines, Asakusa Station (Exit 1).*

$$
✕**Tatsumiya.** Here's a restaurant that's run like a formal ryōtei but has the feel of a rough-cut *izakaya* (Japanese pub). Neither inaccessible nor outrageously expensive, Tatsumiya is adorned—nay, cluttered—with antique chests, braziers, clocks, lanterns, bowls, utensils, and craft work, some of it for sale. The evening meal is in the *kaiseki* style, with seven courses: tradition demands that the meal include something raw, something boiled, something vinegary, and something grilled. The kaiseki dinner is served only until 8:30, and you must reserve ahead for it. Tatsumiya also serves a light lunch, plus a variety of *nabe* (one-pot seafood and vegetable stews, prepared at your table) until 10. The pork nabe is the house specialty. ⊠ *1–33–5 Asakusa, Taitō-ku* ☎ *03/3842–7373* ▭ *MC, V* Ⓜ *Ginza and Asakusa subway lines, Asakusa Station (Exits 1 and 3).*

Azabu-Jūban

American/Casual

$–$$
✕**Homeworks.** Every so often, even on alien shores, you've got to have a burger. When the urge strikes, the Swiss-and-bacon special at Home-

Tips on Dining

• There's no taboo against slurping your noodle soup, though women are generally less boisterous about it than men.

• Pick up the soup bowl and drink directly from it, rather than leaning over the table to sip it. Take the fish or vegetables from it with your chopsticks. Return the lid to the soup bowl when you are finished. The rice bowl, too, is to be picked up and held in your left hand while you eat from it.

• Don't point, lick, or gesture with chopsticks. Also, never take food from a common serving plate with the ends of the chopsticks you've had in your mouth. Never use your chopsticks to take food from someone else's chopsticks, as this denotes a funerary custom. Don't stick your chopsticks upright in your food when you're done using them; instead, allow them to rest on the side of your dish or bowl.

• When drinking with a friend, don't pour into your own glass. Take the bottle and pour for the other person. She will in turn reach for the bottle and pour for you. The Japanese will attempt to top your drink off after every few sips.

• The Japanese don't pour sauces on their rice in a traditional meal. Sauces are intended for dipping foods lightly, not for dunking or soaking.

• Among faux pas that are considered nearly unpardonable, the worst perhaps is blowing your nose. Excuse yourself and leave the room if this becomes necessary.

• Although McDonald's and Häagen-Dazs have made great inroads on the custom of never eating in public, it's still considered gauche to munch on a hamburger (or an ice-cream cone) as you walk along a public street. In particular, avoid eating on trains or you will attract disapproving stares.

works is an incomparably better choice than anything you can get at one of the global chains. Hamburgers come in three sizes on white or wheat buns, with a variety of toppings. There are also hot teriyaki chicken and pastrami sandwiches and vegetarian options like hummus and eggplant. Desserts, alas, are so-so. With its hardwood banquettes and French doors open to the street in good weather, Homeworks is a pleasant place to linger over lunch. There are also branches in Hiro-o and Kyō-bashi. ⊠ *Vesta Bldg. 1F, 1–5–8 Azabu-Jūban, Minato-ku* ☎ *03/3405–9884* ⊟ *AE, MC, V* Ⓜ *Namboku and Ōedo subway lines, Azabu-Jūban Station (Exit 4).*

Korean

$$–$$$$ ✕ **Sankō-en.** With the embassy of South Korea a few blocks away, Sankō-en stands out in a neighborhood thick with Korean-barbecue joints. Customers—not just from the neighborhood but from nearby trendy Roppongi as well—line up at all hours (from 11:30 AM to midnight) to get in. Korean barbecue is a smoky affair; you cook your own food, usually thin slices of beef and vegetables, on a gas grill at your table. The *karubi* (brisket), which is accompanied by a great salad, is the best choice

on the menu. ⊠ *1–8–7 Azabu-Jūban, Minato-ku* ☎ *03/3585–6306* ♠ *Reservations not accepted* ▤ *MC, V* ⊘ *Closed Wed.* Ⓜ *Namboku and Ōedo subway lines, Azabu-Jūban Station (Exit 4).*

Daikanyama

Contemporary

$$–$$$$ ✕ **Tableaux.** The mural in the bar depicts the fall of Pompeii, the ban-
Fodor'sChoice   quettes are upholstered in red leather, and the walls are papered in an-
★   tique gold. Tableaux may lay on more glitz than is necessary, but the service is cordial and professional, and the food is superb. Try Zuwai-crab-and-red-shrimp spring rolls; filet mignon with creamed potatoes, seasonal vegetables, and merlot sauce; or, for dessert, the chocolate soufflé cake. The bar is open until 1:30 AM. ⊠ *Sunroser Daikanyama Bldg. B1, 11–6 Sarugaku-chō, Shibuya-ku* ☎ *03/5489–2201* ▤ *AE, DC, MC, V* ⊘ *No lunch* 🜲 *Jacket and tie* Ⓜ *Tōkyū Tōyoko private rail line, Daikanyama Station (Kita-guchi/North Exit).*

Pan-Asian

¢–$$ ✕ **Monsoon Cafe.** With several locations, Monsoon Cafe meets the de-mand in Tōkyō for "ethnic" food—which by local definition means spicy and primarily Southeast Asian. Complementing the eclectic Pan-Asian food are rattan furniture, brass tableware from Thailand, colorful pa-pier-mâché parrots on gilded stands, Balinese carvings, and ceiling fans. Here, at the original Monsoon, the best seats in the house are on the balcony that runs around the four sides of the atrium-style central space. Try the *satay* (grilled, skewered cubes of meat) platter, coconut-flavored deep-fried calamari, or *nasi goring* (Indonesian fried rice). ⊠ *15–4 Hachiyama-chō, Shibuya-ku* ☎ *03/5489–3789* ⊕ *www.monsoon-cafe.jp* ▤ *AE, DC, MC, V* Ⓜ *Tōkyū Tōyoko private rail line, Daikanyama Station (Kita-guchi/North Exit).*

Ebisu

Japanese

$ ✕ **Afuri.** Ramen is the quintessential Japanese fast food in a bowl: thick Chinese noodles in a savory broth, with soybean paste, diced leeks, grilled *chashu* (pork loin), and spinach. No neighborhood in Tōkyō is with-out at least one ramen joint—often serving only at a counter. In Ebisu, the hands-down favorite is Afuri. Using the picture menu, choose your ramen by inserting coins into a ticket machine, find a seat, and hand over your ticket to the cooks who will prepare your ramen then and there. There's limited seating, and at lunch and dinner, the line of waiting cus-tomers extends down the street. ⊠ *1–1–7 Ebisu, Shibuya-ku* ☎ *03/3571–0957* ▤ *No credit cards* Ⓜ *JR Yamanote Line (Nishi-guchi/West Exit) and Hibiya subway line (Exit 1), Ebisu Station.*

Ginza

Indian

$$–$$$$ ✕ **Ashoka.** Since 1968, Ashoka has staked out the high ground for In-dian cuisine in Tōkyō—with a dining room suited to its fashionable Ginza location. The room is hushed and spacious, incense perfumes the air, the lighting is recessed, the carpets are thick, and the servers wear spiffy uniforms. The best thing to order here is the *thali*, a selection of curries, tandoori chicken, and naan served on a figured brass tray. The Goan fish curry is also excellent, as is the chicken tikka: boneless chunks marinated and cooked in the tandoor. ⊠ *Ginza Inz Bldg. 1, 2nd fl., 3–1 Nishi Ginza, Chūō-ku* ☎ *03/ 3567–2377* 🖃 *AE, DC, MC, V* Ⓜ *Marunouchi and Ginza subway lines, Ginza Station (Exit C9).*

> ### AVOID THE CROWD
>
> Chances are that when you're hungry for dinner, so are hundreds of other people who will flock to the same restaurant districts. It's not uncommon to wait for a table for up to an hour, especially on Friday and Saturday nights. Go a little early, say around 5:30, to bypass the crowds, or reserve ahead to avoid disappointment.

Japanese

$$$$ ✕ **Kappo-Ajioka.** When prepared incorrectly, fugu, the highly poisonous puffer fish, is fatal, yet this doesn't stop people from trying it at this Tōkyō branch of the Kansai fugu ryōtei (puffer-fish restaurant). Licensed chefs prepare the fish in every way imaginable—raw, fried, stewed—using the fresh catch flown in straight from Shimonoseki, a prime fugu-fishing region. The overall flavor is subtle and somewhat nondescript—people are drawn more to the element of danger than the taste (fatalities are rare, but a few people in Japan die each year from fugu poisoning). Try the house specialty of *suppon* (Japanese turtle) and fugu nabe, fugu sashimi, or fugu *no arayaki* (grilled head and cheeks). ⊠ *New Comparu Bldg. 6F, 7–7–12 Ginza, Chūō-ku* ☎ *03/3574–8844* ⌂ *Reservations essential* 🖃 *AE, MC, V* Ⓜ *Ginza, Hibiya, and Marunouchi subway lines, Ginza Station (Exit A5).*

$$$$ ✕ **Ōshima.** The draw at Ōshima is the *Kaga ryōri* cooking of Kanazawa, a small city on the Sea of Japan known as "Little Kyōto" for its rich craft traditions. Waitresses dress in kimonos of Kanazawa's famous Yuzen dyed silk; Kutani porcelain and Wajima lacquerware grace the exquisite table settings. Seafood at Ōshima is superb, but don't ignore the specialty of the house: a stew of duck and potatoes called *jibuni*. Kaiseki full-course meals are pricey, but there's a reasonable lunchtime set menu for ¥1,800. ⊠ *Ginza Core Bldg. 9F, 5–8–20 Ginza, Chūō-ku* ☎ *03/ 3574–8080* 🖃 *AE, MC, V* Ⓜ *Ginza, Hibiya, and Marunouchi subway lines, Ginza Station (Exit A5).*

$$$–$$$$ ✕ **Rangetsu.** Japan enjoys a special reputation for its lovingly raised, tender, marbled domestic beef. Try it, if your budget will bear the weight, at Rangetsu, in the form of this elegant Ginza restaurant's signature shabu-shabu or sukiyaki course. Call ahead to reserve a private alcove, where you can cook for yourself, or have a kaiseki meal brought to your table by kimono-clad attendants. Rangetsu is a block from the Ginza 4-chōme crossing, opposite the Matsuya Department Store. ⊠ *3–5–8 Ginza, Chūō-ku* ☎ *03/3567–1021* 🖃 *AE, DC, MC, V* Ⓜ *Marunouchi and Ginza subway lines, Ginza Station (Exits A9 and A10).*

What's a Vegetarian to Do?

TŌKYŌ IS A GREAT GASTRONOMIC center, but it can be a bit daunting for vegetarians. Most Japanese recipes use fish stock, and it's almost unheard of to ask chefs to tweak their recipes. If you do find a flexible eatery, your choice might still arrive with ham, bacon, or chicken, because in Japanese, none of these words fall semantically under the term "meat."

There are a handful of restaurants in Tōkyō (such as Sasa-no-yuki) that specialize in *shōjin ryōri*. This traditional zen vegetarian food emphasizes natural flavors and fresh ingredients without using heavy spices or rich sauces. The variety and visual beauty of a full-course shōjin ryōri meal offers new dining dimensions to the vegetarian gourmet. *Goma-dōfu*, or sesame-flavored bean curd, for example, is a tasty treat, as is *nasu-dengaku*, grilled eggplant covered with a sweet miso sauce.

The number of veggie-friendly oases is growing, but another safe bet is one of the city's numerous Italian and Indian joints. For a list of vegetarian restaurants, visit **Tōkyō Vegetarian Guide** (⊕ www.vegietokyo.com). Here are four favorites:

Itosho. At this zen restaurant, food arrives in a procession of 13 tiny dishes, each selected according to season, texture, and color. Dinner costs between ¥8,400 and ¥10,500, and reservations must be made at least two days in advance. ⊠ 3–4–7 Azabu-Jūban, Minato-ku ☎ 03/3454–6538 ⊟ No credit cards accepted Ⓜ Namboku and Ōedo subway lines, Azabu-Jūban Station (Exit 1).

Brown Rice Café. Tucked inside a Neal's Yard Remedies store, this café has just 10 tables and closes by 9 PM, but if you're shopping in Harajuku, it's a great place to stop for a tempeh burger or stuffed tofu pouch. In good weather, try the outdoor patio. ⊠ 5–1–17 Jingu-mae, Shibuya-ku ☎ 03/5778–5416 ⊕ www.brown.co.jp ⊟ No credit cards Ⓜ Ginza and Hanzō-mon subway lines, Omotesandō Station (Exit A1).

Pure Café. Though this airy vegan café's menu is limited, the nutritious, organic fare never disappoints. Try the samosas, veggie burgers, or wholesome soups. Pure Café, which is a stone's throw from the upscale fashion hub of Omotesandō, serves breakfast. ⊠ 5–5–21 Minami-Aoyama, Minato-ku ☎ 03/5466–2611 ⊟ No credit cards Ⓜ Ginza and Hanzō-mon subway lines, Omotesandō Station (Exit B3).

Café 8. A short walk from the trendy neighborhood of Naka-Meguro, this cute café serves an inventive fusion of Eastern and Western cuisines. The menu changes often, but might include spring rolls, nutritious curries and soups, or couscous salads. ⊠ 3–17–7 Aobadai, Meguro-ku ☎ 03/5458–5262 ⊟ AE, DC, MC, V Ⓜ Denentoshi subway and private rail lines, Ikejiri-Ohashi Station.

If you plan on staying in town long term, check out **Alishan** (⊕ www.alishan-organic-center.com), a vegetarian mail-order specialist that delivers local and imported flesh-free food.

Higashi-Shinjuku

Japanese

$$$$ ✕ **Kushinobo.** The lively action of the cooks frying kushi-age (skewered meat, fish, and vegetables) coupled with good-value lunch and dinner sets make Kushinobo popular with university students, office workers, and families. For the *omakase* dinner set, you choose skewers, watch the chefs fry them in front of you, and eat them one after another until you're full. There are more than 40 different meats, seafood, and vegetables to choose from, and they're served with traditional and original sauces. Round off your meal with a selection from the extensive list of sake and shōchū. ✉ *1–10–5 Kabuki-chō, Shinjuku-ku* ☎ *03/3232–9744* ▤ *AE, MC, V* ⊙ *Closed Sun.* Ⓜ *Shinjuku Station (Higashi-guchi/East Exit).*

¢–$$ ✕ **Kinkantei.** Opened more than 200 years ago, this hole-in-the-wall soba and udon joint in Tōkyō's gay nightlife area is still a local favorite. The menu changes constantly; when in doubt, order the daily special, or hearty *hoto* (Yamanashi-style udon with vegetables), if it's available. Vegetarian and vegan choices are on the menu, which is rare for Japanese restaurants. The place seats fewer than 30 people, and from the counter you can watch the cooks at work. Open until 4 AM, Kinkantei is a fitting pit stop after a late night out. ✉ *Sunflower Bldg. 1F, 2–17–1 Shinjuku Shinjuku-ku* ☎ *03/3356–6556* ▤ *No credit cards* ⊙ *Closed Sun.* Ⓜ *Shinjuku Station (Higashi-guchi/East Exit).*

Ichiyaga

Italian

$$ ✕ **Ristorante Carmine.** Everybody pitched in, so the story goes, when chef Carmine Cozzolino left his job at an upscale restaurant in Aoyama and opened this unpretentious neighborhood bistro in 1987: friends designed the logo and the interior, painted the walls (black and white), and hung the graphics, swapping their labor for meals. The five-course dinner (¥3,800–¥5,000) here could be the best deal in town. The menu changes weekly; specialties of the house include risotto primavera and Tuscan-style *filetto di pesce* (fish fillet) parmigiano. The wine list is well chosen, and the *torta al cioccolata* (chocolate cake) is a serious dessert. ✉ *Nishikawa Bldg. 1F, 1–19 Saiku-chō, Shinjuku-ku* ☎ *03/3260–5066* ▤ *AE, MC, V* Ⓜ *Ōedo subway line, Ushigome-Kagurazaka Station (Exit 1).*

Ikebukuro

Japanese

$$–$$$ ✕ **Sasashū.** This traditional-style pub is noteworthy for stocking only
Fodor'sChoice the finest and rarest, the Latours and Mouton-Rothschilds, of sake: these
★ are the rice wines that take gold medals in the annual sake competition year after year. It also serves some of the best *izakaya* food in town—the Japanese wouldn't dream of drinking well without eating well. Sasashū purports to be the only restaurant in Tōkyō that serves wild duck; the chefs brush the duck with sake and soy sauce and broil it over a hibachi. It's in a rambling, two-story, traditional-style building, with thick beams and tatami floors. ✉ *2–2–6 Ikebukuro, Toshima-ku* ☎ *03/*

Kanpai!

WHETHER YOU'RE OUT WITH friends, clients, or belting out a tune at the local karaoke bar, you're sure to have a drink at least once during your stay. Things may look a little different, even before you start knocking back a few, so take note on the liquors of this island nation. And remember, shout *Kanpai!* (sounds like "kaan-pie") instead of *Cheers!* when you raise your glass.

BEVERAGE OF THE SAMURAI

Sake, pronounced *sa*-kay, is Japan's number one alcoholic beverage. There are more than 2,000 different brands produced throughout Japan. Like other kinds of wine, sake comes in sweet (*amakuchi*) and dry (*karakuchi*) varieties; these are graded *tokkyū* (superior class), *ikkyū* (first class), and *nikkyū* (second class) and are priced accordingly. (Connoisseurs say this ranking is for tax purposes and is not necessarily a true indication of quality.)

Best drunk at room temperature (*nurukan*) so as not to alter the flavor, sake is also served heated (*atsukan*) or with ice (*rokku de*). It's poured from *tokkuri* (small ceramic vessels) into tiny cups called *choko*. The diminutive size of these cups shouldn't mislead you into thinking you can't drink too much. The custom of making sure that your companion's cup never runs dry often leads the novice astray.

Junmaishu is the term for pure rice wine, a blend of rice, yeast, and water to which no extra alcohol has been added. Junmaishu sake has the strongest and most distinctive flavor, compared with various other methods of brewing, and is preferred by the sake *tsū*, as connoisseurs are known.

Apart from the *nomiya* (bars) and restaurants, the place to sample sake is the izakaya, a drinking establishment that usually serves dozens of different kinds of sake, including a selection of *jizake*, the kind produced in limited quantities by small regional breweries throughout the country.

HEAVENLY SPIRITS

Shōchū is made from grain and particularly associated with the southern island of Kyūshū. It's served either on the rocks or mixed with water and can be hot or cold. Sometimes a wedge of lemon or a small pickled apricot, known as *umeboshi*, is added as well. It can also be mixed with club soda and served cold.

HAVIN' A BIIRU

Japan has four large breweries: Asahi, Kirin, Sapporo, and Suntory. Asahi and Kirin are the two heavyweights, constantly battling for the coveted title of "Japan's No. 1 Brewery," but many beer fans rate Suntory's Malts brand and Sapporo's Yebisu brand as the tastiest brews in the land. Although there are some microbreweries across Japan, locally produced brews can still be hard to find, even when you know they exist.

3971–6796 ⊟ AE, DC, V ☉ Closed Sun. No lunch Ⓜ JR Yamanote Line; Yūraku-chō, Marunouchi, and Ōedo subway lines: Ikebukuro Station (Exit 19).

Kyō-bashi

French

$$$$ ✕ **Chez Inno.** Chef Noboru Inoue studied his craft at Maxim's in Paris and Les Frères Troisgros in Roanne; the result is brilliant, innovative French food. Try fresh lamb in wine sauce with truffles and finely chopped herbs, or lobster with caviar. The main dining room has velvet banquettes, white stucco walls, and stained-glass windows. The elegant Hotel Seiyō Ginza is nearby—making this area the locus of the very utmost in Tōkyō upscale. ⊠ Meiji Seika Honsha Bldg. 1F, 2–4–16 Kyō-bashi, Chūō-ku ☎ 03/3274–2020 ⌣ Reservations essential 🏛 Jacket and tie ⊟ AE, DC, MC, V ☉ Closed Sun. Ⓜ Ginza subway line, Kyō-bashi Station (Exit 2); Yūraku-chō subway line, Ginza-Itchōme Station (Exit 7).

Italian

$$–$$$ ✕ **Attore.** This Italian restaurant in the elegant Hotel Seiyō Ginza is divided into two sections. The "casual" side has a bar counter, banquettes, and a see-through glass wall to the kitchen; the "formal" side has mauve wall panels and carpets, armchairs, and soft recessed lighting. On either side of the room, you get some of the best Italian cuisine in Tōkyō, though the menu is simpler and cheaper on the casual side. Try pâté of pheasant and porcini mushrooms with white-truffle cheese sauce or the walnut-smoked lamb chops with sun-dried tomatoes. ⊠ Hotel Seiyō Ginza, 1–11–2 Ginza, Chūō-ku ☎ 03/3535–1111 ⌣ Reservations essential ⊟ AE, DC, MC, V Ⓜ Ginza subway line, Kyō-bashi Station (Exit 2); Yūraku-chō subway line, Ginza-Itchōme Station (Exit 7).

Meguro

Japanese

★ ¢–$$ ✕ **Tonki.** Meguro, a neighborhood distinguished for almost nothing else culinary, has arguably the best tonkatsu restaurant in Tōkyō. It's a family joint, with Formica-top tables and a server who comes around to take your order while you wait the requisite 10 minutes in line. And people do wait in line, every night until the place closes at 10:45. Tonki is a success that never went conglomerate or added frills to what it does best: deep-fried pork cutlets, soup, raw-cabbage salad, rice, pickles, and tea. That's the standard course, and almost everybody orders it, with good reason. ⊠ 1–1–2 Shimo-Meguro, Meguro-ku ☎ 03/3491–9928 ⊟ DC, V ☉ Closed Tues. and 3rd Mon. of month Ⓜ JR Yamanote and Namboku subway lines, Meguro Station (Nishi-guchi/West Exit).

Thai

★ $$ ✕ **Keawjai.** Blink and you might miss the faded sign of this little basement restaurant a minute's walk from Meguro Station. Keawjai is one of the few places in Tōkyō to specialize in the subtle complexities of Royal Thai cuisine, and despite its size—only eight tables and four banquettes—it serves a remarkable range of dishes in different regional styles. The spicy beef salad is excellent (and *really* spicy), as are the baked rice and crabmeat served in a whole pineapple, and the red-curry chicken in coconut milk with cashews. The service is friendly and unhurried. ⊠ *Meguro Kōwa Bldg. B1, 2–14–9 Kami Ōsaki, Meguro-ku* ☎ *03/ 5420–7727* ▤ *AE, DC, MC, V* Ⓜ *JR Yamanote and Namboku subway lines, Meguro Station (Higashi-guchi/East Exit).*

Niban-chō

Indian

$$ ✕**Adjanta.** In the mid-20th century, the owner of Adjanta came to Tōkyō to study electrical engineering. He ended up changing careers and establishing what is today one of the oldest and best Indian restaurants in town. There's no decor to speak of at this 24-hour restaurant. The emphasis instead is on the variety and intricacy of South Indian cooking—and none of its dressier rivals can match Adjanta's menu for sheer depth. The curries are hot to begin with, but you can order them even hotter. Try the marsala *dosa* (a savory crepe), *keema* (minced beef), or mutton curry. A small boutique in one corner sells saris and imported Indian foodstuffs. ⊠ *3–11 Niban-chō, Chiyoda-ku* ☎ *03/3264–6955* ▤ *AE, DC, MC, V* Ⓜ *Yūraku-chō subway line, Kōji-machi Station (Exit 5).*

Nihombashi

Japanese

$$ ✕**Sasashin.** Like most izakaya, Sasashin spurns the notion of decor: there's a counter laden with platters of the evening's fare, a clutter of rough wooden tables, and not much else. It's noisy, smoky, crowded—and great fun. Like izakaya fare in general, the food is best described as professional home cooking, and is meant mainly as ballast for the earnest consumption of beer and sake. Try the sashimi, the grilled fish, or the fried tofu; you really can't go wrong by just pointing your finger at anything on the counter that takes your fancy. ⊠ *2–20–3 Nihombashi-Ningyōchō, Chūō-ku* ☎ *03/3668–2456* ⚇ *Reservations not accepted* ▤ *No credit cards* ⊙ *Closed Sun. and 3rd Sat. of month. No lunch* Ⓜ *Hanzō-mon subway line, Suitengū-mae Station (Exit 7); Hibiya and Asakusa subway lines, Ningyōchō Station (Exits A1 and A3).*

Omotesandō

Brazilian

$$$$ ✕**Barbacoa Grill.** Carnivores flock here for the great-value all-you-can-eat Brazilian grilled chicken and barbecued beef, which the efficient waiters will keep bringing to your table on skewers until you tell them to stop. Those with lighter appetites can choose the less-expensive salad buffet and *feijoada* (pork stew with black beans); both are bargains. Barbacoa has hardwood floors, lithographs of bull motifs, warm lighting, salmon-color tablecloths, and roomy seating. This popular spot is just off Omotesandō-dōri on the Harajuku 2-chōme shopping street (on the north side of Omotesandō-dōri), about 50 yards down on the left. ⊠ *4–3–24 Jingū-mae, Shibuya-ku* ☎ *03/3796–0571* ▤ *AE, DC, MC, V* Ⓜ *Ginza, Chiyoda, and Hanzō-mon subway lines, Omotesandō Station (Exit A2).*

French

$$$$ ✕ **Le Papillon de Paris.** This very fashion-minded restaurant is a joint venture of L'Orangerie in Paris and couturier Mori Hanae. Muted elegance marks the dining room, with cream walls and deep brown carpets; mirrors add depth to a room that actually seats only 40. The ambitious prix-fixe menus change every two weeks; the recurring salad of sautéed sweetbreads is excellent, as is the grilled Atlantic salmon. This is a particularly good place to be on Sunday between 11 and 2:30, for the buffet brunch (¥3,500), during which you can graze through what is arguably the best dessert tray in town; try the pear tart or the daily chocolate-cake special. ⊠ *Hanae Mori Bldg., 5th fl., 3–6–1 Kita-Aoyama, Minato-ku* ☎ *03/3407–7461* ⌕ *Reservations essential* ▤ *AE, DC, MC, V* ⊘ *No dinner Sun.* Ⓜ *Ginza, Chiyoda, and Hanzō-mon subway lines, Omotesandō Station (Exit A1).*

Japanese

$$–$$$ ✕ **Sakuratei.** Unconventionally located inside an art gallery, Sakuratei defies other conventions as well: eating here doesn't always mean you don't have to cook. At this do-it-yourself *okonomiyaki* (a kind of pancake made with egg, meat, and vegetables) restaurant, you choose ingredients and cook them on the *teppan* (grill). Okonomiyaki is generally easy to make, but flipping the pancake to cook the other side can be challenging—potentially messy but still fun. Fortunately, you're not expected to do the dishes. Okonomiyaki literally means "as you like it," so experiment with your own recipe or try the house special, *sakurayaki* (with pork, squid, and onions), or *monjayaki* (a watered-down variation of okonomiyaki from the Kanto region). ⊠ *3–20–1 Jingū-mae, Shibuya-ku* ☎ *03/3479–0039* ▤ *DC, MC, V* Ⓜ *Chiyoda subway line, Meiji-Jingū-mae Station (Exit 5).*

¢–$$ ✕ **R Style.** Even in some of the swankiest restaurants, Japanese *wagashi* (sweets) aren't up to par. To sample authentic handmade wagashi while sipping green tea, head to this café. The main ingredients in wagashi are adzuki beans, rice, and other grains sweetened slightly by sugarcane—making these treats a fairly healthful dessert. These intricate morsels of edible art are almost too perfectly presented to eat—almost but not quite. Try the *konomi* (rice dumpling with adzuki conserve) or *koyomi* (bracken dumpling with soy custard) set. ⊠ *Omotesandō Hills Main Bldg. 3F, 4–12–10 Jingū-mae, Shibuya-ku* ☎ *03/3423–1155* ▤ *AE, MC, V* Ⓜ *Ginza, Chiyoda, and Hanzō-mon subway lines, Omotesandō Station (Exit A2); Chiyoda subway line, Meiji-Jingū-mae Station (Exit 5).*

Sushi

$$ ✕ **Heiroku-zushi.** Ordinarily, a meal of sushi is a costly indulgence. The rock-bottom alternative is a *kaiten-zushi*, where sushi is literally served assembly-line style. The chefs inside the circular counter maintain a constant supply on the revolving belt on plates color-coded for price; just choose whatever takes your fancy as dishes pass by. Heiroku-zushi is a bustling, cheerful example of the genre, with fresh fish and no pretensions at all to decor. When you're done, the server counts up your plates and calculates your bill (¥126 for staples like tuna and squid to ¥367 for delicacies like eel and salmon roe). ⊠ *5–8–5 Jingū-mae, Shibuya-*

ku ☎ *03/3498–3968* ▤ *No credit cards* Ⓜ *Ginza, Chiyoda, and Hanzō-mon subway lines, Omotesandō Station (Exit A1).*

Roppongi

Contemporary

$$$–$$$$ ╳ **Lovenet.** Within the 33 private theme rooms of Lovenet, you can dine and enjoy Japan's national pastime: karaoke. Go not just for the food but the entire experience. Request the intimate Morocco suite, the colorful Candy room, or the Aqua suite, where you can eat, drink, and take a dip in the hot tub while belting out '80s hits. The Italian-trained chefs prepare Mediterranean and Japanese cuisine in the form of light snacks and full-course meals, which you order via a phone intercom system. Try the duck confit with wine sauce or a salmon-roe rice bowl. The bill is calculated based on what room you use, how long you stay, and what you order. Note that there's a two-person minimum for each room. ⊠ *Hotel Ibis 3F–4F, 7–14–4 Roppongi, Minato-ku* ☎ *03/5771–5511* ⊕ *www.lovenet-jp.com* ⌂ *Reservations essential* ▤ *AE, MC, V* Ⓜ *Ōedo and Hibiya subway lines, Roppongi Station (Exit 4A).*

$$–$$$ ╳ **Roti.** Billing itself a "modern American brasserie," Roti takes pride in the creative use of simple, fresh ingredients, and a fusing of Eastern and Western elements. For an appetizer, try the Vietnamese sea-bass carpaccio with crisp noodles and roasted garlic, or the calamari batter-fried in ale with red-chili tartar sauce. Don't neglect dessert: the espresso-chocolate tart is to die for. Roti stocks some 60 Californian wines, microbrewed ales from the famed Rogue brewery in Oregon, and Cuban cigars. The best seats in the house are in fact outside at one of the dozen tables around the big glass pyramid on the terrace. ⊠ *Piramide Bldg. 1F, 6–6–9 Roppongi, Minato-ku* ☎ *03/5785–3671* ▤ *AE, MC, V* Ⓜ *Hibiya subway line, Roppongi Station (Exit 1).*

Japanese

$$–$$$$ ╳ **Inakaya.** The style here is *robatayaki,* a dining experience that segues
Fodor$Choice into pure theater. Inside a large U-shape counter, two cooks in traditional
★ garb sit on cushions behind a grill, with a cornucopia of food spread out in front of them: fresh vegetables, seafood, skewers of beef and chicken. You point to what you want, and your server shouts out the order. The cook bellows back your order, plucks your selection up out of the pit, prepares it, and hands it across on an 8-foot wooden paddle. Inakaya is open from 5 PM to 5 AM, and fills up fast after 7. ⊠ *Reine Bldg., 1st fl., 5–3–4 Roppongi, Minato-ku* ☎ *03/3408–5040* ⌂ *Reservations not accepted* ▤ *AE, DC, MC, V* ☺ *No lunch* Ⓜ *Hibiya subway line, Roppongi Station (Exit 3).*

$$$$ ╳ **Jidaiya.** The Roppongi branch of this restaurant evokes the feeling of an Edo-period tavern with a good collection of antiques: *aka-dansu* (red-lacquered chests), Nambu ironware kettles, and low *hori-gotatsu* tables, with recesses beneath which you can stretch out your legs. All the tables are for six people or more; you're bound to be sharing yours. The later you dine (the place stays open until 4 AM), the more boisterous and friendly your tablemates will be. Jidaiya serves a bit of everything in its prix-fixe courses: shabu-shabu, tempura, sushi, and steamed rice with seafood. The food is nothing fancy, but it's delicious and filling. ⊠ *Yuni Roppongi Bldg.*

Feasting on a Budget

THERE ARE MANY WONDERFUL restaurants in Tōkyō that provide excellent meals and thoughtful service, without straining the budget. To find them, don't be afraid to venture outside your hotel lobby or try a spot without an English menu; use the point-and-order method. Many restaurants also post menus out front that clearly state the full prices (some do add a 10% tax, and possibly a service charge, so ask in advance).

The following are options that don't cost a fortune and aren't of the international fast-food-chain variety:

The Bentō. This traditional Japanese box lunch is available for takeout everywhere, is extremely portable, and is usually comparatively inexpensive. It has rice, pickles, grilled fish or meat, and vegetables, in an almost limitless variety of combinations to suit the season.

Kushi-age. *Kushi-age* consists of skewered bits of meat, seafood, and vegetables battered, dipped in bread crumbs, and deep-fried. There are many small restaurants serving only kushi-age at a counter, and many of the *robatayaki* serve it as a side dish. It's also a popular drinking snack.

Oden. With *oden*, an inexpensive winter favorite that goes well with beer or sake, various meats and vegetables are slowly simmered in vats. Oden may be ordered piece by piece (*ippin*) from the assortment you see steaming behind the counter or *moriawase*, in which case the cook will serve up an assortment.

Okonomiyaki. Somewhat misleadingly called the Japanese pancake, okonomiyaki is actually a mixture of vegetables, meat, and seafood in an egg-and-flour batter grilled at your table, much better with beer than with butter. It's most popular for lunch or as an after-movie snack.

Robatayaki. Perhaps the most expensive of the inexpensive options is the faithful neighborhood robatayaki (grill). It's easy to order because the selection of food to be grilled is lined up behind glass at the counter. Fish, meat, vegetables, tofu–take your pick. Some popular choices are *yaki-zakana* (grilled fish), particularly *karei-shio-yaki* (salted and grilled flounder), and *asari saka-mushi* (clams simmered in sake). Try the grilled Japanese shiitake mushrooms, *ao-tō* (green peppers), and the *hiyayakko* (chilled tofu sprinkled with bonito flakes, diced green onions, and soy sauce). Yakitori can be ordered in most robatayaki shops, though many inexpensive drinking places specialize in this popular barbecued chicken dish.

Soba and Udon. Soba and udon dishes are lifesaving treats for stomachs (and wallets) unaccustomed to exotic flavors (and prices). Small shops serving soba (thin, brown buckwheat noodles) and udon (thick, white-wheat noodles) in a variety of combinations can be found in every neighborhood in the country. Both can be ordered plain (ask for *o*-soba or *o*-udon), in a lightly seasoned broth flavored with bonito and soy sauce (*dashi*), or in combination with things like tempura shrimp (tempura soba or udon) or chicken (*tori-namban* soba or udon). For a refreshing change in summer, try *zaru* soba, cold noodles to be dipped in a tangy soy sauce. *Nabeyaki*-udon is a hearty winter dish of udon noodles, assorted vegetables, and egg served in the pot in which it was cooked.

B1, 7–15–17 Roppongi, Minato-ku ☎ *03/3403–3563* ▤ *AE, DC, MC, V* Ⓜ *Hibiya subway line, Roppongi Station (Exit 2).*

$$ ╳ **Ganchan.** The Japanese expect their yakitori joints—restaurants that spe-
Fodor'sChoice cialize in bits of charcoal-broiled chicken and vegetables—to be just like
★ Ganchan: smoky, noisy, and cluttered. The counter here seats barely 15,
and you have to squeeze to get to the chairs in back. Festival masks, paper
kites and lanterns, and greeting cards from celebrity patrons adorn the
walls. The cooks yell at each other, fan the grill, and serve up enormous
schooners of beer. Try the *tsukune* (balls of minced chicken) and the fresh
asparagus wrapped in bacon. The place stays open until 1:30 AM (mid-
night on Sunday). ⊠ *6–8–23 Roppongi, Minato-ku* ☎ *03/3478–0092*
▤ *AE, MC, V* Ⓜ *Hibiya subway line, Roppongi Station (Exit 1A).*

Thai

$$–$$$ ╳ **Erawan.** Window tables at this sprawling Thai "brasserie" on the top
floor of a popular Roppongi vertical mall afford a wonderful view of
the Tōkyō skyline at night. Black-painted wood floors, ceiling fans, Thai
antiques, and rattan chairs establish the mood, and the space is nicely
broken up into large and small dining areas and private rooms. The serv-
ice is cheerful and professional. Specialties of the house include deep-
fried prawn and crabmeat cakes, spicy roast-beef salad, sirloin tips with
mango sauce, and a terrific dish of stir-fried lobster meat with cashews.
For window seating, it's best to reserve ahead. ⊠ *Roi Bldg. 13F, 5–5–1
Roppongi, Minato-ku* ☎ *03/3404–5741* ▤ *AE, DC, MC, V* Ⓜ *Hi-
biya subway line, Roppongi Station (Exit 3).*

Shibuya

Japanese

★ **$$–$$$** ╳ **Tenmatsu.** The best seats in the house at Tenmatsu, as in any tempura-
ya, are at the immaculate wooden counter, where your tidbits of choice
are taken straight from the oil and served immediately. You also get to
watch the chef in action. Tenmatsu's brand of good-natured professional
hospitality adds to the enjoyment of the meal. Here you can rely on a
set menu or order à la carte tempura delicacies like lotus root, shrimp,
unagi (eel), and *kisu* (a small white freshwater fish). Call ahead to re-
serve counter seating or a full-course kaiseki dinner in a private tatami
room. ⊠ *1–6–1 Dōgen-zaka, Shibuya-ku* ☎ *03/3462–2815* ▤ *DC,
MC, V* Ⓜ *JR Yamanote Line, Shibuya Station (Minami-guchi/South Exit);
Ginza and Hanzō-mon subway lines, Shibuya Station (Exit 3A).*

Shinagawa

Contemporary

$$–$$$$ ╳ **Manhattan Grill.** Only in hypereclectic Japan can you have a French-
Indonesian meal at a restaurant called the Manhattan Grill in a food court
dubbed the "Foodium." Chef Wayan Surbrata, who trained at the Four
Seasons Resort in Bali, has a delicate, deft touch with such dishes as spicy
roast-chicken salad, and steak marinated in cinnamon and soy sauce, served
with shiitake mushrooms and *gado-gado* (shrimp-flavor rice crackers).
One side of the minimalist restaurant is open to the food court; the floor-
to-ceiling windows on the other side don't afford much of a view. The

square black-and-white ceramics set off the food especially well. ⊠ *Atré Shinagawa 4F, 2–18–1 Konan, Minato-ku* ☎ *03/6717–0922* 🖃 *AE, MC, V* Ⓜ *JR Shinagawa Station (Higashi-guchi/East Exit).*

★ **$$–$$$** ✕ **T. Y. Harbor Brewery.** A converted warehouse on the waterfront houses this restaurant, a Tōkyō hot spot for private parties. Chef David Chiddo refined his signature California-Thai cuisine at some of the best restaurants in Los Angeles. Don't miss his grilled mahimahi with green rice and mango salsa, or the grilled jumbo-shrimp brochettes with tabbouleh. True to its name, T. Y. Harbor brews its own beer, in a tank that reaches all the way to the 46-foot-high ceiling. The best seats in the house are on the bay-side deck, open from May to October. Reservations are a good idea on weekends. ⊠ *2–1–3 Higashi-Shinagawa, Shinagawa-ku* ☎ *03/5479–4555* 🖃 *AE, DC, MC, V* Ⓜ *Tōkyō Monorail or Rinkai Line, Ten-nōz Isle Station (Exit B).*

Shirokanedai

Japanese

$$$$ ✕ **Happo-en.** A 300-year-old-Japanese garden wrapped around a lake is the setting for the palatial complex that houses this upscale restaurant, a shrine, and a traditional teahouse. Beautiful scenery aside, the food is what draws locals and visitors again and again. The grand exterior and pristine banquet rooms are somewhat uninviting and overly formal, but the tables overlooking the garden are a tranquil backdrop for an unforgettable meal. Among the pricey prix-fixe dinners are kaiseki, shabu-shabu, sukiyaki, and tempura, and there's also a buffet dinner. Go in the afternoon for a tour of the grounds, *sado* (tea ceremony), and a seasonal Japanese set lunch for ¥4,500. ⊠ *1–1–1 Shirokanedai, Minato-ku* ☎ *03/5401–2820* 🏛 *Jacket and tie* ⌂ *Reservations essential* 🖃 *AE, MC, V* Ⓜ *Mita and Namboku subway lines, Shirokanedai Station (Exit 2).*

Spanish

$$ ✕ **Sabado Sabadete.** Catalan jewelry designer Mañuel Benito used to rent a bar in Aoyama on Saturday nights and cook for his friends, just for the fun of it. Word got around: eventually there wasn't room in the bar to lift a fork. Inspired by this success, Benito opened this Spanish restaurant. The highlight of every evening is still the moment when the chef, in his bright red cap, shouts out "Gohan desu yo!"—the Japanese equivalent of "Soup's on!"—and dishes out his bubbling-hot paella. Don't miss the empanadas or the *escalivada* (Spanish ratatouille with red peppers, onions, and eggplant). ⊠ *Genteel Shirokanedai Bldg., 2nd fl., 5–3–2 Shirokanedai, Minato-ku* ☎ *03/3445–9353* 🖃 *No credit cards* ⊘ *Closed Sun. and Mon.* Ⓜ *Mita and Namboku subway lines, Shirokanedai Station (Exit 1).*

Shōtō

French

$$$$ ✕ **Chez Matsuo.** With its stately homes, Shōtō, a sedate sort of Beverly Hills, is the kind of area you don't expect Tōkyō to have—at least not so close to Shibuya Station. In the middle of it all is Chez Matsuo, in a lovely two-story Western-style house. The dining rooms overlook the garden, where you can dine by candlelight on spring and autumn evenings. Owner-chef Matsuo studied as a sommelier in London and perfected his culinary finesse in Paris. His pricey French food is nouvelle; among the specialties of the house are *suprême* (breast and wing) of duck, clam-and-tomato mousse, and a fish of the day. ⊠ *1–23–15 Shōtō, Shibuya-ku* ☎ *03/3485–0566* ⚑ *Reservations essential* ▤ *AE, DC, MC, V* Ⓜ *JR Yamanote Line, Ginza and Hanzō-mon subway lines, and private rail lines: Shibuya Station (Exits 5 and 8 for Hanzō-mon, Kita-guchi/North Exit for all others).*

Tora-no-mon

Chinese

$$–$$$$ ✕ **Toh-Ka-Lin.** Business travelers consider the Ōkura to be one of the best hotels in Asia. That judgment has to do with its polish, its human scale, its impeccable standards of service, and, to judge by Toh-Ka-Lin, the quality of its restaurants. The style of the cuisine here is eclectic; two stellar examples are the Peking duck and the sautéed quail wrapped in lettuce leaf. The restaurant also has a not-too-expensive midafternoon meal ($$) of assorted dim sum and other delicacies—and one of the most extensive wine lists in town. ⊠ *Hotel Ōkura Main Bldg. 6F, 2–10–4 Tora-no-mon, Minato-ku* ☎ *03/3505–6068* ▤ *AE, DC, MC, V* Ⓜ *Hibiya subway line, Kamiya-chō Station (Exit 4B); Ginza subway line, Tora-no-mon Station (Exit 3).*

Tsukiji

Sushi

★ $$–$$$ ✕ **Edo-Gin.** In an area that teems with sushi bars, this one maintains its reputation as one of the best. Edo-Gin serves generous slabs of fish that drape over the vinegared rice rather than perch demurely on top. The centerpiece of the main room is a huge tank where the day's ingredients swim about until they are required; it doesn't get any fresher than this. Set menus here are reasonable, especially for lunch, but a big appetite for specialties like sea urchin and *ōtoro* tuna can put a dent in your budget. ⊠ *4–5–1 Tsukiji, Chūō-ku* ☎ *03/3543–4401* ▤ *AE, DC, MC, V* ☉ *Closed Sun. and Jan. 1–4* Ⓜ *Hibiya subway line, Tsukiji Station (Exit 1); Ōedo subway line, Tsukiji-shijō Station (Exit A1).*

¢–$ ✕ **Takeno.** Just a stone's throw from the Tōkyō fish market, Takeno is a rough-cut neighborhood restaurant that tends to fill up at noon with the market's wholesalers and auctioneers and personnel from the nearby Asahi newspaper offices. There's nothing here but the freshest and the best—big portions of it, at very reasonable prices. Sushi and sashimi are the staples, but there's also a wonderful *tendon* bowl, with shrimp and eel tempura on rice. Prices are not posted because they vary with the costs that morning in the market. If you wish to make a reservation, you must telephone before 6:30 PM. ⊠ *6–21–2 Tsukiji, Chūō-ku* ☎ *03/3541–8698* ▤ *No credit cards* ☉ *Closed Sun.* Ⓜ *Hibiya subway line, Tsukiji Station (Exit 1); Ōedo subway line, Tsukiji-shijō Station (Exit A1).*

CLOSE UP

On the Menu

SUSHI—SLICES OF RAW FISH OR shellfish on hand-formed portions of vinegared rice, with a dab of wasabi for zest—is probably the most well known Japanese dish in the Western world. The best sushi restaurants in Tōkyō send buyers every morning to the Central Wholesale Market in Tsukiji for the freshest ingredients: *maguro* (tuna), *hamachi* (yellowtail), *tako* (octopus), *ika* (squid), *ikura* (salmon roe), *uni* (sea urchin), *ebi* (shrimp), and *anago* (conger eel).

Sushi's cousin **sashimi** consists of fresh, thinly sliced seafood served with soy sauce, wasabi paste, ginger root, and a simple garnish like shredded daikon. Though most seafood is served raw, some sashimi ingredients, like octopus, may be cooked. Less common ingredients are vegetarian items such as yuba (bean-curd skin) and raw red meats such as beef or even horse.

Another Japanese dish that may be familiar to you is **tempura**: fresh fish, shellfish, and vegetables delicately batter-fried in oil. Tempura dates to the mid-16th century, with the earliest influences of Spanish and Portuguese culture on Japan, and you find it today all over the world. But nowhere is it better than in Tōkyō, and nowhere in Tōkyō is it better than in the tempura stalls and restaurants of Shitamachi—the older commercial and working-class districts of the eastern wards—or in the restaurants that began there in the 19th century and moved upscale. Typical ingredients are shrimp, *kisu* (smelt), *shirauo* (whitebait), shiitake mushrooms, lotus root, and green peppers. To really enjoy tempura, sit at the counter in front of the chef: these individual portions should be served and eaten the moment they emerge from the oil.

Sukiyaki is a popular beef dish that is sautéed with vegetables in an iron skillet at the table. The tenderness of the beef is the determining factor here, and many of the best sukiyaki houses also run their own butcher shops so that they can control the quality of the beef they serve—the Japanese are justifiably proud of their notorious beer-fed and hand-massaged beef.

Shabu-shabu is another possibility, though this dish has become more popular with tourists than with the Japanese. It's similar to sukiyaki because it's prepared at the table with a combination of vegetables, but the cooking methods differ: shabu-shabu is swished briefly in boiling water (the word *shabu-shabu* is onomatopoeic for this swishing sound), whereas sukiyaki is sautéed in oil and, usually, a slightly sweetened soy sauce.

Nabemono (one-pot dishes), commonly known as nabe, may not be familiar to Westerners, but the possibilities are endless. Simmered in a light, fish-based broth, these stews can be made of almost anything: chicken (*tori-nabe*), oysters (*kaki-nabe*), or the sumō wrestler's favorite, the hearty *chanko-nabe* . . . with something in it for everyone. Nabemono is a popular family or party dish. The restaurants specializing in nabemono often have a casual, country atmosphere.

Uchisaiwai-chō

Chinese

★ $$–$$$$ ✕ **Heichinrou.** A short walk from the Imperial Hotel, this branch of one of Yokohama's oldest and best Chinese restaurants commands a spectacular view of the Imperial Palace grounds. Call ahead to reserve a table by the window. The cuisine is Cantonese; pride of place goes to the *kaisen ryōri,* a banquet of steamed sea bass, lobster, shrimp, scallops, abalone, and other seafood dishes. Much of the clientele comes from the law offices, securities firms, and foreign banks in the building. The VIP room at Heichinrou, with its soft lighting and impeccable linens, is a popular venue for power lunches. ✉ *Fukoku Seimei Bldg., 28th fl., 2–2–2 Uchisaiwai-chō, Chiyoda-ku* ☎ *03/3508–0555* ▭ *AE, DC, MC, V* ⊘ *Closed Sun.* Ⓜ *Mita Line, Uchisaiwai-chō Station (Exit A6).*

Ueno

Japanese

$$$$ ✕ **Sasa-no-yuki.** In the heart of Shitamachi, Tōkyō's old downtown working-class neighborhood, Sasa-no-yuki has been serving meals based on homemade tofu for the past 300 years. The food is inspired in part by *shōjin ryōri* (Buddhist vegetarian cuisine). The basic three-course set menu includes *ankake* (bean curd in sweet soy sauce), *uzumi* tofu (scrambled with rice and green tea), and *unsui* (a creamy tofu crepe filled with sea scallops, shrimp, and minced red pepper). For bigger appetites, there's also an eight-course banquet. The seating is on tatami, and the garden has a waterfall. ✉ *2–15–10 Negishi, Taitō-ku* ☎ *03/3873–1145* ▭ *AE, DC, V* ⊘ *Closed Mon.* Ⓜ *JR Uguisudani Station (Kita-guchi/ North Exit).*

Yūraku-chō

Japanese

$$–$$$ ✕ **Robata.** Old, funky, and more than a little cramped, Robata is a bit daunting at first. But fourth-generation chef-owner Takao Inoue holds forth here with an inspired version of Japanese home cooking. He's also a connoisseur of pottery; he serves his food on pieces acquired at famous kilns all over the country. There's no menu; just tell Inoue-san (who speaks some English) how much you want to spend, and leave the rest to him. A meal at Robata—like the pottery—is simple to the eye but subtle and fulfilling. Typical dishes include steamed fish with vegetables, stews of beef or pork, and seafood salads. ✉ *1–3–8 Yūraku-chō, Chiyoda-ku* ☎ *03/3591–1905* ▭ *No credit cards* ⊘ *Closed some Sun. each month. No lunch* Ⓜ *JR Yūraku-chō Station (Hibiya Exit); Hibiya, Chiyoda, and Mita subway lines, Hibiya Station (Exit A4).*

Fodor'sChoice ★

Points of Interest

RESTAURANTS/AREAS	JAPANESE CHARACTERS
Adjanta	アジャンタ
Afuri	阿夫利.
Akasaka	赤坂
Akasaka-mitsuke	赤坂見附
Aoi-Marushin	葵丸進
Aoyama	青山
Asakusa	浅草
Ashoka	アショカ
Attore	アトーレ
Azabu-Jūban	麻布十番
Barbacoa Grill	バルバッコアグリル
Brown Rice Café	ブラウンライスカフェ
Café 8	カフェエイト
Chez Inno	シェ・イノ
Chez Matsuo	シェ・松尾
Daikanyama	代官山
Ebisu	恵比寿
Edo-Gin	江戸銀
Erawan	エラワン
Ganchan	がんちゃん
Ginza	銀座
Happō-en	八芳園
Heichinrou	聘珍楼
Heiroku-zushi	平禄寿司
Higashi-Shinjuku	東新宿
Higo-no-ya	肥後の屋
Homeworks	ホームワークス
Ichiyaga	市ヶ谷
Ikebukuro	池袋
Inakaya	田舎屋
Itoshō	いと正
Jidaiya	時代屋

2

Kappo-Ajioka	割烹 味岡
Keawjai	ゲウチャイ
Kinkantei	きんかん亭
Kisoji	木曽路
Kushinobo	串の坊
Kyō-bashi	京橋
La Granata	ラ・グラナータ
Le Papillon de Paris	ル・パピヨン・ド・パリ
Lovenet	ラブネット
Maisen	まい泉
Manhattan Grill	マンハッタングリル
Meguro	目黒
Monsoon Cafe	モンスーンカフェ
Moti	モティ
Niban-chō	二番町
Nihombashi	日本橋
Ninja	忍者
Omotesandō	表参道
Ōshima	大志満
Pure Café	ピュアカフェ
R Style	アールスタイル
Rangetsu	らん月
Ristorante Carmine	カルミネ
Robata	炉端
Roppongi	六本木
Roti	ロティ
Sabado Sabadete	サバドサバデテ
Sakuratei	さくら亭
Sankō-en	三幸園
Sasa-no-yuki	笹の雪
Sasashin	笹新
Sasashū	笹周
Sawanoi	澤乃井

Shibuya	渋谷
Shinagawa	品川
Shinjuku	新宿
Shirokanedai	白金台
Shōtō	松濤
T. Y. Harbor Brewery	T.Y.ハーバーブルワリーレストラン
Tableaux	タブローズ
Takeno	たけの
Tatsumiya	たつみや
Tenmatsu	天松
Toh-Ka-Lin	桃花林
Tonki	とんき
Tora-no-mon	虎ノ門
Tsukiji	築地
Uchisaiwai-chō	内幸町
Ueno	上野
Ume no Hana	梅の花
Yūraku-chō	有楽町

Where to Stay

WORD OF MOUTH

"The Westin Tokyo (Ebisu) is truly fabulous. The staff and concierge were very helpful and polite and the rooms were big and had comfortable beds along with gorgeous views of the city."

–Manisha

"Narita has quite a few hotels next to the airport. They all have regular airport pickups and returns as well as a bus that circles the hotels to go into Narita proper and back. I have stayed at the Holiday Inn Narita, which is very Western."

–wintersp

Updated by
Brett Bull

WHEN TŌKYŌ'S DEVELOPERS BUILD, they build big. When the project is a hotel—more often than not, on the upper floors of an office tower—it's invariably at the high end of the market. That begs the question, "Are there bargains to be had?" Probably not. First, it doesn't pay to build small or to convert an existing structure to a moderately priced hotel. Second, hoteliers are banking on research that says most visitors will pay well to be pampered. All that said, developers are taking the spare-no-expense approach to hotels: soaring atriums, concierges, oceans of marble, interior decorators fetched in from London, New York, and Milan. The results rival luxury accommodations anywhere in the world.

Though there are international (full-service) and business hotels, as well as hostels and apartment and home

> **LODGING BOOM**
>
> Recent years have witnessed a construction boom in central Tōkyō. Clusters of skyscrapers have gone up around the city, with many of the projects including foreign-owned luxury hotels as their showpieces. Industry analysts anticipate that by 2008, the number of hotel rooms in Tōkyō will have increased by up to 30%, or roughly 20,000 rooms, over pre-2006 levels and is expected to keep growing.

rentals and exchanges, there are also plenty of Japanese accommodations: *ryokan, minshuku,* "capsule" hotels, homes, and temples.

What to Expect

There are three things you can take for granted almost anywhere you set down your bags in Tōkyō: cleanliness, safety, and good service. Unless otherwise specified, all rooms at the hotels listed in this book have private baths and are Western-style. In listings, we always name the facilities that are available, but we don't specify whether they cost extra. When pricing accommodations, try to find out what's included and what entails an additional charge.

Assume that hotels operate on the European Plan (EP, with no meals) unless we specify that they use the Continental Plan (CP, with a Continental breakfast), Breakfast Plan (BP, with a full breakfast), Modified American Plan (MAP, with breakfast and dinner), or the Full American Plan (FAP, with all meals).

Prices

Deluxe hotels charge a premium for good-size rooms, lots of perks, great service, and central locations. More-affordable hotels that cost less—though not *that* much less—aren't always in the most convenient places, and have disproportionately small rooms as well as fewer amenities. That said, a less-than-ideal location should be the least of your concerns. Many moderately priced accommodations are still within the central wards; some have an old-fashioned charm and personal touch the upscale places can't offer. And, wherever you're staying, Tōkyō's subway and train system—comfortable (except in rush hours), efficient, inexpensive, and safe—will get you back and forth.

HELPFUL VOCAB

Some useful words when checking into a hotel:	pushed together: *kuttsukete*
air-conditioning: *eakon*	queen bed: *kuīn saizu-no-beddo*
double beds: *daburu-beddo*	separate: *betsu*
king bed: *kingu saizu-no-beddo*	showers: *shawā*
private baths: *o-furo*	twin beds: *tsuin-beddo*

WHAT IT COSTS In yen				
$$$$	**$$$**	**$$**	**$**	**¢**
FOR 2 PEOPLE over 40,000	30 to 40,000	20 to 30,000	10 to 20,000	under 10,000

Price categories are assigned based on the range between the least and most expensive standard double rooms in nonholiday high season. Taxes (5%, plus 3% for bills over ¥15,000) are extra.

Lodging Options—Western Style

If culture shock has taken its toll and you're looking for some of the familiar creature comforts of home, try staying in one of these options.

International Hotels

Japan's international hotels resemble their counterparts the world over—expect Western-style quarters, English-speaking staffers, and high room rates. Virtually all these properties also have Western and Japanese restaurants, room service, high-speed Internet, minibars, *yukata* (cotton robe), concierge services, porters, and business and fitness centers. A few also have swimming pools. Some offer a handful of Japanese-style rooms—with tatami mats and futons—but these rooms are more expensive.

Business Hotels

Business hotels are for travelers who only need a place to leave luggage, sleep, and change. Rooms are small; a lone traveler will often take a double rather than suffer the claustrophobia of a single. Each room has a phone, a desk, a TV (often the pay-as-you-watch variety and rarely with English-language channels), slippers, a *yukata* (cotton robe), and a bath with a prefabricated plastic tub, shower, and sink. These bathrooms are scrupulously clean, but if you're basketball-player size, you might have trouble standing up in them. Other than those facilities, you'll probably only find a restaurant and maybe a 24-hour receptionist, who probably doesn't speak English. Business hotels are generally near railway stations. Most fall into the $$ (and sometimes $$$) price category.

Hostels

Hostels offer bare-bones lodging at low prices—often in shared dorm rooms with shared baths—to people of all ages, though the primary market is students. Most hostels serve breakfast; dinner and/or shared cooking facilities may also be available. In some hostels, you aren't allowed to be in your room during the day, and there may be a curfew at night. Nevertheless, hostels provide a sense of community, with public rooms where travelers often gather to share stories.

Many hostels are affiliated with **Hostelling International (HI)**. Membership in any HI association, open to travelers of all ages, allows you to stay in affiliated hostels at special rates. One-year membership is about $28 for adults; hostels charge about $10–$30 per night. Members have priority if the hostel is full; they're also eligible for discounts, even on rail and bus travel in some countries.

Hostels in Japan run about ¥1,500–¥3,200 per night for members, usually ¥1,000 more for nonmembers. The quality of hostels varies a lot in Japan, though the bad ones are never truly terrible, and the good ones offer memorable experiences. Most have private rooms for couples or families, though you should call ahead to be sure. Tourist information offices can direct you to a local hostel. Note that hostels tend to be crowded during school holidays, when university students are traveling around the country.

🗊 **Hostelling International–USA** 🕾 301/495–1240 ⊕ www.hiusa.org. **Japan Youth Hostels, Inc.** 🕾 03/3288–1417 ⊕ www.jyh.or.jp for listings and reservations.

Apartment & House Rentals

Although renting apartments or houses in Japan isn't common, there are agents that can make such arrangements for you. In addition, English-language newspapers and magazines such as the *Japan Times, Daily Yomiuri, Asahi Shimbun,* and *Metropolis,* and Web sites such as ⊕ www.gaijinpot.com may list properties for rent.

🗊 **International Agents Moveandstay** 🕾 02/235–6624 ⊕ www.moveandstay.com. **ReloJapan** 🕾 03/5575–6321 ⊕ www.relojapan.com.

🗊 **Local Agents Ken Corporation** 🕾 03/5413–5666 ⊕ www.kencorp.com. **The Mansions** 🕾 03/5414–7070 or 03/5575–3232 ⊕ www.themansions.jp. **Sakura House** 🕾 03/5330–5250 ⊕ www.sakura-house.com. **Tokyo Apartment** 🕾 03/3368–7117 ⊕ www.tokyoapt.com.

Home Exchanges

With a direct home exchange, you stay in someone else's home while they stay in yours. Some outfits also deal with vacation homes.

🗊 **Exchange Clubs HomeLink International** 🕾 800/877–8723 ⊕ www.homelink.org 🖂 $80 yearly for Web-only membership; $125 with Web access and two directories. **Home Exchange.com** 🕾 800/638–3841 ⊕ www.homeexchange.com 🖂 $59.95 for a 1-year online listing. **Intervac U.S.** 🕾 800/756–4663 ⊕ www.intervacus.com 🖂 $78.88 for Web-only membership; $126 includes Web access and a catalog.

Lodging Options—Japanese Style

Looking for someplace other than the typical Western hotel to rest your head? There are numerous options: ryokan, minshuku, capsule hotels, home visits, or a stay in a traditional temple.

Ryokan

There are two kinds of ryokan. One is an expensive traditional inn, with lots of personal attention, where you're served dinner and breakfast in your room. Rates at such places can be exorbitant—more than ¥30,000 ($255) per person per night with two meals. The other type is an inexpensive hostelry whose rooms come with futon beds, tatami floor mats, a scroll or a flower arrangement in its rightful place, and, occasionally, meal service.

Tōkyō ryokan fall in the latter category. They're often family-run, and service is less a matter of professionalism than of good will. Many have rooms either with or without baths (where tubs are likely to be plastic rather than cedarwood) as well as street, rather than garden, views. Because they have few rooms and the owners are usually on hand to answer questions, these small ryokan are as hospitable as they are affordable (from ¥5,000 [$43] for a single room to ¥7,000 [$60] for a double). Younger travelers love them. ■ TIP➔ Many modern hotels with Japanese-style rooms are now referring to themselves as ryokan, and though meals may be served in the guests' rooms, they are a far cry from the traditional ryokan.

The Japan Ryokan Association has a listing of traditional ryokan all over the country plus literature on ryokan etiquette. You can inquire about reservations at member inns via an online form.

Note that some ryokan do not like to have foreign guests because the owners worry that they might not be familiar with traditional-inn etiquette. For more information on what's expected of guests at traditional ryokan, *see* the Ryōkan Etiquette CloseUp box *in* Chapter 6.

🄵 **Japan Ryokan Association** ☎ 03/3231-5110 ⊕ www.ryokan.or.jp.

Minshuku

Minshuku are essentially bed-and-breakfasts. Usually they cost about ¥6,000 (about $51) per person, including two meals, and you may be expected to lay out and put away your own bedding. Meals are often served in communal dining rooms. Minshuku vary in size and atmosphere; some are in small homes that take in only a few guests, whereas others are more like no-frill inns. Some of your most memorable stays could be at a minshuku, as they often offer a chance to become acquainted with a Japanese family.

To reserve your stay in a minshuku, you must contact the Japan Minshuku Center and fill out a reservation request form, available from the Web site or office.

🄵 **The Japan Minshuku Center** ☎ 03/3216-6556 ⊕ www.minshuku.jp.

Capsule Hotels

Capsule hotels consist of plastic cubicles stacked one atop another. "Rooms" are a mere 3½ feet wide, 3½ feet high, and 7¼ feet long, and they're usually occupied by very junior business travelers, backpackers, or late-night revelers or commuters who have missed the last train home. Each capsule has a bed, an intercom, an alarm clock, and a TV. Washing and toilet facilities are shared. Capsule hotels offer single accommodations only and generally have no facilities for women. Although you may want to try sleeping in a capsule, you probably won't want to spend a week in one.

Home Visits

You can get a good sense of Japanese life by staying (for free) with a local family that has volunteered to participate in a home-visit program. The system is active in many cities throughout the country, including Tōkyō, Yokohama, Nagoya, Kyōto, Ōsaka, Hiroshima, Nagasaki, and Sapporo. ■ TIP➡ **To learn more about the home-visit program, contact the Japan National Tourist Organization (JNTO) before you leave for Japan.**

🖪 The JNTO Tourist Information Center ✉ One Rockefeller Plaza, Suite 1250, New York 10020 ☎ 212/757-5640 ⊕ www.jnto.go.jp.

Temples

Accommodations in Buddhist temples provide a taste of traditional Japan. Some offer instruction in meditation or allow you to observe their religious practices, while others simply offer a room. The Japanese-style rooms are very simple and range from beautiful, quiet havens to not-so-comfortable, basic cubicles. JNTO has lists of temples that accept guests. A stay generally costs ¥3,000–¥9,000 ($26–$77) per night, which includes two meals.

Reservations

The **Japanese Inn Group** is a nationwide association of small ryokan and family-owned tourist hotels. Because they tend to be slightly out of the way and provide few amenities, these accommodations are priced to attract budget-minded travelers. The association has the active support of JNTO.

The **JNTO Tourist Information Center** publishes a listing of some 700 reasonably priced accommodations in Tōkyō and throughout Japan. To be listed, properties must meet Japanese fire codes and charge less than ¥8,000 (about $68) per person without meals. For the most part, the properties charge ¥5,000–¥6,000 ($43–$51). These properties welcome foreigners. Properties include business hotels, ryokan of a very rudimentary nature, and minshuku. It's the luck of the draw whether you choose a good or less-than-good property. In most cases rooms are clean but very small. Except in business hotels, shared baths are the norm, and you are expected to have your room lights out by 10 PM. The JNTO's downtown Tōkyō office is open daily 9–5.

The nonprofit **Welcome Inn Reservation Center** can help you reserve many of the establishments on JNTO's list—and many that are not. Reservation forms are available from the JNTO office. The center must receive reservation requests at least one week before your departure to allow processing time. ■ TIP➡ **If you are already in Tōkyō. JNTO's Tourist Information Centers (TICs) at Narita Airport, Kansai International Airport, and downtown can make immediate reservations for you.**

🖪 Japanese Inn Group ☎ 03/3252-1717 ⊕ www.jpinn.com. JNTO Tourist Information Center ✉ Tokyo Kotsu Kaikan Building, 2-10-1 Yurakucho Chiyoda-ku Tōkyō ☎ 03/3201-3331 ⊕ www.jnto.go.jp. Welcome Inn Reservation Center ☎ 03/3211-4201 ⊕ www.itcj.or.jp.

ACCOMMODATIONS

Akasaka-mitsuke

$$$–$$$$ Akasaka Prince Hotel. Rooms from the 20th to the 30th floor of this hotel, designed by world-renowned architect Kenzō Tange, offer the best views of the city, especially at night. A white-and-pale-gray color scheme accentuates the light from the wide windows that run the length of the rooms. This affords a feeling of spaciousness, though the rooms—oddly shaped because of Tange's attempt to give every accommodation a "corner" location—are a bit small compared to those in other deluxe hotels. The marble and off-white reception areas on the ground floor are pristine—maybe even a bit sterile. ⊠ *1–2 Kioi-chō, Chiyoda-ku 102-8585* ☎ *03/3234–1111* ⊕ *www.princehotelsjapan.com* 🛏 *693 rooms, 68 suites ♿ 9 restaurants, room service, refrigerators, cable TV with movies, pool, massage, 2 bars, laundry service, concierge, in-room broadband, business services, no-smoking floors* ⊟ *AE, DC, MC, V* Ⓜ *Ginza and Marunouchi subway lines, Akasaka-mitsuke Station (Exit 7).*

$$$–$$$$ Hotel New Ōtani Tōkyō and Towers. The New Ōtani is a bustling complex in the center of Tōkyō. When the house is full and all the banquet facilities are in use, the traffic in the restaurants and shopping arcades seems like rush hour at a busy railway station. The hotel's redeeming feature is its spectacular 10-acre Japanese garden, complete with a pond and a red-lacquer bridge. The rooms in the main building are in pleasant pastels, but they lack the outstanding views of those in the Tower, many of which overlook the garden's ponds and waterfalls. Among the many restaurants and bars are La Tour d'Argent, Japan's first Trader Vic's, and The Bar, housed within a revolving lounge on the 40th floor that offers supreme city views. ⊠ *4–1 Kioi-chō, Chiyoda-ku 102-0094* ☎ *03/3265–1111, 0120/227–021 toll-free* ⊕ *www.newotani.co.jp* 🛏 *1,600 rooms, 51 suites ♿ 38 restaurants, room service, in-room safes, refrigerators, cable TV with movies, indoor pool, health club, 5 bars, babysitting, laundry service, in-room broadband, business services, meeting rooms, no-smoking rooms* ⊟ *AE, DC, MC, V* Ⓜ *Ginza and Marunouchi subway lines, Akasaka-mitsuke Station (Exit 7).*

Akihabara

$ Akihabara Washington Hotel. This arch-shaped hotel is an inexpensive choice near Akihabara—Tōkyō's geek paradise containing the city's largest collection of electronic shops and trendy cafés staffed by waitresses in maid uniforms. The small rooms, which are big enough to include a work desk, are simple but comfortable. The subway station is two minutes away on foot. ⊠ *1–8–3 Sakumacho, Chiyoda-ku 101-0025* ☎ *03/3255–3311* ⊕ *www.wh-rsv.com* 🛏 *312 rooms ♿ 4 restaurants, room service, laundry service, business services* ⊟ *AE, DC, MC, V* Ⓜ *JR; Hibiya subway line, Akihabara Station (Exit 5).*

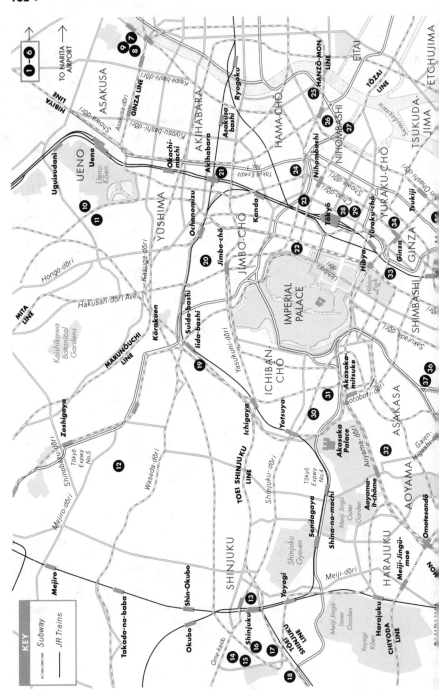

KEY

▬▬ Subway

─── JR Trains

1 - 6

→ TO NARITA AIRPORT

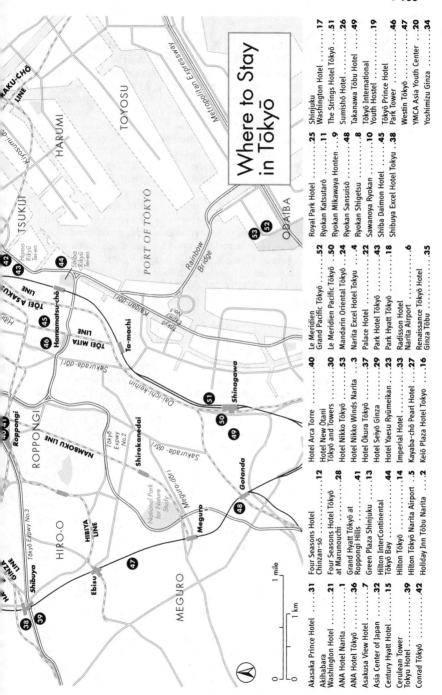

Where to Stay in Tōkyō

Akasaka Prince Hotel **31**
Akihabara
Washington Hotel **21**
ANA Hotel Narita **1**
ANA Hotel Tōkyō **36**
Asakusa View Hotel **7**
Asia Center of Japan **32**
Century Hyatt Hotel **15**
Cerulean Tower
Tōkyū Hotel **39**
Conrad Tōkyō **42**

Four Seasons Hotel
Chinzan-sō **12**
Four Seasons Hotel Tōkyō
at Marunouchi **28**
Grand Hyatt Tōkyō at
Roppongi Hills **41**
Green Plaza Shinjuku **13**
Hilton InterContinental
Tōkyō Bay **44**
Hilton Tōkyō **14**
Hilton Tōkyō Narita Airport . .**5**
Holiday Inn Tōbu Narita . . . **2**

Hotel Arca Torre **40**
Hotel New Ōtani
Tōkyō and Towers **30**
Hotel Nikkō Tōkyō **53**
Hotel Nikkō Winds Narita . . **3**
Hotel Ōkura Tōkyō **37**
Hotel Seiyō Ginza **29**
Hotel Yaesu Ryūmeikan . . . **23**
Imperial Hotel **33**
Kayaba-chō Pearl Hotel . . . **27**
Keiō Plaza Hotel Tokyo . . . **16**

Le Meridien
Grand Pacific Tōkyō **52**
Le Meridien Pacific Tōkyō . . **50**
Mandarin Oriental Tōkyō . . **24**
Narita Excel Hotel Tokyu . . **4**
Palace Hotel **22**
Park Hotel Tōkyō **43**
Park Hyatt Tōkyō **18**
Radisson Hotel
Narita Airport **6**
Renaissance Tōkyō Hotel
Ginza Tōbu **35**

Royal Park Hotel **25**
Ryokan Katsutarō **11**
Ryokan Mikawaya Honten . . **9**
Ryokan Sansuisō **48**
Ryokan Shigetsu **8**
Sawanoya Ryokan **10**
Shiba Daimon Hotel **45**
Shibuya Excel Hotel Tokyu . .**38**

Shinjuku
Washington Hotel **17**
The Strings Hotel Tōkyō . . **51**
Sumishō Hotel **26**
Takanawa Tōbu Hotel **49**
Tōkyō International
Youth Hostel **19**
Tōkyō Prince Hotel
Park Tower **46**
Westin Tōkyō **47**
YMCA Asia Youth Center . . **20**
Yoshimizu Ginza **34**

Asakusa

$$–$$$ 🏨 **Asakusa View Hotel.** Upscale Western-style accommodations are rare in Asakusa, so the Asakusa View pretty much has this end of the market to itself. Off the smart marble lobby, a harpist plays in the tea lounge, and expensive boutiques line the second floor. The communal *hinoki* (Japanese-cypress) baths on the sixth floor, which also houses the Japanese-style tatami suites, overlook a Japanese garden. The best of the Western-style rooms are on the 22nd and 23rd floors, with a view of the Sensō-ji pagoda and temple grounds. There's a top-floor lounge with live entertainment. ✉ *3–17–1 Nishi-Asakusa, Taitō-ku 111-8765* ☎ *03/3847–1111* ⊕ *www.viewhotels.co.jp/asakusa* 🛏 *330 Western-style rooms, 7 Japanese-style suites* ⚭ *4 restaurants, pool, health club, Japanese baths, 2 bars, no-smoking rooms* 🖃 *AE, DC, MC, V* Ⓜ *Ginza subway line, Tawara-machi Station (Exit 3).*

★ **$** 🏨 **Ryokan Shigetsu.** Just off Nakamise-dōri and inside the Sensō-ji grounds, this small inn could not be better located for a visit to the temple. The best options are the rooms with futon bedding and tatami floors; the Western rooms, plain but comfortably furnished, are less expensive. All rooms have private baths; there's also a Japanese-style wooden communal bath on the sixth floor with a view of the Sensō-ji pagoda. ✉ *1–31–11 Asakusa, Taitō-ku 111-0032* ☎ *03/3843–2345* ⊕ *www.roy.hi-ho.ne.jp/shigetsu* 🛏 *14 Western-style rooms, 10 Japanese-style rooms* ⚭ *Restaurant, Japanese baths* 🖃 *AE, MC, V* Ⓜ *Ginza subway line, Asakusa Station (Exit 1/Kaminari-mon Exit).*

★ **¢** 🏨 **Ryokan Mikawaya Honten.** In the heart of Asakusa, this concrete ryokan is just behind the Kaminari-mon, the gateway leading to the Sensō-ji complex. Nearby are the Nakamise souvenir market and the Kappabashi restaurant-supply street, two popular tourist spots. The Japanese-style rooms are small for two people and lack sizable storage areas, but are very clean. Though English-challenged, the staff is attentive and very friendly. ✉ *1–30–12 Asakusa, Taitō-ku 111-0032* ☎ *03/3844–8807* 🛏 *19 Japanese-style rooms, 1 Western-style room* 🖃 *AE, MC, V* Ⓜ *Ginza subway line, Asakusa Station (Exit 1/Kaminari-mon Exit).*

Ebisu

$$$$ 🏨 **Westin Tōkyō.** In the Yebisu Garden Place development, the Westin provides easy access to Mitsukoshi department store, the Tōkyō Metropolitan Museum of Photography, the elegant Ebisu Garden concert hall, and the Taillevent-Robuchon restaurant (in a full-scale reproduction of a Louis XV château). The style of the hotel is updated art nouveau, with an excess of marble and bronze. The rooms are spacious—with bathrooms large enough to accommodate families—and the suites are huge by Japanese standards. The beds are very comfortable. Note, however, that communication with the hotel staff in English can at times be difficult. ✉ *1–4 Mita 1-chōme, Meguro-ku 153-0062* ☎ *03/5423–7000* ⊕ *www.westin-tokyo.co.jp/* 🛏 *438 rooms, 20 suites* ⚭ *6 restaurants, room service, in-room safes, refrigerators, cable TV with movies, gym, massage, bar, dry cleaning, laundry service, in-room broadband, business services, meeting rooms, no-smoking rooms* 🖃 *AE, DC, MC, V* Ⓜ *JR, Hibiya subway line; Ebisu Station (Higashi-guchi/East Exit).*

Ginza

$$–$$$ 🏨 **Renaissance Tōkyō Hotel Ginza Tōbu.** Relatively reasonable prices, friendly service, and comfortable rooms make the Renaissance something of a bargain for the Ginza area. The standard rooms are small and have blond-wood furniture and pastel quilted bedspreads. Larger rooms can be found on the pricier Renaissance Floor. Breakfast, afternoon coffee/tea, and in-room high-speed Internet access are complimentary. Trendy and traditional shopping and the lively Tsukiji fish market are within a short walking distance. ⊠ *6–14–10 Ginza, Chūō-ku 104-0061* ☎ *03/3546–0111* ⊕ *http://marriott.com* 🛏 *197 rooms, 9 suites* ♨ *3 restaurants, room service, refrigerators, cable TV with movies, massage, bar, dry cleaning, laundry service, in-room broadband, business services, no-smoking rooms* ⊟ *AE, DC, MC, V* ¶◯| *CP* Ⓜ *Hibiya and Asakusa subway lines, Higashi-Ginza Station (Exit A1).*

$$
Fodor'sChoice
★
🏨 **Yoshimizu Ginza.** You're expected to fold up your own futon at this modest traditional inn, which was inspired by owner Yoshimi Nakagawa's experience living the simple life at a commune in Woodstock, New York, in the 1970s. The money that isn't spent on service has been spent—with exquisite taste—on simple, natural appointments: wooden floors dyed pale indigo, hand-painted shōji screens, basins of Shigaraki ware in the washrooms. The two stone communal Japanese baths on the ninth floor can be reserved for a private relaxing soak for two. The inn is a few minutes' walk from the Kabuki-za and the fashionable heart of Ginza. Book early. ⊠ *3–11–3 Ginza, Chūō-ku 104-0061* ☎ *03/ 3248–4432* ⊕ *www.yoshimizu.com* 🛏 *11 Japanese-style rooms without bath* ♨ *2 restaurants, Japanese baths; no room phones, no room TVs, no smoking* ⊟ *AE, DC, MC, V* ¶◯| *BP* Ⓜ *Hibiya subway line, Higashi-Ginza Station (Exit 3 or A2).*

Hakozaki

$$$–$$$$ 🏨 **Royal Park Hotel.** For stopovers at Narita, this hotel can't be beat for its airport access and proximity to central Tōkyō. A passageway connects the hotel to the Tōkyō City Air Terminal, where you can catch a bus to Narita without hassle. The comfortable, spacious, marble-clad lobby has wood-panel columns and brass trim. Neutral grays and browns decorate the well-proportioned rooms. The best rooms are those on the executive floors (16–18) with a view of the Sumida River, and those on floors 6–8 overlooking the hotel's delightful Japanese garden. The shopping of Ginza and the Marunouchi business district are a short cab ride away. ⊠ *2–1–1 Nihombashi, Kakigara-chō, Chūō-ku 103-0014* ☎ *03/3667–1111* ⊕ *www.rph.co.jp* 🛏 *450 rooms, 9 suites* ♨ *6 restaurants, room service, refrigerators, cable TV with movies, massage, bar, dry cleaning, laundry service, in-room broadband, business services, no-smoking rooms* ⊟ *AE, DC, MC, V* Ⓜ *Hanzō-mon subway line, Suitengū-mae Station (Exit 4).*

$–$$ 🏨 **Kayaba-chō Pearl Hotel.** Some 90% of the small rooms in the Pearl are singles, designed with the lone (and budget-conscious) Japanese business traveler in mind. Given its location—five minutes' walk across the bridge to Tōkyō City Air Terminal and seven minutes on the subway to Ginza—the hotel is a bargain. Avoid the so-called semi-double: it's a claustrophobic single in disguise. Guest-room floors include vending machines with beer and soft drinks. ✉ *1–2–5 Shinkawa, Chūō-ku 104-0033* ☎ *03/3553–2211* ⊕ *www.pearlhotel.co.jp* ⤺ *268 rooms* ⚒ *Restaurant, refrigerators, TV with movies, massage, laundry facilities, in-room broadband, business services* ▭ *AE, DC, MC, V* Ⓜ *Hibiya and Tōzai subway lines, Kayaba-chō Station (Exit 4b).*

Hibiya

$$$–$$$$ 🏨 **Imperial Hotel.** You can't beat the location of these prestigious quarters: in the heart of central Tōkyō, between the Imperial Palace and Ginza. The finest rooms, on the 30th floor in the New Tower, afford views of the palace grounds. The Old Imperial Bar incorporates elements from the 1923 version of the hotel, which Frank Lloyd Wright designed. The Imperial opened its doors in 1890, and from the outset the hotel has been justly proud of its Western-style facilities and personalized Japanese service. Rooms, complete with walk-in closets and flat-panel TVs, range from standard doubles to suites that are larger than many homes. ✉ *1–1–1 Uchisaiwai-chō, Chiyoda-ku 100-8558* ☎ *03/3504–1111* ⊕ *www.imperialhotel.co.jp* ⤺ *1,005 rooms, 54 suites* ⚒ *13 restaurants, cable TV with movies, indoor pool, health club, massage, 2 bars, in-room broadband, business services, no-smoking rooms* ▭ *AE, DC, MC, V* Ⓜ *Hibiya subway line, Hibiya Station (Exit 5).*

Higashi-Gotanda

¢ 🏨 **Ryokan Sansuisō.** Budgeteers appreciate this basic ryokan, a two-story building near Gotanda Station and the Meguro River, where *sakura* (cherry) trees bloom each April. The proprietor will greet you with a warm smile and a bow and escort you to a small tatami room with a pay TV, a yukata, a Japanese tea set, and a rather noisy heater–air-conditioner mounted on the wall. Some rooms are stuffy, and only two have private baths, but the Sansuisō is clean, easy to find, and only 20 minutes by train from Tōkyō Station or Ginza. The midnight curfew poses a problem for night owls. The Japan National Tourist Organization (JNTO) can help you make reservations at this Japanese Inn Group property. ✉ *2–9–5 Higashi-Gotanda, Shinagawa-ku 141-0022* ☎ *03/3441–7475, 03/3201–3331 for JNTO* ⊕ *www.sansuiso.net* ⤺ *9 rooms, 2 with bath* ⚒ *Room TV with movies, Japanese baths, business services* ▭ *AE, V* Ⓜ *Asakusa subway line (Exit A3) and JR Yamanote Line (Higashi-guchi/East Exit), Gotanda Station.*

Higashi-Shinjuku

★ ¢ 🏨 **Green Plaza Shinjuku.** Male budget travelers in Shinjuku willing to throw claustrophobia to the wind can settle in for a night at the Green Plaza, a capsule hotel in the entertainment district of Kabuki-chō. (As with most capsule hotels, there are no accommodations for women.) Like bees in a honeycomb, patrons sleep in yellow capsules stacked in rows along the halls of each floor. Korean-style massage (on the fifth floor) is an added option not common in the capsule world. Vending machines on three floors dispense drinks, soup, and snacks. Underwear, slacks, and neckties are available for emergency purchases. The environment is not tranquil, but it's clean, safe, and cheap. If you want to try a capsule hotel, this is the place to do it. ⊠ *1–29–3 Kabuki-chō, Shinjuku-ku 160–0021* ☎ *03/3207–4923* ⊕ *www.hgpshinjuku.jp* ⇆ *660 capsules without bath* ⚃ *Massage, sauna, laundry service; no room phones* ⊟ *AE, MC, V* Ⓜ *Shinjuku Station (Higashi-guchi/East Exit).*

Kyō-bashi

$$$$ ⊞ **Hotel Seiyō Ginza.** The grand marble staircase, the thick pile of the carpets, the profusion of cut flowers, the reception staff in coats and tails: all combine to create an atmosphere more like an elegant private club than a hotel. Along with this elegance, location and personalized service are the best reasons to choose the exclusive Seiyō, tucked away on a side street a few minutes from Ginza. Individually decorated rooms have walk-in closets, huge shower stalls, and a direct line to a personal secretary who takes care of your every need. The accommodations, however, are smaller than what you might expect. ⊠ *1–11–2 Ginza, Chūō-ku 104-0061* ☎ *03/3535–1111* ⊕ *www.seiyo-ginza.com* ⇆ *51 rooms, 26 suites* ⚃ *4 restaurants, room service, in-room safes, refrigerators, cable TV with movies, health club, 2 bars, babysitting, dry cleaning, laundry service, concierge, in-room broadband, business services, no-smoking rooms* ⊟ *AE, DC, MC, V* Ⓜ *Ginza subway line, Kyō-bashi Station (Exit 2); Yūraku-chō Line, Ginza-Itchōme Station (Exit 7).*

Marunouchi

$$$$ ⊞ **Four Seasons Hotel Tōkyō at Marunouchi.** A departure from the typical large scale of most properties in the chain, this Four Seasons, set within the glistening Pacific Century Place, has the feel of a boutique hotel. The muted beige-and-bronze reception area resembles a comfortable private club, with deep-pile carpets, plush brocade sofas, and sumptuous armchairs. Chic black-lacquer doors lead to spacious guest rooms, which actually occupy the five floors below the seventh-floor reception area. Beds have brown-leather-covered headboards that continue partway across the ceiling for a canopy effect. Design really *matters* here—but so does high-tech luxury, in touches like plasma-screen TVs and variable lighting. The staff speaks fluent English, and the service is spot-on. ⊠ *1–11–1 Marunouchi, Chiyoda-ku 100-6277* ☎ *03/5222–7222* ⊕ *www. fourseasons.com/marunouchi* ⇆ *48 rooms, 9 suites* ⚃ *Restaurant, room service, in-room safes, refrigerators, cable TV with movies and DVD, health club, Japanese baths, spa, steam room, bar, dry cleaning, laundry service, concierge, Wi-Fi, business services, meeting rooms, no-smoking rooms* ⊟ *AE, DC, MC, V* Ⓜ *JR Tōkyō Station (Yaesu South Exit).*

$$$–$$$$ ⊞ **Palace Hotel.** The service here is extremely helpful and professional; much of the staff has been with the hotel for more than 10 years. The ideal location is only a moat away from the outer gardens of the Imperial Palace, and Ginza and the financial districts of Marunouchi are both a short taxi or subway ride away. An air of calm conservatism bespeaks the Palace's half century as an accommodation for the well-to-do and

well connected. The tasteful, low-key guest rooms are spacious; ask for one on the upper floors, facing the Imperial Palace. ✉ *1–1–1 Marunouchi, Chiyoda-ku 100-0005* ☎ *03/3211–5211* ⊕ *www.palacehotel.co.jp* 🛏 *384 rooms, 5 suites ⚒ 7 restaurants, room service, in-room safes, refrigerators, cable TV with movies and VCR, indoor pool, health club, massage, sauna, bar, dry cleaning, laundry service, concierge, in-room broadband, business services, no-smoking floors* ⊟ *AE, DC, MC, V* Ⓜ *Chiyoda, Marunouchi, Hanzō-mon, Tōzai, and Mita subway lines; Ōte-machi Station (Exit C-13B).*

Nihombashi

★ **$$$$** 🏨 **Mandarin Oriental Tōkyō.** Occupying seven floors of the glistening Nihombashi Mitsui Tower is this hotel, a blend of harmony and outright modernity. The Mandarin's amazing rooms, decorated in dark and light browns, feature large bay windows with exquisite nighttime views of the city lights. The 45-inch flat-panel TVs, 2.1 surround-sound systems, and iPod-docking stations should please tech fans. Corner rooms have sunken marble tubs that allow you to gaze out windows while soaking. The spa devotes nine rooms to the hotel's signature body scrubs and massages. The restaurants are top-of-the-line, but guests weary from overload of superlatives might consider a short stroll toward Tōkyō Station, with its variety of tiny watering holes and *izakaya* (Japanese pubs). ✉ *2–1–1 Nihombashi Muromachi, Chūō-ku 103-8328* ☎ *03/3270–8950* ⊕ *www.mandarinoriental.com/tokyo* 🛏 *157 rooms, 22 suites ⚒ 4 restaurants, in-room safes, TV with DVD, gym, spa, bar, concierge, in-room broadband, Wi-Fi, business center* ⊟ *AE, DC, MC, V* Ⓜ *Ginza and Hanzō-mon subway lines, Mitsukoshi-mae Station (Exit A7).*

Ningyō-chō

$ 🏨 **Sumishō Hotel.** This hotel, in a down-to-earth, friendly neighborhood, is popular with budget-minded foreign visitors who prefer to stay near the small Japanese restaurants and bars of Ningyō-chō. Expect no graces here: even the biggest twin rooms are long and narrow, and the bathrooms are tiny units with low ceilings. The best accommodations are the three tatami rooms on the second floor overlooking a small Japanese garden. Full-course Japanese meals are available in the restaurant. The hotel is a bit hard to find: from Exit A5 of Ningyō-chō Station, turn right and take the first small right-hand street past the second traffic light; the Sumishō is on the left. ✉ *9–14 Nihombashi-Kobunachō, Chūō-ku 103-0024* ☎ *03/3661–4603* ⊕ *www.sumisho-hotel.co.jp* 🛏 *72 Western-style rooms, 11 Japanese-style rooms ⚒ Restaurant, cable TV, Japanese baths, dry cleaning, laundry facilities, in-room data ports, business services, meeting rooms, no-smoking rooms* ⊟ *AE, DC, MC, V* Ⓜ *Hibiya and Asakusa subway lines, Ningyō-chō Station (Exit A5).*

Nishi-Shinjuku

$$$$ 🏨 **Park Hyatt Tōkyō.** An elevator whisks you to the 41st floor, where the hotel—immortalized in the 2003 film *Lost in Translation*—begins with an atrium lounge enclosed on three sides by floor-to-ceiling plate-glass
FodorsChoice
★

windows. The panorama of Shinjuku, gaudy as it can be in the daytime, spreads out in front. Check-in formalities take place at sit-down desks, reached by a pleasant walk through an extensive library. Service is efficient and personal, and the mood of the hotel is contemporary and understated to give a home-away-from-home feel. King-size beds have Egyptian-cotton sheets and down-feather duvets; other appointments include an in-bath TV visible from the tub, black-lacquer cabinets, and huge plasma-screen TVs. Among the hotel's several restaurants is the popular New York Grill, with its open kitchen and steak-and-seafood menu. ⊠ *3–7–1–2 Nishi-Shinjuku, Shinjuku-ku 163-1090* ☎ *03/5322–1234* ⊕ *http://tokyo.park.hyatt.com* ⤳ *155 rooms, 23 suites* ⚒ *4 restaurants, room service, in-room safes, refrigerators, cable TV with movies and DVD, indoor pool, health club, spa, 2 bars, dry cleaning, laundry service, concierge, in-room broadband, business center, airport shuttle, no-smoking rooms* ▭*AE, DC, MC, V* Ⓜ *JR Shinjuku Station (Nishi-guchi/West Exit).*

$$$ 🏨 **Century Hyatt Hotel.** The Century, set amid Shinjuku's skyscrapers, has the trademark Hyatt atrium-style lobby: seven stories high, with open-glass elevators soaring upward and three huge chandeliers suspended from above. The rooms are spacious for the price, though unremarkable in design; the best choices are the View Rooms (10th–26th floors), which overlook Shinjuku Kōen (Shinjuku Park). Tochō-mae Station, beneath the hotel, allows swift access to the nightlife in Roppongi and Shiodome's business towers. ⊠ *2–7–2 Nishi-Shinjuku, Shinjuku-ku 160-0023* ☎ *03/3349–0111* ⊕ *http://tokyo.century.hyatt.com* ⤳ *750 rooms, 16 suites* ⚒ *6 restaurants, room service, in-room safes, refrigerators, cable TV with movies, indoor pool, gym, massage, bar, dry cleaning, laundry service, in-room broadband, business services, no-smoking rooms* ▭ *AE, DC, MC, V* Ⓜ *Marunouchi subway line, Nishi-Shinjuku Station (Exit C8); Ōedo subway line, Tochō-mae Station (all exits).*

$$–$$$ 🏨 **Keiō Plaza Hotel Tōkyō.** This cereal-box-shape hotel, which has a reputation as a business destination, serves its guests with a classic touch. A greeter sporting a black top hat, for example, welcomes you into a lobby of generous marble and high ceilings. Equipped with spacious closets and dressing tables, the standard rooms are plenty big, and the Plaza Premier rooms have the latest in modern furniture design—no shortage of curved wood and metal here. The Sky Pool is actually two pools, one rectangular for laps and the other circular for lounging; both afford views of Shinjuku's steel-and-concrete skyscrapers. ⊠ *2–2–1 Nishi-Shinjuku, Shinjuku-ku 160-8330* ☎ *03/3344–0111* ⊕ *www.keioplaza.co.jp* ⤳ *1,431 rooms, 19 suites* ⚒ *13 restaurants, room service, refrigerators, TV with movies, 2 pools, fitness room, massage, 3 bars, babysitting, in-room broadband, business center, meeting rooms, no-smoking rooms* ▭ *AE, DC, MC, V* Ⓜ *Shinjuku Station (Nishi-guchi/West Exit).*

$$–$$$ 🏨 **Hilton Tōkyō.** The Hilton, which is a short walk from the megalithic Tōkyō Metropolitan Government Office, is a particular favorite of Western business travelers. When it opened in 1984, the gently curved building was the largest Hilton in Asia but opted away from the prevailing atrium-style lobby in favor of more guest rooms and banquet facilities; as a result, the lobby is on a comfortable, human scale. A copper-clad spiral staircase reaching to the mezzanine floor above highlights the bar-lounge. Shōji screens instead of curtains bathe the guest rooms in soft, relaxing light, but overall the accommodations are plain and dated. ☒ *6–6–2 Nishi-Shinjuku, Shinjuku-ku 160-0023* ☏ *03/3344–5111, 0120/489–992 toll-free* ⊕ *www.hilton.com* ⇱ *677 rooms, 129 suites* ⚐ *5 restaurants, room service, some in-room safes, refrigerators, cable TV with movies, pool, gym, massage, sauna, bar, babysitting, dry cleaning, laundry service, concierge, in-room broadband, business services, meeting rooms, no-smoking rooms* ▭ *AE, DC, MC, V* Ⓜ *Shinjuku Station (Nishi-guchi/West Exit); Marunouchi subway line, Nishi-Shinjuku Station (Exit C8); Ōedo subway line, Tochō-mae Station (all exits).*

$ Ⓣ **Shinjuku Washington Hotel.** Both the undulating tower and stouter annex of the Shinjuku Washington represent the typical Japanese business hotel: service is computerized as much as possible, and the rooms—utterly devoid of superfluous features—are just about big enough for the furniture and your luggage. In-room massage chairs, however, are a nice touch. The third-floor lobby has an automated check-in and checkout system; you are assigned a room and provided with a plastic card that opens the door and the minibar. The price is a bargain, but the staff speaks limited English and Shinjuku Station is 10 minutes away or more on foot. ☒ *3–2–9 Nishi-Shinjuku, Shinjuku-ku 160-0023* ☏ *03/3343–3111* ⊕ *www.wh-rsv.com* ⇱ *1,630 rooms, 3 suites* ⚐ *3 restaurants, room service, refrigerators, TV with movies and VCR, massage, some in-room broadband, bar, no-smoking rooms* ▭ *AE, DC, MC, V* Ⓜ *Shinjuku Station (Minami-guchi/South Exit).*

Odaiba

A commercial and entertainment development on reclaimed land within Tōkyō Bay, Odaiba is a bit off the beaten track; although the Rinkai and Yurikamome lines serve the area, Odaiba isn't convenient to the heart of the city. That said, the attractions of the area are a resort quality—with shopping, museums, amusement complexes, and a beach—and proximity to several convention centers. Note that the Hotel InterContinental is near rather than in Odaiba, though it's also accessible by the Yurikamome Line.

$$$–$$$$ Ⓣ **Hotel InterContinental Tōkyō Bay.** Wedged between Tōkyō Bay and an expressway, the InterContinental affords pleasant views, albeit in a slightly isolated setting. Rooms overlooking the river to the north run ¥7,000 more than those pointing to the bay. All of the rooms are large, and the bathrooms include separate showers and tubs. Services and meeting facilities for business travelers are available on the Club InterContinental Floors (the top five floors). The surrounding area is filled with industrial complexes, offering nothing in the way of immediate entertainment options, but the sixth-floor Sunset Lounge is a relaxing place to unwind and view the Rainbow Bridge and surrounding Odaiba. ☒ *1–16–2 Kaigan, Minato-ku 105-8576* ☏ *03/5404–2222* ⊕ *www.ichotelsgroup.com* ⇱ *331 rooms, 8 suites* ⚐ *5 restaurants, refrigerators, fitness room, bar, dry cleaning, in-room broadband, business services, meeting rooms* ▭ *AE, DC, MC, V* Ⓜ *Yurikamome rail line, Takeshiba Station.*

$$$–$$$$ Ⓣ **Hotel Nikkō Tōkyō.** Like the nearby Meridien hotel, the 16-story Nikkō, whose facade follows the curve of the Tōkyō Bay shoreline, pres-

ents itself as an "urban resort" with European style. Dark-wood chairs and golden ornaments adorn the second-floor lobby, where large windows overlook the waterfront. The spacious rooms, which are decorated in yellows and beiges, include a private balcony, and select suites have Jacuzzis. The Captain's Bar serves a large selection of whisky and brandy. Access to the city center from here is cumbersome, but a boardwalk connects the hotel to a small park, an amusement area, and shopping destinations. ⊠ *1–9–1 Daiba, Minato-ku 135-8625* ☎ *03/5500–5500* ⊕ *www.hnt.co.jp* ⤴ *435 rooms, 18 suites* ♿ *8 restaurants, room service, indoor pool, spa, bar, dry cleaning, business center* ☰ *AE, DC, MC, V* Ⓜ *Yurikamome rail line, Daiba Station.*

$$$–$$$$ 🏨 **Le Meridien Grand Pacific Tōkyō.** A sprawling complex at the tip of a human-made peninsula in Tōkyō Bay, the Meridien is a good choice for conventioneers at the nearby Tōkyō Big Site. European-inspired columns, pedestals, and flowery furnishings fill the entrance hall. This theme carries over to the rather sizeable rooms, decorated in shades of gold and brown. Rooms facing Haneda Airport and the Museum of Maritime Science (which resembles a large ship) are ¥6,000 less than those overlooking the Rainbow Bridge and the flat-roofed boats ferrying passengers within the harbor. ⊠ *2–6–1 Daiba, Minato-ku 135-8701* ☎ *03/5500–6711* ⊕ *www.meridien-grandpacific.com* ⤴ *796 rooms, 88 suites* ♿ *8 restaurants, room service, 2 pools, gym, 3 bars, concierge, business center, no-smoking rooms* ☰ *AE, DC, MC, V* Ⓜ *Yurikamome rail line, Daiba Station.*

Roppongi

$$$$ 🏨 **Grand Hyatt Tōkyō at Roppongi Hills.** The Grand Hyatt is a class act—
Fodor'sChoice a hotel designed with every imaginable convenience and comfort. A drawer
★ in the mahogany dresser in each room, for example, has laptop cables and adaptors. The showers have two delivery systems, one through a luxurious "rain-shower" head affixed to the ceiling. No expense has been spared on materials, from the Egyptian-cotton bed linens to the red-granite pool in the spa. Rooms are huge, with high ceilings, touch-panel lighting systems, remote-control blackout blinds, and muted earth tones of brown, beige, and yellow. Guests staying in Grand Club rooms receive complimentary breakfast and evening drinks. Note that the complicated layout of the facilities can make moving around seem like a game of Chutes and Ladders. ⊠ *6–10–3 Roppongi, Minato-ku 106–0032* ☎ *03/4333–8800* ⊕ *www.tokyo.grand.hyatt.com* ⤴ *361 rooms, 28 suites* ♿ *6 restaurants, room service, in-room safes, refrigerators, cable TV with movies and DVD, indoor pool, health club, Japanese baths, spa, 2 bars, babysitting, dry cleaning, laundry service, concierge, in-room broadband, business services, airport shuttle, no-smoking rooms* ☰ *AE, DC, MC, V* Ⓜ *Hibiya subway line, Roppongi Station (Exit 1A); Ōedo subway line, Roppongi Station (Exit 3).*

$ 🏨 **Hotel Arca Torre.** This European-style hotel sits on a coveted location in the heart of one of Tōkyō's premier nightlife quarters, just a few minutes' walk from the Tōkyō Midtown and Roppongi Hills shopping-and-entertainment complexes. Red hanging flags and a faux-stone exterior greet you at the entry. The accommodations are ample for the price (twins are much roomier than doubles), with nice little touches like built-in hot plates for making tea and coffee, and retractable clotheslines in the bathrooms. There are, however, no closets—just some coat hooks on the wall. In keeping with the wild and wooly surroundings, adult channels are offered free of charge. ⊠ *6–1–23 Roppongi, Minato-ku 106-0032* ☎ *03/3404–5111* ⊕ *www.arktower.co.jp* ◌ *77 rooms* ☆ *2 restaurants, refrigerators, cable TV, some in-room broadband, no-smoking floor* ⊟ *AE, MC, V* Ⓜ *Hibiya and Ōedo subway lines, Roppongi Station (Exit 3).*

★ ¢–$ 🏨 **Asia Center of Japan.** Established mainly for Asian students and travelers on limited budgets, these accommodations have become generally popular with many international travelers for their good value and easy access (a 15-minute walk) to the nightlife of Roppongi. The "semi-doubles" here are really small singles, but twins and doubles are quite spacious for the price. Appointments are a bit spartan—off-white walls, mass-market veneer furniture—but the rooms have plenty of basic amenities like hair dryers, electric kettles, and yukatas. ⊠ *8–10–32 Akasaka, Minato-ku 107-0052* ☎ *03/3402–6111* ⊕ *www.asiacenter.or. jp* ◌ *172 rooms, 1 suite* ☆ *Restaurant, refrigerators, cable TV with movies, massage, dry cleaning, laundry service, in-room data ports, meeting rooms, no-smoking rooms* ⊟ *AE, MC, V* Ⓜ *Ginza and Hanzō-mon subway lines, Aoyama-itchōme Station (Exit 4).*

Sekiguchi

$$$$ 🏨 **Four Seasons Hotel Chinzan-sō.** Where else can you sleep in a million-
Fodor'sChoice dollar room? That's about what it cost, on average, to build and fur-
★ nish each spacious room in this elegant hotel with a European flair and a garden setting. Modern touches in the rooms include 32-inch LCD TVs and a bedside control panel for draperies; the large bathrooms have soaking tubs and separate showers. The spectacular fifth-floor Conservatory guest rooms have bay windows overlooking private Japanese-garden terraces. The solarium pool, with its columns, tropical plants, and retractable glass roof, is straight out of Xanadu. Built on the former estate of an imperial prince, Chinzan-sō rejoices in one of the most beautiful settings in Tōkyō; in summer the gardens are famous for their fireflies. Since the hotel occupies a rather isolated section of Tōkyō, the complimentary shuttle service that connects to the subway and Tōkyō Station is very useful. ⊠ *2–10–8 Sekiguchi, Bunkyō-ku 112-0014* ☎ *03/ 3943–2222* ⊕ *www.fourseasons.com/tokyo* ◌ *283 rooms, 51 suites* ☆ *4 restaurants, room service, in-room safes, refrigerators, cable TV with movies, indoor pool, health club, Japanese baths, spa, babysitting, dry cleaning, laundry service, concierge, in-room broadband, business services, no-smoking floors* ⊟ *AE, DC, MC, V* Ⓜ *Yūraku-chō subway line, Edogawa-bashi Station (Exit 1A).*

Shiba Kōen

$$–$$$ 🏨 **Tōkyō Prince Hotel Park Tower.** The surrounding parkland and the absence of any adjacent buildings make the Park Tower a peaceful setting. The atrium lobby is vertically impressive, with two glass elevators giving a clear view of the building's hollow core. Covering almost the en-

CLOSE UP

Match Point

IF YOU LIKE TAKING TO THE courts, you're in luck. There are hundreds of public tennis courts in the central wards of Tōkyō, but you have to sign up for court time in advance (usually in mid-month for a one-hour slot in the following month); for some, you can only sign up by lottery. Another option is choosing a hotel with a court. Availability of the courts at the **Tōkyō Hilton, Hotel New Ōtani Tōkyō**, and **Shinagawa Prince Hotel** goes to guests first and then opens to the public. There are a few private clubs available to nonmembers. The **Taishō Central**

Tennis Club Shinjuku, (✉ 1-55-14HonmachiShibuya-ku ☎ 03/3320-8631 Ⓜ Keiō Shin and Toei Shinjuku lines, Hatsudai Station [North Exit] ◷ Tues.-Sun) has eight hard courts. Visitors fees range from ¥2,100 to ¥51,00 depending on the time of day and day of the week. Courts can be booked for one to three hours, starting at ¥6,300 for an hour of daytime play. **Taishō Central Tennis Club Mejiro** (✉ 3-34-1 TakadaShinjuku-ku ☎ 03/3987-2822) offers 13 recently refurbished hard courts for the same price as The Taishō Central Tennis Club Shinjuku.

tire exterior wall, the guest-room windows afford nice views of nearby Tōkyō Tower and/or Shiba Kōen (Shiba Park). Large flat-panel TVs and bathrooms with full-stall showers and Jacuzzi tubs are nice, modern touches. The relative seclusion limits restaurant choices in the immediate area, though many can be found at the nearby JR Hamamatsu-cho Station, less than 10 minutes away on foot. ✉ 4-8-1 Shiba-kōen, Minato-ku 105-8563 ☎ 03/5400-1111 ⊕ www.princehotelsjapan.com ↘ 633 rooms, 40 suites ♨ 8 restaurants, room service, refrigerators, massage, 2 bars, in-room broadband, business center, no-smoking rooms ☰ AE, DC, MC, V Ⓜ Ōedo subway line, Akabanebashi Station (Akabanebashi Exit).

$ ⛉ **Shiba Daimon Hotel.** This moderately priced hotel a minute's walk from Zōjō-ji temple is popular with Japanese travelers. The staff is a bit ill at ease with guests who cannot speak Japanese but no less willing to help. The ubiquitous blond-veneer-on-pressboard furniture and floral-print bedspreads fill the unremarkable rooms, which are reasonably spacious for the price. A good restaurant on the ground floor serves Japanese and Chinese breakfasts and Chinese fare in the evening. ✉ 2-3-6 Shiba-kōen, Minato-ku 105-0011 ☎ 03/3431-3716 ↘ 92 Western-style rooms, 4 Japanese-style rooms ♨ Restaurant, refrigerators, TV with movies, massage, laundry service, some in-room data ports, no-smoking rooms ☰ AE, DC, MC, V Ⓜ JR Hamamatsu-chō Station (Kita-guchi/North Exit); Asakusa subway line, Daimon Station (Exit A3).

Shibuya

$$$$ ⛉ **Cerulean Tower Tokyu Hotel.** The pricey Cerulean Tower, perched on a slope above Shibuya's chaos, has a cavernous yet bustling lobby filled with plenty of attentive, English-speaking staffers. The rooms af-

ford generous views of Tōkyō, but considering the price, the furnishings are rather plain. Some rooms include windows in the bathroom to allow for bath-time city gazing. Fans of the original Japanese *Iron Chef* TV program might want to dine at Szechwan Restaurant Chen, whose menu is directed by one of the show's combatants, Kenichi Chen. There's a charge (¥2,100 per day) to use the pool, which is off-limits to people with tattoos. ✉ *26–1 Sakuragaoka-cho, Shibuya-ku 150-8512* ☎ *03/ 5457–0109* ⊕ *www.ceruleantower-hotel.com* ⇆ *405 rooms, 9 suites* ⌂ *6 restaurants, room service, refrigerators, massage, 2 bars, in-room broadband, business center, no-smoking rooms* ⊟ *AE, DC, MC, V* Ⓜ *JR Shibuya Station (South Exit).*

> ### BODY ART BEWARE
>
> Think twice about going to take a dip in Tōkyō if you have a tattoo. These personal expressions are strictly forbidden in many of the city's pools, fitness clubs, hot springs, and onsen because of the association between tattoos and the *yakuza* (Japanese mafia). Some places even post signs reading, PEOPLE WITH TATTOOS ARE NOT ALLOWED.

$$–$$$ 🏨 **Shibuya Excel Hotel Tokyu.** The key to this unremarkable but very convenient hotel, which is within the towering Mark City complex, is access: local shopping options are aplenty, Shinjuku is a 5-minute train ride to the north, and the Narita Express departs from nearby Shibuya Station frequently each morning. The rooms, decorated in shades of beige and yellow, are plain but comfortable. North-facing rooms on the 10th floor and above (including the two "ladies-only" floors on levels 23 and 24) afford views of the Shinjuku skyline. The vibrant Estacion Café, above Shibuya's insanely busy "scramble intersection," serves drinks and small snacks. Perhaps equally enjoyable is the lobby vending machine, with its robot-arm dispenser. ✉ *1–12–2 Dogenzaka, Shibuya-ku 150-0043* ☎ *03/ 5457–0109* ⊕ *www.tokyuhotels.co.jp* ⇆ *407 rooms, 1 suite* ⌂ *3 restaurants, refrigerators, massage, in-room broadband, business services, no-smoking rooms* ⊟ *AE, DC, MC, V* Ⓜ *JR Shibuya Station (Hachiko Exit).*

Shinagawa

★ **$$$$** 🏨 **The Strings Hotel Tōkyō.** Like the Conrad up the road in Shiodome, The Strings is all about blending modernity with traditional Japanese aesthetics. From Shinagawa Station, an elevator leads up to the hotel atrium, where a glass bridge spans a pond and cut stone mixes with dark wood. Guest rooms include LCD TVs and awesome views of the Tokyo skyline, (make sure you check it out at night), and the large bathrooms have separate showers and tubs. Prices in the hotel restaurants tend to be high, so a trip to a nearby Western steakhouse or coffee shop might make your wallet smile. ✉ *2–16–1 Konan, Minato-ku 108-8282* ☎ *03/ 4562–1111* ⊕ *www.stringshotel.com* ⇆ *200 rooms, 6 suites* ⌂ *2 restaurants, room service, refrigerators, TV with movies, fitness room, massage, bar, in-room broadband, business center, meeting room* ⊟ *AE, DC, MC, V* Ⓜ *JR Yamanote Line, Shinagawa Station (Konan Exit).*

$$–$$$ 🏨 **Le Meridien Pacific Tōkyō.** Just across the street from JR Shinagawa Station, the Meridien sits on grounds that were once part of an imperial-family estate. The hotel gears much of its marketing effort toward booking banquets, wedding receptions, conventions, and tour groups; the small, unremarkable rooms are quiet and comfortable, but public spaces tend to carry a lot of traffic. The Sky Lounge on the 30th floor has a fine view of Tōkyō Bay. The entire back wall of the ground-floor lounge is glass, the better to contemplate a Japanese garden, sculpted with rocks and waterfalls. ☒ *3–13–3 Takanawa, Minato-ku 108-8567* ☎ *03/3445–6711* ⊕ *www.pacific-tokyo.com* ⇗ *900 rooms, 40 suites* ♨ *6 restaurants, room service, refrigerators, cable TV with movies, pool, massage, bar, dry cleaning, laundry service, concierge, in-room broadband, business services, no-smoking rooms* ☰ *AE, DC, MC, V* Ⓜ *JR Yamanote Line, Shinagawa Station (Nishi-guchi/West Exit).*

$–$$ ☖ **Takanawa Tōbu Hotel.** The Takanawa Tōbu, a five-minute walk from JR Shinagawa Station, provides good value for the price—particularly since the rate includes a buffet breakfast. Rooms are smallish and uninspired, the bathrooms are the claustrophobic prefabricated plastic units beloved of business hotels, and there's no proper sitting area in the lobby, but the hotel atones for these shortcomings with a friendly staff (which speaks a bit of English) and a cozy bar. There's also a small Western restaurant, the Boulogne. ☒ *4–7–6 Takanawa, Minato-ku 108-0074* ☎ *03/3447–0111* ⊕ *www.tobuhotel.co.jp* ⇗ *190 rooms* ♨ *Restaurant, refrigerators, TV with movies, bar, some in-room broadband, meeting room, no-smoking rooms* ☰ *DC, V* ❯◎❮ *BP* Ⓜ *JR Yamanote Line, Shinagawa Station (Nishi-guchi/West Exit).*

Shiodome

$$$$ ☖ **Conrad Tōkyō.** The Conrad welcomes you to the Space Age with a Fodor'sChoice Japanese twist. Elevators shoot upward in the slick, green-hue Tōkyō ★ Shiodome Building to the 28th floor, the location of a lobby of dark oak paneling and bronze lattices. Straight-edge counters in shades of blue and Japanese-lantern illumination come together in the bar areas. The high-ceiling rooms allow for nice views of the bay or the city from a pair of low-back sofas. Motorized blinds and 37-inch plasma TVs with DVD players housed in lacquer boxes are thoughtful touches. Highlights in the bathrooms include dual sinks, rain-shower showerheads, and separate tubs (complete with rubber ducks). The complicated layout of Shiodome can make for difficult access. ☒ *1–9–1 Higashi-Shimbashi, Minato-ku 105-7337* ☎ *03/6388–8000* ⊕ *http://tokyo.conradmeetings. com* ⇗ *222 rooms, 68 suites* ♨ *4 restaurants, room service, in-room safes, refrigerators, TV with DVD, pool, health club, spa, bar, in-room broadband, Wi-Fi, business center, meeting rooms, no-smoking rooms* ☰ *AE, DC, MC, V* Ⓜ *JR Yamanote Line, Shimbashi Station (Shiodome Exit); Oedo subway line, Shiodome Station (Exit 9).*

★ $$ ☖ **Park Hotel Tōkyō.** A panorama of Tōkyō or a bay view, comfortable beds, and large bathrooms greet you in the rooms of this reasonably priced hotel. As is the current trend in Tōkyō, a 10-story atrium of dark-wood paneling sits below a hexagonal skylight ceiling in the lobby. A pillow-fitting service provides advice on how you can change your sleeping habits to get a better night's sleep. If that doesn't work, take a walk to the nearby fish market in Tsukiji—the activity gets started at 5 AM. ☒ *1–7–1 Hi-*

gashi Shimbashi, Minato-ku 105-7227 🕾 *03/6252–1111* 🌐 *www.
parkhoteltokyo.com* ⟿ *272 rooms, 1 suite* ⚭ *5 restaurants, room service, in-room safes, refrigerators, bar, concierge, in-room broadband, business center* ▤ *AE, DC, MC, V* Ⓜ *JR Yamanote Line, Shimbashi Station
(Shiodome Exit); Oedo subway line, Shiodome Station (Exit 10).*

Tora-no-mon

★ **$$$$** 🏨 **Hotel Ōkura Tōkyō.** Understatedly sophisticated and human in its scale,
this hotel is a Tōkyō favorite. Conservative dark wood in the public areas
and the tiered exterior architecture at the entry help the hotel retain the
feel of its early days in the 1960s. Amenities in the tasteful, spacious rooms
include remote-control draperies and terry robes. The odd-number rooms,
871–889 inclusive, overlook a small Japanese landscaped garden. The
on-site museum houses fine antique porcelain, mother-of-pearl, and ceramics; tea ceremonies take place here Monday–Saturday 11–4 (¥1,000).
The main building is preferable to the south wing, which you reach by
an underground shopping arcade. ⊠ *2–10–4 Tora-no-mon, Minato-ku
105-0001* 🕾 *03/3582–0111, 0120/003–751 toll-free* 🌐 *www.okura.
com/tokyo* ⟿ *762 rooms, 96 suites* ⚭ *10 restaurants, room service, in-
room safes, refrigerators, cable TV with movies and VCR, indoor pool,
health club, spa, 3 bars, dry cleaning, laundry service, concierge, in-room
broadband, business services, no-smoking rooms* ▤*AE, DC, MC, V* Ⓜ*Hibiya subway line, Kamiya-chō Station (Exit 4B); Ginza subway line, Tora-
no-mon Station (Exit 3).*

$$$ 🏨 **ANA Hotel Tōkyō.** The ANA typifies the ziggurat-atrium style that seems
to have been a requirement for hotel architecture from the mid-1980s.
The reception floor, with its two-story fountain, is clad in enough mar-
ble to have depleted an Italian quarry. In general, though, the interior
designers have made skillful use of artwork and furnishings to take some
of the chill off the hotel's relentless modernism. Guest rooms are sleek
and spacious. The Astral Lounge on the top (37th) floor and the Exec-
utive floors provide superb views of the city and Mt. Fuji (on clear days).
The hotel is a short walk from the U.S. Embassy. ⊠ *1–12–33 Akasaka,
Minato-ku 107-0052* 🕾*03/3505–1111, 0120/029–501 toll-free* 🌐*www.
anahoteltokyo.jp* ⟿ *882 rooms, 19 suites* ⚭ *14 restaurants, room serv-
ice, refrigerators, cable TV with movies, indoor pool, health club, mas-
sage, sauna, 4 bars, dry cleaning, laundry service, in-room broadband,
business services, meeting room, no-smoking floors* ▤ *AE, DC, MC,
V* Ⓜ *Ginza and Namboku subway lines, Tameike-Sannō Station (Exit
13); Namboku subway line, Roppongi-itchō Station (Exit 3).*

Ueno

¢ 🏨 **Ryokan Katsutarō.** This small, simple, economical hotel is a five-
minute walk from the entrance to Ueno Kōen (Ueno Park) and a 10-
minute walk from the Tōkyō National Museum. The rather spacious
rooms, of which the quietest are in the back, away from the main street,
have traditional tatami flooring and sliding doors. A simple breakfast
of toast, eggs, and coffee is served for only ¥500. To get here, leave the
Nezu subway station by Exit 2, cross the road, take the street running

northeast, and turn right at the "T" intersection; Ryokan Katsutarō is 25 yards along Dōbutsuen-uramon-dōri, on the left-hand side. ⊠ *4–16–8 Ikenohata, Taitō-ku 110-0008* ☎ *03/3821–9808* ⊕ *www.katsutaro. com/ryokan_index.html* ☞ *7 Japanese-style rooms, 4 with bath △ Japanese baths, laundry facilities, in-room data ports; no a/c in some rooms, no TV in some rooms* ⊟ *AE, MC, V* Ⓜ *Chiyoda subway line, Nezu Station (Exit 2).*

Yaesu

★ $ 🏨 **Hotel Yaesu Ryūmeikan.** It's amazing that this ryokan near Tōkyō Station has survived in the heart of the city's financial district, where the price of real estate is astronomical. A friendly, professional staff goes the extra mile to make you feel comfortable; weekday evenings, someone who speaks English is usually on duty. Amenities are few, but for price and location this inn is hard to beat. Room rates include a Japanese-style breakfast; ¥800 per person is deducted from your bill if you'd rather skip it. Checkout is at 10 AM sharp; there's a ¥1,500 surcharge for each hour you overstay. ⊠ *1–3–22 Yaesu, Chūō-ku 103-0028* ☎ *03/ 3271–0971* ⊕ *www.ryumeikan.co.jp* ☞ *21 Japanese-style rooms, 9 Western-style rooms △ 2 restaurants, refrigerators, Japanese baths, in-room broadband* ⊟ *AE, DC, MC, V* ⍵⎮ *BP* Ⓜ *JR Line and Marunouchi subway line, Tōkyō Station (Yaesu North Exit); Tōzai subway line, Nihombashi Station (Exit A3).*

Yanaka

¢ 🏨 **Sawanoya Ryokan.** The Shitamachi area is known for its down-to-earth friendliness, which you get in full measure at Sawanoya. This little inn is a family business: everybody pitches in to help you plan excursions and book hotels for the next leg of your journey. The inn is very popular with budget travelers, so reserve online well in advance. On occasion, the staffers, who manage to keep the facilities and rooms very clean, perform various traditional dances and ceremonies in full costume in the lobby. To get here from Nezu Station, walk 300 yards north along Shinobazu-dōri and take the street on the right; Sawanoya is 180 yards ahead on the right. ⊠ *2–3–11 Yanaka, Taitō-ku 110-0001* ☎ *03/3822–2251* ⊕ *www.sawanoya.com* ☞ *12 Japanese-style rooms, 2 with bath △ Japanese baths, bicycles, laundry facilities, in-room data ports, Internet room* ⊟ *AE, MC, V* Ⓜ *Chiyoda subway line, Nezu Station (Exit 1).*

FodorŚChoice ★

Hostels

¢–$ 🏨 **YMCA Asia Youth Center.** Both men and women can stay here, and all rooms are private and have private baths. Discounts are given to YMCA members, pastors, and students taking university entrance exams. Breakfast is available for ¥200. The hostel is an eight-minute walk from Suidō-bashi Station. ⊠ *2–5–5 Saragaku, Chiyoda-ku 101-0064* ☎ *03/ 3233–0611* ⊕ *http://ymcajapan.org/ayc* ☞ *55 rooms △ Laundry facilities, Internet room, meeting rooms* ⊟ *DC, MC, V* Ⓜ *JR Mita Line, Suidō-bashi Station.*

¢ ▣ **Tōkyō International Youth Hostel.** In typical hostel style, you're required to be off the premises between 10 AM and 3 PM. Less typical is the fact that for an additional ¥1,200 over the standard rate, you can eat breakfast and dinner in the hostel cafeteria. Films are occasionally shown on a 50-inch TV in the lobby, and there's a small convenience store on-site. For those hitting the town, the 11 PM curfew could pose a problem. The hostel is a few minutes' walk from Iidabashi Station. ⊠ *Central Plaza Bldg., 18th fl., 1–1 Kagura-kashi, Shinjuku-ku 162-0823* ☎ *03/3235–1107* ⊕ *www.tokyo-ih.jp* ⊅ *138 bunk beds* � *Japanese baths, Internet room, meeting room* ▤ *AE, MC, V* Ⓜ *JR; Tōzai, Namboku, and Yūraku-chō subway lines: Iidabashi Station (Exit B2b).*

Near Narita Airport

Transportation between Narita Airport and Tōkyō proper takes at least an hour and a half. In heavy traffic, a limousine bus or taxi ride, which could set you back ¥30,000, can stretch to two hours or more. A sensible strategy for visitors with early-morning flights home would be to spend the night before at one of the hotels near the airport, all of which have courtesy shuttles to the departure terminals; these hotels are also a boon to visitors en route elsewhere with layovers in Narita. Many of them have soundproof rooms to block out the noise of the airplanes.

$$ ▣ **Narita Excel Hotel Tokyu.** Airline crews rolling their bags through the lobby are a common sight at the Excel, a hotel with reasonable prices and friendly service. The rooms, which are outfitted with standard water kettles and yukatas, are adequately soundproofed but tend to be very small. The Japanese garden and nearby Shinsho-ji temple are pleasant for walks. ⊠ *31 Oyama, Chiba-ken, Narita-shi 286-0131* ☎ *0476/33–0109* ⊕ *www.narita-e.tokyuhotels.co.jp* ⊅ *710 rooms, 2 suites* ዹ *3 restaurants, cable TV, 2 pools, gym, bar, airport shuttle* ▤ *AE, DC, MC, V.*

$–$$ ▣ **Radisson Hotel Narita Airport.** Set on 28 spacious, green acres, this modern hotel feels somewhat like a resort, with massive indoor and outdoor pools. The standard rooms are comfortable, and those rooms in the hotel's four towers have views of the expansive property. A shuttle bus runs between the Radisson and the airport every 20 minutes or so; the hotel also operates ten buses daily directly to and from Tōkyō Station. ⊠ *650–35 Nanae, Inaba-gun, Chiba-ken, Tomisato-shi 286-0221* ☎ *0476/93–1234* ⊕ *www.radisson.com/tokyojp_narita* ⊅ *493 rooms* ዹ *2 restaurants, room service, refrigerators, cable TV with movies, indoor-outdoor pool, gym, sauna, bar, dry cleaning, laundry service, in-room broadband, meeting rooms, business services, airport shuttle, no-smoking rooms* ▤ *AE, DC, MC, V.*

$ ▣ **ANA Hotel Narita.** With its brass and marble, this hotel, like many others in the ANA chain, aspires to architecture in the grand style. The rooms are small, but the amenities measure up, and the proximity to the airport (about 15 minutes by shuttle bus) makes this a good choice if you're in transit. If you're flying an ANA flight bound for anywhere other than North America, you can check in at a special counter in the lobby. Room views are of the airport or surrounding greenery. ⊠ *68 Hori-no-uchi, Chiba-ken, Narita-shi 286-0107* ☎ *0476/33–1311, 0120/*

029–501 toll-free ⊕ www.anahotel-narita.com ⟳ 434 rooms, 8 suites ♨ 4 restaurants, room service, cable TV with movies, indoor pool, gym, sauna, in-room data ports, Internet room, airport shuttle, no-smoking rooms ▤ AE, DC, MC, V.

$ 🖭 **Hilton Tōkyō Narita Airport.** Given its proximity to the airport (a 10-minute drive), this C-shape hotel is a reasonable choice for people in transit. The deluxe rooms on the three upper floors feature funky orange blackout curtains, a work desk and ergonomic chair, kanji wall art, and a flat-screen TV. The bland furnishings in the remaining rooms, however, could use an upgrade. The top-floor banquet facilities provide a view of the landings and takeoffs on the airport runway. Complimentary buses depart for the airport or the nearby Narita train station a few times each hour. ✉ *456 Kosuge, Chiba-ken, Narita-shi 286-0127* ☎ *0476/33–1121* ⊕ *www.hilton.com* ⟳ *548 rooms* ♨ *3 restaurants, pool, gym, spa, bar, in-room broadband, business center, meeting rooms, airport shuttle, no-smoking rooms* ▤ *AE, DC, MC, V.*

$ 🖭 **Hotel Nikkō Winds Narita.** A regular shuttle bus (at Terminal 1, Bus Stop 14; Terminal 2, Bus Stop 31) makes the 10-minute trip from the airport to the Nikkō Winds. Basic, cheap furnishings fill the rooms in the main building, and there's barely room to pass between the bed and the dresser en route to the bathroom—but the rooms are thoroughly soundproof. Rooms in the "Executive" building are nicer but pricier. The top-floor lounge overlooks the airport. ✉ *560 Tokkō, Chiba-ken, Naria-shi 286-1016* ☎ *0476/33–1111, 0120/582–586 toll-free* ⊕ *www.jalhnn.co.jp* ⟳ *307 rooms, 8 suites* ♨ *4 restaurants, room service, refrigerators, cable TV with movies, pool, massage, in-room data ports, business services, meeting room, airport shuttle, no-smoking rooms* ▤ *AE, DC, MC, V.*

¢–$ 🖭 **Holiday Inn Tōbu Narita.** The modern, Western-style accommodations at this hotel, which is a 5-minute ride by shuttle bus from the airport, are some of the cheapest around. Inquire about specials when making a reservation. ✉ *320–1 Tokkō, Chiba-ken, Narita-shi 286-0106* ☎ *0476/32–1234* ⊕ *www.holidayinntobunarita.com* ⟳ *484 rooms, 5 suites* ♨ *3 restaurants, pool, massage, steam room, in-room broadband, bar, airport shuttle, no-smoking rooms* ▤ *AE, DC, MC, V.*

Points of Interest

HOTELS/AREAS	JAPANESE CHARACTERS
Akasaka-mitsuke	赤坂見附
Akasaka Prince Hotel	赤坂プリンスホテル
Akihabara	秋葉原
Akihabara Washington Hotel	秋葉原 ワシントンホテル
ANA Hotel Narita	成田全日空ホテル
ANA Hotel Tōkyō	東京全日空ホテル
Asakusa	浅草
Asakusa View Hotel	浅草ビューホテル
Asia Center of Japan	アジア会館
Century Hyatt Tōkyō	センチュリーハイアット東京
Cerulean Tower Tokyu Hotel	セルリアンタワー東急ホテル
Conrad Tōkyō	コンラッド東京
Ebisu	恵比寿
Four Seasons Hotel Chinzan-sō	フォーシーズンズホテル椿山荘
Four Seasons Hotel Tōkyō at Marunouchi	フォーシーズンズホテル丸の内東京
Ginza	銀座
Grand Hyatt Tōkyō at Roppongi Hills	グランドハイアット東京
Green Plaza Shinjuku	グリーンプラザ新宿
Hakozaki	箱崎
Hibiya	日比谷
Higashi-Gotanda	東五反田
Higashi-Shinjuku	東新宿
Hilton Tōkyō	ヒルトン東京
Hilton Tōkyō Narita Airport	ヒルトン成田
Holiday Inn Tōbu Narita	ホリデイ・イン東武成田
Hotel Arca Torre	ホテルアルカトーレ
Hotel InterContinental Tōkyō Bay	ホテル インターコンチネンタル 東京ベイ
Hotel New Ōtani Tōkyō and Towers	ホテルニューオータニ
Hotel Nikkō Tōkyō	ホテル日航東京
Hotel Nikkō Winds Narita	ホテル日航ウインズ成田
Hotel Ōkura Tōkyō	ホテルオークラ
Hotel Seiyō Ginza	ホテル西洋銀座

3

The Strings Hotel	ストリングスホテル東京
Sumishō Hotel	住庄ほてる
Takanawa Tōbu Hotel	高輪東武ホテル
Tōkyō International Youth Hostel	東京国際ユースホステル
Tōkyō Prince Hotel Park Tower	東京プリンスホテルパークタワー
Tora-no-mon	虎ノ門
Ueno	上野
Westin Tōkyō	ウエスティンホテル東京
Yaesu	八重洲
Yanaka	谷中
YMCA Asia Youth Center	YMCAアジア青少年センター
Yoshimizu Ginza	銀座吉水

Nightlife &
the Arts

WORD OF MOUTH

"You can spend an enjoyable but exhausting day in Ueno Park, visiting some of the world-class museums and galleries. National Museum has a rich collection of Japanese and other Asian artifacts and has top-rate Western masterpieces."

—Alec

"If you are a museum person, look into the Grutt Pass—it will save you a lot if you go to a number of museums."

—Mara

Updated by
Nicholas
Coldicott

AS TŌKYŌ'S RICH CULTURAL HISTORY entwines itself with an influx of foreign influences, Tōkyōites get the best of both worlds. An evening out can be as civilized as a night of Kabuki or as rowdy as a Roppongi nightclub. In between there are dance clubs, a swingin' jazz scene, theater, cinema, live venues, and more than enough bars to keep the social lubricant flowing past millions of tonsils nightly.

The sheer diversity of nightlife is breathtaking. Rickety street stands sit yards away from luxury hotels, and wallet-crunching hostess clubs can be found next to cheap and raucous rock bars. Whatever your style, you'll find yourself in good company if you venture out after dark.

THE ARTS

An astonishing variety of dance and music, both classical and popular, can be found in Tōkyō, alongside the must-see traditional Japanese arts of Kabuki, Nō, and Bunraku. The city is a proving ground for local talent and a magnet for orchestras and concert soloists from all over the world. Eric Clapton, Yo-Yo Ma, Wynton Marsalis: whenever you visit, the headliners will be here. Tōkyō also has modern theater—in somewhat limited choices, to be sure, unless you can follow dialogue in Japanese, but Western repertory companies can always find receptive audiences here for plays in English. And it doesn't take long for a hit show from New York or London to open. Musicals such as *The Lion King* have found enormous popularity here—although you'll find Simba speaks Japanese.

Japan has yet to develop any real strength of its own in ballet and has only just begun to devote serious resources to opera, but for that reason touring companies like the Metropolitan, the Bolshoi, Sadler's Wells, and the Bayerische Staatsoper find Tōkyō a very compelling venue—as well they might when even seats at ¥30,000 or more sell out far in advance. One domestic company that's making a name for itself is the Asami Maki Ballet, whose dancers are known for their technical proficiency and expressiveness; the company often performs at the Tōkyō Metropolitan Festival Hall. Latin dance also has a strong following and flamenco heartthrob Joaquín Cortés visits regularly to wide acclaim and packed houses.

Tōkyō movie theaters screen a broad range of films—everything from big Asian hits to American blockbusters and Oscar nominees. The increased diversity brought by smaller distributors, and the current vogue for Korean, Chinese, and Hong Kong cinema have helped to develop vibrant small theaters that cater to a sophisticated audience of art house fans. New multiplexes have also brought new screens to the capital, offering a more comfortable film-going experience than some of the older Japanese theaters.

Information & Tickets

Metropolis is a free English-language weekly magazine that has up-to-date listings of what's going on in the city; it's available at hotels, book and music stores, some restaurants and cafés, and other locations. Another source, rather less complete, is the *Tour Companion,* a tabloid visitor guide published every two weeks, available free of charge at hotels and at Japan National Tourist Organization (JNTO) offices. For coverage of all aspects of the performing-arts scene, visit ⊕ www.artindex. metro.tokyo.jp.

If your hotel can't help you with concert and performance bookings, call **Ticket Pia** (☎ 03/5237–9999) for assistance in English. The **Playguide Agency** (✉ Playguide Bldg., 2–6–4 Ginza, Chūō-ku ☎ 03/3561–8821 Ⓜ Yūraku-chō subway line, Ginza Itchōme Station, Exit 4) sells tickets to cultural events via outlets in most department stores and in other locations throughout the city; you can stop in at the main office and ask for the nearest counter, but be aware that you may not find someone who speaks English. Note that agencies normally do not have tickets for same-day performances but only for advance booking.

Dance

Traditional Japanese dance is divided into dozens of styles, ancient of lineage and fiercely proud of their differences. In truth, only the aficionado can really tell them apart. They survive not so much as performing arts but as schools, offering dance as a cultured accomplishment to interested amateurs. At least once a year, these teachers and their students hold a recital, so that on any given evening there's very likely to be one somewhere in Tōkyō. Truly professional performances are given at the Kokuritsu Gekijō and the Shimbashi Enbujō; the most important of the classical schools, however, developed as an aspect of Kabuki, and if you attend a play at the Kabuki-za, you are almost guaranteed to see a representative example.

Ballet began to attract a Japanese following in 1920, when Anna Pavlova danced *The Dying Swan* at the old Imperial Theater. The well-known companies that come to Tōkyō from abroad, perform to full houses that are usually at the Tōkyō Metropolitan Festival Hall in Ueno. There are now about 15 professional Japanese ballet companies, including the Tōkyō Ballet and the up-and-coming Asami Maki Ballet—both of which perform at the Tōkyō Metropolitan Festival Hall—but this has yet to become an art form on which Japan has had much of an impact.

Modern dance, on the other hand, is a different story. The modern Japanese dance form known as Butō, in particular, with its contorted and expressive body movements, is acclaimed internationally and domestically. Butō performances are held periodically at a variety of event spaces and small theaters. For details, check with ticket agencies and the local English-language press.

Film

Fortunately for film fans, Japan's distributors invariably add Japanese subtitles rather than dub their offerings. Exceptions include kids' movies and big blockbusters that are released in both versions—if there are two screenings close to each other, that's a sign that one may be dubbed. The original sound track, of course, may not be all that helpful to you if the film is Polish or Italian, but the majority of first-run foreign films here are made in the United States. Choices range from the usual Hollywood fare to independent movies, but many films take so long to open in Tōkyō that you've probably already seen them. And tickets are expensive: around ¥1,800 ($15) for general admission and ¥2,500–¥3,000 ($21–$25) for a reserved seat, called a *shitei-seki.* Slightly discounted tickets, usually ¥1,200–¥1,600 ($10-$13), can be purchased from the ticket counters found in many department stores.

The Japanese film industry is currently experiencing a renaissance, with high-profile wins at Cannes, the 2001 *Spirited Away*'s Academy Award, and the slew of Hollywood remakes of horror hits such as *The Ring, The Grudge,* and *Dark Water.* Director-actor Takeshi Kitano's works have garnered critical acclaim and a following in Europe. He remains one of the country's foremost auteurs, though that hasn't stopped him from making appearances on some wacky TV shows.

Although many of the major Japanese studios struggle to compete with big-budget U.S. fare, anime remains strong and each year sees several major domestic successes. Unless your Japanese is top-notch, most domestic films will be off-limits, but if you happen to be in town during one of the many film festivals you may be able to catch a screening with English subtitles. Festival season is in the fall, with the Tōkyō International Film Festival taking over the Shibuya district in October and a slew of other more specialized festivals screening more outré fare.

First-run theaters that have new releases, both Japanese and foreign, are clustered for the most part in three areas: Shinjuku, Shibuya, and Yūraku-chō-Hibiya-Ginza. At most of them, the last showing of the evening starts at around 7. This is not the case, however, with the best news on the Tōkyō film scene: the handful of small theaters that take special interest in classics, revivals, and serious imports. Somewhere on the premises will also be a chrome-and-marble coffee shop, a fashionable little bar, or even a decent restaurant. Most of these small theaters have a midnight show—at least on the weekends.

Bunkamura. This complex in Shibuya has two movie theaters, a concert auditorium (Orchard Hall), and a performance space (Theater Cocoon); it's the principal venue for many of Tōkyō's film festivals. ✉ *2–24–1 Dōgenzaka, Shibuya-ku* ☎ *03/3477–9999* Ⓜ *JR Yamanote Line, Ginza and Hanzō-mon subway lines, and private rail lines; Shibuya Station (Exits 5 and 8 for Hanzō-mon Line, Kita-guchi/North Exit for all others).*

Chanter Cine. A three-screen cinema complex, Chanter Cine tends to show British and American films by independent producers but also showcases fine work by filmmakers from Asia and the Middle East. ✉ *1–2–2 Yūraku-chō, Chiyoda-ku* ☎ *03/3591–1511* Ⓜ *Hibiya, Chiyoda, and Mita subway lines, Hibiya Station (Exit A5).*

Cine Saison Shibuya. In addition to popular films, this theater occasionally screens recent releases by award-winning directors from such countries as Iran, China, and South Korea. ✉ *Prime Bldg., 2–29–5 Dōgen-zaka, Shibuya-ku* ☎ *03/3770–1721* Ⓜ *JR Yamanote Line, Shibuya Station (Hachiko Exit).*

Haiyūza. This is primarily a repertory theater, but on the irregularly scheduled Haiyūza Talkie Nights it screens notable foreign films. ✉ *4–9–2 Roppongi, Minato-ku* ☎ *03/3401–4073* Ⓜ *Hibiya subway line, Roppongi Station (Exit 4A).*

Virgin Cinemas. In Roppongi Hills, this complex offers comfort, plus six screens, VIP seats, and late shows on weekends. There are plenty of bars in the area for post-movie discussions. ✉ *Keyakizaka Complex, 6–10–2 Roppongi, Minato-ku* ☎ *03/5775–6090* 📧 *Regular theater ¥1,800; Premier theater ¥3,000* Ⓜ *Hibiya and Ōedo subway lines, Roppongi Station (Roppongi Hills Exit).*

Modern Theater

4

The Shingeki (Modern Theater) movement began in Japan at about the turn of the 20th century, coping at first with the lack of native repertoire by performing translations of Western dramatists from Shakespeare to Shaw. It wasn't until around 1915 that Japanese playwrights began writing for the Shingeki stage, but modern drama did not really develop a voice of its own here until after World War II.

The watershed years came around 1965, when experimental theater companies, unable to find commercial space, began taking their work to young audiences in various unusual ways: street plays and "happenings," dramatic readings in underground malls and rented lofts, tents put up on vacant lots for unannounced performances (miraculously filled to capacity by word of mouth) and taken down the next day. It was during this period that surrealist playwright Kōbō Abe found his stride and director Tadashi Suzuki developed the unique system of training that now draws aspiring actors from all over the world to his "theater community" in the mountains of Toyama Prefecture. Japanese drama today is a lively art indeed; theaters small and large, in unexpected pockets all over Tōkyō, attest to its vitality.

Most of these performances, however, are in Japanese, for Japanese audiences. You're unlikely to find one with program notes in English to help you follow it. Unless it's a play you already know well, and you're curious to see how it translates, you might do well to think of some other way to spend your evenings out if you don't understand Japanese. Language is less of a barrier when you're trying to enjoy a Takarazuka show.

Takarazuka. Japan's all-female theater troupe was founded in the Ōsaka suburb of Takarazuka in 1913 and has been going strong ever since. Today it has not one but five companies, one of which has a permanent home in Tōkyō at the 2,069-seat Tōkyō Takarazuka Theater. Everybody sings; everybody dances; the sets are breathtaking; the costumes are swell. Where else but at the Takarazuka could you see *Gone With the Wind*, sung in Japanese, with a young woman in a mustache and a frock coat playing Rhett Butler? Tickets cost ¥3,800–¥10,000 ($31-$82) for regular performances or ¥2,000–¥5,000 ($16-$41) for debut performances with the company's budding ingenues. ✉ *1–1–3 Yūraku-chō, Chiyoda-ku* ☎ *03/5251–2001* Ⓜ *JR Yamanote Line, Yūraku-chō*

Station (Hibiya Exit); Hibiya subway line, Hibiya Station (Exit A5); Chiyoda and Mita subway line, Hibiya Station (Exit A13).

Music

Information in English about venues for traditional Japanese music (koto, shamisen, and so forth) can be hard to find; check newspaper listings, particularly the Friday and Saturday editions, for concerts and school recitals. Western music poses no such problem: during the 1980s and early 1990s a considerable number of new concert halls and performance spaces sprang up all over the city, adding to what was already an excellent roster of public auditoriums. The following are a few of the most important.

Casals Hall. The last of the fine small auditoriums built for chamber music, before the Japanese bubble economy burst in the early '90s, was designed by architect Arata Isozaki—justly famous for the Museum of Contemporary Art in Los Angeles. In addition to chamber music, Casals draws piano, guitar, cello, and voice soloists. ⊠ *1–6 Kanda Surugadai, Chiyoda-ku* ☎ *03/3294–1229* Ⓜ *JR Chūō Line and Marunouchi subway line, Ochanomizu Station (Exit 2).*

Iino Hall. Built before Japan fell in love with marble, Iino Hall maintains a reputation for comfort, intelligent programming, and excellent acoustics. The venue hosts chamber music and Japanese concert soloists. ⊠ *2–1–1 Uchisaiwai-chō, Chiyoda-ku* ☎ *03/3506–3251* Ⓜ *Chiyoda and Hibiya subway lines, Kasumigaseki Station (Exit C4); Marunouchi subway line, Kasumigaseki Station (Exit B2); Ginza subway line, Tora-no-mon Station (Exit 9); Mita subway line, Uchisaiwai-chō Station (Exit A7).*

Nakano Sun Plaza. Everything from rock to Argentine tango is staged at this hall. ⊠ *4–1–1 Nakano, Nakano-ku* ☎ *03/3388–1151* Ⓜ *JR and Tōzai subway lines, Nakano Station (Kita-guchi/North Exit).*

New National Theater and Tōkyō Opera City Concert Hall. With its 1,810-seat main auditorium, this venue nourishes Japan's fledgling efforts to make a name for itself in the world of opera. The Opera City Concert Hall has a massive pipe organ and hosts visiting orchestras and performers. Large-scale operatic productions such as *Carmen* draw crowds at the New National Theater's Opera House, while the Pit and Playhouse theaters showcase musicals and more intimate dramatic works. Ticket prices range from ¥1,500 to ¥21,000. The complex also includes an art gallery. ⊠ *3–20–2 Nishi-Shinjuku, Shinjuku-ku* ☎ *03/5353–0788, 03/5353–9999 for tickets* ⊕ *www.operacity.jp* Ⓜ *Keiō Shin-sen private rail line, Hatsudai Station (Higashi-guchi/East Exit).*

NHK Hall. The home base for the Japan Broadcasting Corporation's NHK Symphony Orchestra is probably the auditorium most familiar to Japanese lovers of classical music, as performances here are routinely rebroadcast on NHK-TV, the national TV station. ⊠ *2–2–1 Jinnan, Shibuya-ku* ☎ *03/3465–1751* Ⓜ *JR Yamanote Line, Shibuya Station (Hachiko Exit); Ginza and Hanzō-mon subway lines, Shibuya Station (Exits 6 and 7).*

Suntory Hall. This lavishly appointed concert auditorium in the Ark Hills complex has one of the best locations for theatergoers who want to extend their evening out: there's an abundance of good restaurants and bars nearby. ✉ *1–13–1 Akasaka, Minato-ku* ☎ *03/3505–1001* Ⓜ *Ginza and Namboku subway lines, Tameike-Sannō Station (Exit 13).*

Tōkyō Dome. A 55,000-seat sports arena, the dome also hosts big-name Japanese pop acts as well as the occasional international star. ✉ *1–3–61 Kōraku, Bunkyō-ku* ☎ *03/5800–9999* Ⓜ *Marunouchi and Namboku subway lines, Kōraku-en Station (Exit 2); Ōedo and Mita subway lines, Kasuga Station (Exit A2); JR Suidō-bashi Station (Nishi-guchi/West Exit).*

Tōkyō Metropolitan Festival Hall (Tōkyō Bunka Kaikan). In the 1960s and '70s this hall was one of the city's premier showcases for orchestral music and visiting soloists. It still gets major bookings. ✉ *5–45 Ueno Kōen, Taitō-ku* ☎ *03/3828–2111* Ⓜ *JR Yamanote Line, Ueno Station (Kōen-guchi/Park Exit).*

Traditional Theater

Bunraku

Bunraku puppet theater is one of Japan's most accessible traditional arts. Incredibly intricate puppets give performances so realistic that you may soon forget the performers are being guided by black-clad puppet masters. The spiritual center of Bunraku today is Ōsaka, rather than Tōkyō, but there are a number of performances in the small hall of the Kokuritsu Gekijō. Consult *Metropolis* magazine or check with one of the English-speaking ticket agencies for performance schedules.

Kabuki

Kabuki has been entertaining Japanese audiences from all walks of life for more than 300 years. It's the kind of theater—a combination of music, dance, and drama, with spectacular costumes, acrobatics, duels, quick changes, and special effects thrown in—that you can enjoy without understanding a word the actors say.

Fodor's Choice ★ **Kabuki-za.** The best place to see Kabuki is at this theater, built especially for this purpose, with its *hanamichi* (runway) passing diagonally through the audience to the revolving stage. Built in 1925, the Kabuki-za was destroyed in an air raid in 1945 and rebuilt in identical style in 1951. Matinees usually begin at 11 and end at 4; evening performances start at 4:30 and end around 9. Reserved seats are expensive and can be hard to come by on short notice (reserve tickets by at least 6 PM the day before you wish to attend). For a mere ¥800 to ¥1,000, however, you can buy an unreserved ticket that allows you to see one act of a play from the topmost gallery. Bring binoculars—the gallery is very far from the stage. You might also want to rent an earphone set (¥650; deposit ¥1,000) to follow the play in English, but for some this can be more of an intrusion than a help—and you can't use the set in the topmost galleries. ✉ *4–12–15 Ginza, Chūō-ku* ☎ *03/5565–6000 or 03/3541–3131* ⊕ *www.shochiku.co.jp/play/kabukiza/theater* Ⓜ *Hibiya and Asakusa subway lines, Higashi-Ginza Station (Exit 3).*

CLOSE UP

Traditional Japanese Drama

KABUKI

Kabuki emerged as a popular form of entertainment by women dancing lewdly in the early 17th century; before long, the authorities banned it as a threat to public order. Eventually it cleaned up its act, and by the latter half of the 18th century it had become popular with common folks—especially the townspeople of bustling Edo, which would grow into Tōkyō. Kabuki had music, dance, and spectacle; it had acrobatics and sword fights; it had pathos and tragedy, historical romance and social satire. It no longer had bawdy beauties, however—women have been banned from the Kabuki stage since 1629—but in recompense it developed a professional role for female impersonators, who train for years to project a seductive, dazzling femininity. It had—and still has—superstars and quick-change artists and legions of fans, who bring their lunch to the theater, stay all day, and shout out the names of their favorite actors at the stirring moments in their favorite plays.

The Kabuki repertoire does not really grow or change, but stars like Ennosuke Ichikawa and Tamasaburo Bando have put exciting, personal stamps on their performances that continue to draw audiences young and old. If you don't know Japanese, you can still enjoy a performance: Tōkyō's Kabuki-za (Kabuki Theater) has simultaneous English translation of its plays available on headphones.

Nō

Nō is a dramatic tradition far older than Kabuki: it reached a point of formal perfection in the 14th century and survives virtually unchanged from that period. Nō developed for the most part under the patronage of the warrior class; it's dignified, ritualized, and symbolic. Many of the plays in the repertoire are drawn from classical literature or tales of the supernatural, and the texts are richly poetic. Some understanding of the plot of each play is necessary to enjoy a performance, which moves at a nearly glacial pace—the pace of ritual time—as it's solemnly chanted. The major Nō theaters often provide synopses of the plays in English.

The principal character in a Nō play wears a carved wooden mask. Such is the skill of the actor—and the mysterious effect of the play—that the mask itself may appear expressionless until the actor "brings it to life," at which point the mask seems to convey a considerable range of emotions. As in Kabuki, the various roles of the Nō repertoire all have specific costumes—robes of silk brocade with intricate patterns that are works of art in themselves.

Nō is not very *accessible*: its language is archaic, its conventions are obscure, and its pace can put even Japanese audiences to sleep. That said, the best way to see Nō is in the open air, at torchlight performances called Takigi Nō, held in the courtyards of temples. The setting and the aesthetics of the drama combine to produce an eerie theatrical experience. In Tōkyō, as a contrast to the rest of the city, Nō will provide an experience of Japan as an ancient, sophisticated culture.

■ TIP→ *Kyōgen* are shorter, lighter plays that are often interspersed in between Nō performances and are much more accessible than Nō. If Nō doesn't appeal to you, consider taking advantage of opportunities to see kyōgen instead.

BUNRAKU

The third major form of traditional Japanese drama is Bunraku puppet theater. Though its origins date to the 10th century, the golden age of Bunraku didn't occur until the 18th century, when most of the form's great plays were written and the puppets themselves evolved to their present form. These puppets are so large, they cover the puppeteers underneath them, and are so expressive and intricate in their movements, that they require three people at one time to manipulate them. Puppeteers and narrators, who deliver their lines in a kind of high-pitched croak from deep in the throat, train for many years to master this difficult and unusual genre of popular entertainment. Elaborately dressed in period costume, each puppet is made up of interchangeable parts: a head, shoulder piece, trunk, legs, and arms. Various puppet heads are used for roles of different sex, age, and character, and a certain hairstyle will indicate a puppet's position in life.

To operate one puppet, three puppeteers must act in unison. The *omozukai* controls the expression on the puppet's face and its right arm and hand. The *hidarizukai* controls the puppet's left arm and hand along with any props that it's carrying. The *ashizukai* moves the puppet's legs.

This last task is the easiest. The most difficult task belongs to the omozukai. It takes about 30 years to become an expert. A puppeteer must spend 10 years as ashizukai, an additional 10 as hidarizukai, and then 10 more years as omozukai. These master puppeteers not only skillfully manipulate the puppets' arms and legs but also roll the eyes and move the lips so that the puppets express fear, joy, and sadness.

—Jared Lubarsky and David Miles

Kokuritsu Gekijō. This theater hosts Kabuki companies based elsewhere; it also has a training program for young people who may not have one of the hereditary family connections but want to break into this closely guarded profession. Debut performances, called *kao-mise,* are worth watching to catch the stars of the next generation. Reserved seats are usually ¥1,500–¥9,000. Tickets can be reserved by phone up until the day of the performance by calling the theater box office between 10 and 5. ⊠ *4–1 Hayabusa-chō, Chiyoda-ku* ☎ *03/3230–3000* Ⓜ *Hanzō-mon subway line, Hanzō-mon Station (Exit 1).*

Shimbashi Enbujō. Dating to 1925, this theater was built for the geisha of the Shimbashi quarter to present their spring and autumn performances of traditional music and dance. It's a bigger house than the Kabuki-za, and it presents a lot of traditional dance, *kyogen* (traditional Nō-style comic skits), and conventional Japanese drama as well as Kabuki. Reserved seats commonly run ¥2,100–¥16,800, and there's no gallery. ⊠ *6–18–2 Ginza, Chūō-ku* ☎ *03/5565–6000* Ⓜ *Hibiya and Asakusa subway lines, Higashi-Ginza Station (Exit A6).*

Nō

Performances of Nō, with its slow, ritualized movements and archaic language, are given at various times during the year, generally in the theaters of the individual schools. The schools also often teach their dance and recitation styles to amateurs. Consult the *Tour Companion* listings. Tickets to Takigi Nō (held outdoors in temple courtyards) sell out quickly and are normally available only through the temples.

Kanze Nō-gakudō. Founded in the 14th century, this is among the most important of the Nō family schools in Tōkyō. The current *iemoto* (head) of the school is the 26th in his line. ⊠ *1–16–4 Shōtō, Shibuya-ku* ☎ *03/3469–5241* Ⓜ *Ginza and Hanzō-mon subway lines, Shibuya Station (Exit 3A).*

National Nō Theater. This is one of the few public halls to host Nō performances. ⊠ *4–18–1 Sendagaya, Shibuya-ku* ☎ *03/3423–1331* Ⓜ *JR Chūō Line, Sendagaya Station (Minami-guchi/South Exit); Ōedo subway line, Kokuritsu-Kyōgijō Station (Exit A4).*

Rakugo

A *rakugo* comedian sits on a cushion and, ingeniously using a fan as a prop for all manner of situations, relates stories that have been handed down for centuries. With different voices and facial expressions, the storyteller acts out the parts of different characters within the stories. There's generally no English interpretation, and the monologues, filled with puns and expressions in dialect, can even be difficult for the Japanese themselves. A performance of rakugo is still worth seeing, however, for a slice of traditional pop culture.

Suzumoto. Built around 1857 and later rebuilt, Suzumoto is the oldest rakugo theater in Tōkyō. It's on Chūō-dōri, a few blocks north of the Ginza Line's Ueno Hirokō-ji stop. Tickets cost ¥2,800, and performances run continually throughout the day 12:20–4:30 and 5:20–9:10. ⊠ *2–7–12 Ueno, Taitō-ku* ☎ *03/3834–5906* Ⓜ *Ginza subway line, Ueno Hirokō-ji Station (Exit 3).*

NIGHTLIFE

Most bars and clubs in the main entertainment districts have printed price lists, often in English. Drinks generally cost ¥600–¥1,200 ($5-$10), although some small exclusive bars and clubs will set you back a lot more. Be wary of establishments without visible price lists. Hostess clubs and small backstreet bars known as "snacks" or "pubs" can be particularly treacherous territory for the unprepared. That drink you've just ordered could set you back a reasonable ¥1,000 ($8); you might, on the other hand, have wandered unknowingly into a place that charges you ¥15,000 ($124) up front for a whole bottle—and slaps a ¥20,000 ($165) cover charge on top. If the bar has hostesses, it's often unclear what the companionship of one will cost you, or whether she is there just for conversation. Ignore the persuasive shills on the streets of Roppongi and Kabuki-chō, who will try to hook you into their establishment. There is, of course, a certain amount of safe ground: hotel lounges, jazz clubs, and the rapidly expanding Irish pub scene are pretty much the way they are anywhere else. But elsewhere it's best to follow the old adage: if you have to ask how much it costs, you probably can't afford it.

There are five major districts in Tōkyō that have extensive nightlife, and each has a unique atmosphere, clientele, and price level.

Akasaka
Nightlife in Akasaka concentrates mainly on two streets—Ta-machi-dōri and Hitotsugi-dōri—and the small alleys connecting them. The area has several cabarets and nightclubs, plus wine bars, coffee shops, late-night restaurants, pubs, and "snacks"—counter bars that will serve (and charge you for) small portions of food with your drinks, whether you order them or not. It's also renowned for its many Korean barbecue restaurants, which tend to be on the pricey side. Akasaka is sophisticated and upscale—which is not surprising for an old geisha district—but not as expensive as Ginza.

Ginza
Unless you have a bottomless expense account, Ginza is best considered as a window-shopper's destination. Affordable bars and restaurants do exist, but most close around 11 PM. The late-night entertainment spots tend to be exclusive hostess clubs where kimono-clad women pander to politicians and high-rolling businessmen.

Roppongi
Roppongi developed to serve the needs of the post-World War II American occupiers, who picked the area as their base. Some would say little has changed since then, as the area remains a hot spot for American soldiers looking to unwind. Roppongi was traditionally ghostly quiet by day, boisterous and crude by night. But things took an unexpected turn in late 2003 when the city's leading property magnate, Minoru Mori, opened the upscale Roppongi Hills complex a stone's throw from the sleaze. The fancy stores, restaurants, bars, and luxury apartments of the development now draw a more urbane crowd to the area.

CLOSE UP

The Red Lights of Kabuki-chō

TŌKYŌ HAS MORE THAN ITS FAIR share of red-light districts, but the leader of the pack is unquestionably Kabuki-chō, located just north of Shinjuku Station. The land was once a swamp, although its current name refers to an aborted post–World War II effort to bring culture to the area in the form of a landmark Kabuki theater. Nowadays, most of the entertainment is of the insalubrious kind, with strip clubs, love hotels, host and hostess clubs, and thinly disguised brothels all luridly advertising their presence.

The area is also home to throngs of Japanese and Chinese gangsters, giving rise to its image domestically as a danger zone. But in truth, Kabuki-chō poses little risk to even the solo traveler. The sheer volume of people in the area each night, combined with a prominent security-camera presence, means that crime stays mostly indoors.

Despite its sordid reputation, Kabuki-chō does offer something beyond the red lights. There are eateries galore ranging from chain diners to designer restaurants. The impressive 16th-century shrine **Hanazono Jinja** (⊠ 5-17-3 Shinjuku, Shinjuku-ku ☎ 03/3209-5265 ☜ Free ☼ Daily

sunrise–sunset Ⓜ Marunouchi subway line, Shinjuku-san-chōme Station (Exits B2 and B3)) hosts several events throughout the year, but comes alive with two must-see colorful festivals on its grounds. The weekend closest to May 28 brings a shrine festival, in which portable shrines are paraded through the streets. The November Tori-no-Ichi festival (the exact days vary each year) is held here and at several shrines throughout Tōkyō, but Hanazono is the most famous place to buy the festival's *kumade*: big rakes decorated with money, mock fruit, and other items people would like to "rake in." People buy them for luck, and replace them every year.

Also here is Golden Gai, probably Tōkyō's most atmospheric drinking area. The quirky **Koma Gekijō** (Koma Stadium Theater ⊠ 1-19-1 Kabuki-chō, Shinjuku-ku ☎ 03/3200-2213) is a favorite of the pension-drawing crowd, offering variety stage shows starring fading entertainers. Even if a performance here makes little sense, it should still be a memorable experience.

–Nicholas Coldicott

Shibuya

Shibuya is the heart of Tōkyō's vibrant youth culture, with shopping and nightlife geared to the teen and twentysomething crowd. The pedestrian-only Center Gai street is the place to see the latest, quirkiest Tōkyō teen fashion. Shibuya is also a delight for record shoppers, with what is said to be the highest concentration of vinyl of any square mile on the planet.

Shinjuku

Long a favorite drinking spot for artists and businesspeople alike, Shinjuku offers everything from glamorous high-rise bars to sleazy dens. The Golden-Gai area is the haunt of writers, artists, and filmmakers. Nearby

Kabuki-chō is the city's most notorious red-light district, where English-speaking touts offer myriad sordid experiences. The Ni-chōme area (near Shinjuku Gyo-en National Garden) is the center of Tōkyō's diverse and vibrant gay and lesbian scene. The compact area is deserted during the day, but each night more than 250 bars, clubs, and restaurants bring Ni-chōme to life. Thanks in part to its diminutive dimensions, Ni-chōme is said to have more gay bars per block than any other city in the world.

Bars

Absolut Ice Bar. When the world's fourth Ice Bar opened in Tōkyō in early 2006, it proved to be a big hit through the humid summer. The walls, bar counter, and glasses are all crafted from ice shipped from northern Sweden (it's purer, apparently), and the experience is somewhere between Lapland fantasy and being locked in a freezer. Visits are limited to 45 minutes, but only the hardiest will last even that long. The Absolut-vodka-only bar serves a wide range of inventive cocktails. The entrance fee of ¥3,500 includes an ice glass, cocktail, and warming cape. If your glass breaks while you're there and you're in the mood for another cocktail, you have to buy another ice glass for ¥800. And no, you don't get to keep the cloak. ⊠ *4–2–4 Nishi-Azabu, Minato-ku* ☎ *03/5464–2160* ⊕ *www.icebartokyo. com* ☾ *Sun.–Thurs. 6 PM–midnight, Fri.–Sat. 6 PM–4:15 AM* Ⓜ *Hibiya and Ōedo subway lines, Roppongi Station (Exit 1).*

Agave. In most Roppongi hot spots, tequila is pounded one shot at a time so it goes straight into the bloodstream. Not so at Agave: this authentic Mexican cantina treats the spirit with a little more respect, and your palate will be tempted by a choice of more than 400 tequilas and mescals. A single shot can cost between ¥800 and ¥10,000, but most of the varieties here aren't available anywhere else in Japan, so the steep prices are worth paying. ⊠ *7–15–10 Roppongi, Minato-ku* ☎ *03/ 3479–0229* ☾ *Mon.–Thurs. 6:30 PM–2 AM, Fri.–Sat. 6:30 PM–4 AM* Ⓜ *Hibiya and Ōedo subway lines, Roppongi Station (Exit 3).*

Heartland. Depending on how you look at things, this is either a stylish bar for those who've outgrown the cheap thrills of mainstream Roppongi, or a pickup joint for male-expat-banker types and foreigner-infatuated Japanese women. Either way, Heartland is a relentlessly popular drinking spot whose redeeming features are a spacious patio and delicious eponymous microbrew. Drinks start at ¥500. ⊠ *Roppongi Hills West Walk, 1F, 6–10–1 Roppongi, Minato-ku* ☎ *03/5772–7600* ☾ *Daily 11 AM–5 AM* Ⓜ *Hibiya and Ōedo subway lines, Roppongi Station (Roppongi Hills Exit).*

Fodor'sChoice ★ **Montoak.** Positioned halfway down the prestigious shopping street Omotesandō-dōri, within spitting distance of such fashion giants as Gucci, Louis Vuitton, and Tod's, this hip restaurant-bar is a great place to rest after testing the limits of your credit card. With smoky floor-to-ceiling windows, cushy armchairs, and a layout so spacious you won't believe you're sitting on one of Tōkyō's toniest streets, the place attracts a hipper-than-thou clientele but never feels unwelcoming. The bar food con-

Golden Gai

TUCKED AWAY ON THE EASTERN side of Tōkyō's sordid Kabuki-chō district, Golden Gai is a ramshackle collection of more than 200 Lilliputian bars that survived the rampant construction of Japan's bubble-economy years, thanks to the passion of its patrons. In the 1980s, when the *yakuza*, Japan's crime syndicate, was torching properties to sell the land to big-thinking developers, Golden Gai's supporters took turns guarding the area each night.

Each bar occupies a few square meters, and some accommodate fewer than a dozen drinkers. With such limited space, many of the bars rely on their regulars—and give a frosty welcome and exorbitant bill to the casual visitor. And although the timeworn look of Golden Gai captures the imagination of most visitors, many of the establishments are notoriously unfriendly to foreigners. But times change, as do leases, and a new generation of owners is gradually emerging to offer the same intimate drinking experience and cold beers without the unwelcome reception. For a guaranteed warm welcome, try one of the following:

La Jetée. It should come as no surprise that French cinema is the proprietor's big passion: a film lover's paradise, La Jetée is covered in French-cinema posters and was named after a French movie. It struggles to seat 10 customers, but that means intimate conversations—in Japanese, French, and sometimes English—usually about movies. If you want to discuss European cinema with Wim Wenders or sit toe to toe with Quentin Tarantino, this is your best bet. The music, naturally, comes exclusively from film sound tracks. The seating charge is ¥1,000. ⊠ *1-1-8 Kabuki-chō, Shinjuku-ku* ☎ *03/ 3208-9645* ⊘ *Mon.-Sat. 7-early morning* Ⓜ *Marunouchi subway line, Shinjuku-san-chōme Station (Exit B3).*

Albatross G. When it opened in summer 2005, Albatross G quickly built a following with its friendliness and, in Golden Gai terms, affordability. The ¥300 seating charge and drinks starting at ¥600 are a marked contrast to most of its neighbors. ⊠ *5th Ave., 1-1 Kabuki-chō, Shinjuku-ku* ☎ *03/3202-3699* ⊘ *Mon.-Sat. 8 PM-5 AM* Ⓜ *Marunouchi subway line, Shinjuku-san-chōme Station (Exit B3).*

—Nicholas Coldicot

---

sists of canapés, salads, cheese plates, and the like. Drinks start at ¥700. ⊠ *6-1-9 Jingū-mae, Shibuya-ku* ☎ *03/5468-5928* ⊘ *Daily 11:30 AM-midnight* Ⓜ *Chiyoda subway line, Meiji Jingū-mae Station (Exit 4).*

★ **Old Imperial Bar.** Comfortable and sedate, this is the pride of the Imperial Hotel, decorated with elements saved from Frank Lloyd Wright's earlier version of the building—alas, long since torn down. Drinks start at ¥1,000. ⊠ *Imperial Hotel, 1-1-1 Uchisaiwai-chō, Chiyoda-ku* ☎ *03/ 3504-1111* ⊘ *Daily 11:30 AM-midnight* Ⓜ *Hibiya Line, Hibiya Station (Exit 5).*

Fodor'sChoice **Sekirei.** This is simply the best place in Tōkyō to sink a cold one. The pic-
★ ture-perfect summertime beer garden looks like a budget buster, but it's
run by the Asahi brewery and offers refreshments at a price anyone can
afford. Most evenings, kimono-clad *nihon-buyō* dancers perform to the
strains of shamisen music. Sekirei serves Japanese- and Western-style food
to a demure after-work crowd. Drinks start at ¥700. ✉ *2–2–23 Moto-
Akasaka, Minato-ku* ☎ *03/3746–7723* ☾ *June–Sept., weekdays 4:30
PM–10:30 PM, weekends 5:30 PM–10:30 PM; dancers perform two or three
times nightly at varying times* Ⓜ *JR Chūō Line, Shinanomachi Station.*

Vive La Vie. Vive La Vie is exactly what a bar should be: relaxing, friendly,
and stylish, with quality cocktails and good music. You can relax on the
sofas here without any risk of disturbance or sit at the bar and join the
locals' banter. Some weekends the bar hosts local DJs and charges an entrance fee (average ¥1,500). Drinks start at ¥700. ✉ *2–4–6 Shibuya,
Shibuya-ku* ☎ *03/5485–5498* ☾ *Mon.–Thurs. 7 PM–1 AM, Fri.–Sat. 7 PM–3
AM* Ⓜ *Ginza subway line, Omotesandō Station (Exit B1).*

Beer Halls & Pubs

Clubhouse. Rugby is the sport of choice at this pub, but even those with
no interest in watching the game will enjoy the decent food and ami-
able atmosphere. A good mix of locals and foreigners frequents the bar,
and the place is more hospitable than many similar venues. ✉ *3–7–3
Shinjuku 3F, Shinjuku-ku* ☎ *03/3359–7785* ☾ *Daily 5 PM–midnight*
Ⓜ *Marunouchi subway line, Shinjuku-san-chōme Station (Exit 3).*

Ginza Lion. This bar, in business since 1899 and occupying the same stately
Chūō-dōri location since 1934, is remarkably inexpensive for one of
Tōkyō's toniest addresses. Ginza shoppers and office workers alike
drop by for beer and ballast—anything from yakitori to spaghetti. Beers
start at ¥590. ✉ *7–9–20 Ginza, Chūō-ku* ☎ *03/3571–2590* ☾ *Mon.–Sat.
11:30 AM–11 PM* Ⓜ *Ginza, Hibiya, and Marunouchi subway lines,
Ginza Station (Exit A3).*

What the Dickens. This spacious pub is nearly always packed with a fun-
seeking mix of locals and foreigners. It's in a former Aum Shinri Kyō
(the cult held responsible for the gas attack in the Tōkyō subway in 1995)
headquarters in Ebisu. Most Sundays, Mondays, and Tuesdays feature
a mix of live music and DJs. ✉ *Roob 6 Bldg., 4th fl., 1–13–3 Ebisu-
Nishi, Shibuya-ku* ☎ *03/3780–2099* ☾ *Tues.–Wed. 5 PM–1 AM,
Thurs.–Sat. 5 PM–2 AM, Sun. 5 PM–midnight* Ⓜ *Hibiya subway line, Ebisu
Station (Nishi-guchi/West Exit).*

Dance Clubs

Tōkyō's club scene isn't quite up there with the international hot spots
of London or New York, but in many ways it's more enjoyable than
what you find in either of those cities. The scene is markedly less pre-
tentious than other cosmopolitan hubs, with the emphasis on dancing
rather than preening. The crowds are enthusiastic and highly knowledgeable. And most weekends bring more than one world-renowned DJ
to town.

⚠ Dance clubs in Tōkyō are ephemeral ventures, disappearing fairly regularly only to open again with new identities, stranger names, and different selling points, although the money behind them is usually the same. Even those listed here come with no guarantee they'll be around when you arrive, but if the club you seek is gone, a new and better one may have opened up in its place.

★ **Ageha.** This massive bay-side venue has the city's best sound system and most diverse musical lineup. The cavernous Arena hosts well-known house and techno DJs, the bar plays hip-hop, a summer-only swimming-pool area has everything from reggae to break beats, and inside a chill-out tent there's usually ambient or trance music. Because of its far-flung location and enormous capacity, Ageha can be either a throbbing party or an embarrassingly empty hall, depending on the caliber of the DJ. Free buses to Ageha depart every half hour between 11 PM and 4:30 AM from the Shibuya police station on Roppongi-dōri, a three-minute walk from Shibuya Station (there are also return buses every half hour from 11:30 PM to 5 AM). ✉ *2–2–10 Shin-Kiba, Kotō-ku* ☎ *03/5534–1515* ⊕ *www.ageha.com* 🖾 *Around ¥3,500* ◷ *10 PM–early morning* Ⓜ *Yūraku-chō subway line, Shin-Kiba Station.*

La Fabrique. A Continental crowd gathers at the late-night parties at this small, dressy, French restaurant-cum-club in Shibuya's Zero Gate complex. The music is predominantly house. ✉ *B1F, 16–9 Udagawachō, Shibuya-ku* ☎ *03/5428–5100* 🖾 *¥3,000–¥3,500* ◷ *Daily 11 AM–5 AM* Ⓜ *JR Yamanote Line, Ginza and Hanzō-mon subway lines, Shibuya Station (Hachiko Exit for JR and Ginza, Exit 6 for Hanzō-mon).*

Lexington Queen. To Tōkyō's hipster club kids, Lexington Queen is something of an embarrassment: the music hasn't really changed since the place opened in 1980. But to visiting movie stars, fashion models, and other members of the international jet set, the Lex is the place to party hard and go wild—and be seen doing it. ✉ *3–13–14 Roppongi, Minato-ku* ☎ *03/ 3401–1661* ⊕ *www.lexingtonqueen.com* 🖾 *Admission varies* ◷ *Daily 8 PM–5 AM* Ⓜ *Hibiya and Ōedo subway lines, Roppongi Station (Exit 5); Namboku subway line, Roppongi-Itchōme Station (Exit 1).*

911. A great central-Roppongi location and no cover charge make 911 popular as both an early- and late-night singles' spot. Across from the Roi Building, this is a good starting point for a night of barhopping. ✉ *3–14–12 Roppongi, B1F, Minato-ku* ☎ *03/5772–8882* 🖾 *No cover charge* ◷ *Daily 6 PM–6 AM* Ⓜ *Hibiya and Ōedo subway lines, Roppongi Station (Exit 3).*

Ruby Room. The Ruby Room is an expat favorite that plays music of all descriptions. The manager's business card reads "Tasty beats, tough drinks, terrible service," and most patrons would agree. But it omits the main reason people congregate here: the staffers might not mix the best cocktails, but they know how to throw a party. ✉ *2–4 Maruyama-chō, Shibuya-ku* ☎ *03/3461–8806* 🖾 *Admission varies* ◷ *Daily 9 PM–5 AM* Ⓜ *JR Yamanote Line, Ginza and Hanzō-mon subway lines, Shibuya Station (Hachiko Exit for JR and Ginza, Exit 3A for Hanzō-mon).*

Space Lab Yellow. With more than a decade under its belt, this club is the granddaddy of the capital's dance scene. The club—popularly known as just "Yellow"—has been knocked from its perch as young clubbers' venue of choice by Womb, but still regularly draws A-list house DJs (Fatboy Slim, François K, Gilles Peterson) who pack the dancers in like sardines. ☒ *1–10–11 Nishi-Azabu, Minato-ku* ☏ *03/3479–0690* ⊕ *www.club-yellow.com* ✉ *¥3,500–¥4,000* ⊙ *10 PM–early morning* Ⓜ *Chiyoda subway line, Nogizaka Station (Exit 5); Hibiya and Ōedo subway lines, Roppongi Station (Exit 2).*

★ **Womb.** Well-known techno and break-beat DJs make a point of stopping by this Shibuya überclub on their way through town. The turntable talent, including the likes of Danny Howells and Richie Hawtin, and four floors of dance and lounge space make Womb Tōkyō's most consistently rewarding club experience. ☒ *2–16 Maruyama-chō, Shibuya-ku* ☏ *03/5459–0039* ⊕ *www.womb.co.jp* ✉ *Around ¥3,500* ⊙ *Daily 10 PM–early morning* Ⓜ *JR Yamanote Line, Ginza and Hanzō-mon subway lines, Shibuya Station (Hachiko Exit for JR and Ginza, Exit 3A for Hanzō-mon).*

Izakaya

Izakaya (literally "drinking places") are Japanese pubs that can be found on just about every block in Tōkyō. If you're in the mood for elegant decor and sedate surroundings, look elsewhere; these drinking dens are often noisy, bright, and smoky. But for a taste of authentic Japanese-style socializing, a visit to an izakaya is a must—this is where young people start their nights out, office workers gather on their way home, and students take a break to grab a cheap meal and a drink.

Typically, izakaya have a full lineup of cocktails, a good selection of sake, draft beer, and lots of cheap, greasy Japanese and Western food; rarely does anything cost more than ¥1,000. Picture menus make ordering easy, and because most cocktails retain their Western names, communicating drink preferences shouldn't be too difficult.

Amataro. The Center Gai location of this ubiquitous izakaya chain impresses with a huge, dimly lighted interior. On weekends the crowd is young, boisterous, and fun. ☒ *2–3F Tōkyō Kaikan Bldg., 33–1 Udagawachō, Shibuya-ku* ☏ *03/5784–4660* ⊙ *Daily 5 PM–5 AM* Ⓜ *JR Yamanote Line, Ginza and Hanzō-mon subway lines, Shibuya Station (Hachiko Exit for JR and Ginza, Exit 3A for Hanzō-mon).*

Takara. This high-class izakaya in the sumptuous Tōkyō International Forum is a favorite with foreigners because of its English-language menu and extensive sake list. ☒ *B1, 3–5–1 Marunouchi, Chiyoda-ku* ☏ *03/5223–9888* ⊙ *Weekdays 11:30–2:30 and 5–11, weekends 11:30–3:30 and 5–10* Ⓜ *Yūraku-chō subway line, Yūraku-chō Station (Exit A-4B).*

Watami. One of Tōkyō's big izakaya chains—with a half-dozen branches in the youth entertainment district of Shibuya alone—Watami is popular for its seriously inexpensive menu. Seating at this location ranges from a communal island bar to Western-style tables to more private areas. ⊠ *Satose Bldg., 4F, 13–8 Udagawachō, Shibuya-ku* ☎ *03/6415–6516* ◷ *Sun.–Thurs. 5 PM–3 AM, Fri.–Sat. 5 PM–5 AM* Ⓜ *JR Yamanote Line, Ginza and Hanzō-mon subway lines, Shibuya Station (Hachiko Exit for JR and Ginza, Exit 6 for Hanzō-mon).*

Jazz Clubs

Tōkyō has one of the best jazz scenes in Asia. The clubs here attract world-class performers and innovative local acts. On any given night you can choose from more than 20 local live acts, but it'll cost you. Entrance fees start at ¥2,500 for the tiny venues and can be more than five times that for a famous act. The weekly English-language magazine *Metropolis* has listings for the major clubs. For information on jazz events at small venues, a visit to the record shop **Disk Union** (⊠ 3–31–2 Shinjuku, Shinjuku-ku ☎ 03/5379–3551 Ⓜ Marunouchi subway line, Shinjuku-san-chōme Station (Exit A1) is essential. The store has flyers (sometimes in English) for smaller gigs, and the staff can make recommendations.

Blue Note Tōkyō. The Blue Note sees everyone from the Count Basie Orchestra to Herbie Hancock perform to packed houses. The "Sunday Special" series showcases fresh Japanese talent. Prices here are typically high; expect to pay upwards of ¥12,000 to see major acts, and be prepared for shorter sets than you would get at a club in the United States or Europe. ⊠ *6–3–16 Minami-Aoyama, Minato-ku* ☎ *03/5485–0088* ◷ *Shows usually Mon.–Sat. at 7 and 9:30, Sun. at 6:30 and 9* ⊕ *www.bluenote. co.jp* Ⓜ *Chiyoda, Ginza, and Hanzō-mon subway lines, Omotesandō Station (Exit A3).*

Hot House. This could very well be the world's smallest jazz club. An evening here is like listening to live jazz in your living room with five or six other jazz lovers on your sofa. It's so small, in fact, that you can't get through the front door once the pianist is seated, so don't show up late. Live acts are trios at most, with no space for drums or amplifiers. ⊠ *B1 Liberal Takadanobaba, 2–14–8 Takadanobaba, Shinjuku-ku* ☎ *03/3367–1233* ◷ *Daily 8:30 PM–early morning* Ⓜ *JR Takadanobaba Station (Waseda Exit).*

Intro. This small basement bar features one of the best jazz experiences in Tōkyō: a Saturday "jam session" that stretches until 5 AM (¥1,000 entry fee). Other nights of the week occasionally bring unannounced live sets by musicians just dropping by, but usually it's the owner's extensive vinyl and CD collection that the regulars are listening to. Simple Japanese and Western food is available. ⊠ *B1, NT Bldg., 2–14–8 Takadanobaba, Shinjuku-ku* ☎ *03/3200–4396* ◷ *Sun.–Thurs. 6:30 PM–midnight; Fri. 6:30 PM–1 AM; Sat. 5 PM–5 AM* Ⓜ *JR Takadanobaba Station (Waseda Exit).*

Shinjuku Pit Inn. Most major jazz musicians have played at least once in this classic Tōkyō club. The veteran Shinjuku Pit stages mostly mainstream fare with the odd foray into the avant-garde. Afternoon admission is ¥1,300 weekdays, ¥2,500 weekends; evening entry is typically ¥3,000. Better-known local acts are often a little more. ⊠ *B1 Accord*

CLOSE UP

All That Tōkyō Jazz

THE TŌKYŌ JAZZ SCENE IS ONE OF the world's best, far surpassing that of Paris and New York with its number of venues playing traditional, swing, bossa nova, R & B, and free jazz. Though popular in Japan before World War II, jazz really took hold of the city after U.S. forces introduced Charlie Parker and Thelonius Monk in the late 1940s. The genre had been banned in wartime Japan as an American vice, but even at the height of the war, fans were able to listen to their favorite artists on Voice of America radio. In the 1960s Japan experienced a boom in all areas of the arts, and jazz was no exception. Since then, the Japanese scene has steadily bloomed, with several local stars—such as Sadao Watanabe in the 1960s and contemporary favorites Keiko Lee and Hiromi Uehara—gaining global attention.

Today there are more than 120 bars and clubs that host live music, plus hundreds that play recorded jazz. Shinjuku, Takadanobaba, and Kichijōji are the city's jazz enclaves. Famous international acts regularly appear at big-name clubs such as the Blue Note, but the smaller, lesser-known joints usually have more atmosphere. With such a large jazz scene, there's an incredible diversity to enjoy, from Louis Armstrong tribute acts to fully improvised free jazz—sometimes on successive nights at the same venue, so check the schedules before you go.

If you time your visit right, you can listen to great jazz at one of the city's more than 20 annual festivals dedicated to this adopted musical form. The festivals vary in size and coverage, but two to check out are the Tōkyō Jazz Festival and the Asagaya Jazz Street Festival.

In September, the **Tōkyō Jazz Festival** (☎ 03/5777-8600 ⊕ www.tokyo-jazz. com) takes over the Tōkyō International Forum in Marunouchi. Past acts have included Chick Corea, Dave Koz, Hiromi Uehara, and Sadao Watanabe.

The **Asagaya Festival** (☎ 03/5305-5075), held the last weekend of October, is a predominantly mainstream affair, with venues ranging from a Shinto shrine to a Lutheran church (most venues are within walking distance of Asagaya Station). Look for festival staff at the station to help guide you (note that they may not speak English, however). Previous headliners have included the Mike Price Jazz Quintet and vocalist Masamichi Yanō. The festival gets crowded, so come early to ensure entry.

—James Catchpole

Shinjuku Bldg., 2–12–4 Shinjuku, Shinjuku-ku ☎ 03/3354–2024 ⊙ Daily, hrs vary Ⓜ Marunouchi subway line, Shinjuku-san-chōme Station.

Fodor'sChoice ★ **Sweet Basil 139.** An upscale jazz club near Roppongi Crossing, Sweet Basil 139 (no relation to the famous New York Sweet Basil) is renowned for local and international acts that run the musical gamut from smooth jazz and fusion to classical. A large, formal dining area serves Italian dishes that are as good as the jazz, making this spot an excellent choice for a complete night out. With a spacious interior and standing room for 500 on the main floor, this is one of the largest and most accessible jazz bars in town. Prices range from ¥2,857 to ¥12,000 depending on who's headlining. ✉ *6–7–11 Roppongi, Minato-ku* ☎ *03/5474–0139* ⊕ *http://stb139.co.jp* ☺ *Mon.–Sat. 6–11; shows at 8* Ⓜ *Hibiya and Ōedo subway lines, Roppongi Station (Exit 3).*

Karaoke

In buttoned-down, socially conservative Japan, karaoke is one of the pressure valves. Employees, employers, husbands, wives, teenage romancers, and good friends all drop their guard when there's a mike in hand. The phenomenon started in the 1970s when cabaret singer Daisuke Inoue made a coin-operated machine that played his songs on tape so that his fans could sing along. Unfortunately for Inoue, he neglected to patent his creation, thereby failing to cash in as karaoke became one of Japan's favorite pastimes. Nowadays it's the likely finale of any office outing, a cheap daytime activity for teens, and a surprisingly popular destination for dates.

Unlike most karaoke bars in the United States, in Japan the singing usually takes place in the seclusion of private rooms that can accommodate groups. Basic hourly charges vary but are usually less than ¥1,000. Most establishments have a large selection of English songs, stay open late, and serve inexpensive food and drink, which you order via a telephone on the wall. Finding a venue around one of the major entertainment hubs is easy—there will be plenty of young touts eager to escort you to their employer. And unlike most other touts in the city, you won't end up broke by following them.

Big Echo. One of Tōkyō's largest karaoke chains, Big Echo has dozens of locations throughout the city. Cheap hourly rates and late closing times make it popular with youngsters. The Roppongi branch is spread over three floors. ✉ *7–14–12 Roppongi, Minato-ku* ☎ *03/5770–7700* 🍴 *¥500–¥600 per hr* ☺ *Daily 6 PM–5 AM* Ⓜ *Hibiya and Ōedo subway lines, Roppongi Station (Exit 4).*

★ **Lovenet.** Despite the misleading erotic name, Lovenet is actually the fanciest karaoke box in town. Luxury theme rooms of all descriptions create a fun and classy setting for your dulcet warbling. Mediterranean and Japanese food is served. ✉ *7–14–4 Roppongi, Minato-ku* ☎ *03/5771–5511* 🍴 *From ¥2,000 per hr* ☺ *Daily 6 PM–5 AM* ⊕ *www.lovenet-jp.com* Ⓜ *Hibiya and Ōedo subway lines, Roppongi Station (Exit 4A).*

Pasela. This 10-story entertainment complex on the main Roppongi drag of Gaien-Higashi-dōri has seven floors of karaoke rooms with more than 10,000 foreign-song titles. A Mexican-theme bar and a restaurant are also on-site. ✉ *5–16–3 Roppongi, Minato-ku* ☎ *0120/911–086* 🍴 *¥500 per hr* ☺ *Daily 5 PM–10 AM* Ⓜ *Hibiya and Ōedo subway lines, Roppongi Station (Exit 3).*

Shidax. The Shidax chain's corporate headquarters—in an excellent Shibuya location, across from Tower Records—has 130 private karaoke rooms, a café, and a restaurant. ✉ *1–12–13 Jinnan, Shibuya-ku* ☎ *03/ 5784–8881* 💴*¥760 per hr* 🕐 *Daily 11 AM–8 AM* Ⓜ *JR, Ginza and Hanzō- mon subway lines, Shibuya Station (Exit 6).*

Smash Hits. If karaoke just isn't karaoke to you without drunken strangers to sing to, Smash Hits has the answer. An expat favorite, it offers thousands of English songs and a central performance stage. The cover charge gets you two drinks and no time limit. ✉ *5–2–26 Hiro-o, Shibuya-ku* ☎ *03/3444–0432* 💴 *¥3,000* 🕐 *Mon.–Sat. 7 PM–3 AM* 🌐 *www.smashhits.jp* Ⓜ *Hibiya Line, Hiro-o Station.*

Live Houses

Tōkyō has numerous small music clubs known as "live houses." These basement spots range from the very basic to miniclub venues, and they showcase the best emerging talent on the local scene. Many of the best live houses can be found in the Kichijōji, Kōenji, and Nakano areas, although they are tucked away in basements citywide. One of the great things about the live house scene is the variety: a single "amateur night" set can include everything from experimental ethnic dance to thrash rock. Cover charges vary depending on who's performing but are typically ¥3,000–¥5,000 ($25-$41).

Manda-la. Relaxed and intimate, this local favorite in Kichijōji attracts an eclectic group of performers. Cover charges range from ¥1,800 to ¥4,000. ✉*2–8–6 Kichijōji-Minami-cho, Musashino-shi* ☎*0422/42–1579* 🕐 *6:30 PM–varying closing times* Ⓜ *Keiō Inokashira private rail line, JR Chūō and JR Sōbu lines, Kichijōji Station (Kōen-guchi/Park Exit, on Suehiro-dōri).*

Milk. One of the city's larger live houses—it can handle 400 music fans—has three levels and more of a clublike vibe than other venues, right down to the snooty staff. Ticket prices are in the ¥2,500–¥3,000 range. ✉ *1–13–3 Nishi-Ebisu, Shibuya-ku* ☎ *03/5458–2826* 🕐 *Weekends 9 PM–early morning* Ⓜ *JR Yamanote Line and Hibiya subway line, Ebisu Station (Nishi-guchi/West Exit).*

Showboat. A small, basic venue that's been going strong for more than a decade, Showboat attracts both amateur and semiprofessional performers. Ticket prices vary by act but are typically around ¥2,000 and often include one drink. ✉ *B1 Oak Bldg. Kōenji, 3–17–2 Kita Kōenji, Suginami-ku* ☎ *03/3337–5745* 🕐 *Daily 6 PM–early morning* Ⓜ *JR Sōbu and JR Chūō lines, Kōenji Station (Kita-guchi/North Exit).*

Drinks with a View

Bellovisto. This 40th-floor lounge bar atop the Cerulean Tower draws a mixed crowd of tourists and local couples, who come for the grand views out over Shibuya and beyond. Drinks start at ¥1,000. ✉ *26–1 Sakura- gaoka-chō, Shibuya-ku* ☎ *03/3476–3398* 🕐 *Daily 4 PM–midnight* Ⓜ *JR, Ginza, and Hanzō-mon subway lines, Shibuya Station (Minami-guchi/ South Exit for JR and Ginza, Exit 8 for Hanzō-mon).*

Loof. Loof (as in "roof") may be the least high class of Tōkyō's bars with a view, but in summer it's one of the best. The bar sits atop a nine-story Shibuya building and serves an impressive range of world beers. But the real treat is the private table perched above the regular bar. It doesn't have the superlative views of a hotel high-rise bar, but there aren't many other places where you can drink at a private, open-air, rooftop table. Drinks start at ¥800. ⊠ *1–22–12 Dogenzaka, Shibuya-ku* ☏ *03/ 3770–0008* ☉ *Mon.–Sat. 6 PM–4 AM, Sun. 6 PM–1 AM* Ⓜ *JR, Ginza and Hanzō-mon subway lines, Shibuya Station (Hachiko Exit).*

★ **New York Bar.** Even before *Lost in Translation* introduced the Park Hyatt's signature lounge to filmgoers worldwide, New York Bar was a local Tōkyō favorite. All the style you would expect of one of the city's top hotels combined with superior views of Shinjuku's skyscrapers and neon-lighted streets make this one of the city's premier nighttime venues. The quality of the jazz on offer equals that of the view. Drinks start at ¥800, and there's a cover charge of ¥2,000 after 8 PM (7 PM on Sunday). ⊠ *Park Hyatt Hotel 52F, 3–7–1–2 Nishi-Shinjuku, Shinjuku-ku* ☏ *03/5322–1234* ☉ *Sun.–Wed. 5 PM–midnight, Thurs.–Sat. 5 PM–1 AM* Ⓜ *JR Shinjuku Station (Nishi-guchi/West Exit).*

Top of Akasaka. On the 40th floor of the Akasaka Prince Hotel, you can enjoy some of the finest views of Tōkyō. If you can time your visit for dusk, the price of one drink gets you two views—the daylight sprawl of buildings and the twinkling lights of evening. Drinks start at ¥1,000, and there's a table charge of ¥800 per person. ⊠ *Akasaka Prince, 1–2 Kioi-chō, Chiyoda-ku* ☏ *03/3234–1111* ☉ *Mon.–Sat. 5 PM–1 AM, Sun. 5 PM–11 PM* Ⓜ *Ginza and Marunouchi subway lines, Akasaka-mitsuke Station (Exit D).*

Shopping

WORD OF MOUTH

"Visit Tokyu Hands, the most well-stocked department store in the world, where you'll find things you didn't know you needed or existed. Or the chopsticks emporium in Ginza, a narrow shop stuffed to the gills with chopsticks of every variety."
—hobbes

"Visit the shops on Kappabashi Dori that sell the plastic food you see in restaurant windows."
—Lindsey

Updated by
Brett Bull

HORROR STORIES ABOUND ABOUT PRICES IN JAPAN —and some of them are true. Yes, a cup of coffee can cost $10, if you pick the wrong coffee shop. A gift-wrapped melon from a department-store gourmet counter can cost $150. And a taxi ride from the airport to central Tōkyō does cost about $200. But most people take the convenient airport train for $9, and if you shop around, you can find plenty of gifts and souvenirs at fair prices.

You didn't fly all the way to Tōkyō to buy European designer clothing, so shop for items that are Japanese-made for Japanese people and sold in stores that don't cater to tourists. This city is Japan's showcase. The crazy clothing styles, obscure electronics, and new games found here are capable of setting trends for the rest of the country—and perhaps the rest of Asia.

Also, don't pass up the chance to purchase Japanese crafts. Color, balance of form, and superb workmanship make these items exquisite and well worth the price you'll pay. Some can be quite expensive; for example, Japanese lacquerware carries a hefty price tag. But if you like the shiny boxes, bowls, cups, and trays and consider that quality lacquerware is made to last a lifetime, the cost is justified.

The Japanese approach to shopping can be feverish; on the weekends, some of the hipper, youth-oriented stores will have lines that wind down the street as kids wait patiently to pick up the latest trend. But shopping here can also be an exercise in elegance and refinement. Note the care taken with items after you purchase them, especially in department stores and boutiques. Goods will be wrapped, wrapped again, bagged, and sealed. Sure, the packaging can be excessive—does anybody really need three plastic bags for one croissant?—but such a focus on presentation has deep roots in Japanese culture.

This focus on presentation also influences salespeople who are invariably helpful and polite. In the larger stores they greet you with a bow when you arrive, and many of them speak enough English to help you find what you're looking for. There's a saying in Japan: *o-kyaku-sama wa kami-sama*, "the customer is a god"—and since the competition for your business is fierce, people do take it to heart.

Japan has been slow to embrace the use of credit cards, and even though plastic is now accepted at big retailers, some smaller shops only take cash. So when you go souvenir hunting, be prepared with a decent amount of cash; Tōkyō's low crime rates make this a low-risk proposition. The dishonor associated with theft is so strong, in fact, that it's considered bad form to conspicuously count change in front of cashiers.

Japan has an across-the-board 5% value-added tax (V.A.T.) imposed on luxury goods as well as on restaurant and hotel bills. This tax can be avoided at some duty-free shops in the city (don't forget to bring your passport). It's also waived in the duty-free shops at the international airports, but because these places tend to have higher profit margins, your tax savings there are likely to be offset by the higher markups.

Stores in Tōkyō generally open at 10 or 11 AM and close at 8 or 9 PM.

Shopping Districts

Akihabara & Jimbō-chō

Akihabara was at one time the only place Tōkyōites would go to buy cutting-edge electronic gadgets, but the area has lost its aura of exclusivity thanks to the Internet and the big discount chains that have sprung up around the city. Still, for its sheer variety of products and foreigner-friendliness, Akihabara has the newcomers beat—and a visit remains essential to any Tōkyō shopping spree. Salesclerks speak decent English at most of the major shops (and many of the smaller ones), and the big chains offer duty-free and export items. Be sure to poke around the backstreets for smaller stores that sell used and unusual electronic goods. The area has also become the center of the *otaku* (nerd) boom, with loads of shops offering enough video games and *manga* (sophisticated comic books) to satisfy even the most fastidious geek. West of Akihabara, in the used-bookstore district of Jimbō-chō, you'll find pretty much whatever you're looking for in dictionaries and art books, rare and out-of-print editions (Western and Japanese), and prints. Ⓜ *For Akihabara: JR Yamanote, Keihin Tōhoku and Sōbu lines, Akihabara Station (Electric Town Exit); Hibiya subway line, Akihabara Station. For Jimbō-chō: Hanzō-mon, Shinjuku, and Mita subway lines, Jimbō-chō Station.*

Aoyama & Omotesandō

You can find boutiques by many of the leading Japanese and Western designers in Aoyama, as well as elegant, but pricey, antiques shops on Kottō-dōri. Aoyama tends to be a showcase not merely of high fashion but also of the latest concepts in commercial architecture and interior design. The centerpiece of Omotesandō (a short stroll from Aoyama) is the long, wide avenue running from Aoyama-dōri to Meiji Jingū. Known as the Champs-Elysées of Tōkyō, the sidewalks are lined with cafés and designer boutiques, both foreign and domestic. There are also several antiques and souvenir shops here. Omotesandō is perfect for browsing, window-shopping, and lingering over a café au lait before strolling to your next destination. Ⓜ *Chiyoda, Ginza, and Hanzō-mon subway lines, Omotesandō Station (Exits A4, A5, B1, B2, and B3).*

Asakusa

While sightseeing in this area, take time to stroll through its arcades. Many of the goods sold here are the kinds of souvenirs you can find in any tourist trap, but look a little harder and you can find small back-street shops that have been making beautiful wooden combs, delicate fans, and other items of fine traditional craftsmanship for generations. Also here are the cookware shops of Kappabashi, where you can load up on everything from sushi knives to plastic lobsters. Ⓜ *Asakusa subway line, Asakusa Station (Kaminari-mon Exit); Ginza subway line, Asakusa Station (Exit 1) and Tawara-machi Station (Exit 3).*

Daikanyama

Unleash your inner fashionista in Daikanyama. Wedged between Shibuya and Ebisu, this area is a boutique heaven: shelves of funky shoes, stacks of retro t-shirts, and assortments of skate-punk wear. Ⓜ *Tōkyū Tōyoko Line, Daikanyama Station.*

Ginza

This world-renowned entertainment and shopping district dates back to the Edo period (1603–1868), when it consisted of long, willow-lined avenues. The willows have long since gone, and the streets are now lined with department stores and boutiques. The exclusive shops in this area—including flagship stores for major jewelers like Tiffany & Co., Harry Winston, and Mikimoto—sell quality merchandise at high prices. On Sundays the main strip of Chuo-dōri is closed to car traffic and umbrella-covered tables dot the pavement; it's a great place for shoppers to rest their weary feet. Ⓜ *Marunouchi, Ginza, and Hibiya subway lines, Ginza Station (Exits A1–A10); Yūraku-chō subway line, Ginza Itchōme Station; JR Yamanote Line, Yūraku-chō Station.*

Harajuku

The average shopper in Harajuku is under 20; a substantial percentage is under 16. Most stores focus on moderately priced clothing and accessories, with a lot of kitsch mixed in, but there are also several upscale fashion houses in the area—and more on the way. This shopping and residential area extends southeast from Harajuku Station along both sides of Omotesandō and Meiji-dōri; the shops that target the youngest consumers concentrate especially on the narrow street called Takeshita-dōri. Tōkyō's most exciting neighborhood for youth fashion and design lies along the promenade known as Kyū Shibuya-gawa Hodō, commonly referred to as Cat Street. Ⓜ *Chiyoda subway line, Meiji Jingū-mae Station (Exits 1–5); JR Yamanote Line, Harajuku Station.*

Jiyūgaoka
Jiyūgaoka is located at the edge of the well-to-do Meguro Ward. Big chain stores are in abundance here, but the real attractions are the boutiques offering unique bedding, crockery, and furniture items. Ⓜ *Tōkyū Tōyoko line or Oimachi lines, Jiyūgaoka Station.*

Shibuya
This is primarily an entertainment and retail district geared toward teenagers and young adults. The shopping scene in Shibuya caters to these groups with many reasonably priced smaller shops and a few department stores that are casual yet chic. Ⓜ *JR Yamanote Line; Tōkyū and Keiō lines; Ginza and Hanzō-mon subway lines, Shibuya Station (Nishi-guchi/West Exit for JR, Exits 3–8 for subway lines).*

Shimokitazawa
Arguably Tokyo's hippie bastion, the twisting streets and alleyways of Shimokitazawa boast used-clothing shops, record stores, and knick-knack outlets that generally offer low prices. Fans of anime or manga, and their character good offshoots, will be glad that neither is in short supply. Just follow the scent of patchouli oil from the station. Ⓜ *Keiō Inokashira or Odakyū lines, Shimokitazawa Station.*

Shinjuku
Shinjuku is not without its honky-tonk and sleaze, but it also has some of the city's most popular department stores. The shopping crowd is a mix of Tōkyō youth and office ladies. Surrounding the station are several discount electronics and home-appliance outlets. Ⓜ *JR Yamanote Line; Odakyū and Keiō lines; Marunouchi, Shinjuku, and Ōedo subway lines, Shinjuku Station.*

Tsukiji
Best known for its daily fish-market auctions, Tsukiji also has a warren of streets that carry useful, everyday items that serve as a window onto the lives of the Japanese. This is a fascinating area to poke around after seeing the fish auction and before stopping in the neighborhood for a fresh-as-can-be sushi lunch. Ⓜ *Ōedo subway line, Tsukiji-shijō Station (Exit A1); Hibiya subway line, Tsukiji Station (Exit 1).*

Shopping Streets & Arcades

Most Japanese villages have pedestrian shopping streets known as *shotengai,* and Tōkyō, a big city made up of smaller neighborhoods, is no different. But you won't find big-name retailers like pharmacies and grocery stores in these areas—Tōkyō's shotengai are thick with boutiques, accessory shops, and cafés. Just like their surrounding neighborhoods, these streets can be classy, trendy, or a bit shabby.

Ame-ya Yoko-chō Market. Everything from fresh fish to cheap import clothing is for sale on the bustling side streets between Okachi-machi and

Ueno stations. In the days leading up to New Years, the area turns into mosh-pit mayhem as shoppers fight for fish and snacks to serve over the holidays. The name of the market is often shortened to Ameyoko. Most shops and stalls are open daily 10–7. ☒ *Ueno 4-chōme, Taitō-ku* Ⓜ *JR Ueno Station (Hirokō-ji Exit), JR Okachi-machi Station (Exit A7).*

International Shopping Arcade. A somewhat ragtag collection of shops in Hibiya, this arcade holds a range of goods, including cameras, electronics, pearls, and kimonos. The shops are duty-free, and most of the sales staff speaks decent English. If you listen carefully you'll hear the rumble of cars passing above on the freeway that is the roof of the building. ☒ *1–7–23 Uchisaiwai-chō, Chiyoda-ku* Ⓜ *Chiyoda and Hibiya subway lines, Hibiya Station (Exit A13).*

Kyū Shibuya-gawa Hodō. With its avant-garde crafts stores, funky T-shirt shops, and hipster boutiques, this pedestrian strip serves as a showcase for Japan's au courant designers and artisans. Cat Street is the place to experience bohemian Tōkyō in all its exuberance. ☒ *Between Jingū-mae 3-chōme and Jingū-mae 6-chōme, Shibuya-ku* Ⓜ *Chiyoda subway line, Meiji Jingū-mae Station (Exits 4 and 5).*

Nishi-Sandō. Kimono and *yukata* (cotton kimono) fabrics, traditional accessories, swords, and festival costumes at very reasonable prices are all for sale at this Asakusa arcade. It runs east of the area's movie theaters, between Rok-ku and the Sensō-ji complex. ☒ *Asakusa 2-chōme, Taitō-ku* Ⓜ *Ginza subway line, Asakusa Station (Exit 1).*

Takeshita-dōri. Teenybopper fashion is all the rage along this Harajuku mainstay, where crowds of high school kids look for the newest addition to their ever-changing, outrageous wardrobes. ☒ *Jingū-mae 1-chōme Shibuya-ku* Ⓜ *JR Harajuku Station (Takeshita-dōri Exit).*

Malls & Shopping Centers

Most of these self-contained retail zones carry both foreign and Japanese brands and, like the city's department stores, house cafés, bars, and restaurants. If you don't have the time or energy to dash about Tōkyō in search of the perfect gifts, consider dropping by one of these shopping centers, where you can find a wide selection of merchandise. Most are used to dealing with foreigners.

★ **Axis.** Classy and cutting-edge housewares, fabrics, and ceramics are sold at this multistory design center on the main Roppongi drag of Gaien-Higashi-dōri. Living Motif is a home-furnishings shop with exquisite foreign and Japanese goods. Savoir Vivre has an excellent selection of ceramics. The small Yoshikin sells its own brand of professional-grade cutlery. ☒ *5–17–1 Roppongi, Minato-ku* ☎ *03/3587–2781* ⊙ *Most shops Mon.–Sat. 11–7* Ⓜ *Hibiya and Ōedo subway lines, Roppongi Station (Exit 3); Namboku subway line, Roppongi Itchōme Station (Exit 1).*

Coredo. Unlike other big stores in the Ginza and Nihombashi areas, this sparkling mall has a contemporary feel thanks to an open layout and extensive use of glass and wood. Housewares, toys, and fashion can all be found here. ☒ *1–4–1 Nihombashi, Chūō-ku* ☎ *03/3272–4939*

CLOSE UP

Day Spa Escape: May's Garden Spa

IT'S ALL ABOUT PERSONALIZED service at May's, which is located on the third floor of the Roppongi Hills complex. Stone flooring greets visitors in the reception, where just beyond is the waiting room filled with sofas, potted trees, and fashion magazines to flip through while you wait. Herbs used in the foot bath are from the facility's own herb gardens right ourside the windows and much of the nail and hair work is done from seats with views of the Roppongi Hills complex. The full facial treatment includes a one-on-one face consultation with a professional esthetician, as well as a full body immersion in a hydro-jet bath of oxygen foam for some serious cleansing of your pores. Enzyme packs will then be applied to bring the glow back to you complexion, and maybe even peel back a few years. A gentle facial massage completes the service.

Though the package does include a few back rubs, full body work-overs are also available, as are hair, nail, and bridal prep.

Services: Facial treatments, body treatments, waxing, aroma massage, and aroma and germanium baths.

Package Picks: Facial treatments range from ¥13,650 to ¥24,150, depending on the treatment. Body treatments are 120 min ¥28,350; 180 min ¥38,850; 240 min ¥49,350. Waxing ranges from ¥1,050 to ¥16,800, depending on the time and the body part.

General Info: (✉ 6-4-1 Roppongi, Minato-ku ☎ 03/3408-1613 ⊕ www. hollywoodsalon.co.jp ⊙ Daily 9-7 Ⓜ Hibiya and Ōedo subway lines, Roppongi Station (Roppongi Hills Exit).

5

⊙ *Mon.–Sat. 11–9, Sun. 11–8* Ⓜ *Ginza, Tōzai, and Asakusa subway lines, Nihombashi Station (Exit B10).*

Glassarea. Virtually defining Aoyama elegance is this cobblestone shopping center, which draws well-heeled Aoyama housewives to its boutiques, restaurants, and housewares shops. ✉ *5-4-41 Minami-Aoyama, Minato-ku* ☎ *03/5778–4450* ⊙ *Most shops daily 11–8* Ⓜ *Ginza, Chiyoda, and Hanzō-mon subway lines, Omotesandō Station (Exit B1).*

Marunouchi Building. Opened in 2003, this 37-story shopping, office, and dining complex has brought some much-needed retail dazzle to the area between Tōkyō Station and the Imperial Palace. The ground-floor Beams shop is part of the well-respected Tōkyō fashion chain, and the second-floor Aquagirl boutique sells trendy clothes for women. ✉ *2-4-1 Marunouchi, Chiyoda-ku* ☎ *03/5218–5100* ⊙ *Mon.–Sat. 11–9, Sun. 11–8* Ⓜ *Marunouchi subway line, Tōkyō Station (Marunouchi Building Exit); JR Yamanote Line, Tōkyō Station (Marunouchi Minamiguchi/South Exit).*

Omotesandō Hills. Architect Tadao Ando's latest adventure in concrete is Tōkyō's newest monument to shopping. The six wedge-shaped floors include some brand-name heavy hitters (Yves Saint Laurent and Harry Winston) and a wide range of smaller stores whose shelves showcase high-end shoes and bags. ✉ *4–12–10 Jingū-mae, Shibuya-ku* ☎ *03/ 3497–0293* ◷ *Daily 11–8* Ⓜ *Hanzō-mon, Ginza, and Chiyoda subway lines, Omotesandō Station (Exit A2).*

Roppongi Hills. You could easily spend a whole day exploring the retail areas of Tōkyō's newest minicity, opened in 2003. The shops here emphasize eye-catching design and chi-chi brands. Finding a particular shop, however, can be a hassle given the building's Escher-like layout. ✉ *6–10–1 Roppongi, Minato-ku* ☎ *03/6406–6000* ◷ *Most shops daily 11–8* Ⓜ *Hibiya and Ōedo subway lines, Roppongi Station (Roppongi Hills Exit).*

Shibuya 109. This nine-floor outlet is a teenage girl's dream. It's filled with small stores whose merchandise scream kitsch and trend. Many weekend afternoons will see dance groups and fashion shows at the first-floor entrance. ✉ *2–29–1 Dōgenzaka, Shibuya-ku* ☎ *03/3477–5111* ◷ *Daily 10–9* Ⓜ *JR Yamanote Line; Ginza and Hanzō-mon subway lines: Shibuya Station (Hachiko Exit for JR, Exit 3 for subway lines).*

Department Stores

Most Japanese *depāto* (department stores) are parts of conglomerates that include railways, real estate, and leisure industries. The stores themselves commonly have travel agencies, theaters, and art galleries on the premises, as well as reasonably priced and strategically placed restaurants and cafés.

A visit to a Japanese department store is not merely a shopping excursion—it's a lesson in Japanese culture. Plan to arrive just before it opens: promptly on the hour, immaculately groomed young women face the customers from inside, bow ceremoniously, and unlock the doors. As you walk through the store, all the sales assistants will be standing at attention, in postures of nearly reverent welcome. Notice the uniform angle of incline: many stores have training sessions to teach their new employees the precise and proper degree at which to bend from the waist.

On the top floor of many department stores you'll find gift packages containing Japan's best-loved brands of sake, rice crackers, and other food items. Department stores also typically devote one floor to traditional Japanese crafts, including ceramics, paintings, and lacquerware. If you're pressed for time, these are great places to pick up a variety of souvenirs.

Don't miss the *depachika* (food departments) on the lower levels, where you'll encounter an overwhelming selection of Japanese and Western delacacies. Though no locals in their right minds would shop here regularly for their groceries—the price tags on the imported cheeses and hams will cause your jaw to hit the floor—a brief exploration will give you a pretty good picture of what people might select for a special occasion. Many stalls have small samples out on the counter, and nobody will raise a fuss if you help yourself, even if you don't make a purchase.

Major department stores accept credit cards and provide shipping services. Some salesclerks speak English. If you're having communication difficulties, someone will eventually come to the rescue. On the first floor you'll invariably find a general information booth with useful maps of the store in English. Some department stores close one or two days a month. To be on the safe side, call ahead.

Ginza, Nihombashi & Yūraku-chō

Fodor'sChoice **Matsuya.** On the fourth floor, the gleaming Matsuya houses an excel-
★ lent selection of Japanese fashion, including Issey Miyake, Yohji Yamamoto, and Comme Ça Du Mode. The Louis Vuitton shops on the first and second floors are particularly popular with Tōkyō's brand-obsessed shoppers. ⊠ *3–6–1 Ginza, Chūō-ku* ☎ *03/3567–1211* ⊘ *Sat.–Thurs. 10–8:30, Fri. 10–9:30* Ⓜ *Ginza, Marunouchi, and Hibiya subway lines, Ginza Station (Exits A12 and A13).*

Matsuzakaya. The Matsuzakaya conglomerate was founded in Nagoya and still commands the loyalties of shoppers with origins in western Japan. Style-conscious Tōkyōites tend to find the sense of fashion a bit countrified. ⊠ *6–10–1 Ginza, Chūō-ku* ☎ *03/3572–1111* ⊘ *Sun.–Wed. 10:30–7:30, Thur., Fri., and Sat. 10:30–8* Ⓜ *Ginza, Marunouchi, and Hibiya subway lines, Ginza Station (Exits A3 and A4).*

★ **Mitsukoshi.** Founded in 1673 as a dry-goods store, Mitsukoshi later played one of the leading roles in introducing Western merchandise to Japan. It has retained its image of quality and excellence, with a particularly strong representation of Western fashion designers. The store also stocks fine traditional Japanese goods—don't miss the art gallery and the crafts area on the sixth floor. With its own subway stop, bronze lions at the entrance, and an atrium sculpture of the Japanese goddess Magokoro, the remarkable Nihombashi flagship store merits a visit even if you're not planning on buying anything. ⊠ *1–4–1 Nihombashi Muromachi, Chūō-ku* ☎ *03/3241–3311* ⊘ *Daily 10–7:30* Ⓜ *Ginza and Hanzō-mon subway lines, Mitsukoshi-mae Station (Exits A3 and A5)* ⊠ *4–6–16 Ginza, Chūō-ku* ☎ *03/3562–1111* ⊘ *Mon.–Sat. 10–8* Ⓜ *Ginza, Marunouchi, and Hibiya subway lines, Ginza Station (Exits A6, A7, A8).*

Fodor'sChoice **Muji.** This chain features generically branded housewares and clothing
★ at reasonable prices. You'll find a large selection of Bauhaus-influenced furniture, appliances, and bedding at the massive flagship branch in Yūraku-chō. If you're a bit overwhelmed by all the options, relax at the dining area that boasts—what else?—Muji meals. ⊠ *3–8–3 Marunouchi Muro-machi, Chiyoda-ku* ☎ *03/5208–8241* ⊘ *Daily 10–9* Ⓜ *JR Yamanote Line; Yūraku-chō subway line, Yūraku-chō Station (JR Kyobashi Exit, subway Exit A9).*

Takashimaya. In Japanese, *taka* means "high"—a fitting word for this store, which is beloved for its superior quality and prestige. Gift-givers all over Japan seek out this department store; a present that comes in a Takashimaya bag makes a statement regardless of what's inside. The second floor, with shops by Christian Dior, Prada, Chanel, Cartier, and many others, is one of the toniest retail spaces in a shopping district celebrated for its exclusivity. The seventh floor has a complete selection of traditional crafts, antiques, and curios. The lower-level food court carries every gastronomic delight imaginable, from Japanese crackers and green tea to Miyazaki beef and plump melons. ⊠ *2–4–1 Nihombashi, Chūō-ku* ☎ *03/3211–4111* ⊙ *Daily 10–8* Ⓜ *Ginza subway line, Nihombashi Station (Exits B1 and B2)* ⊠ *Takashimaya Times Sq., 5–24–2 Sendagaya, Shibuya-ku* ☎*03/5361–1111* ⊙ *Sun.–Fri. 10–8, Sat. 10–8:30* Ⓜ *JR Yamanote Line, Shinjuku Station (Minami-guchi/South Exit).*

Wako. Wako is well-known for its high-end glassware, jewelry, and accessories, as well as having some of the handsomest, most sophisticated window displays in town. The clock atop this curved 1930s-era building is illuminated at night, making it one of Tōkyō's more recognized landmarks. ⊠ *4–5–11 Ginza, Chūō-ku* ☎ *03/3562–2111* ⊙ *Mon.–Sat. 10:30–6* Ⓜ *Ginza, Marunouchi, and Hibiya subway lines, Ginza Station (Exits A9 and A10).*

Ikebukuro & Shibuya

Parco. Parco, owned by the Seibu conglomerate, is actually not one store but four vertical malls filled with small retail shops and boutiques, all in walking distance of one another in the commercial heart of Shibuya. Parco Part 1 and Part 4 (Quattro) cater to a younger crowd and stock unbranded casual clothing, crafts fabrics, and accessories; Quattro even has a club that hosts live music. Part 2 is devoted mainly to interiors and fashion, and Part 3 sells a mixture of men's and women's fashions, tableware, and household furnishings. The nearby Zero Gate complex houses the basement restaurant-nightclub La Fabrique. ⊠ *15–1 Udagawa-chō, Shibuya-ku* ☎ *03/3464–5111* ⊙ *Parts 1, 2, and 3 daily 10–9; Quattro daily 11–9* Ⓜ *Ginza and Hanzō-mon subway lines, Shibuya Station (Exits 6 and 7).*

Seibu. Even Japanese customers have been known to get lost in this mammoth department store; the main branch is in Ikebukuro. The Shibuya branch, which still carries an impressive array of merchandise, is smaller and more manageable. Seibu has an excellent selection of household goods, from furniture to china and lacquerware, in its stand-alone Loft shops (often next door to Seibu branches, or occasionally within the department store itself). ⊠ *1–28–1 Minami Ikebukuro, Toshima-ku* ☎ *03/3981–0111* ⊙ *Daily 10–9* Ⓜ *JR Yamanote Line; Marunouchi and Yūrakuchō subway lines, Ikebukuro Station (Minami-guchi/South Exit); Seibu Ikebukuro Line, Seibu Ikebukuro Station (Seibu Department Store Exit); Tōbu Tōjō Line, Tōbu Ikebukuro Station (Minami-guchi/South Exit)* ⊠ *21–1 Udagawa-chō, Shibuya-ku* ☎*03/3462–0111* ⊙ *Sun.–Wed. 10–8, Fri.–Sat. 10–9* Ⓜ *JR Yamanote Line; Ginza and Hanzō-mon subway lines, Shibuya Station (Hachiko Exit for JR, Exits 6 and 7 for subway lines).*

Shinjuku

Isetan. One of Tōkyō's oldest and largest department stores, Isetan is known for its mix of high-end and affordable fashions, as well as its selection of larger sizes not found in most Tōkyō stores. The basement's food selection, which includes prepared salads and dried fish, is one of the city's largest in a department store. ⊠ *3–14–1 Shinjuku, Shinjuku-ku* ☎ *03/3352–1111* ⊙ *Daily 10–8* Ⓜ *JR Yamanote Line, Marunouchi subway line (Higashi-guchi/East Exit for JR, Exits B2, B3, B4, and B5 for subway line).*

Marui. Marui, easily recognized by its red-and-white logo, burst onto the department store scene in the 1980s by introducing an in-store credit card—one of the first stores in Japan to do so. Branches typically occupy separate buildings near busy train stations; there are a handful of big shops in Shinjuku with names like Marui Young, Marui City, and Marui Men. Youngsters flock to the stores in search of petite clothing, accessories, and sportswear. ✉ *5–16–4 Shinjuku, Shinjuku-ku* ☎ *03/3354–0101* ✆ *Daily 11–9* Ⓜ *JR Yamanote Line, Shinjuku Station (Higashi-guchi/East Exit); Marunouchi subway line, Shinjuku San-chōme Station (Exit B2).*

Specialty Stores

Antiques

From ornate *tansu* (traditional chests used to store clothing) to Meiji-era Nō masks, Tōkyō's antiques shops are stocked with fine examples of traditional Japanese craftsmanship. The two best areas for antiques are Nishi-Ogikubo (also known as Nishiogi), which is just outside of Shinjuku, and Aoyama. The elegant shops along Kottō-dōri—Aoyama's "Antiques Road"—are the places to hunt down exquisite ¥100,000 vases and other pricey items. The slapdash array of more than 60 antiques shops in Nishi-Ogikubo has an anything-goes feel. When visiting Nishi-Ogikubo, which you can reach by taking the Sōbu Line to Nishi-Ogikubo Station, your best bet is to pick up the free printed area guide available at the police box outside the train station's north exit. Even though it's mostly in Japanese, the map provides easy-to-follow directions to all stores. Dealers are evenly clustered in each of the four districts around the station, so plan on spending at least half a day in Nishi-Ogikubo if you want to see them all.

Antiquers can also find great buys at Tōkyō's flea markets, which are often held on the grounds of the city's shrines.

★ **Fuji-Torii.** An English-speaking staff, a central Omotesandō location, and antiques ranging from ceramics to swords are the big draws at this shop, in business since 1948. In particular, Fuji-Torii has an excellent selection of folding screens, lacquerware, painted glassware, and *ukiyo-e* (wood-block prints). ✉ *6–1–10 Jingū-mae, Shibuya-ku* ☎ *03/3400–2777* ✆ *Wed.–Mon. 11–6; closed 3rd Mon. of month* Ⓜ *Chiyoda subway line, Meiji Jingū-mae Station (Exit 4).*

Hanae Mori Building. The basement floor of this Kenzō Tange–designed emporium houses more than a dozen small antiques shops. The emphasis is on European goods, but Japanese offerings include a tasteful sword shop and ceramics dealers. Upstairs, fashion hounds can shop for designs from Mori Hanae, the doyenne of Japanese designers. ✉ *3–6–1 Kita-Aoyama, Minato-ku* ☎ *03/3406–1021* ✆ *Daily 10:30–7* Ⓜ *Ginza, Chiyoda, and Hanzō-mon subway lines, Omotesandō Station (Exit A1).*

Morita. This Aoyama shop carries antiques and new *mingei* (Japanese folk crafts) in addition to a large stock of textiles from throughout Asia. ✉ *5–12–2 Minami-Aoyama, Minato-ku* ☎ *03/3407–4466* ✆ *Daily 10–7* Ⓜ *Ginza, Chiyoda, and Hanzō-mon subway lines, Omotesandō Station (Exit B1).*

Tōgō Jinja. One of the city's biggest flea markets—where you can often find antiques and old yakuza movie posters—takes place at this shrine near Harajuku's Takeshita-dōri, on the first Sunday of the month from sunrise to sunset. ⊠ *1–5 Jingū-mae, Shibuya-ku* ☎ *03/3425–7965* Ⓜ *Chiyoda subway line, Meiji-Jingū-mae Station; JR Yamanote Line, Harajuku Station (Takeshita-dōri Exit).*

Yasukuni Jinja. Every second and third Sunday of the month, from sunrise to sunset, antique-hunters can search and explore this large flea market. It's located near the Yasukuni shrine, so when you're finished shopping, stroll over to the shrine to learn about the controversy that surrounds it. ⊠ *3–1 Kudan-Kita, Chiyoda-ku* ☎ *03/3791–0006* Ⓜ *Hanzō-mon and Shinjuku subway lines, Kudanshita Station (Exit 1).*

Books

If you want to read while you're in Tōkyō, it's best to bring your books and magazines with you; foreign titles are often marked up considerably. All the shops listed below are open daily.

Bookstores of Jimbō-chō. The site of one of the largest concentrations of used bookstores in the world, the Jimbō-chō area is a bibliophile's dream. In the ½-km (¼-mi) strip along Yasukuni-dōri and its side streets you can find centuries-old Japanese prints, vintage manga, and even complete sets of the *Oxford English Dictionary*. Most shops have predominately Japanese-language selections, but almost all stock some foreign titles, with a few devoting major floor space to English books. Kitazawa Shoten, recognizable by its stately entranceway, carries lots of humanities titles. Tokyo Random Walk is the retail outlet of Tuttle Publishing, which puts out books on Japanese language and culture. The large Japanese publisher Sanseidō has its flagship store here; the fifth floor sells magazines and postcards in addition to books. The stores in the area are usually open 9 or 9:30 to 5:30 or 6, and many of the smaller shops close on Sunday or Monday. Ⓜ *Mita, Shinjuku, and Hanzō-mon subway lines, Jimbō-chō Station (Exit A5).*

Kinokuniya. The mammoth Kinokuniya bookstore near the south exit of Shinjuku Station devotes most of its sixth floor to English titles, with an excellent selection of travel guides, magazines, and books on Japan. ⊠ *Takashimaya Times Sq., 5–24–2 Sendagaya, Shibuya-ku* ☎ *03/5361–3300* ☉ *Sun.–Fri. 10–8, Sat. 10–8:30* Ⓜ *JR Yamanote Line, Shinjuku Station (Minami-guchi/South Exit).*

Maruzen. There are English titles on the fourth floor, as well as art books; this recently relocated flagship branch of the Maruzen chain also hosts the occasional art exhibit. ⊠ *1–6–4 Marunouchi, Chiyoda-ku* ☎ *03/5288–8881* ☉ *Daily 9–9* Ⓜ *JR Yamanote Line, Tōkyō Station (North Exit); Tozai subway line, Otemachi Station (Exit B2C).*

Tower Records. This branch of the U.S.-based chain carries an eclectic collection of English-language books at more reasonable prices than most bookstores in town. It also has the best selection of foreign magazines in Tōkyō. ⊠ *1–22–14 Jinnan, Shibuya-ku* ☎ *03/3496–3661* ☉ *Daily*

10–11 Ⓜ *JR Yamanote Line, Hanzō-mon and Ginza subway lines, Shibuya Station (Hachiko Exit for JR, Exit 6 for subway).*

Yaesu Book Center. English-language paperbacks, art books, and calendars are available on the seventh floor of this celebrated bookstore. ✉ *2–5–1 Yaesu, Chūō-ku* ☎ *03/3281–1811* ◷ *Mon.–Sat. 10–9, Sun. 10–8* Ⓜ *JR Yamanote Line, Tōkyō Station (Yaesu South Exit 5).*

Ceramics

The Japanese have been crafting extraordinary pottery for more than 2,000 years, but this art form really began to flourish in the 16th century with the popularity and demand for tea-ceremony utensils. Feudal lords competed for possession of the finest pieces, and distinctive styles of pottery developed in regions all over the country. Some of the more prominent styles are those of the village of Arita in Kyūshū, with painted patterns of flowers and birds; Mashiko, in Tochigi Prefecture, with its rough textures and simple, warm colors; rugged Hagi ware, from the eponymous Western Honshū city; and Kasama, in Ibaraki Prefecture, with glazes made from ash and ground rocks. Tōkyō's specialty shops and department stores carry fairly complete selections of these and other wares.

At first glance, Japanese ceramics may seem priced for a prince's table, but if you keep shopping, you can find reasonably priced items that are generally far superior in design to what is available back home. Sale items are often amazingly good bargains. Vases, sake sets, and chopstick rests all make good gifts.

Noritake. The Akasaka showroom of this internationally renowned brand carries fine china and glassware in a spacious setting. ✉ *7–8–5 Akasaka, Minato-ku* ☎ *03/3586–0267* ◷ *Weekdays 10–6* Ⓜ *Chiyoda subway line, Akasaka Station (Exit 7).*

Savoir Vivre. In Roppongi's ultratrendy Axis Building, this store sells contemporary and antique tea sets, cups, bowls, and glassware. ✉ *Axis Bldg., 3F, 5–17–1 Roppongi, Minato-ku* ☎ *03/3585–7365* ◷ *Mon.–Sat. 11–7, Sun. 11–6:30* Ⓜ *Hibiya and Ōedo subway lines, Roppongi Station (Exit 3).*

Tsutaya. *Ikebana* (flower arrangement) and *sadō* (tea ceremony) goods are the only items sold at this Kottō-dōri shop, but they come in such stunning variety that a visit is definitely worthwhile. Colorful vases in surprising shapes and traditional ceramic tea sets make for unique souvenirs. ✉ *5–10–5 Minami-Aoyama, Minato-ku* ☎ *03/3400–3815* ◷ *Daily 10–6:30* Ⓜ *Ginza, Chiyoda, and Hanzō-mon subway lines, Omotesandō Station (Exit B1).*

Clothing Boutiques

Japanese boutiques pay as much attention to interior design as they do to the clothing they sell; like anywhere else, it's the image that moves the merchandise. Although many mainstream Japanese designers are represented in the major upscale department stores, you may enjoy your shopping more in the elegant boutiques of Aoyama and Omotesandō—most of which are within walking distance of one another.

Bape Exclusive Aoyama. Since the late 1990s, no brand has been more coveted by Harajuku scenesters than the A Bathing Ape label (shortened to Bape) from DJ–fashion designer Nigo. At the height of the craze, hopefuls would line up outside Nigo's well-hidden boutiques for the chance to plop down ¥7,000 for a T-shirt festooned with a simian visage or a *Planet of the Apes* quote. Bape has since gone above-ground, with Nigo expanding his business empire to Singapore, Hong Kong, and London. Here in Tōkyō, you can see what all the fuss is about at a spacious boutique that houses the Bape Gallery on the second floor. ⊠ *5–5–8 Minami-Aoyama, Minato-ku* ☎ *03/3407–2145* ☉ *Daily 11–7* Ⓜ *Ginza and Hanzō-mon subway lines, Omotesandō Station (Exit A5).*

Busy Workshop Harajuku. This Harajuku spot sells the trendy Bape clothing line and has an avant-garde interior by noted local designers Wonderwall. ⊠ *B1F, 4–28–22 Jingū-mae, Minato-ku* ☎ *03/5474–0204* ☉ *Daily 11–7* Ⓜ *Chiyoda line, Meiji-Jingū-mae Station (Exit 5); JR Yamanote Line, Harajuku Station (Takeshita-dōri Exit).*

★ **Comme des Garçons.** Sinuous low walls snake through Rei Kawakubo's flagship store, a minimalist labyrinth that houses the designer's signature clothes, shoes, and accessories. Staff members will do their best to ignore you, but that's no reason to stay away from one of Tōkyō's funkiest retail spaces. ⊠ *5–2–1 Minami-Aoyama, Minato-ku* ☎ *03/3406–3951* ☉ *Daily 11–8* Ⓜ *Ginza, Chiyoda, and Hanzō-mon subway lines, Omotesandō Station (Exit A5).*

Issey Miyake. The otherworldy creations of internationally renowned designer Miyake are on display at her flagship store in Aoyama, which carries the full Paris line. ⊠ *3–18–11 Minami-Aoyama, Minato-ku* ☎ *03/3423–1407* ☉ *Daily 11–8* Ⓜ *Ginza, Chiyoda, and Hanzō-mon subway lines, Omotesandō Station (Exit A4).*

10 Corso Como Comme des Garçons. Milanese lifestyle guru Carla Sozzani helped create this spacious boutique for designer Rei Kawakubo's Comme des Garçons lines, which include Junya Watanabe menswear and womens wear. Also on offer are Vivienne Westwood and Balenciaga brands, and the staff isn't too busy being hip to help you out. ⊠ *5–3 Minami-Aoyama, Minato-ku* ☎ *03/5774–7800* ☉ *Daily 11–8* Ⓜ *Ginza, Chiyoda, and Hanzō-mon subway lines, Omotesandō Station (Exit A5).*

Under Cover. This stark shop houses Paris' darling Jun Takahashi's cult clothing, with enormously high racks of men's and women's clothing with a tatty punk look. ⊠ *5–3–18 Minami-Aoyama, Minato-ku* ☎ *03/3407–1232* ☉ *Daily 11–8* Ⓜ *Ginza, Chiyoda, and Hanzō-mon subway lines, Omotesandō Station (Exit A5).*

Y's Roppongi Hills. With its glossy surfaces and spare lines, the interior of this Ron Arad–designed shop on Roppongi's Keyakizaka-dōri serves as a suitable showcase for Yohji Yamamoto's austere fashions. ⊠ *6–12–4 Roppongi, Minato-ku* ☎ *03/5413–3434* ☉ *Daily 11–9* Ⓜ *Hibiya and Ōedo subway lines, Roppongi Station (Roppongi Hills Exit).*

CLOSE UP

Day Spa Escape: Canari

PUSHING THROUGH STEADY streams of teenagers on Takeshita-dōri can take its toll on even the most ardent of shoppers. So why not stop by the Swedish spa Canari for a session to soothe your barking dogs? Beyond the entry is a series of relaxation lounges, outfitted with recliners and calming color patterns, to give a friendly welcome. Relax and settle into the very comfortable spa chairs. Your stay begins with a foot bath and ends with a brief leg and foot massage—it's sooo worth it, though extremely muscle-weary shoppers might want to opt for the special package that adds a full foot and leg massage. In addition to foot care, the spa offers equally rejuvenating facials and body treatments.

Services: Facials, reflexology, body and foot massage.

Package Picks: Body care (30 min ¥4,500; 60 min ¥9,000; 90 min ¥13,500), Foot care (60 min ¥8,000; 90 min ¥12,000), Facial (60 min ¥10,000; 75 min ¥12,000), Head Refresh (15 min ¥2,000; 30 min ¥4,000), Reflexology (30 min ¥3,500; 45 min ¥5,000; 60 min ¥6,500).

General Info: (✉ 1-17-5 Jingū-mae, Shibuya-ku ☎ 03/3486-7799 ⊕ www.canari.jp ☉ Mon.-Sat. 11-9, Sun. 11-8 Ⓜ JR Yamanote Line, Harajuku Station (Takeshita-dōri Exit).

5

Clothing Chains

Tokyo street fashion is often profiled in international magazines as being brash and bizarre. The chains tend to line their shelves with a little more restraint than the boutiques, but by nearly any other city's standards, the average Tokyo store still contains plenty of eye-openers.

Beams. Daikanyama features a cluster of Beams stores that provide Japan's younger men and women with extremely hip threads. Shopping here will ensure that you or your kids will be properly attired in street-ready T-shirts and porter bags. ✉ *19–6 Sarugakuchō, Shibuya-ku* ☎ *03/5428–5951* ☉ *Daily 11–8* Ⓜ *Tōkyū Tōyoko line, Daikanyama Station (Komazawa-dōri Exit).*

★ **Journal Standard.** This is not a chain dedicated to outfitting copy editors and reporters in shirts and ties. In fact, this branch is frequented by young couples looking for the season's *it* fashions. ✉ *1–5–6 Jinnan, Shibuya-ku* ☎ *03/5457–0700* ☉ *Daily 11–8* Ⓜ *JR Yamanote Line; Ginza and Hanzō-mon subway lines, Shibuya Station (Hachiko Exit for JR, Exits 6 and 7 for subways).*

Uniqlo. Uniqlo offers customers a chance to wrap themselves in simple, low-priced items from the company's own brand. The vibe of the chain fits well within the relaxed attitudes of the Jiyūgaoka area, but there are locations all over the city as well as overseas. The store focuses on simple men's and women's clothing from its own label. ✉ *1–8–21*

Jiyūgaoka, Meguro-ku ☎ *03/5731–8273* ⊗ *Daily 11–8* Ⓜ *Tōkyū Tōyoko and Oimachi lines, Jiyugaoka Station (South Exit).*

Dolls

There are many types of traditional dolls available in Japan, and each one has its own charm. Kokeshi dolls, which date from the Edo period, are long, cylindrical, painted, and made of wood, with no arms or legs. Daruma, papier-mâché dolls with rounded bottoms and faces, are often painted with amusing expressions. Legend has it they are modeled after a Buddhist priest who remained seated in the lotus position for so long that his arms and legs atrophied. Hakata dolls, from Kyūshū, are ceramic figurines in traditional costume, such as geisha, samurai, or festival dancers.

Beishu. Colorful and often made from precious metals, the delicate dolls hand-crafted at this shop have found their way into some of Japan's larger department stores, museums, and even the Imperial Palace. ⊠ *2–3–12 Taitō-Higashi, Taitō-ku* ☎ *03/3834–3501* ⊗ *Sun.–Fri. 10–6* Ⓜ *Ōedo subway line, Shin-okachimachi Station (Exit A2).*

Kyūgetsu. In business for more than a century, Kyūgetsu sells every kind of doll imaginable. ⊠ *1–20–4 Yanagibashi, Taitō-ku* ☎ *03/5687–5176* ⊗ *Weekdays 9:15–6, weekends 9:15–5:15* Ⓜ *Asakusa subway line, Asakusa-bashi Station (Exit A3).*

Electronics

The area around Akihabara Station has more than 200 stores with discount prices on stereos, digital cameras, computers, DVD players, and anything else that runs on electricity. The larger shops have sections or floors (or even whole annexes) of goods made for export. Products come with instructions in most major languages, and if you have a tourist visa in your passport, you can purchase them duty-free.

★ **Apple Store.** This very stylish showroom displays the newest models from Apple's line of computer products. The Genius Bar on the second floor offers consulting services should you need advice on how to resuscitate a comatose iPod or MacBook. ⊠ *3–5–12 Ginza, Chūō-ku* ☎ *03/5159–8200* ⊗ *Daily 10–9* Ⓜ *Ginza, Hibiya, and Marunouchi subway lines, Ginza Station (Exit A13).*

Bic Camera. A large discount-electronics chain in the Odakyū Halc building, Bic Camera has low prices. ⊠ *1–5–1 Nishi-Shinjuku, Shinjuku-ku* ☎ *03/5326–1111* ⊗ *Daily 10–9* Ⓜ *Marunouchi and Shinjuku subway lines; JR Yamanote Line; Keiō and Odakyū lines, Shinjuku Station (Nishi-guchi/West Exit).*

LAOX. One of the big Akihabara chains, LAOX has several locations in the area. The "Duty Free Akihabara" branch on the main Chūō-dōri strip carries a full six floors of export models. English-speaking staff members are always on call. ⊠ *1–15–3 Soto-Kanda, Chiyoda-ku* ☎ *03/3255–5301* ⊗ *Daily 8–9* Ⓜ *JR Yamanote Line, Akihabara Station (Electric Town Exit).*

Softmap. One Akihabara retailer that actually benefited from the bursting of Japan's economic bubble in the early '90s is Softmap, a used-PC and -software chain with a heavy presence in Tōkyō. Most branches are open daily until 7:30 or 8. ✉ *3–14–10 Soto-Kanda, Chiyoda-ku* ☎ *03/ 3253–3030* 🕙 *Daily 11–8* Ⓜ *JR Yamanote Line, Akihabara Station (Electric Town Exit).*

🕙 **Sony Building.** Test drive the latest Sony gadgets at this retail and entertainment space in the heart of Ginza. Kids will enjoy trying out the not-yet-released PlayStation games, while their parents fiddle with digital cameras and stereos from Japan's electronics leader. ✉ *5–3–1 Ginza, Chūō-ku* ☎ *03/3573–2371* 🕙 *Daily 11–7* Ⓜ *JR Yamanote Line, Yūraku-chō Station (Ginza Exit); Ginza, Hibiya, and Marunouchi subway lines, Ginza Station (Exit B9).*

🕙 **Sukiya Camera.** The cramped Nikon House branch of this two-store operation features enough Nikons—old and new, digital and film—that it could double as a museum to the brand. Plenty of lenses and flashes are available as well. ✉ *4–2–13 Ginza, Chūō-ku* ☎ *03/3561–6000* 🕙 *Mon.–Sat. 10–7:30, Sun. 10–7* Ⓜ *JR Yamanote Line, Yūraku-chō Station (Ginza Exit); Ginza, Hibiya, and Marunouchi subway lines, Ginza Station (Exit B10).*

★ **Y.K. Musen.** Welcome to a world that would truly be Maxwell Smart's dream. From pinhole cameras hidden in cigarette packs to microphones capable of picking up sound through concrete, Y.K. Musen supplies the latest and greatest in snoop technology. ✉ *1–14–2 Soto-Kanda, Chiyoda-ku* ☎ *03/3255–3079* 🕙 *Daily 10–6:45* Ⓜ *JR Yamanote Line, Akihabara Station (Electric Town Exit).*

Yodobashi Camera. This discount-electronics superstore near Shinjuku Station carries a selection comparable to Akihabara's big boys. ✉ *1–11–1 Nishi-Shinjuku, Shinjuku-ku* ☎ *03/3346–1010* 🕙 *Daily 9:30–10* Ⓜ *Marunouchi and Shinjuku subway lines; JR Yamanote Line; Keiō and Odakyū lines, Shinjuku Station (Nishi-guchi/West Exit).*

Folk Crafts

Japanese folk crafts, called *mingei*—among them bamboo vases and baskets, fabrics, paper boxes, dolls, and toys—achieve a unique beauty in their simple and sturdy designs. Be aware, however, that simple does not mean cheap. Long hours of labor go into these objects, and every year there are fewer craftspeople left, producing their work in smaller and smaller quantities. Include these items in your budget ahead of time: the best—worth every cent—can be fairly expensive.

Printed fabric, whether by the yard or in the form of finished scarves, napkins, tablecloths, or pillow coverings, is another item worth purchasing in Japan. The complexity of the designs and the quality of the printing make the fabric, both silk and cotton, special. *Furoshiki*—square pieces of cloth used for wrapping, storing, and carrying things—make great wall hangings.

Bingo-ya. You may be able to complete all of your souvenir shopping in one trip to this tasteful four-floor shop, which carries traditional handicrafts—including ceramics, toys, lacquerware, Nō masks, fabrics, and lots more—from all over Japan. ✉ *10–6 Wakamatsu-chō, Shinjuku-ku*

5

The Power of Tea

CLOSE UP

GREEN TEA IS UBIQUITOUS IN Japan. But did you know that besides being something of the national drink, it's also good for you? Green tea contains antioxidants twice as powerful as those in red wine; these help reduce high blood pressure, lower blood sugar, and fight cancer. A heightened immune system and lower cholesterol are other benefits attributed to this beverage.

Whether drinking green tea for its healing properties, good taste, or as a manner of habit, you'll have plenty of choices in Japan. Pay attention to tea varietals, which are graded by the quality and parts of the plant used, because price and quality runs the spectrum within these categories. For the very best Japanese green tea, take a trip to the Uji region of Kyoto.

Gyokuro (jewel dew). Developed from a grade of green tea called *tencha* (divine tea), the name is derived from the light green color the tea adopts when brewed. Gyokuro is grown in the shade, an essential condition to develop just this type and grade.

Matcha (rubbed tea). Most often used in the tea ceremony, matcha is a high quality, but hard to find, powdered

green tea. It has a thick, paint-like consistency when mixed with hot water. It is also a popular flavor of ice cream and other sweets in Japan.

Sencha (roasted tea). This is the green tea you are most likely to try at the local noodle or bento shop. Its leaves are grown under direct sunlight, giving it a different flavor from cousins like Gyokuro.

Genmai (brown rice tea). This is a mixture, usually in equal parts, of green tea and roasted brown rice.

Bancha (common tea). This second harvest variety ripens between summer and fall, producing leaves larger than those of Sencha and a weaker tasting tea.

Genmaicha (popcorn tea). This is a blend of bancha and genmai teas.

Kabusecha (covered tea). Similar to Gyokuru, Kabusecha leaves are grown in the shade, though for a shorter period, giving it a refined flavor.

Hōjicha (pan fried tea). A pan-fried or oven-roasted green tea.

Kukicha (stalk tea). A tea made from stalks by harvesting one bud and three leaves.

☎ 03/3202–8778 ☺ *Tues.–Sun. 10–7* Ⓜ *Ōedo subway line, Wakamatsu Kawada Station (Wakamatsu-chō Exit).*

★ **Oriental Bazaar.** The four floors of this popular tourist destination are packed with just about anything you could want as a traditional Japanese (or Chinese or Korean) handicraft souvenir: painted screens, pottery, chopsticks, dolls, and more, all at very reasonable prices. ✉ *5–9–13 Jingū-mae, Shibuya-ku* ☎ *03/3400–3933* ☺ *Fri.–Wed. 10–7* Ⓜ *Chiyoda subway line, Meiji Jingū-mae Station (Exit 4).*

Foodstuffs & Wares

This hybrid category includes everything from crackers and dried seaweed to cast-iron kettles, paper lanterns, and essential food kitsch like plastic sushi sets.

Backstreet Shops of Tsukiji. In Tsukiji, between the Central Wholesale Market and Harumi-dōri, among the many fishmongers, you can also find stores selling pickles, tea, crackers, kitchen knives, baskets, and crockery. The area is a real slice of Japanese life. ⊠ *Tsukiji 4-chōme, Chūō-ku* Ⓜ *Ōedo subway line, Tsukiji-shijō Station (Exit A1); Hibiya subway line, Tsukiji Station (Exit 1).*

Tea-Tsu. Some people ascribe Japanese longevity to the beneficial effects of green tea. Tea-Tsu, which has five branches in Tōkyō, sells a variety of leaves in attractive canisters that make unique gifts. The main Aoyama branch also sells tea sets and other ceramics, and the staff will serve you a complimentary cup of *cha* (tea) as you make your selection. ⊠ *3–18–3 Minami-Aoyama, Minato-ku* ☎ *03/5772–2662* ⊙ *Tues.–Sun. 11–8* Ⓜ *Ginza, Chiyoda, and Hanzō-mon subway lines, Omotesandō Station (Exit A4).*

Tokiwa-dō. Come here to buy some of Tōkyō's most famous souvenirs: *kaminari okoshi* (thunder crackers), made of rice, millet, sugar, and beans. The shop is on the west side of Asakusa's Thunder God Gate, the Kaminari-mon entrance to Sensō-ji. ⊠ *1–3 Asakusa, Taitō-ku* ☎ *03/3841–5656* ⊙ *Daily 9–8:45* Ⓜ *Ginza subway line, Asakusa Station (Exit 1).*

Yamamoto Noriten. The Japanese are resourceful in their uses of products from the sea. Nori, the paper-thin dried seaweed used to wrap maki sushi and *onigiri* (rice balls), is the specialty here. If you plan to bring some home with you, buy unroasted nori and toast it yourself at home; the flavor will be far better than that of the preroasted sheets. ⊠ *1–6–3 Nihombashi Muromachi, Chūō-ku* ☎ *03/3241–0261* ⊙ *Daily 9–6:30* Ⓜ *Hanzō-mon and Ginza subway lines, Mitsukoshi-mae Station (Exit A1).*

Housewares

Tōkyōites appreciate fine design, both the kind they can wear and the kind they can display in their homes. This passion is reflected in the exuberance of the city's *zakka* shops—retailers that sell small housewares. The Daikanyama and Aoyama areas positively brim with these stores, but trendy zakka can be found throughout the city.

Idee Shop. Local design giant Teruo Kurosaki's shop, located on the sixth floor of Takashimaya's Futako Tamagawa branch, carries housewares, fabrics, and ceramics by some of Japan's most celebrated young craftspeople. ⊠ *3–17–1 Tamagawa, Setagaya-ku* ☎ *03/5797–3024* ⊙ *Daily 10–9* Ⓜ *Tōkyū Denentoshi and Oimachi lines, Futako Tamagawa Station (West Exit).*

Sempre. Playful, colorful, and bright describe both the products and the space of this Kottō-dōri housewares dealer. Among the great finds here are interesting tableware, glassware, lamps, office goods, and jewelry. ⊠ *5–13–3 Minami-Aoyama, Minato-ku* ☎ *03/5464–5655* ⊙ *Mon.–Sat. 11–8, Sun. 11–7* Ⓜ *Ginza, Chiyoda, and Hanzō-mon subway lines, Omotesandō Station (Exit B1).*

Serendipity. Alessi products and other Western brands are sold at this spacious housewares store in the Coredo shopping center. ⊠ *1–4–1 Nihombashi, Chūō-ku* ☎ *03/3272–4939* ⊙ *Mon.–Sat. 11–9, Sun. 11–8*

CLOSE UP

Kappabashi

A WHOLESALE-RESTAURANT supply district might not sound like a promising shopping destination, but Kappabashi, about a 10-minute walk west of the temples and pagodas of Asakusa, is worth a look. Ceramics, cutlery, cookware, folding lanterns, and even kimonos can all be found here, along with the kitschy plastic food models that appear in restaurant windows throughout Japan. The best strategy is to stroll up and down the 1-km (½-mi) length of Kappabashi-dōgu-machi-dōri and visit any shop that looks interesting. Most stores here emphasize function over charm, but some manage to stand out for their stylish spaces as well. Most Kappabashi shops are open until 5:30; some close on Sunday. To get here, take the Ginza subway line to Tawara-machi Station.

Kappabashi Sōshoku. Come here for *aka-chōchin* (folding red-paper lanterns) like the ones that hang in front of inexpensive bars and restaurants. ☒ *3-1-1 Matsugaya, Taitō-ku* ☎ *03/3844-1973* ⊙ *Mon.-Sat. 9:30-5:30* Ⓜ *Ginza subway line, Tawara-machi Station (Exit 3).*

Kawahara Shōten. The brightly colored bulk packages of rice crackers, shrimp-flavored chips, and other Japanese snacks sold here make offbeat gifts. ☒ *3-9-2 Nishi-Asakusa, Taitō-ku* ☎ *03/3842-0841* ⊙ *Mon.-Sat. 9-5:30* Ⓜ *Ginza subway line, Tawara-machi Station (Exit 3).*

☙ **Maizuru.** This perennial tourist favorite manufactures the plastic food that's displayed outside almost every Tōkyō restaurant. Ersatz sushi, noodles, and even beer cost just a few hundred yen. You can buy tiny plastic key holders and earrings, or splurge on a whole Pacific lobster, perfect in coloration and detail down to the tiniest spines on its legs. ☒ *1-5-17 Nishi-Asakusa, Taitō-ku* ☎ *03/ 3843-1686* ⊙ *Daily 9-6* Ⓜ *Ginza subway line, Tawara-machi Station (Exit 3).*

Noren-no-Nishimura. This Kappabashi shop specializes in *noren*—the curtains that shops and restaurants hang to announce they're open. The curtains are typically cotton, linen, or silk, most often dyed-to-order for individual shops. Nishimura also sells premade noren of an entertaining variety—from white-on-blue landscapes to geisha and sumō wrestlers in polychromatic splendor—for home decorating. They make wonderful wall hangings and dividers. ☒ *1-10-10 Matsugaya, Taitō-ku* ☎ *03/3841-6220* ⊙ *Mon.-Sat. 10-6* Ⓜ *Ginza subway line, Tawara-machi Station (Exit 3).*

Soi Furniture. The selection of lacquerware, ceramics, and antiques sold at this Kappabashi shop is modest, but Soi displays the items in a primitivist setting of stone walls and and wooden floor planks, with up-tempo jazz in the background. ☒ *3-17-3 Matsugaya, Taitō-ku* ☎ *03/ 3843-9555* ⊙ *Daily 10-7* Ⓜ *Ginza subway line, Tawara-machi Station (Exit 3).*

Ⓜ *Ginza, Tōzai, and Asakusa subway lines, Nihombashi Station (Exit B10).*

Sputnik Pad. Sputnik, another of Kurosaki's shops, is Tōkyō's ultimate housewares destination. It carries funky and functional interiors products from big international designers like Marc Newson. Low, a trendy "rice café," is in the basement, and the Vision Network entertainment complex is across the street. ⊠ *5–46–14 Jingū-mae, Minato-ku* ☎ *03/6418–1330* ⊘ *Daily 11–7* Ⓜ *Ginza, Chiyoda, and Hanzō-mon subway lines, Omotesandō Station (Exit B1).*

♻ **Tōkyū Hands.** This housewares chain is dedicated to providing the do-it-yourselfer with all the tools, fabrics, and supplies he or she may need to tackle any job. The selection of plastic models and rubber Godzilla action figures on the seventh floor of the Shibuya branch is amazingly comprehensive. ⊠ *12–18 Udagawa-chō, Shibuya-ku* ☎ *03/5489–5111* ⊘ *Daily 10–8:30* Ⓜ *JR Yamanote Line; Ginza and Hanzō-mon subway lines, Shibuya Station (Hachiko Exit for JR, Exits 6 and 7 for subway).*

Jewelry

Japan has always been known for its craftsmen who possess the ability to create finely detailed work. Jewelry is no exception, especially when cultured pearls are used. Pearls, which have become something of a national symbol, are not inexpensive, but they are a whole lot cheaper in Japan than elsewhere.

Ginza Tanaka. From necklaces to precious metals shaped into statues, this chain of jewelry stores has crafted a reputation as one of Japan's premier jewelers since its founding in 1892. ⊠ *1–7–7 Ginza, Chuo-ku* ☎ *03/5561–0491* ⊘ *Daily 10:30–7* Ⓜ *Yūraku-chō subway line, Ginza 1-Chome Station (Exit 7).*

★ **Mikimoto.** Kōkichi Mikimoto created his technique for cultured pearls in 1893. Since then his name has been associated with the best quality in the industry. Mikimoto's flagship store in Ginza is less a jewelry shop than a boutique devoted to nature's ready-made gems. ⊠ *4–5–5 Ginza, Chūō-ku* ☎ *03/3535–4611* ⊘ *Daily 11–7; occasionally closed on Wed.* Ⓜ *Ginza, Hibiya, and Marunouchi subway lines, Ginza Station (Exit A9).*

Fodor'sChoice **Shinjuku Watch Kan.** Standing a full seven stories, this watch emporium
★ has just about any import brand as well as a wide selection of Casio and Seiko models that are not sold abroad. The top floor offers repair services. ⊠ *3–29–11 Shinjuku, Shinjuku-ku* ☎ *03/3226–6000* ⊘ *Daily 10–9* Ⓜ *Marunouchi and Shinjuku subway lines; JR Yamanote Line; Keiō and Odakyū lines, Shinjuku Station (Higashi-guchi/East Exit).*

Tasaki Pearl Gallery. Tasaki sells pearls at slightly lower prices than Mikimoto. The store has several showrooms and hosts an English-language tour that demonstrates the technique of culturing pearls and explains how to maintain and care for them. ⊠ *1–3–3 Akasaka, Minato-ku* ☎ *03/5561–8880* ⊘ *Daily 9–6* Ⓜ *Ginza subway line, Tameike-Sannō Station (Exit 9).*

Kimonos

Traditional clothing has experienced something of a comeback among Tōkyō's youth, but most Japanese women, unless they work in traditional restaurants, now wear kimonos only on special occasions. Like tuxedos in the United States, they are often rented, not purchased outright, for social events such as weddings or graduations. Kimonos are extremely expensive and difficult to maintain. A wedding kimono, for example, can cost as much as ¥1 million ($8,247).

Most visitors, naturally unwilling to pay this much for a garment that they probably want to use as a bathrobe or a conversation piece, settle for a secondhand or antique silk kimono. You can pay as little as ¥1,000 ($8) in a flea market, but to find one in decent condition, you should expect to pay about ¥10,000 ($82). However, cotton summer kimonos, called *yukata*, in a wide variety of colorful and attractive designs, can be bought new for ¥7,000–¥10,000 ($58–$82).

Hayashi. This store in the Yūraku-chō International Arcade specializes in ready-made kimonos, sashes, and dyed yukata. ⊠ *2–1–1 Yūraku-chō, Chiyoda-ku* ☎ *03/3501–4012* ⊙ *Mon.–Sat. 10–7, Sun. 10–6* Ⓜ *JR Yamanote Line, Yūraku-chō Station (Ginza Exit); Hibiya subway line, Hibiya Station (Exit A5).*

Kawano Gallery. Kawano, in the high-fashion district of Omotesandō, sells kimonos and kimono fabric in a variety of patterns. ⊠ *4–4–9 Jingū-mae, Shibuya-ku* ☎ *03/3470–3305* ⊙ *Daily 11–6* Ⓜ *Ginza, Chiyoda, and Hanzō-mon subway lines, Omotesandō Station (Exit A2).*

Tansu-ya. This small but pleasant Ginza shop, part of a chain with locations throughout Japan and abroad, has attractive used kimonos, yukata, and other traditional clothing in many fabrics, colors, and patterns. The helpful staff can acquaint you with the somewhat complicated method of putting on the garments. ⊠ *3–4–5 Ginza, Chūō-ku* ☎ *03/3561–8529* ⊙ *Mon.–Sat. 11–8, Sun. 11–7* Ⓜ *Ginza, Hibiya, and Marunouchi subway lines, Ginza Station (Exit A13).*

Lacquerware

For its history, diversity, and fine workmanship, lacquerware rivals ceramics as the traditional Japanese craft nonpareil. One warning: lacquerware thrives on humidity. Cheaper pieces usually have plastic rather than wood underneath. Because these won't shrink and crack in dry climates, they make safer—and no less attractive—buys.

Kasumisou Gallery. The gallery's jewelry and collectors boxes are handcrafted from fine wood and make great, but expensive gifts. ⊠ *5–3–29 Minami-Azabu, Minato-ku* ☎ *03/3473–6058* ⊙ *Mon.–Sat. 9:30–5:30, Sun. 10:30–6:30* Ⓜ *Hibiya subway line, Hiroo Station (Exit 3).*

Fodor'sChoice ★ **Yamada Heiando.** With a spacious, airy layout and lovely lacquerware goods, this fashionable Daikanyama shop is a must for souvenir hunters—and anyone else who appreciates fine design. Rice bowls, sushi trays, *bento* lunch boxes, *hashioki* (chopstick rests), and jewelry cases come in traditional blacks and reds, as well as patterns both subtle and bold. Prices are fair—many items cost less than ¥10,000—but these are the kinds of goods for which devotees of Japanese craftsmanship would be willing to pay a lot. ⊠ *Hillside Terrace G Block, 18–12 Sarugakuchō, Shibuya-ku* ☎ *03/3464–5541* ⊗ *Mon.–Sat. 10:30–7, Sun. 10:30–6:30* Ⓜ *Tōkyū Tōyoko line, Daikanyama Station (Komazawa-dōri Exit).*

Paper

What packs light and flat in your suitcase, won't break, doesn't cost much, and makes a great gift? The answer is traditional handmade *washi* (paper), which the Japanese make in thousands of colors, textures, and designs and fashion into an astonishing number of useful and decorative objects.

Items made of paper are one of the best buys in Japan. Delicate sheets of almost-transparent stationery, greeting cards, money holders, and wrapping paper are available at traditional crafts stores, stationery stores, and department stores. Small washi-covered boxes (suitable for jewelry and other keepsakes) and pencil cases are also strong candidates for gifts and personal souvenirs.

Kami Hyakka. Operated by the Ōkura Sankō wholesale paper company, which was founded in the late 19th century, this showroom displays some 512 different types and colors of paper—made primarily for stationery, notes, and cards rather than as crafts material. You can pick up three free samples when you visit. ⊠ *2–4–9 Ginza, Chūo-ku* ☎ *03/3538–5025* ⊗ *Tues.–Sat. 10:30–7* Ⓜ *Yūraku-chō subway line, Ginza-Itchōme Station (Exit 5); Ginza, Hibiya, and Marunouchi subway lines, Ginza Station (Exit B4).*

Kami-no-Takamura. Specialists in washi and other papers printed in traditional Japanese designs, this shop also carries brushes, inkstones, and other tools for calligraphy. ⊠ *1–1–2 Higashi-Ikebukuro, Toshima-ku* ☎ *03/3971–7111* ⊗ *Daily 11–6:45* Ⓜ *JR Yamanote Line; Marunouchi subway line, Ikebukuro Station (East Exit for JR, Exit 35 for subway).*

★ **Kyūkyodō.** Kyūkyodō has been in business since 1663—in Ginza since 1880—selling its wonderful handmade Japanese papers, paper products, incense, brushes, and other materials for calligraphy. ⊠ *5–7–4 Ginza, Chūo-ku* ☎ *03/3571–4429* ⊗ *Mon.–Sat. 10–7:30, Sun. 11–7* Ⓜ *Ginza, Hibiya, and Marunouchi subway lines, Ginza Station (Exit A2).*

Ozu Washi. This shop, which was opened in the 17th century, has one of the largest washi showrooms in the city and its own gallery of antique papers. ⊠ *3–6–2 Nihombashi-Honchō, Chūo-ku* ☎ *03/3662–1184* ⊗ *Mon.–Sat. 10–7* Ⓜ *Ginza and Hanzō-mon subway lines, Mitsukoshi-mae Station (Exit A4).*

Origami Kaikan. In addition to shopping for paper goods at Yushima no Kobayahi's store, you can also tour a papermaking workshop and learn the art of origami. ⊠ *1–7–14 Yushima, Bunkyō-ku* ☎ *03/3811–4025* ⊗ *Mon.–Sat. 9–6* Ⓜ *JR Chūō and Sōbu lines, Ochanomizu Station (West Exit); Chiyoda subway line, Yushima Station (Exit 5).*

Record Stores

Tōkyō is perhaps the premier location in the world to purchase music. The big chains will have all the standard releases, but it is the smaller specialty stores that are the real treat: local music and wide selections of imports from around the world are usually available on both vinyl and CD.

For out-of-print editions and obscurities on vinyl, the prices can run well over ¥10,000 ($82). But collectors will find the condition of the jackets to be unmatched.

Cisco. This small chain offers everything from techno and house to reggae, but at this branch, hip-hop and R&B reign. Make sure you take advantage of the six turntables where you can hone your DJ skills. Well, actually, they are for previewing potential purchases, but feel free to give it a shot. ⊠ *11–1 Udagawa-chō, Shibuya-ku* ☎ *03/3462–0366* ⊗ *Mon.–Sat. 12–10, Sun. 11–9* Ⓜ *JR Yamanote Line; Ginza and Hanzō-mon subway lines, Shibuya Station (Hachiko Exit for JR, Exits 6 and 7 for subway).*

FodorśChoice
★

Disk Union. Vinyl junkies rejoice. The Shinjuku flagship of this chain offers Latin, rock, and indie at 33 rpm. Other stores clustered within the nearby blocks have punk, metal, and jazz. Be sure to grab a store flyer that lists all of their branches since each usually specializes in one music genre or other. Oh, and for you digital folk: CDs are available, too. ⊠ *3–31–4 Shinjuku, Shinjuku-ku* ☎ *03/3352–2691* ⊗ *Daily 11–9* Ⓜ *Marunouchi and Shinjuku subway lines; JR Yamanote Line; Keiō and Odakyū lines, Shinjuku Station (Higashi-guchi/East Exit).*

Manhattan Records. The hottest hip-hop, reggae, and R&B vinyl can be found here and a DJ booth pumps out the jams from the center of the room. Don't expect a lot advice from the staff—no one can hear you over the throbbing tunes. ⊠ *10–1 Udagawa-chō, Shibuya-ku* ☎ *03/3477–7166* ⊗ *Daily 12–9* Ⓜ *JR Yamanote Line; Ginza and Hanzō-mon subway lines, Shibuya Station (Hachiko Exit for JR, Exits 6 and 7 for subway).*

Swords & Knives

Supplying the tools of the trade to samurai and sushi chefs alike, Japanese metalworkers have played a significant role in the nation's military and culinary history. The remarkable knives on offer from the shops below are comparable in both quality and price to the best Western brands. For swords, you can pay thousands of dollars for a good-quality antique, but far more reasonably priced reproductions are available as well. Consult with your airline on how best to transport these items home.

Ichiryō-ya Hirakawa. A small, cluttered souvenir shop in the Nishi-Sandō arcade, Ichiryō-ya carries antique swords and reproductions and has some English-speaking salesclerks. ⊠ *2–7–13 Asakusa, Taitō-ku* ☎ *03/3843–0051* ⊗ *Wed. and Fri.–Mon. 11–6* Ⓜ *Ginza subway line, Asakusa Station (Exit 1) or Tawara-machi Station (Exit 3).*

Kiya. Workers shape and hone blades in one corner of this Ginza shop, which carries cutlery, pocketknives, saws, and more. Scissors with handles in the shape of Japanese cranes are among the many unique gift items sold here, and custom-made knives are available on the second floor. ✉ *1–5–6 Nihombashi-Muromachi, Chūō-ku* ☎ *03/3241–0110* 🕐 *Mon.–Sat. 10–6, Sun. 11:15–5:45* Ⓜ *Ginza subway line, Mitsukoshi-mae Station (Exit A4).*

FodorśChoice ★ **Nippon Tōken** (Japan Sword). Wannabe samurai can learn how to tell their *tōshin* (blades) from their *tsuka* (sword handles) with help from the English-speaking staff at this small shop, which has been open since the Meiji era (1868–1912). Items that range from a circa-1390 samurai sword to inexpensive reproductions will allow you to take a trip back in time, but make sure your wallet is ready for today's prices. ✉ *3–8–1 Toranomon, Minato-ku* ☎ *03/3434–4321* 🕐 *Weekdays 9:30–6, Sat. 9:30–5* Ⓜ *Hibiya and Ginza subway lines, Tora-no-mon Station (Exit 2).*

Tōken Shibata. A tiny, threadbare shop incongruously situated near Ginza's glittering department stores, Tōken Shibata sells well-worn antique swords. ✉ *5–6–8 Ginza, Chūō-ku* ☎ *03/3573–2801* 🕐 *Mon.–Sat. 9:30–6:30* Ⓜ *Ginza, Hibiya, and Marunouchi subway lines, Ginza Station (Exit A1).*

★ **Tsubaya Hōchōten.** Tsubaya sells high-quality cutlery for professionals. Its remarkable selection is designed for every imaginable use, as the art of food presentation in Japan requires a great variety of cutting implements. The best of these carry the Traditional Craft Association seal: hand-forged tools of tempered blue steel, set in handles banded with deer horn to keep the wood from splitting. Be prepared to pay the premium for these items: a cleaver just for slicing soba can cost as much as ¥50,000. ✉ *3–7–2 Nishi-Asakusa, Taitō-ku* ☎ *03/3845–2005* 🕐 *Mon.–Sat. 9–5:45, Sun. 9–5* Ⓜ *Ginza subway line, Tawara-machi Station (Exit 3).*

Toys

Hakuhinkan. The plethora of homegrown-character goods like Hello Kitty make this one of Japan's biggest stores for toys. But the real treat is outside, where a massive vending machine allows shoppers, or customers of one of the nearby hostess clubs, to pick up a stuffed doll or model plane afterhours. It's on Chūō-dōri, the main axis of the Ginza shopping area. ✉ *8–8–11 Ginza, Chūō-ku* ☎ *03/3571–8008* 🕐 *Daily 11–8* Ⓜ *Ginza and Asakusa subway lines, Shimbashi Station (Exit 1).*

Kiddy Land. Commonly regarded as Tōkyō's best toy store, Kiddy Land also carries kitsch items that draw in Harajuku's teen brigade. ✉ *6–1 Jingū-mae, Shibuya-ku* ☎ *03/3409–3431* 🕐 *Daily 11–9* Ⓜ *JR Yamanote Line: Harajuku Station (Omotesandō Exit); Chiyoda subway line, Meiji Jingū-mae Station (Exit 4).*

Traditional Wares

Handmade combs, towels, and cosmetics are other uniquely Japanese treasures to consider picking up while in Tōkyō.

★ **Fuji-ya.** Master textile creator Keiji Kawakami's cotton *tenugui* (teh-*noo*-goo-ee) hand towels are collector's items and are framed instead of used as towels. Kawakami is an expert on the hundreds of traditional towel motifs that have come down from the Edo period: geometric patterns, plants and animals, and scenes from Kabuki plays and festivals. When Kawakami feels he has made enough of one pattern of his own design, he destroys the stencil. The shop is near the corner of Dembō-in-dōri on Naka-mise-dōri. ⊠ *2–2–15 Asakusa, Taitō-ku* ☎ *03/3841–2283* ⊗ *Fri.–Wed. 10–6* Ⓜ *Ginza subway line, Asakusa Station (Exit 6).*

Hyaku-suke. This is the last place in Tōkyō to carry government-approved skin cleanser made from powdered nightingale droppings. Ladies of the Edo period—especially the geisha—swore by the cleanser. These days this 100-year-old-plus cosmetics shop sells little of the nightingale powder, but its theatrical makeup for Kabuki actors, geisha, and traditional weddings—as well as unique items like seaweed shampoo, camellia oil, and handcrafted combs and cosmetic brushes—makes it a worthy addition to your Asakusa shopping itinerary. ⊠ *2–2–14 Asakusa, Taitō-ku* ☎ *03/3841–7058* ⊗ *Wed.–Mon. 11–5* Ⓜ *Ginza subway line, Asakusa Station (Exit 6).*

Jusan-ya. A shop selling handmade boxwood combs, this business was started in 1736 by a samurai who couldn't support himself as a feudal retainer. It has been in the same family ever since. Jusan-ya is on Shinobazu-dōri, a few doors west of its intersection with Chūō-dōri in Ueno. ⊠ *2–12–21 Ueno, Taitō-ku* ☎ *03/3831–3238* ⊗ *Mon.–Sat. 10–6:30* Ⓜ *Ginza subway line, Ueno Hirokō-ji Station (Exit 3); JR Yamanote Line, Ueno Station (Shinobazu Exit).*

Naka-ya. If you want to equip yourself for Sensō-ji's annual Sanja Festival in May, this is the place to come. Best buys here are *sashiko hanten,* which are thick woven firemen's jackets, and *happi* coats, cotton tunics printed in bright colors with Japanese characters. Some items are available in children's sizes. ⊠ *2–2–12 Asakusa, Taitō-ku* ☎ *03/3841–7877* ⊗ *Daily 10–6:30* Ⓜ *Ginza subway line, Asakusa Station (Exit 6).*

Yono-ya. Traditional Japanese coiffures and wigs are very complicated, and they require a variety of tools to shape them properly. Tatsumi Minekawa, the current master at Yono-ya—the family line goes back 300 years—deftly crafts and decorates very fine boxwood combs. Some combs are carved with auspicious motifs, such as peonies, hollyhocks, or cranes, and all are engraved with the family benchmark. ⊠ *1–37–10 Asakusa, Taitō-ku* ☎ *03/3844–1755* ⊗ *Daily 10–7; occasionally closed on Wed.* Ⓜ *Ginza subway line, Asakusa Station (Exit 1).*

Side Trips from Tōkyō

WORD OF MOUTH

"Take a train ride to Yokohama and visit Chinatown and have a wonderful Chinese lunch!"

—peppersalt

"Definitely take a day trip to Kamakura and Hakone."

—Barkinpark

"I prefer Kamakura over Nikko. It's easier to get to from Tōkyō, and I like its small town feel."

—lcuy

Updated by
Katherine
Pham Do

NIKKŌ, WHICH MEANS "SUNLIGHT," is not simply the site of the Tokugawa shrine but also of a national park, Nikkō Kokuritsu Kōen, on the heights above it. The centerpiece of the park is Chūzenji-ko, a deep lake some 21 km (13 mi) around, and the 318-foot-high Kegon Falls, Japan's most famous waterfall. "Think nothing is splendid," asserts an old Japanese proverb, "until you have seen Nikkō."

One caveat: the term "national park" does not quite mean what it does elsewhere in the world. In Japan, pristine grandeur is hard to come by; there are few places in this country where intrepid hikers can go to contemplate the beauty of nature for very long in solitude. If a thing's worth seeing, it's worth developing. This world view tends to fill Japan's national parks with bus caravans, ropeways and gondolas, scenic overlooks with coin-fed telescopes, signs that tell you where you may or may not walk, fried-noodle joints and vending machines, and shacks full of kitschy souvenirs. That's true of Nikkō, and it's true as well of Fuji-Hakone-Izu National Park, southwest of Tōkyō, another of Japan's most popular resort areas.

The park's chief attraction is, of course, Fuji-san—spellbinding in its perfect symmetry, immortalized by centuries of poets and artists. South of Mt. Fuji, the Izu Peninsula projects out into the Pacific, with Suruga Bay to the west and Sagami Bay to the east. The beaches and rugged shoreline of Izu, its forests and highland meadows, and its numerous hot-springs inns and resorts (*izu* means "spring") make the region a favorite destination for the Japanese.

Kamakura and Yokohama, both close enough to Tōkyō to provide ideal day trips, could not make for more contrasting experiences. Kamakura is an ancient city—the birthplace, one could argue, of the samurai way of life. Its place in Japanese history begins late in the 12th century, when Minamoto no Yoritomo became the country's first shōgun and chose this site, with its rugged hills and narrow passes, as the seat of his military government. The warrior elite of the Kamakura period took much of their ideology—and their aesthetics—from Zen Buddhism, endowing splendid temples that still exist today. A walking tour of Kamakura's Zen temples and Shintō shrines is a must for anyone with a day to spend out of Tōkyō. Yokohama, too, can lay claim to an important place in Japanese history: in 1869, after centuries of isolation, this city became the first important port for trade with the West and the site of the first major foreign settlement. Twice destroyed, the city retains very few remnants of that history, but it remains Japan's largest port and has an international character that rivals—if not surpasses—that of Tōkyō. Its waterfront park and its ambitious Minato Mirai bay-side development project draw visitors from all over the world.

About the Restaurants

The local specialty in Nikkō is a soy-bean based concoction known as *yuba* (tofu skin); dozens of restaurants in Nikkō serve it in a variety of dishes you might not have believed possible for so prosaic an ingredient. Other local favorites are soba (buckwheat) and udon (wheat-flour) noodles—both inexpensive, filling, and tasty options for lunch.

Three things about Kamakura make it a good place to dine. It's on the ocean (properly speaking, on Sagami Bay), which means that fresh seafood is everywhere; it's a major tourist stop; and it has long been a prestigious place to live among Japan's worldly and well-to-do (many successful writers, artists, and intellectuals call Kamakura home). On a day trip from Tōkyō, you can feel confident picking a place for lunch almost at random.

Yokohama, as befits a city of more than 3 million people, lacks little in the way of food: from quick-fix lunch counters to elegant dining rooms, you'll find almost every imaginable cuisine. Your best bet is Chinatown—Japan's largest Chinese community—with more than 100 restaurants representing every regional style. If you fancy Italian, Indian, or even Scandanavian, this international port is still guaranteed to provide an eminently satisfying meal.

About the Hotels

Yokohama and Kamakura are treated here as day trips, and as it's unlikely that you'll stay overnight in either city, no accommodations are listed for them. Nikkō is something of a toss-up: you can easily see Tōshō-gū and be back in Tōkyō by evening. But when the weather turns glorious in spring or autumn, why not spend some time in the national park, staying overnight at Chūzenji, and returning to the city the next day? Mt. Fuji and Hakone, on the other hand—and more especially the Izu Peninsula—are pure resort destinations. Staying overnight is an intrinsic part of the experience, and it makes little sense to go without hotel reservations confirmed in advance.

In both Nikkō and the Fuji-Hakone-Izu area, there are modern, Western-style hotels that operate in a fairly standard international style. More common, however, are the traditional ryokan and the Japanese-style *kankō* (literally, "sightseeing") hotels. The main difference between these lodging options is that kanko often have Western-style rooms and are situated in prime tourist locations whereas ryokans stick strictly to Japanese-style rooms and are found in less touristy locations. The undisputed pleasure of a ryokan is to return to it at the end of a hard day of sightseeing, luxuriate for an hour in a hot bath with your own garden view, put on the yukata provided for you, and sit down to a catered private dinner party. There's little point to staying at a kankō, unless you want to say you've had the experience and survived. These places do most of their business with big, boisterous tour groups; the turnover is ruthless and the cost is way out of proportion to the service they provide.

The price categories listed below are for double occupancy, but you'll find that most kankō and ryokan normally quote per-person rates, which include breakfast and dinner. Remember to stipulate whether you want a Japanese or Western breakfast. If you don't want dinner at your hotel, it's usually possible to renegotiate the price, but the management will not be happy about it; the two meals are a fixture of their business. The typical ryokan takes great pride in its cuisine, usually with good reason: the evening meal is an elaborate affair of 10 or more different dishes, based on the fresh produce and specialties of the region, served to you—nay, *orchestrated*—in your room on a wonderful variety of trays and tableware designed to celebrate the season.

WHAT IT COSTS In yen				
$$$$	$$$	$$	$	¢
RESTAURANTS Over 3,000	2,000–3,000	1,000–2,000	800–1,000	under 800
HOTELS Over 22,000	18 to 22,000	12 to 18,000	8 to12,000	under 8,000

Restaurant prices are per person for a main course at dinner. Hotel price categories reflect the range of least- to most-expensive standard double rooms in non-holiday high season, based on the European Plan (with no meals) unless otherwise noted. Taxes (5%) are included.

NIKKŌ

Nikkō is a popular vacation spot for the Japanese, for good reason: its gorgeous sights include a breathtaking waterfall and one of the country's best-known shrines. In addition, Nikkō combines the rustic charm of a countryside village (complete with wild monkeys that have the run of the place) with a convenient location not far from Tōkyō.

Exploring Nikkō

The town of Nikkō is essentially one long avenue—Sugi Namiki (Cryptomeria Avenue)—extending for about 2 km (1 mi) from the railway stations to Tōshō-gū. You can easily walk to most places within town. Tourist inns and shops line the street, and if you have time, you might want to make this a leisurely stroll.

The antiques shops along the way may turn up interesting—but expensive—pieces like armor fittings, hibachi, pottery, and dolls. The souvenir shops here sell ample selections of local wood carvings.

Buses and taxis can take you from Nikkō to the village of Chūzenji and nearby Lake Chūzenji.

> **THE UBIQUITOUS TORII**
>
> Wondering what those gate-like structures are with two posts and two crosspieces? They are toriis and are used as gateways to Japanese Shinto temples.

Numbers in the margin correspond to the Nikkō Area map.

Tōshō-gū Area

The Tōshō-gū area encompasses three UNESCO World Heritage sights—Tōshō-gu Shrine, Futarasan Shrine, and Rinnōji Temple. These are known as *nisha-ichiji* (two shrines and one temple) and are Nikkō's main draw. Signs and maps clearly mark a recommended route that will allow you to see all the major sights, which are within walking distance of each other. You should plan for half a day to explore the area.

A multiple-entry ticket is the best way to see the Tōshō-gū precincts. The ¥1,000 pass gets you entrance to Rinnō-ji (Rinnō Temple), the Taiyū-in Mausoleum, and Futara-san Jinja (Futara-san Shrine); for an extra ¥300 you can also see the Sleeping Cat and Ieyasu's tomb at Taiyū-in

CLOSE UP

Ieyasu's Legacy

IN 1600, IEYASU TOKUGAWA (1543–1616) won a battle at a place in the mountains of south-central Japan called Seki-ga-hara that left him the undisputed ruler of the archipelago. He died 16 years later, but the Tokugawa Shōgunate would last another 252 years.

The founder of such a dynasty required a fitting resting place. Ieyasu (ee-eh-*ya*-su) had provided for one in his will: a mausoleum at Nikkō, in a forest of tall cedars, where a religious center had been started more than eight centuries earlier. The year after his death, in accordance with Buddhist custom, he was given a *kaimyō*–an honorific name to bear in the afterlife. Thenceforth, he was Tōshō-Daigongen: the Great Incarnation Who Illuminates the East. The imperial court at Kyōto declared him a god and his remains were taken in a procession of great pomp and ceremony to be enshrined at Nikkō.

The dynasty he left behind was enormously rich. Ieyasu's personal fief, on the Kantō Plain, was worth 2.5 million *koku* of rice. One koku, in monetary terms, was equivalent to the cost of keeping one retainer in the necessities of life for a year. The

shōgunate itself, however, was still an uncertainty. It had only recently taken control after more than a century of civil war. The founder's tomb had a political purpose: to inspire awe and to make manifest the power of the Tokugawas. It was Ieyasu's legacy, a statement of his family's right to rule.

Tōshō-gū was built by his grandson, the third shōgun, Iemitsu (it was Iemitsu who established the policy of national isolation, which closed the doors of Japan to the outside world for more than 200 years). The mausoleum and shrine required the labor of 15,000 people for two years (1634–36). Craftsmen and artists of the first rank were assembled from all over the country. Every surface was carved and painted and lacquered in the most intricate detail imaginable. Tōshō-gū shimmers with the reflections of 2,489,000 sheets of gold leaf. Roof beams and rafter ends with dragon heads, lions, and elephants in bas-relief; friezes of phoenixes, wild ducks, and monkeys; inlaid pillars and red-lacquer corridors: Tōshō-gū is everything a 17th-century warlord would consider gorgeous, and the inspiration is very Chinese.

6

(separate fees are charged for admission to other sights). There are two places to purchase the multiple-entry ticket: one is at the entrance to Rinnō Temple, in the corner of the parking lot, at the top of the path called the Higashi-sandō (East Approach) that begins across the highway from the Sacred Bridge; the other is at the entrance to Tōshō-gū, at the top of the broad Omote-sandō (Central Approach), which begins about 100 yards farther west.

❶ Built in 1636 for shōguns and imperial messengers visiting the shrine, the original **Sacred Bridge** (Shinkyō) was destroyed in a flood; the present red-lacquer wooden structure dates to 1907. Buses leaving from either railway station at Nikkō go straight up the main street to the bridge, opposite the first of the main entrances to Tōshō-gū. The fare

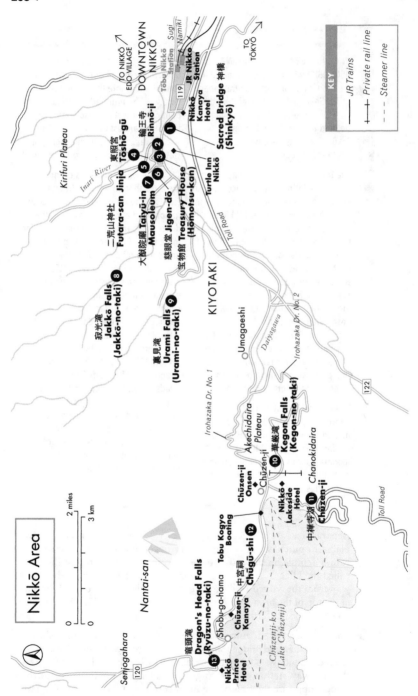

Nikkō Area

KEY
— JR Trains
—⊢ Private rail line
- - - Steamer line

TO NIKKŌ
EDO VILLAGE

DOWNTOWN
NIKKŌ

Tōbu Nikkō Station
JR Nikkō Station
TO
TOKYO

Sugi
Namiki

119

Sacred Bridge 神橋
(Shinkyō)

Nikkō
Kanaya
Hotel

1

輪王寺 Rinnō-ji

東照宮 Tōshō-gū

Kirifuri Plateau

Inari River

二荒山神社 Futara-san Jinja

4
5
7 **6**
3 **2**

大猷院廟 Taiyū-in Mausoleum

慈眼堂 Jigen-dō

宝物館 Treasury House (Hōmotsu-kan)

Turtle Inn
Nikkō

Toll Road

KIYOTAKI

寂光滝 Jakkō Falls
(Jakkō-no-taki) **8**

裏見滝 Urami Falls
(Urami-no-taki) **9**

Umagaeshi

Irohazaka Dr. No. 1

Daiyagawa

Irohazaka Dr. No. 2

122

Akechidaira
Plateau

Chūzenji
Onsen

Chūzen-ji

華厳滝 Kegon Falls
(Kegon-no-taki) **10**

Chanokidaira

Nikkō
Lakeside Hotel

中禅寺湖 Chūzen-ji **11**

Toll Road

Senjogahara

120

Nantai-san

竜頭滝 Dragon's Head Falls
(Ryūzu-no-taki) **13**

Shōbu-ga-hama

Tobu Kogyo
Boating

中宮祠 Chūgū-shi **12**

Chūzen-ji
Kanaya

Nikkō
Prince Hotel

Chūzenji-ko
(Lake Chūzenji)

2 miles

3 km

0

N

is ¥190. The Sacred Bridge is just to the left of a modern bridge, where the road curves and crosses the Daiya-gawa (Daiya River).

The **Monument to Masatsuna Matsudaira**—opposite the Sacred Bridge, at the east entrance to the grounds of Tōshō-gū—pays tribute to one of the two feudal lords charged with the construction of Tōshō-gū. Matsudaira's great contribution was the planting of the wonderful cryptomeria trees (Japanese cedars) surrounding the shrine and along all the approaches to it. The project took 20 years, from 1628 to 1648, and the result was some 36 km (22 mi) of cedar-lined avenues—planted with more than 15,000 trees in all. Fire and time have taken their toll, but thousands of these trees still stand in the shrine precincts, creating a setting of solemn majesty the buildings alone could never have achieved. Thousands more line Route 119 east of Nikkō on the way to Shimo-Imaichi.

> **SEEKING YOUR FORTUNE?**
>
> Make sure you visit **Gohōten-dō**, in the northeast corner of Rinnō Temple, behind the Sanbutsu-dō. Three of the Seven Gods of Good Fortune are enshrined here, which are derived from Chinese folk mythology. These three Buddhist deities are Daikoku-ten and Bishamon-ten, who bring wealth and good harvests, and Benzai-ten, patroness of music and the arts. You might leave Tōkyō rich and musical.

★ ❷ **Rinnō-ji** (Rinnō Temple) belongs to the Tendai sect of Buddhism, the head temple of which is Enryaku-ji, on Mt. Hiei near Kyōto. The main hall of Rinnō Temple, called the **Sanbutsu-dō**, is the largest single building at Tōshō-gū; it enshrines an image of Amida Nyorai, the Buddha of the Western Paradise, flanked on the right by Senju (Thousand-Armed) Kannon, the goddess of mercy, and on the left by Bato-Kannon, regarded as the protector of animals. These three images are lacquered in gold and date from the early part of the 17th century. The original Sanbutsu-dō is said to have been built in 848 by the priest Ennin (794–864), also known as Jikaku-Daishi. The present building dates from 1648.

In the southwest corner of the Rinnō Temple compound, behind the abbot's residence, is an especially fine Japanese garden called **Shōyō-en**, created in 1815 and thoughtfully designed to present a different perspective of its rocks, ponds, and flowering plants from every turn on its path. To the right of the entrance to the garden is the **Treasure Hall** (Hōmotsu-den) of Rinnō Temple, a museum with a collection of some 6,000 works of lacquerware, painting, and Buddhist sculpture. The museum is rather small, and only a few of the pieces in the collection—many of them designated National Treasures and Important Cultural Properties—are on display at any given time. 🎫 *Rinnō Temple ¥1,000, multiple-entry ticket includes admission to the Taiyū-in Mausoleum and Futara-san Shrine; Shōyō-en and Treasure Hall ¥300* ⊘ *Apr.–Oct., daily 8–5, last entry at 4; Nov.–Mar., daily 8–4, last entry at 3.*

❸ An unhurried visit to the precincts of Tōshō-gū should definitely include the **Treasury House** (Hōmotsu-kan), which contains a collection of antiquities from its various shrines and temples. From the west gate of Rinnō Temple, turn left off Omote-sandō, just below the pagoda, onto the cedar-lined avenue to Futara-san Jinja. A minute's walk will bring you to the museum, on the left. 🎫 ¥500 ⊗ Apr.–Oct., daily 9–5; Nov.–Mar., daily 9–4.

❹ With its riot of colors and carvings, inlaid pillars, red-lacquer corridors, and extensive use of gold leaf, **Tōshō-gū**, the 17th-century shrine to Ieyasu Tokugawa, is magnificent, astonishing, and never dull.

Fodor'sChoice ★

The west gate of Rinnō Temple brings you out onto Omote-sandō, which leads uphill to the stone torii of the shrine. The **Five-Story Pagoda** of Tōshō-gū—a reconstruction dating from 1818—is on the left as you approach the shrine. The 12 signs of the zodiac decorate the first story. The black-lacquer doors above each sign bear the three hollyhock leaves of the Tokugawa family crest.

> ### THREE LITTLE MONKEYS
>
> While in the Sacred Stable, take a look at the second panel from the left. Recognize the three monkeys? The trio, commonly referred to as "Hear no evil, Speak no evil, See no evil," is something of a Nikkō trademark and has been reproduced on plaques, bags, and souvenirs. The true origins of this phrase are much debated, but scholars and legend suggest it originated from this shrine as a visual interpretation of the phrase, "If we do not hear, see, or speak evil, we ourselves shall be spared all evil." As for the monkeys, it's been said that a Chinese Buddhist monk introduced the image in the 8th-century.

From the torii a flight of stone steps brings you to the front gate of the shrine—the Omote-mon, also called the Nio-mon (Gate of the Deva Kings), with its fearsome pair of red-painted guardian gods. From here the path turns to the left. In the first group of buildings you reach on the left is the 17th-century **Sacred Stable** (Shinkyū). Housed here is the white horse—symbol of purity—that figures in many of the shrine's ceremonial events. Carvings of pine trees and monkeys adorn the panels over the stable. And where the path turns to the right, you'll find a granite font where visitors can purify themselves before entering the inner precincts of Tōshō-gū. The **Sutra Library** (Rinzō), just beyond the font, is a repository for some 7,000 Buddhist scriptures, kept in a huge revolving bookcase nearly 20 feet high; it's not open to the public.

As you pass under the second (bronze) torii and up the steps, you'll see a belfry and a tall bronze candelabra on the right and a drum tower and a bronze revolving lantern on the left. The two works in bronze were presented to the shrine by the Dutch government in the mid-17th century. Behind the drum tower is the **Yakushi-dō,** which enshrines a manifestation of the Buddha as Yakushi Nyorai, the healer of illnesses. The original 17th-century building was famous for a huge India-ink painting on the ceiling of the nave, *The Roaring Dragon,* so named for the rumbling echoes it seemed to emit when visitors clapped their hands beneath it. The painting was by Yasunobu Enshin Kanō (1613–85), from a family of artists that dominated the profession for 400 years. The Kanō school was founded in the late 15th century and patronized by successive military governments until the fall of the Tokugawa Shōgunate in 1868. The Yakushi-dō was destroyed by fire in 1961, then rebuilt; the dragon on the ceiling now is by Nampu Katayama (1887–1980).

The centerpiece of Tōshō-gū is the **Gate of Sunlight** (Yōmei-mon), at the top of the second flight of stone steps. A designated National Treasure, it's also called the Twilight Gate (Higurashi-mon)—implying that you could gape at its richness of detail all day, until sunset. And rich it is indeed: 36 feet high and dazzling white, the gate has 12 columns, beams, and roof brackets carved with dragons, lions, clouds, peonies, Chinese sages, and demigods, painted vivid hues of red, blue, green, and gold. On one of the central columns, there are two carved tigers; the natural grain of the wood is used to bring out the "fur." As you enter the Yōmei-mon, there are galleries running east and west for some 700 feet; their paneled fences are also carved and painted with nature motifs.

The portable shrines that appear in the Tōshō-gū Festival, held yearly on May 17–18, are kept in the **Shin-yosha**, a storeroom to the left as you come through the Twilight Gate into the heart of the shrine. The paintings on the ceiling, of *tennin* (Buddhist angels) playing harps, are by Tanyu Kanō (1602–1674).

Mere mortals may not pass through this **Chinese Gate** (Kara-mon), which is the "official" entrance to the Tōshō-gū inner shrine. Like its counterpart, the Yomei-mon, on the opposite side of the courtyard, the Kara-mon is a National Treasure—and, like the Yomei-mon, is carved and painted in elaborate detail with dragons and other auspicious figures. The Main Hall of Tōshō-gū is enclosed by a wall of painted and carved panel screens; opposite the right-hand corner of the wall, facing the shrine, is the **Kitō-den,** a hall where annual prayers were once offered for the peace of the nation. For a very modest fee, Japanese couples can be married here in a traditional Shintō ceremony, with an ensemble of drums and reed flutes and shrine maidens to attend them.

The **Main Hall** (Hon-den) of Tōshō-gū is the ultimate purpose of the shrine. You approach it from the rows of lockers at the far end of the enclosure; here you remove and store your shoes, step up into the shrine, and follow a winding corridor to the Oratory (Hai-den)—the anteroom, resplendent in its lacquered pillars, carved friezes, and coffered ceilings bedecked with dragons. Over the lintels are paintings by Mitsuoki Tosa (1617–91) of the 36 great poets of the Heian period, with their poems in the calligraphy of Emperor Go-Mizuno-o. Deeper yet, at the back of the Oratory, is the Inner Chamber (Nai-jin)—repository of the Sacred Mirror that represents the spirit of the deity enshrined here. To the right is a room that was reserved for members of the three principal branches of the Tokugawa family; the room on the left was for the chief abbot of Rinnō Temple, who was always a prince of the imperial line.

Behind the Inner Chamber is the Innermost Chamber (Nai-Nai-jin). No visitors come this far. Here, in the very heart of Tōshō-gū, is the gold-lacquer shrine where the spirit of Ieyasu resides—along with two other deities, whom the Tokugawas later decided were fit companions. One was Hideyoshi Toyotomi, Ieyasu's mentor and liege lord in the long wars of unification at the end of the 16th century. The other was Minamoto no Yoritomo, brilliant military tactician and founder of the earlier (12th-century) Kamakura Shōgunate (Ieyasu claimed Yoritomo for an ancestor).

■ TIP➔ Don't forget to recover your shoes when you return to the courtyard.
Between the Goma-dō and the **Kagura-den** (a hall where ceremonial dances
are performed to honor the gods) is a passage to the **Gate at the Foot
of the Hill** (Sakashita-mon). Above the gateway is another famous symbol of Tōshō-gū, the Sleeping Cat—a small panel said to have been carved
by Hidari Jingoro (Jingoro the Left-handed), a late-16th-century master carpenter and sculptor credited with important contributions to numerous Tokugawa-period temples, shrines, and palaces. A separate
admission charge (¥520) is levied to go beyond the Sleeping Cat, up the
flight of 200 stone steps through a forest of cryptomeria to **Ieyasu's tomb.**
The climb is worth making for the view of the Yomei-mon and Kara-
mon from above; the tomb itself is unimpressive. ▣ *Free; Ieyasu's
tomb ¥520* ☉ *Apr.–Oct. daily 9–5; Nov.–Mar. daily 9–4.*

★ ❺ The holy ground at Nikkō is far older than the Tokugawa dynasty, in
whose honor it was improved upon. To the gods enshrined at the 8th-
century **Futara-san Jinja** (Futara-san Shrine), Ieyasu Tokugawa must
seem but a callow newcomer. Futara-san is sacred to the Shintō deities
Okuni-nushi-no-Mikoto (god of the rice fields, bestower of prosperity),
his consort Tagorihime-no-Mikoto, and their son Ajisukitaka-hikone-
no-Mikoto. Futara-san actually has three locations: the Main Shrine at
Tōshō-gū; the Chūgū-shi (Middle Shrine), at Chūzenji-ko; and the Oku-
miya (Inner Shrine), on top of Mt. Nantai.

The bronze torii at the entrance to the shrine leads to the **Chinese Gate**
(Kara-mon), gilded and elaborately carved; beyond it is the **Hai-den,** the
shrine's oratory. The Hai-den, too, is richly carved and decorated, with
a dragon-covered ceiling. The Chinese lions on the panels at the rear are
by two distinguished painters of the Kanō school. From the oratory of
the Taiyū-in a connecting passage leads to the **Sanctum** (Hon-den)—the
present version of which dates from 1619. Designated a National Treasure, it houses a gilded and lacquered Buddhist altar some 9 feet high,
decorated with paintings of animals, birds, and flowers, in which resides
the object of all this veneration: a seated wooden figure of Iemitsu himself. To get to Futara-san, take the avenue to the left as you're standing
before the stone torii at Tōshō-gū and follow it to the end. ▣*¥200, ¥1,000
multiple-entry ticket includes admission to Rinnō Temple and Taiyū-in
Mausoleum* ☉ *Apr.–Oct., daily 8–5; Nov.–Mar., daily 9–4.*

❻ Tenkai (1536–1643), the first abbot of Rinnō Temple, has his own place
of honor at Tōshō-gū: the **Jigen-dō.** The hall, which was founded in 848,
now holds many of Rinnō Temple's artistic treasures. To reach it, take
the path opposite the south entrance to Futara-san Shrine that passes between the two subtemples called Jōgyō-dō and Hokke-dō. Connected by
a corridor, these two buildings are otherwise known as the Futatsu-dō
(Twin Halls) of Rinnō Temple and are designated a National Cultural
Property. The path between the Twin Halls leads roughly south and west
to the Jigen-dō compound; the hall itself is at the north end of the compound, to the right. At the west end sits the Go-ōden, a shrine to Prince
Yoshihisa Kitashirakawa (1847–95), the last of the imperial princes to
serve as abbot. Behind it are his tomb and the tombs of his 13 predeces-
sors. ▣ *Free* ☉ *Apr.–Nov., daily 8–5; Dec.–Mar., daily 9–4.*

Peaceful Yumoto

LOCATED ON THE NORTHERN shore of peaceful Lake Yunoko, these isolated hot springs were once a popular destination for 14th century aristocrats. Today, the area is still known for its hot springs—being able to soak in an onsen all year long, even when temperatures drop below zero, will always be a major plus—but they are now controlled by separate resorts. Besides the healing and relaxing affects of the baths, visitors come for the hiking trails, fishing, camping, skiing, bird watching, and mountain climbing opportunites. Try to avoid the fall season, as it is peak visitor time and there are always delays. You can get to the Yumoto onsen by taking the Tobu Operated Buses, which leave Tobu Nikko and JR Nikko stations. There are one or two services an hour depending on the time of the day and a one way trip from central Nikko takes about 80 minutes, ¥1,650.

★ ❼ The grandiose **Taiyū-in Mausoleum** is the resting place of the third Tokugawa shōgun, Iemitsu (1604–51), who imposed a policy of national isolation on Japan that was to last more than 200 years. Iemitsu, one suspects, had it in mind to upstage his illustrious grandfather; he marked the approach to his own tomb with no fewer than six different decorative gates. The first is another Niō-mon—a Gate of the Deva Kings—like the one at Tōshō-gū. The dragon painted on the ceiling is by Yasunobu Kanō. A flight of stone steps leads from here to the second gate, the Nitenmon, a two-story structure protected front and back by carved and painted images of guardian gods. Beyond it, two more flights of steps lead to the middle courtyard. As you climb the last steps to Iemitsu's shrine, you'll pass a bell tower on the right and a drum tower on the left; directly ahead is the third gate, the remarkable **Yasha-mon,** so named for the figures of *yasha* (she-demons) in the four niches. This structure is also known as the Peony Gate (Botan-mon) for the carvings that decorate it.

As you exit the shrine, on the west side, you come to the fifth gate: the **Kōka-mon,** built in the style of the late Ming dynasty of China. The gate is normally closed, but from here another flight of stone steps leads to the sixth and last gate—the cast copper **Inuki-mon,** inscribed with characters in Sanskrit—and Iemitsu's tomb. 🎫 *¥1,000 multiple-entry ticket includes admission to Rinnō Temple and Futara-san Shrine* ☉ *Apr.–Oct., daily 8–5; Nov.–Mar., daily 8–4.*

☺ **Nikkō Edo Village** (Nikkō Edo Mura), a living-history theme park a short taxi ride from downtown, re-creates an 18th-century Japanese village. The complex includes sculpted gardens with waterfalls and ponds and 22 vintage buildings, where actors in traditional dress stage martial arts exhibitions, historical theatrical performances, and comedy acts. You can even observe Japanese tea ceremony rituals in gorgeous tatami-floored houses, as well as people dressed as geisha and samurai. Strolling stuffed animal characters and acrobatic ninjas keep kids happy. Nikkō Edo Mura has one large restaurant and 15 small food stalls serving period cuisine like *yakisoba* (fried soba) and *dango* (dumplings). ✉ *470–2 Egura, Fujiwara-chō, Shiodani-gun* ☎ *0288/77–1777* 💰 *¥2,300 general admission, plus extra for rides and shows; ¥6,300 unlimited day pass includes rides and shows* ⊗ *Mid-Mar.–Nov., daily 9–5; Dec.–mid-Mar., daily 9:30–4.*

DID YOU KNOW?

Under the policy of national seclusion, only the Dutch retained trading privileges with Japan. Even then, they were confined to the tiny artificial island of Dejima, in the port of Nagasaki. They regularly sent tokens of their esteem to the shōgunate to keep their precarious monopoly, including the two bronze items found in the Sacred Stable, which were sent in 1636. The 200-year-plus monopoly was dissolved when Japan decided to open its borders to other Western countries in 1858.

To Chūzenji-ko (Lake Chūzenji)

More than 3,900 feet above sea level, at the base of the volcano known as Nantai-san, is Lake Chūzenji, renowned for its clean waters and fresh air. People come to boat and fish on the lake and to enjoy the surrounding scenic woodlands, waterfalls, and hills. If you're looking to sightsee, check out **Tobu Kogyo Boating**, which offers chartered boat rides for 60 minutes. ✉ *2478 Chugushi, Nikkō, Tochigi-ken* ☎ *0288/55–0360* 💰 *Between ¥150–¥1,500 depending on route chosen* ⊗ *Dec.–Mar. 9:30 AM–3:30 PM daily.*

8 Falling water is one of the special charms of the Nikkō National Park area; people going by bus or car from Tōshō-gū to Lake Chūzenji often stop off en route to see **Jakkō Falls** (Jakkō-no-taki), which descend in a series of seven terraced stages, forming a sheet of water about 100 feet high. About 1 km (½ mi) from the shrine precincts, at the Tamozawa bus stop, a narrow road to the right leads to an uphill walk of some 3 km (2 mi) to the falls.

9 "The water," wrote the great 17th-century poet Bashō about the **Urami Falls** (Urami-no-taki), "seemed to take a flying leap and drop a hundred feet from the top of a cave into a green pool surrounded by a thousand rocks. One was supposed to inch one's way into the cave and enjoy the falls from behind." It's a steep climb to the cave, which begins at the Arasawa bus stop, with a turn to the right off the Chūzenji road. The falls and the gorge are striking—but you should make the climb only if you have good hiking shoes and are willing to get wet in the process.

The real climb to Lake Chūzenji begins at **Umagaeshi** (literally, "horse return"). Here, in the old days, the road became too rough for horse riding, so riders had to alight and proceed on foot. The lake is 4,165 feet above sea level. From Umagaeshi the bus climbs a one-way toll road up the pass; the old road has been widened and is used for the traffic coming down. The two roads are full of steep hairpin turns, and on a clear day the view up and down the valley is magnificent—especially from the halfway point at **Akechi-daira** (Akechi Plain), from which you can see the summit of **Nantai-san** (Mt. Nantai), reaching 8,149 feet. Hiking season lasts from May through mid-October; if you push it, you can make the ascent in about four hours. ⚠ Wild monkeys make their homes in these mountains, and they've learned the convenience of mooching from visitors along the route. Be careful—they have a way of not taking no for an answer. Umagaeshi is about 10 km (6 mi) from Tōbu Station in Nikkō, or 8 km (5 mi) from Tōshō-gū.

⑪ The bus trip from Nikkō to the national park area ends at Chūzenji village, which shares its name with the temple established here in 784. **Chūzen-ji** (Chūzen Temple) is a subtemple of Rinnō Temple, at Tōshō-gū. The principal object of worship at Chūzen-ji is the **Tachi-ki Kannon**, a 17-foot-tall standing statue of the

FEELING ADVENTUROUS?

If you want to avoid the hairpin turns, try the **ropeway** that runs from Akechi-daira station directly to the Akechi-daira lookout. It takes 3 minutes and the panoramic views of Nikko and Kegon Falls are priceless. ¥390 ✉ 709-5 Misawa, Hosoo-machi, Nikko ☎ 028/855-0331 ⊙ Apr.–Oct., daily 8:30–4; Nov.–Mar., daily 9–3.

Buddhist goddess of mercy, said to have been carved more than 1,000 years ago by the priest Shōdō from the living trunk of a single Judas tree. You reach the temple grounds by turning left (south) as you leave the village of Chūzenji and walking about 1½ km (1 mi) along the eastern shore of the lake. ¥300 ⊙ Apr.–Oct., daily 8–5; Mar. and Nov., daily 8–4; Dec.–Feb., daily 8–3:30.

⑫ **Chūgū-shi**, a subshrine of the Futara-san Shrine at Tōshō-gū, is the major religious center on the north side of Lake Chūzenji, about 1½ km (1 mi) west of the village. The **Treasure House** (Hōmotsu-den) contains an interesting historical collection, including swords, lacquerware, and medieval shrine palanquins. ✉ Shrine free, Treasure House ¥300 ⊙ Apr.–Oct., daily 8–5; Nov.–Mar., daily 9–4.

⑩ More than anything else, **Kegon Falls** (Kegon-no-taki), the country's most Fodor'sChoice famous falls, are what draw the crowds of Japanese visitors to Chūzenji. ★ Fed by the eastward flow of the lake, the falls drop 318 feet into a rugged gorge; an elevator (¥530) takes you to an observation platform at the bottom. The volume of water over the falls is carefully regulated, but it's especially impressive after a summer rain or a typhoon. In winter the falls do not freeze completely but form a beautiful cascade of icicles. The elevator is just a few minutes' walk east from the bus stop at Chūzenji village, downhill and off to the right at the far end of the parking lot. ✉ 2479-2 Chugushi Nikkō ☎ 028/855–0030 ⊙ Daily 8–5.

NEED A BREAK? Take a breather at the **Ryūzu-no-taki Chaya** (✉ 2485 Chugushi Nikkō ☎ 028/855-0157 ⊙ Daily 11-5): a charming, but rustic, tea shop near the waterfalls. Enjoy a cup of green tea, a light meal, or Japanese sweets like rice cakes boiled with vegetables and *dango* (sweet dumplings) while you gaze at the falling waters.

⑬ If you've budgeted an extra day for Nikkō, you might want to consider a walk around the lake. A paved road along the north shore extends for about 8 km (5 mi), one-third of the whole distance, as far as the "beach" at Shōbu-ga-hama. Here, where the road branches off to the north for Senjōgahara, are the lovely cascades of **Dragon's Head Falls**

(Ryūzu-no-taki). To the left is a steep footpath that continues around the lake to Senju-ga-hama and then to a campsite at Asegata. The path is well marked but can get rough in places. From Asegata it's less than an hour's walk back to Chūzenji village.

Where to Eat

Chūzen-ji

$$–$$$ ✕ **Nantai.** The low tables, antiques, and pillows scattered on tatami flooring makes visitors feel like they're dining in a traditional Japanese living room. Try the Nikkō specialty, *yuba* (tofu skin), which comes with the *nabe* (hot pot) for dinner. It is the quintessential winter family meal. The seafood here is fresh and both the trout and salmon are recommended. Each meal comes with rice, pickles, and selected side dishes like soy-stewed vegetables, tempura, udon, and a dessert. ✉ *2478-8 Chugushi Nikkō* ☎ *028/855–0201* ☱ *MC, V.*

Nikkō

$$$$ ✕ **Gyōshintei.** This is the only restaurant in Nikkō devoted to *shōjin ryōri*, the Buddhist-temple vegetarian fare that evolved centuries ago into haute cuisine. Gyōshintei is decorated in the style of a *ryōtei* (traditional inn), with all-tatami seating. It differs from a ryōtei in that it has one large, open space where many guests are served at once, rather than a number of rooms for private dining. Dinner is served until 7. ✉ *2339–1 Sannai, Nikkō* ☎ *0288/53–3751* ☱ *AE, DC, MC, V* ⊗ *Closed Thurs.*

$$$–$$$$ ✕ **Fujimoto.** At what may be Nikkō's most formal Western-style restaurant, finer touches include plush carpets, art deco fixtures, stained and frosted glass, a thoughtful wine list, and a maître d' in black tie. The menu combines elements of French and Japanese cooking styles and ingredients; the fillet of beef in mustard sauce is particularly excellent. Fujimoto closes at 7:30, so plan on eating early. ✉ *2339–1 Sannai, Nikkō* ☎ *0288/53–3754* ☱ *AE, DC, MC, V* ⊗ *Closed Thurs.*

$$$–$$$$ ✕ **Masudaya.** Masudaya started out as a sake maker more than a century ago, but for four generations now, it has been the town's best-known restaurant. The specialty is yuba, which the chefs transform, with the help of local vegetables and fresh fish, into sumptuous high cuisine. The building is traditional, with a lovely interior garden; the assembly-line-style service, however, detracts from the ambience. Masudaya serves one nine-course kaiseki-style meal; the kitchen simply stops serving when the food is gone. Meals here are prix fixe. ✉ *439–2 Ishiya-machi, Nikkō* ☎ *0288/54–2151* ⚏ *Reservations essential* ☱ *No credit cards* ⊗ *Open 11–3* ⊗ *Closed Thurs.*

$$$–$$$$ ✕ **Meiji-no-Yakata.** Not far from the east entrance to Rinnō Temple, Meiji-no-Yakata is an elegant 19th-century Western-style stone house, originally built as a summer retreat for an American diplomat. The food, too, is Western style; specialties of the house include fresh rainbow trout from Lake Chūzen-ji, roast lamb with pepper sauce, and melt-in-your-mouth filet mignon made from local Tochigi beef. High ceilings, hardwood floors, and an air of informality make this a very pleasant place to dine. The restaurant opens at 11 AM in the summer and 11:30 AM in the winter; it always closes at 7:30. ✉ *2339–1 Sannai, Nikkō* ☎ *0288/53–3751* ☱ *AE, DC, MC, V* ⊗ *Closed Wed.*

$$–$$$ ✕ **Sawamoto.** Charcoal-broiled *unagi* (eel) is an acquired taste, and there's no better place in Nikkō to acquire it than at this restaurant. The place is small and unpretentious, with only five plain-wood tables, and service can be lukewarm, but Sawamoto is reliable for a light lunch or dinner of unagi on a bed of rice, served in an elegant lacquered box. Eel is considered a stamina builder: just right for the weary visitor on a hot summer day. ⊠ *1019 Bandu, Kami Hatsuishi-machi, Nikkō* ☎ *0288/ 54–0163* ▭ *No credit cards* ☽ *No dinner.*

Where to Stay

Nikkō

★ **$$–$$$$** 🏨 **Nikkō Kanaya Hotel.** This family-run operation is a little worn around the edges after a century of operation, but it still has the best location in town: across the street from Tōshō-gū. The main building is a delightful, rambling Victorian structure that has hosted royalty and other important personages—as the guest book attests—from around the world. The long driveway that winds up to the hotel at the top of the hill is just below the Sacred Bridge, on the same side of the street. The hotel is very touristy; daytime visitors browse through the old building and its gift shops. The helpful staff is better at giving area information than the tourist office. Rooms vary a great deal, as do their prices. The more expensive rooms are spacious and comfortable, with wonderful high ceilings; in the annex the sound of the Daiya-gawa murmuring below the Sacred Bridge lulls you to sleep. Horseback riding and golf are available nearby. ⊠ *1300 Kami Hatsuishi-machi, Nikkō, Tochigi-ken 321-1401* ☎ *0288/54–0001* ◹ *77 rooms, 62 with bath* ♨ *2 restaurants, coffee shop, pool, bar* ▭ *AE, DC, MC, V.*

¢ 🏨 **Turtle Inn Nikkō.** This Japanese Inn Group member provides friendly, modest, cost-conscious Western- and Japanese-style accommodations with or without a private bath. Simple, cheap breakfasts and dinners are served in the dining room, but you needn't opt for these if you'd rather eat out. Rates go up about 10% in high season (late July and August). To get here, take the bus bound for Chūzenji from either railway station and get off at the Sōgō Kaikan-mae bus stop. The inn is two minutes from the bus stop and within walking distance of Tōshō-gū. ⊠ *2–16 Takumi-chō, Nikkō, Tochigi-ken 321-1433* ☎ *0288/53–3168* ◹ *7 Western-style rooms, 3 with bath; 5 Japanese-style rooms without bath* ⊕ *www. turtle-nikko.com* ♨ *Restaurant, Japanese baths, Internet* ▭ *AE, MC, V.*

Chūzen-ji

$$$$ 🏨 **Chūzen-ji Kanaya.** A boathouse and restaurant on the lake give this branch of the Nikkō Kanaya on the road from the village to Shōbu-ga-hama the air of a private yacht club. Pastel colors decorate the simple, tasteful rooms, which have floor-to-ceiling windows overlooking the lake or grounds. ⊠ *2482 Chū-gūshi, Chūzen-ji, Nikkō, Tochigi-ken 321-1661* ☎ *0288/51–0001* ◹ *60 rooms, 54 with bath* ♨ *Restaurant, boating, waterskiing, fishing* ▭ *AE, DC, MC, V* ¶◎¶ *MAP.*

$$–$$$ 🏨 **Nikkō Lakeside Hotel.** In the village of Chūzen-ji at the foot of the lake, the Nikkō Lakeside has no particular character, but the views are good and the transportation connections (to buses and excursion boats) are ideal. Prices vary considerably from weekday to weekend and season

6

to season. ✉ 2482 *Chū-gūshi, Chūzen-ji, Nikkō, Tochigi-ken 321-1661* ☎ *0288/55–0321* ↝ *100 rooms with bath* ♿ *2 restaurants, tennis court, boating, fishing, bicycles, bar* ⊟ *AE, DC, MC, V* ⦿I *MAP.*

Shōbu-ga-hama

$$ ⊞ **Nikkō Prince Hotel.** On the shore of Lake Chūzen-ji, this hotel, part of a large Japanese chain, is within walking distance of the Dragon's Head Falls. With many of its accommodations in two-story maisonettes and rustic detached cottages, the Prince chain markets itself to families and small groups of younger excursionists. The architecture favors high ceilings and wooden beams, with lots of glass in the public areas to take advantage of the view of the lake and Mt. Nantai. ✉ *Chū-gūshi, Shōbu-ga-hama Nikkō, Tochigi-ken 321-1692* ☎ *0288/55-1111* ⊕ *www.princehotels.co.jp* ↝ *60 rooms with bath* ♿ *Restaurant, 2 tennis courts, pool, downhill skiing, bar, lounge* ⊟ *AE, DC, MC, V* ⦿I *MAP.*

Nikkō Essentials

BUS TRAVEL

⚠ There is no bus service between Tōkyō and Nikkō. Local buses leave Tōbu Nikkō Station for Lake Chūzen-ji, stopping just above the entrance to Tōshō-gū, approximately every 30 minutes from 6:15 AM until 7:01 PM. The fare to Chūzen-ji is ¥1,100, and the ride takes about 40 minutes. The last return bus from the lake leaves at 7:39 PM, arriving back at Tōbu Nikkō Station at 9:17.

CAR TRAVEL

■ TIP→ It's possible, but unwise, to travel by car from Tōkyō to Nikkō. The trip will take at least three hours, and merely getting from central Tōkyō to the toll-road system can be a nightmare. Coming back, especially on a Saturday or Sunday evening, is even worse. If you absolutely *must* drive, take the Tōkyō Expressway 5 (Ikebukuro Line) north to the Tōkyō Gaikandō, go east on this ring road to the Kawaguchi interchange, and pick up the Tōhoku Expressway northbound. Take the Tōhoku to Utsunomiya and change again at Exit 10 (marked in English) for the Nikkō–Utsunomiya Toll Road, which runs into Nikkō.

TOURS

From Tōkyō, Sunrise Tours operates one-day bus tours to Nikkō, which take you to Tōshō-gū and Lake Chūzen-ji for ¥13,500 (lunch included). The tour schedule varies widely from season to season, so check the Web site or call well in advance.

🚩 Sunrise Tours ☎ 03/5796-5454 ⊕ www.jtb.co.jp/sunrisetour.

TAXIS

Cabs are readily available in Nikkō; the one-way fare from Tōbu Nikkō Station to Chūzen-ji is about ¥6,000.

TRAIN TRAVEL

The limited express train of the Tōbu Railway has two direct connections from Tōkyō to Nikkō every morning, starting at 7:30 AM from Tōbu Asakusa Station, a minute's walk from the last stop on Tōkyō's

Ginza subway line; there are additional trains on weekends, holidays, and in high season. The one-way fare is ¥2,740. All seats are reserved. Bookings are not accepted over the phone; they can only be bought at Asakusa station. During summer, fall, and weekends, buy tickets a few days in advance. The trip from Asakusa to the Tōbu Nikkō Station takes about two hours, which is quicker than the JR trains. If you're visiting Nikkō on a day trip, note that the last return trains are at 4:29 PM (direct express) and 7:42 PM (with a transfer at 7:52 at Shimo-Imaichi).

If you have a JR Pass, use JR (Japan Railways) service, which connects Tōkyō and Nikkō, from Ueno Station. Take the Tōhoku–Honsen Line limited express to Utsunomiya (about 1½ hours) and transfer to the train for JR Nikkō Station (45 minutes). The earliest departure from Ueno is at 5:10 AM; the last connection back leaves Nikkō at 8:03 PM and brings you into Ueno at 10:48 PM. (If you're not using the JR Pass, the one-way fare will cost ¥2,520.)

More expensive but faster is the Yamabiko train on the north extension of the Shinkansen; the one-way fare, including the surcharge for the express, is ¥5,430. The first one leaves Tōkyō Station at 6:04 AM (or Ueno at 6:10 AM) and takes about 50 minutes to Utsunomiya; change there to the train to Nikkō Station. To return, take the 9:43 PM train from Nikkō to Utsunomiya and catch the last Yamabiko back at 10:53 PM, arriving in Ueno at 11:38 PM.

🚉 **Japan Railways** ☎ 03/3423−0111 ⊕ www.japanrail.com.

VISITOR INFORMATION

You can do a lot of preplanning for your visit to Nikkō with a stop at the Japan National Tourist Organization office in Tōkyō, where the helpful English-speaking staff will ply you with pamphlets and field your questions about things to see and do. Closer to the source is the Tourist Information and Hospitality Center in Nikkō itself, about halfway up the main street of town between the railway stations and Tōshō-gū, on the left; don't expect too much in the way of help in English, but the center does have a good array of guides to local restaurants and shops, registers of inns and hotels, and mapped-out walking tours.

🚉 Tourist Information **Japan National Tourist Organization** ✉ Tōkyō Kōtsū Kaikan, 10F, 2-10-1 Yūraku-chō, Chiyoda-ku, Tōkyō ☎ 03/3201-3331 ⊕ www.jnto.go.jp Ⓜ JR Yamanote Line (Higashi-guchi/East Exit) and Yūraku-chō subway line (Exit A-8), Yūraku-chō Station. **Nikkō Tourist Information and Hospitality Center** ☎ 0288/54-2496.

KAMAKURA

Kamakura, about 40 km (25 mi) southwest of Tōkyō, is an object lesson in what happens when you set the fox to guard the henhouse.

For the aristocrats of the Heian-era Japan (794–1185), life was defined by the imperial court in Kyōto. Who in their right mind would venture elsewhere? In Kyōto there was grace and beauty and poignant affairs of the heart; everything beyond was howling wilderness. Unfortunately, it was the howling wilderness that had all the estates: the large grants of land, called *shōen,* without which there would be no income to pay for all that grace and beauty.

By the 12th century two clans— the Taira (*ta*-ee-ra) and the Minamoto, themselves both offshoots of the imperial line—had come to dominate the affairs of the Heian court and were at each other's throats in a struggle for supremacy. In 1160 the Taira won a major battle that should have secured their

TIMING TIP

If your time is limited, you may want to visit only Engaku Temple and Tōkei Temple in Kita-Kamakura before riding the train one stop to Kamakura. If not, follow the main road all the way to Tsuru-ga-oka Hachiman-gū and visit four additional temples en route.

absolute control over Japan, but in the process they made one serious mistake: having killed the Minamoto leader Yoshitomo (1123–1160), they spared his 13-year-old son, Yoritomo (1147–1199), and sent him into exile. In 1180 he launched a rebellion and chose Kamakura—a superb natural fortress, surrounded on three sides by hills and guarded on the fourth by the sea—as his base of operations.

The rivalry between the two clans became an all-out war. By 1185 Yoritomo and his half-brother, Yoshitsune (1159–1189), had destroyed the Taira utterly, and the Minamoto were masters of all Japan. In 1192 Yoritomo forced the imperial court to name him shōgun; he was now de facto and de jure the military head of state. The emperor was left as a figurehead in Kyōto, and the little fishing village of Kamakura became—and for 141 years remained—the seat of Japan's first shogunal government.

The Minamoto line came to an end when Yoritomo's two sons were assassinated. Power passed to the Hōjō family, who remained in control, often as regents for figurehead shōguns, for the next 100 years. In 1274 and again in 1281 Japan was invaded by the Mongol armies of China's Yuan dynasty. On both occasions typhoons—the original kamikaze (literally, "divine wind")—destroyed the Mongol fleets, but the Hōjō family was still obliged to reward the various clans that had rallied to the defense of the realm. A number of these clans were unhappy with their portions—and with Hōjō rule in general. The end came suddenly, in 1333, when two vassals assigned to put down a revolt switched sides. The Hōjō regent committed suicide, and the center of power returned to Kyōto.

Kamakura reverted to being a sleepy backwater town on the edge of the sea, but after World War II, it began to develop as a residential area for the well-to-do. Nothing secular survives from the days of the Minamoto and Hōjō; there wasn't much there to begin with. The warriors of Kamakura had little use for courtiers, or their palaces and gardened villas; the shōgunate's name for itself, in fact, was the Bakufu— literally, the "tent government." As a religious center, however, the town presents an extraordinary legacy. The Bakufu endowed shrines and temples by the score in Kamakura, especially temples of the Rinzai sect of Zen Buddhism. Most of those temples and shrines are in settings of remarkable beauty; many are designated National Treasures. If you can afford the time for only one day trip from Tōkyō, you should probably spend it here.

Exploring Kamakura

There are three principal areas in Kamakura, and you can easily get from one to another by train. From Tōkyō head first to Kita-Kamakura for most of the important Zen temples, including Engaku-ji (Engaku Temple) and Kenchō-ji (Kenchō Temple). The second area is downtown Kamakura, with its shops and museums and the venerated shrine Tsuru-ga-oka Hachiman-gū. The third is Hase, a 10-minute train ride southwest from Kamakura on the Enoden Line. Hase's main attractions are the great bronze figure of the Amida Buddha, at Kōtoku-in, and the Kannon Hall of Hase-dera. There's a lot to see in Kamakura, and even to hit just the highlights will take you most of a busy day.

Numbers in the margin correspond to the Kamakura map.

Kita-Kamakura (North Kamakura)

★ ❶ Hierarchies were important to the Kamakura Shōgunate. In the 14th century it established a ranking system called Go-zan (literally, "Five Mountains") for the Zen Buddhist monasteries under its official sponsorship. The largest of the Zen monasteries in Kamakura, **Engaku-ji** (Engaku Temple), founded in 1282, ranked second in the Five Mountains hierarchy. Here, prayers were to be offered regularly for the prosperity and well being of the government; Engaku Temple's special role was to pray for the souls of those who died resisting the Mongol invasions in 1274 and 1281. The temple complex currently holds 18, but once contained as many as 50, buildings. Often damaged in fires and earthquakes, it has been completely restored.

Engaku Temple belongs to the Rinzai sect of Zen Buddhism. Introduced into Japan from China at the beginning of the Kamakura period (1192–1333), the ideas of Zen were quickly embraced by the emerging warrior class. The samurai especially admired the Rinzai sect, with its emphasis on the ascetic life as a path to self-transcendence. The monks of Engaku Temple played an important role as advisers to the shōgunate in matters spiritual, artistic, and political.

Among the National Treasures at Engaku Temple is the **Hall of the Holy Relic of Buddha** (Shari-den), with its remarkable Chinese-inspired thatched roof. Built in 1282, it was destroyed by fire in 1558 but rebuilt in its original form soon after, in 1563. The hall is said to enshrine a tooth of the Gautama Buddha himself, but it's not on display. In fact, except for the first three days of the New Year, you won't be able to go any farther into the hall than the main gate. Such is the case, alas, with much of the Engaku Temple complex: this is still a functioning monastic center, and many of its most impressive buildings are not open to the public. The accessible National Treasure at Engaku Temple is the **Great Bell** (Kōshō), on the hilltop on the southeast side of the complex. The bell—Kamakura's most famous—was cast in 1301 and stands 8 feet tall. It's rung only on special occasions, such as New Year's Eve. Reaching the bell requires a trek up a long staircase, but once you've made it to

220 <

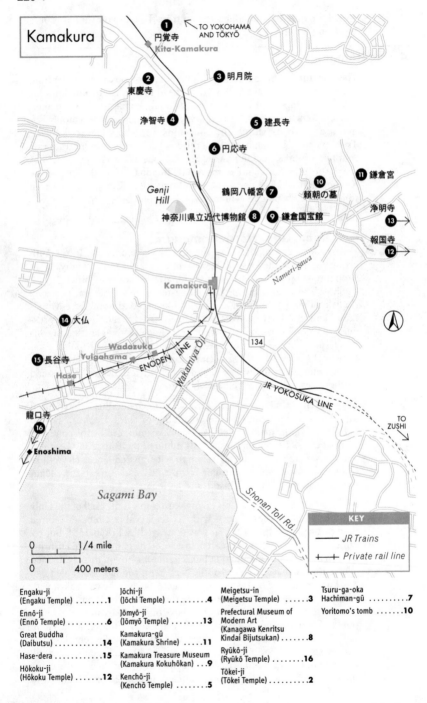

the top you can enjoy tea and traditional Japanese sweets at a small outdoor café. The views of the entire temple grounds and surrounding cedar forest from here are tremendous.

The two buildings open to the public at Engaku Temple are the **Butsunichi-an,** which has a long ceremonial hall where you can enjoy *sado* (Japanese tea ceremony), and the **Ōbai-in.** The latter is the mausoleum of the last three regents of the Kamakura Shōgunate: Hōjō Tokimune, who led the defense of Japan against the Mongol invasions; his son Sadatoki; and his grandson Takatoki. Off to the side of the mausoleum is a quiet garden with apricot trees, which bloom in February. As you exit Kita-Kamakura Station, you'll see the stairway to Engaku Temple just in front of you. ⊠ *409 Yama-no-uchi, Kita-Kamakura* ☏ *0467/22–0478* 🖬 *Engaku Temple ¥300* 🕙 *Nov.–Mar., daily 8–4; Apr.–Oct., daily 8–5.*

★ **❷** **Tōkei-ji** (Tōkei Temple), a Zen temple of the Rinzai sect, holds special significance for the study of feminism in medieval Japan. More popularly known as the Enkiri-dera, or Divorce Temple, it was founded in 1285 by the widow of the Hōjō regent Tokimune as a refuge for the victims of unhappy marriages. Under the shōgunate, a husband of the warrior class could obtain a divorce simply by sending his wife back to her family. Not so for the wife: no matter what cruel and unusual treatment her husband meted out, she was stuck with him. If she ran away, however, and managed to reach Tōkei Temple without being caught, she could receive sanctuary at the temple and remain there as a nun. After three years (later reduced to two), she was officially declared divorced. The temple survived as a convent through the Meiji Restoration of 1868. The last abbess died in 1902; her headstone is in the cemetery behind the temple, beneath the plum trees that blossom in February. Tōkei Temple was later reestablished as a monastery.

The **Matsugaoka Treasure House** (Matsugaoka Hōzō) of Tōkei Temple displays several Kamakura-period wooden Buddhas, ink paintings, scrolls, and works of calligraphy, some of which have been designated by the government as Important Cultural Objects. The library, called the Matsugaoka Bunko, was established in memory of the great Zen scholar D. T. Suzuki (1870–1966).

Tōkei Temple is on the southwest side of the JR tracks (the side opposite Engaku Temple), less than a five-minute walk south from the station on the main road to Kamakura (Route 21–the Kamakura Kaidō), on the right. ⊠ *1367 Yama-no-uchi, Kita-Kamakura* ☏ *0467/22–1663* 🖬 *Tōkei Temple ¥100, Matsugaoka Treasure House additional ¥300* 🕙 *Tōkei Temple Apr.–Oct., daily 8:30–5; Nov.–Mar., daily 8:30–4. Matsugaoka Treasure House Mon.–Thurs. 9:30–3:30.*

❸ **Meigetsu-in** (Meigetsu Temple) is also known as Ajisai-dera, the hydrangeas temple, because when the flowers bloom in June, it becomes one of the most popular places in Kamakura. The gardens transform into a sea of color—pink, white, and blue—and visitors can number in the thousands. A typical Kamakura light rain shouldn't deter you; it only showcases this incredible floral display to its best advantage. Meigetsu-in features Kamakura's largest *yagura,* a tomb cavity enclosing a mural, on which 16 images of Buddha are carved. From Tōkei Temple walk along Route 21 toward Kamakura for about 20 minutes until you cross the railway tracks; take the immediate left turn onto the narrow side street that doubles back along the tracks. This street bends to the right and follows the course of a little stream called the Meigetsu-gawa to the temple gate. ⊠ *189 Yama-no-uchi, Kita-Kamakura* ☎ *0467/24–3437* 🖃 *¥300* ⊗ *Apr., May, and July–Oct., daily 9–4; June, daily 8:30–5; Nov.–Mar., daily 9–4.*

❹ In the Five Mountains hierarchy, **Jōchi-ji** (Jōchi Temple) was ranked fourth. The buildings now in the temple complex are reconstructions; the Great Kantō Earthquake of 1923 destroyed the originals. The garden here is exquisite. Jōchi Temple is on the south side of the railway tracks, a few minutes' walk farther southwest of Tōkei Temple in the direction of Kamakura. Turn right off the main road (Route 21) and cross over a small bridge; a flight of moss-covered steps leads up to the temple. ⊠ *1402 Yama-no-uchi, Kita-Kamakura* ☎ *0467/22–3943* 🖃 *¥200* ⊗ *Daily 9–4:30.*

★ ❺ Founded in 1250, **Kenchō-ji** (Kenchō Temple) was the foremost of Kamakura's five great Zen temples—and lays claim to being the oldest Zen temple in all of Japan. It was modeled on one of the great Chinese monasteries of the time and built for a distinguished Zen master who had just arrived from China. Over the centuries, fires and other disasters have taken their toll on Kenchō Temple, and although many buildings have been authentically reconstructed, the temple complex today is half its original size. Near the Main Gate (San-mon) is a **bronze bell** cast in 1255; it's the temple's most important treasure. The Main Gate and the Lecture Hall (Hattō) are the only two structures to have survived the devastating Great Kantō Earthquake of 1923. Like Engaku Temple, Kenchō Temple is a functioning temple of the Rinzai sect, where novices train and laypeople can come to take part in Zen meditation. The entrance to Kenchō Temple is about halfway along the main road from Kita-Kamakura Station to Tsuru-ga-oka Hachiman-gū, on the left. ⊠ *8 Yama-no-uchi, Kita-Kamakura* ☎ *0467/22–0981* 🖃 *¥300* ⊗ *Daily 8:30–4:30.*

★ ❻ In the feudal period, Japan acquired from China a belief in Enma, the lord of hell, who, with his court attendants, judged the souls of the departed and determined their destination in the afterlife. Kamakura's otherwise-undistinguished **Ennō-ji** (Ennō Temple) houses some remarkable statues of these judges—as grim and merciless a court as you're ever likely to confront. To see them is enough to put you on your best behavior, at least for the rest of your excursion. Ennō Temple is a minute's walk or so from Kenchō Temple, on the opposite (south) side of the main road to Kamakura. A few minutes' walk along the main road to the south will bring you to Tsuru-ga-oka Hachiman-gū in downtown Kamakura. ⊠ *1543 Yama-no-uchi, Kita-Kamakura* ☎ *0467/25–1095* 🖃 *¥200* ⊗ *Mar.–Nov., daily 9–4; Dec.–Feb., daily 9–3:30.*

Kamakura

When the first Kamakura shōgun, Minamoto no Yoritomo, learned he was about to have an heir, he had the tutelary shrine of his family moved to Kamakura from nearby Yui-ga-hama and ordered a stately avenue to be built through the center of his capital from the shrine to the sea. Along this avenue would travel the procession that brought his son—if there were a son—to be presented to the gods. Yoritomo's consort did indeed bear him a son, Yoriie (yo-*ree*-ee-eh), in 1182; Yoriie was brought in great pomp to the shrine and then consecrated to his place in the shogunal succession. Alas, the blessing of the gods did Yoriie little good. He was barely 18 when Yoritomo died, and the regency established by his mother's family, the Hōjō, kept him virtually powerless until 1203, when he was banished and eventually assassinated. The Minamoto were never to hold power again, but Yoriie's memory lives on in the street that his father built for him: Wakamiya Oji, "the Avenue of the Young Prince."

■ TIP→ **A bus from Kamakura Station (Sign 5) travels to the sights listed below, with stops at most access roads to the temples and shrines. However, you may want to walk out as far as Hōkoku-ji and take the bus back; it's easier to recognize the end of the line than any of the stops in between.** You can also go by taxi to Hōkoku-ji—any cab driver knows the way—and walk the last leg in reverse. In any event, downtown Kamakura is a good place to stop for lunch and shopping. Restaurants and shops selling local crafts, especially the carved and lacquered woodwork called Kamakura-*bori,* abound on Wakamiya Oji and the street parallel to it, Komachi-dōri.

★ ❼ The Minamoto shrine, **Tsuru-ga-oka Hachiman-gū,** is dedicated to the legendary emperor Ōjin, his wife, and his mother, from whom Minamoto no Yoritomo claimed descent. At the entrance, the small, steeply arched, vermilion **Drum Bridge** (Taiko-bashi) crosses a stream between two lotus ponds. The ponds were made to Yoritomo's specifications. His wife, Masako, suggested placing islands in each. In the larger **Genji Pond,** to the right, filled with white lotus flowers, she placed three islands. Genji was another name for clan, and three is an auspicious number. In the smaller **Heike Pond,** to the left, she put four islands. Heike (*heh*-ee-keh) was another name for the rival Taira clan, which the Minamoto had destroyed, and four—homophonous in Japanese with the word for "death"—is very unlucky indeed.

On the far side of the Drum Bridge is the **Mai-den.** This hall is the setting for a story of the Minamoto celebrated in Nō and Kabuki theater. Beyond the Mai-den, a flight of steps leads to the shrine's Main Hall (Hon-dō). To the left of these steps is a ginkgo tree that—according to legend—was witness to a murder that ended the Minamoto line in 1219. From behind this tree, a priest named Kugyō leapt out and beheaded his uncle, the 26-year-old Sanetomo, Yoritomo's second son and the last Minamoto shōgun. The priest was quickly apprehended, but Sanetomo's head was never found. Like all other Shintō shrines, the Main Hall is unadorned; the building itself, an 1828 reconstruction, is not particularly noteworthy.

To reach Tsuru-ga-oka Hachiman-gū from the east side of Kamakura Station, cross the plaza, turn left, and walk north along Wakamiya Oji. Straight ahead is the first of three arches leading to the shrine, and the shrine itself is at the far end of the street. ⊠ *2–1–31 Yuki-no-shita* ☎ *0467/22–0315* 🎫 *Free* ☉ *Daily 9–4.*

An Ancient Soap Opera

CLOSE UP

ONCE A YEAR, DURING THE SPRING Festival (early or mid-April, when the cherry trees are in bloom), the Maiden hall at Tsuru-ga-oka Hachiman-gū is used to stage a heartrending drama about Minamoto no Yoritomo's brother, Yoshitsune. Although Yoritomo was the tactical genius behind the downfall of the Taira clan and the establishment of the Kamakura Shōgunate in the late 12th century, it was his dashing half-brother who actually defeated the Taira in battle. In so doing, Yoshitsune won the admiration of many, and Yoritomo came to believe that his sibling had ambitions of his own. Despite Yoshitsune's declaration of allegiance, Yoritomo had him exiled and sent assassins to have him killed. Yoshitsune spent his life fleeing from one place to another until, at the age of 30, he was betrayed in his last refuge and took his own life.

Earlier in his exile, Yoshitsune's lover, the dancer Shizuka Gozen, had been captured and brought to Yoritomo and his wife, Masako. They commanded her to dance for them as a kind of penance. Instead she danced for Yoshitsune. Yoritomo was furious, and only Masako's influence kept him from ordering her death. When he discovered, however, that Shizuka was carrying Yoshitsune's child, he ordered that if the child were a boy, he was to be killed. A boy was born. Some versions of the legend have it that the child was slain; others say he was placed in a cradle, like Moses, and cast adrift in the reeds.

❽ The **Prefectural Museum of Modern Art** (Kanagawa Kenritsu Kindai Bijutsukan) on the north side of the Heike Pond at Tsuru-ga-oka Hachiman-gū, houses a collection of Japanese oil paintings and watercolors, wood-block prints, and sculpture. ✉ 2–1–53 Yuki-no-shita ☎ 0467/22–5000 ☞ ¥800–¥1,200, depending on exhibition ☉ Tues.–Sun. 9:30–4:30.

❾ The **Kamakura Treasure Museum** (Kamakura Kokuhōkan) was built in 1928 as a repository for many of the most important objects belonging to the shrines and temples in the area. Many of these are designated Important Cultural Properties. The museum, located along the east side of the Tsuru-ga-oka Hachiman-gū shrine precincts, has an especially fine collection of devotional and portrait sculpture in wood from the Kamakura and Muromachi periods; the portrait pieces may be among the most expressive and interesting in all of classical Japanese art. ✉ 2–1–1 Yuki-no-shita ☎ 0467/22–0753 ☞ ¥300 ☉ Tues.–Sun. 9–4.

❿ The man who put Kamakura on the map, so to speak, chose not to leave it when he died: it's only a short walk from Tsuru-ga-oka Hachiman-gū to the tomb of the man responsible for its construction, Minamoto no Yoritomo. If you've already been to Nikkō and have seen how a later dynasty of shōguns sought to glorify its own memories, you may be surprised at the simplicity of **Yoritomo's tomb.** To get here, cross the Drum Bridge at Tsuru-ga-oka Hachiman-gū and turn left. Leave the grounds of the shrine and walk east along the main street (Route 204) that forms the T-intersection at the end of Wakamiya Oji. A 10-minute walk will bring you to a narrow street on the left—there's a bakery called Café Bergfeld on the corner that leads to the tomb, about 100 yards off the street to the north and up a flight of stone steps. ⌨ *Free* ☺ *Daily 9–4.*

⓫ **Kamakura-gū** (Kamakura Shrine) is a Shintō shrine built after the Meiji Restoration of 1868 and dedicated to Prince Morinaga (1308–36), the first son of Emperor Go-Daigo. When Go-Daigo overthrew the Kamakura Shōgunate and restored Japan to direct imperial rule, Morinaga—who had been in the priesthood—was appointed supreme commander of his father's forces. The prince lived in turbulent times and died young: when the Ashikaga clan in turn overthrew Go-Daigo's government, Morinaga was taken into exile, held prisoner in a cave behind the present site of Kamakura Shrine, and eventually beheaded. The **Treasure House** (Hōmotsu-den), on the northwest corner of the grounds, next to the shrine's administrative office, is of interest mainly for its collection of paintings depicting the life of Prince Morinaga. To reach Kamakura Shrine, walk from Yoritomo's tomb to Route 204, and turn left; at the next traffic light, a narrow street on the left leads off at an angle to the shrine, about five minutes' walk west. ⌨ *154 Nikaidō* ☎ *0467/22–0318* ⌨ *Kamakura Shrine free, Treasure House ¥300* ☺ *Daily 9–4.*

⓬ Visitors to Kamakura tend to overlook **Hōkoku-ji** (Hōkoku Temple) a lovely little Zen temple of the Rinzai sect that was built in 1334. Over the years it had fallen into disrepair and neglect, until an enterprising priest took over, cleaned up the gardens, and began promoting the temple for meditation sessions, calligraphy exhibitions, and tea ceremony. Behind the main hall are a thick grove of bamboo and a small tea pavilion—a restful oasis and a fine place to go for *matcha* (green tea). The temple is about 2 km (1 mi) east on Route 204 from the main entrance to Tsuru-ga-oka Hachiman-gū; turn right at the traffic light by the Hōkoku Temple Iriguchi bus stop and walk about three minutes south to the gate. ⌨ *2–7–4 Jōmyō-ji* ☎ *0467/22–0762* ⌨ *Hōkoku Temple free, bamboo grove ¥200, tea ceremony ¥500* ☺ *Daily 9–4.*

⓭ **Jōmyō-ji** (Jōmyo Temple) founded in 1188, is one of the Five Mountains Zen monasteries. Though it lacks the grandeur and scale of the Engaku and Kenchō, it still merits the status of an Important Cultural Property. This modest single story monstery belonging to the Rinzai sect is nestled inside an immaculate garden that is particularly beautiful in spring, when the cherry trees bloom. Its only distinctive features are its green roof and the statues of Shaka Nyorai and Amida Nyorai, who represent truth and enlightenment, in the main hall. To reach it from Hōkoku-ji, cross the main street (Route 204) that brought you the mile or so from Tsuru-ga-oka Hachiman-gū, and take the first narrow street north. The monastery is about 100 yards from the corner. ⌨ *3–8–31 Jōmyō-ji* ☎ *0467/22–2818* ⌨ *Jōmyō Temple ¥100, tea ceremony ¥500* ☺ *Daily 9–4.*

Hase

⓮ The single biggest attraction in Hase ("*ha*-seh") is the temple Kōtoku-in's **Great Buddha** (Daibutsu)—sharing the honors with Mt. Fuji, perhaps, as the quintessential picture-postcard image of Japan. The statue of the

FodorsChoice
★

compassionate Amida Buddha sits cross-legged in the temple courtyard, the drapery of his robes flowing in lines reminiscent of ancient Greece, his expression profoundly serene. The 37-foot bronze figure was cast in 1292, three centuries before Europeans reached Japan; the concept of the classical Greek lines in the Buddha's robe must have

> **WHAT IS A BODHISATTVA?**
>
> A Bodhisattva is a being that has deferred their own ascendance into Buddhahood to guide the souls of others to salvation. It is considered a deity in Buddhism.

come over the Silk Route through China during the time of Alexander the Great. The casting was probably first conceived in 1180, by Minamoto no Yoritomo, who wanted a statue to rival the enormous Daibutsu in Nara. Until 1495 the Amida Buddha was housed in a wooden temple, which washed away in a great tidal wave. Since then the loving Buddha has stood exposed, facing the cold winters and hot summers, for more than five centuries.

■ TIP→ **It may seem sacrilegious to walk inside the Great Buddha, but for ¥20 you can enter the figure from a doorway in the right side and explore (until 4:15 PM) his stomach.** To reach Kōtoku-in and the Great Buddha, take the Enoden Line from the west side of JR Kamakura Station three stops to Hase. From the east exit, turn right and walk north about 10 minutes on the main street (Route 32). ✉ 4–2–28 Hase, Hase ☎ 0467/22–0703 💴 ¥200 ⊙ Apr.–Sept., daily 7–6; Oct.–Mar., daily 7–5:30.

⓯ The only Kamakura temple facing the sea, **Hase-dera** is one of the most
FodorsChoice beautiful, and saddest, places of pilgrimage in the city. On a landing part-
★ way up the stone steps that lead to the temple grounds are hundreds of small stone images of Jizō, one of the bodhisattvas in the Buddhist pantheon. Jizō is the savior of children, particularly the souls of the still-born, aborted, and miscarried; the mothers of these children dress the statues of Jizō in bright red bibs and leave them small offerings of food, heartbreakingly touching acts of prayer.

The **Kannon Hall** (Kannon-do) at Hase-dera enshrines the largest carved-wood statue in Japan: the votive figure of Jūichimen Kannon, the 11-headed goddess of mercy. Standing 30 feet tall, the goddess bears a crown of 10 smaller heads, symbolizing her ability to search out in all directions for those in need of her compassion. No one knows for certain when the figure was carved. According to the temple records, a monk named Tokudo Shōnin carved two images of the Jūichimen Kannon from a huge laurel tree in 721. One was consecrated to the Hase-dera in present-day Nara Prefecture; the other was thrown into the sea in order to go wherever the sea decided that there were souls in need, and that image washed up on shore near Kamakura. Much later, in 1342, Ashikaga Takauji—the first of the 15 Ashikaga shōguns who followed the Kamakura era—had the statue covered with gold leaf.

The **Amida Hall** of Hase-dera enshrines the image of a seated Amida Buddha, who presides over the Western Paradise of the Pure Land. Minamoto no Yoritomo ordered the creation of this statue when he reached the age of 42; popular Japanese belief, adopted from China, holds that your 42nd year is particularly unlucky. Yoritomo's act of piety earned him another 11 years—he was 53 when he was thrown by a horse and died of his injuries. The Buddha is popularly known as the *yakuyoke* (good-luck) Amida, and many visitors—especially students facing entrance exams—make a point of coming here to pray. To the left of the main halls is a small restaurant where you can buy good-luck candy and admire the view of Kamakura Beach and Sagami Bay. To reach Hase-dera from Hase Station, walk north about five minutes on the main street (Route 32) towards Kōtoku-in and the Great Buddha, and look for a signpost to the temple on a side street to the left. ⊠ *3–11–2 Hase, Hase* ☎ *0467/22–6300* 🎫 *¥300* ⏰ *Mar.–Sept., daily 8–5:30; Oct.–Feb., daily 8–4:30.*

Ryūkō-ji & Enoshima

🔟 The Kamakura story would not be complete without the tale of Nichiren (1222–82), the monk who founded the only native Japanese sect of Buddhism and who is honored at **Ryūkō-ji** (Ryūkō Temple). Nichiren's rejection of both Zen and Jōdo (Pure Land) teachings brought him into conflict with the Kamakura Shōgunate, and the Hōjō regents sent him into exile on the Izu Peninsula in 1261. Later allowed to return, he continued to preach his own interpretation of the Lotus Sutra—and to assert the "blasphemy" of other Buddhist sects, a stance that finally persuaded the Hōjō regency, in 1271, to condemn him to death. The execution was to take place on a hill to the south of Hase. As the executioner swung his sword, legend has it that a lightning bolt struck the blade and snapped it in two. Taken aback, the executioner sat down to collect his wits, and a messenger was sent back to Kamakura to report the event. On his way he met another messenger, who was carrying a writ from the Hōjō regents commuting Nichiren's sentence to exile on the island of Sado-ga-shima.

Followers of Nichiren built Ryūkō Temple in 1337, on the hill where he was to be executed, marking his miraculous deliverance from the headsman. There are other Nichiren temples closer to Kamakura—Myōhon-ji and Ankokuron-ji, for example. But Ryūkō not only has the typical Nichiren-style main hall, with gold tassels hanging from its roof, but also a beautiful pagoda, built in 1904. To reach it, take the Enoden Line west from Hase to Enoshima—a short, scenic ride that cuts through the hills surrounding Kamakura to the shore. From Enoshima Station walk about 100 yards east, keeping the train tracks on your right, and you'll come to the temple. ⊠ *3–13–37 Katase, Fujisawa* ☎ *0466/25–7357* 🎫 *Free* ⏰ *Daily 6–4.*

THE POWER OF THE JAPANESE BLADE

In the corner of the enclosure where the Chinese Gate and Sanctum are found, an antique bronze lantern stands some 7 feet high. Legend has it that the lantern would assume the shape of a goblin at night; the deep nicks in the bronze were inflicted by swordsmen of the Edo period—on guard duty, perhaps, startled into action by a flickering shape in the dark. This proves, if not the existence of goblins, the incredible cutting power of the Japanese blade, a peerlessly forged weapon.

6

CLOSE UP

Take a Dip

THE SAGAMI BAY SHORE in this area has some of the closest beaches to Tōkyō, and in the hot, humid summer months it seems as though all of the city's teeming millions pour onto these beaches in search of a vacant patch of rather dirty gray sand. Pass up this mob scene and press on instead to Enoshima. The island is only 4 km (2½ mi) around, with a hill in the middle. Partway up the hill is a shrine where the local fisherfolk used to pray for a bountiful catch—before it became a tourist attraction. Once upon a time it was quite a hike up to the shrine; now there's a series of escalators, flanked by the inevitable stalls selling souvenirs and snacks.

The island has several cafés and restaurants, and on clear days some of them have spectacular views of Mt. Fuji and the Izu Peninsula. To reach the causeway from Enoshima Station to the island, walk south from the station for about 3 km (2 mi), keeping the Katase-gawa (Katase River) on your right. To return to Tōkyō from Enoshima, take a train to Shinjuku on the Odakyū Line. From the island walk back across the causeway and take the second bridge over the Katase-gawa. Within five minutes you'll come to Katase-Enoshima Station. Or you can retrace your steps to Kamakura and take the JR Yokosuka Line to Tōkyō Station.

Where to Eat

Kita-Kamakura

★ $$$–$$$$ ✕ **Hachinoki Kita-Kamakura-ten.** Traditional *shōjin ryōri* (the vegetarian cuisine of Zen monasteries) is served in this old Japanese house on the Kamakura Kaidō (Route 21) near the entrance to Jōchi Temple. There's some table service, but most seating is in tatami rooms, with beautiful antique wood furnishings. Allow plenty of time; this is not a meal to be hurried through. Meals, which are prix fixe only, are served Tuesday–Friday 11–2:30, weekends 11–3. ⊠ *7 Yama-no-uchi, Kita-Kamakura* ☎ *0467/23–3722* ▤ *DC, V* ⊘ *Closed Mon. Open weekends only in July and Aug.*

$$–$$$ ✕ **Kyorai-an.** A traditional Japanese structure houses this restaurant known for its excellent Western-style beef stew. Also on the menu are pasta dishes, rice bouillon, homemade cheesecake, and wine produced in the Kita Kamakura wine region. Half the seats are on tatami mats and half are at tables, but all look out on a peaceful patch of greenery. Kyorai-an is on the main road from Kita-Kamakura to Kamakura on the left side; it's about halfway between Meigetsu Temple and Kenchō Temple, up a winding flight of stone steps. Meals are served Mon.–Thurs. 11–3, weekends and holidays 11–5 ⊠ *157 Yamanouchi, Kita-Kamakura* ☎ *0467/24–9835* ▤ *No credit cards.*

Kamakura

$$$ ✕ **Ginza Isomura Kamakuraten.** This branch of the family-style *kushiage* (freshly grilled skewers) restaurant overlooks Komachi-dōri, Kamakura's main shopping street. A place by the window is perfect for people

watching during lunchtime. Since it seats only 21, the place gets crowded during dinnertime, but if you're willing to wait you'll be rewarded with meat, fish, and seasonal vegetable kushiage that's made in front of you. ⊠ *Komachiichibankan Bldg., 2F., 2–10–1 Komachi, Kita-Kamakura* ☎ *0467/22–3792* ⊟ *AE, DC, MC, V* ⊘ *Closed Wed.*

$–$$$ ⋊ **T-Side.** Authentic, inexpensive Indian fare and a second-floor location that looks down upon Kamakura's main shopping street, make this restaurant a popular choice for lunch and dinner. Curries are done well, the various *thali* (sets) are a good value, and the kitchen also serves some Nepalese dishes. T-Side is at the very top of Komachi-dōri on the left as you enter from Kamakura Station. ⊠ *2–11–11 Komachi, Kita-Kamakura* ☎ *0467/24–9572* ⊘ *Daily 10–10* ⊟ *V.*

¢ ⋊ **Kaisen Misaki-kō.** This *kaiten-zushi* (sushi served on a conveyor belt that lets you pick the dishes you want) restaurant on Komachi-dōri serves eye-poppingly large fish portions that hang over the edge of their plates. All the standard sushi creations, including tuna, shrimp, and egg, are prepared here. Prices range from ¥170–¥500. The restaurant is on the right side of the road just as you enter Komachi-dōri from the east exit of Kamakura Station. ⊠ *1–7–1 Komachi, Kita-Kamakura* ☎ *0467/22–6228* ⊟ *No credit cards.*

Hase

$$$–$$$$ ⋊ **Kaiserrō.** This establishment, in an old Japanese house, serves the best Chinese food in the city. The dining-room windows look out on a small, restful garden. Make sure you plan for a stop here on your way to or from the Great Buddha at Kōtoku-in. ⊠ *3–1–14 Hase, Hase* ☎ *0467/22–0280* ⊘ *Daily 11–7:30* ⊟ *AE, DC, MC, V.*

Kamakura Essentials

BUS TRAVEL

A bus from Kamakura Station (Sign 5) travels to most of the temples and shrines in the downtown Kamakura area.

TOURS

Bus companies in Kamakura do not conduct guided English tours. You can, however, take one of the Japanese tours, which depart from Kamakura Station eight times daily, starting at 9 AM; the last tour leaves at 1 PM. Purchase tickets at the bus office to the right of the station. There are two itineraries, each lasting a little less than three hours; tickets, depending on what the tour covers, are ¥2,250 and ¥3,390. These tours are best if you have limited time and would like to hit the major attractions but don't want to linger anywhere or do a lot of walking. Take John Carroll's book *Trails of Two Cities: A Walker's Guide to Yokohama, Kamakura and Vicinity* (Kodansha International, 1994) with you, and you'll have more information at your fingertips than any of your fellow passengers.

■ **TIP→** On the weekend the Kanagawa Student Guide Federation offers a free guide service. Students show you the city in exchange for the chance to practice their English. Arrangements must be made in advance through the Japan National Tourist Organization in Tōkyō. You'll need to be at Kamakura Station between 10 AM and noon.

Sunrise Tours runs daily trips from Tōkyō to Kamakura; these tours are often combined with trips to Hakone. You can book through, and arrange to be picked up at, any of the major hotels. Before you do, however, be certain that the tour covers everything in Kamakura that you want to see, as many include little more than a passing view of the Great Buddha in Hase. Given how easy it is to get around—most sights are within walking distance of each other, and others are short bus or train rides apart—you're better off seeing Kamakura on your own.

🚹 Tour Contacts **Japan National Tourist Organization** ✉ Tōkyō Kōtsū Kaikan, 10F, 2-10-1 Yūraku-chō, Chiyoda-ku, Tōkyō ☎ 03/3201-3331 ⊕ www.jnto.go.jp Ⓜ JR Yamanote Line (Higashi-guchi/East Exit) and Yūraku-chō subway line (Exit A-8), Yūraku-chō Station. **Kanagawa Student Guide Federation** ☎03/3201-3331. **Sunrise Tours** ☎03/ 5796-5454 ⊕ www.jtb.co.jp/sunrisetour.

TRAIN TRAVEL

Traveling by train is by far the best way to get to Kamakura. Trains run from Tōkyō Station (and Shimbashi Station) every 10–15 minutes during the day. The trip takes 56 minutes to Kita-Kamakura and one hour to Kamakura. Take the JR Yokosuka Line from Track 1 downstairs in Tōkyō Station (Track 1 upstairs is on a different line and does not go to Kamakura). The cost is ¥780 to Kita-Kamakura, ¥890 to Kamakura (or use your JR [Japan Railways] Pass). Local train service connects Kita-Kamakura, Kamakura, Hase, and Enoshima.

To return to Tōkyō from Enoshima, take a train to Shinjuku on the Odakyū Line. There are 11 express trains daily from here on weekdays, between 8:38 AM and 8:45 PM; 9 trains daily on weekends and national holidays, between 8:39 AM and 8:46 PM; and even more in summer. The express takes about 70 minutes and costs ¥1,220. Or you can retrace your steps to Kamakura and take the JR Yokosuka Line to Tōkyō Station.

🚹 **Japan Railways** ☎ 03/3423-0111 ⊕ www.japanrail.com.

VISITOR INFORMATION

Both Kamakura and Enoshima have their own tourist associations, although it can be problematic getting help in English over the phone. Your best bet is the Kamakura Station Tourist Information Center, which has a useful collection of brochures and maps. And since Kamakura is in Kanagawa Prefecture, visitors heading here from Yokohama can preplan their excursion at the Kanagawa Prefectural Tourist Association office in the Silk Center, on the Yamashita Park promenade.

🚹 Tourist Information **Enoshima Tourist Association** ☎ 0466/37-4141. **Kamakura Station Tourist Information Center** ☎ 0467/22-3350. **Kamakura Tourist Association** ☎ 0467/23-3050. **Kanagawa Prefectural Tourist Association** ☎ 045/681-0007 ⊕ www.kanagawa-kankou.or.jp.

YOKOHAMA

In 1853, a fleet of four American warships under Commodore Matthew Perry sailed into the bay of Tōkyō (then Edo) and presented the reluctant Japanese with the demands of the U.S. government for the opening of diplomatic and commercial relations. The following year Perry returned and first set foot on Japanese soil at Yokohama—then a small fishing village on the mudflats of the bay, some 20 km (12½ mi) southwest of Tōkyō.

Two years later New York businessman Townsend Harris became America's first diplomatic representative to Japan. In 1858 he was finally able to negotiate a commercial treaty between the two countries; part of the deal designated four locations—one of them Yokohama—as treaty ports. With the agreement signed, Harris lost no time in setting up his residence in Hangaku-ji, in nearby Kanagawa, another of the designated ports. Kanagawa, however, was also one of the 53 relay stations on the Tōkaidō, the highway from Edo to the imperial court in Kyōto, and the presence of foreigners—perceived as unclean barbarians—offended the Japanese elite. Die-hard elements of the warrior class, moreover, wanted Japan to remain in isolation and were willing to give their lives to rid the country of intruders. Unable to protect foreigners in Kanagawa, in 1859 the shōgunate created a special settlement in Yokohama for the growing community of merchants, traders, missionaries, and other assorted adventurers drawn to this exotic new land of opportunity.

The foreigners (predominantly Chinese and British, plus a few French, Americans, and Dutch) were confined here to a guarded compound about 5 square km (2 square mi)—placed, in effect, in isolation—but not for long. Within a few short years the shogunal government collapsed, and Japan began to modernize. Western ideas were welcomed, as were Western goods, and the little treaty port became Japan's principal gateway to the outside world. In 1872 Japan's first railway was built, linking Yokohama and Tōkyō. In 1889 Yokohama became a city; by then the population had grown to some 120,000. As the city prospered, so did the international community and by the early 1900s Yokohama was the busiest and most modern center of international trade in all of east Asia.

Then Yokohama came tumbling down. On September 1, 1923, the Great Kantō Earthquake devastated the city. The ensuing fires destroyed some 60,000 homes and took more than 40,000 lives. During the six years it took to rebuild the city, many foreign businesses took up quarters elsewhere, primarily in Kōbe and Ōsaka, and did not return.

Over the next 20 years Yokohama continued to grow as an industrial center—until May 29, 1945, when in a span of four hours, some 500 American B-29 bombers leveled nearly half the city and left more than half a million people homeless. When the war ended, what remained became—in effect—the center of the Allied occupation. General Douglas MacArthur set up headquarters here, briefly, before moving to Tōkyō; the entire port facility and about a quarter of the city remained in the hands of the U.S. military throughout the 1950s.

By the 1970s Yokohama was once more rising from the debris; in 1978 it surpassed Ōsaka as the nation's second-largest city, and the population is now inching up to the 3.5 million mark. Boosted by Japan's postwar economic miracle, Yokohama has extended its urban sprawl north to Tōkyō and south to Kamakura—in the process creating a whole new subcenter around the Shinkansen station at Shin-Yokohama.

The development of air travel and the competition from other ports have changed the city's role in Japan's economy. The great liners that once docked at Yokohama's piers are now but a memory, kept alive by a museum ship and the occasional visit of a luxury vessel on a Pacific cruise. Modern Yokohama thrives instead in its industrial, commercial, and service sectors—and a large percentage of its people commute to work in Tōkyō. Is Yokohama worth a visit? Not, one could argue, at the expense of Nikkō or Kamakura. But the waterfront is fun and the museums are excellent.

Exploring Yokohama

Large as Yokohama is, the central area is very negotiable. As with any other port city, much of what it has to offer centers on the waterfront—in this case, on the west side of Tōkyō Bay. The downtown area is called Kannai (literally, "within the checkpoint"); this is where the international community was originally confined by the shōgunate. Though the center of interest has expanded to include the waterfront and Ishikawa-chō, to the south, Kannai remains the heart of town.

Think of that heart as two adjacent areas. One is the old district of Kannai, bounded by Basha-michi on the northwest and Nihon-ōdori on the southeast, the Keihin Tōhoku Line tracks on the southwest, and the waterfront on the northeast. This area contains the business offices of modern Yokohama. The other area extends southeast from Nihon-ōdori to the Moto-machi shopping street and the International Cemetery, bordered by Yamashita Kōen and the waterfront to the northeast; in the center is Chinatown, with Ishikawa-chō Station to the southwest. This is the most interesting part of town for tourists.

Numbers in the margin correspond to the Yokohama map.

Central Yokohama

9 Running southwest from Shinko Pier to Kannai is **Basha-michi,** which literally translates into "Horse-Carriage Street." The street was so named in the 19th century, when it was widened to accommodate the horse-drawn carriages of the city's new European residents. This red-brick thoroughfare and the streets parallel to it have been restored to evoke that past, with faux-antique telephone booths and imitation gas lamps. Here you'll find some of the most elegant coffee shops, patisseries, and boutiques in town. On the block northeast of Kannai Station, as you walk toward the waterfront, is **Kannai Hall** (look for the red-orange abstract sculpture in front), a handsome venue for chamber music, Nō, classical recitals, and occasional performances by such groups as the Peking Opera. If you're planning to stay late in Yokohama, you might want to check out the listings. ⊠ *Naka-ku* Ⓜ *JR Line, Kannai Station; Minato Mirai Line, Basha-michi Station.*

★ **17** Yokohama's **Chinatown** (Chūka-gai) is the largest Chinese settlement in Japan—and easily the city's most popular tourist attraction, drawing more than 18 million visitors a year. Its narrow streets and alleys are lined with some 350 shops selling foodstuffs, herbal medicines, cook-

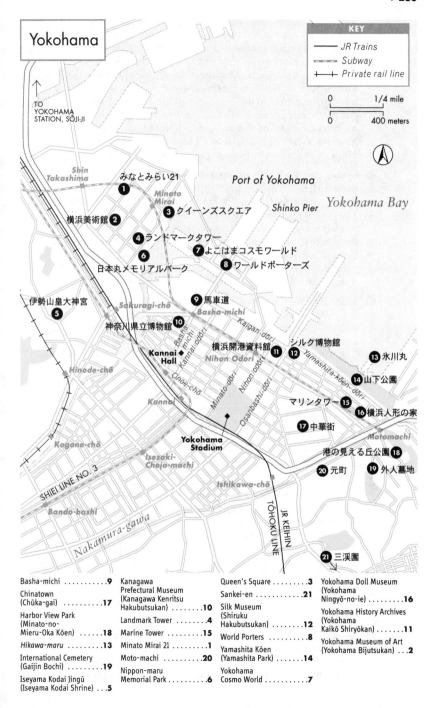

Yokohama

0   1/4 mile

0   400 meters

TO YOKOHAMA STATION, SŌJI-JI

Shin Takashima

みなとみらい21 ①

Minato Mirai

③ クイーンズスクエア

Port of Yokohama

Shinko Pier

Yokohama Bay

横浜美術館 ②

④ ランドマークタワー

⑥

⑦ よこはまコスモワールド

日本丸メモリアルパーク

⑧ ワールドポーターズ

伊勢山皇大神宮

⑤

Sakuragi-chō

⑨ 馬車道

Basha-michi

Kaigan-dōri

神奈川県立博物館 ⑩

Basha-michi

Kannai-ōdori

横浜開港資料館

⑪

⑫ シルク博物館

⑬ 氷川丸

Kannai Hall ◆

Nihon Ōdori

Yamashita-kōen dōri

Nihon-dōri

Minato-dōri

Onoe-chō

Osanbashi-dōri

⑭ 山下公園

Hinode-chō

マリンタワー ⑮

⑯ 横浜人形の家

Kannai

⑰ 中華街

Motomachi

Yokohama Stadium

Kogane-chō

港の見える丘公園 ⑱

Isezaki-Chōja-machi

⑳ 元町

⑲ 外人墓地

SHIEI LINE NO. 3

Bando-bashi

Ishikawa-chō

Nakamura-gawa

JR KEIHIN

TŌHOKU LINE

㉑ 三渓園

ware, toys and ornaments, and clothing and accessories. If China exports it, you'll find it here. Wonderful exotic aromas waft from the spice shops. Even better aromas drift from the quarter's 160-odd restaurants, which serve every major style of Chinese cuisine: this is the best place for lunch in Yokohama. Chinatown is a 10-minute walk southeast of Kannai Station. When you get to Yokohama Stadium, turn left and cut through the municipal park to the top of Nihon-ōdori. Then take a right, and you'll enter Chinatown through the Gembu-mon (North Gate), which leads to the dazzling red-and-gold, 50-foot-high Zenrin-mon (Good Neighbor Gate). ⊠ *Naka-ku* Ⓜ *JR Line, Ishikawa-cho Station; Minato Mirai Line, Motomachi-Chukagai Station.*

⓲ **Harbor View Park** (Minato-no-Mieru-Oka Kōen), once the barracks of the British forces in Yokohama, affords a spectacular nighttime view of the waterfront, the floodlit gardens of Yamashita Park, and the Bay Bridge. The park is the major landmark in this part of the city, known, appropriately enough, as the Bluff (*yamate*). Foreigners were first allowed to build here in 1867, and it has been prime real estate ever since—an enclave of consulates, churches, international schools, private clubs, and palatial Western-style homes. ⊠ *Naka-ku* Ⓜ *JR Line, Ishikawa-chō Station; Minato Mirai Line, Motomachi-Chukagai Station.*

⓭ Moored on the waterfront, more or less in the middle of Yamashita Park, is the ***Hikawa-maru***. It was built in 1929 by Yokohama Dock Co. and was launched on September 30, 1929. For 31 years, she shuttled passengers between Yokohama and Seattle, Washington, making a total of 238 trips. A tour of the ship evokes the time when Yokohama was a great port of call for the transpacific liners. The *Hikawa-maru* has a French restaurant, and in summer there's a beer garden on the upper deck. ⊠ *Naka-ku* ☎ *045/641-4361* 🎫 *¥800; multiple-entry ticket to Hikawa-maru and Marine Tower ¥1,300; multiple-entry ticket to Hikawa-maru, Marine Tower, and Yokohama Doll Museum ¥1,550* ☉ *Apr.–June, daily 9:30–7; July and Aug., daily 9:30–7:30; Sept. and Oct., daily 9:30–7; Nov.–Mar., daily 9:30–6:30* Ⓜ *JR Line, Ishikawa-chō Station; Minato Mirai Line, Motomachi-Chukagai Station.*

⓳ The **International Cemetery** (Gaijin Bochi) is a Yokohama landmark and a reminder of the port city's heritage. It was established in 1854 with a grant of land from the shōgunate; the first foreigners to be buried here were Russian sailors assassinated by xenophobes in the early days of the settlement. Most of the 4,500 graves on this hillside are English and American, and about 120 are of the Japanese wives of foreigners; the inscriptions on the crosses and headstones attest to some 40 different nationalities whose citizens lived and died in Yokohama. From Motomachi Plaza, it's a short walk to the north end of the cemetery. ⊠ *Naka-ku* Ⓜ *JR Line, Ishikawa-chō Station; Minato Mirai Line, Motomachi-Chukagai Station.*

❺ **Iseyama Kodai Jingū** (Iseyama Kodai Shrine) a branch of the nation's revered Grand Shrines of Ise, is the most important Shintō shrine in Yokohama—but it's only worth a visit if you've seen most everything else in town. The shrine is a 10-minute walk west of Sakuragi-chō Station. ⊠ 64

Miyazaki-chō, Nishi-ku ☎ *045/241–1122* 🖙 *Free* ⊙ *Daily 9–7* Ⓜ *JR Line, Sakuragi-chō Station; Minato Mirai Line, Minato Mirai Station.*

❿ One of the few buildings in Yokohama to have survived both the Great Kantō Earthquake of 1923 and World War II is the 1904 **Kanagawa Prefectural Museum** (Kanagawa Kenritsu Hakubutsukan) a few blocks north of Kannai Station (use Exit 8) on Basha-michi. Most exhibits here have no explanations in English, but the galleries on the third floor showcase some remarkable medieval wooden sculptures (including one of the first Kamakura shōgun, Minamoto no Yoritomo), hanging scrolls, portraits, and armor. The exhibits of prehistory and of Yokohama in the early modern period are of much less interest. ✉ *5–60 Minami Naka-dōri, Naka-ku* ☎ *045/201–0926* 🖙 *¥300, special exhibits ¥800* ⊙ *Tues.–Sun. 9–4:30; closed last Tues. of month and the day after a national holiday* Ⓜ *JR Line, Sakuragi-cho and Kannai Stations.*

🄲 ❹ The 70-story **Landmark Tower,** in Yokohama's Minato Mirai, is Japan's tallest building. The observation deck on the 69th floor has a spectacular view of the city, especially at night; you reach it via a high-speed elevator that carries you up at an ear-popping 45 kph (28 mph). The Yokohama Royal Park Hotel occupies the top 20 stories of the building. On the first level of the Landmark Tower is the **Mitsubishi Minato Mirai Industrial Museum,** with rocket engines, power plants, a submarine, various gadgets, and displays that simulate piloting helicopters—great fun for kids.

The Landmark Tower complex's **Dockyard Garden,** built in 1896, is a restored dry dock with stepped sides of massive stone blocks. The long, narrow floor of the dock, with its water cascade at one end, makes a wonderful year-round open air venue for concerts and other events; in summer (July–mid-August), the beer garden installed here is a perfect refuge from the heat. ✉ *3–3–1 Minato Mirai, Nishi-ku* ☎ *045/224–9031* 🖙 *Elevator to observation deck ¥1,000, museum ¥500* ⊙ *Museum Tues.–Sun. 10–5* Ⓜ *JR Line, Sakuragi-chō Station; Minato Mirai Line, Minato Mirai Station.*

⓯ For an older generation of Yokohama residents, the 348-foot-high decagonal **Marine Tower,** which opened in 1961, was the city's landmark structure; civic pride prevented them from admitting that it falls lamentably short of an architectural masterpiece. The tower has a navigational beacon at the 338-foot level and purports to be the tallest lighthouse in the world. At the 328-foot level, an observation gallery provides 360-degree views of the harbor and the city, and on clear days in autumn or winter, you can often see Mt. Fuji in the distance. Marine Tower is in the middle of the second block northwest from the end of Yamashita Park, on the left side of the promenade. ✉ *15 Yamashita-chō, Naka-ku* ☎ *045/ 641–7838* 🖙 *¥700; multiple-entry ticket to Marine Tower and Hikawa-maru ¥1,300; multiple-entry ticket to Marine Tower, Hikawa-maru, and Yokohama Doll Museum ¥1,550* ⊙ *Jan. and Feb., daily 9–7; Mar.–May and Nov. and Dec., daily 9:30–9; June and July and Sept. and Oct., daily 9:30–9:30; Aug., daily 9:30–10* Ⓜ *JR Line, Ishikawa-chō Station; Minato Mirai Line, Motomachi-Chukagai Station.*

❶ If you want to see Yokohama urban development at its most self-as-sertive, **Minato Mirai 21** is a must. The aim of this project, launched in the mid-1980s, was to turn some three-quarters of a square mile of waterfront property, lying east of the JR Negishi Line railroad tracks between the Yokohama and Sakuragi-chō stations, into a model "city of the future." As a hotel, business, international exhibition, and conference center, it's a smash-ing success. ⊠ *Nishi-ku* Ⓜ *JR Line, Sakuragi-chō Station; Minato Mirai Line, Minato Mirai Station.*

> ### BLOOMIN' SEASON
>
> Walking through Sankei-en is es-pecially delightful in spring, when the flowering trees are at their best: plum blossoms in February and cherry blossoms in early April. In June come the irises, followed by the water lilies. In autumn the trees come back into their own with tinted golden leaves.

⓴ Whether you are coming from Tōkyō, Nagoya, or Kamakura, make Ishikawa-chō Station your starting point. Take the south exit from the station and head in the direction of the waterfront. Within a block of Ishikawa-chō Station is the beginning of **Moto-machi,** the street that fol-lows the course of the Nakamura-gawa (Nakamura River) to the har-bor, where the Japanese set up shop 100 years ago to serve the foreigners living in Kannai. The street is now lined with smart boutiques and jew-elry stores that cater to fashionable young Japanese consumers. ⊠ *Naka-ku* Ⓜ *JR Line, Ishikawa-chō Station; Minato Mirai Line, Motomachi-Chukagai Station.*

❻ On the east side of Minato Mirai 21, where the Ō-oka-gawa (Ō-oka River) flows into the bay, is **Nippon-maru Memorial Park.** The centerpiece of the park is the *Nippon-maru,* a full-rigged three-masted ship popu-larly called the "Swan of the Pacific." Built in 1930, it served as a train-ing vessel. The Nippon-maru is now retired, but it's an occasional participant in tall-ships festivals and is open for guided tours. Adjacent to the ship is the **Yokohama Maritime Museum,** a two-story collection of ship models, displays, and archival materials that celebrate the achievements of the Port of Yokohama from its earliest days to the pres-ent. ⊠ *2–1–1 Minato Mirai, Nishi-ku* ☎ *045/221–0280* 🎫 *Ship and museum ¥600* 🕙 *Mar.–June and Sept. and Oct., daily 10–5; July and Aug., daily 10–6:30; Nov.–Feb., daily 10–4:30; closed Mon. (if Mon. is a holiday, closed Tues.) Closed day after a national holiday.* Ⓜ *JR Line, Sakuragi-chō Station; Minato Mirai Line, Minato Mirai Station.*

❸ The courtyard on the northeast side of the ⇨ **Landmark Tower** con-nects to **Queen's Square,** a huge atrium-style vertical mall with dozens of shops (mainly for clothing and accessories) and restaurants. The complex also houses the Pan Pacific Hotel Yokohama and Yokohama Minato Mirai Hall, the city's major venue for classical music. ⊠ *2-3-1 Minato-Mirai Nishi-ku* ☎ *045/222–5015* 🕙 *Shopping 11–8, restaurants 11 AM–11 PM* Ⓜ *JR Line, Sakuragi-chō Station; Minato Mirai Line, Mi-nato Mirai Station* ⊕ *www.qsy.co.jp.*

★ ㉑ Opened to the public in 1906, **Sankei-en** was once the estate and gar-dens of Hara Tomitaro (1868–1939), one of Yokohama's wealthiest men, who made his money as a silk merchant before becoming a patron of the arts. On the extensive grounds of the estate he created is a kind of open-air museum of traditional Japanese architecture, some of which was brought here from Kamakura and the western part of the country. Especially noteworthy is **Rinshun-kaku,** a villa built for the Tokugawa clan in 1649. There's also a tea pavilion, Chōshū-kaku, built by the third Tokugawa shōgun, Iemitsu. Other buildings include a small temple transported from Kyōto's famed Daitoku-ji and a farmhouse from the Gifu district in the Japan Alps (around Takayama). To reach Sankei-en, take the JR Keihin Tōhoku Line to Negishi Station and a local bus (number 54, 58, or 99) bound for Honmoku; it's a 10-minute trip to the garden. Or, go to Yokohama Station (East Exit) and take the bus (number 8 or 125) to Honmoku Sankei-en Mae. It will take about 35 mins. ⊠ *58–1 Honmoku San-no-tani, Naka-ku* ☎ *045/621–0635* 🔒 *Inner garden ¥300, outer garden ¥300, farmhouse ¥100* ⊙ *Inner garden daily 9–4, outer garden daily 9–4:30.*

⑫ The **Silk Museum** (Shiruku Hakubutsukan) pays tribute to the period at the turn of the 20th century when Japan's exports of silk were all shipped out of Yokohama. The museum houses an extensive collection of silk fabrics and an informative exhibit on the silk-making process. People on staff are very happy to answer questions. In the same building, on the first floor, are the main offices of the Yokohama International Tourist Association and the Kanagawa Prefectural Tourist Association. The museum is at the northwestern end of the Yamashita Park promenade, on the second floor of the Silk Center Building. ⊠ *1 Yamashita-chō, Naka-ku* ☎ *045/641–0841* 🔒 *¥500* ⊙ *Tues.–Sun. 9–4* Ⓜ *Minato Mirai Line, Nihon Ōdori Station (Exit 3).*

❽ The **World Porters** shopping center, on the opposite side of Yokohama Cosmo World, is notable chiefly for its restaurants that overlook the Minato Mirai area. Try arriving at sunset; the spectacular view of twinkling lights and the Landmark Tower, the Ferris wheel, and hotels will occasionally include Mt. Fuji in the background. Walking away from the waterfront area from World Porters will lead to **Aka Renga** (Red-brick Warehouses), two more shopping-and-entertainment facilities. ⊠ *2–2–1 Shin-minato-chō, Naka-ku* ☎ *045/222–2000* 🔒 *Free* ⊙ *Daily 10–9, restaurants until 11* Ⓜ *JR Line, Sakuragi-chō Station; Minato Mirai Line, Minato Mirai Station.*

⑭ **Yamashita Kōen** (Yamashita Park) is perhaps the only positive legacy of the Great Kantō Earthquake of 1923. The debris of the warehouses and other buildings that once stood here were swept away, and the area was made into a 17-acre oasis of green along the waterfront. The fountain, representing the Guardian of the Water, was presented to Yokohama by San Diego, California, one of its sister cities. From Harbor View Park, walk northwest through neighboring French Hill Park and cross the walkway over Moto-machi. Turn right on the other side and walk one block down toward the bay to Yamashita-Kōen-dōri, the promenade along the park. ⊠ *Naka-ku* Ⓜ *JR Line, Ishikawa-chō Station; Minato Mirai Line, Motomachi-Chukagai Station.*

🕐 ❼ The **Yokohama Cosmo World** amusement park complex claims—among its 30 or so rides and attractions—the world's largest water-chute ride at 13 feet long and four stories high. It's west of Minato Mirai and Queen's Square, on both sides of the river. ✉ 2-8-1 Shinko, Naka-ku ☎ 045/ 641–6591 ☞ Park free, rides ¥300–¥700 each ⊘ Mid-Mar.–Nov., weekdays 11–9, weekends 11–10; Dec.–mid-Mar., weekdays 11–8, weekends 11–9 Ⓜ JR Line, Sakuragi-chō Station; Minato Mirai Line, Minato Mirai Station.

🕐 ⓰ The **Yokohama Doll Museum** (Yokohama Ningyō-no-ie) houses a collection of some 4,000 dolls from all over the world. In Japanese tradition, dolls are less to play with than to display—either in religious folk customs or as the embodiment of some spiritual quality. Japanese visitors to this museum never seem to outgrow their affection for the Western dolls on display here, to which they tend to assign the role of timeless "ambassadors of good will" from other cultures. The museum is worth a quick visit, with or without a child in tow. It's just across from the southeast end of Yamashita Park, on the left side of the promenade. ✉ 18 Yamashita-chō, Naka-ku ☎ 045/671–9361 ☞ ¥300; multiple-entry ticket to museum, Marine Tower, and Hikawa-maru, ¥1,550 ⊘ Daily 10–6; closed 3rd Mon. of month Ⓜ JR Line, Ishikawa-chō Station; Minato Mirai Line, Motomachi-Chukagai Station.

⓫ Within the **Yokohama History Archives** (Yokohama Kaikō Shiryōkan), housed in what was once the British Consulate, are some 140,000 items recording the history of Yokohama since the opening of the port to international trade in the mid-19th century. Across the street is a monument to the U.S.–Japanese Friendship Treaty. To get here from the Silk Center Building, at the end of the Yamashita Park promenade, walk west to the corner of Nihon-ōdori; the archives are on the left. ✉ 3 Nihon-ōdori, Naka-ku ☎ 045/201–2100 ☞ ¥200 ⊘ Tues.–Sun. 9:30–4:30 Ⓜ Minato Mirai Line, Nihon O-dori Station.

❷ Minato Mirai 21 is the site of the **Yokohama Museum of Art** (Yokohama Bijutsukan) designed by Kenzō Tange. The 5,000 works in the permanent collection include paintings by both Western and Japanese artists, including Cézanne, Picasso, Braque, Klee, Kandinsky, Kishida Ryūsei, and Yokoyama Taikan. ✉ 3–4–1 Minato Mirai, Nishi-ku ☎ 045/221–0300 ☞ ¥500 ⊘ Mon.–Wed. and weekends 10–5:30, Fri. 10–7:30 (last entry); closed Thurs. and the day after a national holiday Ⓜ JR Line, Sakuragi-chō Station; Minato Mirai Line, Minato Mirai Station.

OFF THE BEATEN PATH

SŌJI-JI – One of the two major centers of the Sōtō sect of Zen Buddhism, Sōji-ji, in Yokohama's Tsurumi ward, was founded in 1321. The center was moved here from Ishikawa, on the Noto Peninsula (on the Sea of Japan, north of Kanazawa), after a fire in the 19th century. There's also a Sōji-ji monastic complex at Eihei-ji in Fukui Prefecture. The Yokohama Sōji-ji is one of the largest and busiest Buddhist institutions in Japan, with more than 200 monks and novices in residence. The 14th-century patron of Sōji-ji was the emperor Go-Daigo, who overthrew the Kamakura Shōgunate; the emperor is buried here, but his mausoleum is off-limits to visitors. However, you can see the **Buddha Hall**, the **Main Hall**, and the **Treasure House**. To get to Sōji-ji, take the JR Keihin Tōhoku Line two stops from Sakuragi-chō to Tsurumi. From the station walk five minutes south (back toward Yokohama), passing Tsurumi University on your right. Look out for the stone lanterns that mark the entrance to the temple complex. ✉ *2–1–1 Tsurumi, Tsurumi-ku* ☎ *045/581–6021* 🎫 *¥300* ☉ *Daily dawn–dusk; Treasure House Tues.–Sun. 10–4.*

Where to Eat

★ **$$$$** ✕ **Kaseiro.** Surprisingly, Chinese food can be hit or miss in Japan, but not at Kaseiro. This elegant restaurant, with red carpets and gold-tone walls, is the best of its kind in the city, serving authentic Beijing cuisine, including, of course, Peking Duck and shark-fin soup. The consistently delicious dishes combined with the fact that both the owner and chef are from Beijing, makes this restaurant a well-known favorite among locals and travelers alike. ✉ *186 Yamashita-chō, Chinatown, Naka-ku* ☎ *045/681–2918* 👔 *Jacket and tie* ▣ *AE, DC, V.*

$$$$ ✕ **Motomachi Bairin.** The area of Motomachi is known as the wealthy, posh part of Yokohama; restaurants here tend to be exclusive and expensive, though the service and quality justify the price. This restaurant is an old style Japanese house complete with a Japanese garden and 5 private tatami rooms. The ¥10,000, 27 course banquet includes some traditional Japanese delicacies such as sashimi, shiitake mushrooms and chicken in white sauce, deep fried burdock, and broiled sea bream. ✉ *1-55 Motomachi Naka-ku* ☎ *045/662–2215* 🍴 *Reservations advised* ▣ *No credit cards* ☉ *Close Mon.*

$$$$ ✕ **Scandia.** This Scandinavian restaurant near the Silk Center and the business district is known for its smorgasbord. It's popular for business lunches as well as for dinner. Scandia stays open until midnight, later than many other restaurants in the area. Expect dishes like steak tartar, marinated herring, and fried eel, and plenty of rye bread. ✉ *1–1 Kaigan-dōri, Naka-ku* ☎ *045/201–2262* ▣ *No credit cards* ☉ *No lunch Sun.*

$$$$ ✕ **Serina Romanchaya.** The hallmarks of this restaurant are *ishiyaki* steak, which is grilled on a hot stone, and shabu-shabu—thin slices of beef cooked in boiling water at your table and dipped in one of several sauces; choose from sesame, vinegar, or soy. Fresh vegetables, noodles, and tofu are also dipped into the seasoned broth for a filling, yet healthful meal. ✉ *Shin-Kannai Bldg., B1, 4–45–1 Sumiyoshi-chō, Naka-ku* ☎ *045/681–2727* ▣ *AE, DC, MC, V.*

★ **$$$–$$$$** ✕ **Aichiya.** One of the specialties at this seafood restaurant is fugu (blowfish). This delicacy, which is only served in winter, must be treated with expert care, because the fishes' organs contain a deadly toxin that must be removed before being consumed. The crabs here are also a treat. ✉ *7–156 Isezaki-chō, Naka-ku* ☎ *045/251–4163* ▣ *No credit cards* ☉ *Closed Mon. No lunch.*

$$$–$$$$ ✕ **Rinka-en.** If you visit the gardens of Sankei-en, you might want to have lunch at this traditional country restaurant, which serves kaiseki-style cuisine. Meals here are prix fixe. The owner is the granddaughter of Hara Tomitaro, who donated the gardens to the city. ✉ *52-1 Honmoku San-no-tani, Naka-ku* ☎ *045/621–0318* 👔 *Jacket and tie* ▣ *No credit cards* ☉ *Closed Wed. and Aug. No dinner.*

$$–$$$$ ✕ **Roma Statione.** Opened more than 40 years ago, Roma Statione, between Chinatown and Yamashita Park, remains a popular venue for Italian food. The owner, whose father studied cooking in Italy before returning home to open this spot, is also the head chef and has continued using the original recipes. The house specialty is seafood: the spaghetti *vongole* (with clam sauce) is particularly good, as is the spaghetti pescatora and the seafood pizza. An added bonus is the impressive selection of Italian wines. ✉ *26 Yamashita-chō, Naka-ku* ☎ *045/681–1818* 🚫 *No credit cards* Ⓜ *(Exit 1) Minato Mirai line Motomachi-Chukagai station.*

$$ ✕ **Chano-ma.** This stylish eatery serves modern Japanese cuisine. There are bed-like seats that you can lounge on while eating and a house DJ spins tunes during dinner. While you're there, make sure you try the miso sirloin steak or grilled scallops with tasty citron sauce drizzled on top, served with a salad. It does get crowded here on the weekends, so to avoid a long wait, try coming at lunchtime and you can take advantage of the ¥1,000 set lunch special. ✉ *Red Brick Warehouse Bldg. 2, 3F., 1-1-2 Shinkou Naka-ku* ☎ *045/650–8228* 🚫 *AE, DC, MC, V* Ⓜ *Basha-michi station, Minato Mirai line; Sakuragicho, Kannai stations, JR Negishi line.*

🔥 **$$** ✕ **Yokohama Cheese Cafe.** This is a cozy and inviting casual Italian restaurant, whose interior looks like an Italian country home. There are candles on the tables and an open kitchen where diners can watch the cooks making pizza. On the menu: 18 kinds of Napoli-style wood-fire–baked pizzas, 20 kinds of pastas, fondue and other dishes that include—you guessed it—cheese. The set course menus are reasonable, filling, and recommended. ✉ *2-1-10 Kitasaiwai Nisi-ku* ☎ *045/290–5656* 🚫 *DC, MC, V* Ⓜ *JR Yokohama station.*

Yokohama Essentials

AIRPORTS & AIRPORT TRANSFERS

From Narita Airport, a direct limousine-bus service departs once or twice an hour between 6:45 AM and 10:20 PM for Yokohama City Air Terminal (YCAT). The fare is ¥3,500. YCAT is a five-minute taxi ride from Yokohama Station. JR Narita Express trains going on from Tōkyō to Yokohama leave the airport every hour from 8:13 AM to 1:13 PM and 2:43 PM to 9:43 PM. The fare is ¥4,180 (¥6,730 for the first-class Green Car coaches). Or you can take the limousine-bus service from Narita to Tōkyō Station and continue on to Yokohama by train. Either way, the journey will take more than two hours—closer to three, if traffic is heavy.

The Airport Limousine Information Desk phone number provides information in English daily 9–6; you can also get timetables on its Web site. For information in English on Narita Express trains, call the JR Higashi-Nihon Info Line, available daily 10–6.

🛈 **Airport Limousine Information Desk** ☎ 03/3665-7220 ⊕ www.limousinebus.co.jp. **JR Higashi-Nihon Info Line** ☎ 03/3423-0111.

BUS TRAVEL

Most of the things you'll want to see in Yokohama are within easy walking distance of a JR or subway station, but this city is so much more negotiable than Tōkyō that exploring by bus is a viable alternative. Buses, in fact, are the best way to get to Sankei-en. The city map available in the visitor centers in Yokohama has most major bus routes marked on it, and the important stops on the tourist routes are announced in English. The fixed fare is ¥210. One-day passes are also available for ¥600. Contact the Sightseeing Information Office at Yokohama Station (JR, East exit) for more information and ticket purchases. ☎ 045/465–2077.

EMERGENCIES
The Yokohama Police station has a Foreign Assistance Department.
Ambulance or Fire ☎ 119. **Police** ☎ 110. **Washinzaka Hospital** ✉ 169 Yamate-chō, Naka-ku ☎ 045/623-7688. **Yokohama Police station** ✉ 2-4 Kaigan-dōri, Naka-ku ☎ 045/623-0110.

ENGLISH-LANGUAGE MEDIA
BOOKS Yūrindō has a good selection of popular paperbacks and books on Japan in English. The Minato-Mirai branch is open daily 11–8; the store on Isezaki-chō opens an hour earlier.
Yūrindō ✉ Landmark Plaza 5F, 3-3-1 Minato-Mirai, Nishi-ku ☎ 045/222-5500 ✉ 1-4-1 Isezaki-chō, Naka-ku ☎ 045/261-1231.

SUBWAY TRAVEL
One subway line connects Azamino, Shin-Yokohama, Yokohama, Totsuka, and Shōnandai. The basic fare is ¥200. One-day passes are also available for ¥740. The Minato Mirai Line, a spur of the Tōkyū Tōyoko Line, runs from Yokohama Station to all the major points of interest, including Minato Mirai, Chinatown, Yamashita Park, Moto-machi, and Basha-michi. The fare is ¥180–¥200, and one-day unlimited-ride passes are available for ¥450.

TAXIS
There are taxi stands at all the train stations, and you can always flag a cab on the street. ■ TIP→ Vacant taxis show a red light in the windshield. The basic fare is ¥660 for the first 2 km (1 mi), then ¥80 for every additional 350 meters (⅕ mi). Traffic is heavy in downtown Yokohama, however, and you will often find it faster to walk.

TOURS
Teiki Yuran Bus (☎ 045/465–2077)offers a full-day (9–3:45) sightseeing bus tour that covers the major sights and includes lunch at a Chinese restaurant in Chinatown. The tour is in Japanese only, but pamphlets written in English are available at most sightseeing stops. Buy tickets (¥6,360) at the bus offices at Yokohama Station (east side) and at Kannai Station; the tour departs daily at 9 AM from Bus Stop 14, on the east side of Yokohama Station. A half-day tour is also available, with lunch (9:30–1, ¥3,850) or without (2–5:30, ¥3,000).

The sightseeing boat *Marine Shuttle* makes 40-, 60-, and 90-minute tours of the harbor and bay for ¥900, ¥1,400, and ¥2,000, respectively. Boarding is at the pier at Yamashita Park. Boats depart roughly every hour between 10:20 AM and 6:30 PM. Another boat, the *Marine Rouge,* runs 90-minute tours departing from the pier at 11, 1:30, and 4, and a special two-hour evening tour at 7 (¥2,500).
Tour Contact Marine Shuttle ☎ 045/671-7719. Port Service reservation center.

TRAIN TRAVEL

JR trains from Tōkyō Station leave approximately every 10 minutes, depending on the time of day. Take the Yokosuka, the Tōkaidō, or Keihin Tōhoku Line to Yokohama Station (the Yokosuka and Tōkaidō lines take 30 minutes; the Keihin Tōhoku Line takes 40 minutes and cost ¥450). From there the Keihin Tōhoku Line (Platform 3) goes on to Kannai and Ishikawa-chō, Yokohama's business and downtown areas. If you're going directly to downtown Yokohama from Tōkyō, the blue commuter trains of the Keihin Tōhoku Line are best.

The private Tōkyū Tōyokō Line, which runs from Shibuya Station in Tōkyō directly to Yokohama Station, is a good alternative if you leave from the western part of Tōkyō. ■ TIP→ **The term "private" is important because it means that the train does not belong to JR and is not a subway line. If you have a JR pass you'll have to buy a separate ticket.** Depending on which Tōkyū Tōyoko Line you catch—the Limited Express, Semi Express, or Local—the trip takes between 25 and 44 minutes and costs ¥260.

Yokohama Station is the hub that links all the train lines and connects them with the city's subway and bus services. Kannai and Ishikawa-chō are the two downtown stations, both on the Keihin Tōhoku Line; trains leave Yokohama Station every two to five minutes from Platform 3. From Sakuragi-chō, Kannai, or Ishikawa-chō, most of Yokohama's points of interest are within easy walking distance; the one notable exception is Sankei-en, which you reach via the JR Keihin Tōhoku Line to Negishi Station and then a local bus.

VISITOR INFORMATION

The Yokohama International Tourist Association arranges visits to the homes of English-speaking Japanese families. These usually last a few hours and are designed to give *gaijin* (foreigners) a glimpse into the Japanese way of life.

The Yokohama Tourist Office, in the central passageway of Yokohama Station, is open daily 9–7 (closed December 28–January 3). The head office of the Yokohama Convention & Visitors Bureau, open weekdays 9–5 (except national holidays and December 29–January 3), is in the Sangyō Bōeki Center Building, across from Yamashita Kōen.

🚩 Tourist Information **Yokohama Convention & Visitors Bureau** ✉ 2 Yamashita-chō, Naka-ku ☎ 045/221-2111. **Yokohama International Tourist Association** ☎ 045/641-4759. **Yokohama Tourist Office** ✉ Yokohama Station, Nishi-ku ☎ 045/441-7300.

FUJI-HAKONE-IZU NATIONAL PARK

Fuji-Hakone-Izu National Park, southwest of Tōkyō between Suruga and Sagami bays, is one of Japan's most popular resort areas. The region's main attraction, of course, is Mt. Fuji, a dormant volcano—it last erupted in 1707—rising to a height of 12,388 feet. The mountain is truly beautiful; utterly captivating in the ways it can change in different light and from different perspectives. Its symmetry and majesty have been immortalized by poets and artists for centuries. ■ TIP→ **During spring and summer, Mt. Fuji often hides behind a blanket of clouds. Keep this in mind if seeing the mountain is an important part of your trip.**

Apart from Mt. Fuji itself, each of the three areas of the park—the Izu Peninsula, Hakone and environs, and the Five Lakes—has its own unique appeal. Izu is defined by its dramatic rugged coastline, beaches, and *onsen* (hot springs). Hakone has mountains, volcanic landscapes, and lake cruises, plus onsen of its own. The Five Lakes form a recreational area with some of the best views of Mt. Fuji. And in each of these areas there are monuments to Japan's past.

Although it's possible to make a grand tour of all three areas at one time, most people make each of them a separate excursion from Tōkyō.

Trains will serve you well in traveling to major points anywhere in the northern areas of the national-park region and down the eastern coast of the Izu Peninsula. For the west coast and central mountains of Izu, there are no train connections; unless you are intrepid enough to rent a car, the only way to get around is by bus.

Numbers in the margin correspond to the Fuji-Hakone-Izu National Park map.

Izu Peninsula

6

Atami

❶ *48 min southwest of Tōkyō by Kodama Shinkansen.*

The gateway to the Izu Peninsula is Atami. Most Japanese travelers make it no farther into the peninsula than this town on Sagami Bay, so Atami itself has a fair number of hotels and traditional inns. When you arrive, collect a map from the **Atami Tourist Information Office** (☎ 0557/85–2222) at the train station to guide you to the sights below.

★ The **MOA Museum of Art** (MOA Bijutsukan) houses the private collection of the messianic religious leader Okada Mokichi. Okada (1882–1955), who founded a movement called the Sekai Kyūsei Kyō (Religion for the Salvation of the World), also acquired more than 3,000 works of art; some are from the Asuka period (6th and 7th centuries). Among these works are several particularly fine *ukiyo-e* (Edo-era woodblock prints) and ceramics. On a hill above the station and set in a garden full of old plum trees and azaleas, the museum also affords a sweeping view over Atami and the bay. ✉ *26–2 Momoyama Atami, Shizouka-ken* ☎ *0557/84–2511* 🔊 *¥1,600* ⊙ *Fri.–Wed. 9:30–5.*

The **Ōyu Geyser,** located just a 15-minute walk south east from Atami Station, used to gush on schedule once every 24 hours but stopped after the Great Kantō Earthquake of 1923. Not happy with this, the local chamber of commerce rigged a pump to raise the geyser every five minutes. ✉ *3 Kamijuku-cho Atami, Shizouka-ken.*

The best time to visit the **Atami Plum Garden** (Atami Bai-en) is in late January or early February, when its 850 trees bloom. If you do visit, also stop by the small shrine that's in the shadow of an enormous old camphor tree. The shrine is more than 1000 years old and is popular spot for people who are asking the gods for help with alcoholism. The tree is more than 2,000 years old and has been designated a National Monument. It is believed that if you walk around the tree once, another

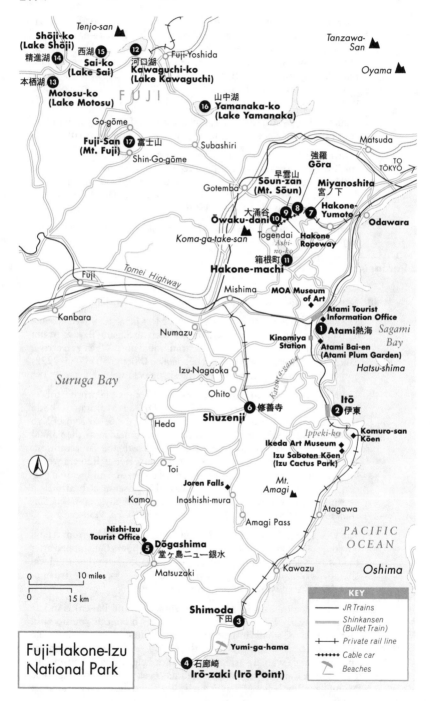

Fuji-Hakone-Izu
National Park

year will be added to your life. Atami Bai-en is always open to the public and is 15 minutes by bus from Atami or an eight-minute walk from Kinomiya Station, the next stop south of Atami served by local trains. ✉ *1169-1 Baien-cho, Atami, Shizouka-ken* ☎ *055/785–2222* ☑ *Free.*

If you have the time and the inclination for a beach picnic, it's worth taking the 25-minute high-speed ferry (round-trip ¥2,340) from the pier over to **Hatsu-shima** (☎ 0557/81–0541 for ferry). There are nine departures daily between 7:30 and 5:20. You can easily walk around the island, which is only 4 km (2½ mi) in circumference, in less than two hours. Use of the **Picnic Garden** (open daily 10–3) is free.

WHERE TO STAY   🏠 **Atami Taikansō.** The views of the sea must have been the inspiration

★ **$$$$**   for Yokoyama Taikan, the Japanese artist who once owned this villa. Now it is a traditional Japanese inn with exquisite furnishings and individualized service. The spacious rooms are classically Japanese, with ceiling to floor windows. The prices are high, but bear in mind that they include a multicourse dinner of great artistry, served in your room, and breakfast the next morning. There are also indoor and outdoor hot-springs baths. The inn is a 10-minute walk west from Atami Station. ✉ *7–1 Hayashi-ga-oka-chō, Atami, Shizuoka-ken 413-0031* ☎ *0557/81–8137* ⊕ *www.atami-taikanso.com* ➥ *44 Japanese-style rooms with bath* ⌂ *Restaurant, pool, sauna, meeting rooms* ▭ *AE, DC, MC, V* ⏐◎⏐ *MAP.*

$$–$$$$ 🏠 **New Fujiya Hotel.** Only the top rooms have a view of the sea at this modern, inland resort hotel that's a great base for sightseeing. Service is impersonal but professional, and a foreign visitor won't fluster the staff. The hotel is a five-minute taxi ride from Atami Station. ✉ *1–16 Ginza-chō, Atami, Shizuoka-ken 413-0013* ☎ *0557/81–0111* ➥ *158 Western-style rooms with bath, 158 Japanese-style rooms with bath* ⌂ *3 restaurants, indoor pool, bar* ▭ *AE, DC, MC, V.*

Itō

❷ *25 min south of Atami by JR local; 1 hr, 40 min southwest of Tōkyō via Atami by Kodama Shinkansen, then JR local.*

There are some 800 thermal springs in the resort area surrounding Itō, 16 km (10 mi) south of Atami. These springs—and the beautiful, rocky, indented coastline nearby—remain the resort's major attractions, although there are plenty of interesting sights here. Some 150 hotels and inns serve the area.

Itō traces its history of associations with the West to 1604, when William Adams (1564–1620), the Englishman whose adventures served as the basis for James Clavell's novel *Shōgun,* came ashore.

Four years earlier Adams had beached his disabled Dutch vessel, *De Liefde,* on the shores of Kyūshū and became the first Englishman to set foot on Japan. The authorities, believing that he and his men were Portuguese pirates, put Adams in prison, but he was eventually befriended by the shōgun Ieyasu Tokugawa, who brought him to Edo (present-day Tōkyō) and granted him an estate. Ieyasu appointed Adams his adviser on foreign affairs. The English castaway taught mathematics, geography, gunnery, and navigation to shogunal officials and in 1604 was ordered to

A Healing Headache

WHILE EARTHQUAKES ARE AN annoying, everyday fact of life in Japan, they also provide one of the country's greatest delights: thermal baths. Wherever there are volcanic mountains—and there are a lot—you're sure to find springs of hot water, called *onsen*, that are rich in all sorts of restorative minerals. Any place where lots of spas have tapped these sources is an *onsen chiiki* (hot-springs resort area). The Izu Peninsula is particularly rich in onsen. It has, in fact, one-fifth of the 2,300-odd officially recognized hot springs in Japan.

Spas take many forms, but the *ne plus ultra* is that small secluded Japanese mountain inn with a *rotemburo* (an open-air mineral-spring pool). For guests only, these pools are usually in a screened-off nook with a panoramic view. A room in one of these inns on a weekend or in high season should be booked months in advance. (High season is late December to early January, late April to early May, the second and third weeks of August, and the second and third weeks of October.) More typical is the large resort hotel, geared mainly to groups, with one or more large indoor mineral baths of its own. Where whole towns and villages have developed to exploit a local supply of hot water, there will be several of these large hotels, an assortment of smaller inns, and probably a few modest public bathhouses, with no accommodations, where you just pay an entrance fee for a soak of whatever length you wish.

build an 80-ton Western-style ship. Pleased with this venture, Ieyasu ordered the construction of a larger oceangoing vessel. These two ships were built at Itō, where Adams lived from 1605 to 1610.

This history was largely forgotten until British Commonwealth occupation forces began coming to Itō for rest and recuperation after World War II. Adams's memory was revived, and since then the Anjin Festival (the Japanese gave Adams the name *anjin*, which means "pilot") has been held in his honor every August. A monument to the Englishman stands at the mouth of the river.

Izu Cactus Park (Izu Saboten Kōen) consists of a series of pyramidal greenhouses that contain 5,000 kinds of cacti from around the world. At the base of Komuro-san (Mt. Komuro), the park is 20 minutes south of Itō Station by bus. ⊠ *1317–13 Futo* ☎ *0557/51–5553* 💴 *¥1,800* ⊙ *Mar.–Oct., daily 9–5; Nov.–Feb., daily 9–4.*

The **Ikeda 20th-Century Art Museum** (Ikeda 20-Seiki Bijutsukan), at Lake Ippeki, houses works by Picasso, Dalí, Chagall, and Matisse, plus a number of wood-block prints. The museum is a 15-minute walk north west from Izu Cactus Park. ⊠ *614 Totari* ☎ *0557/45–2211* 💴 *¥900* ⊙ *Thurs.–Tues., 10–4:30.*

On the east side of **Komuro-san Kōen** (Mt. Komuro Park) are 3,000 cherry trees of 35 varieties that bloom at various times throughout the year. You can take a cable car to the top of the mountain. The park is about

20 minutes south of Itō Station by bus. ✉ *1428 Komuro-cho, Kawana, Ito-shi* ☎ *0557/45–1444* 💰 *Free; round-trip cable car to mountain top ¥400* 🕐 *Daily 9–4.*

WHERE TO STAY

$$$$

🏨 **Hatoya Sun Hotel.** Located along a scenic coastline, Hatoya Hotel is in the Itō onsen resort area. The hotel has an aquarium bath, which has glass walls that let guests gaze at tropical fish in an adjoining aquarium while soaking. The open-air hot springs look out onto the ocean where mountains are visible in the distance. Japanese buffet dinners are available every night. ✉ *572-12 Yukawa Tateiwa, Nagasaki-shi, Shizuoka-ken 414-0002* ☎ *055/736–4126* 🛏 *187 Japanese-style rooms with bath, 3 Western-style rooms with bath, 1 mixed Western-Japanese style room* 🛎 *Minibar, restaurant, parking, bar, swimming pool, sauna* 🖬 *DC, MC, V.*

$$–$$$

🏨 **Hanafubuki.** This traditional Japanese inn, which is located in the Jogasaki forest, was given a modern makeover , but still retains classic elements like tatami mats, screen sliding doors and *chabudai* (low dining ables) with *zabuton* (cushion seating). The onsen are made of wood for rustic appeal. Meals are optional. ✉ *1041 Yawatano Isomichi, Ito-shi, Shizuoka-ken 413-0232* ☎ *055/754–1550* 🛏 *12 Japanese style rooms, 2 Western style rooms, 3 family rooms* 🛎 *Restaurant, bar* 🖬 *MC, V* 🌐 *www.hanafubuki.co.jp.*

EN
ROUTE

South of Itō the coastal scenery is lovely—each sweep around a headland reveals another picturesque sight of a rocky, indented shoreline. There are several spa towns en route to Shimoda. Higashi-Izu (East Izu) has numerous hot-springs resorts, of which **Atagawa** is the most fashionable. South of Atagawa is **Kawazu,** a place of relative quiet and solitude, with pools in the forested mountainside and waterfalls plunging through lush greenery.

Shimoda

3 *1 hr south of Itō by Izu Railways.*

Of all the resort towns south of Itō along Izu's eastern coast, none can match the distinction of Shimoda. Shimoda's encounter with the West began when Commodore Matthew Perry anchored his fleet of black ships off the coast here in 1853. To commemorate the event, the three-day Black Ship Festival (Kurofune Matsuri) is held here every year in mid-May. Shimoda was also the site, in 1856, of the first American consulate.

The **Shimoda Tourist Office** (☎ 0558/22–1531), in front of the station, has the easiest of the local English itineraries to follow. The 2½-km (1½-mi) tour covers most major sights. On request, the tourist office will also help you find local accommodations.

The first American consul to Japan was New York businessman Townsend Harris. Soon after his arrival in Shimoda, Harris asked the Japanese authorities to provide him with a female servant; they sent him a young girl named Saitō Okichi, who was engaged to be married. The arrangement brought her a new name, Tōjin (the Foreigner's) Okichi, much disgrace, and a tragic end. When Harris sent her away, she tried, but failed to rejoin her former lover. The shame brought upon her for working and living with a Westerner and the pain of losing the love of her life drove Okichi to drown herself in 1890. Her tale is recounted in Rei Kimura's biographical novel *Butterfly in the Wind*. **Hōfuku-ji** was Okichi's family temple. The museum annex displays a life-size image of her, and just behind the temple is her grave—where incense is still kept burning in her memory. The grave of her lover, Tsurumatsu, is at Tōden-ji, a temple about midway between Hōfuku-ji and Shimoda Station. ✉ *18–26 1-chōme* ☎ *0558/22–0960* 🎫 *¥300* 🕐 *Daily 8–5.*

Ryosen-ji is the temple in which the negotiations took place that led to the United States–Japan Treaty of Amity and Commerce of 1858. The **Treasure Hall** (Hōmotsu-den) contains some personal articles that belonged to Tōjin Okichi. ✉ *3–12–12 Shimoda* ☎ *0558/22–2805* 🎫 *Treasure Hall ¥500* 🕐 *Daily 8:30–5.*

WHERE TO STAY

$$–$$$$ 🏨 **Shimoda Prince Hotel.** This modern V-shape resort hotel faces the Pacific and is steps away from a white-sand beach. The decor is more functional than aesthetic, but the panoramic view of the ocean from the picture windows in the dining room makes this one of the best hotels in town. The Prince is just outside Shimoda, 10 minutes by taxi from the station. ✉ *1547–1 Shira-hama, Shimoda, Shizuoka-ken 415-8525* ☎ *0558/ 22–2111* ⊕ *www.princehotels.co.jp* 🛏 *70 Western-style rooms with bath, 6 Japanese-style rooms with bath ⚭ 2 restaurants, 3 tennis courts, pool, sauna, bar, nightclub, shops* ☰ *AE, DC, MC, V.*

$$–$$$$ 🏨 **Shimoda Tokyū Hotel.** Perched just above the bay, the Shimoda Tokyū has impressive views of the Pacific from one side (where rooms cost about 10% more) and mountains from the other. Unlike at most Japanese resort hotels, the lobby here is full of character and warmth, with an airy layout and floor-to-ceiling windows overlooking the bay. Prices are significantly higher in midsummer. ✉ *5–12–1 Shimoda, Shimoda, Shizuoka-ken 415-8510* ☎ *0558/22–2411* ⊕ *www.tokyuhotels.co.jp* 🛏 *107 Western-style rooms with bath, 8 Japanese-style rooms with bath ⚭ 3 restaurants, café, pool, bar, shops* ☰ *AE, DC, MC, V.*

¢   🏨 **Pension Sakuraya.** There are a few Western-style bedrooms at this family-run inn just a few minutes' walk from Shimoda's main beach, but the best lodgings are the Japanese-style corner rooms, which have nice views of the hills surrounding Shimoda. The pleasant Japanese couple who runs the pension speaks English, and cheap meals are available in the dining room. ✉ *2584–20 Shira-hama, Shimoda, Shizuoka-ken 415-0012* ☎ *0558/23–4470* 🛏 *4 Western-style rooms with bath, 5 Japanese-style rooms without bath* ⊕ *http://izu-sakuraya.jp/english ⚭ Dining room, Japanese baths, laundry facilities, Internet* ☰ *AE, DC, MC, V.*

Irō-zaki (Irō Point)

❹ *40 min by bus or boat from Shimoda.*

If you visit Irō-zaki, the southernmost part of the Izu Peninsula, in January, you're in for a special treat: a blanket of daffodils covers the cape. From the bus stop at the end of the line from Shimoda Station, it's a short walk to the **Irō-zaki Jungle Park,** with its 3,000 varieties of colorful tropical plants. Beyond the park you can walk to a lighthouse at the edge of the cliff that overlooks the sea, from here you can see the seven islands of Izu. ✉ 546–1 Irō-zaki, Minami-Izu ☎ 0558/65–0050 🎫 ¥900 🕙 Daily 8–5.

Dōgashima

⑤ 1 hr northwest of Shimoda by bus.

The sea has eroded the coastal rock formations into fantastic shapes near the little port town of Dōgashima. A **Dōgashima Marine** (☎ 0558/52–0013) sightseeing boat from Dōgashima Pier makes 20-

---

BATHING BEAUTIES

If you love the sun, make sure you stop at **Yumi-ga-hama**. It's one of the prettiest sandy beaches on the whole Izu Peninsula. The bus from Shimoda Station stops here before continuing to Irō-zaki, the last stop on the route.

---

minute runs to see the rocks (¥920). In an excess of kindness, a recorded loudspeaker—which you can safely ignore—recites the name of every rock you pass on the trip. The **Nishi-Izu Tourist Office** (☎ 0558/52–1268) is near the pier, in the small building behind the bus station.

WHERE TO STAY

$$$$

🏨 **Dōgashima New Ginsui.** Surrounded by its very own secluded beach, every guest room overlooks the sea at the New Ginsui, which sits atop cliffs above the water. Service is first class, despite its popularity with tour groups. The Japanese-style rooms were given a modern makeover and the room rate includes a seafood kaiseki dinner served in your room and a buffet breakfast. For relaxation and pampering, visit the day spa or unwind in the outdoor hot spring. In a town overflowing with up-market hotels, this is by far the best luxury resort on Izu's west coast and though it's a rule that we only include Web sites if they are in English, this one is worth a thousand words. ✉ 2977–1 Nishina, Nishi-Izu-chō, Shizuoka-ken 410-3514 ☎ 0558/52–2211 ⤴ 121 Japanese-style rooms with bath ⚐ Restaurant, 2 pools, spa, nightclub, shops, laundry service, concierge, meeting rooms ▤ AE, DC, MC, V ⊕ www. dougashima-newginsui.jp 🍴 MAP.

Shuzenji

⑥ 2 hrs north of Shimoda by bus, 32 min south of Mishima by Izu-Hakone Railway.

Shuzenji—a hot-springs resort in the center of the peninsula, along the valley of the Katsura-gawa (Katsura River)—enjoys a certain historical notoriety as the place where the second Kamakura shōgun, Minamoto no Yoriie, was assassinated early in the 13th century. Don't judge the town by the area around the station; most of the hotels and hot springs are 2 km (1 mi) to the west.

If you've planned a longer visit to Izu, consider spending a night at **Inoshishi-mura,** en route by bus between Shimoda and Shuzenji. The scenery in this part of the peninsula is dramatic, and the dining specialty at the local inns is roast mountain boar. In the morning, a pleasant 15-minute walk from Inoshishi-mura brings you to **Joren Falls** (Joren-no-taki). Located on the upper part of the Kano River, these falls drop 82 feet into a dense forest below. This area has some nationally protected flora and fauna species and because of the cool temperature, hiking here is popular in summer.

6

$$$$ ⊡ **Ochiairou Murakami.** This traditional ryokan was built in the Showa period and though it has been renovated and modernized, the main wooden structure remains true to its original design. Some Japanese literary figures have stayed in this ryokan while writing their oeuvre with the natural surroundings of Yugashima as the inspiration. The rooms are spacious and comfortable, and look out into the gardens. There is a free pick up from Yugashima bus terminal. ⊠ *1887-1 Yugashima, Izu-shi, Shizuoka-ken 410-3206* ☎ *0558/85–0014* ⤳ *15 Japanese-style rooms* ⚭ *Restaurant, hot spring* ▤ *AE, MC, V.*

★ **$$$$** ⊡ **Ryokan Sanyōsō.** The former villa of the Iwasaki family, founders of the Mitsubishi conglomerate, is as luxurious and beautiful a place to stay as you'll find on the Izu Peninsula. Museum-quality antiques furnish the rooms—the best of which have traditional baths made of fragrant cypress wood and overlook exquisite little private gardens (note that these high-end rooms cost as much as ¥70,000). Breakfast and dinner are served in your room and are included in the rate. The Sanyōsō is a five-minute taxi ride from Izu-Nagaoka Station. ⊠ *270 Mama-no-ue, Izunokuni-shī, Shizuoka-ken 410-2204* ☎ *0559/47–1111* ⤳ *3 Western-style, 30 Japanese-style and 7 mixed Western-Japanese-style rooms with baths* ⚭ *Japanese baths, bar, shops, meeting rooms* ▤ *AE, DC, MC, V.*

$$ ⊡ **Kyorai-An Matsushiro-kan.** Although this small family-owned inn is nothing fancy, the owners make you feel like a guest in their home. They also speak some English. Japanese meals are served in a common dining room. Room-only reservations (without meals) are accepted only on weekdays. The inn is five minutes by bus or taxi from Izu-Nagaoka Station. ⊠ *55 Kona, Izunokuni, Shizuoka-ken 410-2201* ☎ *0559/ 48–0072* ⤳ *14 Japanese-style rooms with bath, 2 without bath* ⚭ *Dining room* ▤ *No credit cards* ⎮⊙⎮ *MAP.*

¢ ⊡ **Goyōkan.** This family-run ryokan on Shuzenji's main street has rooms that look out on the Katsura-gawa, plus gorgeous stone-lined (for men) and wood-lined (for women) indoor hot springs. The staff speaks English and can make sightseeing arrangements for you. ⊠ *765–2 Shuzenji-chō, Tagata-gun, Shizuoka-ken 410-24* ☎ *0558/72–2066* ⊕ *www.goyokan.co.jp* ⤳ *11 Japanese-style rooms without bath* ⚭ *Refrigerators, sauna* ▤ *AE, DC, MC, V.*

Hakone

The national park and resort area of Hakone is a popular day trip from Tōkyō and a good place for a close-up view of Mt. Fuji (assuming the mountain is not swathed in clouds, as often happens in summer). ⚠ **On summer weekends it often seems as though all of Tōkyō has come out to Hakone with you. Expect long lines at cable cars and traffic jams everywhere.**

You can cover the best of Hakone in a one-day trip out of Tōkyō, but if you want to try the curative powers of the thermal waters or do some hiking, then stay overnight. Two of the best areas are around the old hot-springs resort of Miyanoshita and the western side of Koma-ga-take-san (Mt. Koma-ga-take).

The typical Hakone route, outlined here, may sound complex, but this is in fact one excursion from Tōkyō so well defined that you really can't

CLOSE UP

Know the Etiquette

GUESTS ARE EXPECTED TO arrive at ryokan in the late afternoon. When you do, put on the slippers that are provided and a maid will escort you to your room. Remember to remove your slippers before entering your room; never step on the *tatami* (straw mats) with shoes or slippers. Each room will be simply decorated—one small low table, cushions on the tatami, and a scroll on the wall, which will probably be *shōji* (sliding paper-paneled walls).

In ryokan with thermal pools, you can take to the waters anytime, although the pool doors are usually locked from 11 PM to 6 AM. In ryokan without thermal baths or private baths in guest rooms, visits must be staggered. Typically the maid will ask what time you would like to bathe and fit you into a schedule. Make sure you wash and rinse off entirely before getting into the bath. Do not get soap in the tub. Other guests will be using the same bathwater, so it is important to observe this custom. After your bath, change into the yukata provided in your room. Don't worry about walking around in it—other guests will be doing the same.

Dinner is served around 6. At the larger, newer ryokan, meals will be in the dining room; at smaller, more personal ryokan, it is served in your room. When you are finished, a maid will clear away the dishes and lay out your futon. In Japan *futon* means bedding, and this consists of a thin cotton mattress and a heavy, thick comforter, which is replaced with a thinner quilt in summer. The small, hard pillow is filled with grain. The less expensive ryokan (under ¥7,000 for one) have become slightly lackadaisical in changing the quilt cover with each new guest; in an inoffensive a way as possible, feel free to complain—just don't shame the proprietor. Around 8 AM, a maid will gently wake you, clear away the futon, and bring in your Japanese-style breakfast, which will probably consist of fish, pickled vegetables, and rice. If this isn't appealing, politely ask if it's possible to have coffee and toast. Checkout is at 10.

Make sure you call or e-mail as far in advance as possible for a room—inns are not always willing to accept foreign guests because of language and cultural barriers. It is near impossible to get a room in July or August. Many top-level ryokan require new guests to have introductions and references from a respected client of the inn to get a room; this goes for new Japanese guests, too. On the other hand, inns that do accept foreigners without introduction sometimes treat them as cash cows, which means they might give you cursory service and a lesser room. If you don't speak Japanese, try to have a Japanese speaker reserve a room for you; this will convey the idea that you understand the customs of staying in a traditional inn.

6

get lost—no more so, at least, than any of the thousands of Japanese tourists ahead of and behind you. The first leg of the journey is from Odawara or Hakone-Yumoto by train and cable car through the mountains to Tōgendai, on the north shore of Ashi-no-ko (Lake Ashi). The long way around, from Odawara to Tōgendai by bus, takes about an hour—in heavy traffic, an hour and a half. The trip over the mountains, on the other hand, will take about two hours. Credit the difference to the Hakone Tozan Tetsudō Line—possibly the slowest train you'll ever ride. Using three switchbacks to inch its way up the side of the mountain, the train takes 54 minutes to travel the 16 km (10 mi) from Odawara to Gōra (38 minutes from Hakone-Yumoto). The steeper it gets, the grander the view.

7 Trains do not stop at any station en route for any length of time, but they do run frequently enough to allow you to disembark, visit a sight, and catch another train. **Miyanoshita,** the first stop on the train route from Hakone-Yumoto, is a small but very pleasant and popular resort. As well as hot springs, this village has antique shops along its main road and several hiking routes up the half-mile tall Mt. Sengen. If you get to the top, you'll be rewarded with a great view of the gorge.

★ The **Hakone Open-Air Museum** (Hakone Chōkoku-no-mori Bijutsukan), which is only a few minutes walk from the Miyanoshita Station (directions are posted in English), houses an astonishing collection of 19th- and 20th-century Western and Japanese sculpture, most of it on display in a spacious, handsome garden. There are works here by Rodin, Moore, Arp, Calder, Giacometti, Takeshi Shimizu, and Kōtarō Takamura. One section of the garden is devoted to Emilio Greco. Inside are works by Picasso, Léger, and Manzo, among others. ⊠ *1121 Ni-no-taira* ☎ *0460/2–1161* ⊕ *www.hakone-oam.or.jp* ⊡ *¥1,600* ⊘ *Mar.–Nov., daily 9–5; Dec.–Feb., daily 9–4.*

8 **Gōra,** a small town at the end of the train line from Odawara and the lower end of the Hakone Tozan Cablecar, is a good jumping-off point for hiking and exploring. Ignore the little restaurants and souvenir stands here: get off the train as quickly as you can and make a dash for the cable car at the other end of the station. If you let the rest of the passengers get there before you, and perhaps a tour bus or two, you may stand 45 minutes in line.

9 The Hakone Tozan Cablecar travels from Gōra to **Sōun-zan** (Mt. Sōun) and departs every 20 minutes; it takes 10 minutes (¥410; free with the Hakone Free Pass) to get to the top. It's ideal for those wanting to spend a day hiking. There are four stops en route, and you can get off and reboard the cable car at any one of them if you've paid the full fare. The **Hakone Museum of Art** (Hakone Bijutsukan), sister institution to the MOA Museum of Art in Atami, is at the second stop. The museum, which consists of two buildings set in a garden, houses a modest collection of porcelain and ceramics from China, Korea, and Japan. ⊠ *1300 Gōra* ☎ *0460/2–2623* ⊕ *www.moaart.or.jp* ⊡ *¥900* ⊘ *Apr.–Nov., Fri.–Wed. 9:30–4:30; Dec.–Mar., Fri.–Wed. 9:30–4.*

★ **10** At the cable-car terminus of Sōun-zan, a gondola called the **Hakone Ropeway** swings up over a ridge and crosses the valley called Ōwaku-dani, also known as "Great Boiling Valley," on its way to Tōgendai. The landscape here is desolate, with sulfurous billows of steam escaping through holes from some inferno deep in the earth—yet another reminder that Japan is a chain of volcanic islands. At the top of the ridge is one of the

Hakone Freebies

MANY PLACES IN HAKONE ACCEPT the Hakone Free Pass. It's valid for three days and is issued by the privately owned Odakyū Railways. The pass covers the train fare to Hakone and allows you to use any mode of transportation including the Hakone Tozan Cablecar, the Hakone Ropeway, and the Hakone Cruise Boat. In addition to transportation, Freepass holders get discounts at museums such as the Hakone Museum of Art, restaurants, and shops. The list of participants is pretty extensive and it always changes, so it's a good idea to check out the Web site for a complete list of participating companies and terms and conditions.

The Hakone Free Pass (¥5,500) and the Fuji-Hakone Free Pass (¥7,200) can be purchased at the **Odakyu Sightseeing Service Center** inside JR Shinjuku station, near west exit, or by credit card over the phone. Allow a couple of days for delivery to your hotel. If you have a JR Pass, it's cheaper to take a Kodama Shinkansen from Tōkyō Station to Odawara and buy the Hakone Free Pass there (¥4,130) for travel within the Hakone region only ☎ 03/5321-7887 ⊙ 8-8 ⊕ www.odakyu-group.co.jp.

6

two stations where you can leave the gondola. From here, a ¾-km (½-mi) walking course wanders among the sulfur pits in the valley. Just below the station is a restaurant; the food here is truly terrible, but on a clear day the view of Mt. Fuji is perfect. Remember that if you get off the gondola at any stage, you—and others in the same situation—will have to wait for someone to make space on a later gondola before you can continue down to Tōgendai and Ashi-no-ko (but again, the gondolas come by every minute). ⊠ 1-15-1 Shiroyama, Odawara ☎ 046/532–2205 ⊕ www.hakoneropeway.co.jp ☜ ¥970 (without Free Pass) ⊙ Mar.–Nov., daily 8:45–5:15; Dec.–Feb., daily 9:15–4:15.

From Ōwaku-dani the descent by gondola to Tōgendai on the shore of **Ashi-no-ko** (Lake Ashi) takes 25 minutes. There's no reason to linger at Tōgendai; it's only a terminus for buses to Hakone-Yumoto and Odawara and to the resort villages in the northern part of Hakone. Head straight for the pier, a few minutes' walk down the hill, where boats set out on the lake for Hakone-machi. Look out for the **Hakone Sightseeing Cruise.** (⊠ 1-15-1 Shiroyama, Odawara ☎ 046/532–6830 ☜ ¥300 ⊙ Summer, 40 minute intervals. Winter, 50 minute intervals. Mar.–Nov., daily 9:30–5; Dec.–Feb., daily 9:30-4 ⊕ www.hakone-kankosen.co.jp) The ride is free with your Hakone Free Pass; otherwise, buy a ticket (¥970) at the office in the terminal. A few ships of conventional design ply the lake; the rest are astonishingly corny Disney knockoffs. One, for example, is rigged like a 17th-century warship. There are departures every 30 minutes, and the cruise to Hakone-machi takes about 30 minutes.

With still water and good weather, you'll get a breathtaking reflection of the mountains in the waters of the lake as you go. If a cruise is not what you're after, go exploring and fishing with hired boats from **Togendai Boat House** (☎ 090/1448–1834) Ashinoko Fishing Center Oba (☎ 046/04–8984).

⑪ The main attraction in **Hakone-machi** is the **Hakone Barrier** (Hakone Sekisho). The barrier was built in 1618 and served as a checkpoint to control traffic until it was demolished during the Meiji Restoration of 1868. An exact replica was built as a tourist attraction in 1965 and is only a few minutes' walk from the pier, along

> **WHAT THE . . . ?**
>
> No, your eyes are not playing tricks on you. Those are in fact local entrepreneurs boiling eggs in the sulfur pits in Ōwaku-dani. Locals make a passable living selling the eggs, which turn black, to tourists at exorbitant prices. A popular myth suggests that eating one of these eggs can extend your life by seven years. What do you have to loose?

the lakeshore in the direction of Moto-Hakone. Last entry is 30 minutes before closing time. ⊠ *Ichiban-chī, Hakone-machi* ☎ *0460/3–6635* 🎫 *¥300* ☉ *Mar.–Nov., daily 9–5; Dec.–Feb., daily 9–4:30.*

Where to Stay

LAKE ASHI
★ $$–$$$$
🏨 **Hakone Prince Hotel.** The location of this resort complex is perfect, with the lake in front and the mountains of Koma-ga-take in back. The Hakone Prince draws both tour groups and individual travelers, and it's also a popular venue for business conferences. The main building has both twin rooms and triples; the Japanese-style Ryū-gū-den annex, which overlooks the lake and has its own thermal bath, is superb. The rustic-style cottages in the complex sleep three to four guests; these are only open mid-April–November. ⊠ *144 Moto-Hakone, Hakone-machi, Kanagawa-ken 250-0522* ☎ *0460/3–1111* ⊕ *www.princehotels.co.jp* 🛏 *142 Western-style rooms with bath, 116 Western-style cottages with bath* ⟨ *2 restaurants, coffee shop, dining room, room service, 7 tennis courts, 2 pools, Japanese baths, bar, lounge, shops* ⊟ *AE, DC, MC, V* ❑ *CP.*

MIYANOSHITA
★ $$–$$$$
🏨 **Fujiya Hotel.** Built in 1878, this Western-style hotel with modern additions is showing signs of age, but that somehow adds to its charm. The Fujiya combines the best of traditional Western decor with the exceptional service and hospitality of a fine Japanese inn. There are both Western and Japanese restaurants, and in the gardens behind the hotel is an old imperial villa that serves as a dining room. Hot-spring water is pumped right into the guest rooms. ⊠ *359 Miyanoshita, Hakone-machi, Kanagawa-ken 250-0522* ☎ *0460/2–2211* ⊕ *www.fujiyahotel.co.jp* 🛏 *149 Western-style rooms with bath* ⟨ *3 restaurants, room service, 18-hole golf course, 2 pools, bar, convention center, meeting rooms, no-smoking rooms* ⊟ *AE, DC, MC, V.*

SENGOKU
¢
🏨 **Fuji-Hakone Guest House.** A small, family-run Japanese inn, this guesthouse has simple tatami rooms with the bare essentials. The owners, Mr. and Mrs. Takahashi, speak English and are a great help in planning trips off the beaten path. The inn is between Odawara Station and Tōgendai; take a bus from the station (Lane 4) and get off at the Senkyōro-mae stop. The family also operates the nearby Moto-Hakone

The Road to the Shōgun

IN DAYS GONE BY, THE TOWN OF Hakone was on the Tōkaidō, the main highway between the imperial court in Kyōto and the shōgunate in Edo (present-day Tōkyō). The road was the only feasible passage through this mountainous country, which made it an ideal place for a checkpoint to control traffic. The Tokugawa Shōgunate built the Hakone barrier here in 1618; its most important function was to monitor the *daimyō* (feudal lords) passing through—to keep track, above all, of weapons coming into Edo, and womenfolk coming out.

When Ieyasu Tokugawa came to power, Japan had been through nearly 100 years of bloody struggle among rival coalitions of daimyō. Ieyasu emerged supreme because some of

his opponents had switched sides at the last minute, in the Battle of Sekigahara in 1600. The shōgun was justifiably paranoid about his "loyal" barons—especially those in the outlying domains—so he required the daimyō to live in Edo for periods of time every two years. When they did return to their own lands, they had to leave their wives behind in Edo, hostages to their good behavior. A noble lady coming through the barrier without an official pass, in short, was a case of treason.

The checkpoint served the Tokugawa dynasty well for 250 years. It was demolished only when the shōgunate fell, in the Meiji Restoration of 1868. An exact replica, with an exhibition hall of period costumes and weapons, was built as a tourist attraction in 1965.

Guest House, which has five Japanese-style rooms that share a typical Japanese-style bath. ✉ *912 Sengoku-hara (103 Moto-Hakone for Moto-Hakone Guest House), Hakone-machi, Kanagawa-ken 250-0631* ☎ *0460/4–6577 for Fuji-Hakone, 0460/3–7880 for Moto-Hakone* ⌖ *14 Japanese-style rooms without bath in Fuji-Hakone, 5 Japanese-style rooms without bath in Moto-Hakone* ⌂ *All Japanese baths and restrooms are shared* ▭ *AE, MC, V.*

¢ ▦ **Lodge Fujimien.** This traditional ryokan, complete with an onsite onsen, has all the trimmings of an expensive ryokan, for a fraction of the price. Spacious rooms are a little old and dark but have character in the room layout, furniture, and traditional wall hangings, and on clear days, Mt. Fuji is visible from the balcony. The restaurant serves only Japanese food, and its set meals are reasonably priced. Don't forget to pre-book the daily dinner special in advance. Conveniently located near Minami Onsen-sou bus stop, Hakone's main sights are only a five minute ride away. ✉ *1245 Sengoku-hara, Hakone, Kanagawa-ken 250-0631* ☎ *0460/4–8645* ⌖ *21 Japanese-style rooms with bath, 5 Western-style rooms with bath* ⌂ *Restaurant, karaoke, hot spring, parking* ▭ *No credit cards.*

Fuji Go-ko (Fuji Five Lakes)

To the north of Mt. Fuji, the Fuji Go-ko area affords an unbeatable view of the mountain on clear days and makes the best base for a climb to the summit. With its various outdoor activities, such as skating and fishing in the winter and boating and hiking in the summer, this is a popular resort area for families and business conferences.

The five lakes are, from the east, Yamanaka-ko, Kawaguchi-ko, Sai-ko, Shōji-ko, and Motosu-ko. Yamanaka and Kawaguchi are the largest and most developed as resort areas, with Kawaguchi more or less the centerpiece of the group. You can visit this area on a day trip from Tōkyō, but unless you want to spend most of it on buses and trains, plan on staying overnight.

⑫ Kawaguchi-ko (Lake Kawaguchi), a 5- to 10-minute walk from Kawaguchi-ko Station, is the most developed of the five lakes, ringed with weekend retreats and vacation lodges—many of them maintained by companies and universities for their employees. Excursion boats depart from a pier here on 30-minute tours of the lake. The promise, not always fulfilled, is to have two views of Mt. Fuji: one of the mountain itself and the other inverted in its reflection on the water. A gondola along the shore of Lake Kawaguchi (near the pier) quickly brings you to the top of the 3,622-foot-tall **Tenjō-san** (Mt. Tenjō). From the observatory here the whole of Lake Kawaguchi lies before you, and beyond the lake is a classic view of Mt. Fuji.

One of the little oddities at Lake Kawaguchi is the **Fuji Museum** (Fuji Hakubutsukan). The first floor holds conventional exhibits of local geology and history, but upstairs is an astonishing collection of—for want of a euphemism—phalluses (you must be 18 or older to view the exhibit). Mainly made from wood and stone and carved in every shape and size, these figures played a role in certain local fertility festivals. The museum is on the north shore of the lake, next to the Fuji Lake Hotel. ⊠ *3964 Funatsu, Fujikawaguchiko-machi, Kanagawa-ken* ☎ *0555/ 73–2266* 🖼 *1st fl. ¥200, 1st and 2nd fl. ¥500* ☉ *Mar.–Oct., daily 9–4; Nov.–Feb., Sat.–Thurs. 9–4; closed 3rd Tues. of month.*

The largest of the recreational facilities at Lake Kawaguchi is the ☺ **Fuji-kyū Highland**. It has an impressive assortment of rides, roller coasters, and other amusements, but it's probably not worth a visit unless you have children in tow. In winter there's superb skating here, with Mt. Fuji for a backdrop. Fuji-kyū Highland is about 15 minutes' walk east from Kawaguchi-ko Station. ⊠ *5–6–1 Shin Nishi Hara, Fujiyoshida* ☎ *0555/ 23–2111* 🖼 *Full-day pass ¥4,800* ☉ *Weekdays 9–5; weekends 9–8; Sept. only 9–6.*

⑬ Buses from Kawaguchi-ko Station go to all the other lakes. The farthest west is **Motosu-ko** (Lake Motosu), the deepest and clearest of the Fuji Go-ko, which takes about 50 minutes.

⑭ Many people consider **Shōji-ko** (Lake Shōji), the smallest of the lakes, to be the prettiest—not least

> ## THE SHŌJI TRIANGLE
>
> The Aoki-ga-hara (Sea of Trees) seems to hold a morbid fascination for the Japanese. Many people go into Aoki-ga-hara every year and never come out, some of them on purpose. If you're planning to climb Mt. Fuji from this trail, go with a guide.

because it still has relatively little vacation-house development. The **Shōji Trail** leads from Lake Shōji to Mt. Fuji through Aoki-ga-hara (Sea of Trees). Beware. This forest has an underlying magnetic lava field that makes compasses go haywire.

⑮ **Sai-ko** (Lake Sai), between Lakes Shōji and Kawaguchi, is the third-largest lake of the Fuji Go-ko, with only moderate development. From the western shore there is an especially good view of Mt. Fuji. Near Sai-ko there are two natural caves, an ice cave and a wind cave. You can either take a bus or walk to them.

⑯ The largest of the Fuji Go-ko is **Yamanaka-ko** (Lake Yamanaka), 35 minutes by bus to the southeast of Kawaguchi. Lake Yamanaka is the closest lake to the popular trail up Mt. Fuji that starts at Go-gōme, and many climbers use this resort area as a base.

Where to Stay

KAWAGUCHI-KO

$$$–$$$$

Fuji View Hotel. This hotel on Lake Kawaguchi is a little threadbare but comfortable. The terrace lounge affords fine views of the lake and of Mt. Fuji beyond. The staff speaks English and is helpful in planning excursions. Many of the guests are on group excursions and take two meals—dinner and breakfast—in the hotel, but it's possible to opt for the room rate alone. Rates are significantly higher on weekends and in August. ⊠ *511 Katsuyama-mura, Fuji-Kawaguchiko-machi, Yamanashi-ken 401-0310* ☎ *0555/83–2211* ⊕ *www.fujiyahotel.co.jp* ⤳ *40 Western-style rooms with bath, 30 Japanese-style rooms with bath* � *2 restaurants, 9-hole golf course, 3 tennis courts, boating* ▤ *AE, DC, MC, V* ⦿⟨ *MAP.*

YAMANAKA-KO

$$

Hotel Mount Fuji. This is the best resort hotel on Lake Yamanaka and has all the facilities for a recreational holiday including onsite game and karaoke rooms and a nature walk on the grounds. The guest rooms are larger than those at the other hotels on the lake and are modeled after European hotels. The convenient location and large banquet halls make it a favorite among tour groups.The lounges are spacious, and they have fine views of the lake and mountain. Rates are about 20% higher on weekends. ⊠ *1360-83 Yamanaka, Yamanaka-ko-mura, Yamanashi-ken 403-0017* ☎ *0555/62–2111* ⊕ *www.mtfuji-hotel.com* ⤳ *150 Western-style rooms with bath, 1 Japanese-style room with bath* � *3 restaurants, pool* ▤ *AE, DC, MC, V.*

¢

Inn Fujitomita. One of the closest lodging options to the Mt. Fuji hiking trails, this inexpensive inn is a launching point for treks around the Fuji Go-ko area. The inn might not be much to look at from the outside, but the interior is spacious and homey. The staff speaks English and can help you plan an itinerary for visiting the area sights. Meals, including vegetarian options, are available at a very low price. Shuttle service is provided from Fuji Yoshida Station and the Lake Yamanaka bus stop. ⊠ *13235 Shibokusa, Oshinomura, Minami-Tsuru-gun, Yamanashi-ken 401-105* ☎ *0555/84–3359* ⊕ *www.tim.hi-ho.ne.jp/innfuji/* ⤳ *10 Japanese-style rooms, 3 with bath* � *Dining room, 3 tennis courts, pool, fishing, laundry facilities; no TV in some rooms* ▤ *AE, DC, MC, V.*

CLOSE UP

Be Prepared

BEWARE OF FICKLE WEATHER around and atop the mountain. Summer days can be unbearably hot and muggy, and the nights can be a shocking contrast of freezing cold (bring numerous warm layers and be prepared to put them all on). Wear strong hiking shoes. The sun really burns at high altitudes, so wear protective clothing and a hat; gloves are a good idea, too. Bring enough food and water for the climb (remember to take your garbage down with you) and bring a flashlight in case it gets dark. Also, keep altitude sickness in mind. To avoid it, begin your assent at a slow pace and take frequent breaks. Use a backpack to keep your hands free and as a useful tool on the way down: instead of returning to Go-gōme, descend to Shin-Go-gōme on the volcanic sand slide called the **sunabashiri**—sit down on your pack, push off, and away you go.

Fuji-san (Mt. Fuji)

FodorsChoice
★

There are six routes to the summit of the 12,388-foot-high **Fuji-san** (Mt. Fuji), but only two, both accessible by bus, are recommended: from Go-gōme (Fifth Station), on the north side, and from Shin-Go-gōme (New Fifth Station), on the south. The climb to the summit from Go-gōme takes five hours and is the shortest way up; the descent takes three hours. From Shin-Go-gōme the ascent is slightly longer and stonier, but the way down, via the *sunabashiri*, a volcanic sand slide, is faster. The quickest route is to ascend from Go-gōme and descend to Shin-Go-gōme via the sunabashiri.

The Climb

The ultimate experience of climbing Mt. Fuji is to reach the summit just before dawn and be able to greet the extraordinary sunrise. *Go-raikō* (The Honorable Coming of the Light [here *go* means "honorable"]), as the sunrise is called, has a mystical quality because the reflection shimmers across the sky just before the sun itself appears over the horizon. Mind you, there is no guarantee of seeing it: Mt. Fuji is often cloudy, even in the early morning.

The climb is taxing but not as hard as you might think scaling Japan's highest mountain would be. That said, the air *is* thin, and it *is* humiliating to struggle for the oxygen to take another step while some 83-year-old Japanese grandmother blithely leaves you in her dust (it happens). Have no fear of losing the trail on either of the two main routes. Just follow the crowd—some 196,000 people make the climb during the official season, which is July 1–August 26. ⚠ **Outside of this season, the weather is highly unpredictable and potentially dangerous, and climbing is strongly discouraged.** In all, there are 10 stations to the top; hiking purists start at the very bottom but if you want to save time and cheat a little, you can start at the fifth station. There are stalls selling food and drinks along the way, but at exorbitant prices, so bring your own.

Also along the route are dormitory-style huts (about ¥7,000 with two meals, ¥5,000 without meals) where you can catch some sleep. A popular one is at the Hachi-gōme (Eighth Station), from which it's about a 90-minute climb to the top. ⚠ **These huts, which are open only in July and August, should be avoided at all costs. The food is vile, there's no fresh water, and the bedding is used by too many people and seldom properly aired. Sensible folk leave the Go-gōme at midnight with good flashlights, climb through the night, and get to the summit just before dawn. Camping on the mountain is prohibited.**

Fuji-Hakone-Izu National Park Essentials

BUS TRAVEL

Buses connect Tōkyō with the major gateway towns of this region, but except for the trip to Lake Kawaguchi or Mt. Fuji, the price advantage doesn't really offset the comfort and convenience of the trains. If you're interested only in climbing Mt. Fuji, take one of the daily buses directly to Go-gōme from Tōkyō; they run July through August and leave Shinjuku Station at 7:45, 8:45, 10:55, 4:50, 5:50, and 7:30. The last bus allows sufficient time for the tireless to make it to the summit before sunrise. The journey takes about 2 hours and 40 minutes from Shinjuku and costs ¥2,600. Reservations are required; book seats through the Fuji Kyūkō Highway Bus Reservation Center, the Keiō Highway Bus Reservation Center, the Japan Travel Bureau (which should have English-speaking staff), or any major travel agency.

To return from Mt. Fuji to Tōkyō, take an hour-long bus ride from Shin-Go-gōme to Gotemba (¥1,500). From Gotemba take the JR Tōkaidō and Gotemba lines to Tōkyō Station (¥1,890), or take the JR Line from Gotemba to Matsuda (¥480) and change to the private Odakyū Line from Shin-Matsuda to Shinjuku (¥750).

Direct bus service runs daily from Shinjuku Station in Tōkyō to Lake Kawaguchi every hour between 7:10 AM and 8:10 PM (¥1,700). Buses go from Kawaguchi-ko Station to Go-gōme (the fifth station on the climb up Mt. Fuji) in about an hour; there are eight departures a day (9:35, 10:10, 11:10, 12:10, 1:10, 2:10, 3:20, and 5:20) until the climbing season (July and August) starts, when there are 15 departures or more, depending on demand. The cost is ¥1,700.

From Lake Kawaguchi, you can also take a bus to Gotemba, then change to another bus for Sengoku; from Sengoku there are frequent buses to Hakone-Yumoto, Tōgendai, and elsewhere in the Hakone region. On the return trip, three or four buses a day make the two-hour journey from Lake Kawaguchi to Mishima (¥2,130), skirting the western lakes and circling Mt. Fuji; at Mishima you can transfer to the JR Shinkansen Line for Tōkyō or Kyōto. A shorter bus ride (70 minutes, ¥1,470) goes from Lake Kawaguchi to Gotemba with a transfer to the JR local line.

From Lake Kawaguchi, you can also connect to the Izu Peninsula. Take the bus to Mishima and from there go by train either to Shuzenji or Atami.

From Shimoda, the end of the line on the private Izukyū Railway down the east coast of the Izu Peninsula, you must travel by bus around the southern cape to Dōgashima (¥1,360). From there, another bus takes you up the west coast as far as Heda and then turns inland to Shuzenji. From Shimoda, you can also take a bus directly north to Shuzenji through the Amagi Mountains (one departure daily at 10:45 AM, ¥2,180). The Tōkai Bus Company covers the west coast and central mountains of the Izu area well with local service; buses are not especially frequent, but they do provide the useful option of just hopping off and exploring if you happen to see something interesting from the window. Whatever your destination, always check the time of the last departure to make sure that you are not left stranded.

Within the Hakone area, buses run every 15–30 minutes from Hakone-machi buses to Hakone-Yumoto Station on the private Odakyū Line (40 minutes, ¥930), and Odawara Station (one hour, ¥1,150), where you can take either the Odakyū Romance Car back to Shinjuku Station or a JR Shinkansen to Tōkyō Station. The buses are covered by the Hakone Free Pass.

Bus Information from Kawaguchi Fuji Kyūkō Lake Kawaguchi Reservation Center ☎ 055/572-2922. Fuji Kyūkō Gotemba Reservation Center ☎ 055/082-2555. **From Tokyo** Fuji Kyūkō Highway Bus Reservation Center ☎ 03/5376-2222. Keiō Highway Bus Reservation Center ☎ 03/5376-2222. Japan Travel Bureau ☎ 03/3284-7605 ⊕ www.jtb.co.jp. Tōkai Bus Company ☎ 0557/36-1112 for main office, 0557/22-2511 Shimoda Information Center.

CAR TRAVEL

Having your own car makes sense only for touring the Izu Peninsula, and only then if you're prepared to cope with less-than-ideal road conditions, lots of traffic (especially on holiday weekends), and the paucity of road markers in English. It takes some effort—but exploring the peninsula *is* a lot easier by car than by public transportation. From Tōkyō take the Tōmei Expressway as far as Ōi-matsuda (about 84 km [52 mi]); then pick up Routes 255 and 135 to Atami (approximately 28 km [17 mi]). From Atami drive another 55 km (34 mi) or so down the east coast of the Izu Peninsula to Shimoda.

■ TIP→ One way to save yourself some trouble is to book a car through the Nippon or Toyota rental agency in Tōkyō and arrange to pick it up at the Shimoda branch. You can then simply take a train to Shimoda and use it as a base. From Shimoda you can drive back up the coast to Kawazu (35 minutes) and then to Shuzenji (30 minutes). It is possible to drop off the car in Tokyo but only at specific branches, so visit your rental car's Web site or call them in advance.

Nippon Rent-a-Car ☎ 03/3485-7196 English operator available on weekdays 10 AM-5 PM ⊕ www.nipponrentacar.co.jp. Toyota Rent-a-Car ☎ 0070/800-0100 toll-free, 03/5954-8008 English operator available 8-8 ⊕ www.toyota-rl-tyo.co.jp/rentacar/syasyu/info-e.html.

TOURS

Once you are on the Izu Peninsula itself, sightseeing excursions by boat are available from several picturesque small ports. From Dōgashima, you can take the Dōgashima Marine short (20 minutes, ¥920) or long (45 minutes, ¥1,240) tours of Izu's rugged west coast. The Fujikyū Kōgyō company operates a daily ferry to Hatsu-shima from Atami (25 minutes, ¥2,340 round-trip) and another to the island from Itō (23 minutes, ¥1,150). Izukyū Marine offers a 40-minute tour (¥1,530) by boat from Shimoda to the coastal rock formations at Irō-zaki.

Sunrise Tours operates a tour to Hakone, including a cruise across Lake Ashi and a trip on the gondola over Ōwaku-dani (¥15,000 includes lunch and return to Tōkyō by Shinkansen; ¥12,000 includes lunch and return to Tōkyō by bus). ■ TIP→ These tours are an economical way to see the main sights all in one day and are ideal for travelers with limited time. Sunrise tours depart daily from Tōkyō's Hamamatsu-chō Bus Terminal and some major hotels.

🔳 **Dōgashima Marine** ☎ 0558/52-0013. **Fujikyū Kōgyō** ☎ 0557/81-0541. **Izukyū Marine** ☎ 0558/22-1151. **Sunrise Tours** ☎ 03/5796-5454 ⊕ www.jtb.co.jp/sunrisetour.

TRAIN TRAVEL

Trains are by far the easiest and fastest ways to get to the Fuji-Hakone-Izu National Park area. The gateway stations of Atami, Odawara, and Kawaguchi-ko are well served by comfortable express trains from Tōkyō, on both JR and private railway lines. These in turn connect to local trains and buses that can get you anywhere in the region you want to go. Call the JR Higashi-Nihon Info Line (10–6 daily, except December 31–January 3) for assistance in English.

The *Kodama* Shinkansen from JR Tōkyō station to Atami costs ¥3,880 and takes 51 minutes; JR Passes are valid. The JR local from Atami to Itō takes 25 minutes and costs ¥320. Itō and Atami are also served by the JR Odoriko Super Express (not a Shinkansen train) also departing from Tokyo station; for correct platform, check the schedule display board. The Tōkyō–Itō run takes 1¼ hours and costs ¥4,190; you can also use a JR Pass. The privately owned Izukyū Railways, on which JR Passes are not valid, makes the Itō–Shimoda run in one hour for ¥1,570.

The Izu–Hakone Railway Line runs from Tōkyō to Mishima (1 hour, 36 minutes; ¥4,090), with a change at Mishima for Shuzenji (31 minutes, ¥500); this is the cheapest option if you don't have a JR Pass. With a JR Pass, a Shinkansen–Izu Line combination will save about 35 minutes and will be the cheapest option. The Tōkyō–Mishima Shinkansen leg (62 minutes) costs ¥4,400; the Mishima–Shuzenji Izu Line leg (31 minutes) costs ¥500.

Trains depart every 12 minutes from Tōkyō's Shinjuku Station for Odawara in the Hakone area. The ¥5,500 Hakone Free Pass, which you can buy at the station, covers the train fare. Reservations are required for the upscale Romance Car, with comfortable seats and big observation windows, to Hakone (an extra ¥870 with Hakone Free Pass). The Romance Car goes one stop beyond Odawara to Hakone-Yumoto; buy tickets at any Odakyū Travel Service counter or major travel agency, or call the Odakyū Reservation Center. Note that beyond Hakone-Yumoto, you must use the privately owned Hakone Tozan Tetsudō Line or buses.

The transportation hub, as well as one of the major resort areas in the Fuji Five Lakes area, is Kawaguchi-ko. Getting there from Tōkyō requires a change of trains at Ōtsuki. The JR Chūō Line Kaiji and Azusa express trains leave Shinjuku Station for Ōtsuki on the half hour from 7 AM to 8 PM (more frequently in the morning) and take approximately one hour. At Ōtsuki, change to the private Fuji-Kyūkō Line for Kawaguchi-ko, which takes another 50 minutes. The total traveling time is about two hours, and you can use your JR Pass as far as Ōtsuki; otherwise, the fare is ¥1,280. The Ōtsuki–Kawaguchi-ko leg costs ¥1,110. Also available are two direct service rapid trains for Kawaguchi-ko that leave Tōkyō in the morning at 6:08 and 7:10 on weekdays, 6:09 and 7:12 on weekends and national holidays.

The Holiday Kaisoku Picnic-gō, available on weekends and national holidays, offers direct express service from Shinjuku, leaving at 8:10 and arriving at Kawaguchi-ko Station at 10:37. From March through August, JR puts on additional weekend express trains for Kawaguchi-ko, but be aware that on some of them only the first three cars go all the way to the lake. Coming back, you have a choice of late-afternoon departures from Kawaguchi-ko that arrive at Shinjuku in the early evening. Check the express timetables before you go; you can also call either the JR Higashi-Nihon Info Line or Fuji-kyūukō Kawaguchi-ko Station for train information.

🚊 Train Information **Fuji-kyūukō Kawaguchi-ko Station** ☎ 0555/72-0017. **Hakone Tozan Railway** ☎ 0465/24-2115. **Izu-Hakone Railway** ☎ 0465/77-1200. **Izukyū Corporation** ☎ 0557/53-1111 for main office, 0558/22-3202 Izukyū Shimoda Station. **JR Higashi-Nihon Info Line** ☎ 03/3423-0111. **Odakyū Reservation Center** ☎ 03/3481-0130.

VISITOR INFORMATION

Especially in summer and fall, the Fuji-Hakone-Izu National Park area is one of the most popular vacation destinations in the country, so most towns and resorts have local visitor information centers. Few of them have staff members who speak fluent English, but you can still pick up local maps and pamphlets, as well as information on low-cost inns, pensions, and guesthouses.

🚊 Tourist Information **Atami Tourist Association** ✉ 12-1 Ginza-chō, Atami ☎ 0557/85-2222. **Fuji-Kawaguchiko Tourist Association** ✉ 890 Funatsu, Kawakuchiko-machi, Minami-Tsuru-gun ☎ 0555/72-2460. **Hakone-machi Tourist Association** ✉ 698 Yūmoto, Hakone-machi ☎ 0460/5-8911. **Nishi-Izu Tourist Office** ✉ Dogashima, Nishi-Izu-chō, Kamo-gu ☎ 0558/52-1268. **Shimoda Tourist Association** ✉ 1-1 Soto-ga-oka, Shimoda-shi ☎ 0558/22-1531.

Points of Interest

ENGLISH	JAPANESE CHARACTERS
Aichiya	あいちや
Akechi Daira Ropeway	明智平ロープウェイ
Atami	熱海
Atami Plum Garden (Atami Bai-en)	熱海梅園
Atami Taikansō	熱海大観荘
Basha-michi	馬車道
Central Yokohama	横浜市街
Chano-ma	茶の間
Chinatown (Chūka-gai)	中華街
Chūgū-shi	中宮祠
Chūzen Temple (Chūzen-ji)	中禅寺
Chūzen-ji Kanaya Hotel	中善寺金谷ホテル
Dōgashima	堂ヶ島
Dōgashima New Ginsui	堂ヶ島ニュー銀水
Dragon's Head Falls (Ryūzu-no-taki)	竜頭滝
Engaku Temple (Engaku-ji)	円覚寺
Ennō Temple (Ennō-ji)	円応寺
Enoshima	江ノ島
Fuji Five Lakes (Fuji Go-ko)	富士五湖
Fuji Museum (Fuji Hakubutsukan)	富士博物館
Fuji View Hotel	富士ビューホテル
Fuji-Hakone Guest House	富士箱根ゲストハウス
Fuji-Hakone-Izu National Park	富士箱根伊豆国立公園
Fuji-kyū Highland	富士急ハイランド
Fujimoto	ふじもと
Fujiya Hotel	富士屋ホテル
Futara-san Shrine (Futara-san Jinja)	二荒山神社
Garden Arboretum	ガーデン植物園
Ginza Isomura Kamakuraten	ぎんざ磯むら 鎌倉店
Gōra	強羅
Goyōkan	五葉館

Great Buddha (Daibutsu)	大仏
Gyōshintei	尭心亭
Hachinoki Kita-Kamakura-ten	鉢の木北鎌倉店
Hakone	箱根
Hakone Open-Air Museum (Hakone Chōkoku-no-mori Bijutsukan)	箱根彫刻の森美術館
Hakone Prince Hotel	箱根プリンスホテル
Hakone-machi	箱根町
Hanafubuki	花吹雪
Harbor View Park (Minato-no-Mieru-Oka Kōen)	港の見える丘公園
Hase	長谷
Hase-dera	長谷寺
Hatoya Sun Hotel	ホテルサンハトヤ
Hikawa-maru	氷川丸
Hōfuku Temple (Hōfuku-ji)	宝福寺
Hōkoku Temple (Hōkoku-ji)	報国寺
Hotel Mount Fuji	富士山ホテル
Ikeda 20th-Century Art Museum (Ikeda 20-Seiki Bijutsukan)	池田20世紀美術館
Inn Fujitomita	旅館ふじとみた
Inoshishi-mura	いのしし村
International Cemetery (Gaijin Bochi)	外人墓地
Irō Point (Irō-zaki)	石廊崎
Irō-zaki Jungle Park	石廊崎ジャングルパーク
Iseyama Kodai Shrine (Iseyama Kodai Jingū)	伊勢山皇大神宮
Itō	伊東
Izu Cactus Park (Izu Saboten Kōen)	伊豆サボテン公園
Izu Peninsula	伊豆半島
Jakkō Falls (Jakkō-no-taki)	寂光滝
Jigen-dō	慈眼堂
Jōchi Temple (Jōchi-ji)	浄智寺
Jōmyo Temple (Jōmyō-ji)	浄明寺
Kaisen Misaki-kō	海鮮三崎港

Kamakura	鎌倉
Kamakura Shrine (Kamakura-gū)	鎌倉宮
Kamakura Treasure Museum (Kamakura Kokuhōkan)	鎌倉国宝館
Kanagawa Prefectural Museum (Kanagawa Kenritsu Hakubutsukan)	神奈川県立博物館
Kaiserrō	華正樓
Kegon Falls (Kegon-no-taki)	華厳滝
Kenchō Temple (Kenchō-ji)	建長寺
Kita-Kamakura (North Kamakura)	北鎌倉
Kyorai-an	去来庵
Kyorai-an Matsushiro-kan	去来庵 松城館
Lake Ashi (Ashi-no-ko)	芦ノ湖
Lake Kawaguchi (Kawaguchi-ko)	河口湖
Lake Motosu (Motosu-ko)	本栖湖
Lake Sai (Sai-ko)	西湖
Lake Shōji (Shōji-ko)	精進湖
Lake Yamanaka (Yamanaka-ko)	山中湖
Landmark Tower	ランドマークタワー
Lodge Fujimien	ロッジ富士見苑
Marine Tower	マリンタワー
Masudaya	ゆば亭ますだや
Meigetsu Temple (Meigetsu-in)	明月院
Meiji-no-Yakata	明治の館
Minato Mirai 21	みなとみらい21
Miyanoshita	宮ノ下
MOA Museum of Art (MOA Bijutsukan)	MOA 美術館
Monument to Masatsuna Matsudaira	松平正綱の杉並木寄進碑
Moto-machi	元町
Motomachi Bairin	元町梅林
Mt. Fuji (Fuji-san)	富士山
Mt. Komuro Park (Komuro-san Kōen)	小室山公園
Mt. Sōun (Sōun-zan)	早雲山

Mt. Tenjō (Tenjō-san)	天上山
Nantai	なんたい
New Fujiya Hotel	ニュー富士屋ホテル
Nikkō	日光
Nikkō Edo Village (Nikkō Edo Mura)	日光江戸村
Nikkō Kanaya Hotel	日光金谷ホテル
Nikkō Lakeside Hotel	日光レイクサイドホテル
Nikkō Prince Hotel	日光プリンスホテル
Nippon-maru Memorial Park	日本丸メモリアルパーク
Ochiairou Murakami	落合楼村上
Ōwaku-dani	大涌谷
Pension Sakuraya	ペンション桜家
Prefectural Museum of Modern Art (Kanagawa Kenritsu Kindai Bijutsukan)	神奈川県立近代博物館
Queen's Square	クイーンズスクエア
Rinka-en	隣華苑
Rinnō Temple (Rinnō-ji)	輪王寺
Roma Statione	ローマステーション
Ryokan Sanyōsō	旅館三養荘
Ryōsen-ji	了仙寺
Ryūkō Temple (Ryūkō-ji)	龍口寺
Sacred Bridge (Shinkyō)	神橋
Sankei-en	三渓園
Sawamoto	澤本
Scandia	スカンディア
Serina Romanchaya	瀬里奈 浪漫茶屋
Shimoda	下田
Shimoda Prince Hotel	下田プリンスホテル
Shimoda Tokyū Hotel	下田東急ホテル
Shōji Trail	精進 (湖畔)トレイル
Shuzenji	修善寺
Silk Museum (Shiruku Hakubutsukan)	シルク博物館
Sōji-ji	総持寺
Sunabashiri	砂走り

Taiyū-in Mausoleum	大猷院廟
Tōkei Temple (Tōkei-ji)	東慶寺
Tōshō-gū	東照宮
Treasury House (Hōmotsu-kan)	宝物館
Tsuru-ga-oka Hachiman-gū	鶴岡八幡宮
Turtle Inn Nikkō	タートルイン日光
Umagaeshi	馬返し
Urami Falls (Urami-no-taki)	裏見滝
World Porters	ワールドポーターズ
Yamashita Park (Yamashita Kōen)	山下公園
Yokohama	横浜
Yokohama Cheese Café	横浜チーズカフェ
Yokohama Cosmo World	よこはまコスモワールド
Yokohama Doll Museum (Yokohama Ningyō-no-ie)	横浜人形の家
Yokohama History Archives (Yokohama Kaikō Shiryōkan)	横浜開港資料館
Yokohama Museum of Art (Yokohama Bijutsukan)	横浜美術館
Yoritomo's Tomb	頼朝の墓
Yumi-ga-hama	弓ヶ浜
Yumoto Onsen	湯元温泉

6

UNDERSTANDING TŌKYŌ

IN THE 12TH CENTURY, Tōkyō was a little fishing village called Edo (pronounced *eh-doh*). Over the next 400 years, it was governed by a succession of warlords and other rulers. One of them, Dōkan Ōta, built the first castle in Edo in 1457. That act is still officially regarded as the founding of the city, but the honor really belongs to Ieyasu (ee-eh-*ya*-su), the first Tokugawa shōgun, who arrived in 1590. On the site of Ōta's stronghold, he built a mighty fortress of his own—from which, 10 years later, he was effectively ruling the whole country.

By 1680 there were more than a million people here, and a great city had grown up out of the reeds in the marshy lowlands of Edo Bay. Tōkyō can only really be understood as a *jō-ka-machi*—a castle town. Ieyasu had fought his way to the shogunate, and he had a warrior's concern for the geography of his capital. Edo Castle had the high ground, but that wasn't enough; all around it, at strategic points, he gave large estates to allies and trusted retainers. These lesser lords' villas also served as garrisons—outposts on a perimeter of defense.

Farther out, Ieyasu kept the barons he trusted least of all—whom he controlled by bleeding their treasuries. He required them to keep large, expensive establishments in Edo; to contribute generously to the temples he endowed; to come and go in alternate years in great pomp and ceremony; and, when they returned to their estates, to leave their families—in effect, hostages—behind.

All the feudal estates, villas, gardens, and temples lay south and west of Edo Castle in an area known as Yamanote where everything was about order, discipline, and ceremony; every man had his rank and duties and very few women were within the castle's garrisons. Those duties were less military than bureaucratic, and Ieyasu's precautions worked like a charm. The Tokugawa dynasty enjoyed some 250 years of unbroken peace, during which nothing very traumatic happened.

But Yamanote was only the demand side of the economy: somebody had to bring in the fish, weed the gardens, weave the mats, and entertain the bureaucrats. To serve the noble houses, common people flowed into Edo from all over Japan. Their allotted quarters of the city were jumbles of narrow streets, alleys, and cul-de-sacs in the low-lying estuarine lands to the north and east. Often enough, the land assigned to them wasn't even there; they had to *make* it by draining and filling the marshes (the first reclamation project in Edo dates to 1457). The result was Shitamachi—literally "downtown"—the part below the castle, which sat on a hill. Bustling, brawling Shitamachi was the supply side: it had the lumberyards, markets, and workshops; the wood-block printers, kimono makers, and moneylenders set up shop in Shitamachi. The people here gossiped over the back fence in the earthy, colorful Edo dialect. They went to Yoshiwara—a walled and moated area on the outskirts of Edo where prostitution was under official control (Yoshiwara was for a time the biggest licensed brothel area in the world). They supported the bathhouses and Kabuki theaters and reveled in their spectacular summer fireworks festivals. The city and spirit of the Edokko—the people of Shitamachi—have survived, while the great estates uptown are now mostly parks and hotels.

The shogunate was overthrown in 1867 by supporters of Emperor Meiji. The following year, the emperor moved his court from Kyōto to Edo and renamed it Tōkyō: the Eastern Capital. By now the city was home to nearly 2 million people, and the geography was vastly more complex than what Ieyasu had seen. As it grew, it became not one, but many smaller cities, with different centers of commerce, government, entertainment, and transportation. In Yamanote rose the commercial emporia, office buildings, and public halls that made up the architecture of an emerging modern state. The workshops of Shitamachi multiplied, some of them becoming small wholesalers or family-run factories. Still, there was no planning, no grid. The neighborhoods and subcenters were worlds unto themselves, and a traveler from one was soon hopelessly lost in another.

The fire-bombings of 1945 left Tōkyō, for the most part, in rubble and ashes. That utter destruction could have been an opportunity to rebuild on the rational order of cities like Kyōto, Barcelona, or Washington. No such plan was ever made. Tōkyō reverted to type: it became once again an aggregation of small towns and villages. One village was much like any other; the nucleus was always the *shōten-gai*, the shopping arcade. Each arcade had at least one fishmonger, grocer, rice dealer, mat maker, barber, florist, and bookseller. You could live your whole life in the neighborhood of the shōten-gai.

People seldom moved out of these villages. The vast waves of new residents who arrived after World War II—about three-quarters of the people in the Tōkyō metropolitan area today were born elsewhere—just created more villages. People who lived in the villages knew their way around, so there was no particular need to name the streets. Houses were numbered in the order in which they were built, rather than in a spatial sequence. No. 3 might well share a mailbox with No. 12. People still take their local geography for granted—the closer you get to the place you're looking for, the harder it is to get coherent directions. Away from main streets and landmarks, even a taxi driver can get hopelessly lost.

Fortunately, there are the *kōban:* small police boxes, or substations, usually with two or three officers assigned to each of them full time, to look after the affairs of the neighborhood. You can't go far in any direction without finding a kōban. The officer on duty knows where everything is and is glad to point the way. (The substation system, incidentally, is one important reason for the legendary safety of Tōkyō: on foot or on white bicycles, the police are a visible presence, covering the beat. Burglaries are not unknown, of course, but street crime is very rare.)

Tōkyō is still really two areas, Shitamachi and Yamanote. The heart of Shitamachi, proud and stubborn in its Edo ways, is Asakusa; the dividing line is Ginza, west of which lie the boutiques and department stores, the banks and engines of government, the pleasure domes and cafés. Today there are 13 subway lines in full operation that weave the two areas together.

JAPANESE GARDENS

MANY OF THE PRINCIPLES that influence Japanese garden design come from religion. Shintoism, Taoism, and Buddhism, the three major religious influences in Japan, all stress the contemplation and re-creation of nature as part of the process of achieving understanding and enlightenment.

From Shintoism, Japan's ancient religion, comes *genus loci* (the spirit of place) and the search for the divine presence in remarkable natural features: special mountains, trees, rocks, and so forth. You can see the Taoist influence in islands, which act as a symbolic heaven for souls who achieve perfect harmony. Here sea turtles and cranes—creatures commonly represented in gardens—serve these enlightened souls.

Buddhist gardens function as settings for meditation, the goal of which is enlightenment. Shōgun and samurai were strongly drawn to Zen Buddhism, so Zen gardens evolved as spaces to use almost exclusively for meditation and growth. The classic example is the *karesansui* (dry landscape) consisting of meticulously placed rocks and raked gravel.

The first garden designers in Japan were temple priests. Later, tea masters created gardens to refine the tea ceremony experience. A major contribution of the tea masters was the *roji*, the path or dewy ground that leads through the garden to the teahouse. The stroll along the roji emotionally and mentally prepares participants for the tea ceremony.

Gradually gardens moved out of the exclusive realm to which only nobles, *daimyō* (feudal lords), wealthy merchants, and poets had access, and the increasingly affluent middle class began to demand professional designers. In the process, aesthetic concerns came to override those of religion.

In addition to *genus loci*, karesansui style, and the roji mentioned above, here are a few terms that will help you more fully experience Japanese gardens.

Change and movement. Change is highlighted in Japanese gardens with careful attention to the seasonal variations that plants undergo: from cherry blossoms in spring to summer greenery to autumn leaf coloring to winter snow clinging to the garden's bare bones. A water element, either real or abstract, often represents movement, as with the use of raked gravel or a stone "stream."

Mie gakure. The "reveal-and-hide" principle dictates that from no point should all of a garden be visible, that there is always mystery and incompleteness; viewers move through a garden to contemplate its changing perspectives.

Miniaturized landscapes. The depiction of celebrated natural and literary sites has been a frequent design technique in Japanese gardens—Fuji-san, represented by a truncated cone of stones; Ama-no-Hashidate, the famous spit of land, by a stone bridge; or a mighty forest by a lone tree.

Shakkei. "Borrowed landscape" extends the garden's boundaries by integrating a nearby mountain, grove of trees, or a sweeping temple roofline, and framing and capturing the view by echoing it with elements of similar shape or color inside the garden.

Symbolism. Abstract concepts and mythological legends are part of the garden vocabulary. The use of boulders in a streambed can represent life's surmountable difficulties, a pine tree can stand for stability, or islands in a pond for a faraway paradise.

BATHING: AN IMMERSION COURSE

JAPANESE CULTURAL PHENOMENA often confound first-time visitors, but few rituals are as opaque as those surrounding bathing. Baths in Japan are as much about pleasure and relaxation as they are about washing and cleansing. Traditionally, communal bathhouses served as centers for social gatherings, and even though most modern houses and apartments have bathtubs, many Japanese still prefer the pleasures of communal bathing—either at onsen while on vacation or in public bathhouses closer to home.

Japanese bathtubs are deep enough to sit in upright with (very hot) water up to your neck. It's not just the size of the tub that will surprise you; the procedures for using them are quite different from those in the West. You wash yourself in a special area outside the tub first. The tubs are for soaking, not washing—soap must not get into the bathwater.

Many hotels in major cities have only Western-style reclining bathtubs, so to indulge in the pleasure of a Japanese bath you need to stay in a Japanese-style inn or find an *o-furo-ya* (public bathhouse). The latter are clean and easy to find. Japanese bath towels, typically called *ta*-o-ru, are available for a fee at onsen and bathhouses. No larger than a hand towel, they have three functions: covering your privates, washing before and scrubbing while you bathe (if desired), and drying off (wring them out hard and they dry you quite well). If you want a larger towel to dry off, you have to bring one along.

You may feel apprehensive about bathing (and bathing *properly*) in an o-furo, but if you're well versed in bathing etiquette, you should soon feel at ease. And once you've experienced a variety of public baths—from the standard bathhouses found in every neighborhood to idyllic outdoor hot springs—you may find yourself an advocate of this ancient custom.

The first challenge in bathing is acknowledging that your Japanese bath mates will stare at your body. Take solace, however, in the fact that their apparent voyeurism most likely stems from curiosity.

When you enter the bathing room, help yourself to two towels, soap, and shampoo (often included in the entry fee), and grab a bucket and a stool. At one of the shower stations around the edge of the room, use the handheld showers, your soap, and one of your towels to wash yourself thoroughly. A head-to-toe twice-over will impress onlookers. After rinsing, you may enter the public bath. You can use your one dry towel to cover yourself, or you can place it on your head (as many of your bath mates will do) while soaking. The water in the bath is as hot as the body can endure, and the reward for making it past the initial shock of the heat is the pleasure of a lengthy soak in water that is never tepid. All you need to do is lean back, relax, and experience the pleasures of purification.

–David Miles

RITUAL & RELIGION

THERE IS A SAYING that the Japanese are Shintō when they're born, Christian when they marry, and Buddhist when they die. This does not mean they start life as devotees of one religion and change faiths at specific milestones, rather it illustrates their utilitarian view of religion and ritual in daily life and how individuals move back and forth between the different faiths easily.

In Western culture, individuals tend to stay aligned with one religious faith, but the Japanese take advantage of everything a religion has to offer as suits the occasion. Birth of a child is most often commemorated with a Shintō ceremony. While not strictly Christian, Western-style weddings (complete with a chapel and white dress) are very popular. Finally, funerals are usually solemn Buddhist events. Nearly every home has a small shrine dedicated to the gods of Shintō while simultaneously maintaining an area for Buddhist devotion.

Buddhism

Originating in 6th-century India, Buddhism traveled through China, Korea, and eventually to Japan. The foundation of Buddhism is that the only way to be free of the suffering caused by human desire is to realize your true "Buddha nature" through the practices of the Buddhist sect you follow. All Buddhists believe in reincarnation and strive toward reaching nirvana (the Buddhist equivalent of heaven) in the afterlife. Every being (from an ant to an aardvark) possesses Buddha Nature and is on this same path. That's why many strict Buddhists are vegetarians.

Good and bad Karma determine your progress in the spiritual journey and can either hurry you on to nirvana or doom you to repeating innumerable lifetimes on earth. Doing good deeds and living according to Buddhist Tenets like "Boundless love and compassion for all sentient beings" accumulate good Karma. Selfishness, anger, and greed garner bad Karma.

To reach nirvana, you may receive guidance from a Bodhisattva—a being that has achieved nirvana but chooses to return to earth to help those still mired in struggle. Bodhisattvas can appear in any form and offer anything from simple, momentary advice to lifelong guidance.

Buddhist beliefs were initially welcomed by Japan's ruling nobles but not by common people because of complex structure and theories. Different sects evolved, making Buddhism more accessible to everyday folk.

Pure Land Buddhism (Jodo Shinshu) emerged in 1175. Similar to Christianity, it stresses a form of salvation upon death if you follow the rules and believe strongly in Amida, the Buddha of Compassion. Anyone who calls his name, "Namu Amida Butsu," with sincere faith, trust, and devotion, will be granted an eternal life of happiness in the Pure Land.

In 1191, Zen came from China and became popular among the military class, forming a major part of Bushido or the samurai warrior code. Zen Buddhism stresses that each individual must realize his or her own Buddha-hood, achieved through daily practice of meditation, traditional arts like flower arranging, calligraphy, and karate or mundane tasks like chopping wood and carrying water.

Nichiren Buddhism, named after its founder, was established in 1253. It condemned other sects and proclaimed that everyone is guaranteed Buddha-hood in the afterlife by chanting the title of the Lotus Sutra "Nam Myoho Renge Kyo" daily while seated before a devotional object. Nichiren's confrontational attitude twice led to exile but he was eventually allowed to return.

Shintō

Shintō translates as the "Kami Way"— Kami means god or spirit. Devotees believe that all things, animate or inanimate, contain representative spirits. Stones, trees, mountains, waterfalls, even the Japanese islands have spirits honored and worshipped in numerous shrines along with other natural phenomena like the sun, animals, ancestral spirits, the spirits of national heroes, and those who died for the state or community.

This ancient and indigenous faith relates directly to the creation of the islands and lineage of the emperor. As Shintō Mythology outlines creation, in the beginning, from the Kami of the center of heaven (Ame-no-minaka-nushi-no-kami) came the Kami of birth and growth (Takamimusubi-no-mikoto and Kami-musubi-no-mikoto). Then appeared the creative couple Izanagi-no-mikoto and Izanami-no-mikoto who gave birth to the Japanese Islands and the many kami in them. Of these, three were the most important—the Sun Goddess (Amaterasu-o-Mikami); her brother in charge of the Earth (Susa-no-o-no-mikoto); and the Moon Goddess (Tsuki yomi no mikoto), who ruled the realm of darkness.

The grandson of the Sun Goddess (Ninigi-no-mikoto), was instructed to rule the people of Japan with three divine treasures: a mirror, a sword, and a string of jewels. His great grandson, Emperor Jimmu Tenno (literally "Jimmu of heaven") assumed human form and all subsequent emperors of Japan claimed descent from this divine being.

Shintō has since evolved strange symbolism, exotic rites and ceremonies, colorful festivals and mystic atmosphere in the shrines. Shintō shrines are erected on sites where some manifestation of the local Kami has been observed; they are not meant to propagate faith or teach doctrine. Shrines are commonly fronted by a *torri* that marks the boundary between the mundane and the divine. The shrines are usually composed of an inner compartment where the Kami dwells with a space in front for offerings adorned with folded strips of white paper in a zigzag (*gohei*) pattern as a symbolic offering. Actual offerings of salt, rice, water, fruit, flowers, and sake are placed on tables in front of the Kami dwellings.

Basic Shrine and Temple Etiquette

If you are visiting a temple or shrine, follow the behavior of the Japanese visitors. If you're alone, follow these simple rules to avoid being a clumsy foreigner:

Stay out of roped off areas. Some areas are accessible to monks and priests only.

Remove your shoes. When you enter the building, put on a set of slippers at the entrance; they are there for your use.

Bow—always facing the main altar or shrine area—before entering and upon leaving.

When standing before the altar, make some sort of offering. In most Buddhist temples you can buy a stick of incense to light and place in the censor. At Shintō shrines ring the bell, clap your hands twice, and drop a few coins in the offering box.

Don't take flash photographs without asking permission. Many shrines and temples house ancient scrolls or icons that can be damaged by the flash.

Avoid loud and disrespectful behavior. Behave as if you were in a museum or cathedral.

THE TEA CEREMONY

THE TEA CEREMONY is a precisely choreographed program that started more than 1,000 years ago with Zen monks. The ritual begins as the server prepares a cup of tea for the first guest. This process involves a strictly determined series of movements and actions, which include cleansing each of the utensils to be used. One by one, the participants slurp up their bowl of tea, then eat the sweet cracker served with it. Finally, comments about the beauty of the bowls used are exchanged. The entire ritual involves contemplating the beauty in the smallest actions, focusing on their meaning in the midst of the uncertainty of life.

The architecture of a traditional teahouse is also consistent. There are two entrances: a service entrance for the host and server and a low door that requires that guests enter on their knees, in order to be humbled. Tearooms often have tatami flooring and a flower arrangement or artwork in the alcove for contemplation and comment. The three best-known schools of tea ceremonies are the Ura Senke, the Omote Senke, and the Musha Kōji, each with its own styles, emphases, and masters.

Most of your tea experiences will be geared toward the uninitiated: the tea ceremony is a rite that requires methodical initiation by education. If you don't go for instruction before your trip, keep two things in mind: first, be in the right frame of mind when you enter the room. Though the tea ceremony is a pleasant event, some people take it quite seriously, and boisterous behavior beforehand is frowned upon. Instead, make conversation that enhances a mood of serenity and invites a feeling of meditative quietude. Second, be sure to sit quietly through the serving and drinking—controlled slurping is expected—and openly appreciate the tools and cups afterward, commenting on their elegance and simplicity. This appreciation is the ritual's important final step. Above all, pay close attention to the perfect elements of the ceremony, from the art at the entryway and the kimono of the server to the quality of the utensils.

■ TIP→ **Want to experience this ancient and highly ritualized art form firsthand? Stop by the Hotel Ōkura Tōkyō in the heart of Roppongi (⇨ Where to Stay chapter) where one-hour and full-day sessions are available. ☎ 03/3582-0111, 0120/003-751 toll-free, ⊕ www.okura .com/tokyo, ⊗ Mon.–Sat. 11–4.**

–David Miles

GEISHA

IN MODERN JAPAN, geisha are an unusual sight outside of Kyōto, and their numbers have dwindled to around 10,000; in the 1920s there were over 80,000 geisha in Japan. This is partly due to the increase of bar hostesses—who perform a similar function in nightclubs with virtually none of a geisha's training—not to mention the refinement and expense it takes to hire a geisha. Because she is essentially the most personal form of entertainer, the emphasis is on artistic and conversational skills, not solely on youth or beauty. Thus the typical geisha can work to an advanced age.

A geisha typically starts her career as a servant at a house until 13. She continues as a *maiko* (dancing child) until she masters the requisite accomplishments at about 18, including playing the *shamisen* (a traditional Japanese guitar-like instrument) and learning the proper hairstyles and kimono fittings. They are truly a sight to see strolling on the banks of the Kamo-gawa in the Gion district of Kyōto, or in Shimbashi, Akasaka, and Ginza in Tōkyō, especially since these women are of a dying profession. Today geisha unions, restaurant unions, and registry offices regulate the times and fees of geisha. Fees are measured in "sticks"—generally, one hour—which is the time it would take a stick of *senkō* (incense) to burn.

Geisha establish a variety of relations with men. Besides maintaining a dependable amount of favorite customers, one might choose a *danna,* one man for emotional, sexual, and financial gratification. Some geisha marry, most often to an intimate client. When they do, they leave the profession.

Although it's a common misconception in the West, geisha are not prostitutes. The character *gei* in *geisha* stands for arts and accomplishments (*sha* in this case means person); the public image of geisha in Japan is one of high status. To become a geisha, a woman must project perfect grace and have thorough mastery of etiquette. She should have an accomplished singing voice and dance beautifully. She needs a finely tuned aesthetic sense—with flower arranging and tea ceremony—and must excel at the art of conversation. In short, she should be the ultimate companion.

–David Miles

FILMS & LITERATURE

Films

Akira Kurosawa, Japan's best-known film-maker, began directing in 1943. His film *Rashōmon* (1950), a 12th-century murder mystery told by four different and untrustworthy narrators, sparked world interest in Japanese cinema. Among his classic period films are *Seven Samurai* (1954), *The Hidden Fortress* (1958) (also the inspiration for *Star Wars*), *Yōjimbō* (1961), *Red Beard* (1965), *Dersu Uzala* (1975), and *Kagemusha* (1980). The life-affirming *Ikiru* (1952) deals with an office worker dying of cancer. *The Bad Sleep Well* (1960), meanwhile, portrays a nightmare of (then) contemporary Japanese corporate society corruption. Two of Kurosawa's most honored films were adapted from Shakespeare plays: *Throne of Blood* (1957), based on *Macbeth,* and *Ran* (1985), based on *King Lear.* Many of Kurosawa's films star the irrepressible Toshiro Mifune, whose intense character is constantly exploding against a rigid social structure.

Other seminal samurai pics include Teinosuke Kinugasa's *Gate of Hell* (1953), which vividly re-creates medieval Japan and won an Oscar for best foreign film, and *The Samurai Trilogy* (1954), directed by Hiroshi Inagaki, which follows the adventures of a legendary 16th-century samurai hero, Musashi Miyamoto.

In 1962, an immensely popular movie series began about Zatoichi, a blind swordsman who wanders town to town seeking work as a masseur; instead he always finds himself at the center of some bloody intrigue that forces him to kill lots of people. Beginning with *The Tale of Zatoichi*, some 25 movies were made in 11 years. The legend continued in two later films released in 1989 and 2003, both called *Zatoichi.*

A new group of filmmakers came to the forefront in postwar Japan including Kon Ichikawa, Hiroshi Teshigahara, and Shōhei Imamura. Ichikawa directed two powerful antiwar movies, *The Burmese Harp* (1956) and *Fires on the Plain* (1959). Teshigahara is renowned for the allegorical *Woman in the Dunes* (1964), based on a novel by Kōbō Abe. *The Ballad of Narayama* (1983), about the death of the elderly, and *Black Rain* (1989), which deals with the atomic bombing of Hiroshima, are two powerful films by Imamura.

Other Japanese filmmakers worth checking out are Jūzō Itami, Masayuki Suo, Kitano Takeshi, and Iwai Shunji. Itami won international recognition for *Tampopo* (1986), a highly original comedy about food. His other films include *A Taxing Woman* (1987), which pokes fun at the Japanese tax system, and *Mimbō* (1992), which dissects the world of Japanese gangsters. Suo's *Shall We Dance?* (1996) is a bittersweet comedy about a married businessman who escapes his daily routine by taking ballroom dance lessons. (The 2004 film with the same name, starring Richard Gere, Susan Sarandon, and Jennifer Lopez, was based on Suo's original.) Iwai Shunji's *Love Letter* (1995) is a touching story about a girl who receives a lost letter from her boyfriend after he has died.

Akin to the samurai films are Japanese gangster flicks. Though they date back to such Kurosawa classics as *Drunken Angel* (1948) and *Stray Dog* (1949), an edgy gangster genre emerged in the 1990s led by Beat Takeshi Kitano, who wrote, directed, and starred in *Boiling Point* (1990), *Sonatine* (1993), and *Fireworks* (1997). Tasheki is the hard-faced, silent, badass type, and Clint Eastwood fans will appreciate his films. There are many Japanese gangster films, including a whole exploitive subset that mixes extreme violence and basically soft-core porn.

Those interested in Japanese animated or anime movies, should start with the Academy Award-winning picture, *Spirited Away* (2002), which is available in English. *Kiki's Delivery Service* (1989), starring Kirsten Dunst as the voice of Kiki, is another good choice.

Recently, Japanese horror has also enjoyed international popularity. Focusing more on anticipation and psychological horror than blood spurting special effects—though some can be quite gruesome, such as the hair-raising *Audition* (1999)—Japanese horror tends to leave an eerie feeling that's hard to get rid of. Many involve unseen, unstoppable, or difficult to understand threats, like ghosts, poltergeists and inalterable, tragic destiny. Both horror hits, *Ringu* (1998) and *Ju-on: The Grudge* (2003) and their American remakes *The Ring* (2002) and *The Ring Two* (2005) and *The Grudge* (2004) and *The Grudge 2* (2006) are representative of this genre.

Japan has also been the subject of numerous Western movies. For a look at war-time Japan, Steven Spielberg's *Empire of the Sun* (1987) explores the Japanese occupation of China and the Japanese treatment of the Western colonists they replace. The classic *Bridge on the River Kwai* (1957) also explores Japan's treatment of British prisoners of war and the differing cultural perspectives of that treatment.

For something a little lighter, see the classic Bond flick *You Only Live Twice* (1967), which shows Tokyo during the heady growth years of the late sixties. It features Sean Connery who undergoes plastic surgery to disguise himself as a Japanese person; the screenplay is by Roald Dahl. First-time visitors to Tokyo will likely empathize with Sofia Coppola's *Lost in Translation* (2003), about the alienation experienced by an American visitor to Tokyo. It is a compelling and accurate view of life in contemporary Tokyo.

Literature

Fiction. Modern Japanese fiction is widely available in translation. One of the best-known writers is Yukio Mishima, author of *The Sea of Fertility* trilogy and *The Temple of the Golden Pavilion*. His books

often deal with the effects of postwar Westernization on Japanese culture. Two superb prose stylists are Junichirō Tanizaki, author of *The Makioka Sisters, Some Prefer Nettles,* and the racy 1920s *Quicksand*; and Nobel Prize winner Yasunari Kawabata, whose superbly written novels include *Snow Country* and *The Sound of the Mountain*. Kawabata's *Thousand Cranes,* which uses the tea ceremony as a storytelling vehicle, is an elegant page-turner. Jirō Osaragi's *The Journey* is a lucid, entertaining rendering of the clash of tradition and modernity in postwar Japan. Also look for Natsume Sōseki's charming *Botchan* and delightful *I Am a Cat*.

Other novelists of note are Kōbō Abe, whose *Woman in the Dunes* is a 1960s landmark, and Shūsaku Endō, who brutally and breathlessly treated the early clash of Japan with Christianity in *The Samurai*. Seichō Matsumoto's *Inspector Imanishi Investigates* is a superb detective novel with enlightening details of Japanese life. For a fictional retelling of the nuclear devastation of Hiroshima read Ibuse Masuji's classic novel *Black Rain*.

The "new breed" of Japanese novelists is no less interesting. Haruki Murakami's *Wild Sheep Chase* is a collection of often bizarre and humorous stories, and *Hard Boiled Wonderland and the End of the World* paints a vivid and fantastical picture of the frenetic changes of modern Japan. Murakami's *The Wind-up Bird Chronicle,* a dense and daring novel, juxtaposes the banality of modern suburbia with the harsh realities of 20th-century Japanese history. Along with Murakami's books, Banana Yoshimoto's *Kitchen* and other novels are probably the most fun you'll have with any Japanese fiction. Kōno Taeko's *Toddler-Hunting* and Yūko Tsushima's *The Shooting Gallery* are as engrossing and well crafted as they are frank about the burdens of tradition on modern Japanese women. Nobel Prize winner Kenzaburō Ōe's writing similarly explores deeply personal issues, among them his compelling relationship with his disabled son. His most important works are *A Personal Matter* and *Silent Scream*.

The great classic of Japanese fiction is Murasaki Shikibu's *Tale of Genji* written around 1000 AD. Genji, or the Shining Prince, has long been taken as the archetype of ideal male behavior. From the same period, which is often considered Japanese literature's golden age, *The Pillow Book of Sei Shōnagon* is the stylish and stylized diary of a woman's courtly life.

For a selection of Edo period ghost stories try Akinari Ueda's *Ugetsu Monogatari: Tales of Moonlight and Rain,* translated by Leon Zolbrod. The racy prose of late-17th-century Saikaku Ihara is translated in various books, including *Some Final Words of Advice* and *Five Women Who Loved Love.*

Poetry. *Haiku,* the 5-7-5 syllable form that the monk Matsuo Bashō honed in the 17th century, is the flagship of Japanese poetry. Bashō's *Narrow Road to the Deep North* is a wistful prose-and-poem travelogue that is available in a few translations. But there are many more authors and forms of poetry worth exploring. Three volumes of translations by Kenneth Rexroth include numerous authors' work from the last 1,000 years: *One Hundred Poems from the Japanese, 100 More Poems from the Japanese,* and *Women Poets of Japan* (translated with Akiko Atsumi). *Ink Dark Moon,* translated by Jane Hirshfield with Mariko Aratani, presents the remarkable poems of Ono no Komachi and Izumi Shikibu, two of Japan's earliest women poets. The Zen poems of Ryōkan represent the sacred current in Japanese poetry; look for *Dew Drops on a Lotus Leaf.* Other poets to look for are Issa, Buson, and Bonchō. Two fine small volumes that link their haiku with those of other poets, including Bashō, are *The Monkey's Raincoat* and the beautifully illustrated *A Net of Fireflies.*

History & Society. Fourteen hundred years of history are a lot to take in when going on a vacation, but one good survey that makes the task much easier is George Sansom's *Japan: A Short Cultural History.*

Yamamoto Tsunetomo's *Hagakure (The Book of the Samurai)* is an 18th-century guide of sorts to the principles and ethics of the "Way of the Samurai," written by a Kyūshū samurai. Dr. Junichi Saga's *Memories of Silk and Straw: A Self-Portrait of Small-Town Japan* is his 1970s collection of interviews with local old-timers in his hometown outside Tōkyō. Saga's father illustrated the accounts. Few books get so close to the realities of everyday life in early modern rural Japan.

John Hersey's *Hiroshima,* in which he records the stories of survivors, is essential reading.

Karel van Wolferens *The Enigma of Japanese Power* is an enlightening book on the Japanese sociopolitical system, especially for diplomats and businesspeople intending to work with the Japanese. Alex Kerr's *Lost Japan* examines the directions of Japanese society past and present. This book was the first by a foreigner to win Japan's Shinchō Gakugei literature prize. Elizabeth Bumiller's 1995 *The Secrets of Mariko* intimately recounts a very poignant year in the life of a Japanese woman and her family.

If you're interested in the ancient traditions of the tea ceremony, check out *The Book of Tea* by Kakuzo Okakura.

Art & Architecture. A wealth of literature exists on Japanese art. Much of the early writing has not withstood the test of time, but R. Paine and Alexander Soper's *Art and Architecture of Japan* remains a good place to start. A more recent survey, though narrower in scope, is Joan Stanley-Smith's *Japanese Art.*

The multivolume *Japan Arts Library* covers most of the styles and personalities of the Japanese arts. The series includes volumes on castles, teahouses, screen painting, and wood-block prints. A more detailed look at the architecture of Tōkyō is Edward

Seidensticker's *Low City, High City.* Kazuo Nishi and Kazuo Hozumi's *What Is Japanese Architecture?* features the history of Japanese architecture and uses examples of buildings you will see on your travels.

Religion. Anyone wanting to read a Zen Buddhist text should try *The Platform Sutra of the Sixth Patriarch,* one of the Zen classics, written by an ancient Chinese head of the sect and translated by Philip B. Yampolsky. Another Buddhist text of high importance is the *Lotus Sutra;* it has been translated by Leon Hurvitz as *The Scripture of the Lotus Blossom of the Fine Dharma: The Lotus Sutra.* Stuart D. Picken has written books on both major Japanese religions: *Shintō: Japan's Spiritual Roots* and *Buddhism: Japan's Cultural Identity.*

Travel Narratives. Two travel narratives stand out as superb introductions to Japanese history, culture, and people. Donald Richie's classic *The Inland Sea* recalls his journey and encounters on the fabled Seto Nai-kai. Leila Philip's year working in a Kyūshū pottery village became the eloquent *Road Through Miyama.*

Language. There's an overwhelming number of books and courses available for studying Japanese. *Japanese for Busy People* uses conversational situations (rather than grammatical principles) as a means of introducing the Japanese language. With it you will also learn the two syllabaries, *hiragana* and *katakana,* and rudimentary *kanji* characters.

West Meets East. Start with Pico Iyer's *The Lady and the Monk,* a travelogue that starts as a study of temple-life but becomes a book about personal relationships in Japan. For an amusing account of the Gaijin condition, try Will Ferguson's *Hokkaido Highway Blues: Hitchhiking Japan.* Finally, dip into any book by leading Japanologist Donald Ritchie for tales of love, movies, yakuza, islands, and art. Ritchie's *The Image Factory: Fads and Fashions in Japan* is a good introduction to his works.

The emotional realities of Japan life for foreigners are rendered in *The Broken Bridge: Fiction from Expatriates in Literary Japan,* edited by Suzanne Kamata. The enormously popular tale *Memoirs of a Geisha,* by Arthur Golden, recounts the dramatic life of a geisha in the decades surrounding World War II. A film version (2005) is available on DVD.

TŌKYŌ AT A GLANCE

Fast Facts

Type of government: Metropolitan prefecture with democratically elected governor and assembly. There are 47 prefectures in Japan; Tōkyō is the largest. Wards and other subsidiary units have local assemblies.

Population: 12.544 million (city), or 10% of Japan's total population.

Population of foreign residents: 360,000

Population density: 5,736 people per square km; Tōkyō is the most densely populated prefecture in Japan.

Households: 5.866 million; average 2.14 persons per household.

Demographic composition by age: Juveniles (ages 0–14), 1.446 million (11.9%); working age population (ages 15–64), 8.539 million (70.2%); and the elderly (65 years old and over), 2.176 million (17.9%).

Language: Japanese (official)

Geography & Environment

Latitude: 35°N (same as Albuquerque, New Mexico; Kabul, Afghanistan; Memphis, Tennessee).

Longitude: 139° E (same as Adelaide, Australia).

Elevation: 17 meters (59 feet).

Land area: 2,187 square km or 0.6% of the total area of Japan.

Terrain: Tōkyō sits on the Kantō plain, at the head of Tōkyō Bay, near the center of the Japanese archipelago. Edogawa River is to the east, mountains are to the west, and Tamagawa River is to the south. Mount Fuji, Japan's highest mountain, rises up 12,388 feet about 60 mi (100 km) west of Tōkyō.

Natural hazards: Earthquakes, typhoons

Environmental issues: Tōkyō has banned trucks that don't meet strict emissions standards and ordered filters placed on many other diesel vehicles. As a result, the air quality has improved. Studies are being conducted on the so-called heat island effect, which is the raising of temperatures by air-conditioners and other exhausts emitted by buildings in the dense downtown area. Also, finding landfills for the city's garbage is a growing problem.

Economy

Unemployment: 6.1 %

Work force: 6.2 million; clerical, technical, and management occupations 46.3%; sales and services 29.2 %; manufacturing and transportation-related occupations 24%; agriculture, forestry and fisheries 0.5%

Major industries: Automobiles, banking, cameras and optical goods, consumer items, electronic apparatus, equipment, financial services, furniture, publishing and printing, textiles, transport.

Did You Know?

- The average Tōkyō residence is only slightly larger than a two-car garage in the U.S.

- Tōkyō has the lowest population of children aged 0 to 14 of any area of Japan.

- Japanese inventors have created a material that absorbs nitrogen and sulfur oxide gases, reducing smog. The product is now in use on bridges, buildings, and highways across Tōkyō.

- Tōkyō has the second largest home-less population in Japan. In 2003, the city counted 5,927 people. About half are estimated to be sleeping in parks and on the streets, the rest are in government shelters.

- There are eight U.S. military bases within Tōkyō, covering more than 6 square mi.

- Tōkyō's daytime population is 2.7 million people higher than its night-time population. The change is most dramatic in the city's downtown wards—Chiyoda, Chuo, and Minato—which have only 268,000 persons by night and 2.3 million by day.

- The ginkgo is the most common tree in Tōkyō and has even been adopted as the city's symbol. It's fan-shaped green leaves turn yellow every fall.

- Tokyo has served as the capital of Japan only since 1868; before that, Kyoto was capital for more than 1,000 years.

- More than two million people pass through Shinjuku Station, Japan's busiest railway station, every day.

- Tokyo suffers from an overabundance of *jidou hanbaiki* (vending machines) with 2.7 million beverage vending machines alone.

- Tokyo is home to the world's tallest Buddha—standing three times taller than the Statue of Liberty. Cast from bronze, it measures 120 m (394 ft) high, and was completed in January 1993. The joint Japanese and Taiwanese project, which took seven years to make, is 35 m (115 ft) wide and weighs 1,000 tonnes (984 tons).

- The Mega-Float island at Yokosuka Port, Tokyo Bay is the largest artificial island in the world at 1,000 m (3,280 ft 10 in) long, 121 m (396 ft 11.7 in) wide, and 3 m (9 ft 10 in) deep. It was opened to the public on August 10, 1999.

- Japan has the highest density of robots in the world.

CHRONOLOGY

10,000 BC–AD 300 Neolithic Jōmon hunting and fishing culture leaves richly decorated pottery.

AD 300 Yayoi culture displays knowledge of farming and metallurgy imported from Korea.

after 300 The Yamato tribe consolidates power in the rich Kansai plain and expands westward, forming the kind of military aristocracy that will dominate Japan's history.

ca. 500 Yamato leaders, claiming to be descended from the sun goddess, Amaterasu, take the title of emperor.

538–552 Buddhism, introduced to the Yamato court from China by way of Korea, complements rather than replaces the indigenous Shintō religion.

593–622 Prince Shōtoku encourages the Japanese to embrace Chinese culture and has Buddhist temple Hōryū-ji built at Nara in 607. (Its existing buildings are among the oldest surviving wooden structures in the world.)

Nara Period

710–784 Japan has its first permanent capital at Nara; this age marks the great age of Buddhist sculpture, piety, and poetry.

Fujiwara or Heian (Peace) Period

794–1160 The capital is moved from Nara to Heian-kyō (now Kyōto), where the Fujiwara family dominates the imperial court. Lady Murasaki's novel *The Tale of Genji*, written circa 1020, describes the elegance and political maneuvering of court life.

Kamakura Period

1185–1335 Feudalism arises, with military and economic power dominating the provinces and the emperor a powerless, ceremonial figurehead in Kyōto. Samurai warriors welcome Zen, a new sect of Buddhism from China.

1192 After a war with the Taira family, Yoritomo of the Minamoto family becomes the first shōgun; he places his capital in Kamakura.

1274 and 1281 The fleets sent by Chinese emperor Kublai Khan to invade Japan are destroyed by typhoons, praised in Japanese history as kamikaze, or divine wind.

Ashikaga Period

1336–1568 The Ashikaga family assumes the title of shōgun and settles in Kyōto. The Zen aesthetic flourishes in painting, landscape gardening, and tea ceremony. Nō theater emerges. The Silver Pavilion, or Ginkaku-ji, in Kyōto, built in 1483, is the quintessential example of Zen-inspired architecture. The period is marked by constant warfare but also by increased trade with the mainland. Ōsaka develops into an important commercial city, and trade guilds appear.

1467–77 The Ōnin Wars that wrack Kyōto initiate a 100-year period of civil war.

1543 Portuguese sailors, the first Europeans to reach Japan, initiate trade relations with the lords of western Japan and introduce the musket, which changes Japanese warfare.

1549–51 St. Francis Xavier, the first Jesuit missionary, introduces Christianity.

Momoyama Period of National Unification

1568–1600 Two generals, Nobunaga Oda and Hideyoshi Toyotomi, are the central figures of this period. Nobunaga builds a military base with which Hideyoshi unifies Japan.

1592, 1597 Hideyoshi invades Korea. He brings back Korean potters, who rapidly develop a Japanese ceramics industry.

Tokugawa Period

1600–1868 Ieyasu Tokugawa becomes shōgun after the battle of Sekigahara. The military capital is established at Edo (now Tōkyō), which shows phenomenal economic and cultural growth. A hierarchical order of four social classes—warriors, farmers, artisans, then merchants—is rigorously enforced. The merchant class, however, is increasingly prosperous and effects a transition from a rice to a money economy. Merchants patronize new, popular forms of art: Kabuki, haiku, and the ukiyo-e school of painting. Life in the latter part of this era is beautifully illustrated in the wood-block prints of the artist Hokusai (1760–1849).

1618 Japanese Christians who refuse to renounce their foreign religion are persecuted.

1637–38 Japanese Christians are massacred in the Shimabara uprising. Japan, except for a Dutch trading post in Nagasaki harbor, is closed to the outside world.

1853 U.S. commodore Matthew Perry reopens Japan to foreign trade.

Meiji Restoration

1868–1912 Opponents of the weakened Tokugawa Shōgunate support Emperor Meiji and overthrow the last shōgun. The emperor is "restored" (with little actual power), and the imperial capital is moved to Edo, which is renamed Tōkyō (Eastern Capital). Japan is modernized along Western lines, with a constitution proclaimed in 1889; a system of compulsory education and a surge of industrialization follow.

1902–05 Japan defeats Russia in the Russo-Japanese War and achieves world-power status.

1910 Japan annexes Korea.

1914–18 Japan joins the Allies in World War I.

1923 The Great Kantō Earthquake devastates much of Tōkyō and Yokohama including an estimated 575,000 dwellings, and kills more than 142,807 people.

1931   As a sign of growing militarism in the country, Japan seizes the Chinese province of Manchuria.

1937   Following years of increasing military and diplomatic activity in northern China, open warfare breaks out (and lasts until 1945); Chinese Nationalists and Communists both fight Japan.

1939–45   Japan, having signed anti-Communist treaties with Nazi Germany and Italy (1936 and 1937), invades and occupies French Indochina.

1941   The Japanese attack on Pearl Harbor on December 7 brings the United States into war against Japan in the Pacific.

1942   Japan's empire extends to Indochina, Burma, Malaya, the Philippines, and Indonesia. Japan bombs Darwin, Australia. U.S. defeat of Japanese forces at Midway turns the tide of the Pacific war.

1945   Tōkyō and 50 other Japanese cities are devastated by U.S. bombing raids. The United States drops atomic bombs on Hiroshima and Nagasaki in August, precipitating Japanese surrender.

1945–52   The American occupation under General Douglas MacArthur disarms Japan and encourages the establishment of a democratic government. Emperor Hirohito retains his position.

1953   After the Korean War, Japan begins a period of great economic growth.

1964   Tōkyō hosts the Summer Olympic games.

late 1960s   Japan develops into one of the major industrial nations in the world.

mid-1970s   Production of electronics, cars, cameras, and computers places Japan at the heart of the emerging "Pacific Rim" economic sphere and threatens to spark a trade war with the industrial nations of Europe and the United States.

1983   Tokyo Disneyland opens.

1989   Emperor Hirohito, Japan's war-time Emperor, dies.

1990   Coronation of Emperor Akihito. Prince Fumihito marries Kiko Kawashima.

1991   Mount Unzen erupted for the second time since 1792, killing 38 people.

1992   The Diet approves use of Japanese military forces under United Nations auspices.

1993   Crown Prince Naruhito marries Masako Owada, the daughter of a Japanese diplomat and graduate of Harvard University.

1995   A massive earthquake strikes Kōbe and environs. Approximately 5,500 people are killed and 35,000 injured; more than 100,000 buildings are destroyed.

Members of a fringe religious organization, the Aum Shinri Kyō, carry out a series of poison-gas attacks on the transportation networks of Tōkyō and Yokohama, undermining confidence in personal safety in a society that is a model of decorum and mutual respect.

1997 The deregulation of rice prices and the appearance of discount gasoline stations mark a turn in the Japanese economy toward genuine privatization. These small indications constitute a break from traditional price control policies that support small merchants and producers.

1998 The Japanese economy is crippled from slumps throughout Asia. Banks merge or go bankrupt, and Japanese consumers spend less and less.

1999 In the international arena Japanese toys, films, and other accoutrements of pop culture find themselves in the spotlight like never before. The economy, however, continues to suffer as politicians debate economic measures that foreign economists have been recommending for years. Small businesses are most affected, and the attitude of the average Japanese is grim.

A nuclear accident 112 km (70 mi) northeast of Tōkyō injures few but raises many questions about Japan's vast nuclear-power industry.

2001 In support of the U.S. war against terrorism in Afghanistan, the Japanese government extends non-combat military activities abroad for the first time since World War II by sending support ships to the Indian Ocean under a reinterpretation of the existing post-1945, pacifist constitution. Asian leaders express some concern for a first step for Japanese military presence abroad since 1945.

Prime Minister Koizumi visits Yasukuni Shrine, which is dedicated to the memory of Japan's war dead. Koizumi will visit the shrine annually five more times as Japan's Prime Minister, provoking anger and souring relations with neighbors such as Korea and China, who suffered due to Japan's colonial ambitions during the Second World War.

2002 North Korea admits to the kidnapping of 11 Japanese civilians in the 1970s and '80s for use as language teachers. Japan negotiates the return of several of its citizens.

Hayao Miyazaki's *Spirited Away* won the Academy Award for Animated Feature Film.

2003 Prime Minister Koizumi sends Japanese combat troops to Iraq in the first deployment of Japanese troops since WWII.

The Japanese NIKKEI stock market average bottoms up after falling 80% from its 1989 peak, skyrocketing 41% from April to October. Signs are strong that restructuring efforts following the spectacular collapse of Japan's '80's bubble economy are meeting with success.

2006 The Bank of Japan (BOJ) raises interest rates for the first time in six years, from 0% to 0.25%, marking an end to a decade of economic stagnation. The decision brings Japan's monetary policy in line with those of the U.S. and Europe, where central bankers contain inflation by raising rates.

Shinzo Abe is elected as the country's youngest postwar prime minister and the first to be born after World War II.

ABOUT JAPANESE

Japanese sounds and spellings differ in principle from those of the West. We build words letter by letter, and one letter can sound different depending where it appears in a word. For example, we see *ta* as two letters, and *ta* could be pronounced three ways, as in *tat, tall,* and *tale.* For the Japanese, *ta* is one character, and it is pronounced one way: *tah.*

The *hiragana* and *katakana* (tables of sounds) are the rough equivalents of our alphabet. There are four types of syllables within these tables: the single vowels *a, i, u, e,* and *o,* in that order; vowel-consonant pairs like *ka, ni, hu,* or *ro;* the single consonant *n,* which punctuates the upbeats of the word for bullet train, *Shinkansen* (shee-n-ka-n-se-n); and compounds like *kya, chu,* and *ryo.* Remember that these compounds are one syllable. Thus Tōkyō, the capital city, has only two syllables—*tō* and *kyō*—not three. Likewise pronounce Kyōto *kyō-to,* not *kee-oh-to.*

Japanese vowels are pronounced as follows: *a*–ah, *i*–ee, *u*–oo, *e*–eh, *o*–oh. The Japanese *r* is rolled so that it sounds like a bounced *d.*

No diphthongs. Paired vowels in Japanese words are not slurred together, as in our words *coin, brain,* or *stein.* The Japanese separate them, as in mae (ma-eh), which means in front of; *kōen* (ko-en), which means park; *byōin* (byo-een), which means hospital; and *tokei* (to-*keh*-ee), which means clock or watch.

Macrons. Many Japanese words, when rendered in *rōmaji* (roman letters), require macrons over vowels to indicate correct pronunciation, as in Tōkyō. When you see these macrons, double the length of the vowel, as if you're saying it twice: *to-o-kyo-o.* Likewise, when you see double consonants, as in the city name Nikkō, linger on the Ks—as in "bookkeeper"—and on the O.

Emphasis. Some books state that the Japanese emphasize all syllables in their words equally. This is not true. Take the words *sayōnara* and *Hiroshima.* Americans are likely to stress the downbeats: sa-yo-*na*-ra and *hi*-ro-*shi*-ma. The Japanese actually emphasize the second beat in each case: sa-*yō*-na-ra (note the macron) and hi-*ro*-shi-ma. Metaphorically speaking, the Japanese don't so much stress syllables as pause over them or race past them: Emphasis is more a question of speed than weight. In the vocabulary below, we indicate emphasis by italicizing the syllable that you should stress.

Three interesting pronunciations are in the vocabulary below. The word *desu* roughly means "is." It looks like it has two syllables, but the Japanese race past the final *u* and just say "dess." Likewise, some verbs end in -*masu,* which is pronounced "mahss." Similarly, the character shi is often quickly pronounced "sh," as in the phrase meaning "pleased to meet you:" ha-ji-me-*mash(i)*-te. Just like *desu* and -*masu,* what look like two syllables, in this case *ma* and *shi,* are pronounced *mahsh.*

Hyphens. Throughout *Fōdor's Tōkyō,* we have hyphenated certain words to help you recognize meaningful patterns. This isn't conventional; it is practical. For example, *Eki-mae-dōri,* which literally means "Station Front Avenue," turns into a blur when rendered Ekimaedōri. And you'll run across a number of sight names that end in *-jingū* or *-jinja* or *-taisha.* You'll soon catch on to their meaning: Shintō shrine.

Structure. From the point of view of English grammar, Japanese sentences are structured back to front, ie. subject-object-verb instead of subject-verb-object as in English. An English speaker would say "I am going to Tōkyō," which in Japanese would translate literally as "Tōkyō to going."

Note: placing an "o" before words like *tera* (*otera*) and *shiro* (*oshiro*) makes the word honorific. It is not essential, but it is polite.

ESSENTIAL PHRASES

Basics

Yes/No	ha-i/ii-e	はい／いいえ
Please	o-ne-*gai* shi-masu	お願いします
Thank you (very much)	(*dō*-mo) a-*ri*-ga-tō go-*zai*-ma su	(どうも)ありがとう ございます
You're welcome	*dō* i-ta-shi-ma-shi-te	どういたしまして
Excuse me	su-mi-ma-*sen*	すみません
Sorry	*go*-men na-*sai*	ごめんなさい
Good morning	o-*ha*-yō *go*-zai-ma-su	お早うございます
Good day/afternoon	kon-*ni*-chi-wa	こんにちは
Good evening	kom-*ban*-wa	こんばんは
Good night	o-*ya*-su-mi na-*sai*	おやすみなさい
Good bye	sa-*yō*-na-ra	さようなら
Mr./Mrs./Miss	-san	一さん
Pleased to meet you	*ha*-ji-me-*mashi*-te	はじめまして
How do you do?	*dō*-zo yo-*ro*-shi-ku	どうぞよろしく

Numbers

The first reading is used for reading numbers, as in telephone numbers, and the second is often used for counting things.

1	*i*-chi / hi-*to*-tsu	一／一つ	17	*jū*-shi-chi	十七
2	ni / fu-*ta*-tsu	二／二つ	18	*jū*-ha-chi	十八
3	san / *mit*-tsu	三／三つ	19	*jū*-kyū	十九
4	shi / *yot*-tsu	四／四つ	20	*ni*-jū	二十
5	go / i-*tsu*-tsu	五／五つ	21	*ni*-jū-i-chi	二十一
6	*ro*-ku / *mut*-tsu	六／六つ	30	*san*-jū	三十
7	*na*-na / *na*-na-tsu	七／七つ	40	*yon*-jū	四十
8	*ha*-chi / *yat*-tsu	八／八つ	50	*go*-jū	五十
9	kyū / *ko*-ko-no-*tsu*	九／九つ	60	*ro*-ku-jū	六十
10	jū / tō	十／十	70	na-na-jū	七十
11	*jū*-i-chi	十一	80	*ha*-chi-jū	八十
12	*jū*-ni	十二	90	kyū-jū	九十
13	*jū*-san	十三	100	*hya*-ku	百
14	*jū*-yon	十四	1000	sen	千
15	*jū*-go	十五	10,000	*i*-chi-man	一万
16	*jū*-ro-ku	十六	100,000	*jū*-man	十万

Days of the Week

Sunday	*ni*-chi yō-bi	日曜日
Monday	*ge*-tsu yō-bi	月曜日
Tuesday	*ka* yō-bi	火曜日
Wednesday	*su*-i yō-bi	水曜日
Thursday	*mo*-ku yō-bi	木曜日
Friday	*kin* yō-bi	金曜日
Saturday	*dō* yō-bi	土曜日
Weekday	hei-ji-tsu	平日
Weekend	shū-ma-tsu	週末

Months

January	*i*-chi *ga*-tsu	一月
February	*ni* ga-tsu	二月
March	*san* ga-tsu	三月
April	*shi* ga-tsu	四月
May	*go* ga-tsu	五月
June	*ro*-ku *ga*-tsu	六月
July	*shi*-chi *ga*-tsu	七月
August	*ha*-chi *ga*-tsu	八月
September	*ku* ga-tsu	九月
October	*jū* ga-tsu	十月
November	*jū*-i-chi *ga*-tsu	十一月
December	*jū*-ni *ga*-tsu	十二月

Useful Expressions, Questions, and Answers

Do you speak English?	*ei*-go ga wa-*ka*-ri-ma-su *ka*	英語が わかりますか。
I don't speak Japanese.	*ni*-hon-go ga wa-*ka*-ri-ma-*sen*	日本語が わかりません。
I don't understand.	wa-*ka*-ri-ma-*sen*	わかりません。
I understand.	wa-*ka*-ri-ma-shi-*ta*	わかりました。
I don't know.	*shi*-ra-ma-*sen*	知りません。
I'm American (British).	wa-*ta*-shi wa a-*me*-ri-ka (i-*gi*-ri-su) jin *desu*	私はアメリカ (イギリス) 人 です。
What's your name?	o-*na*-ma-e wa *nan* desu *ka*	お名前は何ですか。
My name is . . .	. . . to *mo*-shi-*ma*-su	……と申します。
What time is it?	i-ma *nan*-ji desu *ka*	今何時ですか。

How?	*dō* yat-te	どうやりますか。
When?	*i*-tsu	いつですか。
Yesterday/today/ tomorrow	ki-*nō*/kyō/*ashi*-ta	きのう／きょう／ あした
This morning	*ke*-sa	けさ
This afternoon	*kyō* no go-go	きょうの午後
Tonight	*kom*-ban	こんばん
Excuse me, what?	su-*mi*-ma-*sen, nan* desu *ka*	すみません、 何ですか。
What is this/that?	*ko*-re/*so*-re wa *nan* desu *ka*	これ／ それは何ですか。
Why?	*na*-ze desu *ka*	なぜですか。
Who?	*da*-re desu *ka*	だれですか。
I am lost.	*mi*-chi ni ma-yo-i-*mash*-ta	道に迷いました。
Where is [place]	[place] wa *do*-ko desu *ka*	.....はどこですか。
. . . train station?	e-ki	駅
. . . subway station?	chi-*ka*-te-tsu-no eki	地下鉄の駅
. . . bus stop?	*ba*-su no-ri-*ba*	バス乗り場
. . . taxi stand?	*ta*-ku-shi-i no-ri-*ba*	タクシー乗り場
. . . airport?	kū-kō	空港
. . . post office?	*yū*-bin-*kyo*-ku	郵便局
. . . bank?	*gin*-kō	銀行
. . . the [name] hotel?	[name] ho-*te*-ru	ホテル
. . . elevator?	e-re-bē-tā	エレベーター
Where are the restrooms?	*to*-i-re wa *do*-ko desu *ka*	トイレは どこですか。
Here/there/over there	*ko*-ko/*so*-ko/*a*-so-ko	ここ／そこ／あそこ
Left/right	hi-*da*-ri/*mi*-gi	左／右
Straight ahead	mas-*su*-gu	まっすぐ
Is it near (far)?	chi-*ka*-i (*tō*-i) desu *ka*	近い (遠い) ですか。
Are there any rooms?	*he*-ya *ga* a-ri-masu *ka*	部屋がありますか。
I'd like [item]	[item] ga ho-*shi*-i no desu ga	.....がほしいの ですが。
. . . newspaper	*shim*-bun	新聞
. . . stamp	*kit*-te	切手
. . . key	*ka*-gi	鍵
I'd like to buy [item]	[item] o kai-*ta*-i no desu ke do	.....を買いたいの ですけど。

. . . a ticket to [destination]	[destination] *ma*-de no *kip*-pu	.....までの切符
Map	*chi*-zu	地図
How much is it?	i-*ku*-ra desu *ka*	いくらですか。
It's expensive (cheap).	ta-*ka*-i (ya-*su*-i) de su *ne*	高い (安い) ですね。
A little (a lot)	su-*ko*-shi (*ta*-ku-san)	少し (たくさん)
More/less	*mot*-to o-ku/ *su*-ku-*na*-ku	もっと多く／少なく
Enough/too much	*jū*-bun/*ō*-su-*gi*-ru	十分／多すぎる
I'd like to exchange . . .	. . . *ryō*-ga e shi-*te* i-*ta*-da-ke-masu *ka*	.....両替して 頂けますか。
. . . dollars to yen	*do*-ru o *en* ni	ドルを円に
. . . pounds to yen	*pon*-do o *en* ni	ポンドを円に
How do you say . . . in Japanese?	ni-*hon*-go de . . . wa *dō* i-i-masu *ka*	日本語で.....は どう言いますか。
I am ill/sick.	wa-*ta*-shi wa *byō*-ki desu	私は病気です。
Please call a doctor.	*i*-sha o *yon*-de ku-da-*sa*-i	医者を呼んで 下さい。
Please call the police.	*ke*-i-sa-tsu o *yon*-de ku-da-*sa*-i	警察を 呼んで下さい。
Help!	*ta*-su-*ke*-te	助けて！

Useful Words

Airport	kūkō	空港
Bay	wan	湾
Beach	-hama	浜
Behind	ushiro	後ろ
Bridge	hashi or -bashi	橋
Bullet train, literally "new trunk line"	Shinkansen	新幹線
Castle	shiro or -jō	城
Cherry blossoms	sakura	桜
City or municipality	-shi	市
Department store	depāto (deh-pah-to)	デパート
District	-gun	郡
East	higashi	東
Exit	deguchi or -guchi	出口
Festival	matsuri	祭

Feudal lord	daimyō	大名
Foreigner	gaijin	外人
Garden	niwa	植物園
Gate	mon or torii	門／鳥居
Gorge	kyōkoku	峡谷
Hill	oka	丘
Hot-spring spa	onsen	温泉
In front of	mae	前
Island	shima or -jima/-tō	島
Japanese words rendered in roman letters	rōmaji	ローマ字
Lake	mizumi or -ko	湖
Main road	kaidō or kōdō	街道／公道
Morning market	asa-ichi	朝市
Mountain	yama or -san	山
Museum	hakubutsukan	博物館
North	kita	北
Park	kōen	公園
Peninsula	-hantō	半島
Plateau	kōgen	高原
Pond	ike or -ike	池
Prefecture	-ken/-fu	県／府
Pub	izakaya	居酒屋
River	kawa or -gawa	川
Sea	umi or -nada	海／灘
Section or ward	-ku	区
Shop	mise or -ya	店／屋
Shrine	jinja or -gu	神社／宮
South	minami	南
Street	michi or -dō	道
Subway	chikatetsu	地下鉄
Temple	tera or -ji/-in	寺／院
Town	machi	町
Train	densha	電車
Train station	eki	駅
Valley	tani	谷
West	nishi	西

MENU GUIDE

Restaurants

Basics and Useful Expressions

A bottle of . . .	. . . *ip*-pon	.....一本
A glass/cup of . . .	. . . *ip*-pai	.....一杯
Ashtray	*ha*-i-*za*-ra	灰皿
Bill/check	kan-*jō*	かんじょう
Bread	pan	パン
Breakfast	*chō*-sho-ku	朝食
Butter	ba-*tā*	バター
Cheers!	kam-*pai*	乾杯！
Chopsticks	*ha*-shi	箸
Cocktail	*ka*-ku-*te*-ru	カクテル
Does that include dinner?	*yū*-sho-ku *ga tsu-ki-ma-su-ka*	夕食が付きますか。
Excuse me!	su-mi-ma-*sen*	すみません。
Fork	*fō*-ku	フォーク
I am diabetic.	wa-*ta*-shi wa tō-*nyō*-byō de su	私は糖尿病です。
I am dieting.	*da*-i-et-to *chū* desu	ダイエット中です。
I am a vegetarian.	*saisho*-ku shū-*gi*-sha/ beji-*tari*-an de-su	ベジタリアンです。
I cannot eat [item]	[item] wa *ta*-be-ra-re-ma-*sen*	.....は食べられません。
I'd like to order.	*chū*-mon o shi-*tai* desu	注文をしたいです。
I'd like [item]	[item] o o-ne-*gai*-shi-ma su	.....をお願いします。
I'm hungry.	o-na-ka ga *su*-i-te i-*ma su*	お腹が空いています。
I'm thirsty.	*no*-do ga ka-*wa*-i-te i-*ma su*	喉が渇いています。
It's tasty (not good)	o-i-shi-i (ma-*zu*-i) desu	おいしい (まずい) です。
Knife	*na*-i-fu	ナイフ
Lunch	*chū*-sho-ku	昼食
Menu	me-nyū	メニュー
Napkin	*na*-pu-*kin*	ナプキン
Pepper	ko-*shō*	こしょう
Plate	*sa*-ra	皿
Please give me [item]	[item] o ku-da-*sa*-i	.....を下さい。

Salt	*shi*-o	塩
Set menu	*te*-i-sho-ku	定食
Spoon	su-*pūn*	スプーン
Sugar	sa-tō	砂糖
Wine list	*wa*-i-n *ri*-su-to	ワインリスト
What do you recommend?	o-su-su-me *ryō*-ri wa *nan* desu *ka*	お勧め料理は何ですか。

Meat Dishes

gyōza	ギョウザ	Pork spiced with ginger and garlic in a Chinese wrapper and fried or steamed.
hambāgu	ハンバーグ	Hamburger pattie served with sauce.
hayashi raisu	はやしライス	Beef flavored with tomato and soy sauce with onions and peas over rice.
kara-age	からあげ	Chicken deep-fried without batter
karē-raisu	カレーライス	Curried rice. A thick curry gravy typically containing beef is poured over white rice.
katsu-karē	カツカレー	Curried rice with tonkatsu.
niku-jaga	肉じゃが	Beef and potatoes stewed together with soy sauce.
okonomi-yaki	お好み焼き	Sometimes called a Japanese pancake, this is made from a batter of flour, egg, cabbage, and meat or seafood, griddle-cooked then covered with green onions and a special sauce.
oyako-domburi	親子どんぶり	Literally, "mother and child bowl"—chicken and egg in broth over rice.
rōru kyabetsu	ロール・キャベツ	Rolled cabbage; beef or pork rolled in cabbage and cooked.
shabu-shabu	しゃぶしゃぶ	Extremely thin slices of beef are plunged for an instant into boiling water flavored with soup stock and then dipped into a thin sauce and eaten.
shōga-yaki	しょうが焼	Pork cooked with ginger.
shūmai	シュウマイ	Shrimp or pork wrapped in a light dough and steamed (originally Chinese).
subuta	酢豚	Sweet and sour pork, originally a Chinese dish.

sukiyaki	すき焼き	Thinly sliced beef, green onions, mushrooms, thin noodles, and cubes of tofu are simmered in a large iron pan in front of you. These ingredients are cooked in a mixture of soy sauce, mirin (cooking wine), and a little sugar. You are given a saucer of raw egg to cool the suki-yaki morsels before eating. Using chopsticks, you help yourself to anything on your side of the pan and dip it into the egg and then eat. Best enjoyed in a group.
sutēki	ステーキ	Steak
tanin-domburi	他人どんぶり	Literally, "strangers in a bowl"—similar to oyako domburi, but with beef instead of chicken.
tonkatsu	トンカツ	Breaded deep-fried pork cutlets.
yaki-niku	焼き肉	Thinly sliced meat is marinated then barbecued over an open fire at the table.
yaki-tori	焼き鳥	Pieces of chicken (white meat, liver, skin, etc.) threaded on skewers with green onions and marinated in sweet soy sauce and grilled.

Seafood Dishes

age-zakana	揚げ魚	Deep-fried fish
aji	あじ	Horse mackerel
ama-ebi	あまえび	Sweet shrimp
asari no sakamushi	あさりの酒蒸し	Clams steamed with rice wine
buri	ぶり	Yellowtail
dojo no yanagawa nabe	どじょうの柳川なべ	Loach cooked with burdock root and egg in an earthen dish. Considered a delicacy.
ebi furai	海老フライ	Deep-fried breaded prawns
ika	いか	Squid
iwashi	いわし	Sardines
karei furai	かれいフライ	Deep-fried breaded flounder
katsuo no tataki	かつおのたたき	Bonito cooked slightly on the surface. Eaten with chopped ginger and scallions and thin soy sauce.
maguro	まぐろ	Tuna
nizakana	煮魚	Soy-simmered fish

saba no miso ni	さばのみそ煮	Mackerel stewed with soy-bean paste.
samma	さんま	Saury pike
sashimi	刺身	Very fresh raw fish served sliced thin on a bed of white radish with a saucer of soy sauce and horseradish. Eaten by dipping fish into soy sauce mixed with horseradish.
sawara	さわら	Spanish mackerel
shake	しゃけ	Salmon
shimesaba	しめさば	Mackerel marinated in vinegar.
shio-yaki	塩焼	Fish sprinkled with salt and broiled until crisp.
tako	たこ	Octopus
ten-jū	天重	Deep-fried prawns served over rice with sauce
teri-yaki	照り焼き	Fish basted in soy sauce and broiled
una-jū	うな重	Eel marinated in a slightly sweet soy sauce is charcoal-broiled and served over rice. Considered a delicacy.
yaki-zakana	焼き魚	Broiled fish

Sushi

aji	あじ	Horse mackerel
ama-ebi	甘えび	Sweet shrimp
anago	あなご	Conger eel
aoyagi	あおやぎ	Round clam
chirashi zushi	ちらし寿司	In chirashi zushi, a variety of seafood is arranged on the top of the rice and served in a bowl
ebi	えび	Shrimp
futo-maki	太巻	Big roll with egg and pickled vegetables
hamachi	はまち	Yellowtail
hirame	ひらめ	Flounder
hotate-gai	ほたて貝	Scallop
ika	いか	Squid
ikura	いくら	Salmon roe
kani	かに	Crab

kappa-maki	かっぱ巻	Cucumber roll
kariforunia-maki	カリフォルニア巻	California roll, containing crabmeat and avocado. This was invented in the U.S. but was re-exported to Japan and is gaining popularity there.
kazunoko	かずのこ	Herring roe
kohada	こはだ	Gizzard (shad)
maguro	まぐろ	Tuna
maki zushi	巻き寿司	Raw fish and vegetables or other morsels are rolled in sushi rice and wrapped in dried seaweed. Some popular varieties are listed here.
miru-gai	みる貝	Giant clam
nigiri zushi	にぎり寿司	The rice is formed into a bite-sized cake and topped with various raw or cooked fish. The various types are usually named after the fish, but not all are fish. Nigiri zushi is eaten by picking up the cakes with chopsticks or the fingers, dipping the fish side in soy sauce, and eating.
saba	さば	Mackerel
shake	しゃけ	Salmon
shinko-maki	新香巻	Shinko roll (shinko is a type of pickle)
sushi	寿司	Basically, sushi is rice, fish, and vegetables. The rice is delicately seasoned with vinegar, salt, and sugar. There are basically three types of sushi: nigiri, chirashi, and maki.
tai	たい	Red snapper
tako	たこ	Octopus
tamago	卵	Egg
tekka-maki	鉄火巻	Tuna roll
toro	とろ	Fatty tuna
uni	うに	Sea urchin on rice wrapped with seaweed

Vegetable Dishes

aemono	和えもの	Vegetables dressed with sauces
daigaku imo	大学いも	Fried yams in a sweet syrup

gobō	ごぼう	Burdock root
hōrenso	ほうれん草	Spinach
kabocha	かぼちゃ	Pumpkin
kimpira gobō	きんぴらごぼう	Carrots and burdock root, fried with soy sauce
kyūri	きゅうり	Cucumber
negi	ねぎ	Green onions
nimono	煮もの	Vegetables simmered in a soy- and sake-based sauce
oden	おでん	Often sold by street vendors at festivals and in parks, etc., this is vegetables, octopus, or eggs simmered in a soy fish stock
o-hitashi	おひたし	Boiled vegetables with soy sauce and dried shaved bonito or sesame seeds
renkon	れんこん	Lotus root
satoimo	さといも	Taro root
sumono	酢のもの	Vegetables seasoned with ginger
takenoko	たけのこ	Bamboo shoots
tempura	天ぷら	Vegetables, shrimp, or fish deep-fried in a light batter. Eaten by dipping into a thin sauce containing grated white radish.
tsukemono	漬物	Japanese pickles. Made from white radish, eggplant or other vegetables. Considered essential to the Japanese meal.
yasai itame	野菜いため	Stir-fried vegetables
yasai sarada	野菜サラダ	Vegetable salad

Egg Dishes

bēkon-eggu	ベーコン・エッグ	Bacon and eggs
chawan mushi	茶わんむし	Vegetables, shrimp, etc., steamed in egg custard
hamu-eggu	ハム・エッグ	Ham and eggs
medama-yaki	目玉焼	Fried eggs, sunny-side up
omuraisu	オムライス	Omelet with rice inside, often eaten with ketchup
omuretsu	オムレツ	Omelet
sukuramburu eggu	スクランブル・エッグ	Scrambled eggs
yude tamago	ゆで卵	Boiled eggs

Tōfu Dishes

Tōfu, also called bean curd, is a white, high-protein food with the consistency of soft gelatin.

agedashi dōfu	あげだしどうふ	Lightly fried plain tōfu dipped in soy sauce and grated ginger.
hiya-yakko	冷やっこ	Cold tōfu with soy sauce and grated ginger.
mābō dōfu	マーボーどうふ	Tōfu and ground pork in a spicy red sauce. Originally a Chinese dish.
tōfu no dengaku	とうふの田楽	Tōfu broiled on skewers and flavored with miso.
yu-dōfu	湯どうふ	Boiled tōfu

Rice Dishes

chāhan	チャーハン	Fried rice; includes vegetables and pork.
chimaki	ちまき	Sticky rice wrapped in bamboo.
gohan	ごはん	Steamed white rice
okayu	おかゆ	Rice porridge
onigiri	おにぎり	Triangular balls of rice with fish or vegetables inside and wrapped in a type of seaweed.
pan	パン	Bread, but usually rolls with a meal.

Soups

miso shiru	みそ汁	Miso soup. A thin broth containing tōfu, mushrooms, or other morsels in a soup flavored with miso or soy-bean paste. The morsels are taken out of the bowl and the soup is drunk straight from the bowl without a spoon.
suimono	すいもの	Soy sauce flavored soup, often including fish and tofu.
tonjiru	とん汁	Pork soup with vegetables.

Noodles

hiyamugi	ひやむぎ	Similar to sōmen, but thicker.
rāmen	ラーメン	Chinese noodles in broth, often with *chāshū* or roast pork. Broth is soy sauce, miso, or salt flavored.

soba	そば	Buckwheat noodles. Served in a broth like udon or, during the summer, cold on a bamboo mesh and called *zaru soba*.
sōmen	そうめん	Very thin wheat noodles, usually served cold with a tsuyu or thin sauce. Eaten in summer.
supagetti	スパゲッティ	Spaghetti. There are many interesting variations on this dish, notably spaghetti in soup, often with seafood.
udon	うどん	Wide flour noodles in broth. Can be lunch in a light broth or a full dinner called *nabe-yaki udon* when meat, chicken, egg, and vegetables are added.
yaki-soba	やきそば	Noodles fried with beef and cabbage, garnished with pickled ginger and vegetables.

Fruit

āmondo	アーモンド	Almonds
anzu	あんず／アプリコット	Apricot
banana	バナナ	Banana
budō	ぶどう	Grapes
gurēpufurūtsu	グレープフルーツ	Grapefruit
hoshi-budō	干しぶどう／レーズン	Raisins
ichigo	いちご	Strawberries
ichijiku	いちじく	Figs
kaki	柿	Persimmon
kiiui	キーウィ	Kiwi
kokonattsu	ココナッツ	Coconut
kuri	くり	Chestnuts
kurumi	くるみ	Walnuts
mango	マンゴ	Mango
meron	メロン	Melon
mikan	みかん	Tangerine (mandarin orange)
momo	桃	Peach
nashi	梨	Pear
orenji	オレンジ	Orange
painappuru	パイナップル	Pineapple
papaiya	パパイヤ	Papaya
piinattsu	ピーナッツ	Peanuts

purūn	プルーン	Prunes
remon	レモン	Lemon
ringo	りんご	Apple
sakurambo	さくらんぼ／チェリー	Cherry
suika	西瓜／スイカ	Watermelon

Dessert

aisukuriimu	アイスクリーム	Ice cream
appuru pai	アップルパイ	Apple pie
kēki	ケーキ	Cake
kōhii zeri	コーヒーゼリー	Coffee-flavored gelatin
kurēpu	クレープ	Crepes
purin	プリン	Caramel pudding
shābetto	シャーベット	Sherbert
wagashi	和菓子	Japanese sweets
yōkan	ようかん	Sweet bean paste jelly

Drinks

Alcoholic

bābon	バーボン	Bourbon
biiru	ビール	Beer
burandē	ブランデー	Brandy
chūhai	チューハイ	Shōchū mixed with soda water and flavored with lemon juice or other flavors.
kakuteru	カクテル	Cocktail
nama biiru	生ビール	Draft beer
nihonshu (sake) atsukan hiya	日本酒（酒） あつかん ひや	Sake, a wine brewed from rice. warmed sake cold sake
sake	酒	Rice wine
shampen	シャンペン	Champagne
shōchū	焼酎	Spirit distilled from potatoes
sukocchi	スコッチ	Scotch
uisukii	ウィスキー	Whisky
wain aka shiro roze	ワイン 赤 白 ロゼ	Wine Red White Rose

Nonalcoholic

aisu kōhii	アイスコーヒー	Iced coffee
aisu tii	アイスティー	Iced tea
gyū-nyū/miruku	牛乳／ミルク	Milk
jasumin cha	ジャスミン茶	Jasmine tea
jūsu	ジュース	Juice, but can also mean any soft drink.
kō-cha	紅茶	Black tea
kōhii	コーヒー	Coffee
kokoa	ココア	Hot chocolate
kōra	コーラ	Coca-Cola
miruku sēki	ミルクセーキ	Milk shake
miruku tii	ミルクティー	Tea with milk
nihon cha	日本茶	Japanese green tea
remon sukasshu	レモンスカッシュ	Carbonated lemon soft drink
remon tii	レモンティー	Tea with lemon
remonēdo	レモネード	Lemonade
ūron cha	ウーロン茶	Oolong tea

Tōkyō Essentials

PLANNING TOOLS, EXPERT INSIGHT,
GREAT CONTACTS

There are planners, and there are those who fly by the seat of their pants. We happily place ourselves among the planners. Our writers and editors try to anticipate all the issues you may face before and during any journey, and then they do their research. This section is the product of their efforts. Use it to get excited about your trip to Tōkyō, to inform your travel planning, or to guide you on the road should the seat of your pants start to feel threadbare.

GETTING STARTED

We're really proud of our Web site: Fodors. com, which is a great place to begin any journey. Scan Travel Wire for suggested itineraries, travel deals, restaurant and hotel openings, and other up-to-the-minute info. Check out Booking to research prices and book plane tickets, hotel rooms, rental cars, and vacation packages. Head to Talk for on-the-ground pointers from travelers who frequent our message boards. You can also link to loads of other travel-related resources.

▮ RESOURCES

ONLINE TRAVEL TOOLS

Cultural resources and travel-planning tools abound for the cybertraveler to Japan. Good first stops include the Web sites of Japan's three major English-language daily newspapers, the *Asahi Shimbun* (⊕ www.asahi.com), *Daily Yomiuri* (⊕ www.yomiuri.co.jp) the *Japan Times* (⊕ www.japantimes.co.jp).

For travel updates, visit the Web site of the Japan National Tourist Office (JNTO; ⊕www.jnto.go.jp). You'll also find a links page, which connects you to an amusing and random assortment of sites that somehow relate to Japan.

Online resources abound for information on traveling by public transportation. Visit Jorudan's invaluable "Japanese Transport Guide" (⊕www.jorudan.co.jp), which has a simple, uncluttered interface. You enter the name of the station from which you're departing and your destination, and the planner presents you with the travel time,

fare, and distance for all possible train and bus routes in and outside of Tōkyō. Japan Rail's sites are handy planning tools as well, and provide fare and ticket information. Both the JR East (⊕ www.jreast. co.jp) and the JR West (⊕ www.westjr.co. jp) sites will direct you to detailed information about the Japan Rail Pass (⇨ Train Tickets, *in* Booking Your Trip, *below*). For local info, RATP (⊕www.subwaynavigator. com), the French rail-transit authority, maintains a useful subway navigator, which includes the subway systems in Ōsaka, Tōkyō and Sapporo. The Metropolitan Government Web site (⊕ www.metro. tokyo.jp), incidentally, is an excellent source of information on sightseeing and current events in Tōkyō.

On the Web site of the Japan City Hotel Association (⊕ www.jcha.or.jp), you can search member hotels by location and price and make reservations online. Hotels Japan (⊕ www.hotelsjapan.com) is another online resource that lets you find and book discount lodging.

Japanese-Online (⊕ www.japanese-online. com) is a series of online language lessons that will help you pick up a bit of Japanese before your trip. (The site also, inexplicably, includes a sampling of typical Japanese junior high school math problems.) Kabuki for Everyone (⊕ http://park. org/Japan/Kabuki/kabuki.html) provides a comprehensive and accessible introduction to the dramatic form; on the site you'll find video clips of Kabuki performances, summaries of major plays, an audio archive of Kabuki sounds, and a bibliography for further reading. Finally, for fun, stop by the Web site of Tōkyō's Tsukiji Central Wholesale Market (⊕ www. tsukiji-market.or.jp)—where else online can you see tuna as big as cars?

ALL ABOUT TŌKYŌ

The Tōkyō Convention and Visitors Bureau (⊕ www.tcvb.or.jp) regularly updates details about the city's events, lodging, and more on its Web site. J Mode (⊕ www. jmode.com) offers up-to-date cultural and entertainment news. Japan Guide (⊕ www. japan-guide.com) contains a wealth of information on Tōkyō as well as listing vital resources, while the Web site Picture Tōkyō (⊕ www.picturetokyo.com) has well-cataloged facts, photos, and a whole lot more on the city.

Metropolis (⊕ http://metropolis.co.jp) and *Tōkyō Journal* (⊕ www.tokyo.to) are slick online magazines for the English expat community and will catch you up on the latest capital city goings-on—both have up-to-date arts, events, and dining listings.

Currency Conversion **Google** ⊕ www. google.com does currency conversion. Just type in the amount you want to convert and an explanation of how you want it converted (e.g., "14 Swiss francs in dollars"), and then voilá. **Oanda.com** ⊕ www.oanda.com also allows you to print out a handy table with the current day's conversion rates. **XE.com** ⊕ www.xe.com is a good currency conversion Web site.

Safety **Transportation Security Administration** (TSA) ⊕ www.tsa.gov

Time Zones **Timeanddate.com** ⊕ www. timeanddate.com/worldclock can help you figure out the correct time anywhere in the world.

Weather **Accuweather.com** ⊕ www. accuweather.com is an independent weather-forecasting service with especially good coverage of hurricanes. **Weather.com** ⊕ www. weather.com is the Web site for the Weather Channel.

Other Resources **CIA World Factbook** ⊕ www.odci.gov/cia/publications/factbook/index.html has profiles of every country in the world. It's a good source if you need some quick facts and figures.

VISITOR INFORMATION

For information before you travel, contact the Japan National Tourist Organization (JNTO). But when you arrive in Japan, make a point of dropping by one of the Tourist Information Centers (TIC). The centers advise on trips and have informa-

tion on popular tourist destinations and lodging (same- and subsequent-day bookings can be made for some area hotels at the JNTO center).

The TICs are independently run but Tōkyō's two main TICs are located in the JNTO headquaters and the Tōkyō Metropolitan Government building. Both are great places to get free maps and brochures. Plus, they have helpful, English-speaking staff. You can also find TICs at Narita International and Haneda airports. Many are open weekdays 9–5 and Saturday 9–noon; the JNTO center is open 9–5 every day except January 1. The list of TICs is too extensive (and some say unreliable) to list, so check out the Web site below.

The Asakusa Tourist Information Center, a joint venture of Metro, Asakusa, and neighborhood volunteers, is across from Kaminari-mon and has some English-speaking staff and plenty of maps and brochures; it's open daily 10–5.

INSPIRATION

Want to read up on your travel destination? Start with Pico Iyer's *The Lady and the Monk,* which will guide you through the stereotypical infatuation phases one can have with Japan and leave you with many insights. For an amusing account of the *gaijin* (foreigner) condition, try Will Ferguson's *Hokkaido Highway Blues: Hitchhiking Japan.*

For a visual introduction to Japan, see the Academy Award-winning picture, *Spirited Away* (2002), which is available in English and is a good example of the Japanese phenomenon anime. Both horror hits, *Ringu* (1998) and *Ju-on: The Grudge* (2003) are good representations of the Japan Horror genre and have American remakes, and first-time Tōkyō visitors will likely identify with Sofia Coppola's *Lost in Translation* (2003), about the alienation experienced by an American visitor. For more suggestions *see* Films & Literature *in* Understanding Tōkyō.

Two free weekly magazines, the *Tour Companion* and *Metropolis,* available at hotels, book and music stores, and some restaurants and cafés, feature up-to-date announcements of what's going on in the city. *Metropolis* is the better of the two because it breaks the listings down into separate sections for Art & Exhibitions, Movies, TV, Music, and After Dark.

A monthly magazine with listings similar to *Metropolis,* the *Tōkyō Journal* (¥600) is available at Narita Airport newsstands and at many bookstores that carry English-language books. The Friday edition of *The Japan Times,* a daily English-language newspaper, is yet another resource for entertainment reviews and schedules.

NTT (Japanese Telephone Corporation) can help you find information in English, such as telephone numbers, museum openings, and other information available from its databases. It's open weekdays 9–5.

Japan National Tourist Organization (JNTO)
Japan: ⊠ 10th Floor, Tōkyō Kotsu Kaikan Building, 2-10-1 Yurakucho, Chiyoda-ku, Tōkyō ☎ 03/3201-3331 Ⓜ Yūrakūchō and JR Yamanōte lines, Yūrakūchō. **United States:** ☎ 212/757-5640 in New York, 213/623-1952 in Los Angeles ⊕ www.jnto.go.jp. **Asakusa Tourist Information Center** ⊠ 2-18-9 Kaminari-mon, Taitō-ku ☎ 03/3842-5566 Ⓜ Ginza Line, Asakusa station (Exit 2).

Tourist Information Centers (TIC) **Tōkyō Metropolitan Government Head Office TIC** ⊠ 1st Floor, Tōkyō Metropolitan Government No.1 Building, 8-1 Nishi-Shinjuku 2-chome, Shinjuku-ku, Tōkyō ☎ 03/5321-3077 or 03/5321-3079 Ⓜ Tōei Ōedō line, Tōchōmaé station. **Narita Airport TIC** ⊠ 1st floor passenger terminal No. 2 ☎ 0476-34-6251 Ⓜ Keisei, Sobu/Narita and JR Rappid Airport lines, Airport Terminal 2 station. **Haneda Airport TIC** ⊠ 1st floor Big Bird Bldg. ☎ 03/5757-9345 Ⓜ Keikyu-Kuko and Tōkyō Monorail lines, Haneda Airport Terminal 1 station. **NTT** ☎ 0120/36-4463 toll-free.

GEAR

Because porters can be hard to find and baggage restrictions on international flights

are tight, pack light. What you pack depends more on the time of year than on any dress code. Pack as you would for any major American or European city. The big and tall, however, should weigh the importance of that extra pair of shoes or slacks against the fact that, despite the size of many locals these days, most clothing stores (especially for women) maintain a narrow status quo. At more expensive restaurants and nightclubs, men usually need to wear a jacket and tie. Wear conservative colors (blue, black, or gray) at business meetings. Casual clothes are fine for sightseeing. Jeans are as popular in Japan as they are in the United States and are perfectly acceptable for informal dining and sightseeing.

Although there are no strict dress codes for visiting temples and shrines, you will be out of place in shorts or immodest outfits. For sightseeing leave sandals and open-toe shoes behind; you'll need sturdy walking shoes for the gravel pathways that surround temples and fill parks—if not a long day of trudging up and down subway-station stairs. Make sure to bring comfortable clothing that isn't too tight to wear in traditional Japanese restaurants, where you may need to sit on tatami-mat floors. For beach and mountain resorts pack informal clothes for both day and evening wear.

∎ TIP→ **If you think that toe-revealing hole in your sock or run in the foot of your stocking will remain your own little secret, think again.**

Japanese do not wear shoes in private homes or in many temples or traditional inns. Having shoes you can quickly slip in and out of is also an advantage. Take some wool socks along to help you through those shoeless occasions in winter.

Dietary diversity abounds in Japan, but not without effort. Don't be surprised if accommodating waitstaff is at a loss for dish details—or why you need to know. Diners with allergies or aversions to shellfish and other seafood may want to consider packing with this in mind if a "set menu" is part of a package tour. Most lodgings provide a thermos of hot water and tea in

PACKING 101

Why do some people travel with a convoy of huge suitcases yet never have a thing to wear? How do others pack a duffel with a week's worth of outfits *and* supplies for every contingency? We realize that packing is a matter of style, but there's a lot to be said for traveling light. These tips help fight the battle of the bulging bag.

MAKE A LIST. In a recent Fodor's survey, 29% of respondents said they make lists (and often pack) a week before a trip. You can use your list to pack and to repack at the end of your trip. It can also serve as record of the contents of your suitcase—in case it disappears in transit.

THINK IT THROUGH. What's the weather like? Is this a business trip? A cruise? Going abroad? In some places dress may be more or less conservative than you're used to. As you create your itinerary, note outfits next to each activity (don't forget accessories).

EDIT YOUR WARDROBE. Plan to wear everything twice (better yet, thrice) and to do laundry along the way. Stick to one basic look—urban chic, sporty casual, etc. Build around one or two neutrals and an accent (e.g., black, white, and olive green). Women can freshen looks by changing scarves or jewelry. For a week's trip, you can look smashing with three bottoms, four or five tops, a sweater, and a jacket.

BE PRACTICAL. Put comfortable shoes atop your list. (Did we need to say this?) Pack lightweight, wrinkle-resistent, compact, washable items. (Or this?) Stack and roll clothes, so they'll wrinkle less. Unless you're on a guided tour or a cruise, select luggage you can readily carry. Porters, like good butlers, are hard to find these days.

CHECK WEIGHT AND SIZE LIMITATIONS. In the United States you may be charged extra for checked bags weighing more than 50 pounds. Abroad some airlines don't allow you to check bags over 60 to 70 pounds, or they charge outrageous fees for every excess pound—or bag. Carry-on size limitations can be stringent, too.

CHECK CARRY-ON RESTRICTIONS. Research restrictions with the TSA. Rules vary abroad, so check them with your airline if you're traveling overseas on a foreign carrier. Consider packing all but essentials (travel documents, prescription meds, wallet) in checked luggage. This leads to a "pack only what you can afford to lose" approach that might help you streamline.

RETHINK VALUABLES. On U.S. flights, airlines are liable for only about $2,800 per person for bags. On international flights, the liability limit is around $635 per bag. But items like computers, cameras, and jewelry aren't covered, and as gadgetry can go on and off the list of carry-on no-no's, you can't count on keeping things safe by keeping them close. Although comprehensive travel policies may cover luggage, the liability limit is often a pittance. Your home-owner's policy may cover you sufficiently when you travel—or not.

LOCK IT UP. If you must pack valuables, use TSA-approved locks (about $10) that can be unlocked by all U.S. security personnel.

TAG IT. Always tag your luggage; use your business address if you don't want people to know your home address. Put the same information (and a copy of your itinerary) inside your luggage, too.

REPORT PROBLEMS IMMEDIATELY. If your bags—or things in them—are damaged or go astray, file a written claim with your airline *before leaving the airport*. If the airline is at fault, it may give you money for essentials until your luggage arrives. Most lost bags are found within 48 hours, so alert the airline to your whereabouts for two or three days. If your bag was opened for security reasons in the States and something is missing, file a claim with the TSA.

every room, but for coffee you may have to call room service (which can be expensive), buy coffee in a can from a vending machine, buy instant coffee at a 24-hour convenience store, or find the nearest Starbucks or local equivalent, of which Tōkyō has many. Why not bring along packets of instant coffee, as a precaution?

When it comes to medications, Japan can be a stickler. Even narcotic products sold over the counter in the U.S., such as a Vicks Inhaler, are technically not allowed through customs. And you may find that their counterparts in Japan are less than adequate. No more than a month's supply of prescription drugs, two months of non-prescription, and four months of vitamins and supplements are allowed per passenger. While Japan is no stranger to pornography, such media not meeting government standards are also forbidden. Sunglasses, sunscreen lotions, and hats are readily available, and these days they're not much more expensive in Japan. It's a good idea to carry a couple of plastic bags to protect your camera and clothes during sudden cloudbursts.

Take along small gift items, such as scarves or perfume sachets, to thank hosts (on both business and pleasure trips), whether you've been invited to their home or out to a restaurant.

PASSPORTS & VISAS

There are no passport or visa peculiarities for people traveling to Japan; children need the same documentation as adults. Though it may not be required, it's a good idea to have documentation on hand regarding the relationship between you and the child as well as permission for the child's travel from the parent(s) or legal guardian if they are not present. Having such documentation with you will only facilitate your entry and departure.

Visitors from the United States with passports valid for more than 90 days from their time of arrival can stay in Japan for 90 days; no visa is required so long as your visit does not include paid activities. **Info** For details on diplomatic, working, general (student, trainee or cultural), and other visas contact your local Japanese embassy or consulate. General information is also available at: ⊕ www.mofa.go.jp.

PASSPORTS

We're always surprised at how few Americans have passports—only 25% at this writing. This number is expected to grow in coming years, when it becomes impossible to re-enter the United States from trips to neighboring Canada or Mexico without one. Remember this: A passport verifies both your identity and nationality—a great reason to have one.

U.S. passports are valid for 10 years. You must apply in person if you're getting a passport for the first time; if your previous passport was lost, stolen, or damaged; or if your previous passport has expired and was issued more than 15 years ago or when you were under 16. All children under 18 must appear in person to apply for or renew a passport. Both parents must accompany any child under 14 (or send a notarized statement with their permission) and provide proof of their relationship to the child.

■ TIP→ Before your trip, make two copies of your passport's data page (one for someone at home and another for you to carry separately). Or scan the page and e-mail it to someone at home and/or yourself.

There are 13 regional passport offices, as well as 7,000 passport acceptance facilities in post offices, public libraries, and other governmental offices. If you're renewing a passport, you can do so by mail. Forms are available at passport acceptance facilities and online.

The cost to apply for a new passport is $97 for adults, $82 for children under 16; renewals are $67. Allow six weeks for processing, both for first-time passports and renewals. For an expediting fee of $60 you can reduce this time to about two weeks. If your trip is less than two weeks away, you can get a passport even more rapidly by going to a passport office with the necessary documentation. Private expediters can get things done in as little as 48 hours, but charge hefty fees for their services.

VISAS

A visa is essentially formal permission to enter a country. Visas allow countries to keep track of you and other visitors—and generate revenue (from application fees). You *always* need a visa to enter a foreign country; however, many countries routinely issue tourist visas on arrival, particularly to U.S. citizens. When your passport is stamped or scanned in the immigration line, you're actually being issued a visa. Sometimes you have to stand in a separate line and pay a small fee to get your stamp before going through immigration, but you can still do this at the airport on arrival. Getting a visa isn't always that easy. Some countries require that you arrange for one in advance of your trip. There's usually—but not always—a fee involved, and said fee may be nominal ($10 or less) or substantial ($100 or more).

If you must apply for a visa in advance, you can usually do it in person or by mail. When you apply by mail, you send your passport to a designated consulate, where your passport will be examined and the visa issued. Expediters—usually the same ones who handle expedited passport applications—can do all the work of obtaining your visa for you; however, there's always an additional cost (often more than $50 per visa).

Most visas limit you to a single trip—basically during the actual dates of your planned vacation. Other visas allow you to visit as many times as you wish for a specific period of time. Remember that requirements change, sometimes at the drop of a hat, and the burden is on you to make sure that you have the appropriate visas. Otherwise, you'll be turned away at the airport or, worse, deported after you arrive in the country. No company or travel insurer gives refunds if your travel plans are disrupted because you didn't have the correct visa.

U.S. Passport Information U.S. Department of State ☎ 877/487-2778 ⊕ http://travel.state.gov/passport.

U.S. Passport & Visa Expediters A. Briggs Passport & Visa Expediters ☎ 800/806-0581 or 202/464-3000 ⊕ www.abriggs.com. **American Passport Express** ☎ 800/455-5166 or 603/559-9888 ⊕ www.americanpassport.com. **Passport Express** ☎ 800/362-8196 or 401/272-4612 ⊕ www.passportexpress.com. **Travel Document Systems** ☎ 800/874-5100 or 202/638-3800 ⊕ www.traveldocs.com. **Travel the World Visas** ☎ 866/886-8472 or 301/495-7700 ⊕ www.world-visa.com.

SHOTS & MEDICATIONS

Japan has no issues with serious contagious diseases, but it is worth noting that measles, mumps and rubella (MMR) vaccinations have not been required for a decade. As a result, these mostly once-in-a-lifetime childhood ailments can ebb and flow as minor pandemics (most recently, the mumps in 2006). For more information *see* Health *under* On the Ground in Tōkyō, *below.*

Health Warnings National Centers for Disease Control & Prevention (CDC) ☎ 877/394-8747 international travelers' health line ⊕ www.cdc.gov/travel. **World Health Organization** (WHO) ⊕ www.who.int.

TRIP INSURANCE

What kind of coverage do you honestly need? Do you even need trip insurance at all? Take a deep breath and read on.

We believe that comprehensive trip insurance is especially valuable if you're booking a very expensive or complicated trip (particularly to an isolated region) or if you're booking far in advance. Who knows what could happen six months down the road? But whether or not you get insurance has more to do with how comfortable you are assuming all that risk yourself.

■ TIP→ If you travel a lot internationally—particularly to developing nations—refer to the CDC's *Health Information for International Travel* (aka Traveler's Health Yellow Book). Info from it is posted on the CDC Web site (www.cdc.gov/travel/yb), or you can buy a copy from your local bookstore for $24.95.

Trip Insurance Resources

INSURANCE COMPARISON SITES		
Insure My Trip.com		⊕ www.insuremytrip.com
Square Mouth.com		⊕ www.quotetravelinsurance.com
COMPREHENSIVE TRAVEL INSURERS		
Access America	☎ 866/807-3982	⊕ www.accessamerica.com
CSA Travel Protection	☎ 800/873-9855	⊕ www.csatravelprotection.com
HTH Worldwide	☎ 610/254-8700 or 888/243-2358	⊕ www.hthworldwide.com
Travelex Insurance	☎ 888/457-4602	⊕ www.travelex-insurance.com
Travel Guard International	☎ 715/345-0505 or 800/826-4919	⊕ www.travelguard.com
Travel Insured International	☎ 800/243-3174	⊕ www.travelinsured.com
MEDICAL-ONLY INSURERS		
International Medical Group	☎ 800/628-4664	⊕ www.imglobal.com
International SOS	☎ 215/942-8000 or 713/521-7611	⊕ www.internationalsos.com
Wallach & Company	☎ 800/237-6615 or 504/687-3166	⊕ www.wallach.com

Comprehensive travel policies typically cover trip-cancellation and interruption, letting you cancel or cut your trip short because of a personal emergency, illness, or, in some cases, acts of terrorism in your destination. Such policies also cover evacuation and medical care. Some also cover you for trip delays because of bad weather or mechanical problems as well as for lost or delayed baggage. Another type of coverage to look for is financial default—that is, when your trip is disrupted because a tour operator, airline, or cruise line goes out of business. Generally you must buy this when you book your trip or shortly thereafter, and it's only available to you if your operator isn't on a list of excluded companies.

If you're going abroad, consider buying medical-only coverage at the very least. Neither Medicare nor some private insurers cover medical expenses anywhere outside of the United States besides Mexico and Canada (including time aboard a cruise ship, even if it leaves from a U.S. port). Medical-only policies typically reimburse you for medical care (excluding that related to pre-existing conditions) and hospitalization abroad, and provide for evacuation. You still have to pay the bills and await reimbursement from the insurer, though.

■ TIP→ Japan does not provide foreigners with free outpatient or other medical services. In fact, only partial coverage state insurance is available (it's mandatory) after you've been in the country a year. Before then, you're on your own.

Expect comprehensive travel insurance policies to cost about 4% to 7% of the total price of your trip (it's more like 12% if you're over age 70). A medical-only policy may or may not be cheaper than a comprehensive policy. Always read the fine print of your policy to make sure that you are covered for the risks that are of most concern to you. Compare several policies to make sure you're getting the best price and range of coverage available.

■ TIP→ OK. You know you can save a bundle on trips to warm-weather destinations by traveling in rainy season. But there's also a chance that a severe storm will disrupt your plans. The solution? Look for hotels and resorts that offer storm/hurricane guarantees. Although they rarely allow refunds, most guarantees do let you rebook later if a storm strikes.

BOOKING YOUR TRIP

Unless your cousin is a travel agent, you're probably among the millions of people who make most of their travel arrangements online. But have you ever wondered just what the differences are between an online travel agent (a Web site through which you make reservations instead of going directly to the airline, hotel, or car-rental company), a discounter (a firm that does a high volume of business with a hotel chain or airline and accordingly gets good prices), a wholesaler (one that makes cheap reservations in bulk and then re-sells them to people like you), and an aggregator (one that compares all the offerings so you don't have to)? Is it truly better to book directly on an airline or hotel Web site? And when does a real live travel agent come in handy?

ONLINE

You really have to shop around. A travel wholesaler such as Hotels.com or Hotel-Club.net can be a source of good rates, as can discounters such as Hotwire or Priceline, particularly if you can bid for your hotel room or airfare. Indeed, such sites sometimes have deals that are unavailable elsewhere. They do, however, tend to work only with hotel chains (which makes them just plain useless for getting hotel reservations outside of major cities) or big airlines (so that often leaves out upstarts like jetBlue and some foreign carriers like Air India). Also, with discounters and wholesalers you must generally prepay, and everything is nonrefundable. And before you fork over the dough, be sure to check the terms and conditions, so you know what a given company will do for you if there's a problem and what you'll have to deal with on your own.

TIP➡ To be absolutely sure everything was processed correctly, confirm reservations made through online travel agents, discounters, and wholesalers directly with your hotel before leaving home.

Booking engines like Expedia, Travelocity, and Orbitz are actually travel agents, albeit high-volume, online ones. And airline travel packagers like American Airlines Vacations and Virgin Vacations—well, they're travel agents, too. But they may still not work with all the world's hotels.

An aggregator site will search many sites and pull the best prices for airfares, hotels, and rental cars. Most aggregators compare the major sites such as Expedia, Travelocity, and Orbitz; some also look at airline Web sites, though rarely the sites of smaller budget airlines. Some aggregators also compare other travel products, including complex packages—sometimes you can get the best overall deal by booking an air-and-hotel package.

WITH A TRAVEL AGENT

If you use an agent—brick-and-mortar or virtual—you'll pay a fee for the service. And know that the service you get from some online agents isn't comprehensive. For example Expedia and Travelocity don't search for prices on budget airlines like jetBlue, Southwest, or small foreign carriers. That said, some agents (online or not) do have access to fares that are difficult to find otherwise, and the savings can more than make up for any surcharge.

A knowledgeable travel agent can be a godsend if you're booking a cruise, a package trip that's not available to you directly, an air pass, or a complicated itinerary including several overseas flights. What's more, travel agents that specialize in a destination may have exclusive access to certain deals and insider information on things such as charter flights. Agents who specialize in types of travelers (senior citizens, gays and lesbians, naturists) or types of trips (cruises, luxury travel, safaris) can also be invaluable.

A top-notch agent planning your trip to Russia will make sure you get the correct visa application and complete it on time;

Online Booking Resources

AGGREGATORS		
Kayak	www.kayak.com	looks at cruises and vacation packages.
Mobissimo	www.mobissimo.com	
Qixo	www.qixo.com	compares cruises, vacation packages, and even travel insurance
Sidestep	www.sidestep.com	compares vacation packages and lists travel deals.
Travelgrove	www.travelgrove.com	compares cruises and vacation packages
BOOKING ENGINES		
Cheap Tickets	www.cheaptickets.com	discounter
Expedia	www.expedia.com	large online agency that charges a booking fee for airline tickets
Hotwire	www.hotwire.com	discounter
lastminute.com	www.lastminute.com	specializes in last-minute travel; the main site is for the U.K., but it has a link to a U.S. site
Luxury Link	www.luxurylink.com	has auctions (surprisingly good deals) as well as offers on the high-end side of travel
Onetravel.com	www.onetravel.com	discounter for hotels, car rentals, airfares, and packages
Orbitz	www.orbitz.com	charges a booking fee for airline tickets, but gives a clear breakdown of fees and taxes before you book
Priceline.com	www.priceline.com	discounter that also allows bidding
Travel.com	www.travel.com	allows you to compare its rates with those of other booking engines
Travelocity	www.travelocity.com	charges a booking fee for airline tickets, but promises good problem resolution
ONLINE ACCOMMODATIONS		
Hotelbook.com	www.hotelbook.com	focuses on independent hotels worldwide
Hotel Club	www.hotelclub.net	good for major cities worldwide
Hotels.com	www.hotels.com	big Expedia-owned wholesaler that offers rooms in hotels all over the world
Quikbook	www.quikbook.com	offers "pay when you stay" reservations that allow you to settle your bill when you check out, not when you book
OTHER RESOURCES		
Bidding For Travel	www.biddingfortravel.com	good place to figure out what you can get and for how much before you start bidding on, say, Priceline

the one booking your cruise may get you a cabin upgrade or arrange to have bottle of champagne chilling in your cabin when you embark. And complain about the surcharges all you like, but when things don't work out the way you'd hoped, it's nice to have an agent to put things right.

■ TIP➡ Remember that Expedia, Travelocity, and Orbitz are travel agents, not just booking engines. To resolve any problems with a reservation made through these companies, contact them first.

Travel agents abound in Tōkyō as much as any other major tourist destination. The main advantage to using local agents is that thay can offer foreign travelers deals and options that non-Japanese speakers here or abroad would be hard pressed to do on their own.

Agent Resources American Society of Travel Agents ☎ 703/739–2782 ⊕ www.travelsense. org.

Tōkyō Travel Agents Air1Travel ✉ In Japan: Shinichi Bldg., Suite 602, 2-8 Yotsuya, Shinjuku-ku, Tōkyō ☎ 03/5919–0199 ⊕ www. airltravel.com ✉ In the US: 350 5th Ave., Suite 3304, New York ☎ 212/557–0268 ⊕ www.airltravel.com.

▌ AIRLINE TICKETS

Most domestic airline tickets are electronic; international tickets may be either electronic or paper. With an e-ticket the only thing you receive is an e-mailed receipt citing your itinerary and reservation and ticket numbers. The greatest advantage of an e-ticket is that if you lose your receipt, you can simply print out another copy or ask the airline to do it for you at check-in. You usually pay a surcharge (up to $50) to get a paper ticket, if you can get one at all. The sole advantage of a paper ticket is that it may be easier to endorse over to another airline if your flight is canceled.

■ TIP➡ Discount air passes that let you travel economically in a country or region must often be purchased before you leave. In some cases you can only get them through a travel agent.

10 WAYS TO SAVE

1. Nonrefundable is best. If saving money is more important than flexibility, then non-refundable tickets work. Remember, you'll pay dearly (as much as $100) if you change your plans.

2. Comparison shop. Web sites and travel agents can have different arrangements with the airlines and offer different prices for exactly the same flights.

3. Beware those prices. Many airline Web sites—and most ads—show prices *without* taxes and surcharges. Don't buy until you know the full price.

4. Stay loyal. Stick with one or two frequent-flier programs. You'll rack up free trips faster and you'll accumulate more quickly the perks that make trips easier, i.e., a special reservations number, early boarding, access to upgrades, and more roomy economy-class seating.

5. Watch those ticketing fees. Surcharges are usually added when you buy your ticket anywhere but on an airline Web site. (That includes by phone—even if you call the airline directly—and paper tickets regardless of how you book.)

6. Check early and often. Start looking for cheap fares up to a year in advance. Keep looking till you find a price you like.

7. Don't work alone. Some Web sites have tracking features that will e-mail you immediately when good deals are posted.

8. Jump on the good deals. Waiting even a few minutes might mean paying more.

9. Be flexible. Look for departures on Tuesday, Wednesday, and Thursday, typically the cheapest days to travel. And check on prices for departures at different times and to and from alternative airports.

10. Weigh your options. What you get can be as important as what you save. A cheaper flight might have a long layover, or it might land at a secondary airport, where your ground transportation costs might be higher.

Car Rental Resources

AUTOMOBILE ASSOCIATIONS		
U.S.: American Automobile Association (AAA)	☎ 315/797-5000	⊕ www.aaa.com; most contact with the organization is through state and regional members.
National Automobile Club	☎ 650/294-7000	⊕ www.thenac.com; membership is open to California residents only.
MAJOR AGENCIES		
Alamo	☎ 800/522-9696	⊕ www.alamo.com
Avis	☎ 800/331-1084	⊕ www.avis.com
Budget	☎ 800/472-3325	⊕ www.budget.com
Hertz	☎ 800/654-3001	⊕ www.hertz.com
National Car Rental	☎ 800/227-7368	⊕ www.nationalcar.com
LOCAL AGENCIES		
Ekiren—JR Tōkyō Station Branch	☎ 03/3215-1717	⊕ www.ekiren.co.jp
Nippon Rentacar— JR Tōkyō Station Branch	☎ 03/3271-6643	⊕ www.nipponrentacar.co.jp
Japan Europcar Narita Airport Branch (at the Mazda counter)	☎ 476/30-3318	⊕ www.europcar.jp

Both of Japan's major carriers offer reduced prices for flights within the country, though tickets must be booked outside Japan. JAL offers the Yōkoso Japan Airpass while ANA has the Visit Japan Fare. **Air Pass Info All Asia Pass** ☎ 800/233-2742 Cathay Pacific ⊕ www.cathay-usa.com or www.cathay.ca. **Visit Japan Fare** ☎ 800/235-9262 All Nippon Airways ⊕ www.anaskyweb.com or www.ana.co.jp. **Yōkoso Japan Airpass** ☎ 800/525-3663 Japan Airlines ⊕ www.jal.co.jp.

▌ RENTAL CARS

When you reserve a car, ask about cancellation penalties, taxes, drop-off charges (if you're planning to pick up the car in one city and leave it in another), and surcharges (for being under or over a certain age, for additional drivers, or for driving across state or country borders or beyond a specific distance from your point of rental). All these things can add substantially to your costs. Request car seats and extras such as GPS when you book.

Rates are sometimes—but not always—better if you book in advance or reserve through a rental agency's Web site. There are other reasons to book ahead, though: for popular destinations, during busy times of the year, or to ensure that you get certain types of cars.

▌ TIP→ Make sure that a confirmed reservation guarantees you a car. Agencies sometimes overbook, particularly for busy weekends and holiday periods.

Congestion, the infrequency of road signs in English, and the difficulty—say nothing of the expense—of parking make driving in Tōkyō impractical. And if you think a car will get you somewhere faster within the city than public transportation, you're wrong. If you decide to rent a car be aware that central business offices close at 6 PM or 7 PM, and that you're not guaranteed to reach anybody who can deal with you in English.

As with other travel arrangements, plan well in advance if renting during peak seasons around New Year's, Golden Week (early May) and Obon (mid August)—or avoid it altogether. Expect most car rental agencies to be booked solid at least two months ahead of these seasons. Make your reservation before you come, and budget an extra hour or so when returning a car to an airport you're departing from; it will likely include a shuttle ride from the lot to the terminal. With taxes, the cost of a mid-size sedan is about ¥12,000 ($110) per day with considerably better weekly rates. You'll have a limited selection of newer brand-name automatic makes and models with AC such as Toyotas, Hondas, and Nissans. Minivans may also be available and note that opting for a "compact" model may leave you with even less room than expected. Most agencies require renters to be at least 25 years old and have an International Driver's Permit (IDP), which can be used only in conjunction with a valid driver's license. Check the AAA Web site for more info as well as for IDPs ($10) themselves.

You can hire large and comfortable chauffeured cars (the Japanese call them *haiya*) for about ¥5,000 ($46) per hour for a midsize car, up to ¥18,000 ($164) per hour for a Cadillac limousine. The Imperial, Okura, and Palace hotels also have limousine services.

By law, a car seat must be installed if there is a child under six. Child seats generally cost about ¥500 a day, and must be ordered at the time of reservation.

CAR-RENTAL INSURANCE

Everyone who rents a car wonders whether the insurance that the rental companies offer is worth the expense. No one—including us—has a simple answer. It all depends on how much regular insurance you have, how comfortable you are with risk, and whether or not money is an issue.

If you own a car, your personal auto insurance may cover a rental to some degree, though not all policies protect you abroad; always read your policy's fine print. If you don't have auto insurance, then seriously consider buying the collision- or loss-damage waiver (CDW or LDW) from the car-rental company, which eliminates your liability for damage to the car. Some credit cards offer CDW coverage, but it's usually supplemental to your own insurance and rarely covers SUVs, minivans, luxury models, and the like. If your coverage is secondary, you may still be liable for loss-of-use costs from the car-rental company. Credit-card insurance is not valid unless you use that card for *all* transactions, from reserving to paying the final bill.

■ TIP→ Diners Club offers primary CDW coverage on all rentals reserved and paid for with the card. This means that Diners Club's company—not your own car insurance—pays in case of an accident. It *doesn't* mean your car-insurance company won't raise your rates once it discovers you had an accident.

Some countries require you to purchase CDW coverage or require car-rental companies to include it in quoted rates. Ask your rental company about issues like these in Tōkyō. In most cases it's cheaper to add a supplemental CDW plan to your comprehensive travel-insurance policy (⇨ Trip Insurance *in* Getting Started, *above*) than to purchase it from a rental company. That said, you don't want to pay for a supplement if you're required to buy insurance from the rental company.

■ TIP→ You can decline the insurance from the rental company and purchase it through a third-party provider such as Travel Guard (www.travelguard.com)—$9 per day for $35,000 of coverage. That's sometimes just under half the price of the CDW offered by some car-rental companies.

■ TRAIN TICKETS

If you plan to travel by rail, get a Japan Rail Pass, which offers unlimited travel on Japan Railways (JR) trains and on buses operated by Japan Rail. They aren't valid on the overnight trains or the bullet trains. You can purchase one-, two-, or three-week passes. A one-week pass is less expensive than a regular round-trip ticket from Tōkyō to Kyōto on the Shinkansen.

■ TIP→ **You cannot buy a Japan Rail Pass in Japan. You must obtain a pass voucher prior to your departure and it must be used within three months of purchase.** The pass is available only to people with tourist visas, as opposed to business, student, and diplomatic visas.

Japan Rail Passes are available in coach class and first class (Green Car), and as the difference in price between the two is relatively small, it's worth the splurge for first class, for real luxury, especially on the Shinkansen. A one-week pass costs ¥28,300 coach class, ¥37,800 first class; a two-week pass costs ¥45,100 coach class, ¥61,200 first class; and a three-week pass costs ¥57,700 coach class, ¥79,600 first class. Travelers under 18 pay lower rates. The pass pays for itself after one Tōkyō–Kyōto round-trip Shinkansen ride. Contact a travel agent or the Japan Railways Group to purchase the pass. For more information on train travel *see* By Train, *below.*

About the Pass **Japan Railways Group** ⊠ New York ☎ 212/332-8686 ⊕ www. japanrailpass.net.

Buying a Pass **Japan Airlines** (JAL) ⊠ 655 5th Ave., New York, NY 10022 USA ☎ 212/838-4400. **Japan Travel Bureau** (JTB) ⊠ 810 7th Ave., 34th fl., New York, NY 10019 ☎ 212/698-4900 or 800/223-6104. **Nippon Travel Agency** (NTA) ⊠ 111 Pavonia Ave., Suite 317, Jersey City, NJ 07310 ☎ 201/420-6000 or 800/682-7872.

▌ VACATION PACKAGES

Packages *are not* guided excursions. Packages combine airfare, accommodations, and perhaps a rental car or other extras (theater tickets, guided excursions, boat trips, reserved entry to popular museums, transit passes), but they let you do your own thing. During busy periods packages may be your only option, as flights and rooms may be sold out otherwise. Packages will definitely save you time. They can

also save you money, particularly in peak seasons, but—and this is a really big "but"—you should price each part of the package separately to be sure. And be aware that prices advertised on Web sites and in newspapers rarely include service charges or taxes, which can up your costs by hundreds of dollars.

■ TIP→ **Some packages and cruises are sold only through travel agents. Don't always assume that you can get the best deal by booking everything yourself.** Each year consumers are stranded or lose their money when packagers—even large ones with excellent reputations—go out of business. How can you protect yourself? First, always pay with a credit card; if you have a problem, your credit-card company may help you resolve it. Second, buy trip insurance that covers default. Third, choose a company that belongs to the United States Tour Operators Association, whose members must set aside funds to cover defaults. Finally, choose a company that also participates in the Tour Operator Program of the American Society of Travel Agents (ASTA), which will act as mediator in any disputes. You can also check on the tour operator's reputation among travelers by posting an inquiry on one of the Fodors.com forums.

Organizations **American Society of Travel Agents** (ASTA) ☎ 703/739-2782 or 800/965-2782 ⊕ www.astanet.com. **United States Tour Operators Association** (USTOA) ☎ 212/599-6599 ⊕ www.ustoa.com.

■ TIP→ **Local tourism boards can provide information about lesser-known and small-niche operators that sell packages to only a few destinations.**

▌ GUIDED TOURS

Guided tours are a good option when you don't want to do it all yourself. You travel along with a group (sometimes large, sometimes small), stay in prebooked hotels, eat with your fellow travelers (the cost of meals sometimes included in the price of your tour, sometimes not), and follow a schedule. But not all guided tours are an if-it's-Tuesday-this-must-be-Belgium experience. A knowledgeable guide can take you places that you might never discover on your own, and you may be pushed to see more than you would have otherwise. Tours aren't for everyone, but they can be just the thing for trips to places where making travel arrangements is difficult or time-consuming (particularly when you don't speak the language). Whenever you book a guided tour, find out what's included and what isn't. A "land-only" tour includes all your travel (by bus, in most cases) in the destination, but not necessarily your flights to and from or even within it. Also, in most cases prices in tour brochures don't include fees and taxes. Remember to tip your guide (in cash) at the end of the tour.

Nippon Travel Agency America has theme-focused packages, for Tōkyō alone or in conjunction with Kyōto and Nara as well as an á la carte menu for piecing together custom tours. Travel Oriented offers a variety of package tours to Tōkyō and other Japan destinations. JTB USA has branch offices throughout the U.S. including New York, Chicago, and San Francisco that offer their own five-day package deals to Tōkyō at rock-bottom prices.

Recommended Companies Nippon Travel Agency America ✉ 1 Harmon Plaza, Secaucus, NJ ☎ 800/682-7872 ⊕ www.japanvacation.net. **Travel Oriented** ✉ 15490

S. Western Ave., Gardena, CA ☎ 800/984-8728 ⊕ www.japandeluxetour.com. **JTB USA** ☎ 800/235-3523 in New York, 800 669-5824 in Chicago, 800/882-3884 in San Francisco ⊕ www.jtbusa.com.

▌CRUISES

Many major cruise lines have ships that make stops in Japan's various ports. Cruise Lines makes stops in Tōkyō and Okinawa. Princess Cruises offers port-of-call excursions with day trips in popular Tōkyō and Yōkōhama destinations. Regent Seven Seas Cruises offers occasional stops in Yokohama with overnights in traditional Japanese inns and scenic excursions to nearby onsen, Mount Fuji and more. Cunard Cruises's *Queen Elizabeth* stops in Yokohama and Osaka. Holland America Line offers cruises from Seattle (WA), with extensive day and overnight excursions in Tōkyō.

Cruise Lines Crystal Cruises ☎ 310/785-9300 or 800/446-6620 ⊕ www.crystalcruises.com. **Princess Cruises** ☎ 661/753-0000 or 800/774-6237 ⊕ www.princess.com. **Windstar Cruises** ☎ 206/281-3535 or 800/258-7245 ⊕ www.windstarcruises.com. **Regent Seven Seas** ☎ 877/505-5370 ⊕ www.rssc.com. **Cunard Cruises** ☎ 800/728-6273 ⊕ www.cunard.com. **Holland America Line** ☎ 877/724-5425 ⊕ www.hollandamerica.com.

TRANSPORTATION

Tōkyō is densely packed into 23 municipal wards each with their own distinct neighborhoods. At the heart of the city is the Imperial Palace district near Otemachi and Tōkyō train stations, a major hub of the city's public transportation system. From here, it is relatively easy to plot courses to famed areas such as Ueno and Asakusa to the northeast, east to Tsukiji or Tōkyō Disney Resort, Roppongi in the southwest and westward to Shibuya and Shinjuku. The efficient and user-friendly train and subway systems connect them all and are the best way to get around. With myriad major thoroughfares and byways that are often neither parallel nor perpendicular to one another, proximity to train stations or other major landmarks are relied upon in Tōkyō far more than street names and addresses.

■ TIP→ **Ask the local tourist board about hotel and local transportation packages that include tickets to major museum exhibits or other special events.**

■ BY AIR

Flying time to Tōkyō is 13¾ hours from New York, 12¾ hours from Chicago, 9½ hours from Los Angeles. Japan Airlines' GPS systems allow a more direct routing, which reduces its flight times by about 30 minutes. Your trip east, because of tailwinds, will be about 45 minutes shorter.

■ TIP→ **If you travel frequently, look into the TSA's Registered Traveler program. The program, which is still being tested in several U.S. airports, is designed to cut down on gridlock at security checkpoints by allowing pre-screened travelers to pass quickly through kiosks that scan an iris and/or a fingerprint. How sci-fi is that?**

You can fly nonstop to Tōkyō from Chicago, Detroit, New York, Los Angeles, San Francisco, Portland (OR), Seattle, Minneapolis, and Washington D.C. Because of the distance, fares to Japan from the United States tend to be expensive, usually between $900 and $1,200 for a seat in coach. But it's possible to get a round trip ticket for as low as $700 from a discount travel Web site, depending on the time of year.

Airlines & Airports Airline and Airport Links.com ⊕ www.airlineandairportlinks.com has links to many of the world's airlines and airports.

Airline Security Issues Transportation Security Administration ⊕ www.tsa.gov has answers for almost every question that might come up.

AIRPORTS

Tōkyō has two airports, Narita (NRT) and Haneda (HND). Narita, officially the New Tōkyō International Airport in Narita, is the major gateway to Japan, serving all international flights, except those operated by Taiwan's China Airways, which berths at Haneda. Narita is 80 km (50 mi) northeast of Tōkyō and has two fairly well-developed terminals, plus a central building of shops and restaurants. Traffic in and out of the airport is high, especially in December and August, when millions of Japanese take holidays abroad. Customs clearance delays of an hour or more are not uncommon.

Haneda is just 20 km (12.5 mi) from Tōkyō and despite having been relegated to mainly domestic flights after Narita opened in 1978, it is Japan's biggest and busiest airport and one of the five busiest in the world. In addition to an array of restaurants and other amenities, its Bird View platforms are open 8 to 8 and offer travelers a chance to watch planes come and go. Accommodations such as Haneda Excel Hotel Tokyu (☎ 03/5756–6000) are also nearby.

Both terminals at Narita have ATMs and money exchange counters in the lobbies near Customs. Both terminals also have a JNTO Tourist Information Center, where

FLYING 101

Flying may not be as carefree as it once was, but there are some things you can do to make your trip smoother.

MINIMIZE THE TIME SPENT STANDING IN LINE. Buy an e-ticket, check in at an electronic kiosk, or—even better—check in on your airline's Web site before leaving home. Pack light and limit carry-on items to only the essentials.

ARRIVE WHEN YOU NEED TO. Research your airline's policy. It's usually at least an hour before domestic flights and two to three hours before international flights. But airlines at some busy airports have more stringent requirements. Check the TSA Web site for estimated security waiting times at major airports.

GET TO THE GATE. If you aren't at the gate at least 10 minutes before your flight is scheduled to take off (sometimes earlier), you won't be allowed to board.

DOUBLE-CHECK YOUR FLIGHT TIMES. Do this especially if you reserved far in advance. Schedules change, and alerts may not reach you.

DON'T GO HUNGRY. Ask whether your airline offers anything to eat; even when it does, be prepared to pay.

GET THE SEAT YOU WANT. Often, you can pick a seat when you buy your ticket on an airline Web site. But it's not guaranteed; the airline could change the plane after you book, so double-check. You can also select a seat if you check in electronically. Avoid seats on the aisle directly across from the lavatories. Frequent fliers say those are even worse than back-row seats that don't recline.

GOT KIDS? GET INFO. Ask the airline about its children's menus, activities, and fares. Sometimes infants and toddlers fly free if they sit on a parent's lap, and older children fly for half price in their own seats. Also inquire about policies involving car seats; having one may limit seating options. Also ask about seat-belt extenders for car seats. And note that you can't count on a flight attendant to produce an extender; you may have to ask for one when you board.

CHECK YOUR SCHEDULING. Don't buy a ticket if there's less than an hour between connecting flights. Although schedules are padded, if anything goes wrong you might miss your connection. If you're traveling to an important function, depart a day early.

BRING PAPER. Even when using an e-ticket, always carry a hard copy of your receipt; you may need it to get your boarding pass, which most airports require to get past security.

COMPLAIN AT THE AIRPORT. If your baggage goes astray or your flight goes awry, complain before leaving the airport. Most carriers require this.

BEWARE OF OVERBOOKED FLIGHTS. If a flight is oversold, the gate agent will usually ask for volunteers and offer some sort of compensation for taking a different flight. If you're bumped from a flight *involuntarily*, the airline must give you some kind of compensation if an alternate flight can't be found within one hour.

KNOW YOUR RIGHTS. If your flight is delayed because of something within the airline's control (bad weather doesn't count), the airline must get you to your destination on the same day, even if they have to book you on another airline and in an upgraded class. Read the Contract of Carriage, which is usually buried on the airline's Web site.

BE PREPARED. The Boy Scout motto is especially important if you're traveling during a stormy season. To quickly adjust your plans, program a few numbers into your cell: your airline, an airport hotel or two, your destination hotel, your car service, and/or your travel agent.

NAVIGATING TŌKYŌ

Stepping from a taxi or emerging from the subway onto a bustling Tōkyō street can be disorientating. Those braving it for the first time should take heart in the fact that even locals are not immune to such effects. Follow their lead:

Virtually every Tōkyō business offers a simple map from the nearest train station to their front door on ad flyers, business cards, or Web sites for good reason. Seek one out before venturing off to your destinations.

Similarly, if you have the luxury of a cell phone, call party members upon arriving at a rendezvous point, or phone someone you know lives around that place. You'll be thankful for the time you save. Also ask locals; most are willing to try and help despite, the probable language barrier.

If possible have your destination—whether landmark or address—written in Japanese to make it easier for locals to lend a hand. Even having it written in English can help; many Japanese unable to converse in English can read it.

If hopelessly lost, find a train or subway station; it can be used as a point of reference for commuting back and is likely the best bet for signs, maps, and staff help in English.

Ask the police for help; in Japan uniformed beat officers routinely give directions and those at Kōban (neighborhood police boxes) will consult their maps to help find specific addresses.

When getting directions, never settle for just an address as building numbers and street names are not always easy to see—or are not in English; get the how-to in relation to landmarks.

---

you can get free maps, brochures, and other visitor information. The airport also offers free observation decks facing runways in Terminal 1 and 2. They are open from 8 to 8. If flight delays give you more time than you know what to do with, a 15-minute bus ride from Terminal 2 will get you to the Aviation Museum, which sports a fifth-floor observation deck, restaurants, and open air deck. It's open from 10 AM to 5 PM. Needless to say there's a myriad of nearby hotels including the five-star Hilton Tōkyō Narita Hotel and the Holiday Inn Tōbu Narita.
Airport Information **Haneda Airport (HND)** ☎ 03/5757-8111 ⊕ www.tokyo-airport-bldg. co.jp. **Narita Airport (NRT)** ☎ 0476/34-5000 ⊕ www.narita-airport.or.jp.

FROM NARITA AIRPORT TO TŌKYŌ

Directly across from the customs-area exits at both terminals are the ticket counters for buses to Tōkyō. Buses leave from platforms just outside terminal exits, exactly on schedule; the departure time is on the ticket. The Friendly Airport Limousine offers the only shuttle bus service from Narita to Tōkyō. Different buses stop at various major hotels in the $$$$ category and at the JR Tōkyō and Shinjuku train stations.

A Friendly Airport Limousine bus also goes to Tōkyō City Air Terminal (TCAT), which is in Nihombashi (north-central Tōkyō). It is a bit out of the way, but it offers direct connections with Suitengū station on the Hanzō-mon subway line. From this line, you can go anywhere in the subway network. A taxi from TCAT to most major hotels will cost about ¥3,000 ($27).

Japan Railways trains stop at both Narita Airport terminals. The fastest and most comfortable is the Narita Limited Express (NEX), which makes 23 runs a day in each direction. Trains from the airport go directly to the central Tōkyō station in just under an hour, then continue to Yokohama and Ōfuna. The less elegant *kaisoku* (rapid train) on JR's Narita Line also runs from the airport to Tōkyō station, by way of Chiba.

The Keisei Skyliner train runs between the airport terminals and Keisei-Ueno station. There's also an early train from the airport, called the Morning Liner, which leaves at 7:49 AM and costs ¥1,400. From Ueno to Narita, the first Skyliner is at 6:32 AM, the last at 5:21 PM. All Skyliner seats are reserved. It only makes sense to take the Keisei, however, if your final destination is in the Ueno area; otherwise, you must change to the Tōkyō subway system or the Japan Railways loop line at Ueno (the station is adjacent to Keisei-Ueno station) or take a cab to your hotel.

You can take a taxi to central Tōkyō, but it'll cost you depending on traffic and where you're going. Private car service is also very expensive; from Narita Airport to the Imperial Hotel downtown, for example, will set you back about ¥35,000.

Friendly Airport Limousine a.k.a Airport Limousine ☎ 03/3665-7232 or 03/3665-7220 in Tōkyō, 0476/32-8080 for Terminal 1, 0476/34-6311 for Terminal 2 ⊕ www.limousinebus.co.jp. **IAE Co.** ☎ 0476/32-7954 for Terminal 1, 0476/34-6886 for Terminal 2. **Japan Railways** ☎ 03/3423-0111 for JR East InfoLine ☉ weekdays 10-6. **Keisei Railway** ☎ 03/3831-0131 for Ueno information counter, 0476/32-8505 at Narita Airport.

FROM HANEDA AIRPORT TO TŌKYŌ

The monorail from Haneda Airport to Hamamatsu-chō station in Tōkyō is the fastest and cheapest way into town; the journey takes about 30 minutes, and trains run approximately every 4 to 5 minutes; the fare is ¥470 ($4). From Hamamatsu-chō station, change to a JR train or take a taxi to your destination.

A taxi to the center of Tōkyō takes about 40 minutes; the fare is approximately ¥8,000 ($73).

Tōkyō Monorail Co., Ltd. ☎ 03/3434-3171.

BETWEEN AIRPORTS

The most convenient and affordable way to shuttle between the two airports is by way of **Airport Transport Service Co.**, which is known as Friendly Airport Limousine buses or just Airport Limousine bus. The service runs hourly throughout the day and costs ¥3,000 ($25). The Narita Express train from Narita Airport or the Keikyu-Kuko Line Express and Tōkyō Monorail from Haneda will get you from one airport to the other in 90 minutes for around ¥3,300 ($27) but expect to navigate at least two transfers to different train lines in crowded unfamiliar stations. A taxi will make the trip for about ¥35,000 ($288).

NARITA TO TŌKYŌ			
Transportation	*Fares*	*Times*	*Notes*
Friendly Airport Limousine (buses)	*¥2,400–¥3,800 ($21–$35); (TCAT): ¥2,900 ($26)*	*Every hour, till 11:30 PM; TCAT: Every 10–20 minutes from 6:55 AM to 11 PM*	*70–90 minutes, can be longer in traffic*
Narita Limited Express (NEX)	*One-way fare ¥2,940; Green Car ¥4,980; private compartment (four people) ¥5,380 per person*	*Daily departures begin at 7:43 AM; the last train is at 9:43 PM*	*Reserved seats; fill up fast*
kaisoku (rapid train on JR's Narita Line)	*¥1,280; ¥2,210 Green Car*	*16 departures daily, starting at 7 AM*	*1 hour and 27 minutes*
Keisei Skyliner train	*¥1,920 ($17)*	*Every 20–30 min, 9:21 AM–9:59 PM*	*Reserved seats; 57 minutes*
Taxi	*¥20,000 (about $180) or more*		

Airport Transport Service Co. ☎ 03/3665–7232 or 03/3665–7220 in Tōkyō, 0476/32–8080 for Terminal 1, 0476/34–6311 for Terminal 2 ⊕ www.limousinebus.co.jp.

FLIGHTS

Japan Airlines (JAL) and United Airlines are the major carriers between North America and Narita Airport; Northwest, American Airlines, Continental Airlines, Delta Airlines, and All Nippon Airways (ANA) also link North American cities with Tōkyō. Most of these airlines also fly into and out of Japan's number two international airport, Kansai International Airport, located south of Ōsaka.

Airline Contacts All Nippon Airways ☎ 800/235–9262 in U.S., 0120/02–9709 in Japan for domestic flights, 0120/02–9333 in Japan for international flights ⊕ www.anaskyweb.com. **American Airlines** ☎ 800/433–7300, 0120/000–860 in Japan ⊕ www.aa.com. **Continental Airlines** ☎ 800/231–0856 for international reservations, in Tōkyō 03/5464–5050 ⊕ www.continental.com. **Delta Airlines** ☎ 800/241–4141 for international reservations ⊕ www.delta.com. **Japan Airlines** ☎ 800/525–3663, 0120/255–931 international in Japan, 0120/255–971 domestic in Japan ⊕ www.jal.co.jp. **Northwest Airlines** ☎ 800/225–2525, 0120/120–747 in Japan ⊕ www.nwa.com. **United Airlines** ☎ 800/538–2929 for international reservations, 0120/114–466 in Japan ⊕ www.united.com.

▐ BY BOAT

The best ride in Tōkyō, hands down, is the *suijō basu* (river bus), operated by the Tōkyō Cruise Ship Company from Hinode Pier, from the mouth of the Sumida-gawa upstream to Asakusa. The glassed-in double-decker boats depart roughly every 20–40 minutes, weekdays 9:45–7:10, weekends and holidays 9:35–7:10 (with extended service to 7:50 July 9–September 23). The trip takes 40 minutes and costs ¥660. The pier is a seven-minute walk from Hamamatsu-chō station on the JR Yamanote Line.

The Sumida-gawa was once Tōkyō's lifeline, a busy highway for travelers and freight alike. The ferry service dates to 1885. Some people still take it to work, but today most passengers are Japanese tourists. On its way to Asakusa, the boat passes Tsukiji's Central Wholesale Market, the largest wholesale fish and produce market in the world; the old lumberyards and warehouses upstream; and the Kokugikan, with its distinctive green roof, which houses the sumō wrestling arena, the Sumō Museum, and headquarters of the Japan Sumō Association.

Another place to catch the ferry is at the Hama Rikyū Tei-en (Detached Palace Garden: open daily 9–4:30), a 15-minute walk from Ginza. Once part of the imperial estates, the gardens are open to the public for a separate ¥300 entrance fee—which you have to pay even if you are only using the ferry landing. The landing is a short walk to the left as you enter the main gate. Boats depart every 35–45 minutes every weekday 10:25–4:10; the fare between Asakusa and Hama Rikyū is ¥620.

In addition to the ferry to Asakusa, the Tōkyō Cruise Ship Company also operates four other lines from Hinode Pier. The Harbor Cruise Line stern-wheeler makes a 50-minute circuit under the Rainbow Bridge and around the inner harbor. Departures are at 10:30, 12:30, 1:30, and 3:30 (and 4:45 in August). The fare is ¥800. ■ TIP→ **If you visit in August you should definitely opt for the evening cruise; the lights on the Rainbow Bridge and neighboring Odaiba are spectacular.** Two lines connect Hinode to Odaiba itself, one at 20-minute intervals from 10:10 to 6:10 to Odaiba Seaside Park and the Museum of Maritime Science at Aomi Terminal (¥400–¥520), the other every 25 minutes from 9 to 5:40 to the shopping/amusement center at Palette Town and on to the Tōkyō Big Sight exhibition grounds at Ariake (¥350). The Kasai Sealife Park Line cruise leaves Hinode hourly from 10 to 4 and travels through the network of artificial islands in the harbor to the beach and aquarium at Kasai Rinkai Kōen in Chiba; the one-way fare is ¥800. The Canal Cruise Line connects Hinode with Shinagawa Suizokukan aquarium, south along the harborside. There are six departures daily except Tuesday between 10:15 and 4:50; the one-way fare is ¥800.

Tōkyō Cruise Ship Company ☎ 03/ 3457-7830 at Hinode, 03/3841-9178 at Asakusa ⊕ www.suijobus.co.jp.

▌ BY BUS

Bus routes within Tōkyō are impossibly complicated. The Tōkyō Municipal Government operates some of the lines; private companies run the rest. There's no telephone number even native Japanese can call for help. And buses all have tiny seats and low ceilings. Unless you are a true Tōkyō veteran, forget about taking buses. JR buses can be a viable way to get to and from other parts of the country from Tōkyō but these services are only geared toward locals who are fluent in the language and culture.

Some buses have a set cost, anywhere from ¥100 to ¥200, depending on the route and municipality, in which case you board at the front of the bus and pay as you get on. On other buses cost is determined by the distance you travel. You take a ticket when you board at the rear door of the bus; it bears the number of the stop at which you boarded. Your fare depends on your destination and is indicated by a board at the front of the bus.

Bus Information JR Kantō Bus ☎ 03/ 3844-1950. **Nishinihon JR Bus** ☎ 06/ 6466-9990.

▌ BY CAR

Driving in Tōyō and other Japanese cities is not recommended, as there are many narrow, one-way streets and little in the way of English road signs except on major arteries. Gas is expensive, as is parking—if you're lucky enough to find a spot. Hiring cars with a driver is common. (⇨ Car Rentals *in* Booking Your Trip, *above*)

You need an international driving permit (IDP) to drive in Japan. IDPs are available from the American Automobile Association (AAA). This international permit, valid only in conjunction with your regular driver's license, is universally recognized; having one may save you a problem with local authorities.

Major roads in Japan are sufficiently marked in the Roman alphabet, and on country roads there's usually someone to ask for help. However, it's a good idea to have a detailed map with town names written in *kanji* (Japanese characters) and *romaji* (romanized Japanese).

Car travel along the Tōkyō–Kyōto–Hiroshima corridor and in other built-up areas of Japan is not as convenient as the trains. Within the major cities, the trains and subways will get you to your destinations faster and more comfortably. Roads are congested, gas is expensive, and highway tolls are exorbitant (tolls between Tōkyō and Kyōto amount to ¥10,550). In major cities, with the exception of main arteries, English signs are few and far between, one-way streets often lead you off the track, and parking is often hard to find and usually expensive.

GASOLINE

If you must drive, beware the gas prices. Luckily prices are fairly uniform across the country at about ¥110 per liter ($4.80 per gallon)—still cause for sticker shock!

Gas stations are plentiful along Japan's toll roads, and credit cards are accepted everywhere and are even encouraged—there are discounts for them at some places. Self-service stations have recently become legal, so if you pump your own gas you may get a small discount. Often you pay after pumping, but there are also machines where you put money in first and then use the receipt to get change back. The Japanese word for receipt is *uketori,* but as with every legal transaction in Japan (except for taxis, though if you ask, you can get one) you'll get a receipt without asking. Of course, instructions are in Japanese only and the automated procedure is likely to be quite different from the pumps back home. Even without Japanese skills, however, it should be easy to enlist the aid of an attendant or fellow patron. Tipping is not customary.

PARKING

There's nothing easy about parking in Tōkyō. Parking is often hard to find and authorities have stepped up efforts to ticket and tow illegally parked cars, so be very careful where you park. To top it off, parking is usually very expensive and can range anywhere from ¥100 to ¥800 for an hour or two in a lot or on-street parking to ¥1,500 or more for an off-the-beaten-path overnight lot or half-day stint at a popular attraction. Major attractions and malls usually offer discount parking for purchases of more than ¥3,000; so hang on to your receipts and inquire about discount validation. Meters in lots usually take bills to facilitate long-term parking. ■ TIP➜ On-street meters often have an electronic eye to prevent re-feeding the meter for longer stays; meters won't reboot until the car is moved. Of course, you can pull away and repark at the same meter to extend your stay but that wouldn't be exactly legal.

ROADSIDE EMERGENCIES

Emergency telephones along the highways can be used to contact the authorities. A nonprofit service, JHelp.com, offers a free, 24-hour emergency assistance hotline. Car rental agencies generally offer roadside assistance services—make sure to ask. **Emergency Services Police** ☎ 110. **Fire** ☎ 119. **JHelp.com** ☎ 0570/000-911.

RULES OF THE ROAD

In Japan people drive on the left ■ TIP➜ **Left on red is not allowed.** Speed limits vary, but generally the limit is 80 kph (50 mph) on highways, 40 kph (25 mph) in cities. Penalties for speeding are severe. By law, car seats must be installed if the driver is traveling with a child under six, while the driver and all passengers in cars must wear seat-belts at all times. It is illegal to use hand-held mobile phones while driving.

Many smaller streets lack sidewalks, so cars, bicycles, and pedestrians share the same space. Motorbikes with engines less than 50 cc are allowed to travel against automobile traffic on one-way roads. Fortunately, considering the narrowness of the streets and the volume of traffic, most Japanese drivers are technically skilled. They may not allow quite as much distance between cars as you're used to. Be prepared for sudden lane changes by other drivers. When waiting at intersections after dark, many drivers, as a courtesy to other drivers, turn off their main headlights to prevent glare.

Japan has very strict laws concerning the consumption of alcohol prior to getting behind the wheel. Given the almost zero-tolerance for driving under the influence and the occasional evening police checkpoint set up along the roads, it's best to avoid alcohol entirely if you plan to drive.

■ BY TAXI

In spite of the introduction of ¥340 initial-fare cabs, Tōkyō taxi fares remain among the highest in the world. Most meters start running at ¥660 and after the first 2 km (1 mi) tick away at the rate of ¥80 every 274 meters (about ⅕ mi). Keep in mind that the ¥340 taxis (which are a very small percentage of those on the street) are only cheaper for trips of 2 km (1 mi) or less; after that the fare catches up with the ¥660 cabs. The ¥340 taxis have a sticker on the left-rear window. There is no bargaining or negotiating over prices; you pay the fare indicated on the meter.

There are also smaller cabs, called *kogata*, that charge ¥640 and then ¥80 per 290 meters (⅕ mi). If your cab is caught in traffic—hardly an uncommon event—the meter registers another ¥80 for every 1½ minutes of immobility. Between 11 PM and 5 AM, a 30% surcharge is added to the fare.

You do get very good value for the money, though. Taxis are invariably clean and comfortable. Drivers take you where you want to go by the shortest route they know and do not expect a tip. Tōkyō cabbies are not, in general, a sociable species (you wouldn't be either if you had to drive for 10–12 hours a day in Tōkyō traffic), but you can always count on a minimum standard of courtesy. And if you forget something in the cab—a camera, a purse—your chances of getting it back are almost 100%.

■ TIP→ **Japanese taxis have automatic door-opening systems, so do not try to open the taxi door.** Stand back when the cab comes to a stop—if you are too close, the door may slam into you. When you leave the cab, do not try to close the door; the driver will do it automatically. Only the curbside rear door opens.

Hailing a taxi during the day is seldom a problem. You would have to be in a very remote part of town to wait more than five minutes for one to pass by. In Ginza, drivers are allowed to pick up passengers only in designated areas; look for short lines of cabs. Elsewhere, you need only step off the curb and raise your arm. ■ TIP→ **A red light on the dashboard indicates an available taxi, and a green light indicates an occupied taxi.**

At night, when everyone's been out drinking and wants a ride home, the rules change a bit. Don't be astonished if a cab with a red light doesn't stop for you: the driver may have had a radio call, or he may be heading for an area where a long, profitable fare to the suburbs is more likely. (Or the cab driver may simply not feel like coping with a passenger in a foreign language. Refusing a fare is against the law—but it's done all the time.) Between 11 PM and 2 AM on Friday and Saturday nights, you have to be very lucky to get a cab in any of the major entertainment districts; in Ginza it's almost impossible.

Unless you are going to a well-known destination such as a major hotel, it's advisable to have a Japanese person write out your destination in Japanese. Remember, there's no need to tip.

■ BY RAIL

Tōkyō's subways and trains are the most efficient, safe, and affordable way to get around town. Well maintained with heating and air conditioning, they are inviting enough to nap in, which seated commuters can do with surprising ease. Avoid traveling during rush hours (about 7 AM–9:30 AM and 5 PM–7 PM) when trains can be so crowded attendants must push commuters into cars to close the doors. While most major stations have elevators or escalators, many smaller ones don't; be prepared to hit the stairs. The Metro subway and JR train systems are integrated with mutual, connected, or adjacent stations that make it easy to transfer from one to the other. One transfer—two at most—will take you, in less than an hour, to any part of the city you're likely to visit. At some stations—such as Ōte-machi, Ginza, and Iidabashi—long underground passageways connect the various lines, though it does take time to get from one to another. Directions, however, are clearly marked.

English-language subway and train maps are available for free at most stations. Trains and subways run from 5 AM to 12:30 AM (give or take a half hour depending on the line). Times for the first and last trains are posted outside most stations. It will be in Japanese but it's relatively easy to figure out as the early time will be first train and the late time will be the last (stations where more than one line stops will require Japanese reading or guessing).

Tickets are valid only on the day you buy them. ■ TIP→ **Remember to keep your ticket while traveling; you'll need it to exit the turnstiles.** All stations have charts above the ticket vending machines to check the fare for your destination but those in smaller (especially JR) stations may not be in English. If in doubt, buy the cheapest ticket and pay the difference at the other end. Japan National Tourist Organization offers English-language help on plotting commutes.

Less helpful is the system of signs in larger stations that tell you which of the 15 or 20 exits (exits are often numbered and alphabetized) will take you above ground closest to your destination; most subway stations have such signs in English. When it comes to smaller JR train stations, commuters are left to their own devices. In this book, exit names or numbers have been included in the text where they'll be most useful. You can also try asking the agent when you turn in your ticket; she or he may understand enough of your question to come back with the exit number and letter (such as A3 or B12), which is all you need.

■ TIP→ Electric signboards displaying departure information at platforms or terminals alternate between Japanese and English; be sure the final destination shown matches the direction you want to travel.

BY SUBWAY

The Metro system is especially user friendly, with color-coded lines (the trains are not colored-coded) and a Roman letter and number (such as G 9 for Ginza Station) marking the entrance and interiors of stations along with their names in Japanese and English. ■ TIP→ Metro help desks offer help in English from 9 AM to 5 PM at Ginza, Shinjuku, Harajuku, and Asakusa stations. Thirteen lines serve Tōkyō; nine of them are operated by Tōkyō Metro Co., Ltd. and four by the Tōkyō Municipal Authority (Toei). Trains run roughly every five minutes (5 AM–midnight); except during rush hours, the intervals are slightly longer on the newer Toei lines.

Fares begin at ¥160. Toei trains are generally a bit more expensive than Metro trains, but both are competitive with JR lines. From Ueno across town to Shibuya on the Ginza Line (orange), for example, is ¥190. Metro (but *not* the Toei) has inaugurated an electronic card of its own, called Metro Card. The denominations are ¥1,000, ¥3,000, and ¥5,000. Automatic card dispensers are installed at some stations. For ¥710, you can purchase a one-day open ticket at Metro offices or ticket dispensers that gives you unlimited use of all Metro trains.

BY TRAIN

Japan Railways (JR) trains in Tōkyō are color-coded, making it easy to identify the different lines. The Yamanote Line (green or silver with green stripes) makes a 35-km (22-mi) loop around the central wards of the city in about an hour. The 29 stops include the major hub stations of Tōkyō, Yūraku-chō, Shimbashi, Shinagawa, Shibuya, Shinjuku, and Ueno.

The Chūō Line (orange) runs east to west through the loop from Tōkyō to the distant suburb of Takao. During the day, however, these are limited express trains that don't stop at most of the stations inside the loop. For local cross-town service, which also extends east to neighboring Chiba Prefecture, you have to take the Sōbu Line (yellow).

The Keihin Tōhoku Line (blue) goes north to Ōmiya in Saitama Prefecture and south to Ōfuna in Kanagawa, running parallel to the Yamanote Line between Tabata and Shinagawa. Where they share the loop, the two lines usually use the same platform—Yamanote trains on one side and Keihin Tōhoku trains, headed in the same direction, on the other. This requires a little attention because, for example, if you want to take the loop line from Yūraku-chō around to Shibuya and you board a blue train instead of a green one; four stops later, where the lines branch, you'll find yourself on an unexpected trip to Yokohama.

JR Yamanote Line fares start at ¥130; you can get anywhere on the loop for ¥260 or less. If you plan to use the JR often, pick up an Orange Card, which is available at any station office. The cards come in ¥1,000 and ¥3,000 denominations. Use your card at vending machines with orange panels: you punch in the cost of the ticket and that amount is automatically deducted.

Japan Railways Hotline is an English-language information service, open weekdays 10–6.

Jorudan is an invaluable easy-to-use online source for plotting inner-city train, subway, and bus commutes.

Japan National Tourist Organization Tourist Information Center ☎ 03/3201-3331. **Tōkyō Metro** ⊕ www.tokyometro.jp ☎ 03/3941-2004. **Japan Railways Group** ✉ New York ☎ 212/332-8686. **Japan Railways Hotline** ☎ 03/3423-0111 ⊕ www.jreast.co.jp. **Jorudan** ⊕ www.jorudan.co.jp.

GETTING TO TŌKYŌ BY TRAIN

The Shinkansen (bullet train), one of the fastest trains in the world, connects major cities north and south of Tōkyō. It's only slightly less expensive than flying but is in many ways more convenient because train stations are more centrally located than airports (and, if you have a Japan Rail Pass ⇨ Train Tickets, *above*, it's extremely affordable). On the main line that runs west from Tōkyō, there are three types of Shinkansen. The *Nozomi* makes the fewest stops, which can cut as much as an hour from long, cross-country trips; it's the only Shinkansen on which you cannot use a JR Pass. The *Hikari* makes just a few more stops than the *Nozomi*. The *Kodama* is the equivalent of a Shinkansen local, making all stops along the Shinkansen lines. The same principle of faster and slower Shinkansen also applies on the line that runs north from Tōkyō to Morioka, in the Tōkyō region.

Other trains, though not as fast as the Shinkansen, are just as convenient and substantially cheaper. There are three types of train services: *futsū* (local service), *tokkyū* (limited express service), and *kyūkō* (express service). Both the tokkyū and the kyūkō offer a first-class compartment known as the Green Car. Smoking is allowed only in designated carriages on long-distance and Shinkansen trains. Local and commuter trains are entirely nonsmoking and it is enforced.

■ TIP→ Because there are no porters or carts at train stations, and the flights of stairs connecting train platforms can turn even the lightest bag into a heavy burden, it's a good idea to travel light when getting around by train. Savvy travelers often have their main luggage sent ahead to a hotel that they plan to reach later in their wanderings. It's also good to know that every train station, however small, has luggage lockers, which cost about ¥300 for 24 hours.

Most clerks at train stations know a few basic words of English and can read Roman script. Moreover, they are invariably helpful in plotting your route. The complete railway timetable is a mammoth book written only in Japanese; however, you can get an English-language train schedule from the Japan National Tourist Organization (JNTO). JNTO's booklet *The Tourist's Handbook* provides helpful information about purchasing tickets in Japan.

JAPAN RAIL PASS

When you arrive in Japan, you must exchange your voucher for the Japan Rail Pass. You can do this at the Japan Railways desk in the arrivals hall at Narita Airport or at the JR stations of major cities. When you make this exchange, you determine the day that you want the rail pass to begin, and, accordingly, when it ends. You do not have to begin travel on the day you make the exchange; instead, pick the starting date to maximize use.

The Japan Railways Hotline is an English-language information service, available weekdays 10–6. It's a good resource if you have any questions or problems.

The Japan Rail Pass allows you to travel on all JR-operated trains (which cover most destinations in Japan) but not lines owned by other companies. It does not cover the cost of sleeping compartments on overnight trains (called blue trains), nor does it cover the newest and fastest of the Shinkansen trains, the *Nozomi,* which make only one or two stops on longer runs. The pass covers only the *Hikari*

Shinkansen, which make a couple more stops than the *Nozomi,* and the *Kodama* Shinkansen, which stop at every station along the Shinkansen routes. The JR Pass is also valid on buses operated by Japan Railways (⇨ Bus Travel *in* Transportation, *above*).

Many travelers assume that rail passes guarantee them seats on the trains they wish to ride. Not so. If you're using a rail pass, there's no need to buy individual tickets, but you should book seats ahead. This guarantees you a seat and is also a useful reference for the times of train departures and arrivals. You can reserve up to two weeks in advance or just minutes before the train departs. If you fail to make a train, there's no penalty, and you can reserve again.

Seat reservations for any JR route may be made at any JR station except those in the tiniest villages. The reservation windows or offices, *midori-no-madoguchi,* have green signs in English and green-stripe windows. If you're traveling without a Japan Rail Pass, there's a surcharge of approximately ¥500 (depending upon distance traveled) for seat reservations, and if you miss the train, you'll have to pay for another reservation. If you're traveling with a Japan Rail Pass, you can make seat reservations without paying a fee on all trains that have reserved-seat coaches; there are no reservations made on local service trains. When making your seat reservation, you may request a non-smoking or smoking car. Your reservation ticket shows the date and departure time of your train as well as your car and seat number. On the platform you can figure out where to wait for a particular train car. Notice the markings painted on the platform or on little signs above the platform; ask someone which markings correspond to car numbers. If you don't have a reservation, ask which cars are unreserved. Sleeping berths, even with a rail pass, are additional. Unreserved tickets can be purchased at regular ticket windows. For traveling short distances, tickets are usually sold at vending machines. A platform ticket is required if you go through the wicket gate onto the platform to meet someone coming off a train. The charge is ¥140 (in Tōkyō and Ōsaka, the tickets are ¥130).

Japan Railways Group ✉ New York ☎ 212/332-8686. **Japan Railways Hotline** ☎ 03/3423-0111.

ON THE GROUND

▮ LANGUAGE

One of the best ways to avoid being an Ugly American is to learn a little of the local language. You need not strive for fluency; even just mastering a few basic words and terms is bound to make chatting with the locals more rewarding.

COMMUNICATING IN JAPAN

Communicating can be a challenge because most English speakers know little, if any, Japanese. Take some time before you leave home to learn a few basic words, such as where (*doko*), what time (*nan-ji*), bathroom (*o-te-arai*), thank you (*arigatō goza-imasu*), excuse me (*sumimasen*), and please (*onegai shimasu*).

English is a required subject in Japanese schools, so most Japanese study English for at least six years. However, this does not mean everyone *speaks* English. When asked, "Do you speak English?" many Japanese, out of modesty, say no, even if they understand and speak a fair amount of it. It's usually best to simply ask what you really want to know. If the person understands, he or she will answer or perhaps take you where you need to go.

Although a local may understand your simple question, he or she cannot always give you an answer that requires complicated instructions. For example, you may ask someone on the subway how to get to a particular stop, and he may direct you to the train across the platform and then say something in Japanese that you do not understand. You may discover too late that the train runs express to the suburbs after the third stop; the person who gave you directions was trying to tell you to switch trains at the third stop. To avoid this kind of trouble, ask more than one person for directions every step of the way. You can avoid that trip to the suburbs if you ask someone *on* the train how to get to where you want to go. Also, remember that politeness is a matter of course in

Japan and that the Japanese won't want to lose face by saying that they don't know how to get somewhere. If the situation gets confusing, bow, say *arigatō goza-imashita* ("thank you" in the past tense), and ask someone else. Even though you are communicating on a very basic level, misunderstandings can happen easily. When asking for directions, it's best to ask a "where is" type question—at least the person you've asked can point in the general direction, even if they can't explain themselves to you clearly.

CAN'T READ?

Traveling in Japan can be problematic if you don't read Japanese. Before you leave home, buy a phrase book that shows English, English transliterations of Japanese (*romaji*), and Japanese characters (*kanji* and *kana*). You can read the romaji to pick up a few Japanese words and match the kanji and kana in the phrase book with characters on signs and menus. When all else fails, ask for help by pointing to the Japanese words in your book.

▮ TIP➔ The Japan National Tourist Organization (JNTO) manages a free English-language tourist information line in daily operation 9–5, and if there's an emergency you can always call the free, Tōkyō English Life Line (TELL) between 9 am and 11pm. TELL specializes in counseling services for ex-pats, as well as providing reliable English-language information (referrals) for medical and disaster emergencies, etc.

WESTERN NICKNAMES

Gaijin is used to translate the word "foreigner" throughout this guide for two reasons. First, it's commonly used in books written by Westerners who have lived in Japan, and as such it has wider recognition value. Second, as Japan becomes more global—especially its younger generation—gaijin is losing its negative sense. Many Japanese use gaijin to describe non-Japanese and most often mean no offense by it.

CON OR CONCIERGE?

Good hotel concierges are invaluable—for arranging transportation, getting reservations at the hottest restaurant, and scoring tickets for a sold-out show or entree to an exclusive nightclub. They're in the know and well connected. That said, sometimes you have to take their advice with a grain of salt.

It's not uncommon for restaurants to ply concierges with free food and drink in exchange for steering diners their way. Indeed, European concierges often receive referral *fees*. Hotel chains usually have guidelines about what their concierges can accept. The best concierges, however, are above reproach. This is particularly true of those who belong to the prestigious international society of Les Clefs d'Or.

What can you expect of a concierge? At a typical tourist-class hotel you can expect him or her to give you the basics: to show you something on a map, make a standard restaurant reservation (particularly if you don't speak the language), or help you book a tour or airport transportation. In Asia concierges perform the vital service of writing out the name or address of your destination for you to give to a cab driver.

Savvy concierges at the finest hotels and resorts, can arrange for just about any good or service imaginable—and do so quickly. You should compensate them appropriately. A $10 tip is enough to show appreciation for a table at a hot restaurant. But the reward should really be much greater for tickets to that U2 concert that's been sold out for months or for those last-minute sixth-row-center seats for *The Lion King*.

So if children giggle and point at the *gaijin-san*, know that it's meant with only the kindest fascination. And if you feel that extra politeness is appropriate, use *gaikoku-jin* with colleagues whom you respect—or with whomever might be using gaijin a bit too derogatorily.

Note: There's some disagreement over the use of gaijin ("outside person," or outsider) as opposed to gai-koku-jin ("outside country person," or foreigner) because the former has negative echoes of the days of Japanese isolationism. In the 17th and 18th centuries, when the Japanese had contact only with Dutch traders, Westerners were called *bata-kusai* (literally, "stinking of butter")—obviously a derogatory term. Gai-koku-jin, on the other hand, has a softer, more polite meaning, and many Westerners in Japan prefer it because it has no xenophobic taint.
Japan National Tourist Organization (JNTO) ☎ 0088/22-4800 ⊕ www.jnto.go.jp. **Tōkyō English Life Line (TELL)** ☎ 03/5774-0992 ⊕ www.telljp.com.

▌BUSINESS SERVICES & FACILITIES

As one would expect in the capital of the world's second largest economy, walk-in business centers with copy, fax, professional printing, computer, and Internet services are all over Tōkyō. If you're staying in a major hotel most of these services may be an elevator ride away. There are more than 50 FedEx Kinko's locations in the Tōkyō area alone, not to mention the numerous Kinko's-like businesses. To find the location nearest you, check out the Web site. **FedEx Kinko's** ⊕ http://english.fedexkinkos.co.jp.

▌COMMUNICATIONS

INTERNET

These days, Internet access is as easy to find as water on this island nation, and many Internet cafés operate into the wee hours of the morn to placate those in need of an online fix. Prices range from free online access for paying patrons to ¥500 or more per half hour. Phone jacks are the same in Japan as in the U.S. Many hotels have ADSL or Ethernet connections for high-speed Internet access. Ethernet cables are usually available to buy at hotels if you don't bring your own. Wireless Internet access (Wi-Fi) is popular and available for free in many subway stations, coffee shops and hotel lobbies; so bring that LAN card with your laptop.

Despite its name-brand popularity, Yahoo Café has no available phone numbers and the Web site is only in Japanese, but it has locations in Narita and Haneda airports, as well as the Shingawa Prince Hotel.

Manga Land is another popular Internet café chain that has more than two dozen locations throughout the city.

For a list of Internet café locations in and around the city, visit Enjoy Tōkyō's Web site, which is listed below.

Internet Cafés **Cybercafes** ⊕ www.cybercafes.com lists over 4,000 Internet cafés worldwide. **Manga Land** ☎ 03/3408-3750 **Enjoy Tōkyō** ⊕ www.009.upp.so-net.ne.jp/enjoytokyo/culture/internetcafe2.html.

PHONES

The good news is that you can now make a direct-dial telephone call from virtually any point on earth. The bad news? You can't always do so cheaply. Calling from a hotel is almost always the most expensive option; hotels usually add huge surcharges to all calls, particularly international ones. Calling cards usually keep costs to a minimum, but only if you purchase them locally. And then there are mobile phones (⇨ *below*), which are some-

times more prevalent—particularly in the developing world—than land lines; as expensive as mobile phone calls can be, they are still usually a much cheaper option than calling from your hotel.

The country code for Japan is 81. When dialing a Japanese number from outside of Japan, drop the initial "0" from the local area code.

CALLING WITHIN JAPAN

Payphones come in various colors, including pink and green. Most pink-and-red phones, for local calls, accept only ¥10 coins. Green-and-gray phones accept ¥10 and ¥100 coins as well as prepaid telephone cards. Domestic long-distance rates are reduced as much as 50% after 9 PM (40% after 7 PM). Telephone cards, sold in vending machines, hotels, and a variety of stores, are tremendously convenient because you will not have to search for the correct change.

For directory information on Tōkyō telephone numbers, dial 104; for elsewhere in Japan, dial 105. These services are only in Japanese, but the NTT Information Customer Service Centre, open weekdays 9–5, has service representatives who speak English, French, Spanish, Portuguese, Korean, and Chinese.
NTT Information Customer Service Centre ☎ 0120/364-463 toll-free.

CALLING OUTSIDE JAPAN

Many gray, multicolor, and green phones have gold plates indicating, in English, that they can be used for international calls. Three Japanese companies provide international service: KDD (001), Japan

ACCESS NUMBERS				
	In the U.S.A	KDD (Japan)	IDC (Japan)	JT (Japan)
AT&T Direct	800/222-0300	00/539-111	00/66-55-111	00/44-11-111
MCI WorldPhone	800/444-4444	00/539-9121	00/66-55-121	00/44-11-121
Sprint International Access	800/877-4646	00/539-131	00/66-55-877	00/44-11-131

Telecom (JT) (0041), and IDC (0061). Dial the company code + country code + city/area code and number of your party. Telephone credit cards are especially convenient for international calls. For operator assistance in English on long-distance calls, dial 0051.

The country code for the United States is 1.

CALLING CARDS

For as little as ¥1,000 ($9) pre-paid telephone cards can be bought at station kiosks or convenience stores and can be used in virtually all public telephones. Pre-paid cell phones are also available at some kiosks.

MOBILE PHONES

If you have a multiband phone (some countries use different frequencies than what's used in the United States) and your service provider uses the world-standard GSM network (as do T-Mobile, Cingular, and Verizon), you can probably use your phone abroad. Roaming fees can be steep, however: 99¢ a minute is considered reasonable. And overseas you normally pay the toll charges for incoming calls. It's almost always cheaper to send a text message than to make a call, since text messages have a very low set fee (often less than 5¢).

If you just want to make local calls, consider buying a new SIM card (note that your provider may have to unlock your phone for you to use a different SIM card) and a prepaid service plan in the destination. You'll then have a local number and can make local calls at local rates. If your trip is extensive, you could also simply buy a new cell phone in your destination, as the initial cost will be offset over time.

■■ TIP→ **If you travel internationally frequently, save one of your old mobile phones or buy a cheap one on the Internet; ask your cell phone company to unlock it for you, and take it with you as a travel phone, buying a new SIM card with pay-as-you-go service in each destination.**

Japan is the world leader in mobile phone technology, but overseas visitors cannot easily use their handsets in Japan. So if you really need a cell phone while you're in Tōkyō, rent one. Phones can be rented on arrival at SoftBank (formerly Vodafone) outlets at both Narita and Kansai airports. Rental rates start at ¥525 a day, excluding insurance.

SoftBank ☎ 44/1635-33251 ⊕ www.softbank. co.jp. **Cellular Abroad** ☎ 800/287-5072 ⊕ www.cellularabroad.com rents and sells GMS phones and sells SIM cards that work in many countries. **Mobal** ☎ 888/888-9162 ⊕ www.mobalrental.com rents mobiles and sells GSM phones (starting at $49) that will operate in 140 countries. Per-call rates vary throughout the world. **Planet Fone** ☎ 888/988-4777 ⊕ www.planetfone.com rents cell phones, but the per-minute rates are expensive.

■ CUSTOMS & DUTIES

You're always allowed to bring goods of a certain value back home without having to pay any duty or import tax. But there's a limit on the amount of tobacco and liquor you can bring back duty-free, and some countries have separate limits for perfumes; for exact figures, check with your customs department. The values of so-called "duty-free" goods are included in these amounts. When you shop abroad, save all your receipts, as customs inspectors may ask to see them as well as the items you purchased. If the total value of your goods is more than the duty-free limit, you'll have to pay a tax (most often a flat percentage) on the value of everything beyond that limit.

Japan has strict regulations about bringing firearms, pornography, and narcotics into the country. Anyone caught with these items is liable to be detained, deported, and refused reentry into Japan. Certain fresh fruits, vegetables, plants, and animals are also illegal. Nonresidents are allowed to bring in duty-free: (1) 400 cigarettes or 100 cigars or 500 grams of tobacco; (2) three 760-ml bottles of alcohol; (3) 2 ounces of perfume; (4) other goods up to ¥200,000 value. Proper paperwork is required to export antiques or antiquities, especially antique swords (the cheep tourist replicas are okay).

Information in Japan **Ministry of Finance, Customs and Tariff Bureau** ⊠ Tōkyō ☏ 03/3581-4111 ⊕ www.customs.go.jp/index_e.htm. **U.S. Information U.S. Customs and Border Protection** ⊕ www.cbp.gov.

▊ DAY TOURS & GUIDES

EXCURSIONS

Sunrise Tours, a division of the Japan Travel Bureau, runs a one-day bus tour to Nikkō on Monday, Tuesday, and Friday between April and October, at ¥13,500 (lunch included). Japan Amenity Travel and the Japan Gray Line conduct Mt. Fuji and Hakone tours, with return either by bus or train; one-day trips cost from ¥12,000 to ¥15,000 (lunch included), and two-day tours cost ¥26,500 (meals and accommodation included). Some of these tours include a quick visit to Kamakura. There are also excursions to Kyōto via Shinkansen that cost from ¥49,500 to ¥82,100; you can arrange these Shinkansen tours through Japan Amenity Travel or Japan Gray Line.

ORIENTATION TOUR

April–June and mid-September–November, Sunrise Tours conducts a Thursday-morning (8–12:30) "Experience Japanese Culture" bus-and-walking tour (¥7,000), which includes a calligraphy demonstration, a tea ceremony, and a visit to the Edo-Tōkyō Hakubutsukan. Both Sunrise Tours and the Japan Gray Line operate a number of other bus excursions around Tōkyō with English-speaking guides. The tours vary with the current demands of the market. Most include the Tōkyō Tower Observatory, the Imperial East Garden, a demonstration of flower arrangement at the Tasaki Pearl Gallery, and/or a Sumida-gawa cruise to Sensō-ji in Asakusa. These are for the most part four-hour morning or afternoon tours; a full-day tour (seven

hours) combines most of what is covered in half-day excursions with a tea ceremony at Happō Garden and lunch at the traditional Chinzan-sō restaurant. Costs range from ¥4,000 to ¥12,900. Tours are conducted in large, air-conditioned buses that set out from Hamamatsu-chō Bus Terminal, and there's also free pickup and return from major hotels. (If you travel independently and use the subway, you could probably manage the same full-day itinerary for under ¥3,000, including lunch.)

PERSONAL GUIDES

The Japan Guide Association will introduce you to English-speaking guides. You'll need to negotiate your own itinerary and price with the guide. Assume that the fee will be ¥25,000–¥30,000 for a full eight-hour day.

The Japan National Tourist Organization (JNTO) sponsors a Good-Will Guide program in which local citizens volunteer to show visitors around; this is a great way to meet Japanese people. These are not professional guides; they usually volunteer both because they enjoy welcoming foreigners to their town and because they want to practice their English. The services of Good-Will Guides are free, but you should pay for their travel costs, their admission fees, and any meals you eat with them while you are together. To participate in this program, make arrangements for a Good-Will Guide in advance through JNTO in the United States or through the tourist office in the area where you want the guide to meet you. The program operates in 75 towns and cities, including Tōkyō, Kyōto, Nara, Nagoya, Ōsaka, and Hiroshima.

SPECIAL-INTEREST TOURS

Sunrise Tours also offers a "Geisha Night" tour (4:30–7) of Tōkyō on Tuesday and Friday mid-March–November. Dinner is included. Other evening tours include Kabuki drama at the Kabuki-za, and sukiyaki dinner. Prices are ¥5,000–¥9,500, depending on which portions of the tour you select. Sunrise Tours has a free-schedule trip to Tōkyō Disneyland, but this operates only on Tuesday and Friday and works in only one direction: buses pick you up at major hotels but leave you to manage your own way back to Tōkyō at the end of the day. The cost for the trip is ¥9,500.

It's only possible to visit parts of the Imperial Palace Grounds by making online reservations in advance with the Imperial Household Agency. The guided tour (in Japanese, but with a useful pamphlet and audio guide in English) takes about an hour and 15 minutes, and covers 11 of the buildings and sites on the west side of the Palace grounds, including the Fushimi Yagura watchtower and the Fujimi Tamon armory. ■ TIP→ **Log on to the Imperial Household Agency Web site to make a reservation; do this well in advance, as the available slots fill up quickly.** Visitors under 18 must be accompanied by an adult. The tours are given weekdays at 10:30 AM and 1:30 PM; admission is free. Tours start at the Nijūbashi Bridge, a minute's walk north of the subway; follow the moat to the courtyard in front of the gate.

Recommended Tours/Guides **Imperial Household Agency** ⊕ http://sankan. kunaicho.go.jp. **Japan Amenity Travel** ✉ Chūō-ku ☎ 03/3542-7200. **Japan Gray Line** ✉ Minato-ku ☎ 03/3433-5745. **Japan Guide Association** ☎ 03/3213-2706. **Japan National Tourist Organization** ✉ Chiyoda-ku ☎ 03/3201-3331. **Sunrise Tours Reservation Center, Japan Travel Bureau** ☎ 03/5620-9500.

■ ELECTRICITY

The electrical current in Japan is 100 volts, 50 cycles alternating current (AC) in eastern Japan, and 100 volts, 60 cycles in western Japan; the United States runs on 110-volt, 60-cycle AC current. Wall outlets in Japan accept plugs with two flat prongs, like in the United States, but do not accept U.S. three-prong plugs.

■ TIP→ **Don't use 110-volt outlets marked FOR SHAVERS ONLY for high-wattage appliances such as hair-dryers.**

Consider making a small investment in a universal adapter, which has several types of plugs in one lightweight, compact unit. Most laptops and mobile phone chargers are dual voltage (i.e., they operate equally well on 110 and 220 volts), so require only an adapter. These days the same is true of small appliances such as hair dryers. Always check labels and manufacturer instructions to be sure.

Steve Kropla's Help for World Traveler's ⊕ www.kropla.com has information on electrical and telephone plugs around the world. **Walkabout Travel Gear** ⊕ www. walkabouttravelgear.com has a good coverage of electricity under "adapters."

■ EMERGENCIES

Assistance in English is available 24 hours a day on the Japan Helpline. The Tōkyō English Life Line (TELL) is a telephone service available daily 9 AM–4 PM and 7 PM–11 PM for anyone in distress who cannot communicate in Japanese. The service will relay your emergency to the appropriate Japanese authorities and/or will serve as a counselor. Operators who answer the 119 and 110 hotlines rarely speak English.

The International Catholic Hospital (Seibō Byōin) accepts emergencies and takes regular appointments Monday–Saturday 8 AM–11 AM; outpatient services are closed the third Saturday of the month. The International Clinic also accepts emergencies. Appointments there are taken weekdays 9–noon and 2:30–5 and on Saturday 9–noon. St. Luke's International Hospital is a member of the American Hospital Association and accepts emergencies. Appointments are taken weekdays 8:30 AM–11 AM. The Tōkyō Medical and Surgical Clinic takes appointments weekdays 9–5 and Saturday 9–noon.

The Yamauchi Dental Clinic, a member of the American Dental Association, is open weekdays 9–12:30 and 3–5:30, Saturday 9–noon.

No drugstores in Tōkyō are open 24 hours a day. The American Pharmacy stocks nonprescription Western products; it's open weekdays 9 AM–9 PM and weekends 9 AM–8 PM. The Koyasu Drug Store in the Hotel Okura also offers some Western products and is open Monday–Saturday 8:30 AM–9 PM, Sunday and holidays 10–9. Many grocery and convenience stores carry basics such as aspirin and ibuprofen.

Nagai Yakkyoku is open daily (except Tuesday) 10–7 and will mix a Chinese and/or Japanese herbal medicine for you after a consultation. You can't have a doctor's prescription filled here, but you can find something for a headache or stomach pain. A little English is spoken.

Foreigner Assistance U.S. Embassy ✉ 1-10-5 Akasaka, Minato-ku, Toranomon ☎ 03/3224-500 ⊕ tokyoTōkyō.usembassy.gov/ Ⓜ Namboku Line, Tameike-Sannō station (Exit 13).

General Emergency Contacts Ambulance and Fire ☎ 119. **Japan Helpline** ☎ 0120/461-997 or 0570/000-911. **Police** ☎ 110. **Tōkyō English Life Line (TELL)** ☎ 03/5774-0992.

Hospitals & Clinics International Catholic Hospital (Seibō Byōin) ✉ 2-5-1 Naka Ochiai, Shinjuku District ☎ 03/3951-1111 Ⓜ Seibu Shinjuku Line, Shimo-Ochiai station (Nishiguchi/West Exit). **International Clinic** ✉ 1-5-9 Azabu-dai, Minato-ku, Roppongi District ☎ 03/3582-2646 or 03/3583-7831 Ⓜ Hibiya Line, Roppongi station (Exit 3). **St. Luke's International Hospital** ✉ 9-1 Akashi-chō, Chūō-ku, Tsukiji District ☎ 03/3541-5151 Ⓜ Hibiya Line, Tsukiji station (Exit 3); Yūraku-chō Line, Shintomichō station (Exit 6). **Tōkyō Medical and Surgical Clinic** ✉ 32 Mori Bldg., 3-4-30 Shiba Kōen, Minato-ku ☎ 03/3436-3028 Ⓜ Toei Mita Line, Onarimon station (Exit A1); Hibiya Line, Kamiyachō station (Exit 1); Toei Ōedo Line, Akabane-bashi station. **Yamauchi Dental Clinic** ✉ Shirokanedai Gloria Heights, 1st fl., 3-16-10 Shirokanedai, Minato-ku ☎ 03/3441-6377 Ⓜ JR Yamanote Line, Meguro station (Hi-

gashi-guchi/East Exit); Namboku and Toei Mita lines, Shirokanedai station (Exit 1).

Pharmacies American Pharmacy ✉ Maru Bldg. B1F, 2-4-1 Marunouchi Chiyoda-ku ☎ 03/5220-7716 **Koyasu Pharmacy** ✉ Hotel Okura, Main building 1F, 2-10-4 Toranomon Minato-ku ☎ 03/3583-7958. **Nagai Yakkyoku** ✉ 1-8-10 Azabu Ju-ban, Minato-ku ☎ 03/3583-3889.

▌HEALTH

The most common types of illnesses are caused by contaminated food and water. Especially in developing countries, drink only bottled, boiled, or purified water and drinks; don't drink from public fountains or use ice. You should even consider using bottled water to brush your teeth. Make sure food has been thoroughly cooked and is served to you fresh and hot; avoid vegetables and fruits that you haven't washed (in bottled or purified water) or peeled yourself. If you have problems, mild cases of traveler's diarrhea may respond to Imodium (known generically as loperamide) or Pepto-Bismol. Be sure to drink plenty of fluids; if you can't keep fluids down, seek medical help immediately.

Infectious diseases can be airborne or passed via mosquitoes and ticks and through direct or indirect physical contact with animals or people. Some, including Norwalk-like viruses that affect your digestive tract, can be passed along through contaminated food. If you are traveling in an area where malaria is prevalent, use a repellant containing DEET and take malaria-prevention medication before, during, and after your trip as directed by your physician. Condoms can help prevent most sexually transmitted diseases, but they aren't absolutely reliable and their quality varies from country to country. Speak with your physician and/or check the CDC or World Health Organization Web sites for health alerts, particularly if you're pregnant, traveling with children, or have a chronic illness.

For information on travel insurance, shots and medications, and medical-assistance companies *see* Shots & Medications *in* Getting Started, *above.*

SPECIFIC ISSUES IN TŌKYŌ

Tap water everywhere is safe in Japan. Medical treatment varies from highly skilled and professional treatment at major hospitals to somewhat less advanced procedures in small neighborhood clinics. At larger hospitals you have a good chance of encountering English-speaking doctors who have been educated in the West.

Mosquitoes can be a minor irritation during the rainy season, though you are never at risk of contracting anything serious, like malaria. If you're staying in a ryokan or somewhere without air-conditioning or anti-mosquito coils, an electric-powered spray will be provided. If not, they, along with sunscreen, are available at most stores. Dehydration and heatstroke could be concerns if you spend a long time outside during the summer months, so isotonic sports drinks are readily available from the nation's ubiquitous vending machines.

OVER-THE-COUNTER REMEDIES

It may be difficult to buy the standard over-the-counter remedies you're used to, so it's best to bring with you any medications (in their proper packaging) you may need. Medication can only be bought at pharmacies in Japan, but every neighborhood seems to have at least one. *Kusuriya* is the word for "pharmacy" in Japanese. Pharmacists in Japan are usually able to manage at least a few words of English, and certainly are able to read some, so have a pen and some paper ready, just in case. In Japanese, aspirin is *asupirin* and Tylenol is *Tairenōru.*

▌ HOURS OF OPERATION

General business hours are weekdays 9–5. Many offices also open at least half of the day on Saturday but are generally closed on Sunday.

Banks are open weekdays from 9 to at least 3, with some now staying open until 4 or 5. As with shops, there's a trend toward longer and later opening hours.

Museums generally close on Monday and the day following national holidays. They are also closed the day following special exhibits and during the weeklong New Year celebrations.

There are generally no binding laws about when it is too late to serve alcohol so it's up to the establishments. Last call is not really an applicable concept in Japan.

Department stores are usually open 10–7 but close one day a week, which varies from store to store. Other stores are open from 10 or 11 to 7 or 8. Tōkyō has 24-hour convenience stores, many of which now have ATM facilities.

HOLIDAYS

Below is a list of national holidays.
■ TIP→ Note that when a holiday falls on a Sunday, it's usually observed the following Monday.

January 1 (*Ganjitsu,* New Year's Day); the second Monday in January (*Senjin-no-hi,* Coming of Age Day); February 11 (*Kenkoku Kinen-no-bi,* National Foundation Day); March 20 or 21 (*Shumbun-no-hi,* Vernal Equinox); April 29 (*Midori-no-hi,* Greenery Day); May 3 (*Kempo Kinen-bi,* Constitution Day); May 5 (*Kodomo-no-hi,* Children's Day); the third Monday in July (*Umi-no-hi,* Marine Day); the third Monday in September (*Keirō-no-hi,* Respect for the Aged Day); September 23 or 24 (*Shūbun-no-hi,* Autumnal Equinox); the second Monday in October (*Taiiku-no-hi,* Sports Day); November 3 (*Bunka-no-hi,* Culture Day); November 23 (*Kinro Kansha-no-hi,* Labor Thanksgiving Day); December 23 (*Tennō Tanjobi,* Emperor's Birthday).

MAIL

The Japanese postal service is very efficient. Airmail between Japan and the United States takes between five and eight days. Surface mail can take anywhere from four to eight weeks. Express service is also available through post offices.

Most hotels have stamps and will mail your letters and postcards; they will also give you directions to the nearest post office, or *Yūbinkyoku*. Post offices are open weekdays 9–5 and Saturday 9–noon. Some of the central post offices have longer hours, such as the one in Tōkyō, located near Tōkyō Eki (train station), which is open 24 hours year-round. The main International Post Office is on the Imperial Palace side of JR Tōkyō station. Some of the smaller post offices are not equipped to send packages. You can also buy stamps at convenience stores.

The Japanese postal service has implemented use of three-numeral-plus-four postal codes, but its policy is similar to that in the United States regarding ZIP-plus-fours; that is, mail addressed with the three-numeral code will still arrive at its destination, albeit perhaps one or two days later.

It costs ¥110 (98¢) to send a letter by air to North America and Europe. An airmail postcard costs ¥70 (63¢). Aerograms cost ¥90 (81¢).

To get mail, have parcels and letters sent "poste restante" to the central post office in major cities; unclaimed mail is returned after 30 days.

Main Branch **International Post Office**
✉ 2-3-3 Ōte-machi, Chiyoda-ku ☎ 03/3241-4891 Ⓜ Tōkyō station.

SHIPPING PACKAGES

The Japanese Post Office is very efficient and domestic mail rarely goes astray. To ship a 5 kg/11 lb parcel to the U.S. costs ¥10,150 ($91) if sent by airmail, ¥7,300 ($65) by SAL (economy airmail) and ¥4,000 ($36) by sea. Allow a week for airmail, 2 to 3 weeks for SAL, and up to 6 weeks for packages sent by sea. Large shops usually ship domestically, but not overseas.

FedEx has drop-off locations at branches of Kinko's all over Tōkyō. A 1 kg/2.2 lb package from central Tōkyō to Washing-ton D.C. would cost about ¥7,200 ($64) and take two days to be delivered.

Express Services **FedEx** ☎ 0120/00-320 toll-free, 043/298-1919 ⊕ www.fedex.com/jp.

■ MONEY

In terms of lodging, food, and transportation (except taxis), Tōkyō is about as expensive as New York or Paris. One good way to hold down expenses is to avoid taxis (they tend to get stuck in traffic anyway) and try the efficient, easy-to-use subway system. Restaurants for locals tend to be less expensive than those for tourists, so instead of going to a restaurant with Western-style food and menus in English, go to places where you can rely on your good old index finger to point to the dish you want, and try food that the Japanese eat (⇨ dining *in* Chapter 2).

Prices throughout this guide are given for adults. Substantially reduced fees are almost always available for children, students, and senior citizens.

■ TIP➡ Banks never have every foreign currency on hand, and it may take as long as a week to order. If you're planning to exchange funds before leaving home, don't wait till the last minute.

ATMS & BANKS

Your own bank will probably charge a fee for using ATMs abroad; the foreign bank you use may also charge a fee. Neverthe-

ITEM	Average Cost
Cup of coffee	¥250–¥600 ($2–$5.50)
Bottle of beer	¥350–¥800 ($3–$7)
Bowl of noodles	¥600 ($5.50)
Local dinner	¥2,500 ($22)
McDonald's hamburger	¥84 (75¢)
Two-km (one-mile) taxi ride in Tōkyō	¥660 ($6)
Double room in Tōkyō	¥11,000–¥45,000 ($98–$403)

less, you'll usually get a better rate of exchange at an ATM than you will at a currency-exchange office or even when changing money in a bank. And extracting funds as you need them is a safer option than carrying around a large amount of cash.

■ TIP→ ATMs at many Japanese banks, stores, and post offices do not accept foreign-issued cash or credit cards except for Visa. Citibank has centrally located branches in most major Japanese cities and ATMs that are open 24 hours. Japan's most progressive bank, UFJ, is a member of the Plus network. Some convenience stores also have cash machines in the Plus network. Post offices have ATMs that accept Visa, MasterCard, American Express, Diners Club, and Cirrus cards. Most bank and all post office ATMs will have an English-language user option. Elsewhere, especially in more rural areas, it's difficult to find suitable ATMs. PIN numbers in Japan are comprised of four digits. In Japanese, an ATM is commonly referred to by its English acronym, while PIN is *anshō bangō*.

■ TIP→ PIN numbers with more than four digits are not recognized at ATMs in many countries. If yours has five or more, remember to change it before you leave.

CREDIT CARDS

Throughout this guide, the following abbreviations are used: **AE**, American Express; **DC**, Diners Club; **MC**, MasterCard; and **V**, Visa.

It's a good idea to inform your credit-card company before you travel, especially if you're going abroad and don't travel internationally very often. Otherwise, the credit-card company might put a hold on your card owing to unusual activity—not a good thing halfway through your trip. Record all your credit-card numbers—as well as the phone numbers to call if your cards are lost or stolen—in a safe place, so you're prepared should something go wrong. Both MasterCard and Visa have general numbers you can call (collect if you're abroad) if your card is lost,

but you're better off calling the number of your issuing bank, since MasterCard and Visa usually just transfer you to your bank; your bank's number is usually printed on your card.

If you plan to use your credit card for cash advances, you'll need to apply for a PIN at least two weeks before your trip. Although it's usually cheaper (and safer) to use a credit card abroad for large purchases (so you can cancel payments or be reimbursed if there's a problem), note that some credit-card companies *and* the banks that issue them add substantial percentages to all foreign transactions, whether they're in a foreign currency or not. Check on these fees before leaving home, so there won't be any surprises when you get the bill.

■ TIP→ Before you charge something, ask the merchant whether or not he or she plans to do a dynamic currency conversion (DCC). In such a transaction the credit-card *processor* (shop, restaurant, or hotel, not Visa or MasterCard) converts the currency and charges you in dollars. In most cases you'll pay the merchant a 3% fee for this service in addition to any credit-card company and issuing-bank foreign-transaction surcharges.

Dynamic currency conversion programs are becoming increasingly widespread. Merchants who participate in them are supposed to ask whether you want to be charged in dollars or the local currency, but they don't always do so. And even if they do offer you a choice, they may well avoid mentioning the additional surcharges. The good news is that you *do* have a choice. And if this practice really gets your goat, you can avoid it entirely thanks to American Express; with its cards, DCC simply isn't an option.

MasterCard and Visa are the most widely accepted credit cards in Japan. Many vendors don't accept American Express.

Reporting Lost Cards American Express ☎ 800/992-3404 in the U.S. or 336/393-1111 collect from abroad ⊕ www.americanexpress. com. **Diners Club** ☎ 800/234-6377 in the

U.S. or 303/799–1504 collect from abroad ⊕ www.dinersclub.com. **MasterCard** ☎ 800/ 622–7747 in the U.S. or 636/722–7111 collect from abroad ⊕ www.mastercard.com. **Visa** ☎ 800/847–2911 in the U.S. or 410/581–9994 collect from abroad ⊕ www.visa.com.

CURRENCY & EXCHANGE

The unit of currency in Japan is the yen (¥). There are bills of ¥10,000, ¥5,000, ¥2,000, and ¥1,000. Coins are ¥500, ¥100, ¥50, ¥10, ¥5, and ¥1. Japanese currency floats on the international monetary exchange, so changes can be dramatic. Some vending machines will not accept the newly introduced ¥2,000 bill or the new version of the ¥500 coin, but these older machines are gradually being replaced.

At this writing, the exchange rate was ¥117 for U.S. $1.

■ TIP→ Even if a currency-exchange booth has a sign promising no commission, rest assured that there's some kind of huge, hidden fee. (Oh . . . that's right. The sign didn't say no *fee*.) And as for rates, you're almost always better off getting foreign currency at an ATM or exchanging money at a bank.

Most hotels will change both traveler's checks and notes into yen. However, their rates are always less favorable than at banks. Because Tōkyō is largely free from street crime, you can safely consider changing even hefty sums into yen at any time; two places that may be familiar to you are American Express International and Citibank. The larger branches of most Japanese banks have foreign exchange counters where you can do this as well; the paperwork will be essentially the same. All major branch offices of the post office have ATM machines that accept Visa, MasterCard, American Express, Diners Club, and Cirrus cards. You can also use cards on the Cirrus network at Citibank ATMs. Banking hours are weekdays 9–3.

Exchange Services American Express International ✉ 4-30-16 Ogikubo Suginami-ku ☎ 03/3220-6100. **Citibank** ✉ Ohte Center Bldg., 1F, 1-1-3, Otemachi Chiyoda-ku ☎ 0120/

WORST-CASE SCENARIO

All your money and credit cards have just been stolen. In these days of real-time transactions, this isn't a predicament that should destroy your vacation. First, report the theft of the credit cards. Then get any traveler's checks you were carrying replaced. This can usually be done almost immediately, provided that you kept a record of the serial numbers separate from the checks themselves. If you bank at a large international bank like Citibank or HSBC, go to the closest branch; if you know your account number, chances are you can get a new ATM card and withdraw money right away. **Western Union** (☎ 800/325–6000 ⊕ www.westernunion.com) sends money almost anywhere. Have someone back home order a transfer online, over the phone, or at one of the company's offices, which is the cheapest option. The U.S. State Department's **Overseas Citizens Services** (☎ 202/647–5225) can wire money to any U.S. consulate or embassy abroad for a fee of $30. Just have someone back home wire money or send a money order or cashier's check to the state department, which will then disburse the funds as soon as the next working day after it receives them.

110–330 toll-free for account holders, 03/ 3215–0051 for other inquiries.

TRAVELER'S CHECKS & CARDS

Some consider this the currency of the caveman, and it's true that fewer establishments accept traveler's checks these days. Nevertheless, they're a cheap and secure way to carry extra money, particularly on trips to urban areas. Both Citibank (under the Visa brand) and American Express issue traveler's checks in the United States, but Amex is better known and more widely accepted; you can also avoid hefty surcharges by cashing Amex checks at Amex offices. Whatever you do, keep track of all the serial numbers in case the checks are lost or stolen.

Traveler's checks are widely accepted, though not really used, at major businesses in cities, though not in small businesses or rural areas. Lost or stolen checks can usually be replaced within 24 hours. To ensure a speedy refund, buy your own traveler's checks—don't let someone else pay for them: irregularities like this can cause delays. The person who bought the checks should make the call to request a refund.

American Express now offers a stored-value card called a Travelers Cheque Card, which you can use wherever American Express credit cards are accepted, including ATMs. The card can carry a minimum of $300 and a maximum of $2,700, and it's a very safe way to carry your funds. Although you can get replacement funds in 24 hours if your card is lost or stolen, it doesn't really strike us as a very good deal. In addition to a high initial cost ($14.95 to set up the card, plus $5 each time you "reload"), you still have to pay a 2% fee for each purchase in a foreign currency (similar to that of any credit card). Further, each time you use the card in an ATM you pay a transaction fee of $2.50 on top of the 2% transaction fee for the conversion—add it all up and it can be considerably more than you would pay when simply using your own ATM card. Regular traveler's checks are just as secure and cost less.

American Express ☎ 888/412-6945 in the U.S., 801/945-9450 collect outside of the U.S. to add value or speak to customer service ⊕ www.americanexpress.com.

▋RESTROOMS

The most hygienic restrooms are found in hotels and department stores, while those at most train or gas stations can be considerably less so. All are usually clearly marked with international symbols. ▋TIP➔ You may encounter Japanese-style toilets, with bowls recessed into the floor, over which you squat facing the hood. This may take some getting used to, but it's completely sanitary as you don't come into direct contact with the facility. Train station restrooms often have at least one commode for the less agile at the end-row stall.

In many homes and Japanese-style public places, there will be a pair of slippers at the entrance to the restrooms. Change into these before entering the room, and change back when you exit.

Some public toilets don't have toilet paper, though there are dispensers where packets can be purchased for ¥50 (45¢) or so. Similarly, paper towel dispensers or hand dryers are not always installed, so a small handkerchief is useful to dry your hands. **Find a Loo The Bathroom Diaries** ⊕ www. thebathroomdiaries.com is flush with unsanitized info on restrooms the world over—each one located, reviewed, and rated.

▋SAFETY

Even in its major cities, Japan is a very safe country with one of the lowest crime rates in the world. Most criminals here would back down in the face of a forthright Western response. Shouting for help in English, for example, is likely to scare off any would-be attacker. You should, however, avoid the back street of Kabuki-chō in Tōkyō's Shinjuku district and some of the large public parks at nighttime.

▋TAXES

A 5% national consumption tax is added to all hotel bills. Another 3% local tax is added to the bill if it exceeds ¥15,000 (about $134). You may save money by paying for your hotel meals separately rather than charging them to your bill.

At first-class, full-service, and luxury hotels, a 10% service charge is added to the bill in place of individual tipping. At the more expensive ryokan, where individualized maid service is offered, the service charge is usually 15%. At business hotels, minshuku, youth hostels, and economy inns, no service charge is added to the bill.

There's an across-the-board, nonrefundable 5% consumption tax levied on all sales, which is included in the ticket price. Authorized tax-free shops will knock the tax off purchases over ¥10,000 if you show your passport and a valid tourist visa. A large sign is displayed at such shops. A 5% tax is also added to all restaurant bills. Another 3% local tax is added to the bill if it exceeds ¥7,500 (about $67). At the more expensive restaurants, a 10%–15% service charge is added to the bill. Tipping is not customary.

TIME

All of Japan is in the same time zone. The country is 14 hours ahead of New York and 17 hours ahead of San Francisco. Daylight saving time is not observed.

TIPPING

Tipping is not common in Japan. It's not necessary to tip taxi drivers, or at hair salons, barbershops, bars, or nightclubs. A chauffeur for a hired car usually receives a tip of ¥500 ($4.50) for a half-day excursion and ¥1,000 ($9) for a full-day trip. Porters charge fees of ¥250–¥300 (about $2.50) per bag at railroad stations and ¥200 ($1.80) per piece at airports. It's not customary to tip employees of hotels, even porters, unless a special service has been rendered. In such cases, a gratuity of ¥2,000–¥3,000 ($18–$26) should be placed in an envelope and handed to the staff member discreetly.

INDEX